LABOR RELATIONS IN THE AVIATION AND AEROSPACE INDUSTRIES

LABOR RELATIONS IN THE AVIATION AND AEROSPACE INDUSTRIES

Robert W. Kaps, J. Scott Hamilton, and Timm J. Bliss

Southern Illinois University Press
Carbondale and Edwardsville

Library of Congress Cataloging-in-Publication Data
Kaps, Robert W., 1943–
Labor relations in the aviation and aerospace industries
/ Robert W. Kaps, J. Scott Hamilton, and Timm J. Bliss.
    p. cm.
Includes bibliographical references and index.
ISBN-13: 978-0-8093-3043-0 (cloth : alk. paper)
ISBN-10: 0-8093-3043-1 (cloth : alk. paper)
ISBN-13: 978-0-8093-9001-4 (ebook)
ISBN-10: 0-8093-9001-9 (ebook)
 1. Collective labor agreements—Aeronautics—United
States. 2. Collective bargaining—Aeronautics—United
States. 3. Collective labor agreements—Aircraft indus-
try—United States. 4. Collective bargaining—Aircraft
industry—United States. I. Hamilton, J. Scott. II. Bliss,
Timm J., [date] III. Title.
KF3409.A43K37 2011
344.7301'89042913—dc22   2010043437

The paper used in this publication meets the minimum
requirements of American National Standard for Information Sciences—Permanence of Paper for Printed
Library Materials, ANSI Z39.48-1992. ♾

Contents in Brief

List of Tables xi
List of Case Studies xiii
Preface xv

Part One. Foundations of Labor Law and Policy

1. Public Policy and Labor Law 3
2. The Violent Beginnings of U.S. Labor Law 26
3. Major Collective Bargaining Legislation 53

Part Two. Principles, Practices, and Procedures in Collective Bargaining and Dispute Resolution

4. Elections, Certifications, and Procedures 81
5. Negotiating the Collective Bargaining Agreement 109
6. Unfair Labor Practices 133
7. Grievance Procedures 151

Part Three. The Changing Labor Relations Environment

8. The Airline Industry 165
9. The Aerospace Industry 204
10. General Aviation 227
11. The Public Sector 236

Appendix A: The Railway Labor Act 261
Appendix B: The National Labor Relations Act 294
Notes 323
Glossary 345
Index 353

Contents

List of Tables xi
List of Case Studies xiii
Preface xv

Part One. Foundations of Labor Law and Policy

1. Public Policy and Labor Law 3

Transportation Policy 3
Developmental Policy Initiatives 4
Regulatory Policy Initiatives 5
The Airline Deregulation Act of 1978 6
Labor Regulation 7

The Aviation Industry 9
Aviation/Aerospace Manufacturing 9
Air Transportation 10
General Aviation 16
Public-Sector Aviation 17

Federal Civil Service Labor Law 17
Political Appointment 17
The Merit System 17
The Rise of Public-Sector Unions 18
The Sovereignty Doctrine 19
Executive Orders for Public-Sector
   Collective Bargaining 20
A Brief Comparison: NLRA and Executive
   Order 10988 20
Executive Order 11491 21
The Civil Service Reform Act of 1978 21
National Partnership Council, 1993 22
Public-Sector Labor Unions 22
Public-Sector Collective Bargaining 23

State and Local Government Laws 24

2. The Violent Beginnings of U.S. Labor Law 26
Early Judicial Actions 26
National Railroad System Development 30
National Labor Union 31
Knights of Labor 31

Federation of Organized Trades and Labor
   Unions 32
American Federation of Labor (AFL) 33
Strikes and the Railroads 34

Legislative Beginnings 40
Arbitration Act of 1888 40
Interstate Commerce Act of 1887 41
Sherman Antitrust Act (1890) 41
Erdman Act of 1898 46
Elkins Act of 1903 47
Hepburn Act of 1906 47
Mann Elkins Act of 1910 47
Newlands Act of 1913 47
Adamson Act of 1916 48

Non-Railroad Labor Activities 48
Clayton Antitrust Act of 1914 49
Railroad Labor Gains 50
Transportation Act of 1920 51

Summary 52

3. Major Collective Bargaining Legislation 53

The Railway Labor Act 53
Origins 53
Early Judicial Challenges 55
Depression-Era Unionism 55
Provisions of the RLA 56
National Mediation Board 57
RLA Amendment of 1934 58
RLA Amendment of 1936 58
RLA Amendments of 1940 and 1951 59

The Norris–La Guardia Act of 1932 59

The National Labor Relations Act 62
National Industrial Recovery Act 62
Origins of the NLRA: The Wagner Act 63
NLRA Amendment: The Taft-Hartley Act
   65
NLRA Amendment: The Landrum-Griffin
   Act 71

Other Laws Affecting Labor Relations 72

Summary 76

Part Two. Principles, Practices, and Procedures
in Collective Bargaining and Dispute Resolution

4. **Elections, Certifications, and
   Procedures 81**
   Interstate Commerce 81

**The Process under the Railway Labor Act
   81**
   Jurisdiction 81
   Employees Subject to the RLA 86
   Organizing Employees under the RLA 87
   Procedures of the National Mediation Board
      88
   Class and Craft Determination 93
   Representation Election 95
   Election-Rule Exceptions 98
   Mergers and Acquisitions 101
   Decertification 102

**The Process under the National Labor
   Relations Act 102**
   Employees Subject to the NLRA 102
   Supervisory Personnel Subject to the NLRA
      103
   Managerial Personnel Subject to the NLRA
      103
   Employers Subject to the NLRA 103
   Procedures of the National Labor Relations
      Board 104
   Determining Bargaining Units 105
   Craft, Departmental, or Industrial Units
      106
   Certification Election 106

Summary 108

5. **Negotiating the Collective Bargaining
   Agreement 109**
   Approaches to Bargaining 110

**Procedures in the Airlines under the RLA
   114**
   Contract Status 114
   The Negotiation Time Frame 114
   Mediation 117

The Mediation Process 118
Arbitration 118
Supermediation 119
Emergency Boards 120
Strikes 121
The Mutual Aid Pact 122
Deregulation 124

**Procedures in the Non–Airline/Railroad
   Private Sector under the NLRA 124**
   Bargaining Topics 124
   The Contract-Negotiation Process 125
   Self-Help 125
   Mediation 127
   Arbitration 127
   Actions during a Strike or Lockout 129
   Hiring Replacement Workers under
      Employer Lockout 129
   Hiring Replacement Workers under Union
      Strike 129

**Procedures in the Public Sector under
   Other Federal and State Laws 129**
   Federal-Employee Collective Bargaining
      129
   State and Local Government Employee
      Collective Bargaining 130

Summary 131

6. **Unfair Labor Practices 133**

**Unfair Labor Practices under the NLRA
   133**
   Activities Prohibited under the NLRA 136
   Interference 136
   Penalties 138
   Rulings of the NLRB 138

Unfair Labor Practices under the RLA 139
   Influence, Coercion, and Interference 139
   Rulings of the National Mediation Board
      140
   Interference through Communications 140
   Interference in Certification Elections 142
   Court Decisions 143
   Penalties for Interference in Elections 144
   Featherbedding 145

**Unfair Labor Practices under the CSRA
   and State Laws 145**
   Free-Speech Provisions 146

The Federal Labor Relations Authority 147
State Labor-Relations Agencies 148

Summary 150

7. Grievance Procedures 151

Definition 151
Contract Administration 151
Arbitration 152
Grievance Procedures 153
Grievance Arbitration 154

**Grievance Arbitration under the Railway
Labor Act 156**
The System Board of Adjustment 156
Overruling Arbitration Decisions 157
Arbitration Costs 158

**Grievance Arbitration under the National
Labor Relations Act 159**
Overruling Arbitration Decisions 159
Selecting an Arbitrator 160
Arbitration Costs 161

**Grievance Arbitration under the CSRA
and State Laws 161**

**Statutory Alternatives to Grievance
Procedures 161**

Summary 162

Part Three. The Changing Labor
Relations Environment

8. The Airline Industry 165

**The Era of Economic Regulation by the
CAB 166**
Certificates of Public Convenience 166
Mergers 167
Fare Provisions 167
The Mutual Aid Pact 168
Shuffling toward Deregulation 168

**Deregulation, Competition, and
Consequences 169**
Small-Community Air Service 169
Labor Protective Provisions 170
Legacy Airlines 170
Shifting from Regulation to Competition 170
Fare Wars 171

Managing for Competitiveness 172
The Fuel Crisis of 1979 172
Double-Breasting 174
The First Two-Tier Wage Scales 175
Enter Concessionary Bargaining 176
A Perceptive and Prophetic Assessment 176
The Rate of Change Accelerates,
Consequences Become More Harsh 180
The Braniff Bankruptcy 182
The Quest for Job Security Begins 182
Employees Buy the Company 183
Concessionary Bargaining Snowballs 183
Continental Airlines' Bankruptcy 185
Two-Tier Wage Plans Proliferate 187

**Trends, Issues, and Challenges in Airline
Labor Relations 188**
New Entrants 189
Cost Reduction 190
Bankruptcies 191
Pensions 192
Downsizing 193
Contracting Out and the Globalized
Economy 194
Productivity 195
Mergers and Acquisitions 195

Looming Issues 199
Foreign Ownership of U.S. Airlines 199
Shortages of Pilots and Mechanics 199
Environmental Impacts 201

Summary 202

9. The Aerospace Industry 204

**An Era of Industry Consolidation: Mergers
and Acquisitions 208**
The First Wave Laps Gently 208
The Second Wave Rolls In 208
The Third Wave Crashes Ashore 210
Labor, Weakened, Responds 211

**Lean Manufacturing Boosts Productivity
212**

**Outsourcing and Globalization: Impacts
and Implications 213**
Where the Work Went 214
Confrontation Time 214
A Judicial Rebuke 219

Materials Costs Spike, Currency Fluctuates 220

A Labor Shortage Looms 220

Environmental Factors: Greening the Sky 225

Summary 226

10. General Aviation 227

Jurisdictional Determination 227

Charter and Fractional Operators 230

Ground Support and Maintenance 232

Flight Training 234

Summary 235

11. The Public Sector 236

The Public-Sector Labor-Relations Environment 237
 Management-Rights Clauses 237
 Management Styles 237
 Executive Orders 238

Outsourcing and Privatization 239
 The A-76 Process 239

FAA Flight Service 242
FAA Air Traffic Control 244
Other FAA Employees 245
TSA Airport Security Officers 247

State and Local Government Employees 254
 Airline Woes Straining Airport Budgets 254
 Outsourcing and Privatization of Airports 255
 States Restrict Public-Employee Collective Bargaining 257

Summary 257

Appendix A: The Railway Labor Act 261
Appendix B: The National Labor Relations Act 294
Notes 323
Glossary 345
Index 353

Tables

1.1: Aviation-industry employment in the United States, 2008 9
1.2: Major U.S. and international aviation/aerospace manufacturing companies, 2009 10
1.3: U.S. commercial airlines, 2010 11
1.4: U.S. scheduled passenger regional airlines, July 2010 11
3.1: Major labor-relations laws in the United States, 1926–59 54
3.2: Provisions of the Railway Labor Act 60
3.3: Major provisions of the Wagner Act 64
3.4: Major provisions of the Taft-Hartley Act 66
3.5: Legislative differences between the Railway Labor Act and the National Labor Relations Act 77
4.1: Jurisdictional standards of the National Labor Relations Board 83
5.1: Categories of bargaining subjects assigned by the National Labor Relations Board 126
6.1: Unfair labor practices proscribed by the NLRA for employers and labor organizations 137
6.2: State public-employee-relations boards 149
8.1: Section 401 carrier-certification activity in 1979 173
8.2: Section 401 carrier-certification activity in 1980 173
8.3: Section 401 carrier-certification activity in 1981 175

Case Studies

1.1:   CHAOS 12

2.1:   *Commonwealth v. Hunt* 28

2.2:   The Pinkerton National Detective Agency 35

2.3:   The Colorado Coal Field War—Zenith of Violence in U.S. Labor Relations 37

2.4:   *Hitchman Coal & Coke Company v. Mitchell* 43

3.1:   The Professional Air Traffic Controllers Organization Strike in 1981 69

4.1:   FedEx—Obstacles to Organizing under the Railway Labor Act 85

5.1:   NetJets Aviation—Negotiations through Integrative Bargaining 110

5.2:   Mutual Aid Pact—Northwest Orient Airlines 122

6.1:   The Taft-Hartley Labor Act—A Political Nightmare for the Unions 134

7.1:   Railway Labor Act and Fractional Ownership Companies 158

8.1:   The Goose That Laid Golden Eggs 176

9.1:   Military Contracts Counterbalance Civilian Orders for Boeing 206

9.2:   Preparing for a Strike—2008 216

9.3:   Addressing the Aerospace Labor Shortage—Educational Initiatives 223

10.1: Air Methods Corporation 228

11.1: DynCorp International 241

11.2: Professional Aviation Safety Specialists (PASS) 246

11.3: *National Treasury Employees Union v. Chertoff* 249

11.4: *American Federation of Government Employees v. Stone* 252

Preface

Unlike any other industry, labor-management relations and collective bargaining in aviation encompass the entire range of U.S. labor law. Other current labor-relations texts focus almost exclusively on the National Labor Relations Act of 1935 (NLRA) as administered by the National Labor Relations Board (NLRB) and mention only in passing, if at all, the Railway Labor Act of 1926 (RLA) administered by the National Mediation Board (NMB). (The full texts of the RLA and NLRA are in appendixes A and B, respectively.)

But in the aviation industry, the RLA governs labor relations in "every common carrier by air engaged in interstate or foreign commerce," including not only the major and regional airlines but also charter and even fractional aircraft operators: the lion's share of commercial activity in air transportation.[1]

And the aerospace industry that designs and manufactures the aircraft and components is governed by the NLRA, as are some general aviation activities.

The federal government is deeply involved in establishing standards for civil aircraft certification, flight operations, and airports along with operating the air traffic control system. Its labor relations are governed by yet another set of federal laws administered by another set of federal agencies.

Finally, most air carrier and general aviation reliever airports are owned and operated by local and regional governmental entities whose labor relations are subject to the panoply of differing state laws administered by a variety of state agencies.

All of these laws are executed by administrative agencies that issue and enforce regulations to carry out the legislature's intent. The statutes, regulations, and actions of all of these legislatures, regulators, management, and unions are continuously subject to judicial review in cases that interpret and judge their legality and constitutionality, building a considerable body of case law in the process.

We authors, all university professors teaching the subject, originally came together intending to contribute to updating lead author Robert W. Kaps's 1997 Air Transport Labor Relations, the seminal text, also published by Southern Illinois University Press, on collective bargaining in the airline industry. Our early discussions, however, led to agreement that to more fully serve the needs and interests of our students and our industry, we should expand the scope of the work to include not only the airlines but also the entire aviation and aerospace industry, underlying public airport infrastructure, and related government employers. As we plunged into the research phase, it became quickly apparent that although founded on that earlier work, what we were creating had so outgrown the original concept as to constitute a new book. This is it.

Labor Relations in the Aviation and Aerospace Industries is designed to be used in conjunction with the accompanying study guide both as a university text and as a reference guide for managers, employees, and union representatives in the aviation and aerospace industries, public airports, and aviation-related government service.

Many terms in this book are defined in the glossary, and most of the organizations are also described there. Our use of italics within a sentence may signify the introduction of a new term defined in the glossary, although it is also occasionally used for emphasis.

Unless otherwise noted, opinions expressed are ours and do not purport to represent those of our employers, past or present, or the publisher.

We hope you will find this book both informative and thought provoking.

PART ONE. Foundations of Labor Law and Policy

1. Public Policy and Labor Law

This book is about U.S. transportation labor law and the public policy decisions that shaped it. As is true with many abstract concepts, no single, widely accepted definition of the term *public policy* exists. The term *public* has many connotations, depending on context and perspective. The term *public* is relative, and as Miles' Law states, "Where you stand depends upon where you sit."[1] In the context of policy initiatives as used throughout this book, the term *public* relates to the government.

A standard dictionary definition for the term *policy* is "a definite course of action, adopted as a guiding principle or procedure that is considered expedient, prudent, advantageous, etc."[2] Thomas R. Dye, professor of political science, defines *public policy* as "whatever governments choose to do or not to do."[3] Thus, since it refers to the actions of government and the goals and values that determine those actions, *public policy* can be considered "an intentional course of action (or inaction) followed by the government."[4]

Transportation Policy

The role of transportation is so vital to society in general and to commerce in particular that governments have always treated it as a special industry, one that is particularly affected by the public interest. The famous Supreme Court case *Munn v. Illinois*, 94 U.S. 113 (1877), established the right of the state in the absence of congressional regulation to regulate business enterprises that provide essential public services. In writing for the majority, Chief Justice Morrison Waite cited a common property law principle that was over two hundred years old: "Property does become clothed with a public interest when used in a manner to make it public consequence, and affect the community at large. When therefore, one devotes his property to a use in which the public has an interest, he, in effect, grants to the public an interest in that use, and must submit to be controlled by the public for the common good."[5]

Munn v. Illinois established the constitutionality of state government regulation of private enterprise. However, a few years later, in the 1886 case of *Wabash, St. Louis, & Pacific Railroad Company v. Illinois* (118 U.S. 557), the U.S. Supreme Court made a ruling that severely limited the states' rights to control interstate commerce. Known as the Wabash case, the Court had to decide whether the individual states have the power to regulate railroad rates for interstate shipments. The final decision by the Court stated the commerce clause of the Constitution does not permit individual states the right to regulate railroad rates on the parts of interstate journeys that fall within their borders.[6] With Wabash, the Court barred states from regulating interstate commerce, asserting that only the federal government could do so and, thereby, overturning its 1877 decision in *Munn v. Illinois*, which allowed states to regulate railroads.

As a result of this Court decision, Congress passed the Interstate Commerce Act in 1887,

Figure 1.1. Morrison Waite, chief justice of the U.S. Supreme Court when it heard *Munn v. Illinois* (1877), a case involving corporate rates and agriculture. Ira Munn, a partner in a Chicago warehouse firm, had been found guilty of violating state laws providing for the fixing of maximum charges for grain storage; in his appeal, Munn contended that the fixing of maximum rates constituted a taking of property without due process of law. The Waite court upheld the granger laws, which established as constitutional the principle of public regulation of private businesses involved in serving the public interest. However, the court would abruptly reverse this direction in the Wabash case of 1886. Library of Congress.

which created the Interstate Commerce Commission, the first true federal regulatory agency. It was designed to address the issues of railroad abuse and price discrimination. The creation of this commission signaled the movement of the U.S. government to nationally assume responsibility for economic affairs, which was previously delegated to the states.[7]

Transportation is not only important to the national economy; it is also vital for national defense. This national-defense linkage caused virtually every developed country in the world except the United States to develop publicly owned-and-operated systems of railroads and airlines. Thus, employees of these nationalized transport industries are government employees and fall under their nation's civil service labor laws. Several of these nations have now privatized their transportation systems, and others are now seeking to do so, adding complexity to the global transportation labor relations equation.

Adhering to the philosophy of capitalism and private enterprise, the United States has always had privately owned railroad and airline industries (with the exception of Amtrak). Because of the unique relationship between transportation and the public interest, the U.S. government worked on the principle that it was necessary to pursue different public policy initiatives in the transportation sector than those followed in other sectors of the economy. Whenever government decides to undertake a new public policy directive or alter an existing one, it frequently does so through the legislative process by enacting statutes designed to accomplish its goals. In general, transportation policy can be grouped into two broad categories: developmental (subsidy) policy initiatives and regulatory policy initiatives.

Developmental Policy Initiatives

The federal government has long followed a policy of subsidizing transportation activities to achieve certain national goals and objectives. Public subsidization of the private transportation sector has been justified on the grounds that an efficient rail and air transportation system is an "essential public good" and is "critical to national defense." The essentially private transportation sector has been viewed by the federal government as being in the same class as a pure public good such that when produced, it is available to all citizens without restriction. It is this "public good" philosophy that has also led to federal subsidization of the nation's system of airports and airways.

Transportation is also subsidized because it is essential for economic growth. Significant direct and indirect benefits are associated with efficient private transportation systems that warrant public investment. For example, the U.S. government promoted both railroad transportation and air transportation because of their ability to carry the mail, which is closely linked to commerce. The railroads had reached their maturity by 1925, but the fledgling aviation industry needed assistance from the federal government. The Air Mail Act of 1925, also known as the Kelly Act, helped to regulate prices charged for hauling mail and freight. The U.S. Congress finally demonstrated its intent to regulate this growing aviation industry with the enactment of the Air Commerce Act of 1926, the first comprehensive attempt by the federal government to regulate the aviation industry. The act called for the promotion of air commerce, charged the federal government with the operation and maintenance of an airway system, required the federal government to operate and maintain all air-navigation aids, and called for the regulation of air safety.[8]

Regulatory Policy Initiatives

Laws that establish standards of conduct and affect the behavior of other governmental organizations or private organizations through legally enforceable methods are called *regulation*, as is a rule by which conduct is regulated and which an authority develops to administer the principles of a given law. Regulation is the favored governmental policy instrument to achieve its primary transportation goal—stability. The government finds regulation an appealing policy instrument because it can promulgate regulations at little cost to itself. Regulatory costs incurred are transferred from the government to the regulated industry. The affected industry then passes these costs on to its customers. Regulation thus generates a lumpy distribution of costs and benefits. As shown in later chapters, the traveling public

Figure 1.2. First U.S. air mail flight taking off from Washington, D.C., May 15, 1918. In 1925, the Congress passed HR 7064, titled "An Act to encourage commercial aviation and to authorize the Postmaster General to contract for Air Mail Service" (aka the Kelly Act), which directed the U.S. Post Office to contract with commercial air carriers to fly the mail over designated routes. Thirty-four contract air mail routes would eventually be awarded and opened in the United States between February 15, 1926, and October 25, 1930. However, with the 1934 air mail scandal, the U.S. Post Office cancelled all the contracts effective February 19, 1934. U.S. Army photo.

has absorbed the brunt of the cost of regulating the air transport industry, and air transport labor has been a prime beneficiary of that same governmental regulation.

Transportation is regulated because of the positive and negative externalities often associated with it. An *externality* is a consequence of the activity of an individual or firm that is incidental (or "external") to but indivisible from its main activity and that affects the utility of another individual or firm favorably or unfavorably.[9] For example, an airline allows passengers to travel long distances quickly, but it also produces noise and air pollution—typical external costs.

The U.S. government imposed comprehensive economic regulation on the airline and railroad industries until the late 1970s. Economic regulation was also deemed necessary because of negative "public good" externalities—in this case because of the oligopolistic imperfections extant in the air- and rail-transport market structures. Federal economic regulation was imposed on the air transport industry in 1938 because of the belief that the industry was prone to either "destructive competition," on the one hand, or "monopoly abuse," on the other.

The most widely recognized type of regulation associated with the airline industry is safety regulation. Both the Federal Aviation Administration (FAA) and the National Transportation Safety Board (NTSB) are primarily devoted to safety in the aviation industry. Another well-known type of government regulatory activity that was once present in the aviation industry was economic regulation via the Civil Aeronautics Board (CAB), which had three primary functions: award air routes to the airlines, limit the entry of airlines into new markets, and regulate passenger airfares. The CAB was created under the Civil Aeronautics Act (CAA) of 1938 and was authorized to supervise the U.S. air transport industry, as well as develop and promote it. The CAA provided for a separate entity to regulate aviation by establishing three separate but interrelated air agencies: the Civil Aeronautics Authority, the Administrator of Aviation, and the Air Safety Board.[10] Later, the Civil Aeronautics Authority and the Air Safety Board merged to form the CAB in 1940.[11]

The established goals of the CAB were to provide Americans with the least-expensive, most efficient, safest, and widest-ranging air service possible. The CAB achieved these goals by regulating entry and exit from individual air markets, passenger airfares, subsidies to airlines flying on less-profitable routes, mergers, and intercarrier agreements. However, this level of government regulation ended with the passage of the Airline Deregulation Act of 1978.

The Airline Deregulation Act of 1978

The push to deregulate the U.S. air transportation industry was initiated by President Jimmy Carter, who appointed economist Alfred E. Kahn, a strong supporter of deregulation, to head the CAB in 1977. By November of 1977, Congress deregulated air cargo, and in late 1978, Congress passed the Airline Deregulation Act (ADA) (see fig. 1.3).[12] Opposition to the act was stiff. The major airlines in the U.S. feared free competition, and the labor unions feared nonunion employees. Safety advocates feared that air safety would be compromised with the passage of this bill. However, under regulation, the government provided and continues to provide under deregulation subsidies for essential air service, particularly to small communities. All communities served by scheduled air carriers are guaranteed continued service. According to Steven Morrison and Clifford Winston, subsidies in force during regulation were supplemented in 1979 by a new program that guaranteed service to a far greater number of communities than under the regulated era.[13] And for the first time in forty years, each airline had the freedom to expand its markets and to set its own airfares. On January 1, 1985, the CAB was officially abolished since regulating the economics of the airline industry was no longer necessary because it was no longer an infant industry.[14]

Much has been written concerning the positive and negative aspects of the Airline Deregulation Act of 1978. The full implications and effects are still unfolding and remain a subject of debate. However, two things are certain. The act ended years of government control of the

Figure 1.3. President Jimmy Carter signing the Airline Deregulation Act (or ADA) into U.S. federal law on October 24, 1978. The main purpose of the act was to remove government control from commercial aviation and expose the passenger airline industry to market forces. National Archives and Records Administration.

airline industry, particularly economic control of fares and route structures. And the increased exposure to competition led to heavy losses and to conflicts with labor unions at a number of airlines. Between 1978 and 2001, nine major carriers (including America West, Braniff, Continental, Eastern, Pan Am, and TWA) and over one hundred smaller airlines went bankrupt or were liquidated, including most of the new airlines founded in deregulation's aftermath. No airline in the history of the United States had gone bankrupt prior to 1982, but despite the success of the aviation industry under the regulatory system in place in the 1970s, Braniff was the first to do so.[15] The airline ceased operations on May 12, 1982, a victim of escalating fuel prices, aggressive expansion, and fierce competition. Mergers and acquisitions among the surviving airlines have created oligopolistic conditions in U.S. markets as well as a select group of "megacarriers."

In 1978, after forty years of strict economic regulation, the industry was deregulated on the rationale that the fears of destructive competition and monopoly abuse were unwarranted. A majority of the transportation policymakers and elected officials believed that the market characteristics of the airline industry would allow it to operate in a fashion approaching pure competition without governmental economic regulation. The elimination of most economic regulations, without any adjustment to other interrelated air transport regulatory statutes, has had important and profound consequences on the collective bargaining process in the air transport sector because labor represents the single-largest operating cost of major carriers. The government's approach to labor-management relations also involves regulation.

Labor Regulation

Although the Airline Deregulation Act cannot be considered a labor law per se, its pervasive impact on the industry created new frontiers in labor-management relations. The relatively stable labor relations environment prior to deregulation of the airline industry has become an arena where the forces of economic pressure have created untold labor problems. Several have argued that without the established norms of the Railway Labor Act (RLA) of 1926, total chaos would have ensued.

Regulation of the employment relationship in the United States is divided between the federal government and the states. The federal government's authority to regulate the behavior of private parties is limited to matters affecting interstate commerce. Since 1937, Congress's power to legislate under the commerce clause of the Constitution has been given an expansive reading, but because Congress has regulated only in certain defined areas, the states also play an important role in filling out the terms of the employment relationship. Each state administers unemployment insurance and workers' compensation systems; maintains its own safety, minimum-wage, overtime, and maximum-hour rules; and sets the terms for hiring and firing workers. Even where Congress has legislated in the area, with the exception of laws governing labor relations and employee benefits, most federal statutes allow the states to enact more-protective worker standards.

In the area of labor relations, however, the states generally have limited authority over employees and employers that are within the reach of two major labor statutes, the Railway Labor Act of 1926, which covers the airlines and railroads, and the National Labor Relations Act of 1935 (NLRA), which covers all other industries affecting commerce, including general aviation and aerospace manufacturing. These laws broadly preempt any state regulation of activity they arguably protect or prohibit, any conduct that Congress wishes to leave entirely unregulated (such as peaceful economic strikes), or any claims whose adjudication requires the interpretation of collective bargaining agreements.

States may regulate where federal labor boards cede jurisdiction back to them or where they deal with aspects of conduct that reflect deeply held state concerns and are only peripherally the concern of the federal statutes. Examples in this category include state regulation of violent or mass picketing and libel actions for knowingly or recklessly making false statements in the course of labor disputes.

The Railway Labor Act of 1926 established the regulatory framework for the labor relations process in the railroad industry. The primary purpose of the act was to define a specific process that railroad management and union labor would use to satisfactorily negotiate labor contracts and settle disputes without resorting to the ultimate self-help weapons: the strike and the lockout. The importance of airmail transportation, coupled with a strong lobby by the Air Line Pilots Association (ALPA), led the government to amend the RLA in 1936 to encompass the airline industry engaged in interstate commerce.

In the early twentieth century, the federal courts were often hostile to union activity. The Norris–La Guardia Act of 1932 narrowed the grounds on which federal judges could issue injunctions in labor disputes, thereby reducing the role of the judiciary. In part as a consequence of this history, administrative agencies play an important role in the administration of both of the federal labor laws. In the case of the NLRA, the National Labor Relations Board (NLRB) has exclusive authority over the representation procedures and unfair labor practice provisions of the NLRA. The role of the courts is limited to judicial review of final NLRB orders in unfair labor practice cases and suits to enforce collective bargaining agreements. In the case of the Railway Labor Act, the National Mediation Board (NMB) conducts representation elections and plays an important role in mediating disputes.

Under the NLRA, charges of unfair labor practices (ULPs) are filed with regional offices of the NLRB. If after investigation the charges are believed to be meritorious, the general counsel issues a complaint on the government's behalf. An adversary, trial-type proceeding is then conducted before an administrative law judge (ALJ), who after hearing the testimony and reviewing the evidence makes initial findings of fact and conclusions of law. If no appeal is taken, the ALJ's determination becomes the ruling of the agency. If a party appeals, the five-member NLRB (usually sitting in panels of three members) considers the record and briefs. The final decision of the NLRB is reviewable in the federal courts of appeals. The reviewing court must uphold the agency's decisions if the agency's findings of fact are supported by "substantial evidence" on the record "considered as a whole" and if its rulings of law are in conformity with the NLRA. Further review is possible on writ of certiorari to the U.S. Supreme Court (a writ of certiorari is a granting of a hearing at the Supreme Court level; failure to obtain a writ of certiorari means a case will not be heard). Such writs of certiorari are rarely granted.

Under the RLA, the NMB's adjudicative authority is limited to representational disputes; the parties go directly to the federal district court to enforce other statutory obligations. Both statutes are based on the principles of:

- *exclusivity.* Employees have a right to be exclusively represented in bargaining by representatives chosen by a majority of the employees in a unit or craft and class.
- *legally mandated duty to bargain.* Both the exclusive bargaining representative and the employer are legally obligated to bargain in "good faith" (good-faith bargaining).
- *free collective bargaining.* After exhaustion of the duty to bargain, the parties are free to press their disagreements in the form of strikes and lockouts.
- *arbitration of disputes.* The means for resolving disputes arising under collective

bargaining agreements are provided for by contract rather than statute.

The provisions embodied in the RLA precede labor legislation affecting the rest of the major industrial economy by almost ten years. Many aspects of railway labor legislation served as an example for subsequent federal legislation designed to reduce the number of labor disputes in other parts of the economy. The guarantee of the right to organize and bargain collectively came later for all workers who could be reached by Congress. Insistence on collective bargaining as the "first line of defense" also came later for other workers. Government action to mediate disputes has been favored for a long time and strongly urged in recent laws. Finally, the idea of a cooling-off period, during which efforts are made to try to settle the issues involved, came in the Taft-Hartley Act. The precedent of the RLA in this type of provision is clear. Railway labor legislation has therefore maintained a considerable degree of continuity of operation and has set patterns in other laws.[16]

Not until the passage of the National Labor Relations Act of 1935 (the Wagner Act) did the federal government enact successful nationwide federal labor legislation. The NLRA was built on the basic concepts of the RLA, and although the two acts are similar in some respects, there are substantive differences between them. These differences in rules and procedures are discussed in later chapters.

The Aviation Industry

The "aviation industry" consists of several distinct segments including aviation/aerospace manufacturing, air transportation, general aviation, and government (public sector) aviation. Each segment of the U.S. aviation industry is subject to its own labor laws and practices. No single labor statute, organization, or agency encompasses all workers in the aviation industry. Any given law may or may not apply to an aviation employee or employer.

Aviation/Aerospace Manufacturing

The aviation/aerospace manufacturing segment is involved in several areas of production: aircraft; guided missiles; space vehicles; aircraft engines and propulsion units; and aircraft overhaul, rebuilding, and conversion. In 2008, aviation/aerospace manufacturers employed slightly more than the air transportation segment, according to the U.S. Bureau of Labor Statistics (see table 1.1).

The major companies involved in aviation/aerospace manufacturing include such familiar names as Boeing (McDonnell-Douglas merged with Boeing in 1997), Lockheed Martin (merged in 1996), General Dynamics, and General Electric (see table 1.2).

Organized labor employed in the United States by these industrial giants falls under the jurisdiction of the National Labor Relation Act. Rank-and-file employees of many of these firms are represented by such well-known labor organizations as the United Auto Workers (UAW), the International Brotherhood of Teamsters (IBT), and the International Association of Machinists and Aerospace Workers (IAMAW). Workers at several of these firms are not represented by

Table 1.1.
Aviation-industry employment in the United States, 2008

Segment of the industry	Total employment
Aviation/aerospace manufacturing	503,900
Air transportation	492,000

Source: Bureau of Labor Statistics

Table 1.2.

Major U.S. and international aviation/aerospace manufacturing companies, 2009

Industry component	Major manufacturers
Civil/commercial	Airbus, Boeing, Bombardier, Embraer,
General aviation	Bell Helicopter, Bombardier, Cessna, Cirrus Design, Diamond Aircraft, Eurocopter, Hawker Beechcraft, MD Helicopters, Mooney, Piper, Robinson Helicopter, Sikorsky
Military/defense	Bell Helicopter, Boeing, EADS, Eurocopter, General Dynamics, Honeywell, Lockheed Martin, , MD Helicopters, Northrop Grumman, Raytheon, Sikorsky
Space	ArianeSpace, Boeing, EADS Space, General Electric, Lockheed Martin, Northrop Grumman, Raytheon, Rockwell International, Thiokol Propulsion, Tietronix

Source: Aerospace Industries Association

any union. Labor, in this segment of the aviation industry, falls under the jurisdiction of the NLRA and not the RLA.

Air Transportation

From 2001 to 2004, a series of global and economic events resulted in air transportation employment remaining below the 2001 level. The U.S. air transportation segment provided 487,000 jobs in 2006. During this period, the U.S. air transportation sector endured terrorist attacks, a national recession, and concerns about pandemics. The impacts of these events were devastating to the U.S. commercial airline industry. However; air travel in the United States remains one of the most popular modes of transportation, expanding from 172 million passengers in 1970 to 770 million in 2007.[17]

Commercial airlines in the United States are classified on the basis of annual revenue generation. Major airlines generate more than $1 billion in annual operating revenues, national airlines from $100 million to $1 billion, and regional and commuter airlines up to $100 million. Table 1.3 lists the major and national commercial airlines (mainline); table 1.4 lists the regional airlines.

Major and national airlines. Employees of major and national airlines fall under the jurisdiction of the RLA. Airline labor unions are craft unions, meaning that no single union represents all of an airline's employees; for instance, pilots, flight attendants, and mechanics are usually represented by separate labor organizations. No hard-and-fast rule dictates which particular labor union will represent each of the employee groups or crafts, but air transport employees typically belong to one of only a handful of major labor unions. For example, most air transport pilots are represented by the ALPA, flight attendants by the Association of Flight Attendants (AFA), and mechanics by the IAMAW, although recently the Aircraft Mechanics Fraternal Association (AMFA) has been making major headway in organizing the mechanics classification. Other craft-specific air transport unions represent other classifications, such as stores personnel, customer service agents, clerical employees, dispatchers, and so on.

Case study 1.1 demonstrates the disruptive effect the dissatisfaction of one such craft union can have on an airline.

Table 1.3.
U.S. commercial airlines, 2010

Major airlines (>$1 billion in operating revenues)		National airlines ($100 million to $1 billion in operating revenues)	
AirTran	Frontier	Air Wisconsin	Pinnacle
Alaska	Hawaiian	Allegiant	PSA
American	JetBlue	Colgan	Republic
American Eagle	Northwest	Compass	Ryan
Atlantic Southeast	SkyWest	Executive	Shuttle America
Comair	Southwest	ExpressJet	Spirit
Continental	United	GoJet	Sun Country
Delta	US Airways	Horizon	USA 3000
		Mesaba	USA Jet
		Miami Air	Virgin America
		North American	World
		Omni Air	

Source: "World Airline Report," *Air Transport World,* July 2010

Table 1.4.
U.S. scheduled passenger regional airlines, July 2010

Air Midwest	Frontier Flying Service	New Mexico Airlines
AeroLitoral	GoJet Airlines	Pacific Airways
Air Sunshine	Grand Canyon Airlines	Pacific Wings
Air Wisconsin Airlines	Grant Aviation	Peninsula Airways
American Eagle Airlines	Great Lakes Aviation	Piedmont Airlines
Atlantic Southeast Airlines	Gulfstream International Airlines	Pinnacle Airlines
Bering Air	Hageland Aviation	PM Air
Cape Air	Hawaii Island Air	PSA Airlines
Chautauqua Airlines	Homer Air	Seaborne Airlines
Colgan Air	Horizon Air	Shuttle America
Comair	Jazz Air	Skyway Airlines
CommutAir	Iliamna Air Taxi	SkyWest Airlines
Compass Airlines	Kenmore Air	Taquan Air Service
ERA Aviation	Lynx Air International	Vieques Air Link
Executive Airlines	Mesa Airlines	Warbelows Air Ventures
ExpressJet Airlines	Mesaba Aviation	Wings of Alaska
Freedom Airlines	Mokulele Airlines	Wright Air
Frontier Alaska	New England Airlines	Yute Air

Source: Regional Airline Association, 2010

Case Study 1.1: CHAOS

In May 1993, Association of Flight Attendants (AFA; see fig. CS1.1.1) members at Alaska Airlines were facing a thirty-day cooling-off period after three years of negotiations and additional months of mediation under the National Mediation Board's supervision. In the past, the airline had taken a series of strikes in pursuit of its bargaining demands and seemed prepared to take another one. For years, the airline had kept all of its front-office personnel trained as flight attendants just so they could be used as replacements for striking flight attendants.[18] Thus, a traditional strike by the flight attendants clearly was doomed to fail. Historically, thousands of TWA flight attendants represented by a different union had been permanently replaced by corporate raider Carl Icahn in a disastrous traditional strike in 1986.

Figure CS 1.1.1. Logo of the Association of Flight Attendants–Communications Workers of America (AFA-CWA). Courtesy of AFA-CWA.

The Railway Labor Act (RLA) is the federal law that governs labor relations in the airline industry. The RLA is a different law from the National Labor Relations Act, which governs most other industries in the United States. The Railway Labor Act is designed to deal with the unique nature of the transportation industry. When it comes to labor disputes, the RLA, during traditional contract negotiations, calls for a process that includes a thirty-day cooling-off period prior to a strike. Once that thirty-day period is over, the RLA allows the parties involved to engage in self-help. Striking is a form of self-help, and the RLA provides strikers options that are not available to workers in other industries.

Instead of a traditional strike, the Alaska flight attendants designed and executed a unique campaign that featured surprise tactics and intermittent strikes, called CHAOS (create havoc around our system).

The flight attendants rallied around CHAOS as airline management had to deal with the fact that travelers could only count on uncertainty if they risked flying during CHAOS. Eventually, Alaska Airlines flight attendants, by executing the following summary of the CHAOS strategy, won a fair contract.

In June 1993, the cooling-off period mandated by the Railway Labor Act had expired without AFA and Alaska Airlines reaching agreement in the negotiations. Four days later, Alaska Airlines management implemented its imposed work rules. For six weeks, flight attendants were free to strike, but instead, AFA imposed a huge impact on the airline purely through the threat of CHAOS, AFA's trademarked strategy of intermittent strikes designed to maximize the impact of an industrial action and place pressure on airline management while minimizing the risk for striking flight attendants (see figs. CS1.1.2 and CS1.1.3).

CHAOS is a strategically planned and targeted set of actions designed to put pressure on airline management. Unlike a traditional strike, airline management will not be able to predict when and where flight attendants will strike. Management will not know if flight attendants will conduct a long-term mass company-wide strike, strike certain flights, or strike in certain cities, or conduct a mass strike for

Figure CS 1.1.2. AFA flight attendants picketing Northwest Airlines at the San Francisco International Airport, August 15, 2006.

Figure CS 1.1.3. Alaska Airlines 737-400 combi aircraft in Barrow, Alaska.

fifteen minutes. CHAOS may call for a mass walkout for a day or a week at a time, with no advanced notice to the airline or to the passengers.

CHAOS also allows flight attendants to continue to work and receive a paycheck right up until the strategic strike and then return to work again. By selectively striking only on layovers, at certain airports or on certain days when staffing is at a minimum and there is a lack of available flight attendants, even a single striking crewmember can shut down a flight. Targeted strikes against specific types of aircraft or specific routes on a given day make it very difficult for airline management to plan its schedule and react to CHAOS actions.

Alaska Airlines paid office personnel to fly as passengers on every flight and be ready at a moment's notice to perform flight attendants' duties in the event the working crew initiated a CHAOS strike. During this time, off-duty AFA members participated in informational picketing and other activities that included the biggest labor rally in many years. These activities kept the threat of CHAOS in the minds of management, the media, and passengers. The first CHAOS strike took place in Seattle, when three flight attendants walked off an Alaska Airlines flight just before passengers boarded the aircraft.[19] Simultaneously, a notice was faxed to the airline's front office announcing the CHAOS strike had begun on that particular flight. Twenty minutes later, the union faxed a notice to the company explaining the strike was over and that the flight attendants had offered to unconditionally return to work. Management at Alaska Airlines could not decide what to do so they suspended (with pay) the three flight attendants until management simply let them return to work a few weeks later.

A month later, another crew of Alaska flight attendants struck the last flight that night out of Las Vegas.[20] Rather than allowing these flight attendants to come back to work thirty minutes later when the intermittent strike ended, Alaska management told this crew they were "permanently replaced," much like a traditional strike. These flight attendants were placed on a recall list, which the airline was required to call from before hiring "off the street," and after about eight weeks, each of the flight attendants was recalled with full seniority. During the time they were out of work, they were fully supported through AFA's CHAOS strike donations with the pay they would have earned working as flight attendants.

A few weeks later, AFA struck five flights simultaneously in the San Francisco area.[21] Alaska Airlines management suspended these flight attendants and threatened to terminate any other flight attendant who participated in CHAOS strikes. This forced AFA to go to court, where the union's attorneys ultimately won a preliminary injunction. In the injunction ruling, the court stated the airline could not threaten, discipline, or terminate flight attendants for engaging in intermittent strikes. The only permissible action Alaska Airlines could take would be to replace the flight attendants and put them on a recall list. The suspended strikers were ordered reinstated with full back pay. AFA also financially supported these strikers during the time of their suspension through the CHAOS strike donations.

While more CHAOS strikes were anticipated, Alaska Airlines' CEO made a new bargaining proposal. The company offered to enter into a new bargaining agreement with AFA that included as much as a 60 percent raise and addressed all of the other issues sought by the Alaska flight attendants during the campaign for a new contract. Within an hour, a tentative agreement was signed. The flight attendants later ratified the new agreement by an overwhelming margin. After striking only seven flights in a period of nine months, AFA had executed the most successful strike in airline history without financially harming a single union member.

In the years since the Alaska Airlines CHAOS strike, flight attendants at numerous other AFA carriers have used CHAOS or the threat of CHAOS to increase their bargaining leverage and win favorable contracts. America West, AirTran, and US Airways all settled with AFA by the end of a thirty-day cooling-off period in the 1990s.[22] The threat of CHAOS forced management at each of those airlines to settle on terms favorable to the flight attendants, without a single flight ever being struck. In 2002, AFA flight attendants at Midwest Express (now Midwest Airlines) completed a cooling-off period without reaching a new bargaining agreement. After three weeks of a CHAOS campaign and on the eve of CHAOS strikes, management agreed to terms that were ratified by the flight attendants. United Airlines flight attendants used the threat of CHAOS to leverage their negotiations during the airline's bankruptcy, succeeding in doubling the value of the replacement retirement plan management had proposed.[23]

Flight attendants at Northwest Airlines, locked in bankruptcy negotiations, deployed a CHAOS campaign days after joining AFA in July 2006. Days later, union negotiators concluded a new tentative agreement with millions of dollars in improvements but which was voted down by a narrower margin. AFA continued preparations for CHAOS strikes at Northwest pending the outcome of negotiations and litigation surrounding the case.[24]

The bankruptcy court ruled in favor of the union, denying the strike injunction sought by management. But on appeal, the federal district court and the court of appeals ruled that workers under the Railway Labor Act cannot strike in response to rejection of a collective bargaining agreement in bankruptcy, effectively preempting the threat of CHAOS

strikes.[25] Northwest and AFA returned to negotiations and reached a new tentative agreement, which was narrowly ratified by the flight attendants on May 29, 2007.[26] The new contract provided Northwest with $195 million in annual cuts through 2011 and secured a $182 million equity claim for the flight attendants before the airline's exit from bankruptcy.[27]

Organized in 1945, the AFA is the world's largest flight attendant union, representing more than fifty-five thousand flight attendants at twenty airlines. In 2004, the AFA merged with the seven-hundred thousand-member Communications Workers of America (CWA) to form an affiliate of the nine-million-member AFL-CIO.

Although the IAMAW is highly visible in these classifications, so are the International Brotherhood of Teamsters, the Transport Workers Union (TWU), and several of the larger carrier-specific unions, such as the Allied Pilots Association (APA) representing the pilots at American Airlines and the Southwest Airlines Pilots' Association (SWAPA) representing the flight crews of Southwest Airlines (see fig. 1.4). No matter which union organization they belong to, employees of the major and national airlines fall under the legal framework of the RLA.

Foreign-flag carriers are not considered part of the U.S. aviation community. They do, however, employ a significant number of U.S. citizens in gateway cities, and with the advent of open-skies bilateral agreements, employment at other U.S. locations is on the increase. Although regulation of such airlines resides in their home countries' air transport regulatory legislation, they must obey U.S. FAA air regulations if they seek entry to U.S. airports. They are also subject to U.S. labor regulations and to other employment regulations that govern their workers based in the United States. When union representation is sought on U.S. soil by employees of these foreign carriers, the tenets of the RLA apply. For example, clerical employees

Figure 1.4. Classified as a U.S. major airline, Southwest Airlines is a low-cost carrier based in Dallas, Texas. In 2010, Southwest was the largest airline in the United States by number of passengers carried domestically per year and maintained the sixth-largest fleet (more than 550 aircraft) among the world's commercial airlines. Southwest operates more than thirty-one-hundred flights a day. One of the world's most profitable airlines, Southwest in 2010 posted a profit for the thirty-seventh consecutive year. Courtesy of www.erikhenne.com.

of Air India, Alitalia, Egypt Air, and Mexicana are represented by the IAMAW; El Al (the Israeli airline) mechanics are also represented by the IAMAW.

Regional and commuter airlines. The regional and commuter airline industry has a relatively short history of operation in comparison to the overall aviation industry in the United States. Although the CAB had long exempted a class of small commercial air taxis from the requirements for Section 401 certification, it was not until 1969 that the board recognized the growing need to establish a class of small scheduled airlines; thus, the commuter airlines were born.[28] In that year, the CAB amended part 298 of the Civil Aeronautics Act to allow airlines that operated at least five scheduled round-trips per week between two or more points to receive exemptions from 401 economic regulation. To meet CAB requirements, such carriers, called Part 298 operators, could not operate aircraft exceeding 12,500 pounds maximum gross weight, which effectively limited the size of aircraft to

those seating nineteen passengers. These passenger and load limitations were eased over the years, allowing aircraft seating up to thirty passengers by 1972. Passage of airline deregulation in 1978 established a new classification for these commuters, classifying them as regional airlines and permitting these carriers to operate aircraft having sixty seats or less.

Today, about seventy U.S. regional airlines (regionals) play an increasingly important role in the national air transportation system. They continue to provide new city pairs, increase frequencies on existing routes, and transfer passengers from their mainline partners. The vast majority of airports in North America receive scheduled service from regional airlines. In 1990, 811 airports were served by regionals; 71 percent of these airports were exclusively dependent on their service needs. At that time, the major airlines served only 32 percent, or 275 airports.[29] At the end of 2007, 666 U.S. commercial airports were served by regional airlines, with 465 airports served exclusively by regional airlines.[30]

In 1990, regional airlines employed about thirty-five thousand people.[31] By the end of 2007, regional airlines employed approximately sixty thousand workers.[32] Like employees of major and national air carriers, these workers fall under the jurisdiction of the RLA. It is difficult to determine in general whether these employees are represented by a labor union, both because of the diversity of the industry itself and because of the number of mergers and code-sharing arrangements that characterize the regional airline industry.

In 1991, forty-two of the top fifty regional carriers, which accounted for 96 percent of the regional service for that year, had formalized code-sharing agreements and had begun to use the two-letter code of a larger airline to list their flights.[33] By late 2005, regional and major/national airlines had fifty-three code-sharing agreements between them, varying from outright ownership by major or national carriers to partial ownership by major airlines to pure marketing alliances devoid of any ownership by major airlines.

The regional airline industry's integration into the U.S. air transportation system and its importance within that system are growing. The importance of regional airlines is expected to increase in the future because the growth that characterized the 1980s has continued throughout the 1990s and into the twenty-first century. In 2008, one in four domestic airline passengers traveled on regionals. Operating more than twenty-four hundred aircraft, the regional fleet constitutes about one-third of the U.S. commercial airline fleet.[34] As the regionals continue to integrate with the majors and the level of industry concentration increases, it is likely that employees of the regionals will be represented by the same unions that represent employees working in the same crafts for the regionals' major partners or parents.

General Aviation

An important, yet largely overlooked component of the aviation industry is general aviation. There is no legal definition for the term *general aviation*. Rather, it is generally used to denote a type of aircraft or aviation activities. The term often has a negative context when it is used to make inferences concerning all segments of the aviation industry (except for air carrier and military operations).[35] It encompasses a diverse range of aviation activities, from ab initio flight training to the intercontinental jet transportation of executives and public officials. General aviation includes fixed-base operators, business and executive transport, and operations involving helicopters and light aircraft. It includes not only recreational pilots but also the emergency air ambulance and the police officer or radio newsperson observing traffic.

In number of aircraft, number of pilots, and number of airports and communities served,

general aviation is the largest segment of aviation. It is important not only as a key component of the aviation system but also as a contributor to national, state, and local economies. It provides aviation services that commercial airlines cannot provide. The production and sale of general aviation aircraft, avionics, and other aviation equipment, along with the provision of support services (flight schools, fixed-base operators, finance, and insurance), make the general aviation industry an important contributor to the nation's economy.[36]

General aviation is the dominant force in the sky, accounting for 92 percent of the civil aircraft fleet, 81 percent of civil operations (departures), and almost 60 percent of the total hours flown by the U.S. civil aircraft fleet.[37] However, it is largely unnoticed and unappreciated. Yet, general aviation supports 1.3 million jobs and more than $100 billion of total economic activity in the United States each year. These jobs range from pilot to mechanic to dispatcher to executive chef.[38]

The estimated thirty-six-hundred-plus fixed-base operators are the "front line" or "grass roots" of aviation.[39] They are the privately owned-and-operated businesses that offer a wide range of services, including aircraft sales and service, maintenance, and fuel; aircraft storage; and a variety of other support services to pilots of general aviation. Of the estimated thirty-six hundred fixed-base operators, approximately three out of four fall in the category of small fixed-base operators, or mom-and-pop shops. There are several large, multimillion-dollar fixed-base operators (such as MillionAir, Signature Flight Support), but even they are small when compared to a commercial airline operation. Most, if not all, employees of fixed-base operators work as "employees at will" or as independent contractors, and the vast majority are not represented by any labor union.

The same is true for pilots and other personnel of corporate flight departments and other business aviation operations. It appears unlikely that any of these professions will be pursued by organized labor in the foreseeable future. Although general aviation plays a critical role in the nation's air transportation system, it remains largely invisible to the general public. Should any unions seek to organize the general aviation segment, any activities would be governed by the NLRA, except for common carriers by air (such as air charter operations conducted under the provisions of FAR (Federal Aviation Regulations in 14 C.F.R, Part 135).

Public-Sector Aviation

Approximately a hundred thousand federal employees are directly involved in aviation. Some of these, such as FAA inspectors and air traffic controllers, are federal employees who are members of public unions. Federal employees, union or otherwise, do not fall under the jurisdiction of either the RLA or the NLRA. Rather, all federal employee labor relations issues are governed by the Civil Service Reform Act of 1978. This enabling legislation established the Federal Labor Relations Authority (FLRA) to oversee most civil service labor relations matters. Additionally, thousands of others, such as airport management and operations personnel, are employed by state and local governments. State and local civil service employees working in the transportation sector are governed by their state's or city's version of civil service regulations.

Federal Civil Service Labor Law

Although not directly related to the air transport sector, any discussion of federal labor legislation would be incomplete without an examination of federal civil service labor laws. This section provides a brief overview of the history of the enabling legislation and processes and procedures used by the government and the various public union organizations in the civil service collective bargaining environment.

About fifteen million people are employed in all capacities by the three branches of government in the United States. Approximately one-third of these government employees are members of public unions. Government organizations in the United States use two different personnel-appointment-and-management systems. The first is political appointment and election. The second is objective-merit-determination systems.

Political Appointment

Political appointment and election have a long history in the United States at the federal, state, and local levels. No other country in the world elects or appoints as many of its administrators as does the United States.[40] The political-appointment system dates back to colonial times and was known as the spoils system under President Andrew Jackson. Jackson believed that to the victor go the spoils and that patronage appointments were a practical and appropriate way of rewarding loyal political supporters. The political-appointment system still exists for some federal positions and for many state positions. But the patronage system caused such a serious decline in administrative ethics, efficiency, and performance during its heyday that politicians were forced to heed the calls for reform of the system.

The Merit System

The Pendleton Act. In 1883, the Pendleton Act introduced the merit system, an alternative method of recruitment. This legislation established a systematic procedure for hiring and employing all categories of civil servants. The merit principle has continued to flourish and today embraces over 90 percent of all federal positions, including employees of the Department of Transportation, the FAA, the National Transportation Safety Board, the National Mediation Board, and the National Labor Relations Board. In addition, increasing numbers of state and local government employees are hired and managed under the merit system, including employees of state and local aviation agencies and local airports.[41] Today, approximately two-thirds of the states have merit systems that cover most of their employees.

The public personnel system adopted under the Pendleton Act involved the selection of public employees based on open competitive examinations (civil service exams), the establishment of tenure (job protection), and the creation of strict job classifications and procedures for advancement and promotion. The act remained in force until 1978, when reform issues were addressed.

The Civil Service Reform Act of 1978. The Civil Service Reform Act constitutes the centerpiece of present federal personnel policy. The act governs federal employer and employee labor relations and specifically declares labor organizations and collective bargaining in the civil service to be in the public interest. The principal achievements of the act were the separation of many of the managerial, political, and legal aspects of federal employment practices and procedures. These functions, once administered by a single organization, the Civil Service Commission, are now divided among three separate personnel organizations.

- *Office of Personnel Management (OPM).* The agency is charged with establishing the rules governing federal civilian employment procedures and practices and reports directly to the president of the United States.
- *Merit System Protection Board (MSPB).* The Reorganization Plan No. 2 of 1978, codified by the Civil Service Reform Act of 1978, established the MSPB, which assumed the employee appeals function of the Civil Service Commission and is charged with resolving all appellate and quasi-judicial issues arising from federal employment procedures and practices. This board deals with the legal concerns of federal personnel management. It decides most complaints and appeals, issues regulations regarding the nature and scope of its review, and establishes time limits for settlement of appeals. It also orders corrective and disciplinary action against employers or departments and agencies, if required.

- *Federal Labor Relations Authority (FLRA).* The Civil Service Reform Act of 1978 created the FLRA, which oversees the process of collective bargaining in the federal sector. The FLRA represents the federal government's consolidated approach to its labor-management relations and makes a variety of rulings concerning fair and unfair labor practices and those aspects of employment that are allowable for collective bargaining. It has the authority to resolve questions concerning the representation of federal employees by labor unions and can play a role in the resolution of disputes between the unions and government.

The Rise of Public-Sector Unions

In the early years of the twentieth century, labor unions in the railroad industry flourished under the protection of the Railway Labor Act of 1926. During the 1930s and 1940s, private-sector unionization also prospered under the protection of the National Labor Relations Act. These unions sought job security, higher wages, improved benefits, grievance procedures, arbitration rights, and more important, recognition as participants in the decision-making process. Whereas at this same time, many public employees already had similar, if not better working conditions, unionization probably held little or no attraction for them. In point of fact, lobbying efforts for wage/salary and benefit improvement seemed more plausible. The successes of private unions, however, began to surpass the public employees' ability to lobby, and changes in their job classifications and numbers gave an impetus to public sector, or governmental, unionization.

In the private sector, wages and benefits improved year after year, and job security was increased through the establishment of grievance and arbitration procedures in collective bargaining agreements. The organized worker also became cognizant of the respect a union could demand from an employer. Because strikes were protected under the act, the employer did not hold all the bargaining strength.

Public employees discovered that lobbying efforts alone could not provide them with the controls and benefits of collective bargaining. Their swelling ranks made the lobbying process increasingly cumbersome and, as David Lewin and Shirley Goldenberg contend, contributed to the rise of public-sector unionism.[42] In an article published in the *Monthly Labor Review,* one author is more definitive about the rationale for the insistent nature of the labor movement in government.[43] The late U.S. labor leader Jerry Wurf was president of the American Federation of State, County, and Municipal Employees (AFSCME). Wurf squarely places blame on the civil service systems: "It is the labor-management inadequacy of the civil service system that has been a prime cause of the remarkable thrust of union organization among public employees in recent years."[44]

The Sovereignty Doctrine

When considering the lessening of total management rights at the recognition of a union, a distinct difference is involved between that of the government and that of private industry.

Such difference has to do with the consideration of authority and resistance. In the private, nongovernmental sector, the key to employers' resistance to collective bargaining was, and still is, the desire to protect their private-property rights. Both the Railway Labor Act and the National Labor Relations Act tried to balance the employer's private-property rights against the employee's right to organize and to bargain collectively. Although the purpose of each of the foregoing acts was to place employees in an equal bargaining position, employers still held all rights not reduced or eliminated by the collective bargaining process.

In the public sector, governments were able to resist collective bargaining because of the doctrine of sovereignty. According to Henry Campbell Black, *sovereignty* is defined as "the supreme, absolute, and uncontrollable power by which an independent state is governed."[45] In a democracy, the source of that supreme power is the people who have vested their government with rights and responsibilities as caretakers of that power. The sovereignty doctrine requires that the government exercise its power unfettered by any force other than the people, all the people. Collective bargaining was seen as a threat to that sovereignty doctrine if government was to share decision-making authority with employees. Obviously, decisions made at the collective bargaining table would affect the way government provides services and the amount those services would cost the taxpayer. Wouldn't it be a nightmare if a member of the military, for example, was permitted to use a job description as a reason not to "charge that machine-gun nest"? Or, members of the air force could refuse to fly missions because they exceeded prescribed hours of operation? In many areas of operation, the sovereignty principle must be paramount.

Over time, however, the doctrine has been eroded, and the Supreme Court has allowed citizens to claim civil rights, torts, and contract violations against state and local governments, subjecting such institutions to monetary damages and remedial actions, thus minimizing the sovereignty exclusive rights. The establishment of governmental unions by the federal government has become one of those areas in which the sovereignty issue has become soft.

Executive Orders for Public-Sector Collective Bargaining

In January 1962, the President's Task Force on Employee-Management Relations reported that one-third of the federal employees belonged to labor organizations. It recommended that the government officially acknowledge this fact and respond affirmatively to employees' desire for collective bargaining. President John F. Kennedy signed Executive Order (E.O.) 10988, which recognized the rights of federal employees to join or to refrain from joining labor organizations. In addition, it granted recognition to those labor organizations selected by employees and detailed bargaining subjects. This executive order can be cited as having established the framework for labor-management relations in the federal government.

What is important about the Kennedy order of 1962 is the lightning effect it had on organizing drives among federal, state, and municipal employees. The order served as an entrée to the organization of public workers, much as Wagner had done more than a quarter of century prior in the private sector.

The effect of Executive Order 10988 was to send public sector union-membership rolls soaring. In his book *The Birth of Modern Public Employee Unions*, Robert Wechsler indicates that before 1962, only 26 union or association units in the executive branch of the federal government had union shops, and they represented only 19,000 workers.[46] Six years after the Kennedy order, 2,305 bargaining units held a total membership of 1.4 million employees. A number of unions represented federal workers, the largest being the American Federation of Government Employees (AFGE). From 1962 to 1972, the AFGE grew from 84,000 members to 621,000. The American Postal Workers Union (APWU) and the National Association of Letter Carriers (NALC) also experienced growth in that period.

For state and local public employees, the 1962 Kennedy order also spawned growth in unionization, although the order did not apply to them directly. The fact that union membership grew, however, did not mean that all state or local governments recognized or bargained with unions.

An interesting side note is that the right to organize under Executive Order 10988 was granted to federal civilian employees. However, the head of an agency could determine that a bureau or office was primarily performing intelligence, investigative, or security functions, and the employees of that bureau or office could be excluded from the executive order for national security reasons.

A Brief Comparison: NLRA and Executive Order 10988

Under the National Labor Relations Act, a labor organization receiving a majority vote of the members of the bargaining unit gains exclusive recognition. Under Executive Order 10988, exclusive recognition could be gained in the same manner, but two other types of recognition were also extended.

The first granted formal recognition if there was no exclusive representative for the bargaining unit and the group seeking recognition had at least 10 percent of the employees in the unit. Such an organization would represent only its members.

The second type consisted of informal recognition of an employee organization that did not meet the majority vote or 10 percent of membership qualifications. Albeit a part of the executive order, this system generated a great deal of confusion. Under such an arrangement, an agency might have to deal with two unions representing the same class of employees. For example, 10 percent of the service personnel could gain formal recognition, whereas a different 8 percent could claim informal recognition. The agency would be negotiating with two unions consisting of 18 percent of one class of employee.

In the private sector, bargaining subjects protected by the act included wages, hours, and conditions of employment. Under Executive Order 10988, bargaining subjects are limited. Employees or their unions could not mandate negotiations on economic issues. A management-rights clause reserved the government's power to direct and discipline employees. A grievance procedure could not result in binding arbitration.

A major deficiency in Executive Order 10988 was its failure to define a central authority to determine bargaining-unit recognition and to resolve disputes. Many decisions were left to agency heads, who were the immediate employers of the labor organization's members. The most significant difference between the National Labor Relations Act and Executive Order 10988 was the right to engage in work stoppages. Strikes are specifically denied to public labor organizations. Such is the nature of dealing with the sovereign.

Executive Order 11491

While successful in establishing a beachhead for union activity within the federal government, it would be President Richard M. Nixon's order, effective in January 1970, that would elevate union organization to the next level.

Executive Order 11491 abolished the types or union recognition identified in Executive Order 10988. Rather than identifying informal and formal union recognition, it provided instead that any union could gain recognition similarly to that of the Wagner Act. In other words, exclusive recognition was dependent on receiving majority recognition of the employees in a bargaining unit through a secret-ballot process.

While the right to strike and federal employees' proscription from strikes remained an issue with the unions, Executive Order 11491 established an impartial Federal Services Impasse Panel to settle disputes arising during contract negotiations. Decisions of this panel were final and binding. For the time being, this new system for arbitration neutrals seemed equitable and acceptable. Executive Order 11491 would lay the foundation for the more liberal Federal Labor Relations Authority established in 1978.

The Civil Service Reform Act of 1978

Currently, Title VII of the Civil Service Reform Act of 1978 and Reorganization Plan No. 2 of 1978 govern federal employee labor relations. Title VII, known as the Federal Labor Relations Act, is modeled after the National Labor Relations Act. Central authority is placed in a three-member panel, the Federal Labor Relations Authority. This panel oversees labor-management relations within the federal government; its three members are appointed by the president of the United States. The president also appoints a general counsel empowered to investigate alleged unfair labor practices and to file and prosecute complaints.

The FLRA oversees creation of bargaining units, conducts elections, decides representation cases, determines unfair labor practices, and seeks enforcement of its decisions in the federal courts. The Federal Service Impasse Panel was continued by the act and provides assistance in resolving negotiation impasses. The unfair labor practice provision of Title VII generally mirrors the unfair labor practice provision in legislation for private employers and employees. The government is prohibited from the following practices:

- Restraint and coercion in the exercise of their organizational rights
- Encouragement or discouragement of union membership
- Sponsorship of labor organizations
- Refusal to bargain in good faith with a recognized organization
- Refusal to cooperate in impasse procedures
- Discipline of a union member who files a complaint

- Enforcement of a new regulation that conflicts with an existent collective bargaining agreement

The union is prohibited from the following practices:

- Interference with an employee's right to organize or to refrain from organizing
- Discrimination against or causing the employer to discriminate against employees because of union activity
- Refusal to cooperate in impasse procedures
- Refusal to bargain in good faith
- Calling for or engaging in a work stoppage, strike, or slowdown

Unlike private-sector labor laws, Title VII mandates inclusion of a grievance procedure with binding arbitration as a final step in all federal collective bargaining agreements. Accordingly, any negotiated grievance procedure referred to will:

- Be fair and simple
- Provide for expeditious processing
- Include procedures that:
  - Assure an exclusive representative the right, in its own behalf or on behalf of any employee in the unit represented by the exclusive representative, to present and process grievances
  - Assure such an employee the right to present a grievance on the employee's own behalf and assure the exclusive representative the right to be present during the grievance proceeding
  - Provide that any grievance not satisfactorily settled under the negotiated grievance procedure shall be subject to binding arbitration, which may be invoked by either the exclusive representative or the agency

Title VII also codifies presidential policies toward federal labor-management relations.

National Partnership Council, 1993

In 1993, President William Jefferson Clinton enacted Executive Order 12871 as part of the reengineering of government programs. It was hailed as a significant and fundamental change in federal-sector labor-management relations. The goal was to change the relationship and alter the process by which the managers and unions reached decisions. A team of federal managers and union representatives worked on the plan. It created the National Partnership Council (NPC) to advise the president on labor-management issues. The NPC was made up of union leaders, representatives from the Federal Labor Relations Board, the Federal Mediation and Conciliation Service, and executive-branch directors.

The executive order directed each agency to establish labor-management partnerships at appropriate levels to change the way government operates. The 1993 NPC allowed federal unions to organize new bargaining units and increase membership, as well as design and implement methods of increasing productivity. In 2001, however, President George W. Bush issued Executive Order 13203, which abolished the NPC and the labor-management partnerships. The Bush order ended a period of federal union growth (61 percent) of all federal workers and 80 percent of all federal employees eligible for union representation. This change came at a critical time for federal unions; over half of their membership would retire before 2010. According to Robert Tobias, this seems to imply that the unions will need to appeal to younger workers, 70 percent of whom work in "knowledge" positions, or the white-collar industry.[47] In general, this caliber of worker has been reluctant to join the union movement and has not been an easy target for the unions' organization campaigns.

Public-Sector Labor Unions

Until the 1960s and the Great Society program of President Lyndon Baines Johnson, collective bargaining in the public sector was considered antithetical to a constitutional democracy. It was considered absurd that organized public employees could bargain with the government as coequals or that matters of public personnel policy would be determined in any forum other than the legislative, executive, or judicial. In particular, strikes were feared because they represented a breakdown of the public order and, consequently, could lead to chaos. Many states considered collective bargaining a threat to their sovereignty, and the federal government had no general policy or practice for collective bargaining with its employees.[48]

These attitudes toward collective bargaining changed with remarkable rapidity. In large part, the rise of public collective bargaining has been related to the growth of public employment and the political pressure exerted by the unions. Many unions view the public sector as a promising recruiting ground from which they can draw new members to offset the decline in union membership in the private sector. The 1960s and 1970s were times of unprecedented growth in public-sector unionism. Today, public-sector collective bargaining is found throughout the federal government and in most states. It does, however, remain a patchwork of practices and procedures. As yet, no comprehensive law covers all aspects and levels of government unionism. Despite these nonuniform practices, a basic bargaining pattern has emerged in the public sector, patterned after private-sector procedures.

Public-Sector Collective Bargaining

The basic public-sector pattern for collective bargaining is as follows. Civil servants in the same occupations and classifications organize into bargaining units through an election or through submission of union membership cards to the appropriate government agency. Exclusive recognition of a union occurs when a majority of the employees in that bargaining unit want rep-resentation by a single union that will bargain for all employees in that unit. Precisely what can and cannot be bargained over is called the *scope of bargaining*. It may be relatively comprehensive and include wages, benefits, hours, position classification, promotion procedures, overtime assignments, and working conditions. Or it may be very restrictive and confined largely to issues of discipline and the issuance of safety equipment, coffee breaks, and parking spaces. The scope of bargaining is composed of:

- Items over which bargaining is mandatory
- Items over which bargaining is permitted
- Items over which bargaining is prohibited

An impasse results when labor and management cannot agree on matters that are subject to mandatory bargaining. Resolution of the impasse can take many forms, including mediation, fact-finding, and arbitration.

Several limitations placed on public-sector labor relations make the collective bargaining process quite different from private-sector practices. Most notable are serious restrictions on the scope of bargaining and the virtual prohibition on strikes. Many governmental agencies have enacted strong management rights clauses that severely limit the items over which collective bargaining can take place. These limitations often encompass the fundamental conditions of work. For example, in some agencies and jurisdictions, schoolteachers cannot bargain over the number of pupils in a classroom. At the federal level, most non–postal workers are prohibited from bargaining over wages and hours. These restrictions are the legacy of constitutional sovereignty—the government remains the supreme representative of the citizenry, including those represented by a labor union.

In addition to the limitations on the scope of bargaining, there is a virtual prohibition on the right to strike in the federal government. In 1981, the Professional Air Traffic Controllers (PATCO) challenged this prohibition when its members went on strike August 3, 1981, over working conditions, including better pay and a thirty-two-hour workweek (see fig. 1.5).[49] In doing so, the union violated a 1955 law that banned strikes by government unions. President Ronald Wilson Reagan declared the PATCO strike a peril to national safety and ordered the strikers back to work under the terms of the Taft-Hartley Act of 1947. Following their refusal to return to work, Reagan fired the 11,359 striking air traffic controllers who had ignored the order, and he permanently banned them from federal service. In the end, Reagan sent the PATCO controllers and the entire public labor force a sobering message: "There is a law that federal unions cannot strike against their employers, the people of the United States. What they did was terminate their own employment by quitting."[50]

State and Local Government Laws

Title VII of the Civil Service Reform Act of 1978 does not cover state and local employees,

Figure 1.5. Some of the more than twelve thousand members of the Professional Air Traffic Controllers Organization (PATCO) who walked off the job on August 3, 1981. The strike set off a chain of events that would redefine labor relations in America. Two days later, President Ronald Reagan fired thousands of the unionized air traffic controllers for illegally going on strike, an event that marked a turning point in labor relations in America with lasting repercussions. Courtesy of Professional Air Traffic Controllers Organization.

whose collective bargaining rights, if granted, come from the individual state where situated. According to Arthur Sloane and Fred Whitney, virtually all states have sanctioned collective bargaining for at least some type of public workers.[51] And forty states have enacted legislation conferring protection upon all state and local employees. More than two-thirds of the states have enacted legislation granting public-sector collective bargaining rights to some groups, such as teachers, police, and firefighters. Local, county, and municipal governments may also adopt collective bargaining laws or, by practice, recognize and bargain with employee organizations.

Although state and local laws differ as to particulars, some patterns do emerge. Legislation is more favorable to collective bargaining in the northern, northeastern, midwestern, and far-western parts of the United States. The sunbelt states located along the lower Atlantic coast, the southeast, the southwest, and the southwestern Rocky Mountain states generally do not have comprehensive public-sector labor laws.

State legislation usually includes bargaining over wages, hours, terms of employment, and working conditions. Unfair labor practices and limits on or prohibitions of the right to strike also are legislated. The bargaining obligation is enforced by an administrative agency, and procedures are established should there be an impasse.

A developing campaign to include state and municipal employees under federal legislation was substantially undermined by the U.S. Supreme Court in a 1976 decision of *National League of Cities v. Usery* (426 U.S. 833). That case reconfirmed the specific state's sovereignty over its own employees and denied that the commerce power of the federal government could be invoked to regulate that relationship. A recent study of the growth of teacher bargaining concluded that although teacher bargaining in large cities typically starts before collective bargaining laws are passed, the passage of the laws spurs subsequent union growth.

Like the federal government, all but eight states (Alaska, Hawaii, Minnesota, Montana, Oregon, Pennsylvania, Vermont, and Wisconsin) have absolute prohibitions against the right of public workers to strike or create work stoppages of any kind. Employee bargaining units that violate these restrictions generally face statutory and court-ordered penalties. Although not always effective, these restrictions raise the costs of strikes and stoppages to the unions and the employees and deter such activities. Many people question what purpose and use a public union is without the right to strike. George Meany, former president of the American Federation of Labor and Congress of Industrial Organizations (AFL-CIO), once stated, "[A] free and collective bargaining system contemplates that at the end of the road there can be a strike. . . . If you don't like that idea, then take out the word free."[52] In the absence of the right to strike, other means of resolving disputes are required. Thus, arbitration, mediation, and fact-finding are endemic to federal civil labor relations procedures. They are also part and parcel of the RLA and the NLRA but to a lesser degree.

2. The Violent Beginnings of U.S. Labor Law

The railroads and airlines are intertwined in both background and regulation. Their evolutions in the United States parallel each other. Thomas Moore comments, "The current situation of railways is only intelligible in the context of history."[1] This holds for the air industry as well.

The first nationwide economic regulation of transportation in the United States occurred in the railway sector. Because of such attention to the railways from a regulatory standpoint, initial airline labor regulations, one would assume, would also follow. Oftentimes, the regulatory aspects coincided with activity commencing in the economic environment.

Most historians trace the American labor movement to the early 1800s. During the 1820s and 1830s, carpenters, masons, painters, and other skilled workers established citywide organizations to obtain better pay.[2] The objective of these early organizations was to uphold the price of labor against the encroachment of the employers.[3] These associations focused on disputes involving working hours and apprenticeship programs designed to ensure the hiring of members of a particular trade. The first organizing efforts took place among groups of isolated workers in Philadelphia in the late 1820s.

In actions not unanticipated—because of the adversarial relationship between management and labor at this time—workers agreed to a certain wage level and pledged not to work for any employer who refused to pay this amount.

Proving themselves willing to strike, although usually for only a short time; the citywide organizations were both aggressive and quite successful at achieving their goals.[4] Employers and the courts viewed early trade-union attempts as common-law criminal conspiracies whose activities damaged commerce and trade.

Early Judicial Actions

Under common law, such actions as the withholding of services by employees were deemed illegal conspiracies, and workers were often prosecuted when strikes occurred. Under both English common law and statutory law, the very existence of unions was unlawful. Because English law provided the precedent for the early American courts, such an attitude became prevalent in the U.S. system.[5] The success of employers in resisting union organizing efforts was most pronounced in the Federal Society of Cordwainers decision, in which cordwainers (shoemakers) in a strike in 1806 were found guilty of joining a conspiracy in restraint of trade. In the cordwainers decision *Commonwealth v. Pullis*, Mayor's Court of Philadelphia (1806), the justice stated, "The rule in this case is pregnant with sound sense and all the authorities are clear on the subject. Hawkins, the greatest authority on criminal law, has laid it down, that a combination to maintain one another, carrying a particular object, whether true or false, is criminal."[6] This decision established the conspiracy doctrine by which courts could forestall unionization activities whenever they deemed such activities illegal.

Although local unions achieved minor victories despite the cordwainers decision, and the economic depression in the 1830s crushed much of the labor movement, the fledgling labor movement was not vanquished. As movement and growth continued, the unions found themselves facing another legal adversary, the state courts.

Case study: Commonwealth v. Hunt. The decisions of these courts often went against early unionization attempts until March 1842 when the Massachusetts Supreme Judicial Court, led by Chief Justice Lemuel Shaw (see fig. 2.1), ruled in *Commonwealth v. Hunt* that trade unions were lawful and had the right to organize and that strikes for a closed shop were legal.[7] Although Justice Shaw's decision was not binding outside Massachusetts, judges in other states accorded it substantial weight as a precedent, and his decision marked an important liberalization of judicial tolerance for union activities. This landmark decision cleared the way for labor unions to operate freely in the commonwealth.[8]

In *Commonwealth v. Hunt,* the discernible intent of the supreme judicial court was to encourage all those engaged in the same occupation to become members of the labor union and that joining this organization was not a criminal conspiracy under the law. Before this decision, based on *Commonwealth v. Pullis,* labor unions attempting to create a unionized workplace could be charged with conspiracy.[9] So, in effect in *Commonwealth v. Hunt,* the unions were asking the court to interpret the meaning of *criminal conspiracy,* which Shaw's court defined as "a combination of two or more persons, by some concerted action, to accomplish some criminal or unlawful purpose, or to accomplish some purpose, not in itself criminal or unlawful, by criminal or unlawful means."

The rule of law determined by the court in *Commonwealth v. Hunt* and subsequent

Figure 2.1. Lemuel Shaw (1781–1861), a chief justice of the Massachusetts Supreme Court and a major legal figure of the early industrial revolution in the United States. In his thirty years of service on the bench, Shaw handed down more than two thousand opinions, many of which are still cited in the courts today. In *Commonwealth v. Hunt,* he established a revolutionary precedent by ruling that it was not criminal for a combination of employees to refuse to work for an employer who hires nonunion labor.

determinations has been that a labor union is not a criminal conspiracy if it is formed for lawful purposes and if it employs allowable means to achieve its purposes and that it is not unlawful for a labor organization to seek to achieve security by suggesting all in the same occupation to be members and by refusing to work for a person who employs nonmembers.

Though judges throughout the decade would become more anti-union, *Commonwealth v. Hunt* freed the state's unions from the prevailing judicial application of the law of criminal conspiracy to labor actions. In the twentieth century, the opinion has been hailed as the foremost nineteenth-century ruling on labor unions because it freed them from the risk of criminal prosecution for conspiracy. Since this decision, common-law criminal conspiracy has never played an important part in the control of labor unions by the U.S. court system, and the right of American workers to organize has not been seriously questioned.[10]

Case study 2.1 more fully examines this landmark decision.

Case Study 2.1: *Commonwealth v. Hunt*

The Boston Journeymen Bootmakers' Society was an early trade union of journeymen bootmakers (a journeyman is one who has learned a trade or craft through successful completion of an apprenticeship and is competent and qualified for employment in that trade or craft). John Hunt was the principal leader of the union. Union members, in an effort to create a closed or union shop, agreed not to work for any employer who employed or continued to employ nonmembers after the union notified the employer to discharge the nonunion employee.

Journeyman bootmaker Jeremiah Horne was not a union member, but his employer, master bootmaker Isaac B. Wait's shop, was otherwise fully staffed with members of the union although no collective bargaining agreement was yet in place. Horne did not have an employment contract, either. When the union notified Wait to discharge Horne, Wait did so rather than risk a strike or walkout by his other workers. Horne then complained to the district attorney, who, on behalf of the people of the Commonwealth of Massachusetts and in keeping with the prevailing understanding of the law at the time, brought criminal-conspiracy charges against Hunt and other union leaders.

Hunt was convicted at trial to a jury and appealed to the Massachusetts Supreme Judicial Court. The issue on appeal was whether the union's activities by causing Horne's employer to discharge him from employment constituted a criminal conspiracy.

Writing for the court in its decision, Chief Justice Shaw summarized the controlling legal definition of *conspiracy* as "a combination of two or more persons, by some concerted action, to accomplish some criminal or unlawful purpose, or to accomplish some purpose, not in itself criminal or unlawful, by criminal or unlawful means." Excerpts from the reasoning of this landmark decision merit reading today, over a century and a half after the writing, for what it reveals of the court's humane consideration of the legal right of employees to act collectively and limits on that right:

> The manifest intent of the association is, to induce all those engaged in the same occupation to become members of it. Such a purpose is not unlawful. It would give them a power which might be exerted for useful and honorable purposes, or for dangerous and pernicious ones. . . . Such an association might be used to afford each other assistance in times of poverty, sickness and distress; or to raise their intellectual, moral and social condition; or to make improvement in their art; or for other proper purposes. Or the association might be designed for purposes of oppression and injustice. But in order to charge all those, who become members of an association, with the guilt of a criminal conspiracy, it must be averred and proved that the actual, if not the avowed object of the association, was criminal. An association may be formed, the declared objects of which are innocent and laudable, and yet they may have secret articles, or an agreement communicated only to the members, by which they are banded together for purposes injurious to the peace of society or the rights of its members. Such would undoubtedly be a criminal conspiracy, on proof of the fact, however meritorious and praiseworthy the declared objects might be. The law is not to be hoodwinked by colorable pretences. It looks at truth and reality, through whatever disguise it may assume. But to make such an association, ostensibly innocent, the subject of prosecution as a criminal conspir-

acy, the secret agreement, which makes it so, is to be averred and proved as the gist of the offence. But when an association is formed for purposes actually innocent, and afterwards its powers are abused, by those who have the control and management of it, to purposes of oppression and injustice, it will be criminal in those who thus misuse it, or give consent thereto, but not in the other members of the association. In this case, no such secret agreement, varying the objects of the association from those avowed, is set forth in this count of the indictment.

Nor can we perceive that the objects of this association, whatever they may have been, were to be attained by criminal means. The means which they proposed to employ . . . were, that they would not work for a person, who, after due notice, should employ a journeyman not a member of their society. Supposing the object of the association to be laudable and lawful, or at least not unlawful, are these means criminal? The case supposes that these persons are not bound by contract, but free to work for whom they please, or not to work, if they so prefer. In this state of things, we cannot perceive, that it is criminal for men to agree together to exercise their own acknowledged rights, in such a manner as best to subserve their own interests. One way to test this is, to consider the effect of such an agreement, where the object of the association is acknowledged on all hands to be a laudable one. Suppose a class of workmen, impressed with the manifold evils of intemperance, should agree with each other not to work in a shop in which ardent spirit was furnished, or not to work in a shop with any one who used it, or not to work for an employer, who should, after notice, employ a journeyman who habitually used it. The consequences might be the same. A workman, who should still persist in the use of ardent spirit, would find it more difficult to get employment; a master employing such as one might, at times, experience inconvenience in his work, in losing the services of a skilful but intemperate workman. Still it seems to us, that as the object would be lawful; and the means not unlawful such an agreement could not be pronounced a criminal conspiracy.

From this count in the indictment, we do not understand that the agreement was, that the defendants would refuse to work for an employer, to whom they were bound by contract for a certain time, in violation of that contract; nor that they would insist that an employer should discharge a workman engaged by contract for a certain time, in violation of such contract. It is perfectly consistent with every thing stated in this count, that the effect of the agreement was, that when they were free to act, they would not engage with an employer, or continue in his employment, if such employer, when free to act, should engage with a workman, or continue a workman in his employment, not a member of the association. If a large number of men, engaged for a certain time, should combine together to violate their contract, and quit their employment together, it would present a very different question. Suppose a farmer, employing a large number of men, engaged for the year, at fair monthly wages, and suppose that just at the moment that his crops were ready to harvest, they should all combine to quit his service, unless he would advance their wages, at a time when other laborers could not be obtained. It would surely be a conspiracy to do an unlawful act, though of such a character, that if done by an individual, it would lay the foundation of a civil action only, and not of a criminal prosecution. It would be a case very different from that stated in this count.

Suppose a baker in a small village had the exclusive custom of his neighborhood, and was making large profits by the sale of his bread. Supposing a number of those neighbors, believing the price of his bread too high, should propose to him to reduce his prices, or if he did not, that they would introduce another baker; and on his refusal, such other baker should, under their encouragement, set up a rival establishment, and sell his bread at lower prices; the effect would be to diminish the profit of the former baker, and to the same extent [as Horne] to impoverish him. And it might be said and proved, that the purpose of the associates was to diminish his profits, and thus impoverish him, though the ultimate and laudable object of the combination was to reduce the cost of bread to themselves and their neighbors. The same thing may be said of all competition in every branch of trade and industry; and yet it is through that competition, that the best interests of trade and industry are promoted. It is scarcely necessary to allude to the familiar instances of opposition lines of conveyance, rival hotels, and the thousand other instances, where each strives to gain custom to himself, by ingenious improvements, by increased industry, and by all the means by which he may lessen the price of commodities, and thereby diminish the profits of others.

We think, therefore, that associations may be entered into, the object of which is to adopt measures that may have a tendency to impoverish another, that is, to diminish his gains and profits, and yet so far from being criminal or unlawful, the object may be highly meritorious and public spirited. The legality of such an association will therefore depend upon the means to be used for its accomplishment. If it is to be carried into effect by fair or honorable and lawful means, it is, to say the least, innocent; if by falsehood or force, it may be stamped with the character of conspiracy.[11]

National Railroad System Development

The introduction and expansion of railroads in the United States was the principal reason behind the transformation of the union movement from city organizations into nationwide labor organizations. In America, railroads were the essential means of transportation after the middle of the nineteenth century. Both passenger and freight rail service played a crucial role in the transformation of the United States from a sparsely settled nation, largely composed of self-sufficient and isolated farm communities, to an industrialized, urbanized giant.[12] With the expansion of the railroad system, the groundwork was laid for the birth of bona fide national labor organizations.[13] Because railroads cast such a large shadow across the nation during the post–Civil War industrialization movement, early legislative attempts at creating public policy toward organized labor focused on the railroad workplace.[14]

Goods delivered ever more widely by the expanding rail transportation system from newly accessible manufacturing centers flowed into formerly stable and profitable markets. The flow of these new goods pressured employers to develop cost-cutting measures to remain competitive. The resultant labor atmosphere was like that in the post–airline-deregulation era. To decrease labor costs, employers introduced women and children into the workplace, farmed out work to prison inmates, and generally reduced wages while increasing working hours.[15]

Predictably, labor reacted by escalating and institutionalizing union activities to improve its bargaining position. Early attempts at national unionization began in the 1850s and 1860s with such organizations as the National Typographers Union (1852), the Hat Finishers (1854), the Stone Cutters (1855), the United Cigarmakers (1856), and the Iron Molders (1859). Most national unions had humble beginnings and lasted for only a short while. In the early 1870s, national unions numbered approximately thirty, and total union membership was around three hundred thousand.[16] Although employer opposition and the continual economic depression of the 1800s caused some of these groups to wane, they did not disappear. Over time, they stressed and pressed for negotiation with employers and for arbitration of disputes.

Though generally separate and distinct from other workers, railroad workers organized in the 1860s and 1870s to deal collectively with the problems of hazardous employment, long hours, and low wages. Between 1880 and 1893, four large brotherhoods emerged as the leading representatives of railroad labor, and they have subsequently become known as the Big Four: the Brotherhood of Locomotive Engineers, the Brotherhood of Locomotive Firemen and Enginemen, the Order of Railway Conductors, and the Brotherhood of Railroad Trainmen. A fifth large union, the Switchman's Union of North America, organized in 1894. In these formative years of railroad unionism, efforts to recruit all railroad workers into an all-embracing labor organization called the Knights of Labor were unsuccessful, as was an attempt in 1894 to organize all railroad workers into a single comprehensive union known as the American Railway Union.[17]

National Labor Union

The National Labor Union (NLU) was the first large-scale national labor federation in the United States. Founded in 1866, it paved the way for other organizations, such as the American Federation of Labor (AFL) and the Knights of Labor.

The NLU followed the unsuccessful efforts of labor activists to form a national coalition of local trade unions. The union's objective was to bring together all of the national labor organizations in existence, to mandate the eight-hour workday, to create a national federation that could press for labor reforms, and to help create national unions in those areas where none existed.[18]

The NLU drew much of its support from construction unions and other groups of skilled employees but also invited the unskilled and farmers to join. And yet, the union campaigned for the exclusion of Chinese workers from the United States and made only halting efforts to defend the rights of women and black workers. African American workers established their own Colored National Labor Union, but their support of the Republican Party and the racism of white unionists prevented the two unions from working together.

The union boasted 650,000 members at its height. It collapsed when it adopted the policy that third-party politics was the only means for advancing its agenda. The organization was unsuccessful at the 1872 presidential election polls and lost virtually all of its union supporters, many of whom moved on to the newly formed Knights of Labor. The depression of the 1870s, which drove down union membership (Americans needed *any* wages, not better wages), was the final factor contributing to the end of the NLU in 1872.[19] Although the National Labor Union failed to persuade Congress to shorten the workday, its efforts heightened public awareness of labor issues and increased public support for labor reform throughout the 1870s and 1880s.

Knights of Labor

Despite the major railroad unions' disinterest in including themselves in an all-embracing labor organization, the first national federation to remain active for more than a few years was the Noble Order of the Knights of Labor. This organization was founded in secrecy in December 1869 by a group of Philadelphia tailors led by Uriah S. Stephens. Even though it was established by a group of garment workers, membership after 1883 also included farmers and merchants as well as women and African Americans. However, bankers, lawyers, stockholders, liquor dealers, and stockbrokers were excluded because they were considered unproductive members of society.[20] The Knights' main platform was to attack the problems created by an industrial society and to protect the rights of the workers. The goals of the group included the abolition of child labor, equal pay for equal work, and an eight-hour workday.

Even though the leadership of the organization was essentially idealistic, favored social reform, and preferred arbitration over strikes, the Knights of Labor achieved national attention when the group won a strike in 1865, under the guidance of Terrence Powderly (see fig. 2.2), against railroads owned by millionaire Jay Gould. Most conspicuous was a successful strike against the Wabash Railroad in 1885, which took place after Gould attempted to break the union by laying off its

Figure 2.2. Terence Powderly (1849–1924), who led the Knights of Labor, a powerful advocate for the eight-hour day, in the 1870s and early 1880s. Under Powderly's leadership, the union discouraged the use of strikes and advocated restructuring society along cooperative lines. At first, the Knights of Labor was a secret organization, but Powderly ended the group's secrecy upon assuming control of the organization in 1879. U.S. Department of Labor.

members. This strike, over wages, was not won easily, and it was characterized by violence. But the national publicity it received added impetus to the organization, so that by the middle of 1886, membership in the Knights of Labor reached seven hundred thousand.[21]

The Knights were unsuccessful in the Missouri Pacific strike in 1886 and lost many craft unionists that same year when the rival nonsectarian American Federation of Labor was founded. Because of other unsuccessful strikes and the aftereffects of the Haymarket Square riot, the group's effectiveness waned. Membership declined with the additional problems of an autocratic structure and mismanagement. The organization had less than a hundred thousand members at the end of 1889.[22] By 1900, the organization had ceased to exist.[23] The Knights of Labor disappeared from the labor scene almost as quickly as the group had come onto it.

Federation of Organized Trades and Labor Unions

The Federation of Organized Trades and Labor Unions was the immediate predecessor of the AFL and represented a transition stage of labor unions in the United States. Founded in November 1881 at a convention attended by representatives of a number of labor unions and chapters of the Knights of Labor, its original goals were to encourage the alliance of national and international unions and to obtain legislation, such as the enforcement of the statutory eight-hour day, the abolition of child labor, and repeal of the conspiracy laws.[24] Samuel Gompers of the Cigar Makers National Union was chosen as the chairman of its Committee on Organization (see fig. 2.3).

The federation made some efforts to obtain favorable legislation but had little success in organizing or chartering new unions. It came out in support of the proposal, attributed to Peter J. McGuire of the Carpenters Union, for

Figure 2.3. Samuel Gompers (1850–1924), who helped found the Federation of Organized Trades and Labor Unions in 1881 as a coalition of like-minded unions. In 1886, it was reorganized into the American Federation of Labor (AFL), with Gompers as its president. Gompers's insistence against political affiliation and radicalism in the AFL, combined with the AFL's tendency to cater to skilled labor over unskilled, led indirectly to the formation of the Industrial Workers of the World organization in 1905, which tried with limited success to organize unskilled workers. Library of Congress.

a national Labor Day holiday on the first Monday in September and threw itself behind the eight-hour movement, which sought to limit the workday.

In 1886, as the relations between the trade union movement and the Knights of Labor worsened, McGuire and other union leaders called for a convention at Columbus, Ohio, on December 8. The Federation of Organized Trades and Labor Unions merged with the new organization, known as the American Federation of Labor, formed at that convention.[25]

American Federation of Labor (AFL)

Despite the dissolution of the Knights of Labor, the impact of the national union and the strike weapon had been established; following the example of that early organization, other national unions took its place. The most vigorous organization in pursuit of the national union concept was the American Federation of Labor, whose main platform insisted on the strike as the ultimate weapon to achieve its aims and goals.

Begun in 1886, the AFL, under the guidance of Gompers, later known as the father of the American labor movement, had a significant impact on the course of American unionism. The new AFL distinguished itself from the Knights by emphasizing the autonomy of each trade union affiliated with it and limiting membership to workers and organizations made up only of workers, unlike the Knights, who also admitted employers as members.

While the Knights disappeared, the AFL grew steadily in the late nineteenth century and eventually became the largest union grouping in the United States for the first half of the twentieth century. Under Gompers, the AFL sought to unite all workers in singular occupations (job classifications). The goal of the organization was to organize craft (skilled) workers only and to focus on gaining strength through the political process. Gompers created a platform that, in many respects, survives present day:

- Establishing one union for each craft, each union having its own sphere of jurisdiction into which no other union could trespass
- Permitting each national union to be autonomous
- Concentrating on wage-centered gains through collective bargaining
- Avoiding political alliances with any particular party, using instead collective union votes to defeat politicians with anti-union bias
- Utilizing the strike as labor's ultimate weapon when collective bargaining does not produce desired results

With the establishment of the AFL platform, the labor movement had taken root, and by 1914, the AFL-represented unions had more than two million members.

Strikes and the Railroads

As rail service grew, the goods the trains carried and the transportation they provided became less of a luxury and more of a necessity. Rail strikes and work disputes became commonplace, impacting strongly on the public interest by denying consumers basic goods and services that they had come to expect and demand. Opposition to union organizations increased during the late 1800s. Employers exchanged blacklists of workers suspected of union membership, preventing them from finding employment. Factory owners hired strikebreakers and armed guards to crush strikes. In the public interest, the state or federal government often approved the use of federal troops to quell strikes, claiming that strikes were still illegal because they restrained trade. Many states passed laws to restrict union activity.[26] The 1880s and 1890s saw a series of bitter labor disputes accompanied by violent strikes and even death.

The most notable violent activities of this era and some of most serious in U.S. history were several strikes and union-related activities that severely impeded the unions' ability to generate supportive legislation. For example, the Haymarket Riot of 1886 increased antilabor feelings throughout the country (see fig. 2.4). Starting out as a peaceful rally of workers held in Haymarket Square in Chicago to protest police activity against strikers in a local industrial plant, an unknown person threw a bomb into an assemblage of police officers, killing eight of them. The remaining police officers fired on the crowd, sparking a riot. Three additional persons were killed, and more than a hundred others were injured. The nation's press blamed the labor movement for the violence and condemned unionists as anarchists. Responsibility for the police deaths were quickly pinned on leaders of the group. These eight leaders were immediately tried in court; seven were ordered hanged, and the eighth was imprisoned for fifteen years. Four of the leaders were actually hung a year later in 1887; however, in 1893, all eight defendants were pardoned by the Illinois governor after concluding they were innocent.[27] The public was shaken by the entire ordeal, and the trial is often referred to as one of the most serious miscarriages of justice in United States history.

Several other bitter and damaging strikes hurt the labor movement during this period.

Figure 2.4. Engraving of the seven anarchists (labor-union activists) sentenced to die for murder. An eighth defendant, not shown, was sentenced to fifteen years in prison. The Haymarket Affair on May 4, 1886, in Chicago began as a rally in support of striking union workers that became violent when an unknown person threw a bomb at police as they marched to disperse the public meeting. The bomb blast and ensuing gunfire resulted in the deaths of eight police officers and an unknown number of civilians. In the publicized legal proceedings that followed, eight labor activists were tried and convicted of murder. From *Frank Leslie's Illustrated Newspaper.*

One was the Homestead Strike of 1892, which involved the Carnegie Steel Company and the Amalgamated Association of Iron, Steel, and Tin Workers. The Homestead Strike (see the Pinkerton National Detective Agency case study) was a labor confrontation lasting 143 days in 1892 and one of the most serious in the history of the United States. Andrew Carnegie, who attempted to project a prolabor image, left the country for a trip to Scotland before the strike occurred, leaving the situation in the hands of his manager, Henry Clay Frick, who was well known to be anti-union. The company attempted to cut the wages of the skilled steel workers; when the workers refused the pay cut, management locked the union out. The company hired guards from the Pinkerton National Detective Agency for protection. As violence erupted between the strikers and three hundred Pinkerton guards armed with Winchester rifles, several people were killed.

The Pinkerton National Detective Agency. The Pinkerton National Detective Agency was a security guard agency established in the United States in 1850 by Allan Pinkerton, who became famous when he foiled a plot to assassinate President Abraham Lincoln.[28]

Pinkerton agents performed services that ranged from the nineteenth-century equivalent of both a private military contractor and a security guard. During the height of their existence, the Pinkerton Agency had more men than the U.S. Army; the state of Ohio outlawed the agency due to the possibility of it being hired as a private army. During labor unrest in the late 1800s, businessmen hired Pinkerton guards to keep strikers and suspected unionists out of their factories, the most notorious example being the Homestead Strike of 1892. Pinkerton agents were also used as guards in coal, iron, and lumber disputes, as well as the railroad strikes of 1877.[29]

Case study 2.2 examines the Pinkertons more fully.

Case Study 2.2: The Pinkerton National Detective Agency

Allan Pinkerton, born in Glasgow, Scotland, in 1819, immigrated at the age of twenty-three to the United States in 1842 (see fig. CS2.2.1). His detective career began by chance in 1847 when he witnessed counterfeiters making coins in a secluded area where he was gathering tree saplings for his barrel-making business. His assistance in arresting these men led to his appointment in 1849; he was Chicago's first full-time detective.[30]

Figure CS 2.2.1. Portrait of Allan Pinkerton from *Harper's Weekly*, 1884.

In the 1850s, formed the North-Western Police Agency, later known as the Pinkerton National Detective Agency.[31] One of the first of its kind in the United States, Pinkerton's detective agency flourished from the start. By the mid-1850s, businessmen desired greater control over their employees; their solution was to hire Pinkerton's private detective agency.

As the United States expanded in territory, the rail transportation system also increased. In February 1855, Pinkerton signed lucrative contracts to protect six railroads' property from train robbers. By the end of the decade, the Pinkerton Agency had become national in scope and an indispensable clearinghouse for information on criminal activity.[32]

By the 1870s, the Pinkerton agency had the world's largest collection of mug shots and extensive criminal files. The agency's logo, "the All-Seeing Eye," inspired the phrase *private eye*.[33]

Following the outbreak of the Civil War, Pinkerton served as head of the Union Intelligence Service (forerunner of the U.S. Secret Service) from 1861 to 1862. In 1861, while investigating a railway case, Pinkerton uncovered an assassination plot against president-elect Abraham Lincoln. It was believed that conspirators intended to kill Lincoln in Baltimore during a stop along the way to his inauguration. President Lincoln later hired Pinkerton to organize a "secret service" to obtain military information in the Southern states during the Civil War (see fig. CS2.2.2). While Pinkerton sent undercover agents into the Southern states, he traveled under the pseudonym "Major E. J. Allen" and performed his own investigative work in Tennessee, Georgia, and Mississippi.[34]

Following his service with the Union army, Pinkerton resumed the management of his detective agency, pursuing train robbers and opposing labor unions. The agency experienced significant growth between the end of the war in 1865 and the turn of the twentieth century as business owners hired the Pinkerton Agency to provide security at work sites. At one point during the late nineteenth century, the agency was larger than the standing army of the United States, causing the legislature in Ohio to outlaw the agency over fears it could be hired out as a private army or militia.[35]

The economic depression of 1873 left Allan Pinkerton groping for work as business activity declined dramatically. While wondering how he would be able to fund his agency, an opportunity arose in Pennsylvania's coal region. Labor strikes were commonplace as mine workers and owners frequently battled over wages. These strikes severely crippled the coal industry as well as the railroad owners, who had a financial

Figure CS 2.2.2. (*Left to right*) Allan Pinkerton, President Abraham Lincoln, and Major General John A. McClernand. This photo was taken not long after the Civil War's first battle on Northern soil in Antietam, Maryland, on October 3, 1862. Library of Congress.

stake in the coal mines because of their freight monopolies. When the railroad owners heard that the striking miners were destroying railroad property, the owners hired the Pinkerton Agency to infiltrate the coal-mining communities and expose the perpetrators. Thus began the Pinkerton Agency's involvement in the U.S. labor movement. Pinkerton's men were also used as guards in coal, iron, and lumber disputes, as well as the railroad strikes of 1877.[36]

After Allan Pinkerton's death in 1884, businessmen hired Pinkerton agents to infiltrate labor unions and as guards to keep strikers and suspected unionists out of factories. The agents were involved in numerous strikebreaking activities against labor during the late nineteenth century. The most notorious example was the Homestead Strike of 1892 (see fig. CS2.2.3). Homestead, a Pennsylvania town of ten thousand people, supplied the labor force for the Carnegie, Phipps

Figure CS 2.2.3. Shield used by the strikers when firing the cannon and watching the Pinkerton men at the Carnegie Steel Works.

Steel Company. When a labor strike threatened in 1892, Henry Clay Frick, the plant manager, bypassed local police and hired agents from the Pinkerton Agency. On July 4, 1892, 376 Pinkerton agents secretly arrived in Youngstown, Ohio, and boarded barges to sail to Homestead. The steelworkers thought the agents were scabs (replacement workers) and fired upon the boats. The Pinkerton agents returned fire; ten steelworkers and three Pinkerton agents were killed during the gunfight. The Homestead Strike of 1892 became one of the most famous labor strikes in American history, touching economic, political, and popular culture.

These strikebreaking efforts tarnished the image of the Pinkerton's for years. Many labor sympathizers accused the Pinkerton's agents of inciting riots in order to discredit unions and justify police crackdowns. The Pinkerton reputation was harmed by its agents' protection of scabs and the business property of the major industrialists. Due to the Pinkerton Agency's conflicts with labor unions, the name *Pinkerton* remains in the vocabulary of labor organizers and union members as a derogatory reference to authority figures who side with management.[37]

Another violent dispute, the Pullman strike, occurred in 1894. In this instance, three thousand Pullman Palace Car Company workers struck to protest a wage cut by company owner George Pullman. Many of the discontented workers joined the American Railway Union (ARU), led by Eugene V. Debs. The strike effectively shut down production in the Pullman factories and led to a lockout. In sympathy, an estimated 250,000 members of the American Railway Union supported the strike by refusing to handle the company's cars. With a historic use of an injunction, the strike was eventually broken up by U.S. marshals and over two thousand U.S. Army troops sent in by President Grover Cleveland on the basis that the strike interfered with the delivery of U.S. mail. By the end of the strike, thirteen strikers were killed, and fifty-seven were wounded. An estimated $80 million worth of property was damaged, and Debs was found guilty of conspiracy to obstruct the mails and sent to jail for six months.[38]

The late nineteenth century witnessed a flurry of strike action. According to government records, 509 rail strikes involving 218,000 striking workers occurred between 1881 and 1905.[39] In number of strikes, railroads are fourteenth on a list of eighty-one industries; the coal industry is first with 3,403 strikes.[40]

Case study 2.3 describes the most violent strike in U.S. history.

Case Study 2.3: The Colorado Coal Field War—Zenith of Violence in U.S. Labor Relations

A turning point in relations between labor and management in the United States came in the form of the bloody Colorado Coal Field war of 1913–14. The Colorado Fuel & Iron Corporation (CF&I), owned by wealthy New York industrialist John D. Rockefeller, operated mines in coal fields in Colorado and northern New Mexico.

Working conditions were harsh and dangerous, particularly in the southern Colorado fields, where fatality rates were double the national average, due largely to CF&I disobedience to state laws requiring timber shoring in the mine shafts (managers were said to be making a profit on the side by selling timbers intended for mine shoring to others).[41] Miners were paid $1.68 per day, and even that modest amount came not in U.S. dollars but in the form of company scrip, which could be used only at the company-owned store, where prices were exorbitant, or to pay rent for company-owned housing, which was the only housing close to the mines.

The United Mine Workers of America (UMWA) had been secretly working to organize the CF&I miners and in late 1913 demanded recognition as the miners' bargaining agent, along with higher wages (to be paid in real money) and improved working conditions. The company refused. A union activist was murdered. The union called a strike on September 17, 1913, and ten thousand to twelve thousand miners, representing 90 percent of the CF&I workforce, walked off the job, shutting down the mines.

Within the week, all striking miners and their families were evicted from company housing into the rain and snow of an early, approaching Colorado winter. Anticipating this, the UMWA had leased private lands nearby (usually astride entrance roads to the mines where they might be able to block strikebreakers from entering) and set up tent colonies. The strikers and their families moved into the tents (see fig. CS2.3.1).

CF&I then hired the Baldwin-Felts Detective Agency, which provided a force of gunmen to augment the company's own force of armed guards, who built an armored car equipped with a machine gun. Christening it "the Death Special," they then went about shooting up the strikers' camps, indiscriminately killing and wounding the occupants (see fig. CS2.3.2). Striking miners dug cellars under their tents for their families to hide in for protection and

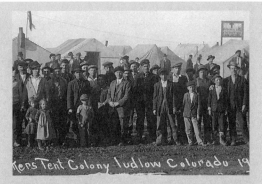

Figure CS 2.3.1. A group of Ludlow strikers in front of the Ludlow Tent Colony Site. Western History/Genealogy Department, Denver Public Library.

Figure CS 2.3.2. Company guards in "the Death Special" armored car with mounted machine gun.

returned fire. Additional deaths resulted from clashes between strikers and strikebreakers, leading Colorado's governor to call out the state militia (forerunner to today's National Guard).[42]

Thinking the soldiers had been sent to protect them, cheering strikers greeted the militiamen waving flags. They soon learned that the militia had been ordered to break the strike. The soldiers escorted replacement workers through the camps to the mines and beat and arrested hundreds of striking miners. On the main street of Trinidad, the principal city in the area, a militia cavalry troop swinging unsheathed sabers galloped into a parade of women lead by famed labor organizer Mother Jones marching in a peaceful show of support for the strikers, breaking up the demonstration and jailing some of the women, including Jones (see CS2.3.3).

Yet, the strikers held their ground as the winter worsened, and the calendar flipped to 1914. That January 1, half a continent away in warmer Florida and connected only by a timeline, America's first airline, the St. Petersburg–Tampa Airboat Line, commenced passenger service across Tampa Bay with one pilot, Tony Jannus, and one airplane, the Benoist Type XIV flying boat (see fig. CS2.3.4).

Meanwhile, back in Colorado, the striking coal miners held out through the winter, and as spring approached, Rockefeller brought pressure on Colorado's governor to take even more forceful measures to break the strike. Two militia companies were positioned overlooking the strikers' tent colony at Ludlow, the largest in the area and home to a thousand men, women, and children. On April 20, the miners (largely immigrants from a great variety of nations) were celebrating Greek Easter when at 10:00 A.M., the militia commander ordered riflemen and a machine gun crew to commence firing on the camp. Women and children took shelter in the cellars, and men returned fire.

After a few hours of firing, Louis Tikas (the leader of the miners) came out under a flag of truce to meet with militia commander and two of his men. As they conferred, the officer suddenly knocked Tikas out with the butt of his rifle, and the soldiers fatally shot the fallen union leader to death at point-blank range. The battle resumed but paused as a passing freight train stopped to offer the families a ride out of the line of fire. Hundreds escaped this way. Once the train departed, the shooting recommenced. At nightfall, militiamen carrying torches swept down on the camp, shooting and setting the tents ablaze. The remaining strikers scattered into the hills.

In the fighting that raged for fourteen hours, at least thirteen strikers were killed by gunfire. In the morning, a worker going through the ruins of the camp moved aside a burned set of bedsprings that had served as a lid to one of the cellars. In the pit below were the bodies of two women and eleven children, suffocated by the fire. The event came to be known as the Ludlow Massacre.[43]

Figure CS 2.3.3. Mother Jones, known to working folk during her lifetime as "the miners' angel." Persevering in her efforts despite the many tragic events she witnessed, her fierce determination was expressed in her famous declaration, "Pray for the dead and fight like hell for the living." When she was denounced on the Senate floor as the "grandmother of all agitators," she replied in typical fashion, "I hope to live long enough to be the great-grandmother of all agitators." Library of Congress.

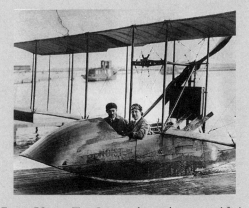

Figure CS 2.3.4. Tony Jannus piloting the inaugural flight of the Benoist Type XIV flying boat biplane on January 1, 1914. Then-mayor of St. Petersburg, Florida, Abram C. Pheil was a passenger on the inaugural flight. Florida Photographic Collection.

News of the massacre spread quickly, and the UMWA issued a call to arms, urging its members to "gather together for defensive purposes all arms and ammunition legally available." From other tent camps in the area, three hundred armed mine workers marched into Ludlow and cut telephone and telegraph wires. They were joined by three hundred more from Colorado Springs, anticipating further battle. Other unions volunteered to send five hundred armed men and four hundred nurses to support the embattled UMWA members. In Trinidad, the funeral procession for the Ludlow victims stretched for miles. After the funeral ceremony, mourners took up arms and moved into the hills along a forty-mile stretch of the Front Range of the Rockies, where they rampaged for ten days, killing mine guards who opposed them and dynamiting the mine shafts, putting the mines out of service.

When additional militiamen were ordered in, some refused to go, and railroad workers refused to transport others. Protests and demonstrations occurred nationwide, and protesters were clubbed by police. Colorado's governor requested President Woodrow Wilson send federal troops to restore order. Wilson complied, and the strike was broken. The union failed to gain recognition. Congressional committees held hearings, generating thousands of pages of testimony. All told, sixty-six men, women, and children had been killed in the violence. No one was indicted for their murders. There is no report of the number of wounded.[44]

Meanwhile down in Florida, the wealthy snowbird clientele had returned north with the coming of spring to New England, and America's first airline went out of business. Although the union lost its fight for recognition and the strike was crushed, the effort is recognized today as a victory in the broad sense for the union movement because it galvanized public opinion that lead to a progressive era of reforms in labor relations.

A monument erected by the UMWA stands on the Ludlow site today, a few miles west of Interstate 25 between Trinidad and Pueblo.[45] There, visitors can still gaze down into that fateful cellar.

Legislative Beginnings

As early as 1882, the U.S. Senate, concerned about the substantial strike activity, sought to remove the cause of strikes and prevent their reoccurrence by directing a Committee on Labor to establish a Senate commission to investigate labor issues. The result was four volumes of testimony on labor strife but no legislative action.[46] Similarly, a House of Representatives committee was also considering legislation to curtail strike activity. Although failing to provide any action, the House committee did recommend voluntary arbitration for the settlement of disputes.

Arbitration Act of 1888

In 1886, another bloody dispute arose against the Gould Railway System, followed by similar occurrences against the Chicago, Burlington, and Quincy Railroad in 1888.[47] In response, the government attempted to reduce disputes in the railroad industry by establishing the Arbitration Act of 1888. This act, although virtually unused, was the first federal statute to address labor issues in the railroad industry. The tenets of the act provided for adjustment of disputes through voluntary arbitration and an investigative commission. To facilitate the handling of disputes, the act called for the establishment of a panel of three arbitrators to whom disputing parties could bring the issue for resolution. The act intended to settle the differences between railroad corporations and other common carriers engaged in transportation of property or passengers and their employees.

However, the relationship between labor and management was so strained during this period, with virtually no good-faith bargaining by either of the parties, that the arbitration act went unused. The act was a complete failure, and only one panel was ever convened under it, and that one, in the case of the Pullman Strike, only issued its report after the strike had been crushed by a federal court injunction backed by federal troops.

Following closely on the heels of the attempt to mitigate labor unrest, Congress set out to begin the economic regulation of the rail industry. This activity would have lasting impact on the future of relations between labor and management.

Interstate Commerce Act of 1887

This act was the first piece of economic regulation that set the stage for nearly a century of regulation and provided:

- All rail charges for passenger and freight should be reasonable and just.
- Geographic discrimination (rates favoring one port or state over another) was prohibited.
- The Munn Act was now outdated concerning the railroads.
- Long-haul rates were not allowed to be charged at rates less than short-haul rates.
- All rates should be charged as published (that is, no under-the-table dealings).
- The Interstate Commerce Commission was created to oversee the regulation and to collect and publish information.

Although Congress had some sense of the economic rationale (or "irrationale") for the legislation, the overwhelming motivating force was political perception, and those perceptions exist today. In overall expectations and beliefs of the unions representing both rail and airline and for many years into the early twenty-first century, the perceptions indicated above persisted.[48] In 1989, Eric Bashers in an article written for the World Bank calls this perception "the myth of the miraculous railroad," the belief that all railroads were rich, powerful, and unscrupulous and that they were probably earning exorbitant profits from their monopoly positions.[49] It is a short step from this railroad analogy to that of the airlines during the twentieth century.

Sherman Antitrust Act (1890)

While labor was vying for its place in the sun, the business industry was feeling strong public pressure to curtail its own monopolistic tendencies, having achieved tremendous economic power. In 1890, Congress passed new legislation presumably aimed at big-business monopoly excesses: the Sherman Antitrust Act, designed to make monopolies that restrained trade illegal.

Initially conceived to curb monopolistic abuses of large business combinations, the act proved more successful against organized labor. Violation of the Sherman Act warranted the issuance of an injunction, with enforcement and fines, jail terms, and damage restitution up to triple the amount of actual damages. Sections 1 and 2 of the act state, "Every contract, combination . . . or conspiracy, in restraint of trade or commerce . . . is . . . illegal."[50] Violators of Sections 1 and 2 were subject to fine and/or imprisonment. Section 4 provided for the use of injunctions to curtail picketing, boycotts, trespass, and the use of force.

Based on the body of this act, management found a new weapon in its arsenal for combating union activities: the injunction. These antitrust provisions were first used against organized labor, rather than business entities. Opponents of labor turned to civil actions to thwart and curtail unionism, primarily initiating lawsuits to enjoin certain labor activities. The courts had previously recognized a general right to advance the interest of workers (*Commonwealth v. Hunt*), as Chief Justice Lemuel Shaw ruled that unions were legal organizations and had the right to organize and strike. But this right was narrowly interpreted. In the mind of the courts, any action that impacted on the public welfare was a legitimate subject of injunction.

In *Plant v. Woods*, decided in 1900, this attitude was clearly demonstrated when the court enjoined striking and picketing that attempted to enforce a demand that an employer could hire only union members. The court held that the demands of the union were not sufficient to justify interference with the employer's right to be "free of molestation."[51] In this same opinion, however, the elements of judicial discord were indicated in Associate Justice Oliver Wendell Holmes's dissenting opinion: "Unity of organization is necessary to make the contest of labor effectual, and [labor unions] lawfully may employ in their preparation the means which they might use in the final contest."[52]

Use of the injunction later made a significant appearance in the Pullman Strike, a dispute that brought a variety of legislative laws into play to quell strike activities. In that dispute, employees of the Pullman Palace Car Company, manufacturers of railroad cars, struck to protest a wage cut. Layoffs and wage reductions of 40 percent, made necessary by financial losses at Pullman's production facilities, caused workers to strike on May 11, 1894.[53] Members of the ARU declared a sympathy strike and refused to handle the company's cars (see fig. 2.5).

Figure 2.5. Striking American Railway Union members confronting Illinois National Guard troops outside the Arcade Building in Chicago during the Pullman Strike in 1894. Abraham Lincoln Historical Digitization Project.

Since the strike involved railroad workers, it was hoped that the enactment of the Arbitration Act of 1888 would work to resolve the differences. Unfortunately, the legislation was found to be without teeth, and it became necessary to utilize the provisions of the Sherman Act to secure injunctions against ARU president Debs and against the union itself. The U.S. attorney general sought the injunction on grounds of interference with the delivery of the mail by train. Debs and other union leaders were ultimately sent to prison, and the ARU was so weakened that it dissolved three years later. After the Pullman strike, labor injunctions were commonly issued. Prior to 1931, state and federal courts issued 1,845 injunctions in labor disputes.[54]

The best example of management's usage of the Sherman Act occurred in 1902, in a case called the *Danbury Hatters*, or *Loewe v. Lawlor*. During a strike against Loewe and Company, a hat manufacturer in Danbury, Connecticut, the union called a boycott. Unrelated unions, in a secondary action, struck against Loewe's suppliers to try to compel unionization of the company's manufacturing operations. The United Hatters union, in conjunction with the AFL, began primary and secondary boycotts of dealers who sold Loewe's hats. An unfair list sent to union members appreciably reduced Loewe's sales and effectively stopped Loewe and Company from receiving raw goods that would have permitted the company to continue operations despite direct union action against them. Injunctions were ordered requiring the union to return to work, and, more significant, lawsuits were filed for losses incurred due to "restraint of trade."

In a sweeping U.S. Supreme Court decision, a judgment was given in favor of the company for over $250,000.[55] This award was a staggering setback for unions. In addition, the decision outlawed the use of secondary boycotts, a provision that remained effective and made secondary boycotts illegal until the 1932 passage of the Norris–La Guardia Act. It was then reactivated by the passage of the Taft-Hartley Act in 1947 and applied to all industries except those under the RLA.

By the time of *Loewe v. Lawlor*, the balance of power in disputes had decidedly swung to management. In the management arsenal were the use of injunctions, strikebreakers (i.e., organizations similar to the Pinkerton Agency), federal troops, and a new anti-union agreement, the yellow-dog contract.

Yellow-dog contracts. Beset by continuous strike activity, employers set out to find ways to discourage their employees from involvement and membership in union activities. The yellow-dog contract, or union-free agreement, provided such relief. This contract, entered into between employers and employees, bound the employees to refrain from becoming members of a union or engaging in union activity while employed by a company. It became a de facto condition of employment. Though the yellow-dog contract was believed by unions to be unconstitutional, the Supreme Court not only upheld its validity in 1917 but also further permitted lower courts to issue injunctions for enforcement.[56]

In the particulars of the *Hitchman Coal & Coke Company v. Mitchell*, the company required a yellow-dog contract of its mining personnel. The union, the United Mine Workers of America, believed the contracts were unconstitutional and struck the company over their usage. The court found that the union strike was legal and a good defense against the company contention that it was illegal and thus not enjoinable. The court said that the defense of the strike itself was good, but the defense was not good inasmuch as the court held that the end sought caused an illegal breach of contract—the yellow-dog

contract itself. In short, the court held that the union did have the right to form a labor organization at the company but that the right was subject to employer acquiescence, and because the company had valid "yellow-dogs" in place, the employer had not acquiesced. Under the premise of "constitutional rights of personal liberty and private property," the yellow-dog contract was upheld.

As a result, a company could require a yellow-dog contract as a condition of employment and could also terminate an employee if he or she refused to sign one. Beyond employee enforcement, injunctions could also be issued against any union attempting to persuade workers to violate their agreements.[57]

Case study 2.4 examines the details of this episode.

Case Study 2.4: *Hitchman Coal & Coke Company v. Mitchell*

By 1907, the United Mine Workers of America (UMWA), then the largest and most powerful affiliate of the American Federation of Labor (AFL), had successfully unionized the entire coal-mining industry in Ohio, Indiana, and Illinois, along with parts of West Virginia and Pennsylvania. Under the leadership of its president, John Mitchell, the union launched a campaign to organize the workers in the remaining mines in the West Virginia and Pennsylvania.

Hitchman Coal & Coke Company operated a mine in the panhandle of West Virginia. The mine had previously been unionized by the UMWA, and the relationship between the company and the union had been bitter, with strikes in 1903, 1904, and 1906. Those strikes had been extremely costly to the company in lost business and for obtaining coal from other sources to fulfill its contract with the Baltimore & Ohio Railroad, which operated a coaling station for its locomotives beside the Hitchman mine.

During the 1906 strike at the mine, the union failed to provide strike benefits (replacement income) to its striking members, largely poor, recent immigrants from Eastern Europe. The result was that about a month and a half into the strike, a committee of the miners acting without the union's knowledge or consent met with the company's president to ask the company's terms to allow them to resume work. The company's conditions were that the strikers could return to work only if they would not be members of any union, that the mine would be operated non-union, and that the company would deal with each miner individually. The miners orally agreed to this yellow-dog contract and went back to work. The agreement was later put in writing and signed by each of them.

When the UMWA launched its 1907 offensive, it sent an organizer into the panhandle to organize all of the mines there. Management of the Hitchman and several other mines in the area having similar yellow-dog contracts with their employees put the organizer on notice of these agreements and asked the union to honor those contracts and leave them alone. This did not deter the organizer in the slightest, as he continued to meet with miners in secret and collect the names of miners who agreed to join the union. The organizer expressed the intent to paralyze each mine with a surprise strike to force the company to recognize the union and create a closed shop as soon as he had enough names at a mine to do so. He claimed to have almost enough names to initiate such an action at the Hitchman mine.

Determined to defend against a resumption of disruptive and costly battles with the union, the company took preemptive action, filing a lawsuit in federal court seeking an injunction against the union to prohibit it from activities that would interfere with the company's contract with its employees. The trial court issued a temporary injunction against the union and its staff, followed by a permanent injunction. The case would ultimately make its way up to the Supreme Court of the United States, which would hear argument on it twice before rendering its final decision over ten years later. The case presented the court the challenge of resolving conflicting

legal rights: the by-then well-acknowledged rights of workers to form unions and for such unions to seek to enlarge their membership by inviting other workmen to join against the right (of the company, in this case) to hold people to their contractual bargains and prevent outsiders from interfering with those obligations.

In a case such as this, seeking an equitable remedy, a court may consider a great number of factors in order to reach the decision it deems most fair under the facts and circumstances of the case. (An injunction is an *equitable remedy*, an order for a defendant to do or refrain from doing something, as distinguished from a *remedy at law*, such as a judgment that the defendant pay the plaintiff money for damages caused by the plaintiff's unlawful actions or inaction.) From the language of its decision, it is clear that a majority of the Supreme Court was offended by the union's methods, its disregard of the company's contract with its employees, the disloyalty of the employees, and the tactics of the union's organizer, Thomas Hughes. The Court even questioned the union's motives. Here are some examples, excerpted from the majority's lengthy decision:

The evidence shows that he [Hughes] had distinct and timely notice that membership in the union was inconsistent with the terms of employment at all three mines, and a violation of the express provisions of the agreement at Hitchman and Glendale. Having unsuccessfully applied to Koch and McKinley [operators of those mines] for their cooperation, Hughes proceeded to interview as many of the men as he could reach and to hold public meetings in the interest of the union. There is clear and uncontradicted evidence that he did not confine himself to mere persuasion, but resorted to deception and abuse. In his public speeches he employed abusive language respecting Mr. Pickett, William Daugherty, and Jim Jarrett. [Pickett was superintendent of the Hitchman and Glendale mines and the company representative with whom the miners had made their yellow dog contract, while Daugherty and Jarrett were miners at Hitchman who had been president and secretary of the union local, respectively, at Hitchman at the time of the 1906 strike, when the local deserted the UMWA.] He prophesied, in such a way that ignorant, foreign-born miners, such as he was addressing, naturally might believe him to be speaking with knowledge, that the wages paid by the Hitchman would be reduced unless the mine was unionized. The evidence as to the methods he employed in personally interviewing the miners, while meager, is significant. Myers, a Hitchman miner, testified:

> He told me that he was a good friend of Mr. Koch, and that Mr. Koch had nothing against having the place organized again. He said he was a friend of his, and I made the remark that I would ask Mr. Koch and see if it was so; and he said no, that was of no use because he was telling me the truth.

He did not confine his attentions to men who were in plaintiff's employ but in addition dissuaded men who had accepted employment from going to work.

A highly significant thing, giving character to Hughes' entire course of conduct, is that while his solicitation of the men was more or less public, as it necessarily had to be, he was careful to keep secret the number and the names of those who agreed to join the union. Meyers, being asked to allow his name to be entered on a book that Hughes carried, tried to see the names already entered, "but he would not show anything; he told me he had it, and I asked how many names was on it, and set said he had about enough to 'crack off.'" To Stewart, another Hitchman miner, he said, that "he was forming a kind of secret order among the men."

Every Hitchman miner who joined Hughes' "secret order" and permitted his name to be entered upon Hughes' list was guilty of a breach of his contract of employment and acted a lie whenever thereafter he entered plaintiff's mine to work. Hughes not only connived at this but must be deemed to have caused and procured it for it was the main feature of the defendants' plan, the sine qua non of their program.

In any aspect of the matter, it cannot be said that defendants were pursuing their object by lawful means The question of their intention—of their bona fides—cannot be ignored. It enters into the question of malice. [Citing a British case:]

> Intentionally to do that which is calculated in the ordinary course of events to damage, and which does, in fact, damage another in that person's property or trade, is actionable if done without just cause or excuse.

And the intentional infliction of such damage upon another, without justification or excuse, is malicious in law. Of course, in a court of equity, when passing upon the right of injunction, damage threatened, irremediable by action at law, is equivalent to damage done. And we cannot deem the proffered excuse to be a "just cause or excuse," where it is based, as in this case, upon an assertion of conflicting rights that are sought to be obtained by unfair methods, and for the very purpose of interfering with plaintiff's rights, of which defendants have full notice.

In our opinion, any violation of plaintiff's legal rights contrived by defendants for the purpose of inflicting damage, or having that as its necessary effect, is as plainly inhibited by the law as if it involved a breach of the peace. A combination to procure concerted breaches of contract by plaintiff's employees constitutes such a violation.

Upon all the facts, we are constrained to hold that the purpose entertained by defendants to bring about a strike at plaintiff's mine in order to compel plaintiff, through fear of financial loss, to consent to the unionization of the mine as the lesser evil, was an unlawful purpose, and that the methods resorted to by Hughes—the inducing of employees to unite with the union in an effort to subvert the system of employment at the mine by concerted breaches of the contracts of employment known to be in force there, not to mention misrepresentation, deceptive statements, and threats of pecuniary loss communicated by Hughes to the men—were unlawful and malicious methods, and not to be justified as a fair exercise of the right to increase the membership of the union.[58]

The Court's majority opinion (Justice Brandeis, joined by others, dissenting) approved the injunction originally issued by the district court, with a slight modification, thus enshrining the yellow-dog contract in the common law of labor relations in the United States at least until, as chapter 3 shows, Congress reconsidered the practice through the legislative process. The reader may well wonder if the Court's decision was not affected by the horrors of the recent Colorado Coal Field War of 1913–14, as well as the fact that the United States had entered into World War I, an endeavor heavily dependent on a large and uninterrupted supply of coal to power ships and trains moving equipment and personnel toward the battlefield in Europe, midway through the year between argument of the case and announcement of the Court's decision. It is unlikely any jurist would admit the influence of external events on a court's decision process, but equally unlikely the public would believe or expect the minds of members of the judiciary to be so compartmentalized as to be unaffected in their work by such epochal events going on around them.

Erdman Act of 1898

Although the vast majority of union activity was outside the railroad industry, the preservation of public interest remained paramount. As a result, greater legislative emphasis was applied to labor relations issues involving the operation of interstate train service.

Recognizing the inadequacies of the Arbitration Act of 1888 in the Pullman strike, Congress set out to consider other alternatives to resolve railroad disputes. In 1898, it passed the Erdman Act, introducing for the first time the possibility of mediation between the parties. This law, with its mediation provision, was less abrasive to both parties to a dispute, allowing for a third party to help reach an accord. Should such attempts at mediation fail, the act provided that the mediators were to urge the parties to submit to voluntary arbitration of the dispute. The modus vivendi would be to establish a three-party panel: one member who represented labor, one who represented management, and a third, neutral party. When convened, both parties to a dispute were to maintain the status quo or to continue working under the old agreement until the arbitration session culminated. Under the Arbitration Act of 1888, the parties may have been forced into an agreement.

Because of the broad use of yellow-dog contracts by railroad employers, the original Erdman Act included a section prohibiting railroad discrimination against a worker because of union membership. This section clearly ran contrary to the anti-union feeling of the majority of employers and did not go unchallenged. It was later declared unconstitutional. In the view of the Supreme Court, the act violated the Fourteenth Amendment by depriving the employer of "property without due process of the law." In addition, the commerce clause of the Constitution did not empower Congress to regulate employer-employee relationships.[59]

Despite its enactment, the Erdman Act went virtually unused for seven years and only became operational when management voluntarily chose to recognize a union. But from 1906 until the act was amended in 1913, sixty-one disputes were settled under the act's mediation provisions. A successor statute, the Newlands Act, passed in 1913 proved more effective but was largely superseded when the federal government nationalized the railroads in 1917.

In other areas of railroad legislation, chinks in the protective covering of regulation were being observed. In this spirit, the 1887 Interstate Commerce Act was undergoing political modifications. According to Nash, Wardman, Button, and Nijkamp, "the equity goals, along with the interest groups that passed the law, were inconsistent with economic efficiency." Nash et al. go on to say that the reason it was not fixed for almost one hundred years, or with deregulation activity, was because the political myth cited by bashers was much stronger than reality.[60]

Elkins Act of 1903

The Elkins Act of 1903 was the first attempt to fix the ailing Interstate Commerce Act. In doing so, it made it a punishable offense for railway corporations to offer or engage in rebates or concessions, made it unlawful for shippers to solicit or receive rebates, and made it a misdemeanor to depart from published rates.

The regulatory aspect of these elements made it difficult for a carrier of the times to operate efficiently, due to the social burdens placed upon them combined with the burdens of a regulatory milieu. Thus, the rails, and to an extent the future airlines, were thought to be protected from undue competition, and thus they could always afford a little more of a social burden than other industries.

Hepburn Act of 1906

The next piece of legislation, the Hepburn Act of 1906, addressing the interstate commerce act

and its rule-making authority over the railroads spoke to a number of issues. This act:

- Allowed the Interstate Commerce Commission (ICC) to set maximum rates
- Required a thirty-day notice of rate changes
- Prohibited railroads from shipping commodities they or their subsidiaries produced to prevent them from gaining a competitive advantage
- Extended ICC jurisdiction to pipelines and express companies
- Permitted the ICC to set through rates and joint rates for shipments that traversed two or more railroads
- Increased the penalty for offering rebates

The airplane had three years earlier made its debut with the Kitty Hawk flight, and its future and that of the companies owning planes were being established. It would not be until the late 1930s that the Civil Aeronautics Authority, later the Civil Aeronautics Board (CAB), would make its appearance, but some of its procedural tenets were already being written.

Mann Elkins Act of 1910

It only took four years before another ICC modification, the Mann Elkins Act of 1910, came forward. This new legislation:

- Permitted ICC to suspend the implementation of rate changes for up to six months
- Permitted ICC to have control over the classification of commodities shipped
- Reinvigorated the long haul/short haul clause of the 1906 amendment

Newlands Act of 1913

By 1913, railroad labor disputes were being considered separate and distinct from union activity in other areas of commerce. Legislative policy was evolving similarly. Recognizing the success of the latter years of the Erdman Act—that mediation rather than arbitration was leading to the resolution of labor disputes—Congress amended the Erdman Act. The Newlands Act of 1913 established a permanent board for handling railway labor disputes.

The Board of Mediation and Conciliation became responsible for all activities under the Newlands Act and for the interpretation of agreements when submitted to the board's authority. Like the panel stipulated in the Erdman Act, this permanent board of mediation also consisted of three members, one being a neutral party. In addition, the act created a permanent, voluntary arbitration board, which was instructed to confine its decisions to the specific matters of each case. Unlike the Erdman Act, the Newlands Act permitted the mediation board to offer its services without first having been invited into the dispute by either the labor unions or the railroad company.[61]

Adamson Act of 1916

Usage of the Newlands Act by the railroads and the unions was widespread and met with a high degree of success. But in March 1916, the Big Four brotherhoods presented a uniform demand for eight-hour workdays to all American railroad companies. Their demand called for a standard day of eight hours or one hundred miles of travel, whichever came first, and time-and-a-half pay for overtime. The response from the railroads was predictably negative, and the parties entered into protracted negotiations over the issue. Frustrated in their attempt to secure contractual language through direct negotiation with the railroad management, the unions refused to submit the matter to the Board of Mediation and Conciliation, settling instead on the strategy of calling for a nationwide strike.

Seeking to avert the consequences of a national rail strike, the Chamber of Commerce of the United States petitioned Congress to direct the ICC to investigate union wage-and-hour demands. At the same time, President Wilson appealed to the carriers and unions to find some commonality in their respective positions. A strike call, to become effective on Labor Day 1916, was the reply. One day prior to the scheduled strike, the workers and their unions agreed to forgo their action if federal law was enacted allowing for a workday to be only eight hours long. In response, Congress enacted the Adamson Act, which provided for an eight-hour workday on the railroads only. On September 5, 1916, the Adamson Act was passed and signed by President Wilson.[62]

Immediately after its passage, railroads' ownership contested the Adamson Act on the grounds that it was unconstitutional. In retaliation, the railroad unions prepared for and rescheduled another nationwide strike. The Supreme Court, weighing the evidence, concluded that the law was not in conflict with constitutional or congressional rights to regulate trade.[63] The decision was handed down the very day the brotherhoods had selected for commencement of strike action. Railroad labor policy was evolving at a more rapid pace than the legislation affecting other industries.

Non-Railroad Labor Activities

Though strides in labor-management relations were being made in the railroad industry, labor in general was not faring as well in the legislative arena. The Sherman Act was a definite barrier to non–rail unions' ability to organize and bargain collectively. Later, in the early 1900s, the movement suffered a number of setbacks. In a 1905 ruling, the Supreme Court held that minimum-wage laws were unconstitutional because they restricted the right of an individual to contract for employment. The decision was based on the principle of "liberty of contract," derived from the Fourteenth Amendment of the Constitution.[64] This decision and the extensive usage of yellow-dog contracts made union activism problematic.

Despite setbacks, the movement continued to struggle and gained hard-won congressional support. In 1914, Congress enacted legislation that on the surface appeared to have prolabor qualities and that was in fact designed to side with labor concerns. Pressure from the AFL after the *Loewe v. Lawlor* (Danbury Hatters) Supreme Court decision led Congress to pass the Clayton Act. So sweeping were some of the act's reforms favoring the labor movement that it was hailed as labor's Magna Charta. Gompers said Section 6 of the Clayton Act was "a sledge hammer blow to the wrongs and injustices so long inflicted upon the workers. The declaration is the industrial Magna Charta upon which the working people will rear their construction of industrial freedom."[65]

Clayton Antitrust Act of 1914

The Clayton Antitrust Act of 1914 was designed to supplement existing laws against unlawful restraints and monopolies (see fig. 2.6). The law was intended to remove ambiguities in the Sherman Antitrust Act by making certain specific practices illegal. Price discrimination among buyers was forbidden along with exclusive selling and tying contracts if their effect was to lessen competition. The Clayton Act also specifically stated there was no provision in antitrust law to forbid the formation of labor unions.

Specifically addressing the plight of the worker, the Clayton Act notes, "The labor of humans is not a commodity or article of commerce." Accordingly, unions were not illegal per se, and injunctions against unions could not be made unless they were necessary to prevent irreparable injury to property. The right to strike for "economic gains" was also addressed. Section 6 provided that antitrust laws, such as the Sherman Act, should not be interpreted or construed to prevent labor unions "from lawfully carrying out the legitimate

objects thereof." Section 20 went further, barring the use of federal injunctions in disputes involving the terms and conditions of employment.[66]

On the surface, the passage of the Clayton Act was a striking victory for the proponents of labor. But in subsequent interpretations, the courts ruled in ways that diminished labor's favorable position. The courts limited the use of boycotts and allowed unions to be sued, even though they were not incorporated or legally recognized organizations.

In 1921, the Supreme Court all but destroyed Sections 6 and 20 of the Clayton Act. Such cases

Figure 2.6. "Trusts—The Main Issue," a cartoon by C. Gordon Moffat, 1899. On October 15, 1914, Congress passed the Clayton Antitrust Act to clarify and supplement the Sherman Antitrust Act of 1890. The Clayton Act outlawed trusts formed by two companies with interlinking boards of directors, price-fixing with businesses offering competing products, making agreements with other businesses to control the supply of a product, and abusing power to gain or maintain a monopoly. *Verdict*, July 10, 1889.

as *Duplex Printing v. Deering* and *Bedford Cut Stone Co. v. Journeymen Stone Cutters Association of North America* provided the death knell of the favorable position originally afforded labor under that act.

In the Duplex case, the International Association of Machinists (IAM) sought to secure an eight-hour day and a union wage scale. In doing so, the IAM told its members not to install and service Duplex equipment. The union also threatened customers with sympathy strikes, influenced trucking companies not to haul the Duplex products, and notified repair shops not to service Duplex presses.[67] Regarding the decision, which favored Duplex, the court held that Section 6 of the Clayton Act was inapplicable to this case because the IAM had departed "from its normal and legitimate objects and engaged in a conspiracy in restraint of trade." In sweeping decisions, the court determined, "Unions were not exempt from the provisions of the Sherman Anti-Trust Act and injunctions could be issued against employees engaging in boycotts of employers, other than their own,"[68] and "Where striking activity or boycotts involve 'interstate commerce' the provisions of the Sherman Anti-Trust Act are applicable."[69]

Despite judicial setbacks, the continuing validity of yellow-dog contracts, and negative publicity, labor organizations outside the railroad industry continued to work toward their goals and increase their membership roles. But it was almost twenty years before parity was reached with the railroad unions.

Railroad Labor Gains

During World War I, union activity took a backseat to the war effort. But a significant occurrence during this period had a profound impact on railroad labor relations. World War I is an interesting interlude in the regulatory and labor stories. During this period, the federal government took over the direction of the railroads in the name of promoting the war effort. Because rail service was important to the war effort, labor disputes were viewed as an ill-afforded inconvenience. To minimize rail disputes and curtail possible loss of rail service, the federal government took control of the nation's railroads in January 1918, placing them under a general director for railroad administration.

The Army Appropriation Act of 1916 provided legislation permitting the president of the United States to take possession of any transportation system in time of war.[70] The act failed to establish an expiration time for such conversion. One major responsibility of the government was to ensure that compensation rates were "fair" and "just." This placed all labor-related activity under the direct control and purview of the U.S. government.

At the beginning of the war, the brotherhoods lacked both legal protection for the right to organize and procedures for settling grievances arising over the interpretation of collective bargaining agreements. On February 21, 1918, the director general of railroads issued Order No. 8, which protected workers from discrimination because of union membership. The government further strengthened the brotherhoods by entering national collective bargaining agreements with railroad unions.

During the two years of government control, the right to organize became an accomplished fact. The wartime establishment of regional railway boards of adjustment to settle grievances over the interpretation of collective bargaining agreements gave collective bargaining a new recognition and permanence.[71] The government had unilaterally implemented what management had sought to avoid. Yellow-dog contracts were being systematically eliminated, and third parties were making decisions on matters of railway disputes without being asked—in the name of the war effort.[72] The Railroad Administration and its director general encouraged union membership by:

- Prohibiting discrimination of any sort against the union worker[73]
- Increasing wages across the board to levels double those at the time of the takeover
- Standardizing wages and working conditions on a national basis
- Imposing restrictive work rules over the objections of management[74]

The resultant changes to the structure of the railroad industry were pervasive. Prior to federal controls, only 50 percent of all rail workers were unionized. But by 1920, the proportion of workers who were unionized had climbed to 85 percent.[75] The results of the quasi-nationalization of the railroad industry by the federal government were overwhelming. In a time of booming traffic, a $568 million profit in 1917 was turned into a loss of $1.5 billion by 1920.[76] This was an expensive, but depressingly familiar, lesson.

The results for organized labor were overwhelming. Never before in history had so much been received by labor in a short period of time. A monumental public policy shift had occurred. The apparent government-union adversarial relationship embodied in previous conspiracy doctrines and restraint of trade analyses was now moving away from indifference toward outright promotion. This public policy shift ignited and fueled legislation of a pro-union nature. The 1920s and 1930s witnessed this shift with the development of the Railway Labor Act (RLA), the Norris–La Guardia Act, the ill-fated National Industrial Recovery Act, the Wagner Act, and the Fair Labor Standards Act. The railroads, their unions, and governmental action toward the parties combined to lay the track for not only rail labor legislation but also its spur, the remainder of industrial America.

Transportation Act of 1920

The ill-fated venture into the government's quasi-ownership of the railroad industry sent shivers down the back of many congressional incumbents of the time. As a result, Congress wanted to make the railroads financially sound and stable, as they had been prior to the government involvement in the managerial aspects of the railroads. Once again, the ICC practices were modified. The transportation act provided that the ICC should:

- Set "just and reasonable" rates so that railroads could earn a 6 percent rate of return on assets (railroads earning more than 6 percent would have to set aside additional amounts so that other, non–6-percent-producing carriers could partake of the returns
- Consider the revenue needs of the weaker railroads when deciding the division of joint rates and how to divide the revenues (this ultimately led to subsidization)
- Establish minimum rates
- Control interstate rates and entry and exit into the railroad business
- Approve traffic and rate pooling
- Develop railway lines in order to keep as much mileage in operation as possible

The last provision was used in merger cases. All of these provisions will be revisited when the airlines become a reality, and regulation is controlled by the Civil Aeronautics Board.

Upon return of the railroads to private ownership, other industrial sectors showed varying degrees of interest in the activities that had taken place during the war period. The railroad unions, content with the government handling of a nationalized workplace, sought, unsuccessfully, to officially and permanently nationalize the rail industry. Since relative stability existed in the railroads during this period, Congress was anxious to continue a harmonious labor-management relationship for the public interest. Labor was anxious to retain the gains they had made, and management was equally anxious to erode these union windfalls.

The legislation Congress enacted—the Transportation Act—was a compromise between

House and Senate versions desirous to retain elements of government control. All unresolved disputes were to be referred to the U.S. Railroad Labor Board for hearing and decision. This newly created board was to carry out both mediation and arbitration of disputes. The one-sided nature of the act was totally opposed by both labor and management because it left the decision of their fates in the hands of a disinterested third party. Further, the act required that adjustment boards, created for the purpose of resolving grievances, be established between the parties to contracts. Title III of the Transportation Act created a tripartite Railroad Labor Board to recommend settlement in labor disputes. This provision permitted the voluntary establishment of boards of adjustment to handle grievances. The right to organize was not given statutory protection. Neither the unions nor the carriers were satisfied with the new law.[77]

When enacted, the U.S. Railroad Labor Board was immediately inundated with cases. As might have been expected, the parties contested the binding nature of the board's decisions and contended the nonvoluntary nature of the act. In several court decisions, enforcement powers were struck down. The labor board was to act as a board of arbitration, and no constraint was to be placed on the parties to do what the board decided.[78] The ultimate decision of the board therefore was not compulsory, and no process was furnished to enforce it.[79] These decisions and the resultant problems eventually discredited the board, despite that during the five years of its life, it handled more than thirteen thousand disputes, for the most part successfully.[80]

Summary

Title III of the Transportation Act, thoroughly discredited by the courts, joined its predecessors in the dustbin of failed labor legislation. The laws enacted between the 1880s and 1920 were proven defective or inadequate when applied to the important labor issues of the day. A befitting epithet for Title III was given by a union president in testimony before a Senate committee. The president of the Brotherhood of Locomotive Firemen and Enginemen told Congress that the principal defect of Title III was that it was a "compromise between compulsion and persuasion. It established a board to take the place of mediators who should be persuaders and then required them to decide disputes which made them arbitrators. As soon as they began deciding disputes they immediately lost standing as mediators. Their peace-power became dependent on force and they had no force to exert."[81] Labor, management, and government had come full circle. The framework for labor relations remained a minefield strewn with ineffective legislation, uncertainty, and adversarial attitudes.

3. Major Collective Bargaining Legislation

Labor movement formation peaked in the mid-1920s for the railroad industry and in the mid-1930s for the remainder of the industrialized workforce. The government's segregated approach to labor-relations legislation allowed the railroad-industry unions to emerge and evolve at a more rapid pace than the other craft and industrial associations. Despite the plethora of legislative and judicial setbacks experienced by the unions in the early 1900s, several developments in the mid- to late 1920s had a positive impact on the union movement. For example, in 1924, an isolated piece of legislation called the Immigration Act was signed into law limiting the number of immigrants admitted to the United States. The restriction on immigration reduced the number of new arrivals competing for jobs and significantly increased the bargaining power of the American worker.

This chapter focuses primarily on legislation from the 1920s through the 1950s that affected union development. Table 3.1 lists these acts and their functions within the labor-relations environment. Detailed discussion of these acts follows.

The Railway Labor Act
Origins

Within the railroad industry, union dissatisfaction with the Transportation Act of 1920 caused the railroad brotherhoods to support the independent candidacy of Robert M. La Follette for president in 1924 (see fig. 3.1). The brotherhoods were disappointed by the failure of the Transportation Act to establish grievance machinery and angered by appointments to the Railroad Labor Board. The railroad unions felt the existing board constituency had management leanings. La Follette's advocacy of government ownership of the railroads raised hopes for a return to the wartime prosperity the unions had enjoyed.

Figure 3.1. President Calvin Coolidge and Mother Jones. During the 1924 presidential election, the American Federation of Labor (AFL) solicited funds for independent candidate Robert M. La Follette's presidential campaign. On September 16, 1924, the AFL issued a press release stating that Coolidge and the Ku Klux Klan were "running neck and neck as the spokesmen of God and the Constitution." That same day, however, Mother Mary Jones, an outspoken proponent of organized labor, showed her support for Coolidge by posing with him outside the White House. Library of Congress.

Table 3.1.
Major labor-relations laws in the United States, 1926–59

Act	*Function*
Railway Labor Act (1926)	Established the rights of railroad employees to engage in union activities; codified the collective bargaining process
Norris–La Guardia Act (1932)	Restricted the right of courts to issue injunctions against unions engaging in various activities; forbade yellow-dog contracts
Railway Labor Act (1934 amendment)	Amended the act to create the National Mediation Board; mandated mediation and secured union-representation privileges
National Labor Relations Act (1935)	Established the rights of workers to form unions, bargain collectively, and strike; forbade employers from engaging in unfair labor practices; established National Labor Relations Board to administer the act
Railway Labor Act (1936 amendment)	Amended the act to include all interstate commercial air carriers
Fair Labor Standards Act (1938)	Established a minimum wage and maximum work week; outlawed child labor
Railway Labor Act (1940 amendment)	Amended the act to clarify coverage of railroad activity in the coal industry
Taft-Hartley Act (1947)	Amended the National Labor Relations Act to prohibit unfair union practices; established provisions for right-to-work laws; established procedures for emergency dispute resolutions
Railway Labor Act (1951 amendment)	Amended the act to eliminate the bar against closed shops
Landrum-Griffin Act (1959)	Amended the National Labor Relations Act; required unions to hold democratic elections; required unions to make annual financial disclosure to the Department of Labor

After La Follette's defeat, the brotherhoods began to muster nonpartisan support for the repeal of the Transportation Act. Ironically, railroad management became their most potent political ally.[1] The dissatisfaction with the Transportation Act of 1920 came because both management and labor had concerns about forced arbitration and the Railroad Labor Board's inability to enforce its decisions. Congress agreed that the labor provisions of the Transportation Act needed revision. As a result, various bills were proposed, one of which—the Howell-Barkley Bill—received a very favorable response. Interestingly, this proposal was prepared by the attorney for the railroad unions and thus had the consent of the union membership.[2] Management, also recognizing the need to preserve certain elements of the voluntary dispute resolution, submitted its own version of legislation.

In 1925, a committee of management and labor representatives convened to draft a joint approach that they hoped would satisfy both labor and management. After repeated conferences, a shared draft bill similar to the Howell-Barkley proposal, the Watson-Parker Bill, received a consensus and in January 1926 was presented to Congress. Having the support of both railroad management and unions, it passed Congress with a wide margin of victory (the Senate vote was 69-13, and the House vote was 381-13).[3]

The only opposition came from the National Association of Manufacturers, and President Calvin Coolidge attempted to persuade the railroads to accept amendments proposed by that association. On May 20, 1926, failing to convince the railroads to accept the amendments, Coolidge signed the Railway Labor Act (RLA). The new act repealed the Erdman and Newlands Acts and Title III of the 1920 Transportation Act. The RLA, with a number of amendments, remains valid and operative legislation today. As such, it is the oldest federal collective bargaining legislation in the nation's history.[4]

Early Judicial Challenges

The year 1926 saw the birth of the first national labor-relations statute ever formulated to sanction and codify union-management collective bargaining. The statute provides for cooling-off periods and mediation and conciliation in disputes over the terms of new agreements. Since both management and labor opposed compulsory arbitration and the final determination of wages, hours, and working conditions by government edict, the act provided for a less-restrictive procedure. The law preserved the right to strike after extended negotiations and mediation. To the disappointment of the unions, the act did not provide for national adjustment boards to handle grievance disputes. This deficiency was removed by amendment in 1934.

Labor and management had worked together on the joint drafting of the original act, but the question of constitutionality remained. In 1930, when the U.S. Supreme Court upheld the provisions of the act, the constitutionality issue was resolved. The issue in *Texas and New Orleans Railroad v. the Brotherhood of Railway and Steamship Clerks* was the railroad's discharging employees because of their union membership. Contrary to the decision rendered in *Adair v. United States*, which challenged the Erdman Act provisions that made it a criminal offense to discharge employees for union membership, the *Texas* decision states, "The RLA does not interfere with the normal exercise of the right of the carrier to select its employees or to discharge them. The statute is not aimed at this right of the employers, but at the interference of the right of the employees to have a representative of their own choosing. As the carriers subject to the Act have no constitutional right to interfere with the freedom of the employees in making their selection, they cannot complain of the statute on constitutional grounds."[5]

The change in the philosophical reasoning of the court is more evident when the decision on the *Adair* case is placed side by side with that of the *Texas* decision. In *Adair*, the court ruled, "The right of a person to sell his labor upon such terms as he deems proper, is, in its essence, the same as the right of the purchaser to prescribe the conditions upon which he will accept such labor from the person offering to sell it."[6]

Depression-Era Unionism

The Great Depression of 1929, which left millions of American workers jobless, had its own special impact on the labor movement and on subsequent legislation. The Great Depression changed the attitude of many Americans. Both workers and nonworkers came to embrace the labor movement. Before 1929, most people regarded the heads of American business to be benevolent national leaders, capable of resolving any of the nation's ills. Members of the union movement were identified as dangerous radicals. Despite such contrastive stereotypes, people began losing faith in managerial leadership when business could not revive the economy. Many Americans began to believe that the way to fight the slump was to increase the purchasing power of wage earners, a philosophy espoused by most unions. The political climate changed from one favoring management to one favoring labor.

The RLA allowed the railroad unions and employees to weather the Great Depression far better than their counterparts in other industries. Wage rates were not cut, but the unions allowed the carriers to deduct 10 percent from wages during the period from February 1, 1932, through June 10, 1934. On April 1, 1935, wages were restored to their January 1932 level. The railroad employees were also helped by the Federal Emergency Railroad Transportation Act of 1933, which forbade railroad mergers that would result in job loss.[7]

Provisions of the RLA

For many years, the RLA was widely proclaimed as "ideal" labor-relations legislation. It avoided compulsory arbitration and encouraged industrial peace in an essential industry. Its cooling-off period, emphasis on mediation and conciliation, and provision for emergency boards offered multiple pathways for managing and defusing disputes in these essential national industries.

Only recently has there been an outcry to repeal the act—in particular, its secondary-boycott provision. Adding to the secondary-boycott dilemma is a Supreme Court ruling favoring the use of secondary picketing as a proper means of self-help during disputes with carriers. Despite such outcries, "any assessment of the RLA must be kept in proper perspective . . . and any measure

of the RLA's effectiveness must be made with reference to its [original] objectives to promote free collective bargaining and to protect the public from interrupted flows of commerce."[8]

Public policy objectives. The RLA impacts broadly on the collective bargaining process in the rail and air transport industries. As stated by the act, the five general public policy purposes are:

- Avoid interruption to interstate commerce in the railroad and airline industries
- Ensure the right of employees to freely determine whether they wish to be represented for collective bargaining purposes
- Ensure the independence of labor and management for self-organization to carry out the purposes of the act
- Provide for the prompt and orderly settlement of collective bargaining disputes
- Provide for the prompt and orderly settlement of disputes over the interpretation of existing collective bargaining agreements

The act, which created procedures and mechanisms for adjusting differences, imposes duties on carriers (rail and air) and on employees and their representatives, defines rights and provisions for their protection, and prescribes methods for settling various types of disputes.[9]

Major and minor disputes. To facilitate implementation of the general objectives of the RLA, two distinct dispute categories were defined: "major" and "minor" disputes. Major disputes deal with union certification elections and the development of a new agreement or a change in an existing agreement. (The process and procedures for handling major disputes are examined in chapters 4 and 5 of the current volume.) Minor disputes deal with the resolution of grievances and the interpretation or application of the existing terms of a labor agreement. (Minor dispute procedures are examined in chapter 7 of the current volume.) Congress established the National Railroad Adjustment Board (NRAB) to settle minor disputes arising out of grievances or application of contracts. This board, confined to the railroad industry, has final and binding authority in resolving minor disputes. Because the board is congressionally established, the cost of its operation is paid from government coffers.

In the airline industry, the mechanism for minor dispute resolution is different. A board similar to that in the railroad industry was never established, although the 1934 amendment authorized one. Title II of the RLA requires each carrier and its employees to set up a system board of adjustment for the purpose of adjudicating minor disputes. Title II also gives the National Mediation Board (NMB) the authority when the board deems such action necessary to establish a National Air Transport Adjustment Board (NATAB), which would function substantially the same as the National Railroad Adjustment Board. To date, no such board has been established in the airline industry.[10]

National Mediation Board

The NMB was established by Congress in 1934 to administer the RLA. Its functions are categorized as largely ministerial, and therefore it lacks the ability to make decisions involving the interpretation of the act. These decisions remain the sole province of Congress.[11]

The NMB comprises three members, whom the president of the United States appoints and the Senate confirms. These members must be persons with no current labor, airline, or railroad employment. No more than two members may have the same political affiliation. Each member is appointed for a term of three years, and each acts as chairperson on an annual rotation. The board may designate one or more of its members to exercise its functions in mediation proceedings and has the power to administer oaths and affirmations. The board is authorized to appoint experts and assistants to act in any capacity essential to required transactions and

can assign or refer any portion of its work or functions to individual members or employees. It also has the authority to provide for salaries and expenditures necessary to complete these actions.[12]

The NMB provides the following services to parties of a dispute:

- Mediation of disputes relating to the changing of existing agreements affecting rates of pay, rules, and/or working conditions
- Determination or certification of the representatives of a class or craft of employees
- Election monitoring
- Interpretation of agreements made under its mediation program

The purpose of the NMB is to take measures that will avoid any interruption of interstate commerce, to enforce the limitations of the freedom of choice or association by the employees of an air or rail carrier, and to provide a means for the prompt and orderly settlement of disputes.[13]

The RLA relies almost entirely on the use of collective bargaining to settle labor disputes, but unlike the NLRA, it mandates mediation by the NMB if the parties reach an impasse in the negotiation process. If mediation fails, the RLA provides for a proffer of arbitration by the NMB. Although either party to the dispute is free to refuse arbitration, the costs of which the board pays, the RLA further provides that the president of the United States may convene an emergency board to investigate the dispute and recommend procedures and terms for the agreement.[14]

The long-term effect of this required mediation procedure is that contractual negotiations can, and often do, take an exorbitant amount of time before a settlement is reached. During the mediation process, the provisions of the existing contract remain in effect, eliminating any ability on the part of the carrier or the unions to impose financial pressure. If a strike occurs, the provisions of the act do not prohibit secondary boycotts, as does the NLRA. This singular provision may at some time in the future cause either a congressional revision of the act or its demise altogether.

RLA Amendment of 1934

By 1934, with the advent of the Norris–La Guardia Act and the National Industrial Recovery Act (NIRA), Congress recognized that the RLA required modifications to keep pace with the growing labor movement. The initial passage of the act had been designed to produce peaceful settlement of contract disputes, but it failed to establish freedom of association in various labor unions that were not in existence in 1926. As late as 1933, for example, 147 of the 233 largest railroads still maintained company unions.[15] Interest in applying the provisions of the Norris–La Guardia Act to the RLA was so strong that Joseph B. Easton, the federal coordinator of transportation, suggested they be written directly into the act.[16]

In 1934, the first of five amendments to the RLA occurred. Major importance was centered on three particular areas. Company-sponsored unions were banned from existence, as were unions dominated by railroad companies. This elimination provided the protection of the right of employees to organize for collective bargaining purposes without interference by the employer. This proscription also permanently put an end to the concept of yellow-dog contracts in the railroad industry.

Another important provision was the establishment of the National Railroad Adjustment Board, a forum to which grievances could be submitted by either party to a dispute. This board was empowered to interpret the application of bargaining agreements in existence and settle minor disputes over working conditions and contract interpretation. Thus, the 1934 amendment made arbitration of such disputes compulsory. This requirement is one of the RLA's unusual features.

RLA Amendment of 1936

In 1936, Congress, prodded by a strong lobbying effort by the fledgling Air Line Pilots Association (ALPA), decided to put the tiny airline industry (twenty-four carriers with a total of 4,200 employees and 433 aircraft) under the RLA. Ten years after the original enactment of the RLA, Congress passed the Title II amendment, which applied most of the provisions of the act to air carriers engaged in interstate commerce. In the spirit of the times, Congress decided that the traveling and shipping public had to be protected against work stoppages and interruption of airborne commerce. Thus, the RLA, already successful in the railroad industry for a decade, was extended to airlines. The history of the statute reveals that airmail transportation was the legislative issue in the minds of the politicians.[17]

Prior legislative issues. Prior to their inclusion under the RLA, the air carriers that were in existence were subject to the provisions of the 1932 Norris–La Guardia Act and the 1933 National Industrial Recovery Act (NIRA). The NIRA coverage resulted in one of the major standing decisions of airline labor work rules, Decision 83 of the National Labor Board, which set maximum flying hours and incremental pay plans for mileage and speed. This fundamental work rule was issued outside the purview of the RLA but remains in force because of grandfather rights.

This National Labor Board decision, the only airline determination made outside the purview of the RLA, has historically influenced pilot labor relations and negotiations. Its formula for the establishment of hourly and mileage pay rates relative to aircraft speed has led to increased wages and related benefits whenever aircraft productivity and technology improvements were made by manufacturers. The essential components of this pay formula still apply to airline pilots today.[18]

The decision to place the nation's airlines under the provisions of the RLA seemed so unimportant that two decades later, it drew only a small footnote in a college textbook covering labor-union history.[19] In most labor textbooks today, the RLA occupies less than two pages. Table 3.2 lists a summary of the provisions of the RLA after passage of the 1934 and 1936 amendments.

RLA Amendments of 1940 and 1951

In 1940, a minor amendment was added to the RLA to clarify coverage of the act in relation to rail operations in coal mines. In 1951, the union shop was made a permissible form of required union membership.

Right-to-work laws. Section 14(b) of the Taft-Hartley Act affirms the right of states to enact right-to-work laws (see fig. 3.2). A right-to-work law guarantees that no person can be compelled, as a condition of employment, to join or not to join or to pay dues to a labor union. This, however, is not applicable to those under the Railway

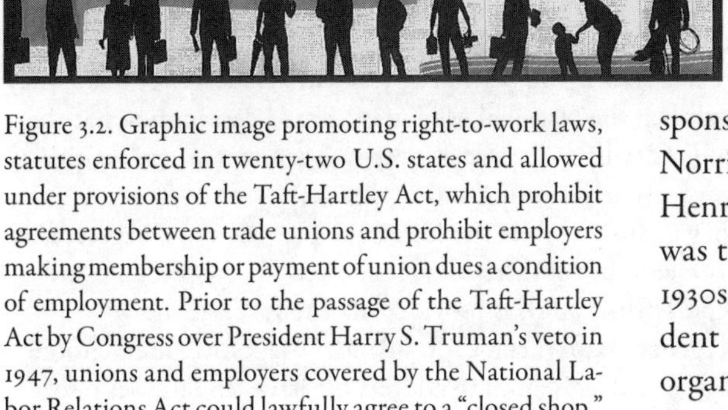

Figure 3.2. Graphic image promoting right-to-work laws, statutes enforced in twenty-two U.S. states and allowed under provisions of the Taft-Hartley Act, which prohibit agreements between trade unions and prohibit employers making membership or payment of union dues a condition of employment. Prior to the passage of the Taft-Hartley Act by Congress over President Harry S. Truman's veto in 1947, unions and employers covered by the National Labor Relations Act could lawfully agree to a "closed shop," in which employees are required to be union members as a condition of employment. Courtesy of National Right to Work.

Labor Act as the 1951 RLA amendment requiring union membership is in direct conflict with the National Labor Relations Act and subsequently right-to-work laws in twenty-two states.

If a union is certified as a bargaining representative in a state that has passed right-to-work laws, and no provisions have been made between the employer and the union, an airline or railroad employee is compelled to join or financially support the union certified by the NMB. Section 2, Eleventh, of the RLA specifically preempts states from making laws favoring employee rights over those of union membership.

Questioning the constitutionality of this provision, the Supreme Court stated, "[W]e pass narrowly on paragraph 2, eleventh of the Railway Labor Act. We only hold that the requirements for financial support of the collective bargaining agency by all who receive benefits of its work are within the power of Congress under the Commerce Clause and do not violate either the First or the Fifth Amendments."[20] This means that railroad and airline employees do not enjoy the benefits of a state's right-to-work legislation because, at the minimum, they will be required to pay dues to the union for benefits received attributable to the negotiation process.

The Norris–La Guardia Act of 1932

In 1932, Congress enacted one of the first prolabor laws outside the railroad industry. The law acquired its name from the sponsors of the original bill, Senator George W. Norris of Nebraska and Representative Fiorello Henry La Guardia of New York (see fig. 3.3). It was the first of several statutes enacted in the 1930s, a time when both Congress and the president favored collective bargaining and union organization. The preamble of the Norris–La Guardia Act makes clear the public policy of the United States and reflects the prolabor attitude of the nation during this period: "Whereas

Table 3.2.
Provisions of the Railway Labor Act

Category	Provisions
Purpose	To avoid interruption to interstate commerce.
	To provide prompt settlement of disputes in covered industries.
	Provisions for major dispute resolution include certification of election results from organizational activities and mediation of disputes arising under the collective bargaining process for contract renewal.
	Provisions for minor dispute resolution include interpretation, through system boards of adjustment, of existing contracts.
Extent of coverage	All railroads and subsidiaries of railroads covered under the original passage in 1926.
	All U.S. airlines operating under Interstate Commerce provisions and all foreign-flag airline carriers operating on U.S. soil; added to Railway Labor Act by 1936 amendments.
Negotiation procedures	Section 6 notice, as outlined by the act, requires thirty days' notice of intended change to contract, working conditions, wages, and the like.
	Conferences between the parties to be held within ten days of the Section 6 notice.
	Strikes not permitted during meetings between the parties until parties have been released by the National Mediation Board or for ten days after direct meetings between the parties have passed.
Mediation	Upon impasse in negotiations between the parties, either party may request mediation from the National Mediation Board. The National Mediation Board may impose mandatory mediation without a request from either party if, in the determination of the board, a labor emergency exists.
	No time limit exists for mediation. The timing of the mediation process is at the discretion of the National Mediation Board.
	The contract under discussion remains in effect during the mediation process and for thirty days after a proffer of arbitration has been refused by either party (status quo).
Arbitration	As noted above, if mediation fails, the National Mediation Board must offer voluntary arbitration to the parties.
	When arbitration is accepted, arbitration will provide a final and binding agreement.
	Refusal by either party to arbitration will cause the board to withdraw from the case and the status quo provision will remain in effect for thirty days (cooling-off period).
Emergency provisions	Upon recommendation and report to the president of the United States, after the parties have been released and are in a cooling-off period, a presidential emergency board may be established. This occurs when the National Mediation Board determines that the dispute could "threaten substantially to interrupt interstate commerce" or "deprive any section of the country of essential transportation service."
	Establishment of an emergency board preserves the status quo provision of an agreement an additional sixty days. A maximum of thirty days is allowed for the special board to make investigation and report. Thirty days is provided after report is made.
	Possible outcomes of the emergency board include: presidential suggestive intervention, congressional enactment of special legislation to address the issue, and parties resort to self-help.

Source: National Mediation Board

under prevailing economic conditions, developed with the aid of governmental authority for owners of property to organize in corporate forms of ownership association, the individual unorganized worker is commonly helpless. . . . [W]herefore . . . it is necessary to have full freedom of association . . . for the purpose of collective bargaining or other mutual aid."[21]

Figure 3.3. Fiorello Henry La Guardia (1882–1947). In 1932, U.S. Representative La Guardia, along with U.S. Senator George W. Norris, secured passage of the pro-union Norris–La Guardia Act, which outlawed the practice of requiring prospective employees not to join a labor union as a condition of employment (yellow-dog contract) and limited the use of court injunctions against strikes. Library of Congress.

Passage of the act curtailed management's ability to receive federal injunctions during labor disputes. Prior to enactment of the Norris–La Guardia Act, it was only necessary for management to apply for such injunctions to receive them. Temporary restraining orders would generally be issued and received before the unions could respond, making the injunction ex parte (the court could issue an injunction without first

allowing the union or its attorneys to be heard) to the unions. This ex parte injunctive relief effectively created a unilateral right of management to deter or dampen the unions' activities. The Norris–La Guardia Act closed this loophole and provided unions with the opportunity to appear in court and present opposing arguments on why injunctions should not be issued. This eliminated the issuance of ex parte injunctions, which management had been adept at using with the full knowledge and concurrence of the courts. The other provision of the act was equally important because it eliminated management's ability to use the yellow-dog contract. No longer would it be a risk for union organizers to approach employees who had been forced to sign such agreements. Thus, the door was opened for union expansion. The act placed no affirmative obligation on employers to negotiate with or recognize unions. Rather, it sought to aid union organizing and collective bargaining. Its main impact was to permit the unions to exert effective economic pressure against employers. Years earlier, Samuel Gompers had proclaimed the Clayton Act to be labor's Magna Charta, but his proclamation may have been premature. With the signing of the Norris–La Guardia Act, a wide range of aggressive tactics were given to the unions and dramatically increased their ability to achieve their objectives.

Railroad workers received a bonus from the act when Congress refused arguments calling for the exemption of railroads from coverage. Not only were the railroad employees and their unions covered by the RLA but under the Norris–La Guardia Act, they also were permitted the use of such economic weapons as strikes, picketing, and boycotts.

In summary, the provisions of the Norris–La Guardia Act are to:

- Forbid federal courts to issue injunctions against the following specifically described union activities:

- Stopping or refusing to work
- Union membership
- Paying or withholding strike benefits, unemployment benefits, and so on to those engaging in a labor dispute
- Publicizing a labor dispute in a nonviolent manner
- Assembly to organize
- Aid or assistance for persons suing or being sued
- Agreeing to engage or not engage in any of the foregoing
- Forbid employers to require employees to sign yellow-dog contracts

The National Labor Relations Act

National Industrial Recovery Act

With the country in the throes of depression in 1933, Franklin D. Roosevelt assumed the position of president in January of that year and immediately set in motion the New Deal, his proposal to bring the nation back to prosperity. Included in his plan was the passage of several laws that benefited labor. One of the most important was the National Industrial Recovery Act (NIRA).

The NIRA became effective in 1933 and set minimum wages and maximum hours of work and implemented Section 7(a), which provided for the right of labor to organize and to engage in collective bargaining.[22] The act provided for the establishment of codes for "fair competition" in the industries covered. Its most important labor feature made it mandatory that any activity emanating from the act contain the following conditions:

[E]mployees shall have the right to organize and bargain collectively through representatives of their own choosing, and shall be free from the interference, restraint, or coercion of employers of labor, or their agents, in the designation of such representatives or in self organization or in other concerted activities for the purpose of collective bargaining or other mutual aid or protection. That no employee and no one seeking employment shall be required as a condition of employment to join any company union or to refrain from joining, organizing or assisting a labor organization of his own choosing.[23]

To handle labor disputes, President Roosevelt created the National Labor Board, later renamed the National Labor Relations Board. The latter, commencing its operation in July 1934, functioned to investigate the facts in labor disputes arising under the NIRA. The board was given the right to conduct elections among employees to determine their bargaining representatives and to certify those desired by the majority of employees.

The program was greeted with enthusiasm at first but began to run into serious administrative difficulties and faced growing opposition. The act was to expire, unless renewed, on June 16, 1935. The government claimed its power to institute the NIRA was founded on interstate commerce jurisdiction and thus that the act was constitutionally appropriate. But in *Schechter v. United States*, a case directly emanating from the act, the Supreme Court determined, "If the commerce clause were construed to reach all enterprises and transactions which could be said to have an indirect effect upon interstate commerce, the federal authority would embrace practically all the activities of the people and the authority of the state over its domestic concerns would exist only by sufferance of the federal government."[24]

The code structure of the NIRA—which had only three weeks to go unless renewed—collapsed with the *Schechter* decision. The code had proved too cumbersome and unworkable.[25] The NIRA had, however, with its codes of fair competition, encouraged voluntary collective bargaining by employers and, like the RLA, indicated the need for federal intervention in labor disputes. The movement toward government involvement was incontrovertible, and the NIRA had laid the groundwork for the enactment of future regulation.

Origins of the NLRA: The Wagner Act

Immediately following the collapse of the NIRA, Senator Robert F. Wagner of New York set in motion replacement language contained in the Wagner Bill, which later became the Wagner Act, the foundation of the NLRA. The NLRA, enacted on July 5, 1935, applied to all workers in interstate commerce and created the National Labor Relations Board. This act set forth the right of employees to self-organization and collective bargaining, defined unfair labor practices, and laid down rules about the representation of employees for the purpose of collective bargaining. The act also empowered the National Labor Relations Board to prevent those described unfair labor practices that affected commerce.[26] The board was given power to punish unfair labor practices and to determine which union should represent workers at various companies falling under its provisions.[27] Table 3.3 summarizes the provisions of the Wagner Act.

The intent of the NLRA is to equalize the bargaining power of the employee. Its regulatory aspects are contained in the following statement of policy:

> Experience has proved that protection by law of the right of employees to organize and bargain collectively safeguards commerce from injury, impairment, or interruption, and promotes the flow of commerce by removing certain recognized sources of industrial strife and unrest, by encouraging practices fundamental to the friendly adjustment of industrial dis-

putes arising out of differences as to wages, hours, or other working condition, and by restoring equality of bargaining power between employers and employees. . . .

> It is hereby declared to be the policy of the United States to eliminate the causes of certain substantial obstructions to the free flow of commerce and to mitigate and eliminate these obstructions when they have occurred by encouraging the practice and procedure of collective bargaining and by protecting the exercise by workers of full freedom of association, self-organization, and designation of representatives of their own choosing, for the purpose of negotiation the terms and conditions of their employment or other mutual aid or protection.[28]

The primary objectives of the NLRA are twofold. Section 7 guarantees employees:

- Freedom to form, join, and/or assist labor organizations
- Freedom to bargain collectively with employers
- Freedom to engage in concerted activity to enhance collective bargaining

Section 8 seeks to keep the rights of the employees inviolate by imposing affirmative duties on the employer to deal in good faith with unions. In this area, the act lists five employer labor practices that were to be considered unfair:

- Interference with employees' rights to self-organization
- Discrimination against employees because of their affiliation with a labor union
- Refusal to bargain with a labor organization of the employees' choice
- Attempts to dominate or contribute to the support of a labor organization or to form company unions to deter the legitimate attempt by employees to select a representative of their choice

Table 3.3.
Major provisions of the Wagner Act

Category	Provisions
Policy	To protect the right of employees to organize and bargain collectively. To make a policy of the United States to encourage the practice and procedure of collective bargaining and the exercise by employees of their right to organize and negotiate.
Rights of employees	To organize into unions of the employees' choice. To bargain collectively with their employer through representatives of their own choosing. To strike or take similar concerted action. To assist labor unions in the encouragement of membership.
Establishment of the National Labor Relations Board	The five board members are appointed by the president of the United States. The board conducts elections to determine employee representatives. The board has exclusive power to prevent employer unfair labor practices.
Employer unfair labor practices	Interfering with employee rights guaranteed under the act. Discrimination against employees or labor unions pursuing their rights guaranteed under the act. Refusal to bargain in good faith with the representatives of the employees' choice. Any attempt to interfere with the employees' choice to join a union.
Elections	The National Labor Relations Board (NLRB) conducts secret-ballot elections to determine employee representatives. The National Labor Relations Board determines the appropriate unit (collective bargaining group) for purpose of representation and elections. Employee representatives shall be the exclusive representatives of the defined unit.
Limitations	The act was primarily concerned with the organizing phase of labor relations. The act dealt exclusively with employer tactics (unfair labor practices) and did not address union activities.

- Retaliation against any employee for filing a complaint against a company or giving testimony against an employer

In view of the failure of the NIRA and the history of union-representation movements, many employers took umbrage with the NLRA's passage and refused to comply with its procedures. Once again, the constitutionality issue was raised.

Judicial challenge. Opponents argued that the NLRA went beyond the commerce clause and invaded the Tenth Amendment rights of the sovereign states. A second constitutional issue presented was that employers' due process of law was denied by imposing restriction on their freedom of contract. In a 1937 landmark decision, *National Labor Relations Board v. Jones & Laughlin Steel Corporation*, the Supreme Court upheld constitutionality by enforcing a National Labor Relations Board cease and desist order against a company for unfair labor practices of interfering with employees' rights to organize and bargain collectively (see fig. 3.4).[29] This decision held that the law was proper extension of the commerce clause to manufacturing workers and that it was not in violation of the constitutional due-process clause. The rationale for the extension of the commerce clause was that a reduction in labor strife would promote commerce among the states.

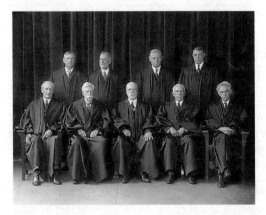

Figure 3.4. U.S. Supreme Court that upheld the Wagner Act, the first federal law to regulate disputes between capital and labor. Chief Justice Charles Hughes (center, bottom row) on April 12, 1937, read the majority opinion in *National Labor Relations Board v. Jones & Laughlin Steel Corporation*. U.S. Supreme Court.

No previous period in the history of American trade unionism other than the Great Upheaval of 1886 matched the epochal importance of the 1930s in the development of collective bargaining and industrial government for the worker. With the passage of the NIRA in 1933 and the NLRA in 1935, collective bargaining received a degree of public respectability that a century and a half of private efforts had been unable to achieve. The impact on the organizing and collective bargaining activities of the trade-union movement was nothing short of phenomenal.[30]

The Wagner Act, in its desire to provide for union parity with management's rights, created a significant number of requirements for the employer. In the exuberance to pass Wagner, Congress placed restrictions on the employer and did not address similar issues relating to union activities. Only the employers were prohibited from engaging in unfair practices. This failure to incorporate the duties and responsibilities of unions went unchecked for twelve years, and it was not until the passage of the Taft-Hartley amendment in 1947 that unions were placed under similar restraints.

NLRA Amendment: The Taft-Hartley Act

The Labor-Management Relations Act of 1947, better known as the Taft-Hartley Act, was intended to limit some of the activities of labor unions in the United States (see table 3.4 for a summary of the Taft-Hartley Act). It amended the NLRA of 1935, which had defined unions' rights to organize and to bargain with employers.

Initially, the NLRA was the Wagner Act. But it has been amended and supplemented by additional legislation: the Labor-Management Relations Act of 1947 (Taft-Hartley), the Labor-Management Reporting and Disclosure Act of 1959 (Landrum-Griffin), and Public Law 93-36 (health-care industry) in 1974.[31] Today, all these amendments make up the NLRA.

Subsequent to World War II, during which all wage increases were prohibited by the government, the United States entered its greatest period of economic growth. Unions, with their newfound freedoms, attempted to secure a large portion of this new wealth for their membership. Waves of strikes began, and in 1946, the number of work stoppages reached an all-time high. From 1945 to 1947, the country experienced nationwide strikes in the automobile, coal, oil, lumber, textiles, maritime, and rail transportation industries.

Although unions scored some of their most impressive victories during this time, many members of Congress felt that the balance of the labor-management–relations equation had become too

Table 3.4.
Major provisions of the Taft-Hartley Act

Category	Provisions
Policy	To determine certain practices of labor organizations that obstruct the free flow of commerce. To eliminate union practices necessary to guarantee free flow of commerce. To create the Federal Mediation and Conciliation Service, which assists in any dispute affecting interstate commerce and requires parties to notify the service when any change in the terms and conditions of employment is desired.
Rights of employees	Right to refrain from union activities, except provisions contained in union-shop collective bargaining agreements.
Right to work	Established state rights to outlaw union-shop requirements in collective bargaining agreements. Employees in right-to-work states can refrain from joining the union representing their bargaining unit.
Union unfair labor practices	Refusal to bargain in good faith with the employer. Discriminating against employee for not engaging in union activities. Restraint or coercion of employees in their rights. Prohibition on closed shops.
Restriction on certain activities	Elimination of secondary boycotts and secondary strikes. Prohibition of strikes during the term of a valid collective bargaining agreement. Elimination of strikes to force employer to make work for union members. Outlawed featherbedding. Prohibition of strikes to force dislocation of one union in favor of another.
Provides for presidential intervention	The president intervenes where an industry-wide dispute could "imperil the national health or safety." The president appoints a board of inquiry to Investigate and report on the facts of the dispute and the parties' positions. Make recommendations and issue injunction for eighty days if "national health or safety" is in jeopardy. After the first sixty days, give a report on the status of the dispute to the president. Within the next fifteen days, a poll is taken by employees on management's final offer. After eighty days, the injunction expires, and the parties are free to exercise self-help. The president considers the possibility of congressional legislation to halt the dispute.

heavily weighted in favor of the unions. They believed that employers and employees needed protection against unfair labor practices of unions and that the public needed protection against labor disputes that threatened the national health and security. The 1946 Congress was the first since 1930 with a Republican majority, and in 1947, it passed a law, the Taft-Hartley Act, that amended the NLRA by placing greater restrictions on unions' behavior.[32] The act, built on the framework of the Wagner Act, retained the provisions for exclusive representation of employees and established new code of conduct for unions and their agents.

Sections 8(a) and 8(b) redefined unfair labor practices, recognizing that both parties to collective bargaining needed protection from wrongful interference from each other. Though the unfair labor practices on the part of management remained similar to those outlined in the Wagner Act, the Taft-Hartley amendments provided greater power to combat unfair labor practices. Some unfair labor practices added were:

- Restraining or coercing employees in their selection of a bargaining or grievance representative
- Causing or attempting to cause an employer to discriminate against an employee because of the employee's membership or nonmembership in a labor organization
- Refusing to bargain in good faith with an employer
- Inducing or encouraging employees to stop work to force an employee to join a union

Right-to-work laws. Taft-Hartley also permitted right-to-work laws that allowed the states to determine whether their citizens must join a union when that union is certified by the employees of a company (see fig. 3.5). The right to work without requiring union membership had been nationwide until restricted by the NLRA of 1935. It was recognized again by Taft-Hartley, which made the closed shop illegal and, in Section 14(b), allowed state laws against union security measures to supersede the federal law: "Nothing in this Act shall be construed as authorizing the execution or application of agreements requiring membership in a labor organization as a condition of employment in any State or Territory in which such execution or application is prohibited by State or Territorial law."

The states then had a free choice to make union security agreements illegal. Within two years after the passage of the act, fourteen

Figure 3.5. Map showing states with right-to-work laws versus those that enforce union membership. A right-to-work law secures the right of employees to decide for themselves whether to join or financially support a union. However, employees who work in the railway or airline industries are not protected by a right-to-work law. Copyright © National Right to Work Committee (NRTWC.org). Used with permission.

states enacted laws providing that the right of a person to work could not be denied or abridged on account of membership or nonmembership in a labor union. Organized labor denounced these right-to-work laws as management efforts to put a stop to the growth of union membership and undertook campaigns to repeal both Section 14(b) and state legislation based on it. Labor's success was minute until 1958, when the American Federation of Labor–Congress of Industrial Organizations (AFL-CIO) faced the National Right-to-Work Committee in a campaign to extend the law to six more states. The AFL-CIO won all but one of the encounters. Since then, the campaigns to repeal or extend have declined in number and intensity, and the lineup of states with right-to-work laws has reached twenty-two.

Unions have sought to curb the effect of these laws by developing the agency shop, which requires employees, whether members or not, to pay fees to the union, particularly where such employees are receiving the negotiated benefits of union workers. Such shops are generally determined by the negotiating process between union and management. But in 1963, the Supreme Court ruled that states have the authority to make such practices illegal.[33]

Small businesses are the strongest supporters of right-to-work laws. In 1966, the states that supported the right to work were primarily located in the south and west. No major industrial states were or are included. Today, the right-to-work states are: Alabama, Arizona, Arkansas, Florida, Georgia, Idaho, Iowa, Kansas, Louisiana, Mississippi, Nebraska, Nevada, North Carolina, North Dakota, Oklahoma, South Carolina, South Dakota, Tennessee, Texas, Utah, Virginia, and Wyoming.

Other provisions. Other major provisions of Taft-Hartley are the elimination of featherbedding, or the creation of nonexistent jobs; the right of unions to insist on closed shops; permission for federal intervention in national emergencies; and the exemption of supervisory personnel from coverage. Taft-Hartley also limits the authority of the National Labor Relations Board.

While the act upheld collective bargaining as the preferred method of settling labor disputes, it also recognized that these procedures could often break down. Since failure to reach agreement could seriously damage the economy when national issues are concerned, alternate processes were established. In this regard, Taft-Hartley created the Federal Mediation and Conciliation Service (FMCS) to assist in any dispute affecting interstate commerce. To maintain control of contracts being negotiated, the act also required that labor or management notify the service when any changes in the terms or conditions of employment are desired by the parties.

Emergency boards. Following the lead of the RLA, Taft-Hartley also provided for a National Emergency Board. When the president of the United States believes that an industry-wide dispute could have an impact on the national health or safety, a board of inquiry may be convened to investigate and report on the facts of the dispute. The board is precluded from making recommendations, but if it believes the national health or safety is in jeopardy, the president of the United States can seek a federal injunction, effectively stopping a strike or lockout for a period of eighty days.

After the first sixty days of the injunction, a status report of the dispute is provided to the president, and within the next fifteen days, the employees of the union are be provided the opportunity to vote on management's final offer. Failing to reach any accord, the union is then free to strike after the eighty-day expiration. At this point, the only possible action to prevent a major work stoppage would require special emergency legislation on the part of Congress.

One of the foremost examples of presidential intervention in a labor dispute occurred in August 1981, when nearly thirteen thousand members of the Professional Air Traffic Controllers Organization (PATCO) walked off the job, setting off a chain of events that redefined labor relations in America. By going on strike, the union technically violated a 1955 law that banned strikes by government unions. In response to the walkout, President Ronald Reagan took an uncompromising stand against the striking air traffic controllers, who threatened to shut down the nation's airlines. The president warned that striking is illegal for public employees and that anyone who did not return to work within forty-eight hours would be terminated under the terms of the Taft-Hartley Act of 1947.

After the two-day period, President Reagan fired the striking air traffic controllers and banned them from ever being rehired by the FAA. The FAA immediately began accepting applications for new air traffic controllers; the Federal Labor Relations Authority decertified PATCO. Later, new air traffic controllers, hired in the wake of the strike, organized a new union to represent them, the National Air Traffic Controllers Association (NATCA). In June 1987, NATCA was certified as the sole bargaining unit for air traffic controllers employed by the FAA.

President Reagan's firing of thousands of unionized air traffic controllers for illegally going on strike marked a turning point in labor relations in America that has had lasting repercussions. In the decades before 1981, major work stoppages averaged around three hundred per year; today, that number is fewer than thirty.[34]

Case study 3.1 explores the PATCO strike and its consequences.

Case Study 3.1: The Professional Air Traffic Controllers Organization Strike in 1981

One of the toughest battles in the history of organized labor was the 1981 Professional Air Traffic Controllers Organization (PATCO) strike (see fig. CS3.1.1). On August 3, 1981, nearly 13,000 of the 17,500 members of the Professional Air Traffic Controllers Organization went on strike, hoping to disrupt the nation's air transportation system to the extent that the federal government would accede to its demands for higher wages, a shorter workweek, and better retirement benefits.[35]

Figure CS 3.1.1. Professional Air Traffic Controllers Organization (PATCO) logo. Courtesy of Professional Air Traffic Controllers Organization.

The PATCO strike was organized to take place during the airlines' busiest quarter of the year in an effort to impact the operating revenues of major U.S. carriers including American, Braniff, Eastern, and TWA. These airlines were relying on increased summer revenues to turn a profit to make up for losses due to airline deregulation, which had spurred the growth of new and smaller low-cost carriers that effectively competed with these major legacy carriers. Also, there was concern that the strike would entirely cripple the nation's air transportation system. Every day the U.S. airline industry (340,000 employees) was operating fourteen thousand scheduled U.S. commercial flights carrying eight hundred thousand passengers. Revenue losses due to the strike forced U.S. airlines to cancel flights resulting in wage reductions or laying off employees.[36]

When management-labor negotiations began in February of 1981, Robert Poli, PATCO president, explained the union's major demands as a $10,000 across-the-board raise, a thirty-two-hour workweek, a better retirement package after twenty years of service, and updated computer equipment.

Even though these demands carried a $750 million price tag, the union argued that its members deserved these considerations due to the highly stressful nature of their job. Air traffic controllers in the United States were required to work forty-hour weeks, and often twenty hours of mandatory overtime were added on each week.[37]

The FAA made a $40 million counteroffer that only included a shorter workweek and a 10 percent pay hike for those controllers who doubled as instructors and for controllers who worked night shifts (see fig. CS3.1.2). When Poli presented the FAA's terms to the union membership, 95 percent voted to reject the terms.[38] The FAA refused to make any further concessions, and on August 3, 1981, 85 percent of PATCO's members went on strike.

Figure CS 3.1.2. Federal Aviation Administration (FAA) logo.

Unknown to PATCO members, the FAA had been working on a contingency plan that would go into effect if the union struck. When the FAA implemented its backup plan, it functioned smoothly and minimized the strike's overall effects. Approximately three thousand supervisors joined two thousand nonstriking controllers and nine hundred military controllers in manning the nation's airport towers. U.S. airlines were ordered to reduce scheduled flights at major airports by 50 percent during peak hours for safety reasons, and sixty small airport towers were shut down indefinitely. The FAA's training school in Oklahoma City, which produced fifteen hundred graduates per training class, considered plans to increase that number to fifty-five hundred graduates.[39]

PATCO strikers made dismal predictions about reduced air safety as a consequence of the sixty-hour workweek put in by their replacements, but with limited traffic and the monitoring efforts of nearly thirty-five thousand Air Line Pilots Association members, the FAA soon realized they could fully operate with one-third less air traffic controllers; therefore, the PATCO strike really achieved the opposite of what the union had intended.

On the first day of the strike, August 3, 1981, President Ronald Reagan responded with an ultimatum: the strikers were to return to work within forty-eight hours or face termination (see fig. CS3.1.3). As federal employees, the controllers were violating the no-strike clause of their employment contracts. In 1955 Congress had made strikes by federal employees punishable by fines and incarceration, a provision that was upheld by a judicial decision in 1971.[40]

Before the Reagan administration, the FAA under President Jimmy Carter's administration organized a management campaign of harassment against unionized controllers. And twelve months before the PATCO contract was scheduled to expire, Carter's administration formed a Management Strike Contingency Force to prepare for a labor walkout, including the use of scabs (replacement workers).[41]

But PATCO members stood their ground. Eighty-five percent of the controllers walked out on the first

Figure CS 3.1.3. President Ronald Reagan making a statement to the press regarding the air traffic controllers strike (PATCO) from the White House Rose Garden, 1981. White House Photo Office.

day of the strike, and more than six thousand daily flights were immediately canceled by the FAA. Two days later, President Reagan fired 11,350 striking controllers who had not returned to work and declared a lifetime ban on the rehiring of the PATCO strikers by the FAA.

During the walkout, the FAA was able to keep scheduled flights at 70 percent of prestrike levels, as a result of its contingency plan for replacing the striking controllers. The Reagan administration was determined to teach PATCO a lesson. PATCO leaders were hauled off to jail for ignoring federal injunctions and federal judges levied million-dollar-a-day fines against the union. Over ten thousand strikers had their employment terminated; only twelve hundred were allowed to go back to work within a week's time. Morale among the strikers was shaky. "I thought Reagan was bluffing," lamented one controller.[42] In October 1981, the Federal Labor Relations Authority decertified PATCO because of its promotion of an illegal strike.

Overwhelmingly, the public supported President Reagan's decisive action and exhibited little sympathy for controllers whose earnings were already well above the national average. Union leaders accused President Reagan of overkill in firing the strikers and complained that the president was engaged in union busting; however labor strategists criticized Poli for calling an ill-advised strike that damaged labor's overall image.

Two months after the strike, a congressional committee report indicated that only two-thirds of the air traffic controllers needed for full and safe operation of air traffic in the U.S. would be in place by January 1983 and recommended rehiring some of the strikers. However, the Reagan administration refused, and Transportation Secretary Drew Lewis declined even to meet with Poli. By 1984, air traffic had increased by 6 percent; 20 percent fewer air traffic controllers were on the job than prior to the strike.

Even though President Reagan handled the PATCO strike in a swift and decisive manner, he emphasized that he derived no satisfaction from firing the controllers and pointed out that he was the first president to be a lifetime member of the AFL-CIO. In his memoirs, he wrote, "I supported unions and the rights of workers to organize and bargain collectively, but no president could tolerate an illegal strike by Federal employees."[43]

In summary, the Taft-Hartley Act forbids unions to force employees to become members. It also bans both secondary boycotts and closed shops that require union membership as a condition of being hired. It authorizes the president of the United States to impose an eighty-day delay on any strike found to imperil the national health or safety. The act allows employers to replace striking workers. It imposed a ban on union contributions to political campaigns that was nullified later by a court ruling holding that the ban infringed on the constitutional right of citizens to free expression. The act retains the provisions of the Wagner Act for voting by employees on whether they wish to be represented by a union, but it restricts representation elections for craftworkers, professionals, supervisors, and custodial employees.[44]

NLRA Amendment: The Landrum-Griffin Act

Senate investigations by the McClellan Committee during the 1950s uncovered corruption in some unions and a lack of democratic procedures in others. As happened in response to events preceding the passage of the Taft-Hartley Act, public sentiment was aroused, and legislation was demanded to protect individual workers and the public from union activities. This corruption included embezzlement from union treasuries, violence toward union members, undemocratic practices, and conversion of union resources to the personal interests of union officials.[45]

As a direct result, the Labor-Management Reporting and Disclosure Act (Landrum-Griffin Act) was passed in 1959 under the commerce clause. In its preamble, the position of Congress is clearly enunciated:

> Congress . . . finds, from recent investigations in the labor and management fields, that there have been a number of instances of breach of trust, corruption, disregard of the rights of individual employees, and other failures to observe high standards of responsibility and ethical conduct which require further and supplementary legislation that will afford necessary protection of the rights and interests of employees and the public generally as they relate to the activities of labor organizations, employers, labor relations consultants, and their officers and representatives.[46]

The act seeks to impose regulation of the internal affairs of unions and to establish rights for union members. Title I of the act has been called the Bill of Rights of union members. It gives union members the following rights:

- To nominate candidates, to vote in elections, to attend union meetings, and to have a voice in business transactions
- Free expression in union meetings and business discussions
- Vote on an increase of dues or fees
- Sue and testify against the union and to receive all rights by law prior to any disciplinary action against them by the union

- Obtain a copy of the collective bargaining agreement under which they work

These rights and remedies granted to union members are in addition to any other rights that the members may have under other laws or under union bylaws and constitutions. If a member's rights are violated, this act allows the member to bring civil action for relief in the U.S. district courts where the violation occurred or where the main offices of the union are located.

The provisions of the Landrum-Griffin Act apply to the carriers and unions covered under the RLA. In summary, the Landrum-Griffin Act:

- Establishes a Bill of Rights for members of union organizations, which
  - Includes freedom of speech and assembly
  - Protects from an increase in dues without a vote
  - Protects against the taking of inappropriate disciplinary action by union officials against rank-and-file members
- Requires reporting by labor organizations to the secretary of labor about union financial dealings and thus regulates union finances and administration

Other Laws Affecting Labor Relations

Besides the RLA and the NLRA, other statutes and executive orders influence the labor-relations process either directly or indirectly. A brief discussion of legislation applicable to all industries follows. This discussion highlights major provisions only; labor-relations specialists find that a detailed knowledge of the legislation is essential.

The Interstate Transportation of Strikebreakers Act (or Byrnes Act, 1936) makes it illegal to transport or travel in interstate commerce for the purpose of interfering by force or threats with peaceful picketing by employees or with other employment rights and guarantees.

The Fair Labor Standards Act of 1938 (FLSA) is administered by the Wage and Hour Division of the United States Department of Labor (US-DOL). The FLSA outlawed oppressive child labor, established a national minimum wage, and a maximum workweek.[47] All private employers employing a specified minimum number of employees and conducting business in interstate commerce are required to compensate employees with time-and-a-half pay for work beyond forty hours in a workweek.

Exemptions were originally given to protect traditional pay practices in small, rural businesses; however, most of them have been repealed. Currently, the most important issues relate to white-collar exemptions applicable to professional, administrative, and executive employees. Contentious issues in recent years have related to technical employees who have a significant degree of specialized knowledge without formal academic credentials. Such employees often exercise no direct management or even administrative authority and so are arguably ineligible for any of the FLSA white-collar exemptions. By legislative amendment, some employees of this sort are now exempt from the overtime provisions of the FLSA, but many unsettled issues remain.[48]

Controversial changes to the FLSA's overtime laws went into effect in August 2004 that modified the definition of an exempt employee. These changes were sought by the George W. Bush administration, which claimed that the laws needed clarification and that few workers would be affected. But business organizations, including the AFL-CIO, claimed the changes would make millions of additional workers ineligible to obtain relief under the FLSA for overtime pay.[49]

The Bankruptcy Amendment Act of 1984 includes standards for the rejection of collective bargaining agreements when companies file for bankruptcy under a Chapter 11 reorganization plan. In cases where no agreement can be reached between the parties, the act specifies the requirements for terminating or altering a provision of a collective bargaining agreement.

In the 1984 case of *NLRB v. Bildisco & Bildisco*, a debtor-in-possession requested permission from the bankruptcy court to reject its collective bargaining agreement with a labor union. The bankruptcy court granted permission to reject the agreement, and the district court upheld the bankruptcy court order. The labor union filed unfair labor practice charges, and the National Labor Relations Board found that the company violated the National Labor Relations Act by unilaterally changing the terms of the collective bargaining agreement and by refusing to negotiate with the union. The U.S. Court of Appeals for the Third Circuit held that the collective bargaining agreement was subject to rejection if the debtor could show that the agreement was burdensome and the equities balanced in favor of rejection. The U.S. Supreme Court ruled that it was legal for a company to petition for bankruptcy and immediately reject the terms and conditions of an existing collective bargaining labor agreement without waiting for approval of its petition by the bankruptcy court.[50] A similar case occurring in the airline industry centered on the abrogation of contracts in a bankruptcy proceeding by Continental Airlines under the leadership of Francisco A. (Frank) Lorenzo (see fig. 3.6).

Disagreeing with the court's decision, Congress amended the Bankruptcy Reform Act of 1978. At present, a company may not reject the terms of a valid labor agreement until the bankruptcy judge has approved the firm's bankruptcy petition. To obtain such approval, the company seeking to obtain debtor-in-possession status must demonstrate to the court that the following conditions have been met:

- The company must make a proposal to the union to modify the existing labor

Figure 3.6. Francisco A. Lorenzo, who created Texas Air Corporation, a holding company that in 1981 initiated the takeover of Continental Airlines. Lorenzo's existing airline, Texas International, was merged into Continental Airlines in 1982. Lorenzo took Continental into Chapter 11 bankruptcy in September 1983 after negotiations with labor unions proved unsuccessful. Bankruptcy, up to 1984, allowed immediate cessation of union contracts and imposition of new labor conditions, subject to later court approval and revision. A more streamlined Continental emerged out of bankruptcy shortly after the original filing, and the bankruptcy court approved management's measures. Courtesy of Joe Wright and Harris Herman.

agreement based on the most complete and reliable information available at the time.

- The company's proposed contract modifications must represent only those changes necessary to permit the successful reorganization of the firm and avoidance of bankruptcy risk.
- The proposed contract modifications must treat all creditors, the debtor firm, and other affected parties fairly and equitably.
- Between the time when the proposed modifications are presented to the union and the court hearing on the firm's bankruptcy petition is held, the company must bargain in good faith with the union concerning the proposed contract modifications.
- The company must provide the union with all relevant information necessary for the union to evaluate the firm's proposed contract modifications.
- The union must have rejected the company's proposed contract modifications without good cause. The burden of proof

is on the union to show why the company's proposal is unreasonable or unnecessary, thereby giving the union good cause for rejecting the company's proposal.

- In the court's judgment, a review of all the factors must demonstrate that the balance of equities clearly favors approval of the company's rejection of the existing labor agreement.

The Bankruptcy Reform Act of 1978 created a number of legal controversies. As a result, many amendments and judicial clarifications of the 1978 act were made throughout the 1980s. One significant event was a 1982 Supreme Court ruling that the bankruptcy court's enlarged jurisdiction, established by the 1978 act, was unconstitutional, that is, the Supreme Court ruling stated that bankruptcy judges had been given too much power by Congress, and their duties overlapped with those of other branches of the federal government. This 1982 ruling led to the Bankruptcy Amendment Act of 1984.[51]

During the 1980s and 1990s, record numbers of bankruptcies were filed. Many well-known commercial airlines filed for Chapter 11 bankruptcy reorganization including Eastern Airlines, Continental Airlines, and Pan Am. These massive bankruptcies created challenges for the court system. The 1990s also witnessed a rise in the use of examiners and mediators, particularly in large bankruptcy cases. These professionals are expected to expedite the resolution of contentious matters and reduce the time and money expended on complex bankruptcy cases.

The Bankruptcy Reform Act of 1994, the most comprehensive bankruptcy legislation since the 1978 act, was signed in October 1994 by President William Jefferson Clinton. The 1994 act contains many provisions, including:

- Provisions to expedite bankruptcy proceedings

- Provisions to encourage individual debtors to use Chapter 13 to reschedule their debts rather than use Chapter 7 to liquidate
- Provisions to aid creditors in recovering claims against bankrupt estates
- Creation of a National Bankruptcy Commission to investigate further changes in bankruptcy law[52]

The Equal Pay Act (1963) provides that employers cannot pay different rates of pay for the same job on the basis of gender or race (see fig. 3.7). Congress believed gender discrimination stifled the maximum utilization of labor resources and caused labor disputes, thereby burdening, affecting, and obstructing commerce and the free flow of goods in commerce. It also constitutes an unfair method of competition. The law provides that:

> No employer having employees subject to any provisions of this section shall discriminate, within any establishment in which such employees are employed, between employees on the basis of sex by paying wages to employees in such establishment at a rate less than the rate at which he pays wages to employees of the opposite sex in such establishment for equal work on jobs, the performance of which requires equal skill, effort, and responsibility, and which are performed under similar working conditions, except where such payment is made pursuant to (i) a seniority system; (ii) a merit system; (iii) a system which measures earnings by quantity or quality of production; or (iv) a differential based on any other factor other than sex.[53]

The Civil Rights Act of 1964, amended by the Equal Employment Opportunity Act of 1972, prohibits employment decisions that discriminate on the basis of race, sex, religion, color, or national origin. Originally conceived to protect the rights of black men, the bill was amended

Figure 3.7. President John F. Kennedy signing the Equal Pay Act (EPA) into law on June 10, 1963, as Business and Professional Women members look on. The EPA prohibits discrimination on the basis of sex in the payment of wages or benefits where men and women perform work of similar skill, effort, and responsibility for the same employer under similar working conditions. Courtesy of Business and Professional Women/USA.

prior to passage to protect the civil rights of all men and women. The act transformed American society. It prohibits discrimination in public facilities, in government, and in employment. Furthermore, it is illegal to compel segregation of the races in schools, housing, or hiring. Enforcement powers were initially weak, but they grew over the years, and later programs (affirmative action) were made possible by the act.

The Age Discrimination in Employment Act (1967, 1984, and 1986) prohibits employment discrimination against those over the age of forty and prohibits mandatory retirement except for specified occupations. At present, pilot mandatory retirement at age sixty-five is excluded from the act.

The Vocational Rehabilitation Act (1973) and the Disabilities Act of 1991 require holders of federal government contracts in excess of $2,500 to develop affirmative action programs to employ and advance qualified physically and mentally handicapped individuals.

Executive Order 11246 (1965) requires contractors underutilizing minorities and women to specify goals and develop timetables for affirmatively recruiting, selecting, training, and promoting individuals from underutilized groups. Since 1965, the U.S. Department of Labor's Office of Federal Contract Compliance Programs (OFCCP) has been committed to ensuring that government contractors comply with the equal-employment-opportunity (EEO) and the affirmative-action provisions of their contracts through the enforcement of Executive Order 11246.

The Occupational Safety and Health Act (OSHA; 1970) imposes an affirmative duty on employers to provide working conditions that will not harm their employees. Regulations are published by the U.S. Department of Labor and include procedures for the issuance of citations for corrections or fines where adherence to regulations is lacking. OSHA's authority extends to most nongovernmental workplaces where there are employees. State and local government workers are excluded from federal coverage; however, states operating their own state workplace-safety-and-health programs under plans approved by the USDOL cover most private-sector workers and are also required to extend their coverage to public-sector (state and local government) workers in the state.

The Worker Adjustment and Retraining Notification Act (WARN; 1988) requires employers with one hundred or more employees to give advance notice of sixty days to employees who will be affected by a plant closing or major layoff. This notice must be provided to either affected workers or their labor union, to the state dislocated-worker unit, and to the appropriate unit of local government. Employees entitled to notice under WARN include hourly and salaried workers, as well as managerial and supervisory employees.

The Racketeering Influenced and Corrupt Organizations Act (RICO; 1970) forbids anyone involved in racketeering from investing in or controlling through racketeering activities any enterprise (business or labor unions) engaged in interstate commerce.

The Military Selection Act (1967) requires employers to reemploy veterans to the position they held before entering the armed services. Such restoration must be to positions of like seniority, status, and pay. Also, the Military Selective Service Act of 1967 requires all men between the ages of eighteen and twenty-six to register for service.

The Vietnam Era Veteran Readjustment Assistance Act (1974) requires employers with government contracts or subcontracts of $25,000 or more to take affirmative action to employ and promote qualified and disabled veterans from the Vietnam War, as well as veterans who served on active duty during a war or in a campaign or expedition for which a campaign badge has been authorized.

The Americans with Disabilities Act (1990) provides for access to and protection in the workplace for those with physical impairments. This law prohibits discrimination in employment opportunities against disabled people; requires equal accessibility to all services provided by state and local government, including transportation; and prohibits discrimination in public accommodations. It provides similar protections against discrimination to Americans with disabilities as the Civil Rights Act of 1964, which made discrimination based on race, religion, sex, national origin, and other characteristics illegal.

Other laws important to labor relations include state and local ordinances, such as wage-and-hours regulations, the Employee Retirement Income Security Act of 1974, and the Social Security Act of 1935 and its amendments.

Summary

Two principal pieces of labor legislation and their respective amendments affect employees and employers in the air transport sector: the RLA and the NLRA, which have many similarities and many fundamental differences. Table 3.5 offers a side-by-side comparison of the major provisions of each act and the applicable influences of the Norris–La Guardia Act on each.

One fundamental overriding question remains in the current examination of the two major labor acts. Is it necessary to have two distinct sets of labor legislation, one of which, the RLA, governs only two industrial sectors employing less than a million workers total? Poignant and adroit arguments can be offered in support of either side of this issue. Any legislative attempts to combine the existing bifurcated system by elimination of the RLA and the transference of the railroad and air transport sectors into the NLRA must be filtered through the lens of operational history.

Several crippling unified national strikes have occurred under the NLRA, notably in the steel and coal industries. To date, no unified national strikes have taken place under the RLA. The public policy goals and objectives of the RLA, to avoid interruption of interstate commerce and to promote collective bargaining, seem to have been achieved. Despite the relatively small number of employees covered under the RLA, an untold number of labor agreements are in place in the rail and air transport sector. Transferring these agreements to the NLRA would be a truly complex and expensive task that might not be worth the cost and effort.

Table 3.5.
Legislative differences between the Railway Labor Act and the National Labor Relations Act

| Category | Provisions | |
	RLA	NLRA
Contract	Amendable; continued in perpetuity unless modified by parties	Terminable expiration date acts as drop-dead provision unless modified
Decertification procedure	None listed; one union may be replaced by another	Specific procedure allowing for change of union or return to nonunion status
Featherbedding	No proscription but distinct possibility	Made unlawful by Taft-Hartley
Grievance arbitration	Mandatory	Subject to agreement between the parties
Injunctive relief under Norris–La Guardia	Applicable to date of airline incorporation	Yes
Judicial review of board decision	No	Yes
Mediation	Mandatory	On request to the Federal Mediation and Conciliation Service
Requirement for representation election	No particular citation; subject to discretion of the National Mediation Board	30 percent signatory cards from covered employees
Right-to-work	None	Provided and applicable in twenty-two states
Secondary boycott	No provision for restriction	Outlawed by Taft-Hartley
Unfair labor practices	None listed in the act	Enumerated and proscribed by Taft-Hartley

Some of the provisions of the RLA, notably the proscription of right-to-work and the inclusion of secondary-boycott provisions, need to be revised to ensure worker rights are consistent between the two acts. This can certainly be achieved more cost effectively by congressional amendment than by repeal. But unless and until unions, management, and the American people generate sufficient political pressure on their elected representatives, these issues will remain unresolved, and the question of the necessity for bifurcated labor legislation will remain unanswered. The supplemental readings in the accompanying *Study Guide & Supplemental Readings* include two articles that discuss this dualistic labor environment.

PART TWO. Principles, Practices, and Procedures in Collective Bargaining and Dispute Resolution

4. Elections, Certifications, and Procedures

The election and certification process under the RLA and the NLRA require an understanding of the bargaining unit from an employees' point of view. The two acts are broad in nature and are federally mandated, but their coverage does not necessarily extend to all employers or employees. This chapter specifies the jurisdiction of the various statutes of both acts. Whether workers, unions, and employers are covered by the provisions of the acts depends on the statutory definitions of the terms *interstate commerce*, *carrier*, and *employee*.

Interstate Commerce

The Supreme Court has defined commerce in a series of cases in which the federal government has the ability to apply legislation affecting industries that are engaged in interstate commerce. The interpretation of Article I, Section 8, of the Constitution, was challenged in the case of *Gibbons v. Ogden*. The interpretation of "Congress shall have the power to regulate commerce with foreign nations, and among the several States, and with Indian Tribes" was clarified by Chief Justice John Marshall's court opinion: "It is the power to regulate; that is, to prescribe the rule by which commerce is to be governed. This power, like all others vested in Congress, is complete in itself, may be exercised to its utmost extent and acknowledge no limitation, other than in the Constitution."[1] The cases that followed established the authority and constitutionality of

Congress to enact the RLA and the NLRA (see fig. 4.1).[2]

In enacting these two sets of labor legislation, Congress applied the rulings of commerce and extended the definition to mean interstate commerce. The reach of the acts was based on the Supreme Court rulings of what affected commerce. This extended definition of commerce, when applied to the two labor acts, implied and established that business must be conducted across state lines in order for the acts to apply. Products do not have to be physically shipped across state lines. It is sufficient that raw materials, power, or communications are used between states. The operating agencies of the two acts, the National Mediation Board (NMB) and the National Labor Relations Board (NLRB), were therefore given authority to exercise their jurisdiction over all but the smallest of businesses or airlines, particularly those airlines operating as intrastate carriers only. So pervasive is the coverage under the interstate commerce definition that the NLRB has found it necessary to limit its jurisdiction. Table 4.1 lists the jurisdictional limitations of the NLRB.

The Process under the Railway Labor Act
Jurisdiction

One might assume that there is a clear understanding of who is covered under the Railway Labor Act: employees of airlines and railroads. However, this is not entirely the case. The United

Figure 4.1. Employees relaxing during the United Auto Workers' sit-down strike in Flint, Michigan, in the mid-1930s. The National Labor Relations Act (NLRA), also known as the Wagner Act, passed through Congress in 1935. Reversing years of federal opposition to organized labor, the statute guarantees the right of employees to organize, form unions, and bargain collectively with their employers. It assures that workers have a choice on whether to belong to a union and promotes collective bargaining as the major way to ensure peaceful industry-labor relations. The act also created a National Labor Relations Board (NLRB) to arbitrate deadlocked labor-management disputes, guarantee democratic union elections, and penalize unfair labor practices by employers. However, many unions did not use the NLRB in the first few years of its passage, choosing instead to strike for recognition, using methods such as the sit-down strike. Library of Congress.

The term "carrier" includes any express company, sleeping car company, carrier by railroad, subject to the Interstate Commerce Act (24 Stat. 379, as amended; 49 U.S.C. 1 et seq.), and any company which is directly or indirectly owned or controlled by or under common control with any carrier by railroad and which operates any equipment or facilities or performs any service (other than trucking service) in connection with the transportation, receipt, delivery, elevation, transfer in transit, refrigeration or icing, storage, and handling of property transported by railroad, and any receiver, trustee, or other individual or body, judicial or otherwise, when in the possession of the business of any such "carrier."[3]

Title II extended the RLA to "every common carrier by air engaged in interstate or foreign commerce, and every carrier by air transporting mail for or under contract with the United States Government." Where no U.S. mail is transported, purely intrastate operations are not subject to the RLA.

These definitions imply that not only are airlines and railroad carriers bound by the RLA but also "any company which is directly or indirectly owned or controlled by or under common control with any carrier." In 1934, Congress expanded the definition of *carrier* to include carrier affiliates and transportation-related services in order to avoid the possibility that a strike could interfere with the flow of commerce and to prevent a carrier covered by the RLA from evading the purposes of the act by spinning off components of its operation into subsidiaries.[4] It is only when the activities of a carrier affiliate are vital to the operation of that carrier and when

States is a country bound by laws, and these laws are written in words; therefore, we are bound by these words. It is in the deliberation of the meaning of certain words that we find contention in RLA coverage.

The RLA was originally crafted to cover railroads, and the jurisdictional language in the act reflects this. The definition of *carrier* in the RLA refers to the railroad industry and not the airlines. This definition is essential in determining what employers and employees are subject to the RLA. The original definition in Title I of the RLA by reference to the Interstate Commerce Act reads as follows:

Table 4.1.

Jurisdictional standards of the National Labor Relations Board

Jurisdiction	*Standard*
Employer associations	Any member meets any jurisdictional standard or the combined operations of all members meet any such standard
Gambling casinos	Gross annual revenues exceed $500,000
Hospitals	At least $250,000 gross annual revenue
Hotels, motels, apartments, and condominiums	Gross revenues of $500,000 or more per year
Law firms and legal-assistance programs	Gross annual revenues are $250,000 per year
Links and channels of interstate commerce	Gross revenue of at least $50,000 per year derived from furnishing interstate transportation services or functioning as essential links in such transportation of passengers or commodities
National-defense enterprise	Substantial impact on the national defense, irrespective of whether the operations satisfy any other jurisdictional standard
Newspapers	Gross business volume of at least $200,000 per year
Nonretail enterprises	Gross outflow or inflow of revenue of at least $50,000, whether such outflow or inflow is regarded as direct or indirect
Nursing homes and related facilities	At least $100,000 gross annual revenue
Office buildings and shopping centers	Gross revenue of at least $100,000 per year, of which at least $25,000 derived from organizations whose operations meet any of the board's jurisdictional standards other than the nonretail standard
Public utilities	Gross business volume of at least $250,000 per year or an interstate outflow or inflow of goods, materials, or services of $50,000 or more per year, whether directly or indirectly
Radio and television stations; telephone and telegraph systems	Gross business volume of at least $100,000 per year.
Restaurants and country clubs	Gross annual volume of at least $500,000
Retail establishments	Gross business volume of at least $500,000 per year and substantial purchases from or sales to other states on a direct or indirect basis. When an employer's operations are both retail and nonretail, the nonretail jurisdictional standards are applied unless the nonretail portion is de minimis.
Secondary employers	In cases involving union conduct with respect to secondary employers, if the primary employer meets any of the jurisdictional standards or if the combined operations of the primary employer and the business of any secondary employers at the location affected by the conduct meet such standards
Single employer engaged in multiple enterprises	The employer's overall operations meet any jurisdictional standard
Symphony orchestras	Gross annual revenue of at least $1,000,000
Taxicab companies and other transit systems	Gross volume of at least $250,000 per year

a labor dispute could prohibit those operations that the affiliate is covered by the RLA.[5]

Title II also fails to give a definition of what a common carrier is. This lack of a clear definition and the inclusion of loosely defined subsidiaries and affiliates have left the NMB and the courts on their own to decipher who is bound by the RLA: "When an employer is not a rail or air carrier engaged in the transportation of freight or passengers, the NMB applies a two-part test in determining whether the employer and its employees are subject to the RLA."[6] This test has two central considerations:

- Whether there is common ownership or control between the entity in question and the RLA carrier
- Whether the work performed by the entity's employees is traditionally performed by the employees of an airline or railroad

Both components of this test must be satisfied for the NMB and the courts to conclude that the entity is covered by the RLA. The NMB defines *control* as established by ownership. With this, all airline subsidiaries satisfy the first prong of the test. If there is no ownership, an entity such as a ground-service contractor or other affiliate can still be "controlled" by a carrier that exercises de facto control over manner in which the entity does business.[7] Significant factors include:

- Whether the entity's employees are supervised by railroad or airline employees in how they perform their jobs
- Whether the carrier's managers make effective recommendations regarding hiring, firing, or discipline of the entity's employees
- Ownership of equipment
- Training of the entity's employees
- Holding out the entity's employees as employees of the carrier[8]

As for the second part of the test, work traditionally performed by a carrier, the following activities have been found to come under the RLA:

- Air taxi services and charter operations
- Maintenance, servicing, and refueling of aircraft
- Screening and security
- In-flight food catering
- Sky-cap service
- Ground service (including directing, parking, starting, and towing aircraft, transporting cargo or baggage, and cleaning aircraft)[9]

Information services are another area of contention. The courts and the NMB have been inconsistent with their rulings on this matter. The area of debate is whether information-technology companies provide service that is work traditionally performed by airlines. The NLRB decided in one case that an IT company was not covered by the RLA because the work performed was not traditional airline work.[10]

In contrast, one court determined that an information-technology company was covered by the RLA because its service was "an integral part of the air carriers' transportation function" that historically had been performed by airline employees.[11]

Trucking. The RLA does not cover trucking services under its carrier definition. Therefore, a company that is affiliated with a carrier and performs trucking operations is excluded from coverage. However, the NMB has been inconsistent with its decisions. The board found in one case involving Federal Express that all of its sorting employees and truck drivers were covered under the RLA.[12]

In contrast to this, the NLRB has made the opposite determination regarding United Parcel Service (UPS). The NLRB determined that a trucking subsidiary of UPS was not covered by the RLA.[13] The courts affirmed this decision, based on the NLRB's use of NMB criteria that to be covered by the RLA, a trucking company must:

- Perform services principally for an RLA carrier with which it is affiliated

- Be an integral part of the RLA carrier
- Provide services essential to the RLA carrier's operations

The deciding factor in this case was that UPS only received a fraction of its business from the subsidiary. Therefore, it was not an integral part of the carrier.[14]

Case study 4.1 examines the different labor laws affecting FedEx and its principal competitor, UPS, the effects of this difference on their competition for market share, and lobbying efforts by UPS to eliminate the difference.

Case Study 4.1: FedEx—Obstacles to Organizing under the Railway Labor Act

Since its inception in 1973, FedEx has been governed by the RLA, and so it is different from United Parcel Service (UPS), which started out in 1907 as a messenger and ground package-delivery trucking company and has been covered under the National Labor Relations Act (NLRA) since that act became law (see figs. CS4.1.1 and CS4.1.2). Many FedEx subsidiaries are also under the NLRA, including its freight and ground-delivery units; however, FedEx is still governed by the RLA.

Therefore, in FedEx's case, a union would have to organize the workers on a "national basis" instead of by local terminals or ramps. It is easier for unions to organize under the NLRA because members can enroll at individual work sites. Believing this difference put UPS at a competitive disadvantage against FedEx, UPS and the Teamsters Union sought a legislative change to bring FedEx under the NLRA. Beginning in 2007, the tactic was to persuade legislators to insert the change as a rider to the annual FAA Reauthorization Act (the legislation that funds the FAA).[15]

During the legislative maneuverings, FedEx stated, "FedEx believes in its great history of growing the company customer by customer, unlike our

competition who wants to grow its business by a legislative bailout. . . . We hope the House will remove the amendment so the U.S. consumers rather than the Congress will decide who the marketplace winner will be." "UPS is attempting to change the rules by harming the competition through legislation." said David J. Bronczek, president and CEO of FedEx. "FedEx thrives on competition. We just think it should be done in the marketplace, not the halls of Congress."[16]

The UPS-FedEx fight is rooted in the fact that most UPS workers are covered by the NLRA, while FedEx is classified as an air carrier under the RLA. Workers

Figure CS 4.1.1. FedEx Airbus A310–200. Courtesy of Adrian Pingstone.

Figure CS 4.1.2. A UPS MD-11F aircraft taxiing at Honolulu International Airport in Hawaii. Photographer: Polihale. Source: Wikipedia; GNU Free Documentation License, Version 1.3.

under the RLA may only organize nationally—a higher hurdle to forming a union. Aside from its pilots, FedEx workers are not unionized, so shifting FedEx to the RLA could be a huge victory for organized labor, given that UPS is the largest employer of members of the International Brotherhood of Teamsters, who drive its trucks.

UPS said it did not sponsor the legislation but strongly supported it. "Workers performing the same tasks in the express delivery industry should fall under the same labor laws," said Malcolm Berkley, UPS spokesperson. "We're talking about drivers for express delivery companies who perform non–airline-related functions. These people pass each other in courier vans every day. They make deliveries on the same streets, often to same addresses. They do the same job." Berkley, insisting this is not a UPS versus FedEx fight, stated, "This is not something that UPS drummed up and is driving." But lobbyists tracking the issue said UPS had been pressing lawmakers to make the change behind the scenes and that FedEx sees itself as under attack by a rival seeking to injure it. Although FedEx has a revenue advantage over UPS in express-delivery market share, FedEx has gained on UPS in ground deliveries, which make up the bulk of the UPS business.[17]

FedEx founder Frederick W. Smith testified before a Senate subcommittee that he took exception to the amendment in the house bill and the method used to pass it. He testified that the FedEx pickup and delivery operations are "an integral part of its air operation."[18]

On several occasions, one or the other house of Congress has sided with UPS and added the change to the annual FAA Reauthorization Act, but each time the other house has rejected the change. As recently as February 2011, the provision had to be removed in conference before the bill could pass the Senate. Backers have vowed to try again, hardly surprising since together the two carriers and the Teamsters spent at least $72.5 million on Washington lobbying efforts on the issue between 2007 and the end of 2010.[19]

Employees Subject to the RLA

The RLA expressly includes in its definition of *employee* every person in the service of a carrier who performs the work of a "subordinate official." This definition is in direct contradiction with that of the NLRA, which excludes "any individual employed as a supervisor." Consequently, under the RLA, foremen and other members of the supervisory staff are considered employees and have the attendant rights of self-organization, representation, and freedom from interference and coercion by employers. The NMB reviews the following factors in determining if an employee is in a supervisory position:

- Power to hire, fire or discipline, or to effectively recommend the same
- Authority to supervise
- Authority over other job elements such as overtime, work assignments, and transfers
- Exercise of independent judgment
- Formulation of carrier policy and budget
- Rank in the management hierarchy
- Compensation common to upper management
- Authority to commit carrier funds and resources with outside parties[20]

Applying these criteria, the board must consider these elements in their totality. Considered only on a separate basis, they may not be determinant of whether an employee is a management official. However, when considered on a cumulative basis, they tend to remove an individual from that of either employee or subordinate official.

The term *subordinate official* was applicable to the railroad industry when the RLA was enacted. It was never a part of airline labor terminology. Consequently, the majority of cases questioning the definition and duties of a subordinate official comes from the airline industry. As a result, the NMB adjudicates these particular questions.[21]

Unfortunately, the NMB has a history of deciding these questions on an ad hoc basis that tends to reflect the attitudes and political leanings of the board members then serving. The board has never developed a specific and consistent definition for *subordinate official*. The board does, however, tend to follow the argument that the union attempting to organize a particular segment carries the burden of proof if and when the employer puts the status of individuals in question by asserting that they are managers who do not "perform work as an employee or subordinate official."[22] The board's present position is that "the burden of proof required to persuade the Board to overrule the mediator's preliminary determination rests with the carrier or organization appealing the determination."[23]

Oftentimes, the definition of *employee* becomes blurred by interrelated job aspects. Two classes of individuals beg the question: When does an individual officially become an employee under the RLA? Applicants and trainees raise this issue frequently due to the ambiguity in the definition of *applicant*, *trainee*, and *employee*.

Applicant. Those persons who apply for jobs at an airline or railroad are not covered by the RLA. The courts affirmed this determination in a case involving a strikebreaker seeking employment with a different airline. The pilot applied for a position at Piedmont Aviation while he was on strike at Wien Air Alaska. After being denied employment at Piedmont, the pilot filed a lawsuit claiming he had been blackballed by the pilots union and his rights were violated under the RLA. The court held that the RLA only protects employees of airlines. Since he was no longer employed by either Wien Air Alaska or Piedmont, his rights had not been violated. The NLRA, however, does have specific language that protects against hiring discrimination.[24]

Trainee. Trainees, although they may be paid by the carrier, are also not covered by the RLA. During a strike in 1986, TWA hired eight hundred new flight attendants to fill the positions of striking workers. The trainees were still in the midst of instruction when the strike ended. The eight hundred positions originally intended for the new hires went to the returning strikers. In the subsequent lawsuit, the court found that the trainees were not yet employees. The language of the RLA defines an employee as one "who renders service" for the gain of the carrier. Since the trainees had not yet "rendered service" that resulted in benefits to the carrier, they were not covered under the RLA.[25]

Organizing Employees under the RLA

Under the RLA, the NMB is charged with the responsibility of certifying the representatives of the employees' choice. NMB certification of a union makes that union the exclusive bargaining agent for those employees. The board's certification is final and nonreviewable.[26] In determining who is eligible to represent employees, the RLA defines *representative* as "any person or persons, labor union, organization, or corporation designated either by a carrier or group of carriers or by its or their employees, to act for it or them."[27] The duties of the board with respect to the selection of employee representatives are defined as follows:

> If any dispute shall arise among a carrier's employees as to who are the representatives of such employees[,] . . . it shall be the duty of the Mediation Board, upon request of either party to the dispute, to investigate such a dispute and to certify to both parties, in writing, the name or names of the individuals or organizations that have been designated and authorized to represent the employees involved in the dispute, and certify the same to the carrier. . . . In such an investigation, the Mediation Board shall be authorized to take a secret ballot of the employees involved or to utilize any other appropriate method of ascertaining the names of their duly

designated and authorized representatives in such a manner as shall insure the choice of representatives by the employees without interference, influence, or coercion exercised by the carrier.[28]

Procedures of the National Mediation Board

The duties outlined in the preceding quote from Section 2, Ninth, of the RLA set forth the activities and procedures to be followed by the board in certification proceedings. Figure 4.2 shows the summary of the representation process under the RLA. A list and discussion of each procedure follows, in the order in which the procedures are implemented by the board.

Disputes concerning representation. The NMB is responsible for disputes concerning representation. In such disputes, only the employees or employee groups are party to any question of rep-

resentation. The employer has no statutory rights as a party, and the Supreme Court has explicitly held that the employer is not entitled to be heard at any proceedings convened to resolve the dispute.[29] Consequently, the employer has no role or voice in determining the existence of a dispute. In contrast, an employer is an interested party under the NLRA and may under certain circumstances initiate an investigation by petitioning the NLRB. Section 2, Ninth, was added to the RLA in 1934. It gave the NMB the authority to control all aspects of a representation dispute. A growing trend of the airlines was their beginning to create their own unions in an attempt to control and manipulate them. This amendment, added to thwart this movement, states that the employer's involvement may consist of only providing information necessary to determine eligibility of employees. Any other employer involvement

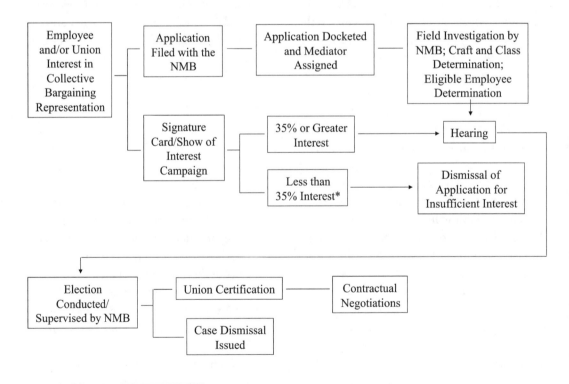

* At least a majority of the craft or class is required if the employees are represented by another person.

Figure 4.2. Railway Labor Act representation process.

risks a board determination of interference with an employee's right of selection.[30]

Application for investigation of representation dispute. Figure 4.3 is the two-page NMB application for investigation of a representation dispute. Application procedures are specified at Section 1203.2 of the RLA and provide that application cards must be received from interested parties along with a formal application from the party interested in representing the employees. Contained in the application must be the name or description of the craft or class of employees involved, the name of the invoking organization, the name of the organization currently representing the employees, if any, the estimated number of employees in each craft or class involved, and the number of signed authorizations submitted from employees in each craft or class. The RLA stipulates that "the applications should be signed by the chief executive of the invoking organization, or other authorized officer of the organization. These disputes are given docket numbers in series 'R.'"[31]

If the employees are not represented by an individual or labor organization, "a showing of proved authorizations from at least 35 percent of the employees in the craft or class" must be made before the NMB will take any further action.[32] Employees who are represented by a valid contract must have a showing of cards from at least a majority of the craft or class.[33]

The NMB procedures, particularly in the percentage required to obtain board intervention, are much different from the NLRB's requirements of 30 percent for either a representation or decertification election. The RLA implies that 35 percent is required to obtain a certification election and at least 50 percent to change present representation. No language in the RLA allows employees to decertify a union or representative and return to a nonrepresented state: "The only effect of certification by the Board of a new representative is that the employees have chosen other agents to represent them in dealing with the management under the existing agreement."[34]

This rationale clearly shows that contracts under the RLA are amendable, whereas contracts under the NLRA are terminable. The current chapter's supplemental readings in the accompanying study guide contain a salient example of this contract difference between the RLA statute and the NLRA one. In 1986, Trans World Airlines (TWA) and its owner, Carl Icahn, attempted to replace striking union flight attendants by hiring replacements and offering the replacements a different, nonunion employment contract. The union filed a dispute with the NMB. The board intervened and ruled that TWA must recognize the existing union as the "duly authorized and elected representative for all flight attendants at TWA."[35] This case clearly established that both elections and contracts under RLA can only be amended, not eliminated.

Investigation. The NMB reviews all applications it receives to confirm that the craft and class determinations are correct. The board also determines whether bar rules are applicable and whether there is sufficient employee interest. Unless the application is improper, it is given an "R" docket number (the "R" designation is the NMB's indication for a case indicating a potential representation election) and assigned to a mediator for field investigation. The investigating mediator will accept authorization cards from employees up until the time he or she reports back to the board.[36]

Bar rules. The NMB will refuse to accept an application under certain circumstances:

- Where an application has previously been made and a representative certified, a two-year moratorium will exist for the same craft or class of employees on the same carrier.
- Where an election was held on a carrier and where less than a majority of eligible voters participated in the election, the board will require a one-year moratorium.

Form NMB - 1 OMB No. 3140-0001 (Expiration Date 04/30/2009)

Application for Investigation of Representation Dispute

Date: _____

TO THE NATIONAL MEDIATION BOARD, Washington, D. C. 20572: A dispute has arisen among the employees of:

Name of Carrier:		Address:	
Contact:		City, State, Zip Code:	
Telephone Number:		Fax Number:	

as to who is the representative of these employees designated and authorized in accordance with the requirements of the Railway Labor Act. The undersigned, one of the parties to the dispute, hereby requests the National Mediation Board to investigate this dispute, and to certify the name or names of the individuals or organizations authorized to represent the employees involved in accordance with Section 2, Ninth, of the Act.

PARTIES TO DISPUTE

Petitioning organization or representative:	
Organization holding existing agreement, if any:	Date:
Other organization or representatives involved in dispute:	

CRAFT OR CLASS of Employees Involved – (If more than one craft or class, list separately)

	Craft or Class	Number of Employees
1.		
2.		
3.		
4.		
5.		
6.		

EVIDENCE OF REPRESENTATION – this application is supported by (check applicable box):

	At least a majority, if the employees are represented and there is a valid collective bargaining agreement.
	At least 35%, if the employees are unrepresented.

Name and Signature:			
Title:			
Address:		Telephone:	
City, State, Zip Code:		Fax:	

Revised October 31, 2005   Page 1 of 2

Figure 4.3. Application for Investigation of Representation Dispute, National Mediation Board. U.S. Government Printing Office.

• Where dismissal of a prior docketed application lacked a sufficient showing of interest, the moratorium will last one year.[37]

The NMB is not required to hold an election to determine representatives. The act specifically provides that the board "shall be authorized to take a secret ballot or to utilize any other appropriate method."[38] The board holds sole discretion in deciding to hold an election or certify on the basis of authorization cards.

Instructions: Continue to page 2.
Form NMB - 1 OMB No. 3140-0001 (Expiration Date 04/30/2009)

Application for Investigation of Representation Dispute

APPLICANT NOTICE OF APPEARANCE

The _____ hereby enters the following names, addresses,
(Applicant Organization)

phone numbers, fax numbers, and email addresses for the individual(s) designated as the representative(s)

of _____ in connection with the Application for Investigation
(Applicant Organization)

of Representation Dispute:

Name & Title:		Telephone:	
Address:		Fax:	
City, State, Zip Code		Email:	
		Alternate Telephone:	

Name & Title:		Telephone:	
Address:		Fax:	
City, State, Zip Code		Email:	
		Alternate Telephone:	

Name & Title:		Telephone:	
Address:		Fax:	
City, State, Zip Code		Email:	
		Alternate Telephone:	

Filing Instructions: File this application in duplicate.   **Additional Sheets:** Use and attach additional sheets as needed.

According to the Paperwork Reduction Act of 1995, no persons are required to respond to a collection of information unless it displays a valid OMB control Number. The valid OMB control number for this information collection is 3140-0001. The time required to complete this information collection is estimated to average 15 minutes per response, including the time to review instructions, search existing data resources, gather the data needed, and complete and review the information collection.

Revised October 31, 2005   Page 2 of 2

Figure 4.3, continued.

The board cannot be compelled or required to divulge the names of the employees signing cards. The board is obligated to reveal only the number of proved authorizations.[39] If there are allegations of fraud, the board has the sole authority to make a determination, provided the board does not abuse that discretion.

A U.S. Court of Appeals decision in 1977 demonstrates the problems inherent when the NMB certifies a representative without an election. The Teamsters Union, which was attempting to organize employees of the International In-flight Catering Company, a Hawaiian-based subsidiary of Japan Airlines, produced and distributed an employee-signature card that read, "I authorize the Airline Division of the International Brotherhood of Teamsters to request the National Mediation Board to conduct an investigation and a representation election, also to represent me in all negotiations of wages, hours and working conditions in accordance with the Railway Labor Act."[40] The NMB compared signatures on the signed cards against signatures found in the employer's records and certified the Teamsters as representative without an election. The district court set aside the certification and was highly critical of the NMB's process. The NMB merely checked signatures and refused to explain to the court what further investigation it conducted. The court held that cards asking for an election were incompetent evidence that the employees had chosen the Teamsters as their sole bargaining agent. The court stated:

> It is not a usual practice of the NMB to resolve representation disputes without an election. Plaintiff's un-contradicted evidence . . . establishes that the NMB used a check of authorizations as a means of resolving representation disputes in 12 out of 462 representation cases in the airline industry, involving less than ½ of 1% of eligible employees. On the facts before the court, Defendant NMB issued the certification to Plaintiff IICC and Defendant Teamsters in case R 4476 without conducting the investigation of choice of representative required by the statute, and without any competent evidence that a majority of IICC's employees had designated or selected Defendant Teamsters as their bargaining representative. The NMB's certification in this case failed to comply with the requirements of Section 2, Ninth of the Act and constituted an act contrary to the statute and in excess of its authority there under, and is therefore null, void and of no effect. We do fault the NMB for its pertinacious adherence to a position that flatly contradicts the intended meaning of the employees who had signed the Request for Election card, the plain language on the card itself, and the spirit of the RLA. It is a perversion of the search for truth and the policy of the RLA for the NMB to continue to insist, in these circumstances, that it conducted an investigation and discharged its duty under the RLA.[41]

Unfortunately for management, this case does not stand for the proposition that certification without an election is legally prohibited. As noted earlier, the board is free to make its determinations at will. Furthermore, it does so in its own time. Although the act requires the investigation and the identity of the representative thirty days after receipt of the application, the actual practice of the board has been to exceed that requirement whenever the facts of the case or the board's workload require.

The Supreme Court has stated that the board's duty to investigate requires the finding of certain facts to support the ultimate finding of fact that a certain group is the employee representative. These certain facts are:

- The number of eligible voters
- The number participating in the election
- The choice of the majority of those who participate[42]

Although these basic facts would appear to require an election, one is not required. If an election is not held, the NMB's alternate method must ascertain similar, analogous findings.

A showing of interest must be present to fulfill the board's basic requirements for certification. No specific format is required for such a showing, but the universal approach generally rests with authorization cards. Interestingly, there is no standard format for authorization cards. Cards are acceptable in any form as long as they are valid. To be valid, the cards must be dated and signed by the employee, and the date on the cards must be no more than one year before the date of the application. After reviewing the report of the mediator's field investigation, the NMB either dismisses an application or finds that a dispute does exist and orders a determination of the choice of a majority of the employees.

Participation. The RLA provides that if an election is to be held, then the NMB is to make the designation of the eligible employees. Two relevant board rules govern the designation of eligible employees:

- "In the conduct of a representation election, the Board shall designate who may participate in the election, which may include a public hearing on craft or class, and establish the rules to govern the election."
- "When disputes arise between parties to a representation dispute, the National Mediation Board is authorized by the Act to determine who may participate in the selection of employees representatives."[43]

Class and Craft Determination

The determination of class or craft dominates employees' choice of a representative under the RLA. This single decision of class or craft is paramount to determining which employees can vote in a representation election because it determines the bounds and/or positions for which the representing party may seek coverage. The NMB must first define who can vote: "In the conduct of any election for the purposes herein indicated[,] the Board shall designate who may participate in the election and establish the rules to govern the election, or may appoint a committee of three neutral persons who after hearing shall within ten days designate the employees who may participate in the election."[44] This determination establishes the class of employees or the particular craft to be represented. The policy of the board is based on the language of the act: "The majority of any craft or class of employees shall have the right to determine who shall be the representative of the craft or class."[45] This language has consistently been interpreted to mean that all employees of any single carrier who belong to the same craft or class must constitute a single unit for the purpose of selecting one representative. For example, all the airframe- and power plant–certified mechanics employed by a single carrier throughout its system make up a unit for selection of a representative.

The board has taken the position that a class or craft must be carrier-wide in its scope, but the board still has to determine the makeup of the appropriate unit. In making these determinations, history indicates a heavy reliance on customary and established practices indigenous to that group. In a 1940 decision regarding the Seaboard Air Line Railroad, guidelines were established that have remained the hallmark for decisions to this day. From that decision, the following five elements are present in the determination:

- Composition and relative permanency of the groupings along craft or class lines for representation purposes which the employees have voluntarily developed in the past among themselves
- The extent, nature, and effectiveness of the collective bargaining arrangements and labor agreements developed by the employees interested in the dispute with the carriers employing them
- Duties, responsibilities, skill, training, and experience of the employees involved and the nature of their work
- Usual practices of promotion, demotion, and seniority observed or developed for the employees concerned

- Nature and extent of the communities of interest existing among the employees[46]

The class or craft terminology was added to the RLA when the act was amended in 1934. The act implies that the two terms are synonymous. But the terms were identified thus: "While 'craft' and 'class' may not be synonymous as used in the Act, this could only be because 'class' may be more comprehensive."[47]

The term *craft* has been defined as "those engaged in any trade, taken collectively." The term *class* has been defined as "a group of individuals ranked together as possessing common characteristics or as having the same status." Federal Coordinator of Railroads Joseph Eastman, the author of the bill, explained the term *craft* or *class*, as he had used it before a congressional committee, as "all of the employees of the carrier, no matter in what shop they were located, who did that particular kind of work."[48]

The determination of crafts and classes has always been the exclusive prerogative of the NMB. This has been demonstrated by the hearings the board has convened to determine jurisdiction: "At the conclusion of such hearings the Board customarily invites all interested parties to submit briefs supporting their views, and after considering the evidence and briefs, the Board makes a determination or finding, specifying the craft or class of employees eligible to participate in the designation of representatives."[49] This statement indicates that the determination of eligible employees is equivalent to the determination of the craft or class to be represented. A hearing on this matter is only required if the interested parties to the dispute request one and then only if the board itself does not intend to designate the class or craft. The implications are that a hearing will not be held if the contesting parties agree on the employees eligible to participate. If the board decides to hold a hearing, it appoints a committee of three neutral persons, who will usually invite the employer to present factual information. However,

because the employer is not an interested party under the RLA, "whether, and to what extent, carriers will be permitted to present their views on craft or class questions is a matter that the Act leaves solely to the discretion of the Board."[50]

This ambiguity and vagueness of terminology has proved frustrating to the carriers. Determining the divisions within their workforce, who may represent that workforce, and which positions may or may not be included has been problematic for carriers. To the board's credit, attempts have been made to define the terminology more precisely. The board's attempt for the airline industry follows:

> [A] "craft or class" in the air transport industry means a well-knit and cohesive occupational group which has been developed over a period of years in the course of general voluntary association of the employees into collective bargaining units. The fact that a number of rather well defined occupational groups may now be covered in one working agreement is not conclusive evidence that such coverage determines the "Craft or Class" in that particular instance. Accordingly, it becomes necessary to examine the occupational groupings as they have emerged over a period of years in the airline industry, and to determine whether such groupings are uniform to the extent that they might now be termed "crafts or classes" under the provisions of the Railway Labor Act.[51]

The generally recognized "crafts and classes" referred to in the board's definition were in existence in the railroad industry when the act was passed in 1926, and the determinations were basic to the act itself. But a long-standing history was not evident in the air industry in 1936, when the RLA was amended to cover air carriers. Consequently, the majority of representation activity in the years prior to deregulation of the air transport industry was from the airlines. A 1977 ruling indicates the continuing dilemma: "Two issues affecting the Carrier's employees have been addressed by this proceeding: (1) whether personnel of United Air Lines, described as Passenger Service Employees, are properly an independent craft or class for the purposes of Section 2, Ninth, of the Railway Labor Act; and (2) which classifications are appropriately incorporated within such craft or class should it be identified as a separate and distinct grouping for collective bargaining purposes."[52]

Present determinations. The NMB, in making determinations for the airline industry, has taken two steps forward and one backward in its attempts to apply the origins of the class or craft determinations from the railroad industry to the airlines. The industries differ significantly, but short of new issues arising, a fair separation has been made.

The flight personnel class has been easily defined by its own nature to include flight deck personnel in the pilot category. Although this category appears today to be homogeneous, in one NMB determination, the board held that flight engineers were essentially flying mechanics and were to be listed under the craft of the airline mechanic. In a separate NMB determination, however, flight engineers were listed neither separately nor with the mechanics but instead with the pilot craft or class.[53] The flight attendants' class (stewards, stewardesses, and pursers) seems to be well understood as a class and craft encompassed by flight personnel.

The majority of class-and-craft-determination controversy stems from the area of ground personnel. The controversy has stemmed from the commingling of a variety of different groups, including mechanics, clerical workers, office employees, stores workers, fleet and passenger service workers, and stocks and stores employees. Despite the controversy, recent cases have shown that a basic degree of uniformity exists.[54]

The class of airline mechanics and related personnel includes aircraft mechanics, aircraft cleaners, parts washers, plant maintenance mechanics, and the service group known variously as "ground service personnel," "fleet service personnel," and "utility personnel."[55] The latter can include fuelers, internal and external aircraft cleaners, and janitorial workers in airport hangars and buildings.

In a decision rendered in 1934 pertaining solely to the railroad industry, the craft or class of clerical, office, station, and storehouse employees (including office janitors, ticket agents, and freight and baggage handlers) was recognized. With the exception of the following classification, this definition holds today.

The final class is that of stocks and stores employees. Originally, employees whose chief functions are to receive, issue, check, store, and inventory supplies were placed in the clerical class or craft. In 1953, two unpublished NMB cases changed this to include stocks and stores employees in a separate craft or class.[56]

Many unions, principally the International Association of Machinists and Aerospace Workers, have been the beneficiaries of such a huge classification of employees, particularly the category of mechanics and related employees. Still, despite the broad coverage, other unions—namely, the Aircraft Mechanics Fraternal Association (AMFA)—believe that mechanics in the industry are and should be a distinct class. Historically, the AMFA has lobbied for this change, albeit unsuccessfully to this point. Recently, AMFA petitioned for separation of the mechanics at Continental and United. In late 1994, the board refused to separate the mechanic classification from the airline mechanics and related class and craft.

Representation Election

The RLA provides that when an election is called, "[t]he majority of any craft or class of employees shall have the right to determine who shall be the representative of the craft or class for the purposes of this chapter."[57] Beginning with an NMB interpretation of a 1935 amendment to the RLA, the board's election procedures were unique, providing that in order for the union to be certified, at least a majority of the eligible voters (not simply a majority of those casting valid ballots) must vote for the union, and nonvotes were treated as votes against union representation. For the union to win, the valid "yes" votes cast had to equal at least 50 percent of the eligible voters plus one vote. So if a union sought to be recognized as the bargaining representative of an airline's 1,000 aircraft mechanics, it needed 501 valid "yes" votes to win the election.

In comparison, both the NLRA and CSRA provide that if a simple majority of those casting valid ballots vote for the union, the union wins. So if a union seeks to be recognized as the bargaining representative of an aerospace manufacturer's 1,000 aircraft mechanics, small voter turnout is inconsequential. If, for example, only 300 eligible voters voted, 151 valid "yes" votes would yield a union win.

In *Virginian Railroad Company v. System Federation No. 40*, the policy was established that although a majority of eligible voters must participate, a requirement fulfilled by the mere fact that the craft or class is under an organizational attempt, the board will consider an election valid if a majority of the craft class participated in the election.[58] If 501 of 1,000 employees cast a vote during the election, and if 251 vote for a particular representative, that representative could be certified as the official bargaining representative of all the craft or class, with as little as 26 percent of the employees actually casting a vote in favor of that particular representative.

Moreover, when the votes are cast, for whom or what they are cast also has its own special implications. If votes are supposed to be cast concerning only one union, votes for "no union" and write-in votes for any other organization or individual will be considered a vote for unionism. Figure 4.4 shows the NMB standard ballot used in most elections.

In a March 1991 election at Command Airways, a feeder carrier for American Airlines, the Transport Workers Union (TWU) won an election where they did not receive an actual majority of votes cast. Seven write-in votes were made in favor of the Association of Professional Flight Attendants, making the actual final outcome 32 in favor of representation, 25 against, and 7 for another union. The TWU had received exactly 50 percent of the eligible votes cast. The NMB ruled that the 7 votes for the other union were, in fact, votes for unionism and held that the final election outcome was therefore 39 for and 25 against. The NMB then certified the TWU as representatives of the flight attendants. A true majority in favor of the particular union on the ballot is not the only criteria for certification.

The Supreme Court, in hearing the 1965 *Brotherhood of Railway and Steamship Clerks* case, established the rules concerning the board's conduct in elections:

- The details of an election are to be left to the final determination of the board.
- Board election rules are not subject to judicial review unless there is a showing that it has acted in excess of its statutory authority.
- The election ballot does not have to contain a box allowing employees to vote for "no union."
- Employees do have the option of rejecting collective representation, and this option is sufficiently satisfied by the board policy of effectively treating nonvoters as having voted for no representation.

In this same Supreme Court finding, a specific ballot provision was approved that implies that a minority can certify a representative: "No employee is required to vote. If less than a majority of employees cast valid ballots, no representative

Form NMB-R-2(a)
Rev. 7/89

UNITED STATES OF AMERICA

OFFICIAL BALLOT OF NATIONAL MEDIATION BOARD

Involving   CASE NO. _____

Employees of

_____

A dispute exists among the above named craft or class of employees as to who are the representatives of such employees designated and authorized in accordance with the requirements of the Railway Labor Act. The National Mediation Board is taking a SECRET BALLOT in order to ascertain and to certify the name or names of organizations or individuals designated and authorized for purposes of the Railway Labor Act.

INSTRUCTIONS FOR VOTING

No employee is required to vote. If less than a majority of the employees cast valid ballots, no representative will be certified. Should a majority vote to be represented, the representative which receives a majority of the votes cast will be certified.

If you desire to be represented by:

Mark an "X" in this square. . . . .

If you desire to be represented by:
ANY OTHER ORGANIZATION OR INDIVIDUAL
Write name of such organization or individual on the line below:
_____, AND

Mark an "X" in this square. . . . .

NOTICE

1. This is a SECRET BALLOT. DO NOT SIGN YOUR NAME.
2. Marks in more than one square make ballot void.
3. Do not cut, mutilate or otherwise spoil this ballot. If you should accidentally do so, you may return the spoiled ballot at once to the Mediator and obtain a new one.

☆U.S. GPO: 1989—246-341

Figure 4.4. National Mediation Board standard ballot. U.S. Government Printing Office.

will be certified."[59] Although the board had in its history conformed to the proposition that a nonvote would be considered a vote against representation, it was apparent that the precedent could be changed at the board's discretion.

The NMB's initial approach of treating nonvotes as votes against union representation led to three-quarters of a century of a culture of intense company efforts to suppress voter turnout in union-representation elections. Kate Bronfenbrenner, director of Labor Education Research at Cornell University's School of Industrial and Labor Relations, conducted a study of data collected from a sample of all ninety-four certification elections and card-check campaigns supervised by the NMB that occurred in bargaining units with fifty or more eligible voters during the five-year period between January 1, 1999, and December 31,

2003. Bronfenbrenner's study found that in elections under the RLA, employer suppression of voter participation takes many forms. Employer tactics identified included positive changes in the workplace, such as granting unscheduled pay raises, making positive changes in personnel and working conditions, paying bribes and granting special favors, promising further improvements, and establishing an employee-involvement program. Tactics to impede the union's organizing effort included discharging union activists, laying off bargaining-unit employees, assisting anti-union committees, attempting to infiltrate the union's organizing committee, distributing union promise coupon books, and distributing pay stubs showing union dues deducted. Prevalent voter-suppression tactics included urging workers to tear up ballots (the most effective tactic and one also legal) and misleading workers on the voting procedures. Coercive, intimidating, harassing and retaliatory tactics by employers included holding captive-audience meetings of bargaining-unit employees, threatening to file for bankruptcy, threatening to close workplaces, unilaterally altering employee benefits and working conditions, harassment and discipline of activists, and bringing police into the workplace.[60]

In written comments submitted to the NMB on December 7, 2009, Bronfenbrenner characterizes the long-standing RLA certification process as "contrary to US democratic traditions," noting that her study revealed that in close to half of the RLA campaigns sampled, employers used five or more of the listed anti-union tactics, and in 27 percent of the campaigns, employers used ten or more. Charts of study data submitted suggested that for campaigns under the RLA, increases in voter suppression tactics yield lower voter turnout and lower union win rates, while for campaigns under the NLRA, where to win employers must get a majority of actual "no" votes, more-aggressive and coercive employer tactics tend to yield much higher voter turnout

and union win rates. In her concluding remarks, Bronfenbrenner states:

> Perhaps the most disturbing of all is that the single most effective strategy being used by employers to suppress union votes is legal—namely campaigns urging voters to destroy their ballots. It is also pervasive. We found that employers used this tactic with at least one or more voters in 67 percent of our sample. Ripping up ballots is a perfect example of just how undemocratic the current RLA process is.[61]

On May 10, 2010, after completing the Administrative Procedure Act process of notification and public comment, the NMB changed its long-standing interpretation of the 1935 amendment to the RLA to bring its election rules into line with those of the NLRB.[62] Immediately following the board's reinterpretation, some Republican members of Congress indicated their intention to sponsor proposed legislation to override the board's new interpretation, but that drive lost momentum in November 2010 when Delta Air Lines defeated the Association of Flight Attendants in a representation election decided under the new process. The union had previously failed to win elections to represent Delta's cabin crews in 2002 and 2008 (elections held under the board's old process), and the outcome of this election under the new process demonstrated that the change had not insurmountably stacked the deck in favor of unions.[63]

Election-Rule Exceptions

Since the establishment of the NMB in 1934, only two cases have surfaced where it was not necessary for the majority of employees to cast ballots for the election to be declared valid and where the majority of valid ballots actually cast determined the outcome. In both cases, commonly referred to as the Laker and Key ballot cases, the board's position was predicated on the belief that management had interfered with the employees' right of organization and representation to such an extent that they made the normal procedure invalid.

The RLA, unlike the NLRA, does not provide the NMB with specific authority to make a finding of unfair labor practices in federally supervised elections. Creation of the Laker and Key ballots is the method employed by the board's presidential appointees to provide what amounts to redress of unfair labor practices in RLA cases. The Laker ballot (see fig. 4.5) was the NMB's first attempt to provide a modified ballot for cases where management interference or coercion of employees was found.

In the Laker Airways case, the NMB found that management had influenced the certification election by telling all eligible employees to return

UNITED STATES OF AMERICA

OFFICIAL BALLOT OF NATIONAL MEDIATION BOARD

CASE NO.

Involving

Employees of

A dispute exists among the above named craft or class of employees as to who are the representatives of such employees designated and authorized in accordance with the requirements of the Railway Labor Act. The National Mediation Board is taking a SECRET BALLOT in order to ascertain and to certify the name or names of organizations or individuals designated and authorized for purposes of the Railway Labor Act.

INSTRUCTIONS FOR VOTING

No employee is required to vote. The majority of valid ballots actually cast will determine the outcome of the election. Mark an "X" in the appropriate square:

YES ☐

Do you desire to be represented by
the   ?

NO ☐

NOTICE

1. This is a SECRET BALLOT. DO NOT SIGN YOUR NAME.
2. Marks in more than one square make ballot void.
3. Do not cut, mutilate or otherwise spoil this ballot. If you should accidentally do so, you may return the spoiled ballot at one to the Mediator and obtain a new one.

Figure 4.5. National Mediation Board Laker ballot. U.S. Government Printing Office.

the ballots to the director of human resources instead of mailing them to the NMB. Management also sent letters and held meetings telling employees not to vote for representation. The offenses on the part of Laker's management lead to the creation of the Laker ballot in 1981. Unlike the standard ballot, which has boxes for write-ins, the Laker ballot is a "yes" or "no" ballot. The Laker ballot does not require a majority of employees to cast ballots for the election to be declared valid, and the majority of valid ballots actually cast determines the outcome of the election.

In the Key Airlines case, the NMB said that events surrounding the election in question were "disturbingly similar" to a 1986 case involving the carrier. In the earlier Key Airlines case, the board had also found management guilty of illegal interference and coercion of employees in a unionizing effort. To provide the Teamsters with redress in that 1986 case, the NMB ordered use of the Laker ballot in a second election, which the union also lost. NMB members decided that even stronger measures were required to redress these new instances of management interference and created the Key ballot (see fig. 4.6).

In a Key election, all eligible employees who fail to cast a ballot are automatically counted by NMB officials as having voted "yes" for

---

UNITED STATES OF AMERICA

OFFICIAL BALLOT OF NATIONAL MEDIATION BOARD

Involving   CASE NO. _____

Employees of

A dispute exists among the above named craft or class of employees as to whether such employees desire representation in accordance with the requirements of the Railway Labor Act. To resolve this dispute the National Mediation Board (NMB) is taking a SECRET BALLOT in order to ascertain and to certify the name of the organization or individual, if any, designated and authorized to represent said employees for purposes of the Railway Labor Act.

INSTRUCTIONS FOR VOTING

You may exercise your choice in either of the two following ways. If you wish to be represented by the United Transportation Union, do not return your ballot to the NMB. Should less than a majority of the eligible employees return valid ballots, the will be certified. However, if you are opposed to representation by the , mark an "X" in the box below and return your ballot to the NMB before p.m., . Should a majority of employees return valid ballots opposing representation, no representative will be certified.

If you are opposed to representation by the

Mark an "X" in this space . . . .

NOTICE

1. This is a SECRET BALLOT. DO NOT SIGN YOUR NAME
2. Do not cut, mutilate or otherwise spoil this ballot. If you should accidentally do so, you may return the spoiled ballot at once to the Board representative to obtain a new one.
3. Ballots to be counted must be received at the NMB before p.m.,

Figure 4.6. National Mediation Board Key ballot. U.S. Government Printing Office.

representation by the union seeking to represent. The opposite is true for the normal ballot; employees who want a specific union representative have to cast a ballot in favor of the union of their choice; and for the election to be declared valid, a majority of the eligible employees have to cast ballots. The winner is the party receiving the majority of the votes cast. The election would be declared invalid if less than a majority of the employees cast votes, and the board has ruled in the past that the employees then would not be represented by any union because they failed to produce a majority interest in any representation.

In the actual balloting under a Key ballot election, all eligible employees receive a ballot marked, for example, "Are you opposed to representation by the International Brotherhood of Teamsters–Airline Division?" The employee, if opposed, places an X next to the question and mails the ballot back to the NMB. This procedure considers all eligible employees as voting in favor of the union unless a ballot is returned to the board. Under these guidelines, for the union to be disavowed, the union seeking to represent would have to do something that causes the rank-and-file employees to vote against it.

This form of voting does not follow the traditional method of "one person, one vote." Instead, it stacks the deck in favor of the union. "One person, one vote" only applies to a dissenter. The remainder of the employees, if apathetic to the entire affair, is considered in favor of unionization.

Another indication of the NMB's authority in this area occurred in 1990 in a representation dispute at America West Airlines. In that case, the board found that the Phoenix-based carrier violated its employees' right to freedom of choice. The board held that during an election campaign, the company contaminated the laboratory conditions necessary for a fair election. According to the board, America West "improperly interfered

with, influenced, and coerced its flight attendants in their freedom of choice by the 'totality' of its conduct, by announcing and implementing certain work rule changes, by implementing increases in layover benefits and distributing profit-sharing bonuses during the election." The board ordered that the election be rerun, distributed to all employees' special notices concerning the company's conduct, and sent new ballot materials to each affected employee.

Mergers and Acquisitions

Since the Airline Deregulation Act of 1978, the elements of mergers and takeovers have dominated the industry. Comparing the names of the airlines in existence before deregulation with the names of those flying today reveals that a variety of well-known carriers has vanished or has been acquired by others. In mergers and takeovers, the NMB has followed a policy of acquiescing to the union or nonunion status of the surviving carrier. For example, when one carrier was merged into another and the result was a mixture of union and nonunion employees in a particular craft or class, the board determined that the new class was to be either totally union or totally nonunion. When the majority of the merged classification was nonunion, the union status of the merged carrier was abolished. Likewise, when the majority of the merged classification was unionized, the nonunion status was abolished, and the labor union representing the majority of the employees became the representative for all.

This approach was evident in the Delta Air Lines and Western Airlines merger (see fig. 4.7). Delta was the surviving carrier and employed larger numbers of nonunion employees than did Western, a unionized carrier. Western's unions were decertified. In the same case, Western's pilots and Delta's pilots were both unionized, so the Air Line Pilots Association continued as the certified representative.

The Londoner

Figure 4.7. Western Airlines DC-10. On April 1, 1987, a San Francisco federal appeals court blocked the $860 million merger of Western Airlines and Delta Air Lines. The appeals court ruled the merger would be prohibited until a union representation dispute could be settled through arbitration. About 10 percent of Delta's employees were represented by unions versus 92 percent of Western's employees. However, on April 7, 1987, the U.S. Supreme Court rejected an emergency request by a Western Airlines' union, refusing to interfere with the merger. The court let stand a previous order issued by Justice Sandra Day O'Connor that cleared the way for the merger. The merger made Delta the nation's fourth-largest airline at that time.

More recently, the board has shifted its position away from its precedent. In two cases of merger, USAir and Piedmont (1987) and Federal Express and Flying Tiger (1989), the board, citing inability to determine precise numbers, did not decertify any unions, and the surviving carriers were forced to consider the possibility of having their workforce unionized or, worse yet, having a payroll split by craft. This occurred in the Federal Express–Flying Tiger merger, despite the statistics provided by the surviving carrier, Federal Express, that indicated it had almost two hundred more nonunion pilots than Flying Tiger, the merged carrier. In both cases, the NMB ruled that the mix of union and nonunion employees would be temporary until arrangements could be made for an election among all the employees. One close observer of airline labor relations said, however, that "the actual numbers [of union and nonunion employees] could have been determined for the purpose of deciding the representation issue. The mediation

board decision was considered 'a back door way to keep the pilots' union alive.'"[64]

These actions, coupled with the board's actions in the Laker and Key cases, indicate a major difference between the NLRA and the RLA. In theory, at least, the NLRB is structurally forced to be impartial. Such is not the case with the NMB under the RLA. In a 1988 federal court of appeals decision, the board's partiality was at issue. In the decision rendered, the appeals judge upheld the NMB's right to be biased: "[T]here is no expressed statutory duty of neutrality."[65]

Decertification

No language in the Railway Labor Act provides guidance for the decertification of a union. The NMB historically has taken the position that the act itself favors the organization of labor and decertification prohibits this right. The courts have overruled this stance on the grounds that the act also protects labor's freedom of choice.[66]

In 1985, the Chamber of Commerce of the United States filed a petition suggesting the NMB develop formal decertification procedures. The NMB determined that this was not necessary due to the availability of the straw-man election. A *straw-man election* works by voting for a representative in an election for the sole purpose of ousting the incumbent. Once elected, the new representative revokes his or her status with the NMB, which results in unrepresented employees.[67]

The Process under the National Labor Relations Act
Employees Subject to the NLRA

Section 2 of the Taft-Hartley Act defines *employee* as a person currently on an employer's payroll and also a person whose work has ceased because of a current strike or an unfair labor practice. The definition specifically excludes:

• Agricultural laborers
• Persons employed in the domestic service of a family or persons at their home

- Independent contractors
- Supervisors
- Persons covered under the RLA
- Government employees, including those employed by the U.S. government, any government corporation or Federal Reserve Bank, or any state or political subdivision such as a city, town, or school district

Employees who fall under the jurisdiction of the act and who appeal for union coverage may still be ignored by the NLRB because the board limits the cases it will accept based on established employee standards.

Supervisory Personnel Subject to the NLRA

The unique personnel definition under the NLRA is that of supervisor. Prior to the 1947 Taft-Hartley amendments, a supervisor was not excluded from the definition of employee, and the employer could not discriminate against him or her for engaging in union activities. Since 1947, however, supervisors have not been protected under the act. Supervisors may join unions but may be discharged for doing so. Additionally, no provisions in the law compel an employer to deal with any union designated by the supervisors to represent them.[68] Supervisor is defined in Section 2 of the NLRA as a person with the authority "to hire, transfer, suspend, lay off, recall, promote, discharge, assign, reward, or discipline other employees, or responsibly to direct them, or to adjust their grievances, or effectively to recommend such action . . . [that] requires the use of independent judgment." The NLRB, in the case of *Ohio Power Company v. Utilities Workers Union of America*, ruled that the responsibility to direct other employees is enough in itself to classify a person as a supervisor.[69]

Managerial Personnel Subject to the NLRA

Other personnel, such as "managerial" and "confidential" personnel, are not specifically excluded by the Taft-Hartley Act. But the Supreme Court ruled that a managerial employee is not covered by the act if he or she "formulates and executes management decisions."[70] Furthermore, the NLRB has ruled that confidential workers, defined as those workers with access to personnel and labor relations records and files, must also be excluded from employee bargaining units.[71]

Thus, secretaries otherwise covered by a union contract are excluded from coverage and representation if they are employed in the labor relations or personnel departments of a business.

Employers Subject to the NLRA

Employer is defined in Section 2 of the Taft-Hartley Act as an organization or its personnel—other than "employees"—who act in behalf of the organization and whose operations affect, or fall within, the definition of interstate commerce. Specifically exempted from the act are the following organizations:

- The federal government or any wholly owned government corporation or any federal reserve bank (except the U.S. Postal Service)
- Employers subject to the RLA
- Any state or political division of a state
- Labor organizations, except when acting as employers

In 1958, the NLRB revised its own standards to establish basic guidelines for employees and employers falling under the act. This was done in an effort to reduce excessive case loads. The following year, amendments under the Landrum-Griffin Act forbade the board from changing these standards solely as a way of reducing its workload. These standards are based on the annual amount of business done by the employer, that is, the amount of its sales or purchases stated in terms of total dollar volume of business. The amount differs for various kinds of businesses.[72]

Procedures of the National Labor Relations Board

The NLRA provides that the NLRB is responsible for the certification of elections only when a petition requesting one has been filed. A petition for certification may be filed by an employee, a group of employees, a union, or an employer. The petition must be signed, sworn to, or affirmed under oath at the regional office of the NLRB. Figure 4.8 shows the various steps required for certification of a union under the NLRA, and figure 4.9 shows a typical NLRB authorization card.

Union petition. A union may file a petition when it seeks recognition as exclusive bargaining agent and the employer refuses to recognize the union or when it has been recognized by the employer but desires to obtain the benefits of certification by the board.[73] Accompanying the petition should be proof that at least 30 percent of the employees in the unit are interested in having the union represent them.

Individual petitions. Individuals, excluding supervisors, may file petitions. Such petitions must also be backed by proof that 30 percent of the employees are interested in having the nominated bargaining agent represent them.[74]

Employer requests. A formal request by an employer is not required. Employer requests are generally made when confronted by a union that

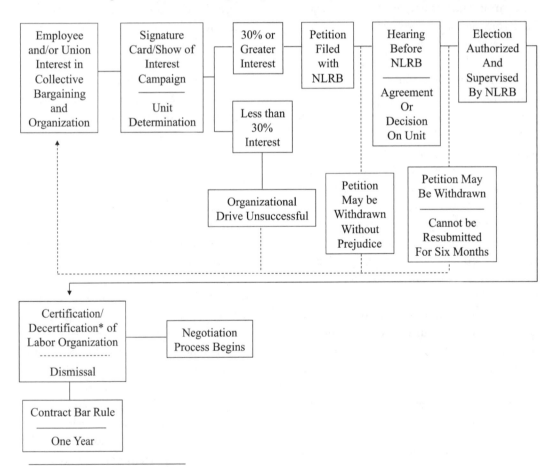

* Process may also be used to decertify an existing union or to change union representation

Figure 4.8. National Labor Relations Board representation process.

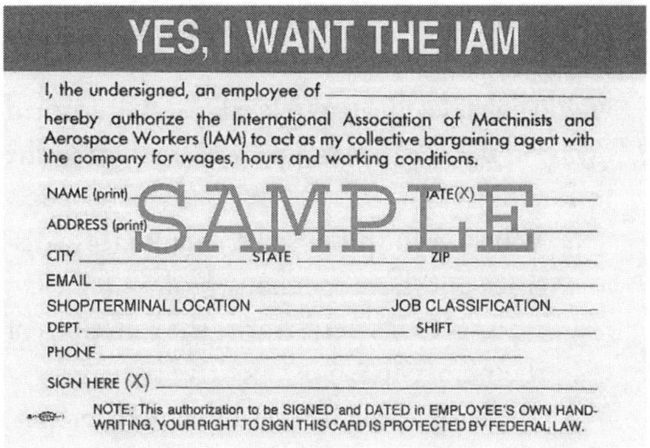

YES, I WANT THE IAM

I, the undersigned, an employee of ______

hereby authorize the International Association of Machinists and Aerospace Workers (IAM) to act as my collective bargaining agent with the company for wages, hours and working conditions.

NAME (print) ______ DATE(X) ______

ADDRESS (print) ______

CITY ______ STATE ______ ZIP ______

EMAIL ______

SHOP/TERMINAL LOCATION ______ JOB CLASSIFICATION ______

DEPT. ______ SHIFT ______

PHONE ______

SIGN HERE (X) ______

NOTE: This authorization to be SIGNED and DATED in EMPLOYEE'S OWN HANDWRITING. YOUR RIGHT TO SIGN THIS CARD IS PROTECTED BY FEDERAL LAW.

SAMPLE

Figure 4.9. International Association of Machinists authorization card.

contends that the majority of employees desire representation. The board will direct an election even if it is claimed that no reasonable basis exists for questioning the union's majority.[75]

Investigation. Upon receipt of a petition, the NLRB is required to determine if a question of representation actually exists. The investigation is to determine:

- If the board has jurisdiction to conduct the election
- Whether there is enough showing of employee interest in a collective bargaining representative to justify an election
- Whether there actually is a question about representation
- Whether the election is sought in the appropriate unit of employees
- Whether the representative named in the petition (ordinarily a union) is qualified
- Whether there are any legal barriers to an election

Often, a legal barrier to an election takes the form of an existing bona fide collective bargaining agreement covering the employees in question. Such an agreement may constitute a contract bar to an election. Another legal impediment is the certification by the NLRB of a bargaining unit within the previous year. Such a certification bars an election, as does a previous election within the prior twelve months.[76]

Determining Bargaining Units

Subject to certain limitations, Section 9(B) of the NLRA provides that the NLRB determine the bargaining unit "in order to assure to employees the fullest freedom in exercising the rights guaranteed by this act, the unit appropriate for the purpose of collective bargaining shall be the employee unit, *craft unit*, plant unit or subdivision thereof."

The Taft-Hartley amendments, however, placed limitations on the NLRB's authority:

- Professional employees may not be included in a unit with nonprofessionals unless a majority of the professional employees vote for this inclusion in a separate self-determination election.
- Supervisors are excluded from inclusion.
- Plant guards may not be included in a unit of production and maintenance workers.
- The extent to which employees have organized a union shall not be controlling. The NLRB may not direct an election among particular employees just because the union has not been able to organize employees elsewhere in the plant.[77]

In addition, the act requires that certain types of employees be excluded from a unit. The principal exclusions consist of individuals identified with management interests. Excluded are supervisors, domestic servants, independent contractors, and employees covered by the RLA. The NLRB also excludes confidential employees "who assist and act in a confidential capacity to persons who formulate, determine and effectuate management policies in the field of labor relations."[78] Not excluded are probationary employees, regular part-time employees, employees on vacation or authorized leave of absence, laid-off employees, and those absent because of illness.[79]

The board has generally sought to determine the appropriateness of a bargaining unit on the grounds of common employment interests of the employees involved. Among the principal factors the board considers are:

- The similarity of duties, skills, wages, and working conditions
- The pertinent bargaining history, if any, among the employees involved
- The employees' own wishes in the matter
- The appropriateness of the unit's purpose in relation to the organizational structure of the company itself[80]

Craft, Departmental, or Industrial Units

A significant and persistent problem has been the desire of craft employees (carpenters, mechanics, etc.) not to be included, absorbed, or lost in industrial or departmental bargaining units. Because of the trade nature of these positions, many craft employees wish to have their own separate and distinct representation rather than to be covered under an umbrella union that represents a variety of different workers.

In its 1948 *National Tube* decision,[81] the NLRB decided that craft-severance elections should not be permitted in the basic steel industry because of the integrated nature of these business operations and the history of bargaining on an industrial rather than craft basis. Later, in separate decisions, this denial of craft-severance election was extended to the aluminum, lumber, and wet-milling industries for the same reasons. The NLRB reversed its *National Tube* decision in the 1954 *American Potash* decision, which held that craft units must be split off from an established industrial unit when the unit seeking severance was a "true craft group" or the union seeking to represent the unit had traditionally represented that craft.[82] This decision did not extend to the industries previously barred in the 1948 *National Tube* case.

In 1966, the board again changed its position on craft severance. The decision in the *Mallinckrodt Chemical* case is now controlling and applies to all industries, including those

eliminated from consideration in 1948.[83] In the *Mallinckrodt* decision, the board stated that it would consider all areas relevant to an informed decision in craft-severance cases, including the following:

- Whether the proposed unit embraces a distinct and homogeneous group of skilled crafts persons performing the functions of their craft on a nonrepetitive basis
- The bargaining history of employees
- The extent to which the employees have maintained their separate identity during their inclusion in the broader unit
- The history and pattern of bargaining in the industry
- The degree of integration of the employer's production process
- The qualifications of the union seeking to represent the severed unit

Certification Election

To appropriately conduct an election, the NLRB may require an employer to provide a list of the names and addresses of all employees eligible to vote so that the NLRB may determine if the petitioning unit is appropriate. If the unit in the petition is not appropriate, an election is not conducted. If the unit is appropriate and there is no present bargaining unit or contract bar rule, the board sets in motion the machinery for holding an election. Figure 4.10 shows an NLRB notice of election.

Preparing for an election involves the establishment of polling places, preparation of ballots, and provision of representatives to monitor the election and tabulate votes. The election is conducted through secret ballots tabulated by NLRB personnel. The union or unions seeking certification are listed on the ballots, which also include a section to vote for "no union." Figure 4.11 shows the ballot used by the NLRB in its elections.

If the union wins the election, gaining a majority of the votes, it is duly certified as the

NOTICE TO EMPLOYEES

FROM THE
National Labor Relations Board

A PETITION has been filed with this Federal agency seeking an election to determine whether certain employees want to be represented by a union.

The case is being investigated and NO DETERMINATION HAS BEEN MADE AT THIS TIME by the National Labor Relations Board. IF an election is held Notices of Election will be posted giving complete details for voting.

It was suggested that your employer post this notice so the National Labor Relations Board should inform you of your basic rights under the National Labor Relations Act.

YOU HAVE THE RIGHT under Federal Law

- To self-organization
- To form, join, or assist labor organizations
- To bargain collectively through representatives of your own choosing
- To act together for the purposes of collective bargaining or other mutual aid or protection
- To refuse to do any or all of these things unless the union and employer, in a state where such agreements are permitted, enter into a lawful union-security agreement requiring employees to pay periodic dues and initiation fees. Nonmembers who inform the union that they object to the use of their payments for nonrepresentational purposes may be required to pay only their share of the union's costs of representational activities *(such as collective bargaining, contract administration, and grievance adjustments).*

It is possible that some of you will be voting in an employee representation election as a result of the request for an election having been filed. While NO DETERMINATION HAS BEEN MADE AT THIS TIME, in the event an election is held, the NATIONAL LABOR RELATIONS BOARD wants all eligible voters to be familiar with their rights under the law IF it holds an election.

The Board applies rules that are intended to keep its elections fair and honest and that result in a free choice. If agents of either unions or employers act in such a way as to interfere with your right to a free election, the election can be set aside by the Board. Where appropriate the Board provides other remedies, such as reinstatement for employees fired for exercising their rights, including backpay from the party responsible for their discharge.

NOTE:

The following are examples of conduct that interfere with the rights of employees and may result in the setting aside of the election.

- Threatening loss of jobs or benefits by an employer or a union
- Promising or granting promotions, pay raises, or other benefits to influence an employee's vote by a party capable of carrying out such promises
- An employer firing employees to discourage or encourage union activity or a union causing them to be fired to encourage union activity
- Making campaign speeches to assembled groups of employees on company time within the 24-hour period before the election
- Incitement by either an employer or a union of racial or religious prejudice by inflammatory appeals
- Threatening physical force or violence to employees by a union or an employer to influence their votes

Please be assured that IF AN ELECTION IS HELD every effort will be made to protect your right to a free choice under the law. Improper conduct will not be permitted. All parties are expected to cooperate fully with this Agency in maintaining basic principles of a fair election as required by law. The National Labor Relations Board, as an agency of the United States Government, does not endorse any choice in the election.

NATIONAL LABOR RELATIONS BOARD
an agency of the
UNITED STATES GOVERNMENT

THIS IS AN OFFICIAL GOVERNMENT NOTICE AND MUST NOT BE DEFACED BY ANYONE

Figure 4.10. National Labor Relations Board notice of election.

exclusive bargaining agent for the workers in the bargaining unit.[84] To be certified as a bargaining representative, a labor union must receive a majority of the votes cast in an election. Majority is 50 percent plus one person. The majority rule does not take into consideration the total unit. Only those employees actually voting are considered. If a clear majority is not received by any party when three or more choices are on the ballot, run-off elections are held for the two parties or categories receiving the most votes.

Within thirty days of the election, the NLRB notifies the company of the vote outcome. If a union wins, it is certified as the exclusive bargaining representative of the employees in the unit. Immediately following, the parties meet to engage in the negotiation of the initial agreement. But if the employer prevails, no election petition is honored by the NLRB for one year. In effect, certification guarantees the union or nonunion status of a bargaining unit for at least one year after an election.[85]

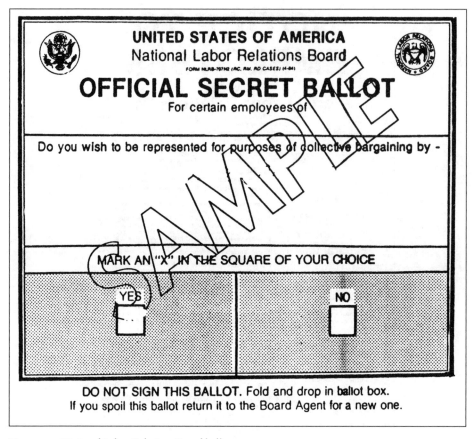

Figure 4.11. National Labor Relations Board ballot.

Summary

The principal differences between the RLA and the NLRA in handling union certification elections center on the two respective governing bodies, the NMB and the NLRB. The NMB has far greater discretionary power for dictating and manipulating election rules and conditions than the NLRB, and the very fabric of the RLA is pro-union, whereas the NLRA legislation possesses a more balanced view of workers' desires regarding unionization. No mechanism under the RLA allows represented airline employees to decertify and work as unrepresented employees. They are only allowed by law to change unions or representatives, not to eliminate them.

Because of this statutory prohibition on decertification, once a craft is unionized under the RLA, that craft, by law, must always remain unionized or represented. Thus, bargaining agreements under the RLA are only amendable, not terminable as under the NLRA. In essence, the RLA has created a set of union contracts that are valid in perpetuity. The terms and conditions can be, and are, negotiated every few years, but the existence of the agreement, like union representation itself, can never be eliminated. The financial impact of these provisions of the RLA and on the enforcement power of the NMB on the carriers covered under that act is significant.

5. Negotiating the Collective Bargaining Agreement

Management and labor are mutually dependent for their continued existence, but within this dependent relationship is a pervasive philosophic conflict. One of management's primary objectives is to minimize costs, particularly labor costs. Naturally, labor seeks the highest wages and fringe benefits possible. Furthermore, management believes that it has the duty and responsibility to make all decisions concerning the business, but labor argues for a voice in these decisions.

Management's view is founded on the argument that the ownership of capital carries with it the right and responsibility of deciding how that capital is used. Management argues that it bears the risk of loss of capital. Labor claims the right to participate, founded on the philosophy of industrial democracy, in business decisions.[1] This philosophy argues that employees have an inherent right to participate in the decisions that directly affect their work lives, especially those that involve wages, work hours, and employment conditions. Labor also argues that capital owned by the business is of little value without the services of its employees.

Historically, this basic conflict between labor and management has led to the disruption of the free flow of commerce and to many social and economic problems for society. In disputes between labor and management, a third party to the dispute is often overlooked: the general public. All labor law must be designed to reflect the conflicting concerns of all three parties.[2] The present labor laws were crafted to resolve these disputes and to protect the public from undue harm through the provisions for *emergency boards*. These boards, contained in both the RLA and the NLRA, are the legislative means to protect the public from damaging and protracted labor disputes. Emergency boards are particularly important because both the RLA and the NLRA legislation encourage collective bargaining and the settlement of disagreements by negotiation, and the emergency boards promote negotiation by providing for the suspension of self-help options until they become absolutely necessary.[3]

Issues about and attitudes toward negotiations in the airline industry have changed dramatically following the passage of the Airline Deregulation Act of 1978. This act and other labor-oriented developments in the air transport sector—the Professional Air Traffic Controllers Organization's strike (that also put public-employee labor unions on clear notice), the first bankruptcy of Continental Airlines, the demise of Eastern Airlines, and most recently, the post–September 11, 2001, bankruptcies of numerous major U.S. airlines—have altered the traditional approaches taken by both management and unions at the negotiating table. But the negotiation procedures and statutory time constraints remain the same.

This chapter introduces alternative approaches to bargaining and compares the contract negotiation procedures that must be followed under the RLA, the NLRA, or the Civil Service Reform Act and similar state laws. Before delving into these issues, however, it is necessary to identify several terms used frequently in the labor negotiations environment that are often used incorrectly by the news media in reporting on those very same negotiations: *arbitration*, *conciliation*, *lockout*, *mediation*, *self-help*, *strike*, and *supermediation*. The glossary in the current volume provides the correct definition for each of these terms.

Approaches to Bargaining

The two basic approaches to the bargaining process are: *distributive bargaining* (also known as *zero-sum bargaining*) and *integrative bargaining* (also known as *interest-based bargaining*).

Distributive bargaining is the classic, old-school approach in which the parties (union and management) view the process of collective bargaining as negotiation to divide up a pie of a fixed size. Any gain by one side necessarily comes at the expense of the other, so the interests of each side are seen as being in direct conflict. Distributive bargaining is always highly adversarial and confrontational, typically characterized by mutual hostility, belligerency, posturing, histrionic ranting, table-pounding, threatening, bluffing, secrecy, deceit, and distrust. At the negotiating table, only the lead negotiator for each party has a speaking role. This has been the prevailing model for collective bargaining in the United States since its inception, but it is not well suited to today's extremely competitive global marketplace.

In contrast, parties to integrative bargaining view the process of collective bargaining as a concerted effort to enlarge the pie so that labor's demands may be met while improving productivity to at least pay for labor's gains (or in a company in peril, to avoid labor's giving further concessions), so that the result may be seen as a win for both labor and management. Thus, the interests of the parties are seen as being compatible in that both are working to make the company more competitive. Integrative bargaining is highly cooperative, requiring full disclosure and truthful and open communication between the parties in a mutually respectful "Come, let us reason together" atmosphere of trust. At the negotiating table, all members of both negotiating teams are typically free, even encouraged, to speak out in a brainstorming-style process. This more modern approach, more positive and typically more productive, is beginning to take hold in the context of today's fiercely competitive environment in the airline, aerospace, general aviation, and other industries and should also be considered in public-employee collective bargaining, given the pressures on government agencies at all levels to contain and reduce costs. For example, in late 2007, NetJets Aviation, a major fractional business-jet operator, reached a new collective bargaining agreement with its pilots (represented by International Brotherhood of Teamsters Local 1108), said to be the most generous in the industry, through integrative bargaining.

Case study 5.1 describes this successful use of integrative bargaining.

Case Study 5.1: NetJets Aviation—Negotiations through Integrative Bargaining

NetJets, formerly Executive Jet Aviation, was founded in 1964 as one of the first private business-jet charter and aircraft-management companies. The NetJets program was created in 1986 by Richard Santulli, the chairman and CEO of NetJets, as the first fractional aircraft-ownership program. In 1998, after being a NetJets customer for three years, Warren Buffett, chairman and CEO of the Berkshire Hathaway Company, acquired NetJets (see fig. CS5.1.1). NetJets' fleet comprises approximately 650 business jets. Jets in the company's fleet are classified by cabin size: light, midsized, and large.

The International Brotherhood of Teamsters Professional Aviators Local 1108 is dedicated to professional

Figure CS 5.1.1. Warren Buffett, an American investor, businessman, and philanthropist. He is one of the world's most successful investors and the largest shareholder and CEO of Berkshire Hathaway. He was ranked by *Forbes Magazine* as the third-richest person in the world in 2010, with an estimated net worth of $47 billion. Courtesy of Mark Hirschey.

union representation for professional aviators. Their mission is to remove pilot job security, wages, benefits, and working conditions from the competitive consumer market by advocating a "safety first" work environment and establishing professional collective bargaining agreement standards across the industry. Strong union representation neutralizes management pressures that focus on profits at the expense of safety. Professional career opportunities attract the best pilots, and only professional collective bargaining agreements provide stable professional career opportunities. Local 1108 is a union organization of professional pilots united under the banner of the International Brotherhood of Teamsters for the purpose of addressing needs that are specific to the pilots of shared aircraft-ownership programs.[4]

In December 2007, NetJets Aviation and International Brotherhood of Teamsters Professional Aviators Local 1108 (IBT 1108; see fig. CS5.1.2) announced that the pilot group had approved a major amendment to their collective bargaining agreement. The NetJets Aviation Pilot Union represents more than twenty-six hundred pilots. Seventy-six percent of eligible members voted in favor of the amendment,

with voter participation reaching an unprecedented 96 percent.[5]

By mutual agreement, union and company officials began negotiations in late April 2007, worked with an aggressive deadline to ensure focus on completion, and used a process called *integrative bargaining*—a style of contract negotiating that is rarely successful in the aviation industry.

Integrative bargaining (also called *interest-based bargaining*) is a negotiation strategy in which parties collaborate to find a "win-win" solution to their dispute. This strategy focuses on developing mutually beneficial agreements based on the disputants' interests. Interests include the concerns, desires, needs, and fears important to each side. These interests are the underlying reasons why people initially become involved in a conflict. Integrative bargaining is important because it produces more-satisfactory outcomes for the parties involved than does positional bargaining. Positional bargaining is based on fixed, opposing viewpoints and tends to result in a compromise and not necessarily an agreement. Oftentimes,

Figure CS 5.1.2. Logo of the International Brotherhood of Teamsters Professional Aviators Local 1108. Courtesy of International Brotherhood of Teamsters Professional Aviators Local 1108.

compromises do not satisfy the true interests of the disputants. Instead, compromises simply split the difference between the two positions, giving each side half of what they want. Integrative bargaining, on the other hand, can potentially give everyone all of what they want.[6]

NetJets Chairman Richard T. Santulli praised the results: "The overwhelming turnout and strong approval of the agreement is a testament to the fact that both sides negotiated in good faith using integrative [interest-based] bargaining. This agreement would not have been reached without the true spirit of cooperation and dedication union leadership displayed throughout the process. With this contract, NetJets Aviation offers its pilots career opportunities and a quality of life that are unmatched in the industry. This agreement maintains NetJets' leadership position and enables us to continue to provide the best service available in private aviation."[7]

The new collective bargaining agreement will become amendable in 2012; however, a provision was included in the contract that allows for a three-year extension should NetJets meet certain requirements. These requirements include NetJets giving NetJets Aviation (NJA) 85 percent of all international flying, maintaining the same level of health care at no cost to pilots, opening ten additional crew bases, and adding cost-of-living adjustments to pay tables each year of the extension. Perhaps the most important of these requirements is the 85 percent international-flying provision. If met, this would guarantee that pilots flying for NetJets International (the nonunion division that operates NetJets' Gulfstreams) would be integrated into NJA and thus be unionized under IBT 1108.[8]

NetJets' first officers, as well as captains, benefit greatly from the new agreement. First-year pay for first officers climbs from $39,000 to $56,875 a year under the seven-days-on–seven-days-off schedule. This eclipses the previous industry-leading annual salary for new-hire first officers of $40,000 at CitationShares. After ten years of service, a first officer's salaries will top out at $81,081. First-year captain salaries increased from $52,500 to $87,500, a significant step beyond the previous high of $64,000 at CitationShares. Under the new pay scale, five-year captains will earn six figures.[9]

The other fractionals seem to be unfazed by the new NetJets' pilot agreement. A CitationShares spokesperson stated that its executives "do not make business decisions based upon what others in the industry are doing. We believe we have established a premium compensation package for all of our employees that includes competitive wages and excellent benefits, as well as work rules which we believe are the most attractive in the industry." However, industry scuttlebutt was that CitationShares is preparing a pay increase in response to the NetJets' integrative bargaining.[10]

Figure CS 5.1.3. NetJets International Gulfstream IV-SP N477QS. The larger NetJets aircraft all wear this paint scheme, and those based in the United States have the letters *QS* as part of their registrations. Source: Wikipedia, GNU Free Documentation License, Version 1.3.

The transition from the distributive to the integrative approach, however, is difficult at best in established enterprises and agencies with long histories of confrontation between labor and management and in unions whose members have come to expect their representatives to put up a good, loud, theatrical fight akin to the entertainment of professional wrestling in all negotiations. Indeed, where members perceive (whether rightly or wrongly) that their union is not putting up the best possible fight on their behalf, they may oust that union and replace it with one they deem more pugnacious. For example, when America West Airlines and US Airways merged, pilots of both carriers were represented by Air Line Pilots Association (ALPA) under separate contracts (see fig. 5.1). A major issue in the merger was the details of merging the seniority lists of the two carriers. *Seniority* is a major quality-of-life issue among airline pilots because it governs such matters as what aircraft, routes, and schedules they fly, where they are based, and when they may take vacations. When in 2008, approximately three years into the merger, ALPA's recommendation for the pilot-seniority merger methodology outraged a majority of the pilots; they formed a new union (the US Airline Pilots Association) and voted ALPA out.

Likewise, where past practices have fostered deep distrust between labor and management, the transition to integrative bargaining will prove especially difficult. For example: to avoid bankruptcy, in 2003 American Airlines was able to negotiate concessions (give-backs) in wages and benefits totaling $1.6 billion from many of its employee unions, including pilots, flight attendants, mechanics, and ground workers. After these deals were struck, enabling the company to avoid the bankruptcy route taken by such competitors as United, Northwest, and Delta, the employees learned that $42 to 160 million (the company has refused to reveal the exact amount) of these savings were then used to pay bonuses

Figure 5.1. Logo of the Air Line Pilots Association, International (ALPA), the largest airline-pilot union in the world, representing nearly fifty-three thousand pilots at thirty-eight U.S. and Canadian airlines. The AFL-CIO and the Canadian Labor Congress charter the association founded in 1931. ALPA provides three critical services to its pilot group members: airline safety and security, representation, and advocacy. The pilot group at each airline decides its own internal affairs, such as negotiating contracts, enforcing those contracts, and discussing issues of concern with its airlines. ALPA.org. Courtesy of Air Line Pilots Association, International.

to top company executives for their coup in obtaining these concessions. This outraged the employees, leaving them (and their unions) deeply distrustful of American's managers and assuring that present and future negotiations (at least so long as that management remains in office) will be anything but collaborative. On the eve of new contract negotiations in April 2008, the Association of Professional Flight Attendants (APFA), representing American's flight attendants, called on American's top five executives to either decline their bonuses or resign. APFA President Laura Glading stated, "Should they choose to accept the bonuses they will have lost their credibility and destroyed the good faith that underlies all successful negotiations. At that point, they will no longer be able to serve as effective leaders of American Airlines."[11]

Making the transition to integrative bargaining (or beginning the collective bargaining process in that fashion in a new enterprise) is facilitated by *attitudinal structuring*, the process of developing close professional relationships between members of the negotiating teams, building the mutual respect and trust necessary to a more cooperative, less-adversarial working relationship.

Procedures in the Airlines under the RLA
Contract Status

The RLA has a number of features that distinguish negotiations and dispute resolution in airlines from negotiations in enterprises governed by the NLRA. One of the most striking differences between the RLA and the NLRA is that contracts under the RLA are not terminable (have no fixed expiration dates) but continue in time without end unless replaced by another contract,[12] while contracts negotiated under the NLRA expire at their termination date unless they are renewed. Although contracts under the RLA are negotiated for a specified period of time and have amendable dates (open to renegotiation), they continue in existence after their amendable dates, with all provisions of the existing contract remaining in effect until settlement or modification. This statutory contractual aberration under the RLA is generally unknown to the public and is often misrepresented by the news media, who routinely announce that airline employees are working without a contract. This misinterpretation often occurs in reports on the airline industry, where it is common for negotiations to extend beyond the amendable date of contracts negotiated under the RLA. This media-spin interpretation could not be further from the truth, because under the RLA, no self-help action may be taken by either party during the negotiation process. The terminology used by the news media is proper when used in reference to contractual activities under the NLRA but not the RLA.

The statutory procedures for opening renegotiation under the RLA are given in Section 6 of the act:

In case of a dispute . . . it shall be the duty of the designated representative or representatives . . . , within ten days after the receipt of notice of desire on the part of either party to confer in respect of such dispute, to specify a time and place at which such conference shall be held: Provided, (1) that the place so specified shall be situated upon the line of the carrier involved or mutually agreed upon; and (2) that the time so specified shall allow the designated conferees reasonable opportunity to reach such place of conference, but shall not exceed twenty days from the receipt of such notice.

The party seeking renegotiation must serve notice, at least thirty days prior to the contract amendable date of the existing agreement, of their intent to negotiate changes in the contract. Thirty days is the required minimum notification period under the RLA. It is important to understand that under Section 6, notice of desire to renegotiate can be given at any time during the life of the contract whenever a party is interested in reopening negotiation on the rates of pay, work rules, or working conditions.

Figure 5.2 shows the required steps for contract negotiation under the RLA.

The Negotiation Time Frame

Once negotiations begin, the RLA places no time constraint on either party. The contract under negotiation continues in force until either the existing contract is amended or an impasse is reached, and mediation by the National Mediation Board (NMB) is requested by the parties. Section 6 provides that during the negotiation time period, "rates of pay, rules or working conditions shall not be altered by the carrier." The

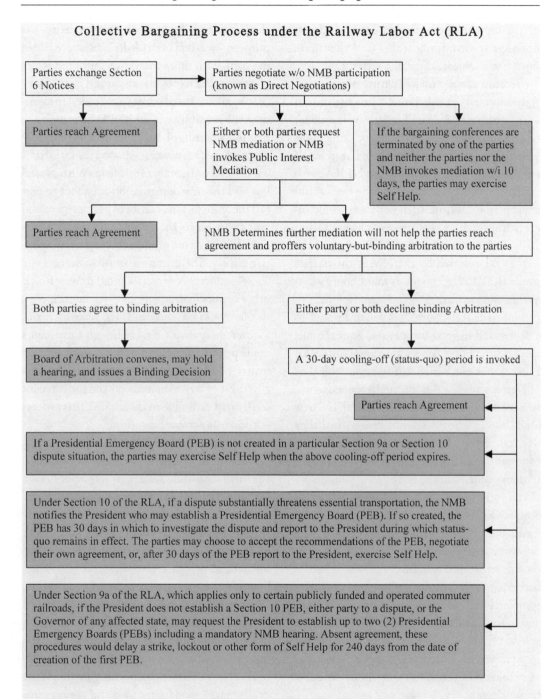

Collective Bargaining Process under the Railway Labor Act (RLA)

Parties exchange Section 6 Notices	Parties negotiate w/o NMB participation (known as Direct Negotiations)

Parties reach Agreement

Either or both parties request NMB mediation or NMB invokes Public Interest Mediation

If the bargaining conferences are terminated by one of the parties and neither the parties nor the NMB invokes mediation w/i 10 days, the parties may exercise Self Help.

Parties reach Agreement

NMB Determines further mediation will not help the parties reach agreement and proffers voluntary-but-binding arbitration to the parties

Both parties agree to binding arbitration

Either party or both decline binding Arbitration

Board of Arbitration convenes, may hold a hearing, and issues a Binding Decision

A 30-day cooling-off (status-quo) period is invoked

Parties reach Agreement

If a Presidential Emergency Board (PEB) is not created in a particular Section 9a or Section 10 dispute situation, the parties may exercise Self Help when the above cooling-off period expires.

Under Section 10 of the RLA, if a dispute substantially threatens essential transportation, the NMB notifies the President who may establish a Presidential Emergency Board (PEB). If so created, the PEB has 30 days in which to investigate the dispute and report to the President during which status-quo remains in effect. The parties may choose to accept the recommendations of the PEB, negotiate their own agreement, or, after 30 days of the PEB report to the President, exercise Self Help.

Under Section 9a of the RLA, which applies only to certain publicly funded and operated commuter railroads, if the President does not establish a Section 10 PEB, either party to a dispute, or the Governor of any affected state, may request the President to establish up to two (2) Presidential Emergency Boards (PEBs) including a mandatory NMB hearing. Absent agreement, these procedures would delay a strike, lockout or other form of Self Help for 240 days from the date of creation of the first PEB.

Note: this is a synopsis of the applicable procedures; refer to the RLA itself for exact guidance.

Figure 5.2. Railway Labor Act collective bargaining process. National Mediation Board.

carrier must maintain the status quo and may not alter working conditions, and the union must not engage in any strike activity.

Because of the timeless nature of the negotiating process at this point, both the unions and the carriers have a well-established tendency of bringing wish lists to the negotiating table, sometimes consisting of hundreds of items. If this situation occurred under the NLRA, with contract-termination dates coming due within short periods of time, such wish lists would increase the likelihood of strikes or lockouts. But strikes are unlawful under the RLA until the parties are released by the NMB; the parties under the RLA often seek as many concessions as they can get during forced negotiations.

Unfortunately, wish lists generally lead to a protracted negotiation period. For example, the Air Line Pilots Association and United Air Lines agreement, which had an amendable date of October 1988, was not actually amended until September 1990. Because of this delay, new aircraft (747-400s) were not flown until they were covered under the terms of the amended contract. Another example of prolonged negotiations occurred at the FedEx Corporation between 1993 and 1999. According to Frederick Smith, CEO of FedEx, two tentative labor agreements with FedEx pilots' unions failed before they were able to reach a satisfactory settlement on a five-year deal. On both occasions, FedEx had to reestablish the bargaining process with a completely new union-negotiations committee, and it took almost six years before they were able to get a new contract in place. During that six-year period, FedEx pilots' pay and benefits were locked in place, causing understandable frustration.

Another example of protracted negotiation under the RLA occurred between Ozark Air Lines and their mechanics, represented by the Aircraft Mechanics Fraternal Association (AMFA). In May 1978, the agreement between

the parties was due for renegotiation. After the proper notices had been filed, negotiations began in April, with more than three hundred issues placed on the table by the union and forty-five by management. Small issues were settled to eliminate the possibility of an impasse through the first four months of direct negotiation. Neither party wanted to invoke mediation for fear that it would lead ultimately to self-help. With capital low and the new deregulation act about to curtail the ability of the carrier to pass its increased labor cost on to the public, Ozark Air Lines feared that a strike would devastate its competitive ability. The union, wishing to receive the "best" industry contract, wanted to wait for all other airlines in negotiations to sign agreements, so they could use those airlines' wage increases as leverage against Ozark. Though agreements made prior to deregulation were negotiated on a carrier-by-carrier basis, the union based its negotiation of new demands on the most recent settlement favorable to the union. This process is known as *pattern bargaining*.

The parties agreed to nonbinding interest arbitration to eliminate the prospect of mediation and a possible release to self-help. Ozark executives believed that any reasonable arbitrator would agree with their position, especially since the union was seeking wage increases in excess of 25 percent, while the industry standard was 9 to 10 percent. According to O. V. Delle-Femine, the national director of the AMFA, "Since we didn't want a release from the Board at that time because of too many other airlines in negotiation and since every agreement I've been involved with in the industry has only gotten better, we felt we had nothing to lose. If the decision was good for us, we could always agree to it. If it was bad, we could just refuse it and wait for the other agreements to be settled. In any event, we get the time we want."[13]

Contrary to the company's belief, the arbitrator in this decision awarded the union the wage increases and a change in work rules that would have severely penalized the company. The decision was refused by the company, and the parties returned to the table. The union wasted no time before pressing for the awards of the decision, however, and an impasse occurred. An NMB mediator was assigned to the case, and negotiations continued for another eight months. Mediation in this particular case did not provide a solution, and the eventual outcome was a release by the NMB and a strike by the AMFA.[14]

The parties eventually came to terms, eighteen months after the amendable date of the original contract. Because the new contract provisions were retroactive to the original amendable date of the previous contract, which continued in force during the entire negotiation and mediation period, and because the new contract, like most airline contracts, included an amendable date three years after its effective date, the parties were again in negotiation within a year and a half.[15]

Mediation

Mediation is a fundamental procedure under the RLA. Unlike the NLRA, which offers optional mediation for the nonrail and nonairline private sector by the Federal Mediation and Conciliation Service (FMCS), the courts have established that under the RLA, mediation is mandatory under the guidance of the NMB. Therefore, before new contract terms can be imposed unilaterally and strikes or lockouts can be initiated, both parties are required to progress through several procedural steps regulated by the NMB. This procedure is often referred to by airline and railroad labor lawyers and negotiators as the Kabuki theater, after the ancient Japanese style of drama that consists of ritual in the extreme, exalting form over substance. If the parties are unable to reach an agreement in direct negotiations and conclude that a deadlock or impasse has been reached, either party is free to request mediation by the board.

In *Machinists v. National Mediation Board*, the court held the following:

The legislature provided procedures purposefully drawn out, the Board's process may draw them even to the point that the parties deem them almost interminable. What is voluntary about mediation, including mediation under this Act, is the decision to accept or reject the result available from the mediation process. What is involuntary about mediation under this Act is the obligation to engage in the mediation process even though a party is not unreasonable from his point of view in his conviction that further mediation is futile. The court's inquiry cannot go beyond an examination of the objective facts and determination thereon whether there is a reasonable possibility of conditions and circumstances (including attitudes and developments), available to the Board, consistent with the objective facts, sufficient to justify the Board's judgment that the possibility of settlement is strong enough to warrant continuation of the mediation process.[16]

Mediation is mandatory under the RLA, but no time frame is mandated. The duration of time the parties will be held in mediation is at the sole discretion of the NMB's assigned mediator, who alone decides when the dispute has reached an impasse. Once in mediation, just how long the process will take to complete negotiations and create a tentative contract agreement can be influenced by how many unresolved issues are brought by both parties. A 2003 study on labor negotiations in the airline industry indicated that the airline industry's labor negotiations took 1.3 years, on average, to conclude. Furthermore, only approximately 10 percent of labor contracts are concluded by one month after the amendable date. The study also found that half of airline labor negotiations go into federal mediation.[17]

NMB expertise in the mediation process ensures that bargaining disputes between parties rarely worsen into disruptions of passenger service and commercial transportation. Historically, approximately 97 percent of all NMB mediation cases have been resolved without interruptions to public service.[18] From 2001 to 2006, the NMB successfully helped the parties reach tentative contract agreements in over 550 airline mediation cases, with only five instances of self-help involving a strike, work stoppage, or lockouts.

The Mediation Process

When an application for mediation is received in Washington, D.C., the NBM dockets it and then reviews it to verify that the parties are actually at impasse. When the NMB believes that such is the case, a mediator is assigned to the dispute, generally assigned on an availability basis. The NMB employs approximately ten full-time mediators, based throughout the country. A mediator can be of invaluable service to the negotiation process if the parties are willing to use the mediator's services and experience. The mediator does not settle the bargaining impasse but assists the parties (union and management) in reaching an acceptable agreement. This assistance may involve one or more of the following functions:

- Arranging and scheduling joint or separate meetings between the bargaining parties or the mediator
- Presiding over and maintaining order at meetings (e.g., determining issues to be discussed, order of speaking, record keeping)
- Influencing the duration or location of bargaining meetings
- Facilitating the adoption of procedures for contract extensions or postponement of strike deadlines

- Continuing negotiations between the parties after a strike has occurred
- Keeping communication channels open
- Exploring the underlying interests behind each party's position (e.g., how realistic are the party's expectations regarding an acceptable settlement? Is the party aware of the potential costs involved with nonsettlement relative to settlement? How flexible is each party's position?)
- Helping the parties to define or redefine their respective bargaining priorities
- Offering creative suggestions on a specific issue or alternative settlement terms
- Offering creative suggestions to one or both parties on how each might "save face" or create opportunities for settlement that might allow their opponent to agree and still save face in the eyes of constituents, other employers, a union, or the general public[19]

If and when the mediator concludes that his or her efforts are failing to produce results (length of time is solely at the mediator's discretion) and an impasse exists where the parties are no longer talking, the mediator may inform the board of the situation by a private report based on his or her conclusions drawn from the meetings with the parties.

If and when the board concludes that further mediation would be pointless, it works to obtain the parties agreement to submit the dispute to binding arbitration by submitting to each party a formalized proffer of arbitration. A proffer of arbitration made by the NMB under Section 7 of the RLA is an offer to submit the deadlock or impasse to a neutral judge to decide the conditions of the final agreement.

Arbitration

If either of the parties rejects the proffer of arbitration, the board notifies both parties in writing that its mediation efforts have failed, and it releases the parties from the procedure after a thirty-day cooling-off period. The cooling-off period is designed to allow both parties the opportunity to reevaluate their positions. Nothing precludes the parties from reconvening negotiations during this period.

In September 2006, the president of the ALPA requested federal arbitration for the pilots at Atlantic Southeast Airlines. He reportedly cited as reasons for mediation the carrier's ongoing financial success, the currently imposed recess on contract talks, and the fact that pilots and management have been negotiating without results for more than four years. As per the terms of Section 6 of the Railway Labor Act, which governs airline-employee labor negotiations, the NMB can extend a proffer of arbitration, which is an offer to the parties to arbitrate any remaining issues. This arbitration is binding, requiring both parties to agree in advance to the results.

Supermediation

As a final effort to resolve an issue, the NMB will usually request the parties to attempt to reach an agreement through supermediation. This procedure, although not a statutory part of the RLA, is often employed to avert a strike. The offer of supermediation is rarely refused by either labor or management.

America West and the Association of Flight Attendants (AFA) met in March 1999 in a final negotiating session just two days before the expiration of a thirty-day cooling-off period. The supermediation session came at the request of the NMB to discuss a $6 million salary gap between the demands of the union and management for twenty-four hundred flight attendants. The AFA was looking for its first contract with America West, and negotiations had been dragging on since 1994. In October 1997, flight attendants overwhelmingly defeated a tentative pact; talks resumed in March 1998 but broke off in January 1999 with an impasse and thirty-

day cooling-off period declared in February 1999. The AFA had made clear it would not call an indefinite strike of its full membership but would order partial or limited walkouts. In return, America West threatened to shut down the airline if the AFA strikes. The day after the thirty-day cooling-off period, March 20, 1999, America West announced that the airline had reached a tentative agreement with AFA on a five-year collective bargaining agreement.

In supermediation, the parties generally meet with one of three members of the NMB, who are appointed by the president of the United States. This meeting is designed to bring visibility and political pressure on the parties to reevaluate their positions one final time. If a breakdown in this procedure becomes eminent, the board may again suggest arbitration before withdrawing from the case and effectively leaving the parties to their own devices. Withdrawal at this point does not mean that the NMB can never again reenter the dispute, even after a strike or lockout has occurred. Section 5 of the act states that the NMB may reenter at any time it deems necessary.

After the thirty-day cooling-off period, the parties are free to resort to self-help, which includes strikes, lockouts, a company's implementation of its final offer, or any other legal means, unless the president of the United States establishes an emergency board. The length of the negotiation period is critical to an airline because a number of unions are present on the property to represent the many craft and class determinations. Theoretically, with protracted negotiations, a contract dispute may be resolved only to become the subject of immediate renegotiation because agreements under the RLA are retroactive to the amendable dates. Because of protracted negotiations and the number of unions on the property, a company or its labor-relations department can be, and often is, in labor negotiations with a variety of unions on a nonstop basis.

Emergency Boards

The RLA, like the NLRA, has provisions for assisting in the settlement of disputes that "threaten substantially to interrupt interstate commerce to a degree such as to deprive a section of the country of essential transportation service."[20] In a 1981 amendment, the RLA permitted the creation of specialized presidential emergency boards for collective bargaining disputes at commuter railroads. This amendment permits the president of the United States to intervene and create an emergency board to investigate the dispute and report on it to the president within thirty days from the date of the board's establishment. During those thirty days and for thirty days following the report, neither the union nor management may make any change in the contract. Once the recommendations of the emergency board are submitted to the president and to the parties, the parties have the option, under the RLA, of rejecting the emergency board's recommendations, and the parties are free to resort to self-help to resolve the dispute. Thus, the emergency board provisions of the RLA provide the president with little more than a method of postponing a strike or lockout for at least sixty days, and after that, the act is silent on further government intervention.

The creation of emergency boards to handle disputes in the airline industry was common during the 1950s and 1960s. Since that time, government has made it clear that threatened or actual strikes will not result in the invocation of the RLA emergency-board procedures, particularly since other air carriers in the market can transport most goods and people. Since 1966, there have been only three RLA-based presidential emergency boards: American Airlines and the Allied Pilots Association in 1997, Northwest Airlines and the Aircraft Mechanics Fraternal Association in 2001, and United Air Lines and the International Association of Machinists and Aerospace Workers in 2002. Because of the economic impact of deregulation, a reevaluation of this procedure may be necessary in the future if a return to protracted negotiations occurs. Consolidation is leading to fewer airlines available to pick up the slack.

The president does have one other alternative available under executive privilege: introducing legislation, which if passed by both houses and signed, binds the union and management to the terms of the legislation. Such legislation would generally follow the emergency board's recommended solution.

In late 1993, President William Jefferson Clinton used his office to intercede in a strike by flight attendants against American Airlines (see fig. 5.3). The president telephoned both union and management and asked both to reconsider their positions, stressing quick settlement. Management and the union agreed to send the dispute to binding arbitration.

In February 1997, American Airlines pilots walked off the job after waiting months to be in a legal strike position as RLA rules describe. Within five minutes of their walkout, Clinton intervened with an emergency decree ordering them back to work. Facing the threat that Congress might impose an even-worse deal, the pilots ratified an unfavorable agreement that government-appointed negotiators supervised. But Clinton did not step in when pilots struck in 1998 against Northwest Airlines, saying in both cases that the national economy was not immediately endangered. Northwest lost an estimated $600 million.

President George W. Bush issued an order in March 2001 blocking a strike by Northwest Airlines mechanics, cleaners, and custodians. The workers, members of AMFA, were set to strike following the expiration of a federally mandated cooling-off period. By intervening in the Northwest dispute in advance of a strike that would otherwise be legally sanctioned under

Figure 5.3. President William Jefferson Clinton. On November 22, 1993, the president stated, "I am pleased to announce that I have spoken with both parties involved in the American Airlines strike, and that both have agreed in principle to end the strike and to return to the bargaining table immediately. They've also agreed to resolve all matters under dispute through binding arbitration. All American Airlines flight attendants will be reinstated." Painting by Simmie Knox. Displayed in the White House.

the terms of the RLA, Bush became only the second president since 1966 to order workers at a major airline to stay on the job. The president also made a blanket statement that he would block all airline strikes at the three other major carriers (Delta, United, and American) currently involved in contract disputes. In the late 1990s, these four airlines carried approximately 70 percent of total passengers traveling annually by air in the United States.

Even without presidential intervention, the RLA severely restricts the right of rail and airline workers to strike, imposing mediation procedures and other requirements that have the effect of delaying possible strike action for months on end. Once the mediation process is

exhausted, however, the workers are legally free to strike in pursuit of a new contract. The president can, however, intervene under the terms of the RLA to outlaw strike action by declaring an emergency. He then appoints a three-member emergency board to make recommendations for a settlement.

Strikes

The vast majority of self-help action in the airline industry has centered on the strike, which represents the unions' ultimate weapon to resolve the issues when the parties are unable to agree (see fig. 5.4). It has been far more prevalent in the air transport sector than the lockout, primarily because an airline requires a highly sophisticated workforce of specialists (pilots, cabin crew, aircraft mechanics, and reservationists), all of whom must have some degree of aviation-related knowledge to perform their appointed tasks. Because replacements may be hard to get, a lockout could result in economic

Figure 5.4. United Airlines (UAL) flight attendants and other union supporters picketing at UAL departure gates at San Francisco International Airport. "We are working at 1994-wage levels after suffering wage cuts, staff reductions, and rising health care costs," Chris Black, SFO Council 11 president, Association of Flight Attendants (AFA-CWA), told several hundred workers on January 8, 2010. Photo by Carl Finamore. Courtesy of Association of Flight Attendants–CWA.

suicide, a total loss of cash flow. Consequently, the strike by employees is the dominant form of self-help activity, which is not to say that only the unions are responsible for strikes. In many instances, the company has literally forced the unions to strike.

A U.S. General Accounting Office (GAO) report in 2003 indicates that since airline deregulation in 1978, labor contract negotiations have protracted but have been marked less by strikes and more by nonstrike work actions such as sickouts. Some U.S. airlines—Continental, Southwest, Alaska, and United—have been more successful than other air carriers at reaching agreement with their labor unions in much less time. For example, the average length of time to negotiate contracts at US Airways in the 1990s was thirty-four months. By contrast, the length of time to negotiate contracts at Southwest Airlines was thirteen months. Of the sixteen airline strikes of major U.S. carriers after deregulation, twelve took place from 1978 to 1989, and the other four took place since 1990. These strikes ranged from as short as twenty-four minutes to more than two years.[21]

The Mutual Aid Pact

Prior to deregulation in 1978, carriers held a distinct advantage in forcing a strike rather than become involved in a lockout. In 1958, the airlines formed the Mutual Aid Pact (MAP), designed as a form of insurance for airlines under strike. The provisions of the pact included recovery by struck carriers of a portion of the windfall-revenue profits experienced by other carrier members of the pact. *Windfall revenue* was the increased revenue of the carrier member of the pact that was attributable to the strike minus the added expense of carrying the additional traffic. In return, the airline under strike was required to make every reasonable effort to provide the public with information concerning air service offered by other carriers in the pact.

The airline unions had been urging Congress to outlaw this pact ever since a group of the nation's largest air carriers joined in establishing it in 1958. Labor believed the pact violated the intent of the RLA by undermining collective bargaining and prolonging strikes. However, Congress did not consent to outlaw MAP until it thoroughly destabilized relationships between management and labor. It was not until 1978, with the passage of the Airline Deregulation Act, all existing mutual aid agreements were declared void. During its twenty-year history, over half a billion dollars in mutual aid was paid under the agreements.[22]

Case Study 5.2 describes one airline's experience in benefitting from the MAP.

Case Study 5.2: Mutual Aid Pact— Northwest Orient Airlines

The collective bargaining structure that developed within the airline industry is decentralized and separated by craft (pilots, mechanics, and so forth) Before airline deregulation in 1978, unions and airline management engaged in carrier-by-carrier bargaining, whereby the last labor contract signed by one carrier generally served as the starting point for the next airline (known as *pattern bargaining*). During regulation, labor-management relations were generally good because the Civil Aeronautics Board's fare setting allowed airlines to pass their increased labor costs on to passengers.[23] Furthermore, an airline's bargaining position was improved by the Mutual Aid Pact (MAP), a strike-insurance plan created in 1958, through which an airline under strike was compensated by other airlines based on increases in traffic volume the others received during the strike.

Six of the nation's twelve domestic major airlines organized a MAP to soften the impact of strikes against individual airlines. These original six airline signatories and four other airlines that later joined the MAP accounted for approximately 90 percent of the annual domestic traffic carried in the United States.[24]

At its inception, the MAP provided only for "windfall payments" resulting from the strike. A strikebound airline received payments from other MAP airlines equal to their increase in revenues resulting from the strike minus their added operating expenses in servicing the new business. In March 1962, MAP members changed the agreement so that a struck airline member was guaranteed at least 25 percent of its normal operating expenses for operations shut down by the strike. In 1969, an amendment raised this percentage to a downward sliding scale from 50 to 35 percent depending on the length of the strike: 50 percent during the first fourteen days of the strike and then dropping by stages to 35 percent after a strike period of four weeks or longer.[25] Each airline member in the proportion that its air-transport operating revenues bore to the total revenue for all members contributed these additional supplemental payments over windfall.[26]

According to a 1972 *Time Magazine* article, no airline benefited more from the Mutual Aid Pact than Northwest Orient Airlines (the rebranded name of Northwest Airlines), which strikes had shut down airline operations about one day in every ten since 1960

Figure CS 5.2.1. Northwest Orient's B727-51C N498US at Boston's General Edward Lawrence Logan International Airport with the new Eastern Airlines terminal as a backdrop on a gray Christmas Eve, 1974. Courtesy of Tom Hildreth Photography.

(see fig. CS5.2.1). In 1970, Northwest Orient received $46 million in aid from other MAP airlines, resulting in a profit of $44 million for the year. In that same year, United Air Lines lost $40 million but paid nearly $17 million to Northwest Orient under MAP.

In October 1972, Northwest settled another strike and received so much in strike benefits that it actually showed a profit. The financial reports indicated that Northwest collected about $39 million from other MAP airlines during the strike and showed a profit of $1 million during the third quarter of 1972. During the same period of the preceding year, when there was no strike at Northwest, the airline earned about $14 million and a quarterly profit of $700,000.

During the 1972 strike, Northwest pilots finally agreed to a three-year contract calling for a 29 percent increase in salary and benefits. The wage adjustment increased junior officer's pay from $15,564 to $18,504, annually, and captains' salary rose to $66,816 per year. ALPA compromised its primary demand that the airline rehire all 1,619 pilots employed before the strike and accepted Northwest's offer to rehire 1,425 immediately and set up a recall schedule for the rest. During the fourteen years that MAP existed (1958 to 1972), Northwest Orient Airlines paid only $4,000,000 into the fund but collected $90,000,000 from it.[27]

The Mutual Aid Pact was eventually repealed with the promulgation of the Airline Deregulation Act of 1978, which enhanced airline labor's bargaining power in contract negotiations. But, over its lifetime, the MAP transferred more than $610 million dollars among its airline members.

Until deregulation, the outcome of strikes was relatively predictable. It was just a matter of time until the parties reached some sort of agreement on terms and conditions. The cost of any wage or benefit increases could be passed on to the consumer in the form of fare increases granted by the Civil Aeronautics Board. Since the industry was highly regulated, competition by fares was virtually nonexistent and was not a factor in a particular market or airline. Since deregulation, however, all aspects of the air transport labor environment have changed, but none more so than the negotiating approach taken by management in the event of a strike.

Deregulation

The RLA places many limitations on a company during a strike or lockout, but with a one-week notice, a company can hire either temporary or permanent replacement workers.[28] Until deregulation, the thought of replacement workers was foreign to airline management for many reasons. Hiring replacement workers would deny the carrier the opportunity to partake in revenue sharing under the Mutual Aid Pact. More significant, a sufficient pool of labor to accomplish replacement hiring was virtually nonexistent. Deregulation and the subsequent demise of many carriers and craft positions changed this equation by creating a previously unavailable pool of skilled labor.

In August 1983, the International Association of Machinists and Aerospace Workers struck Continental Airlines. Continental replaced many of the strikers with permanent employees. A new union contract was negotiated very quickly, and the event ushered in a new era and approach to airline labor relations. Another new element was added later, when Francisco "Frank" A. Lorenzo, chairman of the board for Texas Air Corporation and the owner of Continental Airlines, declared a chapter 11 bankruptcy. No case brings the postderegulation changes of labor relations in the air transport sector into sharper focus than the actions of Continental. The effects of this dispute were so profound that the government was forced to change the bankruptcy rules regarding the abrogation of existing contracts.

Procedures in the Non–Airline/Railroad Private Sector under the NLRA

Bargaining Topics

As previously noted, there are similarities as well as differences between negotiation procedures in the airlines under the RLA and in all other private-sector enterprises under the NLRA. The NLRA declares it the policy of the United States to encourage collective bargaining. Section 8(a)(5) makes it an unfair labor practice for an employer to refuse to bargain collectively with the employees' representatives. Similarly, Section 8(b)(3) requires the employees' representatives to bargain with the employer's representative. Section 10(c) provides the National Labor Relations Board the authority to enforce these provisions.

Additionally, the act requires the parties to meet and confer in "good faith," at "reasonable times," with respect to wages, hours, and other terms and conditions of employment. Defining *good faith* has been the subject of many articles, NLRB rulings, and court decisions. The definition generally rests on the interpretation of the action, or lack of action, by either party to the negotiating process. Accordingly, determining the validity of a charge of "lack of good-faith bargaining" rests on interpretation of the particular activity involved. According to *The Labor Board and the Collective Bargaining Process*, a Bureau of National Affairs publication, good faith is attained if both parties have a "sincere" desire to reach an agreement. Three examples of "bad faith" are:

- Failing to give negotiators sufficient authority to bind the employer
- Refusing to sign an agreement already reached
- Unilaterally granting wage increases or changing other benefits without consulting the union[29]

Under the NLRA, certain topics are, by law, the subject of mandatory negotiations, others have been declared illegal, and a third group is the subject of voluntary negotiations. Illegal topics of bargaining are those mentioned directly in the NLRA statutory language. These topics are expressly forbidden, and attempts to bring them to the negotiating table are subject to fines and penalties. Examples of prohibited topics are closed shops, featherbedding, and a union security clause in a right-to-work state. Voluntary topics of bargaining become a part of negotiations only through the joint agreement of both parties. Neither party can be compelled, by law, to negotiate over voluntary subjects. Adamant refusal to bargain about a voluntary subject or to include it in the final agreement is not illegal under the rules of the NLRA.[30] Nor do these subjects have to be bargained in good faith.[31] Mandatory topics of bargaining are those over which the parties must bargain if either party at the table introduces the topics. The courts and the NLRB have placed approximately seventy items into this category. Table 5.1 lists examples of the subjects the NLRB assigned to each of the three categories.

The Contract-Negotiation Process

The Labor Management Relations Act requires that for an existing contract to be legally opened for renegotiation under the NLRA, the party requesting renegotiation must serve written notice to the opposing party sixty days prior to the termination date of the existing contract. The sixty-day notice is a minimum requirement. If a timely notice has not been served by the party seeking to renegotiate, the other party has no obligation, under the NLRA, to bargain, modify, amend, or extend the existing contract. The contract can be allowed to lapse. The company can then implement any changes it wishes with regard to wages, benefits, or work conditions, and any workers who continue to work must accept these new, unilaterally introduced terms and conditions.

The NLRA places certain limitations on employers and unions during the negotiating process. Neither party has the option to strike or lockout at will. No party to a collective bargaining agreement can terminate or modify a contract, unless the party desiring the termination or modification complies with the following procedure:

- The party must notify the other party to the contract in writing about the proposed termination or modification sixty days before the date on which the contract is scheduled to expire. If the contract is not scheduled to expire on any particular date, the notice in writing must be served sixty days before the time when it is proposed that the termination or modification take effect.

- The party must offer to meet and confer with the other party for the purpose of negotiating a new contract or a contract containing the proposed changes.

- The party must, within thirty days after the notice to the other party, notify the FMCS of the existence of a dispute if no agreement has been reached by that time. Said party must also notify at the same time any state or territory where the dispute occurred.

- The party must continue in full force and effect, without resorting to strike or lockout, all the terms and conditions of existing contracts until sixty days after the notice to the other party was given or until the date the contract is scheduled to expire, whichever is later.[32]

Self-Help

Under the NLRA, the ability to strike or lockout is contingent on a request for mediation or arbitration and also faces the possibility of presidential intervention. Should the president of the United States determine that a strike and or lockout will threaten "an entire industry

Table 5.1.

Categories of bargaining subjects assigned by the National Labor Relations Board

Mandatory subjects	Permissive subjects
Arbitration	Ground-rule negotiations
Bargaining unit work	Internal union matters such as how and when a
Bereavement leave	tentative agreement is ratified
Bonuses	The price of meals furnished or sold to employees
Clothing and tool allowances	by an independent caterer
Cost of living adjustments	Granting the employer the right to use the union
Dental and vision plans	label
Discharge and discipline	Demanding that a union settle all grievances
Discounts on company products	that are arbitrated that arose under the previ-
Dues check-off clauses	ous contract
Equity-pay adjustments	Settlement of unfair labor practice charges
Grievance procedures	Pension benefits for retired members
Holiday pay	
Hours of work	
Incentive pay	*Illegal subjects*
Jury-duty pay	Closed-shop provisions (requires an employee to
Layoffs and recalls	be a union member in order to be hired for a
Legal-services plans	job)
Life insurance	Provisions that discriminate against employees
Management's rights clauses	because of race, creed, sex, and the like
Medical insurance	Hot-cargo clauses (language that prohibits
Overtime premiums	an employer from dealing with any other
Pay for time spent on union business	employer, typically those involved in a labor
Pay for training	dispute)
Pension for current employees	
Premium pay for Sundays and holidays	
Profit-sharing	
Promotions	
Red-circle pay	
Rest and lunch periods	
Salaries	
Shop or plant rules	
Sickness and accident plans	
Testing of employees	
Transfers	
Tuition reimbursement	
Union shop or other union-security clauses	
Vacation pay	
Wages	
Work schedules	
Workloads	

or substantial part thereof engaged in trade, commerce, transportation, or communication among the several states or with foreign nations, or engaged in the production of goods for commerce" or that it "will, if permitted to occur or continue, imperil the national health or safety,"[33] he or she may appoint a review board to study the strike or lockout. If it is determined that the national health is indeed affected, the president, through the U.S. Attorney General, may seek an injunction ordering a suspension of the strike or lockout.[34]

The strike or lockout is delayed for a period of eighty days if the injunction is granted, during which time the FMCS works with the two parties to resolve the dispute. Should the reconciliation effort fail and the injunctive cooling-off period expire, new hearings may be held by the NLRB, at which time the final company offer to the union is presented. The members of the union are allowed to vote on this final management proposal. If they vote for the proposal, the dispute is over, and work continues under the new terms and conditions. If the employees vote against the proposal, they may then be called out on strike by the union. The strike may continue indefinitely until the disagreement is resolved or until other arrangements are made by the parties. Figure 5.5 shows the steps in the NLRA's collective bargaining process.

This type of cooling-off period and injunctive suspension of self-help options is not used in all situations; it is statutorily limited, under the NLRA, to national-emergency disputes. Most strikes or lockouts do not receive or deserve this level of attention. Consequently, at the termination of a contractual agreement, most parties are able to utilize self-help immediately.

Mediation

Self-help may also be delayed by a request for mediation or arbitration. Mediation is generally the first step. Mediation may begin prior to a contract's expiration. The NLRA does not list a specified time limit for the mediation process but rather follows the doctrine of "reasonable time frame." The FMCS may proffer its services either on its own motion or on the request of one or more parties to the dispute.[35]

Although the FMCS performs a mediation role similar to that of the NMB under the RLA, there are significant differences in their roles. Unlike mediation by the NMB, mediation by the FMCS is a separate function of that service, and mediators do not have any power or authority to make recommendations or determinations on when an impasse between the parties occurs or on whether to force the parties to continue negotiations. Moreover, the time frame for mediation is broadly defined under the NLRA, but no such time frame exists under the RLA, where a mediator could literally hold the parties in mediation, against their will, for as long as he or she desires.

Under the NLRA, the mediator acts only as a guide to assist the parties. If, within a "reasonable time frame," mediation fails, other courses of action may be suggested, such as arbitration. Mediation is not binding in any way, and a rejection of mediation procedure by either party is not deemed a violation of the NLRA or an unfair labor practice.[36]

Arbitration

Arbitration is a method of dispute resolution used as an alternative to litigation. It is commonly used in collective bargaining agreements between management and labor as the way to resolve disputes. There are major differences between mediation and arbitration. Arbitration is defined as "a process by which an answer is provided for issues in a dispute."[37] The focus in mediation is to bring the parties to an agreement. Arbitration determines exactly what the actual agreement will be. Even though arbitration is a quasi-judicial procedure, it can be accepted

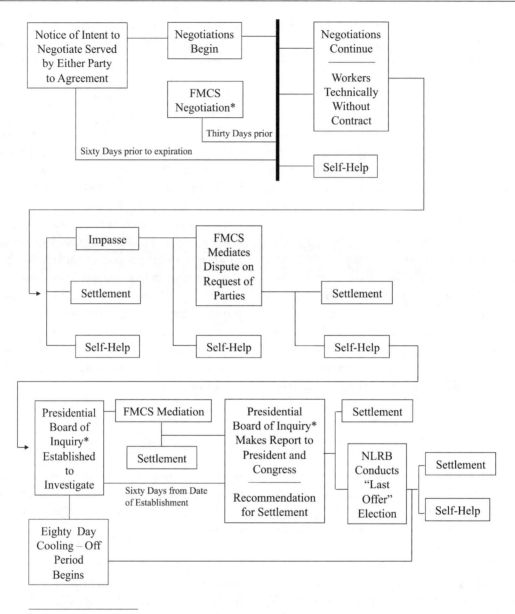

* May occur if dispute threatens interstate commerce, a large portion of society, or national security.

Figure 5.5. National Labor Relations Act collective bargaining process.

or rejected under the NLRA.[38] Acceptance requires both parties' approval.

Under the NLRA, two types of arbitration may be entered into by the parties. Final arbitration settles the dispute on the basis of the arbitrator's decision. Advisory or interest arbitration provides a decision that the parties will use as a guideline in the negotiation process.

Arbitration is conducted by a neutral party, and the process has no specified time limits. Arbitration is usually used as a last resort to settle disputes. Final or binding arbitration will end the dispute. Advisory or interest arbitration may not settle the dispute, and if it does not, a strike or lockout may commence or continue.

Actions during a Strike or Lockout

The intent of either a strike or a lockout is to apply economic pressure on the opposing party and to bring that party to agreement at the negotiating table. Both activities are legal under the NLRA, after the administrative procedures have been exhausted.

Hiring Replacement Workers under Employer Lockout

An employer may lockout employees only after the bargaining agreement has terminated. After doing so, if the company desires to continue operations, it can continue on a reduced scale with temporary employees not covered by the terminated contract.[39] When the dispute is resolved, the temporary replacement workers, being temporary, are expected to end their employment relationship with the company.

Permanently replacing employees who have been locked out questions the very fiber of the NLRA, particularly in the area of unfair practices. In a 1977 decision rendered in a lockout at Johns-Manville Products Corporation, the NLRB held that a company's lockout becomes illegal when during the lockout, the employer unilaterally decides to hire permanent replacements without first consulting the union. This unilateral act violates Section 8(a)(3) of the NLRA. Furthermore, permanently replacing all employees in a bargaining unit who are locked out is a violation of Section 8(a)(5) because it completely destroys the bargaining unit and constitutes an unlawful withdrawal of recognition of a duly-designated union. The board also noted and cited the absence of evidence that the union had engaged in an in-plant strike or other improper statutory conduct that might justify the employer's hiring of permanent replacements.[40]

Hiring Replacement Workers under Union Strike

The hiring of replacement workers (called *scabs*) during a strike is treated differently. The hiring of replacement workers on either a temporary or a permanent basis by the employer is legal when the employees are engaged in a strike solely designed to bring economic pressure on the employer to resume negotiations with the striking union. The only condition is that the employer did not cause the strike by engaging in an unfair labor practice, in which case the hiring of replacements is prohibited.

Because permanent replacements are permitted when a union strikes for economic purposes, the strikers may never return to work. The major strikes that unions have lost in the United States in recent years share the characteristic that the employer has been able to obtain replacements and operate indefinitely despite the strike. Examples of this circumstance include the Florida East Coast Railway strike in 1963 against an intrastate rail carrier covered under the NLRA, the *Washington Post* Pressmen strike in 1975, the Caterpillar strike of 1991–92, and the Giant Cement Company strike in 2005.

Procedures in the Public Sector under Other Federal and State Laws

Federal-Employee Collective Bargaining

Federal, state, and local government workers are excluded from coverage under the NLRA. Most federal employees, however, have collective bargaining rights under the Civil Service Reform Act of 1978 and the Federal Service Labor Management Relations statute. Not covered are employees of the Federal Bureau of Investigation (FBI), Central Intelligence Agency (CIA), National Security Agency (NSA), Transportation Security Agency (TSA), and others, whose numbers total about one-third of the federal civilian workforce. It is illegal for military personnel to unionize.

Like private-sector employees covered by the NLRA or RLA, federal employees covered by these statutes have the right to form unions and bargain collectively. A union selected by a majority of the workers in that craft or class (for example, the National Air Traffic Controllers Association for FAA air traffic controllers) is recognized as the exclusive bargaining agent of all of those employees agency-wide. Even a union not representing a majority of the workers has the right to be consulted by management before making changes to working conditions, so long as the union has the support of at least 10 percent of those workers.

The scope of bargaining for federal employees is far narrower than that afforded employees in the private sector under the NRLA or RLA. Issues on which federal employees are precluded from bargaining include the agency's mission, budget, organization, number of employees, and internal security practices, along with the hiring, direction, discipline, assignment of employees, and their wages and benefits and the contracting out of agency work. Thus, the scope of bargaining for covered federal employees is generally confined to agency policies and procedures such as for air traffic controllers, facility staffing, and workload (including the numbers, types, and grades of employees or positions assigned along with the technology, methods, and means of performing the work).

Federal employees are prohibited from striking. In the event collective bargaining reaches an impasse, either party may request the FMCS mediate the matter. If mediation fails, either party may request the FMCS refer the issue(s) to its Federal Services Impasse Panel for consideration. The panel considers the impasse and may conduct fact-finding and recommend a resolution. If the resolution is not accepted by both parties, the panel may hold hearings and take final action to resolve the impasse, and such action binds the parties unless they reach agreement to the contrary.

The Office of Personnel Management (OPM) establishes the rules regulating federal civilian employment practices and procedures. The Federal Labor Relations Authority (FLRA) is responsible to oversee representation elections and collective bargaining of federal employees, while the Merit System Protection Board (MSPB) hears and decides the appeals from agency decisions on employee grievances, such as those that were filed by many of the air traffic controllers who were terminated for participation in the PATCO strike.

State and Local Government Employee Collective Bargaining

The collective bargaining rights of public employees (and others not covered by the NLRA) at the state and local level vary widely from state to state. Twenty-six states and the District of Columbia have enacted statutes (often referred to as "little Wagner Acts") providing collective bargaining rights to almost all public employees. These states include Alaska, California, Connecticut, Delaware, Florida, Hawaii, Illinois, Iowa, Maine, Massachusetts, Michigan, Minnesota, Montana, Nebraska, New Hampshire, New Jersey, New York, Ohio, Oregon, Pennsylvania, Rhode Island, South Dakota, Vermont, Washington, and Wisconsin.[41]

Twelve states have provided collective bargaining rights to specific groups of employees, such as teachers or firefighters, or for state but not local government employees through legislation or gubernatorial executive orders. These states include Georgia, Indiana, Idaho, Kansas, Kentucky, Maryland, Missouri, Nevada, North Dakota, Oklahoma, Tennessee, and Wyoming. Local ordinances may provide collective bargaining rights to local government employees, such as public-airport workers, where states laws are silent.[42]

Eleven states (Alabama, Arizona, Arkansas, Colorado, Louisiana, Mississippi, New Mexico, North Carolina, South Carolina, Virginia, and West Virginia) have no laws providing collective bargaining rights to state and local government employees. The remaining state, Texas, specifically prohibits most groups of public employees from bargaining collectively (with the exception that local firefighters and police may bargain with approval of a majority of the voters in that jurisdiction).[43]

However, as this book goes to press in 2011 during the Great Recession, numerous cash-strapped states are considering proposed legislation to strip state employees of their collective bargaining rights and reduce their pay and benefits.[44]

The American Federation of State, County, and Municipal Employees (AFSCME) reports that eleven states allow some public employees the right to strike. Most states that allow collective bargaining by public employees prohibit most covered workers from striking, providing instead for resolution of major disputes through binding arbitration.

Summary

The issues surrounding amendable contracts under the RLA versus contract termination under the NLRA and the difficult and pervasive question of permanent replacement-worker status represent the most troublesome points of contention between management and labor today. That contracts under the RLA remain in force even after their amendable dates essentially means that management, at best, can only achieve maintenance of the status quo. Under the RLA, the unions have a tremendous bargaining advantage over management, both because highly specialized skill levels are inherent in the air transport industry and because pro-union language is extant in the RLA. Under the RLA, the best-case scenario for management,

maintenance of the status quo, is the worst-case scenario for unions. Unless the company files for bankruptcy protection, the worst a union can do under an RLA-governed dispute is achieve what it already has. There is little downside statutory risk to the union under the RLA. This statutory concept of a "contract in perpetuity" represents management's "crown of thorns" under the RLA and significantly impacts management's self-help options.

Equally problematic for management under the RLA is the lack of statutory privilege to hire permanent replacement craft workers under terms different from the existing contract. The RLA expressly states, and the NMB and the courts have expressly held, that any replacement craft workers are "automatically represented by the very union that is on strike" and "must be compensated under the terms of the contract that is being negotiated."

This latter issue presents a very different set of concerns when viewed through the legislative lens of the NLRA. Employers under the NLRA can and do hire permanent replacement workers, and they do so under terms decidedly different from the striking union's terminated contract. Under the NLRA, replacement workers are the "crown of thorns" for unions. So important is this issue to labor that heavy lobbying efforts take place in Washington, D.C., to prevent management from hiring permanent replacements during strikes under the NLRA. (Airline and railroad management also lobby in the nation's capital to be allowed to utilize permanent replacements under the RLA.)

Round 1 of this issue took place in mid-1993, when Congress considered legislation that would bar employers from permanently replacing employees who walked off the job for economic reasons. It was argued by both the secretary of labor and the American Federation of Labor and Congress of Industrial Organizations (AFL-CIO) that the Workforce Fairness Act, as the issue became titled, would level the playing field between management and labor. According to an article in *Aviation Daily*, the bill had strong support in the House of Representatives, with at least 162 cosponsors.[45] Thus, in June 1993, the House of Representatives passed the Cesar Chavez Workplace Fairness Act, renamed after the hero of the California agriculture union movement. However, the Senate version of the same bill (S. 55), known simply as the Workplace Fairness Act, failed to muster the votes and died on the Senate floor after a Senate filibuster held it up.[46] Twice before, in 1992, the threat of a Senate filibuster blocked action on a striker-replacement ban.

The issue is unquestionably foggy and needs some finality. The NLRA is unclear on procedural application, the RLA has questionable applicability, and the Supreme Court has never really addressed the question except indirectly. In 1938, the court's decision in *NLRB v. Mackay Radio & Telegraph Co.* has some relevance.[47] In that two-sided ruling, the court decided that it is illegal to fire strikers but that it is not illegal to fail to rehire them. Such a nonsensical position leaves both management and unions in a quandary as to interpretation.

Airline and labor officials said that the fate of the striker-replacement bill would set the stage for labor-management relations in the airline industry well into the future. Had it eventually passed both houses of Congress and received presidential approval, it would have made it an unfair labor practice for airlines to give hiring preference to employees who worked or were willing to work during a legitimate walkout (e.g., TWA flight attendants in 1986). Airline officials feared that such a provision would threaten an already-weakened industry. Some labor experts argued that the issue is moot because none of today's megacarriers is in a position to withstand a strike.[48]

Faced with a narrow scope of bargaining and deprived of the right to withhold their services (that is, to strike), public employees have far less bargaining power than employees in the public sector. Public-sector employees have historically enjoyed better benefits and job security than their counterparts in private industry, although wages have typically been somewhat lower. Economic pressures are now driving government at all levels to reduce costs. This has led some state legislatures to consider eliminating state employees' collective bargaining rights.[49] Governments at all levels—federal, state, and local—are facing major budget shortfalls and considering major reductions in public employee wages and benefits and in the size of government agencies, programs, and workforces. These trends may eliminate the job security and benefits that once attracted job seekers to public employment, putting public agencies at a disadvantage in competing with the private sector to attract the most-talented employees once the private sector recovers from the Great Recession. Indeed, there is already some evidence of this happening at the FAA.

6. Unfair Labor Practices

Unfair labor practices apply to the entire collective bargaining process from initial election of a bargaining representative through negotiation of the bargaining agreement to application and interpretation of the agreement in practice. This chapter deals primarily with the involvement of such practices in the selection of a representative and in the organizational process.

The term *unfair labor practice* has statutory meaning only under the NLRA and the Civil Service Reform Act of 1978. The Wagner and Taft-Hartley amendments to the NLRA identified certain practices that were deemed unfair and prohibited their use. These two acts also created the National Labor Relations Board (NLRB) to adjudicate unfair labor practice complaints. Similar provisions were included in the Civil Service Reform Act of 1978 that also created the Federal Labor Relations Authority (FLRA) to adjudicate unfair labor practice complaints in federal employment. The RLA contains no "unfair labor practice" provisions. Despite the absence of unfair labor practice provisions in the RLA, courts confronted with disputes requiring interpretation under the RLA often cite the NLRB's rulings on unfair practices as precedent.

The RLA does contain strict provisions of conduct regarding organizational representation election and collective bargaining activities. The National Mediation Board (NMB) possesses significant investigative and enforcement authority in these areas. Because of the judicial weight afforded NLRB rulings when interpreting RLA activities, it is essential that both air transport management and union personnel be cognizant of the unfair labor practices contained in the NLRA, which provides a solid foundation for practical guidance under the RLA.

Unfair Labor Practices under the NLRA

With the passage of the Wagner Act in 1935, Congress attempted not only to recognize unions officially but to also inject a degree of control into the organization process by making certain actions illegal (see fig. 6.1). These illegal actions were initially, and almost exclusively, aimed at management and were the "thou shalt nots" that management was forced to abide by when dealing with unions, employees, and the collective bargaining process.

To many critics, the language of the Wagner Act provided a one-sided approach to labor relations law. As a matter of public policy, Congress mandated, "It is hereby declared to be the policy of the United States to eliminate the causes of certain substantial obstructions to the free flow of commerce and to mitigate and eliminate these obstructions when they have occurred by encouraging the practice and procedure of collective bargaining and by protecting the exercise by workers of full freedom of association . . . for the purpose of negotiating the terms and conditions of their employment or other mutual aid or

Figure 6.1. Frances Perkins. When President Franklin D. Roosevelt tapped Perkins as labor secretary in 1933, she drew on the New York state experience as the model for new federal programs. She put all of her energy into securing benefits for American workers. Her vision found concrete expression in such landmark reforms as the Wagner Act (or National Labor Relations Act), which gave workers the right to organize unions and bargain collectively. Franklin D. Roosevelt Library.

protection."[1] Under the Wagner Act, management was required to recognize unions, bargain collectively, and not interfere with an employee's freedom to join a union.

The Taft-Hartley Act corrected the Wagner Act's one-sided approach by holding the unions to the same standards of conduct originally assigned to management in the Wagner Act. These union standards of conduct became incorporated into the NLRA through the Taft-Hartley Amendment of 1947, which "both amended and added to the NLRA of 1935. Its purpose was to bring organized labor to responsibility by law in the same way that employers had been treated in 1935, specifically singling out certain activities of unions for regulation and establishing additional

procedures for the resolution of labor-management conflict."[2]

Case study 6.1 examines the causes and effects of the Taft-Hartley Act.

Case Study 6.1: The Taft-Hartley Labor Act—A Political Nightmare for the Unions

According to labor journalist Peter Gilmore, Republicans and spineless Democrats dominated the Congress during the late 1940s. In the White House sat a Democratic president, Harry S. Truman, who apparently identified more with business than with labor. The political mood was aggressively antilabor. Conservative legislators called for new or amended laws to reign in "big labor." More than 250 antilabor bills were pending in both houses of Congress in 1947.

This congressional antilabor campaign focused on two primary bills: a House bill introduced by Republican Representative Fred Hartley and a Senate bill, similar to the House bill, introduced by Republican Senator Robert A. Taft (see fig. CS6.1.1). Both bills were written by corporate lobbyists representing the interests of General Electric, Allis-Chalmers, Inland

Figure CS 6.1.1. Portrait of Senator Robert A. Taft, 1953. Taft served as U.S. senator from Ohio from 1939 until 1953, when he died in office. Painting by Rudolf Anton Bernatschke, 1953.

Steel, J. I. Case, and Chrysler.[3] As a response to rising union radicalism, the bills were seen as a response by business to the post–World War II labor upsurge of 1946. During the twelve months after World War II ended, more than five million American workers were involved in strikes, which lasted on average four times longer than those occurring during the war.[4]

On April 17, 1947, the House passed the Hartley bill. And on May 13, 1947, the Senate adopted the Taft bill. President Truman, under heavy constituent pressure, vetoed the bill at the last minute but did little to influence the override vote that followed in both the House and Senate.

As Gilmore states, the Taft-Hartley Act was seen as a means of demobilizing the labor movement by imposing limits on labor's ability to strike and by removing radical leadership from union activities. Within a ten-year span (1935 to 1945), the number of union members in the United States had grown from less than 4 million to over 15 million. After World War II ended in 1945, the labor unions began to deploy their power with a series of strikes aimed at increasing living standards for their members. Steel, auto, electrical, oil, and packinghouse workers, among others, went on strike simultaneously, bringing the United States to the verge of a general industry strike. Their motive: to redistribute corporations' wartime profits. So, it is of little surprise that U.S. corporations sought action against the labor unions.[5]

The Taft-Hartley Act amended much of the National Labor Relations Act of 1935 and nullified parts of the Norris–La Guardia Act of 1932. The act established better control of labor disputes by enlarging the National Labor Relations Board and providing that the union or the employer must serve notice on the other party and on a government mediation service before terminating a collective bargaining agreement.

The unions called the Taft-Hartley Act "a workers' nightmare" because it restored

- antistrike injunctions
- limited labor's ability to mass picket
- prohibited secondary boycotts
- restricted political contributions by unions
- authorized employer interference in organizing
- denied strikers the right to vote in union elections
- allowed management to terminate workers for certain types of union activity
- outlawed the closed shop
- authorized states to ban the union shop
- interfered in internal union politics by requiring officers to sign affidavits that they were not communists[6]

Larger unions pledged not to cooperate with the new Taft-Hartley labor board. But within a few years, unions were forced to comply with the act. As a result, union membership in the early 1950s steadily declined, aided heavily by the employer tools supplied by Taft-Hartley.

An effort to get part of the Taft-Hartley Act repealed during the Jimmy Carter administration (1977–81) failed miserably—despite a Democratic majority in both houses. The return of a Democratic president and Democrat-controlled Congress (1992–94) did not raise real hope of repealing Taft-Hartley.[7]

In a 2002 article, Ralph Nader wrote that the passage of the Taft-Hartley Act was one of the great blows to American democracy (see CS6.1.2). He added that the act fundamentally infringed on workers' human rights. And legally, it impeded employees' right to join together in labor unions, undermined the power of unions to effectively represent workers' interests, and authorized anti-union activities by employers[8]

According to Nader, "Taft-Hartley entrenched significant executive tyranny in the workplace, with ramifications that are more severe today than ever. And as a result, union membership is at historic sixty-year lows, with only 10 percent of the private economy's workforce unionized." Nader wrote that repealing Taft-Hartley would be one of the most important steps in restoring workers' right to organize into unions and in revitalizing American democracy.[9]

Figure CS 6.1.2. Ralph Nader. An American attorney, author, lecturer, and political activist, Nader was an independent candidate for president of the United States in 2004 and 2008 and a Green Party candidate in 1996 and 2000. Source: Wikimedia Commons; photo by Don LaVange; Creative Commons Attribution Share-Alike 2.0 license.

Although most attempts to repeal the Taft-Hartley Labor Act have been unsuccessful, the 1959 Landrum-Griffin Act did amend some features of the act.

Activities Prohibited under the NLRA

Section 8(a) of the NLRA proscribes certain activities by management. Section 8(b) of the NLRA proscribes certain activities by unions and employees. Table 6.1 lists the activities in which management and the unions are prohibited to engage.

Most issues of unfair labor practice are raised during union-organization campaigns, although others can occur outside an organizational drive. The NLRA establishes certain ground rules of conduct and makes certain actions by employers unfair. The law prohibits employers from restraining, interfering with, or coercing employees in their choice of a bargaining representative.

The employer is not legally precluded from informing, persuading, or urging employees to join or not join a union. An employer has the right of free speech under the First Amendment, and this right has been codified in Section 8(e) of the NLRA. Further, the NLRA does not prohibit all employer activities that may obstruct organizing efforts by employees. The act recognizes that an employer has certain rights, including freedom of speech on matters affecting the operation of the business.

Accordingly, section 8(e) provides that the mere expression of views, arguments, or opinion does "not constitute an unfair labor practice . . . if such expression contains no threat of reprisal, or force, or promise of benefit." Some of these liberties, which would clearly be questionable under the RLA, rest on the methods the employer uses to make his or her position known to the employees. In this context, whether a practice is considered unlawful and/or illegal depends on definition of interference, threats, and behavior designed to eliminate an employee's choice.

Interference

Interference in union elections can take many forms. For example, questioning employees about union activities or union membership in a manner that restrains or coerces is considered interference. Prior to 1967, the NLRB held that questioning employees about their union activities, though not unlawful per se, was subject to very close scrutiny.[10] Under current policy, questioning is still considered unlawful unless its purpose is to determine the truth of a union's claim or to determine if the majority of the employees are in favor of the union. This type of questioning, however, will also be held unlawful unless several other elements are present:

- The employees are advised that the questioning is solely for polling purposes.

Table 6.1.

Unfair labor practices proscribed by the NLRA for employers and labor organizations

Charges against employer

8(a)1—Interfering with, restraining, or coercing employees in the exercise of their rights to join or assist labor organizations or not to join or assist

8(a)2—Dominating or interfering with the formation or administration of any labor organization or contributing financial or other support to it

8(a)3—Discriminating in regard to hire or tenure of employment or any term or condition of employment to encourage or discourage membership in any labor organization

8(a)4—Discharging or otherwise discriminating against an employee because he or she has filed charges or given testimony under this act

8(a)5—Refusing to bargain collectively with the representatives of his employees

Charges against labor organization

8(b)1—Restraining or coercing employees in the exercise of their choice of a union representative

8(b)2—Causing an employer to discriminate against an employee with respect to whom membership in such organization has been denied or terminated

8(b)3—Refusing to bargain collectively with an employer

8(b)4—Encouraging or engaging in certain types of strikes or boycotts

8(b)5—Requiring employees to pay excessive or discriminatory initiation fees or dues to become a member of a labor organization

8(b)6—Requiring employees to pay for services not performed (featherbedding)

8(b)7—Requiring an employer to bargain with a labor organization as the representative of his employees, or requiring employees to accept such labor organization as their collective bargaining representative

- The employees are advised that there will be no reprisal.
- The question is asked in a secret ballot.
- A coercive atmosphere has not otherwise been created.[11]

Threatening to close or move a plant if a union should be certified has been determined an unfair labor practice. An employer has the absolute right to close his or her entire business for any reason. This right includes the employer's right to close because he or she is totally against unionism. But this right does not extend to closing only a part of the business in an effort to thwart unionization; it is an unfair labor practice to close a plant whose employees are seeking representation or are already unionized and transfer that work to another, nonunion facility.[12]

Granting wage increases or unilateral increases of wages or benefits during a union organizing campaign, whether planned prior to the beginning of the campaign or not, is considered a prima facie case of unlawful interference and an unfair labor practice. Conversely, charges of unfair labor practice could be sought if the postponement of a planned wage or benefit increase were construed as an attempt to chill a unionist movement.[13] In an airline case heard under the auspices of the NLRB in which the carrier operated intrastate and was covered under the NLRA, not the RLA, it was ruled that the employer may not withhold a general wage increase customary at a specified time each year because the employees had elected to seek union representation.[14] But an employer may be permitted under section 8(c) to announce during a campaign, to influence the election, benefits that would take effect later, as long as the benefits were planned or in motion prior to the beginning of the campaign.[15]

Sending a management or supervisory employee to a union meeting, asking employees particulars about union organizing meetings, and other types of surveillance have been found unlawful interference of union activities.[16] So has the use of spies or informers in connection with any phase of the employees' right to self-organization.[17] The pre-1966 attitude of the NLRB was that if an election was lost by a union due to allegations of surveillance, the election could be set aside.[18] A subsequent decision indicates that proof must exist that the employer both authorized and conducted the surveillance.[19]

Threatening employees with loss of jobs or benefits should they join a union or vote for a union is a direct violation of Section 8(a).[20] An employer may not hire or fire an employee on the basis of the employee's membership or lack of membership in a union or to encourage or discourage union membership.[21] A violation of section 8(a)(3) has been found in one case in which an employer discharged a nonunion employee solely because the employee attended a union organizational meeting and in another in which the employer discharged an employee who refused to join a company-dominated union.[22] An exception to this provision does exist where agreements that permit an employer (at the request of the union) to discharge an employee for nonpayment of dues or initiation fees are allowed.[23]

Establishing rules that forbid union solicitation by employees during nonworking time, even if such rules are limited to working areas, may also be considered an unfair labor practice, depending on the past practices of the employer.[24]

Penalties

The penalties set against management for engaging in an unfair labor practice can range from a minor cease-and-desist order to reimbursing a union and the NLRB for their expenses in investigating, preparing, presenting, and conducting a case[25] to certification of a union representative without the necessity of an election. The theory behind certification without election is that a union would win an election if not for the unfair practice of management. In 1969, in *NLRB v. Gissel Packing Company*, the Supreme Court sustained the right of the NLRB to certify a representative without an election, holding that because of the actions of the company, an election would not reflect the actual sentiment of the employee.[26]

Rulings of the NLRB

The NLRB has two major functions: supervising and conducting representative elections and ruling on employer and union unfair labor practices. In unfair labor practice proceedings, the NLRB, through its general counsel, actually prosecutes the offending party, and the board functions in the role of a judge. After evidence has been considered and if a belief exists that an unfair practice has taken place, orders to cease and desist are issued, and appropriate affirmative-action measures are introduced. The actions taken by the NLRB are remedial, not punitive. Automatic compliance by an offending party is not always a reality. Consequently, court reviews of decisions are available under the NLRA, with ultimate appeal to the U.S. Supreme Court.

In what appears to be the most exhaustive research to date on the subject of employer compliance with the law of unfair labor practices in elections under the NLRA, Kate Bronfenbrenner, director of Labor Education Research at Cornell University's School of Industrial and Labor Relations, found that "it is standard practice for workers to be subjected to threats, interrogation, harassment, surveillance, and retaliation for union activity. [E]mployers threatened to close the plant in 57% of elections, discharged workers in 34%, and threatened to cut wages and benefits in 47% of elections. Workers were forced to attend anti-union one-on-one sessions with a supervisor at least weekly in two-thirds of elections. In 63% of elections employers used supervisor one-on-one meetings to interrogate workers about who they or other workers supported, and in 54% used such sessions to threaten workers."[27] The authors consider this study so important that it is reproduced in its entirety in the study guide accompanying this volume.

Unfair Labor Practices under the RLA

Because the RLA contains no unfair labor practice provisions, the NMB does not have the investigatory and enforcement power to regulate employer, employee, or union conduct that may violate the tenets or guaranteed rights of the act. It is, however, a federal crime to violate the act's provisions.[28] The penalties for such violations are set forth in Section 2, Tenth: "The willful failure or refusal of any carrier, its officers or agents, to comply with the terms of the third, fourth, fifth, seventh, or eighth paragraph . . . shall be a misdemeanor . . . subject to a fine of not less than $1,000, nor more than $20,000 or imprisonment for not more than six months, or both . . . for each offense, and each day during which . . . [the] carrier . . . shall fail or refuse to comply . . . ." The mechanism for enforcement of these provisions is through the federal court system."

The provisions cited in the third, fourth, fifth, seventh, and eighth paragraphs of the RLA state that any conduct by a carrier that interferes with, influences, or coerces employees in any manner in the designation of their collective bargaining representative is a violation of the act itself. These provisions do not preclude the carrier from

making any comments on organizational activities during a campaign. The weight rests with the truthfulness of company-directed statements.

Influence, Coercion, and Interference

Two cases before the Supreme Court have interpreted the provisions of the RLA in dealing with the question of carrier management influence, coercion, or interference. In *Texas and New Orleans Railroad v. Brotherhood of Railway and Steamship Clerks,* the company formed a company union and urged its employees and members of the Brotherhood of Railway and Steamship Clerks to join the new union. The question before the courts was whether the formation of a company union interfered with the employees' exercise of their rights of self-organization.

In the decision rendered in the *Texas* case, the Court noted "that the railroad company and its officers were actually engaged in promoting the organization of the association in the interest of the company and in opposition to the Brotherhood, and that these activities constituted an actual interference with the liberty of the clerical employees in the selection of their representatives."[29] With reference to the meaning of the statutory prohibition against influence, interference, or coercion in Section 2 of the RLA, the Court held:

the intent of Congress is clear with respect to the sort of conduct that is prohibited. "Interference" with freedom of action and "coercion" refer to well understood concepts of the law. "Influence" in this context plainly means pressure, the use of the authority of power of either party to induce action by the other in derogation of what the statute calls "self-organization." The phrase covers the abuse of relation or opportunity so as to corrupt or override the will, and it is no more difficult to appraise conduct of this sort in connection with selection of representatives for the purpose of this act than in relation to well known applications of the law with respect to fraud, duress, and undue influence.

The decisions in the *Texas* case and another major Supreme Court case—*Virginian Railroad Company v. System Federation No. 40*—provide the majority of judicial weight for interpreting the influence, coercion, and interference provisions of the RLA.[30] At the very least, these decisions indicate that management efforts to form company unions interfere with the act. But the decisions do not answer other questions of conduct to any degree. Questions concerning communication to employees and other tactics by management during union elections are answered by the administrative decisions of the NMB itself.

Rulings of the National Mediation Board

The NMB is vested with the authority to interpret and enforce the RLA. Consequently, any interpretations by the board carry significant weight—particularly because most board rulings, especially those dealing with certification, are not judicially reviewable. The absence of judicial review grants tremendous power to the NMB.

Interference through Communications

The original intent of the RLA was to foster collective bargaining between the parties. Given this basic policy goal, it is reasonable to assume that any communication of a negative or hostile nature between a carrier and its employees regarding any aspect of the collective bargaining process, particularly certification elections, would be viewed as running counter to the intent of the act. But would such communications necessarily be illegal under the act?

A partial answer to this question was delivered by the NMB in a ruling on actions by

Allegheny Airlines (see fig. 6.2).[31] The board was called upon to determine whether communications and conduct of a carrier influenced employees not to participate in a union-certification election.

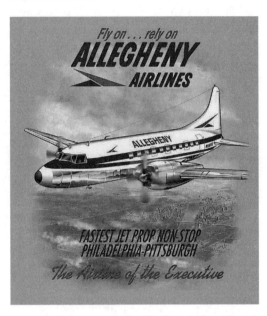

Figure 6.2. Advertisement for Allegheny Airlines. Founded in 1939 as All-American Aviation Company by two du Pont family brothers, Allegheny, like several other airlines, began by carrying airmail. In 1949, the company was renamed All-American Airways as it switched from airmail to passenger service. The company was again renamed, to Allegheny Airlines, in 1952. Allegheny Airlines became one of the first airlines to create an affiliated branded network of regional airline carriers. However; after deregulation, Allegheny changed its name to USAir on October 28, 1979, in an effort to shed its image as a regional air carrier. Lastly, in 1997, USAir was renamed US Airways.

The alleged interference was a letter the carrier sent to its employees when a union-certification vote was about to be taken. Excerpts of the letter state such things as, "Almost every day, from your newspapers or TV, you learn of destructive actions on the part of labor union leaders. Hindrances, shut-downs, strikes, violence, and similar disturbances have been in the news. . . . Merit promotions and merit raises are out. . . . Is this what you want? Do you want to be held back in that way? Remember that professional union organizers work to get your dues. Are they really trying to help you? Do they honestly have the welfare of Allegheny employees at heart? Are they the men whom you respect, whom you look up to, and in whose hands you can place your future? Are they the kind of people who would advance through their own abilities, without politics and union pressure?" The letter concludes, "If you vote for the union, your whole future may be altered; the whole future of Allegheny may be altered. An outside minority will seize your rights."[32]

In its decision, the board dealt with interference as follows:

> In so far as the Carrier's letter to its employees is concerned, we entertain no doubt that it was designed by the carrier to induce its employees to vote "No Union." It is equally clear that the employees would read the letter fully appreciative of the power and authority which the Carrier exercised over them with respect to their day-to-day assignments and security of their jobs. It would be completely unrealistic to believe that under such circumstances employees would not be particularly susceptible to the arguments advanced by the carrier against union representation. It was pure and simple pressure to interfere with a free choice of a representative.

In addition to sending the letter, the airline held meetings with the employees who were eligible to vote. At these meetings, the carrier urged employees to vote and then pointed out how to vote "no union." The board concluded:

> [T]he Carrier's meeting with its employees constituted activity prohibited by the Act. . . . The coercive effect may be subtle, but it is nonetheless present. Such a technique in and of itself is conduct which interferes

with a free choice by employees of a representative. When it is supplementary to other conduct already specified, there can be no doubt that the Carriers totality of conduct in the course of this representation election prevented this Board from fulfilling its obligation under Section 2, Ninth, to insure the choice of representatives by the employees without interference, influence or coercion exercised by the Carrier.

The implications of the Allegheny Airlines case were staggering. By determining, without further delineation, that the "totality of conduct" of the carrier was unlawful, the NMB offered little insight about what is permissible by a carrier in an election campaign. Unlike the NLRA, any and all actions on the part of the carrier appear to be highly suspect, which underscores the need for a carrier to exercise caution.

The RLA prohibits conduct or communication by a carrier that "interferes" with employees rights to self-organization. As the Supreme Court noted in the *Texas* and *Virginian Railroad* cases, the act prohibits communication or conduct by a carrier that, in effect, pressures employees into joining or not joining a union. In this respect, the prohibitions of the act are analogous to the prohibitions of the NLRA.

Any communication or conduct that would be an unfair labor practice under the NLRA would also be unlawful under the RLA. Because no specific illegal communications practices are contained in the RLA, interpretation of interference and its extent is open. NLRB decisions appear to have served as precedents for many NMB rulings and have subsequently been reinforced by the federal courts.

But a review of cases decided by the NMB also clearly indicates that a carrier's election communication or conduct may be ruled unlawful even though the NLRB would not find the same conduct and communication unlawful or sufficient to overturn the results of a certification election. Such conduct and communication by an employer as holding meetings, discrediting the union, telling employees its position concerning an upcoming election, and urging employees to vote "no union" are not permissible under the RLA, but they are permissible under the NLRA.

Interference in Certification Elections

The language of the RLA provides very little guidance on what kinds of election-related conduct are prohibited. Therefore, the NMB has established procedures to ensure that elections are conducted fairly and in a manner that restricts both parties from exercising undue influence or coercion over employee voting. As a part of this process, the NMB is also charged with the responsibility of determining the methods and forms used in the election process and in the conduct of the actual election. The NMB has sole jurisdiction over election procedures and has at times exhibited incongruity in applying these procedures.

Several cases regarding carrier interference with certification elections have been decided. Most notable are the rulings in the *Laker* and *Key Airlines* cases, where direct air carrier involvement was observed. The supplemental readings in the study guide for chapter 4 of the current volume contain the full text of the NMB rulings in the *Laker*, *Key*, and *America West* certification-election interference cases, as well as two examples of management guidelines that have been used during the election process.

In a 1955 ruling involving an election scheduled for Linea Aeropostal Venezolana, implication, not direct action, was the key factor in determining carrier interference. On May 16 and 17, 1955, voting was to take place for the mechanics of the airline. Prior to the vote, all eligible employees were notified that if they could not

be available for the voting process, they would be sent an absentee ballot by mail. On the days scheduled for the vote, no voters (eligible employees) appeared at the polls. In accordance with the previous instructions, ballots were mailed to the eligible employees. Only 8 of the 108 total ballots mailed were returned. The union then filed an objection with the NMB concerning company actions.

According to company records, on the days of the scheduled vote, no mechanics reported for work. The record also indicated that no mechanic suffered loss of pay for the days in question or was disciplined for his or her failure to report for a scheduled workday. Based on these facts, the board concluded that the employer had tainted the election process and interfered with the employees' rights. The board was convinced "that in view of all of the circumstances surrounding this election . . . the employees were not afforded an opportunity to freely express whether they desire representation for collective bargaining purposed in accordance with the Railway Labor Act."[33]

In a 1990 decision, America West Airlines was cited by the NMB for election interference during a representation-election campaign. At America West, the customer-service representatives who were eligible to vote in a representation election contended that the airline violated the rules for a fair election. The union seeking election, the Association of Flight Attendants (AFA), filed an action with the NMB. On January 16, 1990, the NMB rendered the decision supporting the AFA position. The NMB ruled that America West's conduct in the February 1989 election had interfered with the election process. The NMB also stated that America West influenced many customer-service representatives by announcing and implementing certain changes in work rules that were favorable to the employees. The airline implemented increases in layoff benefits and distributed profit-sharing bonuses to the affected class of employees. On June 30, 1990, the NMB ordered a new election.

Court Decisions

In addition to the cases decided by the NMB, the courts have examined the question of the communication process and whether carriers have interfered with or coerced employees in their choice of a bargaining representative. In *Teamsters v. Braniff Airways Inc.*, heard in 1969, the International Brotherhood of Teamsters (Teamsters) sought an injunction to prohibit the airline from preelection communication. The union's motion for an injunction was denied. In its ruling, the court found the following:

[T]he Teamsters and Braniff have issued written communications and have had oral communications with the affected employees, designed to communicate to such employees information and their respective positions, arguments, and beliefs with respect to the issues in the election. On the preliminary record before the Court, the communications complained of in the Complaint and Motion for Preliminary Injunction appear to communicate information, Braniff's position, arguments, and beliefs with respect to issues involved in the proposed election and do not contain threats or promises. Such communications, therefore, are not prohibited by the Railway Labor Act. Such communications are protected by the First Amendment to the United States Constitution protecting free speech. On the preliminary record before the Court, such communications were not shown to be false or misleading or to have had a corrupting or undue effect on the outcome of the election. The Railway Labor Act [does] not prohibit a carrier involved in a representation dispute and

election, which is being conducted by the National Mediation Board, from communicating to the affected employees information, its positions, arguments, and beliefs with respect to the issues involved in the election.

The Teamsters belief that Braniff had interfered with employees' representative choice was based on certain memos and alleged oral communications by Braniff management.[34]

In a more recent federal decision, rendered in Portland, Oregon, the court ruled that Horizon Airlines had "bargained in a manner designed to frustrate negotiations and engaged in illegal bad faith bargaining under the Railway Labor Act." In this case, the court ordered the company to cease and desist from any conduct designed to forestall the reaching of an agreement. In addition, Horizon was charged with "intimidation, arrogance and intractability" at the bargaining table and was ordered to pay the attorney's fees and costs incurred by the union during the lawsuit. The court determined that Horizon Air had strongly opposed the AFA when the union conducted an organization drive in 1987. The court found that after the NMB had certified the AFA to represent Horizon's flight attendants, Horizon had repeatedly delayed and canceled negotiations, consistently refused to make counterproposals during the negotiation process for a first agreement, and "engaged in the mere pretense of negotiating with a completely closed mind." The parties remained in negotiations under the auspices of the NMB. AFA sued the airline in April 1989, alleging that the company had engaged in bad-faith bargaining with the union.[35]

Despite the ruling of the court in this instance, the decisions of the NMB are not subject to judicial review. The ruling in this case only came about as a result of the Teamsters' insistence that an injunction be issued outside the

NMB's jurisdiction. Consequently, the board's decision concerning the propriety or impropriety of Horizon's conduct may not have reached the same conclusion as the court.

The lack of case law on RLA communication issues makes employer communication uncertain and consequently hazardous. The broad principle that a carrier can communicate with its employees about the choice of a bargaining representative is easily stated and well established. But as the foregoing examples demonstrate, the content of that right is very difficult to define with precision, particularly because of the nonreviewable nature of NMB decisions and the statutory scheme of the RLA, which encourages both unionization and collective bargaining. Because their rights are not clearly defined, carriers have gone to great lengths to advise their supervisory employees of the responsibilities they have during a union-organizing campaign.

Penalties for Interference in Elections

When any airline conducts an aggressive election campaign to offset the efforts of an organization attempt, the airline and its officers risk potential criminal prosecution as outlined in Section 2, Tenth, of the RLA:

The willful failure or refusal of any carrier, its officers or agents to comply with the terms of the third, fourth, fifth, seventh, or eighth paragraph of this section shall be a misdemeanor, and upon conviction thereof the carrier, officer, or agent offending shall be subject to a fine of not less than $1,000 nor more than $20,000 or imprisonment for not more than six months, or both fine and imprisonment, for each offense, and each day during which such carrier, officer, or agent shall willfully fail or refuse to comply with the terms of the said paragraphs of this section shall constitute a separate offense. It shall be the duty of any district attorney of the United States [U.S. Attorney] to whom any duly designated representative of a carrier's employees may apply to institute in the proper court and to prosecute under the direction of the Attorney General of the United States, all necessary proceedings for the enforcement of the provisions of this section, and for the punishment of all violations thereof and the costs and expenses of such prosecution shall be paid out of the appropriation for the expenses of the courts of the United States: Provided, That nothing in the Act shall be construed to require an individual employee to render labor or service without his consent, nor shall anything in this Act be construed to make the quitting of his labor by an individual employee an illegal act; nor shall any court issue any process to compel the performance by an individual employee of such labor or service, without his consent.

Rather than invoke this section, the NMB has so far either set aside an election, certified a union representative without an election, or taken some action similar to that in the *Key Airlines* case discussed earlier in this chapter. The NMB's failure to institute the actions under Section 2, Tenth, does not imply that such actions will not be instituted in the future.

There is a decided lack of airline case rulings under this provision. Only two have been brought before the board: one was settled before the board sent it to trial, and fines were imposed in the other. In *United States v. Taca Airways Agency Inc.*, defendants G. R. Moody and Rudolph O. Duscoe were indicted for firing certain employees who had been obtaining employee signatures to authorize a union to act as the legal bargaining representative.[36] Prior to any decision, an out-of-court settlement was reached.

In the only other case, *United States v. Jerry Winston & Broome County Aviation Inc. d/b/a/ Commuter Airlines Inc.*, the Department of Justice issued indictments, and the defendants were convicted of "interfering with, influencing and coercing employees in their choice of a representative."[37] Specifically, in a union-organization drive in which the pilots had secured the services of the NMB and an election was being conducted, the defendants

- Discharged from their services the chief organizers
- Called a meeting for all pilots and copilots where the employees were told that they, the employees, would have tough check rides if they favored organization
- Requested the employees to deliver their ballots to the employer rather than to the NMB, which in effect constituted a no vote because the cards were not turned in

As a direct result of these actions, the president, Jerry Winston, was sentenced to a prison term of fifteen days and fined $75,000 on various counts. In addition, the defendant corporations separately received fines of $1,000 on fifteen counts. The total amount of the fines equaled $105,000. As previously noted in chapter 4, Bronfenbrenner's research demonstrates a pervasive pattern of employers disregarding the law in union certification elections conducted under the RLA and accepting any penalties that may eventually be imposed as a reasonable cost of preventing or delaying union certification.[38]

Featherbedding

Unlike the NLRA, the RLA does not contain any provisions for the elimination of featherbedding, contractual requirements that employees be hired into positions for which their services are not required. The usage of firemen on the railroads years after the technical elimination of the position is a perfect example that the practice exists under the RLA.

Within the air transport industry, the Air Line Pilots Association (ALPA) sought to require a three-man flight-deck crew in the B-737 and DC-9 jetliners, even though the manufacturers had designed and the FAA had certified these aircraft (along with the competing British-designed BAC-111) for a two-person flight-deck crew, and the flight decks of these aircraft had no flight engineer (second officer) station. ALPA was nonetheless able to maintain collective bargaining agreement provisions with United Air Lines requiring a third flight-deck crewmember in these aircraft for years, riding in the folding "jump seat."[39]

Although ALPA presented this issue under the guise of safety concerns, the author of *Flying the Line: The First Half-Century of the Air Line Pilots Association* indicates that other motives might be present:

> Featherbedding is an ugly word. It conjures up images of cynical union bosses extorting wages from helpless employers on behalf of lazy, corrupt workers. From the very beginning, ALPA's crew compliment policy has suffered from charges that it was pure featherbedding, merely an attempt to make work for pilots who would otherwise be unemployed. The third man in the cockpit, critics said, might as well be at home in a featherbed. Only a fool would deny that ALPA was worried about technological unemployment when the crew compliment case arose. In an economic sense, airline pilots were attached to the "Three" because its relatively low productivity meant jobs.[40]

Unfair Labor Practices under the CSRA and State Laws

The Civil Service Reform Act of 1978, which governs federal-employee collective bargaining rights, sets out unfair labor practices for agencies and unions similar to those found in the NLRA. Under that section of the Act, it is an unfair labor practice for a *federal agency* to:

- Interfere with, restrain, or coerce any employee in the exercise of any right granted by the Act
- Encourage or discourage membership in any labor organization by discrimination in connection with hiring, tenure, promotion, or other conditions of employment
- Sponsor, control, or otherwise assist any labor organization, other than to furnish, upon request, customary and routine services and facilities if the services and facilities are also furnished on an impartial basis to other labor organizations having equivalent status
- Discipline or otherwise discriminate against an employee because the employee has filed a complaint, affidavit, or petition, or has given any information or testimony under the Act
- Refuse to consult or negotiate in good faith with a labor organization as required by the Act
- Fail or refuse to cooperate in impasse procedures and impasse decisions as required by the Act
- Enforce any rule or regulation that is in conflict with any applicable collective bargaining agreement if the agreement was in effect before the date of the regulation

or

- Fail or refuse to comply with any provision of the Act

Similarly, it is an unfair labor practice for a *union* to:

- Interfere with, restrain, or coerce any employee in the exercise of any employee right under the Act
- Cause or attempt to cause an agency to discriminate against any employee in the exercise of any such right

- Deny membership to any represented employee who meets reasonable occupational standards uniformly required for admission and who tenders dues uniformly required as a condition of acquiring and retaining membership
- Coerce, discipline, fine, or attempt to coerce a member of the labor organization as punishment, reprisal, or for the purpose of hindering or impeding the member's work performance or productivity as an employee or the discharge of the member's duties as an employee
- Discriminate against an employee with regard to the terms or conditions of membership in the labor organization on the basis of race, color, creed, national origin, sex, age, preferential, or nonpreferential civil service status, political affiliation, marital status, or handicapping condition
- Fail or refuse to cooperate in impasse procedures and impasse decisions as required by the Act
- Call, or participate in, a strike, work stoppage, or slowdown or picketing of an agency in a labor-management dispute if such picketing interferes with an agency's operations
- Condone any such activity by failing to take action to prevent or stop such activity (informational picketing that does not interfere with agency operations is not considered an unfair labor practice) or
- Fail or refuse to comply with any provision of the Act[41]

Free-Speech Provisions

Section 7116 (like Section 8 of the NLRA) further provides that the expression of any personal view, argument, opinion, or the making of any statement that either publicizes the fact of a representational election and encourages employees to exercise their right to vote in the election, corrects the record with respect to any false or misleading statement made by any person, or informs employees of the government's policy relating to labor-management relations and representation is not considered an unfair labor practice so long as the statement was not made under coercive conditions and contains no threat of reprisal or force or promise of benefit.

The Federal Labor Relations Authority

The Federal Labor Relations Authority (FLRA) is an independent federal administrative agency created by the Civil Service Reform Act. One of the agency's primary responsibilities is resolving complaints of unfair labor practices.

The FLRA's Office of General Counsel (OGC) is the agency's independent investigator and prosecutor. Charges of unfair labor practices are initially filed with the appropriate OGC regional office, where they are investigated and a determination made as to whether to dismiss or prosecute the charges. That decision is subject to being overruled by the FLRA general counsel.

If charges are filed, the union or agency against which they are filed may appeal and have a trial-type evidentiary hearing before an FLRA administrative law judge (ALJ). The losing party may then appeal the ALJ's decision to the three members of the FLRA (appointed by the president with the advice and consent of the Senate). The FLRA's decision can then be appealed to the appropriate U.S. Court of Appeals. FLRA administrative appeals must first be exhausted before a court will consider the matter. Because the unfair labor practice provisions of the Civil Service Reform Act so closely track those of the NLRA, it is not surprising that FLRA and judicial decisions under the act usually reach the same result as those under the NLRA.

Consider, for example, the case of Professional Airways System Specialists (PASS) and U.S. Department of Transportation, Federal Aviation Administration. On December 31, 1981,

the Professional Airways Systems Specialists, AFL-CIO, was certified as the exclusive nationwide bargaining agent for FAA airways-facility-service employees, replacing the previous representative, the Federal Aviation Science and Technological Association (FASTA) (see fig. 6.3). The collective bargaining agreement negotiated with the FAA by FASTA had expired, and PASS had put the agency on notice that it wished to negotiate a new agreement, but no negotiations had begun. PASS filed a complaint with the FLRA alleging that the FAA had committed an unfair labor practice under Section 7116 by unilaterally implementing a change in the basic watch schedule for represented electronic technicians at its Sonora sector field office without notifying the union, without providing it an opportunity to negotiate the change, and by bypassing the union to deal directly with unit employees concerning the matter. OGC prosecuted the case as an unfair labor practice. On appeal from the initial decision and order

Figure 6.3. Logo of the Professional Airways Systems Specialists (PASS). The union represents more than eleven thousand employees of the Federal Aviation Administration (FAA) and Department of Defense (DOD). In 1977, PASS was formed to provide exclusive representation for the FAA's technician bargaining unit. PASS members certify the safety and the efficiency of the National Airspace System (NAS), maintain and support the United States' air-traffic-control system, and ensure the reliability and the safety of the commercial- and general-aviation industries. Courtesy of Professional Aviation Safety Specialists.

of the ALJ, the FLRA found that the FAA had a statutory obligation to negotiate the proposed change in watch schedule but had refused to notify PASS's designated representative of the proposed change and had refused to bargain in good faith with the union over the change.[42]

The FLRA found that these actions of the FAA constituted unfair labor practices and ordered the FAA to: cease and desist from "changing the basic watch schedule" of the Sonora office employees without giving prior notice to the PASS representative, which would let the representative negotiate the change; to cease and desist from bypassing the PASS and dealing directly with employees about their working conditions; and to cease and desist from any interference with, restraint, or coercion of its employees who are exercising their rights. The FLRA also ordered the FAA to take several steps: to negotiate with PASS about the basic watch schedule, post for sixty days FLRA-furnished forms at Sonora's office and the Austin Airways Facility Sector, and notify in writing the regional director of region 7 about what steps were taken to comply with the order.

The FAA order states in part:

1. Cease and desist from:
   a. Changing the basic watch schedule of unit employees at the Sonora Sector Field Office without providing prior notice to the representative designated by the Professional Airways Systems Specialists, AFL-CIO, the exclusive representative of its employees, and affording such representative the opportunity to negotiate over such change.
   b. Bypassing the Professional Airways Systems Specialists, AFL-CIO, the exclusive bargaining representative of its employees, by dealing directly with unit employees concerning personnel policies, practices and matters affecting their working conditions.

   c. In any like or related manner interfering with, restraining, or coercing its employees in the exercise of their rights assured by the Federal Service Labor-Management Relations Statute.

2. Take the following affirmative action in order to effectuate the purposes and policies of the Federal Service Labor-Management Relations Statute:
   a. Upon request, negotiate with the Professional Airways Systems Specialists, AFL-CIO, concerning changes in the unit employees' basic watch schedule.
   b. Post at its facilities at the Austin Airways Facility Sector and the Sonora Sector Field Office copies of the attached Notice on forms to be furnished by the Federal Labor Relations Authority. Upon receipt of such forms, they shall be signed by the Manager of the Austin Airways Facility Sector, or a designee, and shall be posted and maintained for 60 consecutive days thereafter, in conspicuous places, including all bulletin boards and other places where notices to employees are customarily posted. Reasonable steps shall be taken to insure that such notices are not altered, defaced, or covered by any other material.
   c. Pursuant to section 2423.30 of the Authority's Rules and Regulations, notify the Regional Director, Region VII, Federal Labor Relations Authority, in writing, within 30 days from the date of this Order, as to what steps have been taken to comply herewith.

State Labor-Relations Agencies

Most states that allow public employees to organize and bargain collectively have state public-employee-relations boards that are more or less equivalent to the FLRA. The names, authority, responsibilities, jurisdiction, and procedures of these state agencies vary widely. Table 6.2 lists

Table 6.2.
State public-employee-relations boards

State	Agency
Alaska	Alaska Labor Relations Agency
California	Public Employment Relations Board
Connecticut	State Board of Labor Relations
Delaware	Public Employee Relations Board
District of Columbia	Public Employee Relations Board
Florida	Public Employee Relations Commission
Hawaii	Labor Relations Board
Illinois	Illinois Labor Relations Board Illinois Educational Labor Board
Indiana	Indiana Education Employment Relations Board
Iowa	Public Employment Relations Board
Kansas	Public Employee Relations Board
Kentucky	Office of Labor-Management Relations and Mediation
Maine	Maine Labor Relations Board
Maryland	Maryland State Labor Relations Board Maryland State Higher Education Relations Board
Massachusetts	Labor Relations Commission
Michigan	Michigan Civil Service Commission Employment Relations Commission
Minnesota	Bureau of Mediation Services
Missouri	Missouri Labor & Industrial Relations Commission
Montana	Labor Standards Bureau Collective Bargaining Unit
Nebraska	Nebraska Commission of Industrial Relations
Nevada	Local Government Employee-Management Relations Board
New Hampshire	Public Employee Labor Relations Board
New Jersey	Public Employment Relations Commission
New Mexico	Public Employee Labor Relations Board
New York	Public Employment Relations Board
Ohio	State Employment Relations Board
Oklahoma	Public Employees Relations Board
Oregon	Employment Relations Board
Pennsylvania	Pennsylvania Labor Relations Board
Puerto Rico	Comision de Relaciones del Trabajo del Servicio Publico
Rhode Island	State Labor Relations Board
South Dakota	South Dakota Department of Labor Division of Labor and Management
Vermont	Labor Relations Board
Washington	Public Employment Relations Commission
Wisconsin	Wisconsin Employment Relations Commission

these state agencies and those of Washington, D.C., and Puerto Rico. States that do not provide for public employees to organize and bargain collectively are not listed. Some states have separate boards for public-education employees.

Summary

Though there are differences between the RLA and the NLRA, a carrier can work on the assumption that what is applicable under the NLRA concerning unfair labor practices will also have application and weight under the RLA. Both management and labor are responsible for dealing fairly with one another. Air carriers and their unions, though subject to no legislation describing unfair labor practices, are in essence bound by the precedents of the NLRB cases because they have significant weight in the eyes of the courts.

This relationship between NLRB precedents and RLA cases was specifically emphasized in a 1967 district court decision involving Pan American World Airways and the Teamsters. In that case, covered by the RLA, the court attempted to provide an analogy between the activities specifically proscribed by the NLRA and the actions of the Clerks Union (IBT) and the airline under the RLA: "[C]ases under the NLRA are not controlling under the Railway Labor Act which is different in scheme, structure and enforcement machinery. However, they offer cogent analogy in the solution of similar problems arising under the RLA and the courts have frequently drawn on NLRA cases for guidance."[43]

For federal government employees, unfair labor practices under the Civil Service Reform Act are very similar to those under the NLRA for the private sector. For state and local government employees, state laws and regulations vary widely, and seventeen states do not provide collective bargaining rights to their employees.

7. Grievance Procedures

Grievance procedures are a fundamental component of any union contract. Under the RLA, arbitration of grievances is mandatory for the airline (and railroad) industry. For other industries, the NLRA lists grievance procedures as one of the mandatory bargaining issues, but the language of the NLRA is not explicit about the procedures that must be employed in resolving grievance disputes, leaving the parties to agree to standard grievance procedures in their contract. Under the Civil Service Reform Act, grievance procedures meeting certain prescribed minimum standards are required to be set forth in the contract.

Under the NLRA, a union has a statutory duty to represent the employees fairly in both contract negotiations and contract administration. This duty is derived from the union's exclusive representative rights in Section 9(a) of the Wagner Act. In Section 203(d) of the Landrum-Griffin Act, Congress declares, "Final adjustment by a method agreed upon by the parties is the desirable method for the settlement of grievance disputes arising over the application or interpretation of an existing collective bargaining agreement."

Definition

Generally, a *grievance* exists when an employee or union alleges that there has been:
- A violation of the agreement
- A violation of the law (for which a statutory alternative is available)
- A violation of rules or regulations contained either specifically in the agreement or in other company action
- A change in working conditions
- A violation of past practice
- A violation of health or safety standards (for which a statutory alternative is available)

Many contracts specifically limit the grievance procedure to matters involving the "meaning and application" of the contract. But when matters not directly related to the meaning and application of the contract are brought up, it is permissible for the appropriate board or arbitrator to hear these types of complaints and grievances. Both management and the union can use the established grievance procedures to handle these noncontract issues, and by doing so, they may possibly avoid early appeal to arbitration or external statutory investigation. The early steps of the grievance procedure provide for factual discussion, exchange, and consideration of the issues. Although time may be wasted dealing with these noncontract issues, "it is better to waste time than leave a sore spot unattended."[1]

Contract Administration

When agreements are reached in contract negotiations, the parties generally announce, through informal and formal statements, that a new understanding between the parties exists and that peace will again prevail. In airline negotiations, the ratification process is lengthy because the membership is generally spread throughout the country. Because the ratification process is prolonged, the company allows the unions to make the first announcements about what they attained during negotiations. To do otherwise may work against the ratification process and cause a workable agreement to become moot.

With all the exuberance and enthusiasm generated by the signing of a new agreement, a sense of optimism is established concerning the workings of the new agreement. It takes some period of time, however, before it is determined whether this optimism is justified. Once the contract is signed, management and union officials have the job of implementing it in the workplace.

The new agreement establishes the framework for which labor relations are to exist during the term of the contract. Although the negotiators, through compromise and statesmanship, believe they are totally aware of what was negotiated, questions of interpretation and application develop almost immediately. To minimize these questions, negotiators sometimes keep "minutes of negotiation" for reference at a later date. But these documents tend to lose their value by the time the contract is finalized, especially in protracted negotiations, which are found often in the airline industry. Both the company and the union must begin to administer the contract on a daily basis.

Normally, management and the unions devote a considerably larger amount of their time to the administration of the agreement than to its negotiation. The formal signing of the agreement, not the negotiating process, identifies the true beginning of union-management relations. Contract administration is not an event that takes place just once or every three years—it is an ongoing process.

Many administrative problems result from the interpretation of the language of the agreement. Because of the nature of the bargaining procedure—clauses and amendments being written in the haste of the eleventh hour, when negotiators compromise, modify, and change position to reach an agreement before the possibility of a work stoppage—many clauses are written in rather broad and ambiguous terms. Consequently, each side to the agreement may have a different interpretation of the meaning and application of these clauses.

It is unrealistic to believe that a labor agreement that fully ensures against ambiguous language can be written. At the bargaining table, the parties may have differences of opinion on which they are not willing to compromise. In the interest of reaching an agreement, they may agree on language that is vague, general, and even contradictory. Written agreements only take on shape and operational meaning when management makes decisions about how it intends to apply meaning to the terms and conditions and when the union and employees react to these decisions.[2] Contract administration works through these issues.

Arbitration

The Railway Labor Act (RLA) provides for two types of arbitration:

- *interest arbitration*: arbitration of collective bargaining negotiations when the parties do not reach agreement through NMB mediation and both agree to binding arbitration, or
- *grievance arbitration*: arbitration of grievances as specified in a collective bargaining agreement over wages, hours, benefits, and working conditions

Interest arbitration. Interest arbitration establishes the terms of a collective bargaining agreement through arbitration, rather than through negotiations. Although the RLA provides an effective process for interest arbitration, it is not statutorily required. The NMB offers the parties the opportunity to use interest arbitration when it has been determined that further mediation efforts will not be successful. In addition, the parties may directly agree to resolve their collective bargaining dispute through interest arbitration. The NMB provides the parties with panels of potential arbitrators from which they select the individuals to resolve the dispute. An interest arbitration decision is final and binding with very narrow grounds for a judicial appeal.

Grievance arbitration. Grievance arbitration, involving existing collective bargaining agreements, is mandatory under the RLA. In the railroad industry, the NMB has significant administrative responsibilities for the three avenues of grievance arbitration. These sources are the National Railroad Adjustment Board established under the RLA, as well as the arbitration panels established directly by the labor-management parties at each railroad (Public Law Boards and Special Boards of Adjustment). In the airline industry, grievance arbitration is accomplished at the various System Boards of Adjustment created jointly by labor and management at the parties' expense. The NMB furnishes panels of prospective arbitrators for the parties' selection in both the airline and railroad industries. The NMB also has substantial financial responsibilities for railroad arbitration proceedings in that it pays the salary and travel expenses of the arbitrators. As discussed later, Congress never chose to provide such financial support to arbitration in the airline industry. Arbitration decisions under the RLA are also final and binding with very limited grounds for judicial review.

Grievance Procedures

Arbitrator Michael I. Komaroff refers to the grievance procedure as the "life blood of a collective bargaining relationship,"[3] and Gerald G. Somers writes that the grievance machinery "is not a mere adjunct of the collective bargaining process; it is the very heart of the process."[4] In the initial implementation stages following ratification of the contract, the parties meet to iron out differences that may have developed. But because most contracts have a three-year time frame, the interpretation eventually becomes the responsibility of the labor-relations-department personnel and the union officials (committeemen, stewards, etc.), who may or may not have participated in the formal negotiations.

Problems of interpretation are generally handled through the grievance procedure of the contract. Such procedures can be formalized or impersonal and may contain a variety of steps allowing for appeal to a higher authority if the complaining party is not in agreement with the decision rendered. The actual number of steps in the procedure and its machinery and formality are subjects of the negotiation process and are mandatory subjects of bargaining under the NLRA.

The grievance procedure provides an orderly approach for union and management to determine whether a contract has been violated. In very few cases are the alleged violations willful or in complete disregard of the terms and conditions negotiated. More frequently, unions and employers pursue a course they believe to be in conformity with that agreed on at the table. Differences between the way labor and management interpret how the contract applies to continued working relationships are the province of the grievance procedure.

Not all collective bargaining contracts provide for the same structural arrangements, as can be seen by comparing the information in the study guide for the current volume, which contains a typical procedure for airline grievances handled by a system board of adjustment and a typical grievance procedure found in NLRA contracts. Some grievance procedures contain only one step, and others have many more, but the basic characteristics of the procedures are similar. A time limit is placed on each step for both parties to file, appeal, and answer grievances. Failure to adhere to these time limits could result in the matter being summarily resolved against the tardy or inattentive party.

Grievance answers can be precedent setting both in the in-house stages and, more important, in the arbitration stage. For this reason, the ultimate decision in small-plant operations should rest with a member of the management team who has final and binding authority for the plant. In cases where the organization is large and spread over many work locations, as is the airline industry, the grievance decision makers at the local level should clear their decisions with an ultimate authority, such as the vice president of labor relations, before rendering a decision. This approach maintains consistency and continuity in the process throughout larger companies.

Ultimately, the grievance procedure will be exhausted. The party filing the grievance either agrees with the decision or takes the matter to a higher authority. If it has been agreed to in the contract under the NLRA, or in the case of the RLA, this higher authority is an arbitrator.

Grievance Arbitration

A typical grievance and arbitration procedure includes several steps (see fig. 7.1). Generally, the employee and his or her union steward present the grievance to the employee's immediate supervisor. Usually, this first step is not formalized—that is, a written complaint is not initiated. If a satisfactory settlement cannot be reached, the union and employee can appeal to progressively higher levels of management. At these higher stages, the union usually has exclusive control over whether to pursue the grievance further, settle it, or dismiss it. At this point, the union is insulated from suit by the employee, unless he or she can establish that any unilateral action by the union amounts to a refusal or breach of the union's duty of fair representation.

When the bilateral process of the grievance procedure breaks down and the parties cannot agree, provisions are made between the parties

to place the matter with an impartial arbitrator selected by the parties to decide the controversy. The arbitrator determines the outcome of the dispute. The contract invariably stipulates that the arbitrator's final decision is binding.

Typically, arbitration begins by a submission agreement or by a notice invoking an arbitration clause in a collective bargaining agreement. The submission agreement generally describes the dispute and the relief sought by the petitioning party and is jointly signed by the parties to the dispute. The document may also include details concerning the procedures to be followed by the arbitrator, the limits of the arbitrator's authority, and the deadline for rendering a decision.

Irrespective of whether arbitration is initiated by submission or demand, the arbitrator frequently requests a statement of the issues in the case at the outset of the hearing. If the parties are unable to agree on the specifics, the arbitrator may simply request separate statements from each party and may infer from these statements the nature of the dispute.

Arbitrator authority and limits. Most arbitrators draw their authority to decide on contract issues from the contract they are asked to interpret. If there are limits, they are usually defined in clear and unambiguous terms. Most contracts provide that the arbitrator has no power or authority to alter, change, or modify the provisions or intent of the contract.

When a company and union seek arbitration, they have already made an agreement between themselves to disagree on a particular issue. Consequently, they seek an arbitrator to rule on what the language of the contract means and on whether it has been applied correctly under the circumstances. The parties are not seeking innovative ideas outside the scope of the agreement. Thus, the arbitrator becomes an instrument of the contract. Should a decision expose flaws in a collective bargaining agreement, the correction

GRIEVANCE RELEASE FORM

I, _____

Print Name

Hereby authorize my AFA Union Representative(s) to file and represent a grievance on my behalf.

Signature_____

Base and Employee Number_____

Date_____

Contact Number_____

Email_____

Figure 7.1. Association of Flight Attendants Grievance Release Form. It is the employee's responsibility to know his or her labor contract and to contact a union representative in a timely manner regarding a grievance. Time limits are strictly enforced, and once an employee's time limits have expired, the grievance cannot be filed; whether or not the employee has a legitimate grievance, the case is over based on expiration of time limits alone. Association of Flight Attendants.

of such inconsistencies is the responsibility of the company and the union at the next round of negotiations. It is not within the scope of the arbitrator's authority to render a decision that amends the contract to repair the flaw.

Grievance Arbitration under the Railway Labor Act

Arbitration is mandatory under the RLA. Although the RLA is silent with respect to specific grievance procedures between the parties, it does state in Section 3 that disputes "shall be handled in the usual manner up to and including the chief operating officer of the carrier designated to handle such disputes; but failing to reach an adjustment in this manner, the disputes may be referred by petition of the parties or by either party to the appropriate Division of the Adjustment Board." In 1934, the act was amended to establish the National Railroad Adjustment Board (NRAB). This amendment required grievances to be handled on the rail-carriers property and, when not resolved, to be submitted to the NRAB for final decision.

In 1936, the National Mediation Board (NMB) was empowered to create for the air transport sector an adjudicating authority similar to the NRAB. This grievance authority was to be the National Air Transport Adjustment Board

(NATAB) and was to be composed of two members selected by the carriers and two members selected by the unions. A neutral referee was to be the fifth member of the board. The decisions rendered by this board were to be final and binding on the parties to a dispute.

Up to the present time, it has not been considered necessary to establish the National Air Transport Adjustment Board. Instead, the courts have interpreted Section 204 of Title II—which mandates that each air carrier and labor organization establish grievance machinery and a system board of adjustment.[5] A system board's decisions are subject to the same judicial review as those of the NRAB. Consequently, the airlines and the unions evolved their own grievance machinery, similar in concept to the NATAB but different in its structure. Each airline agreement provides for a system board of adjustment and a negotiated procedure for resolving disputes. Figure 7.2 shows a typical airline grievance procedure under the RLA.

The System Board of Adjustment

When the machinery of grievance resolution is exhausted, a case is eligible for submission to a system board of adjustment. The composition of system boards varies among airlines. Some system boards are composed of members from man-

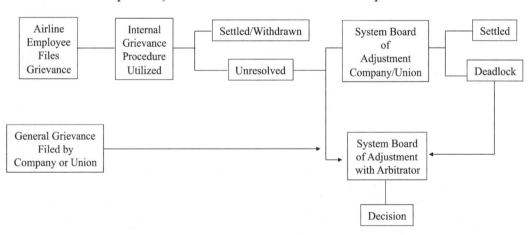

Figure 7.2. Railway Labor Act airline grievance procedure.

agement and labor. For example, when coauthor J. Scott Hamilton was in private practice, the collective bargaining agreement between Frontier Airlines and the Air Line Pilots Association created a system board comprising two representatives from management and two from labor. System boards decide the outcome of grievance hearings on a case-by-case basis. If a majority of the members of the system board agrees, the decision is final and binding. If, however, a deadlock occurs, a neutral referee is required. In this case, the parties may ask the NMB to submit a panel of arbitrators from which the parties will select an arbitrator, or they may proceed on their own to select an arbitrator without the assistance of the NMB. An example of grievance procedures included in an airline collective bargaining agreement is included in the supplemental materials relating to this chapter in the study guide.

A variation on the provision for a system board of adjustment is the empanelment of a neutral party from the very beginning of the arbitration process, and in some cases, provisions have been made for the system board to be bypassed in favor of a single, neutral arbitrator used on a case-by-case basis. The provision to bypass the system board, although not conforming to the language of the RLA or to the court-ordered requirements, has been allowed by the NMB because it still provides a system for peaceful settlements of minor disputes.

Overruling Arbitration Decisions

The arbitration methodology in the airline sector is varied, but in most cases, it conforms to the spirit and intent of the RLA. The advantage of a board approach is that in an industry with unique practices and nomenclatures, the appointed union and management parties can help a neutral adjudicator understand the issues more clearly so that he or she may reach an equitable solution. Occasionally, however, even with such assistance, an impartial arbitrator reaches a decision that is clearly "out in left field." When this happens, the management and union board members may agree to dissent from and overrule the arbitrator's decision. But when a system board of adjustment is not convened and only an arbitrator is making the final and binding decision, no appeal for judicial review may be made unless language contained in the contract stipulates that the arbitrator may not exceed the intent of the parties to the agreement.

Prior to the 1966 amendment to the RLA, a carrier that disagreed with an arbitration decision could unilaterally set the decision aside and refuse to comply. The union involved could accept the carrier's decision and let the award go unenforced, or the union could bring action in federal court to enforce the award. In addition, prior to 1956, the union could strike to force the carrier to honor the decision. But in 1956, in *Brotherhood of Railroad Trainmen v. Chicago River & Indiana Railroad Co.*, the Supreme Court eliminated the ability of a union to strike to enforce a decision by stating, "Congress had intended Section 3 to be a mandatory comprehensive and exclusive system for resolving disputes over grievances and claims."[6]

The 1966 amendment also provided that the award of a system board was enforceable in federal court. This amendment thus limited the courts' power to review the decisions of the arbitration machinery and required the courts to use the same standards for reviewing awards under the RLA as employed in the *Enterprise Wheel & Car* decision affecting the NLRA. In the *Enterprise Wheel* decision, the court stated that as long as the arbitrator's award drew its essence from the collective bargaining agreement, a court could not set aside the award.[7]

In 1969, the U.S. Circuit Court of Appeals construed the 1966 amendment to imply that the power of judicial review was limited to awards that had no foundation in reason or fact. The court further held that an award could not be overruled because the court's interpretation of contractual language was different from that of the arbitrator. In a decision similar to that in the *Enterprise Wheel* case, the court concluded that "the parties had bargained for the arbitrator's construction of the contract rather than the court's."[8]

In the 2006 case *NetJets Aviation v. Teamsters*, NetJets, a company covered by the RLA, dismissed an employee for posting an obscene video on the union website. The union grieved the employee's dismissal, and an arbitrator ordered NetJets to reinstate the employee. The aviation company sued to set aside the arbitrator's award, arguing that reinstating the employee would violate the public policy favoring safety in air travel and workplace safety. However, the court stated that "public policy" does not constitute a basis for reviewing the award under the RLA.

The court's ruling was quite simple. It believed that the RLA only states three grounds for overturning an award: failure to comply with the RLA, exceeding jurisdiction, and fraud or corruption. Public policy is not on the list. Some critics of the court's ruling found it interesting because courts frequently hold that public policy is a ground for vacating an award under the Federal Arbitration Act, even though that act has a specific list of grounds that does not include public policy.

Case study 7.1 explores the recent application of these RLA grievance-resolution procedures to companies conducting fractional aircraft operations under subpart K of FAR Part 91.

Case Study 7.1: Railway Labor Act and Fractional Ownership Companies

The Railway Labor Act (RLA) applies not only to railroads and airlines but also to any company that is directly or indirectly owned or controlled by or under common control with a railroad or airline and that performs a transportation service.

The National Mediation Board (NMB) applies a two-part test to determine if an entity that is not an airline or railroad is covered by the RLA:

- Is there is common ownership or control between the entity in question and an RLA carrier?
- Is the work performed by the entity's employees is traditionally performed by the employees of an airline or railroad?

Both components of the test must be satisfied for the NMB to conclude that the entity is covered by the RLA.

As for the second part of the test, the following airline-related entities have been found to come under the RLA: air taxi services and charter operations that are not negligible or sporadic.

In a 2006 action filed by NetJets Aviation Inc. (NetJets) against the International Brotherhood of Teamsters, Airline Division, and the International Brotherhood of Teamsters, Local 1108 (collectively referred to as the union), the complaint sought to vacate an arbitration award finding that NetJets violated the collective bargaining agreement between NetJets and the union.

This particular case was found to be governed by the RLA. NetJets operates both an air-charter service carrying persons and property for hire under the provisions of FAR Part 135 and fractional operations under Subpart K of FAR Part 91. The conduct of charter operations renders NetJets and other "fractional ownership companies" common carriers within the jurisdiction of the federal Railway Labor Act.[9]

Arbitration Costs

Costs associated with arbitration in the airline industry depend on the arbitrator selected and his or her background and reputation. It is not unusual for fees to exceed $1,000 per day plus expenses. The arbitrator's fee and the costs of witness transportation, hotel expenses, time away from work, conference-room expense, and other incidentals can make grievance arbitration very expensive. The size and makeup of the system board create additional expenses.

An interesting aspect of the RLA is that arbitration held under the NRAB is paid by the federal government. Although this expense has been under attack by various government agencies and presidential administrations for many years, the railroad unions have argued that government coverage in this area was part of their agreement to accept statutory, mandated, binding grievance arbitration as a part of the 1926 act.

The RLA provided the airline industry with the NATAB, and one might logically and correctly assume that grievance arbitration in the air transport sector would be at the government's expense if the NMB ever authorized its use. Mediators accustomed to the railroad industry and involved in airline negotiations have espoused the virtues of the NRAB and have suggested that airline management press for the installation of the NATAB, if for no other reason than to reduce expenses. But enactment of the NATAB is highly unlikely for two reasons. First, the system presently utilized by the airline industry and its unions, albeit expensive, is comfortable and familiar. Second, because of the pressures of a federal budget deficit, the government is not likely to approve the additional expenditures by the NMB.

Grievance Arbitration under the National Labor Relations Act

Under the NLRA, no statutory language exists to force the parties to a dispute into arbitration. Without specific contractual language to the contrary, usually embodied in a provision to submit unresolved grievances to arbitration, the parties might use strikes or lockouts to settle such problems. Because these methods are costly to both parties, most negotiated contracts contain some procedure for arbitration. At the present time, approximately 95 percent of all U.S. labor agreements provide for arbitration as the final step in the grievance procedure.[10] Figure 7.3 shows a typical grievance procedure under an NLRA contract.

Although the NLRA does not contain language requiring arbitration, the Supreme Court has stated, "In the absence of any express provision excluding a particular grievance from arbitration, we think only the most forceful evidence of a purpose to exclude the claim from arbitration can prevail, particularly where, as here, the exclusion clause is vague and the arbitration clause quite broad."[11] Consequently, the courts may impose arbitration if the parties do not specifically exclude it in contractual terms.

Overruling Arbitration Decisions

In many decisions rendered by arbitration, one of the parties may contend that the arbitrator overstepped his or her authority in the interpretation of the contract. Contention is less likely to occur in airline disputes than in those of other industries because in the airlines' board of adjustment approach, more than one party is involved in the final decision. In some situations where contention has occurred, companies have ignored the decisions. In others, both

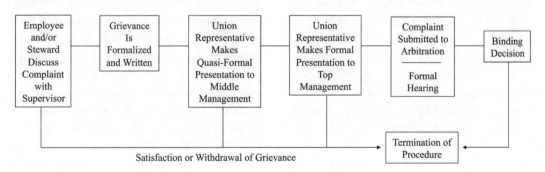

Figure 7.3. National Labor Relations Act airline grievance procedure.

management and the unions have jointly petitioned the courts to set the decisions aside. The arbitrator's decision-making authority and the binding nature of the arbitrator's decision were outlined in the 1960 decision by the Supreme Court preserving the integrity of the arbitrator's award. Upholding an arbitration decision, the Court stated, "Interpretation of the collective bargaining agreement is a question for the arbitrator. It is the arbitrator's construction which was bargained for; and so far as the arbitration decision concerns construction of the contract, the courts have no business overruling him because their interpretation of the contract is different from his."[12]

The importance and significance of this decision is clear. Unions and/or management may not use the courts to set aside an arbitrator's award. In an attempt to alleviate this problem, for both union and management, some agreements contain contractual language stating that in the arbitration process, the arbitrator cannot interpret the contract beyond the intentions of the parties to the agreement. But this language itself can be subject to interpretation. The simplest and most common method of dealing with a decision that is contrary to both union and management interpretation is for them to decide between themselves to disregard the finding.

Selecting an Arbitrator

Most labor agreements provide for the method in which an arbitrator will be selected by the parties. This process generally utilizes the services of the Federal Mediation and Conciliation Service or the American Arbitration Association (see fig. 7.4). When called on, these organizations provide a list of arbitrators, complete with a brief description of their background and a quote of their daily fees. Often, the parties are familiar with several arbitrators on the list, making the selection procedure less trou

Figure 7.4. Logo of the Federal Mediation and Conciliation Service (FMCS), an independent agency of the U.S. government. Founded in 1947, it provides mediation services to industry, community, and government agencies worldwide. The FMCS offers a comprehensive package of services and programs designed to strengthen collective bargaining relationships and reduce conflict. These services include collective bargaining mediation, grievance mediation, programs for repairing broken bargaining relationships, and training in communication and dispute resolution. World Intellectual Property Organization.

blesome. If the arbitrators are unknown, useful information concerning their prior decisions on similar issues may be available from a number of sources, including legal and labor-relations services or reporters. Reports from these sources review an arbitrator's decisions and provide an analysis of the arbitrator's methods and decisions on an issue-by-issue basis.

If the parties cannot agree on an arbitrator who is mutually acceptable, they may resort to a variety of different methods for selection. The most common is the "first strike" method, which employs the flip of a coin. The party that wins the coin toss is allowed to eliminate from the list the name of the arbitrator least desirable to it, and then the opposing side makes the second strike. This process continues, back and forth, until only one name remains. This method, although not scientific, sometimes employs a degree of gamesmanship and maneuvering to arrive at the choice least objectionable to both parties.

Arbitration Costs

Costs associated with the arbitration process under the NLRA do not vary much from those under the RLA, which are listed earlier in this chapter. But under the NLRA, the parties must pay for arbitration out of their own pockets. Usually, these costs are divided equally between the parties.

Grievance Arbitration under the CSRA and State Laws

Under Subchapter III of the Civil Service Reform Act (CSRA), 5 U.S.C. sections 7121–23, federal-employee collective bargaining agreements are required to include procedures for the settlement of grievances, including questions of arbitrability. Such contract procedures are the exclusive procedures for resolving grievances under the contract. The CSRA requires that any such negotiated grievance procedure:

- Be fair and simple
- Provide for expeditious processing
- Assure the union the right to present and process grievances on behalf of employees it represents
- Assure employees the right to bring grievances on their own behalf and assure the union the right to be present during such grievance proceedings
- Provide that any grievance not satisfactorily settled under the negotiated grievance procedure shall be subject to binding arbitration at the request of either party

Either party may file an exception to an arbitrator's award with the Federal Labor Relations Authority (FLRA). The FLRA's statutory scope of review of arbitral awards is narrow, allowing the authority to overturn the award only if it finds at least one of the following:

- The award is contrary to a law, rule, or regulation.
- The award fails to draw its essence from the collective bargaining agreement

- The award is not based on fact.
- The award violates public policy.
- The arbitrator denied the party a fair hearing.
- The arbitrator exceeded his or her authority.
- The award shows bias on the part of the arbitrator.
- The award is ambiguous, incomplete, or contradictory.

FLRA final orders on review of arbitrators' grievance awards are final and not subject to judicial review. The FLRA may petition the appropriate U.S. Court of Appeals for enforcement of its order, if needed.

Among those states that provide union organizing and collective bargaining rights to state and/or local government employees, laws are not uniform but generally prefer binding arbitration of grievances.

Statutory Alternatives to Grievance Procedures

Several pieces of federal legislation have had a significant impact on grievance procedures under both the RLA and the NLRA. Grievances that were adjudicated solely under the agreed provisions of the NLRA or under the statutory mandates of the RLA now have alternative means of redress.

Of major significance is the legislation passed in the areas of Equal Employment Opportunity (EEO), the Occupational Safety and Health Act (OSHA), and the Americans with Disabilities Act (ADA). When an employee files a charge with one of the agencies responsible to administer one of these acts, company and union policies and even the contract's grievance procedure itself are subject to outside scrutiny. The existence of these statutory alternatives inserts the government as a fourth party to the proceedings and makes the entire process more formalized and legalistic. The parties must be more objective in their relationship regarding those areas where a statutory alternative exists.[13]

In cases of dismissal, the employee can seek statutory relief if there is the least indication that the discharge is discriminatory. The employee has the right to include the union as a codefendant if the union refuses to arbitrate the discharge,[14] placing an added incentive on the union to arbitrate even if it does not feel the case has merit.[15] Statutory or contractual grievance machinery and outside agency review can occur simultaneously. These simultaneous reviews can place the grievance adjudicator in an awkward position when deciding complaints because the adjudicator's decision may be overruled by the outside government agency considering the same complaint.

Aggrieved federal employees covered by the Civil Service Reform Act have the option of pursuing statutory relief either through statutory procedures or through the contract's negotiated grievance procedure. They are prohibited from pursuing both routes. For example, a federal employee who believes he or she has suffered discrimination in employment based on race, color, religion, sex, or national origin may complain to the Equal Employment Opportunity Commission (EEOC) or submit the issue as a grievance under the collective bargaining agreement. An employee who is disciplined for unacceptable performance under 5 U.S.C. sec. 7513(d) may seek review by the Merit System Protection Board (MSPB) or submit the matter as a grievance through contract procedures. In federal employment, this either/or requirement serves to promote efficiency and avoid the possibility of conflicting results described above.

Summary

Grievance procedures under the RLA are a matter of law. Under the NLRA, they are purely a matter of contract. Under the CSRA, they are largely a matter of contract, so long as the contractual grievance procedures comply with statutory requirements. Under the RLA, air carriers and their unions must have a system board of adjustment or some other formal, NMB-accepted mechanism for resolving grievances. Over 95 percent of all NLRA-based contracts have some formal grievance-resolution provisions.

When a grievance exhausts the available procedures under the RLA, the issue is submitted to binding arbitration by statute. The CSRA requires that contracts include a provision for resolution of grievances by binding arbitration. Arbitration is optional under the NLRA. The arbitration decision can be set aside by agreement of the parties but not through the courts, because the Supreme Court has ruled that such decisions are beyond the scope of the courts to interpret.

The cost of grievance resolution and arbitration for the railroads under the RLA is provided by the federal government through the NRAB. But grievance and arbitration costs for the airlines and their unions are not government sponsored under the RLA because the duly-authorized NATAB has never been activated by the NMB. Consequently, the cost of grievance resolution and arbitration is provided by the airline and the union equally. The situation is identical for grievance resolution and arbitration costs incurred under NLRA contracts. For federal, state, and local government employees, unless the contract provides or the parties agree otherwise, the arbitrator may assign responsibility for payment of the costs of arbitration in his or her award.

PART THREE. The Changing Labor Relations Environment

8. The Airline Industry

The airline industry is a major component of the U.S. economy, with annual operating revenues of almost $155 billion in 2009. Airlines are both capital intensive, requiring hundreds of billions of dollars of investment in equipment and facilities, and labor intensive, with U.S. airlines employing over 536,000 people in 2009.[1]

Between the passage of the Title II Railroad Labor Act (RLA) amendment in 1936 and the passage of the Airline Deregulation Act of 1978, the U.S. airline industry and the air transport unions developed a workable set of procedures for handling disputes. During this time period, agreements between the carriers and the unions, although at times reached only after protracted strikes, were generally very favorable to the unions in the areas of wages, benefits, and working conditions yet without undue financial impact on the carrier. This latter point seems paradoxical but was the result of a public policy decision to heavily regulate the economics of the air transport sector and the unique nature of that regulation.

Since economic deregulation, the U.S. airline industry has experienced a wild roller-coaster ride with the fluctuations of business cycles, undisciplined excess capacity industry-wide, disruption caused by the terrorist attacks of September 11, 2001 (9/11), and skyrocketing fuel prices beginning in late 2007 (see fig. 8.1). An initial rush of new entries by upstart airlines operating with nonunion labor brought a sudden shock of competition to the market at the dawn of deregulation, and management of established (legacy) carriers struggled to find ways to compete in this rough-and-tumble new business environment. Many of the legacy airlines failed and either reorganized or disappeared through bankruptcy, the latter a route also taken by many failed upstarts. Others were swallowed up in mergers and acquisitions, characterized by extensive reliance on hostile takeovers and leveraged buyouts. To help the airlines survive, labor unions granted wage and benefit concessions or had such concessions forced upon them by the bankruptcy courts. Then the economy perked up, and the industry earned record profits. Unions looked to recoup concessions given in the hard times, with interest. But the highly profitable period again passed, its passing hastened by the consequences of 9/11. In the wake of 9/11, several already struggling carriers turned again to bankruptcy reorganization to survive. No sooner had airline passenger traffic finally returned to pre–9/11 levels than oil prices began to climb at a rate and to heights without precedent, triggering (among other factors) a serious downturn in the U.S. economy.

Historically, fuel expenses have ranged between 10 percent and 15 percent of U.S. passenger airline operating costs, but by mid-2008, they were running between 30 percent and 50 percent. With oil prices doubling within the year between June of 2007 and June of 2008, fuel costs surpassed labor costs for the first time in the history of the industry. Although fuel

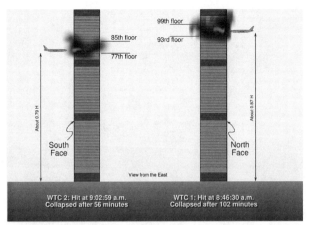

Figure 8.1. Graphic illustration of levels at which airliners struck the World Trade Center on September 11, 2001. Early that morning, nineteen hijackers took control of four commercial airliners en route to San Francisco and Los Angeles from Boston, Newark, and Washington, D.C. The hijackers flew two of the airliners, American Airlines Flight 11 (Boeing 767) and United Airlines Flight 175 (Boeing 767), into the North Tower and South Tower of the World Trade Center in New York City. Another group of hijackers flew American Airlines Flight 77 (Boeing 757) into the Pentagon. A fourth flight, United Airlines Flight 93 (Boeing 757), whose ultimate target was either the U.S. Capitol or the White House, crashed near Shanksville, Pennsylvania. Wikimedia Commons; GNU Free Documentation License, Version 1.3.

prices dropped for the first few months of 2009, they then resumed an inexorable climb, according to the Air Transport Association of America, a trade association of the U.S. airline industry, each dollar's increase in the price of a barrel of oil increases the annual fuel costs of the U.S. airline industry by $465 million.[2] In the spring of 2008, U.S. airlines began serious capacity reductions: retiring hundreds of older, less–fuel-efficient aircraft; dropping unprofitable routes; reducing workforces; and looking again toward mergers and acquisitions (and reorganization in bankruptcy) for routes to survival. Through it all, airline workers have seen reductions in pay, benefits, and job security as they have granted negotiated concessions in efforts to help their airlines survive or had such losses forced upon them by the

bankruptcy courts. Others have lost jobs to cutbacks (downsizing) and outsourcing. Airline management and employees alike may feel that they're on the receiving end of the ancient Chinese curse "May you live in interesting times."

The Era of Economic Regulation by the CAB

Air transport economic regulation had its formal beginnings with the passage of the Civil Aeronautics Act of 1938. This act created the Civil Aeronautics Authority, the Administrator of Aeronautics, and the Air Safety Board. In 1940, the Civil Aeronautics Authority and the Air Safety Board were combined into the Civil Aeronautics Board (CAB). The CAB was granted broad economic regulatory power, and until the board began moving toward a deregulated posture in 1976, it controlled virtually every aspect of airline economic operation.

Certificates of Public Convenience

In 1938, when industry regulation began, the Civil Aeronautics Authority granted only sixteen Certificates of Public Convenience and Necessity to airlines that the authority felt were financially strong enough to survive. Under the 1938 act, a carrier was required to have such a certificate before it could operate scheduled air service or carry U.S. mail. A regulated and controlled airline environment was put in place.

The authority to issue and rescind operating certificates and the other economic policy tools available to the CAB allowed it to:

- Control the number of carriers permitted to operate in the U.S.
- Control the entrance or exit from a particular city pair market (no carrier could enter or stop serving a market without CAB approval)
- Control fares by approving, modifying, or rejecting the fare requests of individual

carriers or by directly setting the exact fare or a narrow range of permissible fares in each city pair market

- Regulate the rate of return and profit an airline could earn[3]

In addition, only the CAB could award new routes, and it had absolute authority over mergers and acquisitions. In general, the CAB took a restrictive view of mergers, and often, instead of allowing a financially distressed carrier to merge, it would grant monopoly route awards to that airline in an attempt to strengthen the carrier and maintain stability in the industry.[4] According to Nawal K. Taneja, professor and chairman of the Department of Aviation at the Ohio State University, this regulation had a profound impact on labor-management relations in the industry, specifically in the areas of certification rejection, mergers, fare provisions, and the existence of the Mutual Aid Pact, which was a CAB-authorized program.[5]

Certification rejection. The CAB's powers were enhanced substantively by the passage of the 1958 Federal Aviation Act, which contained the provision that a carrier holding a Certificate of Public Convenience and Necessity had to be in full compliance with the RLA. This provision had great impact on the labor-relations process and placed the CAB in the position of deciding whether a carrier was acting in good faith in terms of the RLA. A carrier's failure to bargain in good faith with its unions could allow the CAB to rescind the carrier's operating certificate. For example, in 1962, the Air Line Pilots Association (ALPA) presented arguments to the CAB that Southern Airlines had failed to engage in good-faith negotiations. In that case, the board demanded that Southern begin negotiating in good faith with ALPA or face the consequences of losing its operating certificate.

This broad, discretionary power remained a part of the CAB until it ceased operations, or sunset, in 1984. It placed the collective bargaining

efforts of the carriers under the scrutiny of not only the National Mediation Board and the union itself but also a third party, the CAB. The CAB could independently consider whether the carrier's negotiating styles were in good faith and thus enforce statutory remedies that were not available to the National Mediation Board through the RLA.

Mergers

The CAB controlled not only whether carriers could merge but also the terms and provisions of any mergers and/or route transfers. Consequently, the board could, and often did, provide job protection for the employees and the unions affected by any mergers. These CAB-managed mergers and transfers provided an umbrella of protection for craft positions, wage and benefit levels, and seniority rights during mergers. For example, in the 1961 merger of United Air Lines and Capital Airlines, provisions for integration of seniority lists, based on length of service, were standardized.[6] Thus, an employee of an acquired airline could bump employees of the surviving airline if he or she had more seniority in a particular craft or class determination.

Fare Provisions

The CAB was given the dual role of both regulating and promoting the air transportation industry. Therefore, if the industry faced cost increases because of high wage-settlement agreements with the unions, these cost increases would usually be passed on to the consumers through a tariff-adjustment application—submitted to the CAB by the carrier—for a series of fare increases that would cover the increases in labor costs. The existence of this financial security blanket tended to increase the bargaining power of the unions.[7] In airline terminology, a *tariff* encompasses the total agreement between the airline and the passenger or shipper, although the price is the predominant factor in most tariff discussions.[8]

The Mutual Aid Pact

The airline Mutual Aid Pact, approved and supported by the CAB, was designed to increase the bargaining power of airline management by increasing the ability of a carrier to withstand a strike. Prior to the existence of the pact, consensus among airline management was that labor had far greater bargaining power than management. This opinion was based partially on the nature of the industry and partially on the language of the RLA. To shift the balance in favor of management, the airlines began as early as 1947 to look for ways to cooperate among themselves. By 1958, Capital Airlines, faced with a strike by the International Association of Machinists, convinced six airlines to agree to the initial Mutual Aid Pact, a form of strike insurance.

The provisions of the Mutual Aid Pact included recovery by the struck carrier of "windfall revenues" to other carriers if the strike resulted from one or more of the following:

- Union demands in excess of those recommended by the emergency board
- A strike called prior to the exhaustion of prestrike procedures under the RLA
- An otherwise unlawful strike

Windfall revenue is the increase in traffic and revenues received by the unaffected carriers. If three airlines served the Charlotte, North Carolina–Washington, D.C., route, and one of these carriers was struck, its competitors could expect to pick up the struck carrier's passengers during the term of the strike. The Mutual Aid Pact was designed to return to the struck carrier a portion of the increased revenue received by the pact carriers attributable to the strike less the added expense of carrying the additional traffic. The carrier struck, in return, was to make every reasonable effort to provide the public with information concerning air service offered by the other carriers in the pact.[9]

Shuffling toward Deregulation

A general move away from excessive government regulation of industry began to emerge in the early 1970s. Proponents of industry deregulation cited the banking industry, the telecommunications industry, and the transportation industry—more specifically, the trucking and the airline sectors—as industries in which government regulation actually worked to the disservice of the American public.[10] Conceptually, the proponents of deregulation cited consumer welfare and freedom of choice as the driving factors, believing that free and competitive markets would provide more and better products, promote greater efficiency, and lower prices for comparable competitive services. In some instances, this belief was correct, as the deregulation of the telephone industry has proved. Certainly, the antithetical result was the banking industry, where unbridled, undisciplined, and illegal activities resulted in a bailout that cost the taxpayers $500 billion. Whether these expanded services and products have improved the lot of the average citizen is a point of conjecture and continuing argument.

On October 8, 1975, President Gerald R. Ford proposed legislation that would reduce the authority of the CAB to regulate the airlines. The proposed legislation was based on the premise that the airline industry had outgrown the need for protective regulation by the government. In a message to Congress, Ford adamantly stated, "[T]he rigidly controlled regulatory structure now serves to stifle competition, increase costs to travelers, makes the industry less efficient than it could be and denies large segments of the American public access to lower cost air transportation."[11] To accommodate the American public, Ford suggested that the CAB's control over the availability and pricing of airline services be relaxed.

In 1976, the CAB, under the chairmanship of John Robson, began to move away from the restrictive policy posture of the previous thirty-eight years. Under Robson, the board reversed its policy of not allowing discount fares and permitted Texas International Airlines to begin its "Peanuts" fare and American Airlines to begin its "SuperSaver" fare. These discount fares were quickly followed by similar discount fares offered by other airlines. Robson also became the first CAB chairman to advocate airline deregulation.

When Alfred E. Kahn became CAB chairman on June 10, 1977, the board accelerated its move toward less economic regulation. The CAB gave airlines even wider latitude to experiment with discount fares. In addition, the CAB expressly stated and stressed fare reductions as an important factor in the selection of applicants for new route authorities—a major shift from the CAB's previous policies.

Under Kahn, the CAB also no longer considered a carrier's financial need in making route awards. The board no longer forced cross-subsidization by awarding long-haul routes to subsidized short-haul carriers. The CAB shifted the burden of proof in route proceedings from the applicant to those opposing the new route authorities. Diversion of traffic and revenue from an incumbent carrier was no longer a sufficient reason for denying new route authority in markets with little or no competition. Kahn suggested that the CAB eventually allow all applicants found "fit, willing, and able" to compete on any routes they wished to serve.[12]

Deregulation, Competition, and Consequences

Whatever the rationale or intent behind the push for deregulation, Congress enacted the Airline Deregulation Act on October 24, 1978, which ended the CAB's economic regulation of the airline industry. If the case for deregulation stressed concerns for the welfare and choices of the public, it had little or no concern with the affected labor markets or collective bargaining agreements in the industry. In the intellectual world, the case was established for deregulation of product markets—for example, fares, rates, entry, and quality of service—but there was no consideration of its consequences or impact in the short run or over a longer term, or on labor markets, the collective bargaining process, wage and benefit levels, unemployment, and so on. This lack of foresight had significant impact in the years to come.[13] A highly sophisticated system had developed under regulation. The failure to manage the transition from regulation to deregulation led to a fragmented labor-relations system.

The Airline Deregulation Act of 1978 prescribed the process by which the gradual removal of economic control over the industry was to occur. The 1978 act did not mandate the immediate and total deregulation of the industry that then president Jimmy Carter had suggested. The act was directed toward redesigning the existing regulatory structure to ease the transition to eventual removal of regulatory controls. All the entry and pricing barriers were not eliminated until 1983, and the CAB did not cease operations, or sunset, until December 1984.

Small-Community Air Service

Prior to passage of the act, certain compromises were made to satisfy concerns over the consequences of deregulation. There were major concerns that deregulation would have adverse effects on aviation safety. The act's declaration of policy contained a clause emphasizing the preeminence of safety. In addition, many in Congress believed that the abrupt elimination of regulations was too drastic a measure, so the act provided for a slow transition period, which included a sunset provision. Small communities feared losing air service. The act guaranteed air service for ten years to all communities served at the time of passage. The program has continued unabated for thirty years, but its efficacy has been called into question by the DOT, and at this writing

Congress is considering possible reforms to this program as part of its larger reauthorization of aviation programs.

Labor Protective Provisions

Lastly, Congress was aware that deregulation could have negative impacts on airline employees who "entered the industry and shaped their careers in reliance on a regulatory system which gave them a measure of job security."[14] Therefore, the legislation contained labor-protection provisions to ensure safeguards for employees.

In March 1979, the Department of Labor initiated a program designed to accomplish this policy objective. It provided a ceiling of $1,800 a month for a "protected employee" who lost his or her position due to the effects of deregulation. The DOL defined one group of protected employees as those with four years' continuous service who lost their jobs for reasons other than just cause. Benefits would include monthly allotment checks, relocation funds, and first right-of-hire at another airline. A second group of protected employees included those who worked for an airline that had lost at least 7.5 percent of its workforce or that had filed bankruptcy. To initiate benefits for the latter, the CAB would be required to rule that the layoffs or the bankruptcy had been caused by deregulation before benefits could begin. The program for unemployed airline employees included referrals to state agencies, and the DOL was the focal point for information, compiling lists of those affected for regular release to state agencies.

Immediately prior to the intended implementation date, the program came under fire. Captain John O'Donnell, then president of ALPA, immediately took issue with the $1,800 ceiling for an ex–airline employee. An ALPA spokesman stated, "[T]hat amount is simply not enough for a pilot."[15] That argument was made moot, however, because Congress never appropriated any money to fund the program, and as a result,

the statute's promised financial assistance was never forthcoming. Finally, carriers were less than enthusiastic about being forced to hire employees of other airlines, and this portion of the plan met with only moderate success. All these concerns had an impact on the airlines. But the question of job security became the most important and vigorously negotiated item by the employees and their union representatives.

Legacy Airlines

According to data from the U.S. Department of Transportation, forty-two Section 401 carriers were grandfathered into the act in October 1978 as preexisting carriers:

Airlift	Flying Tiger	Reeve
Air Micronesia	Frontier	Rich
Air Midwest	Hawaiian	Seaboard
Air New England	Hughes Airwest	Southern
	Kodiak	Texas
Alaska	Munz	International
Aloha	National	Transamerica
American	New York	Trans World
Aspen	North Central	United
Braniff	Northwest	USAir
Capitol	Overseas	Wien
Continental	National	Western
Delta	Ozark	World
Eastern	Pan American	Wright
Evergreen	Piedmont	Zantop

Shifting from Regulation to Competition

Prior to deregulation, the CAB was responsible for setting fare levels based on actual industry costs. This system enabled the existing airlines to place the expense of each carrier's new labor agreement into the overall rate structure, which allowed the carriers to recover the increased costs. These fares were used by all domestic airlines, and a certain level of consistency and understanding was instilled in the minds of those responsible for running the airline industry. With strict levels of conformity, there was little incentive for a company to resist excessive union demands, which, if not acceded to, could result in a potentially expensive strike for the airline. Because of this management mindset, airlines generally made the allowances requested by the labor organizations and passed the costs through the adjusted general-fare level set by the CAB.[16]

With the advent of deregulation, there was no longer a regulated route franchise to protect high-yield domestic routes from free entry by competing carriers. Carriers added new routes and city pairs rapidly because restrictions on entry were lifted and because the CAB had implemented and expedited procedures that significantly opened the air transport route structure. Deregulation also meant the demise of the Mutual Aid Pact. Airline managers found themselves without a tool to offset strike losses. The fundamental problem faced by the airlines was the inability, directly or indirectly, to defer the high costs of the labor-contract structure per unit, let alone any increases demanded by the unions. With the demise of the Mutual Aid Pact, there was also no way to mitigate the cost of a strike. This appeared to strengthen the unions' bargaining power.

The passage of the act gave the airline industry many options. Managers were free to restructure their networks and gain control over their product lines. These new freedoms required carriers to make fundamental decisions about their future decisions that some were willing to make quickly. Others took a wait-and-see attitude.

Most airline management concerns and activities in the first year of deregulation were directed not at learning how to compete in a deregulated market but at how to prevent the new entrants from eroding market share. The existing majors began to develop defensive marketing plans.

One year after the act was passed, and while the CAB still maintained control over pricing arrangements, the CAB responded to the concerns of the higher unit costs faced by the industry by matching them with increases of the standard industry fare level. But starting in mid-1979, the airline industry suffered serious financial losses that were primarily due to effects beyond the CAB's control or influence. The principal culprit creating sharply reduced airline net profits in late 1979 appears to have been "a managerial lag in reducing capacity offerings and cost structures rather than a regulatory lag. However, this managerial lag is eminently understandable. The industry was confronted with many developments that departed sharply from historical precedents."[17]

In 1979, nineteen new carriers entered the marketplace. The first wave of mergers took place, with North Central Airlines and Southern combining to form Republic and with National being absorbed by Eastern. Two other carriers, Apollo and New York Air, ceased operation. Table 8.1 lists the new carriers that entered the marketplace and the old carriers that exited. The new market entries triggered a series of fare wars that had disastrous consequences on income and profitability and directly impacted the collective bargaining process. These fare wars eventually forced the airlines to negotiate aggressively for lowered labor costs.

Also in 1979, a massive profit decline driven by this fare competition began. In 1978, the trunk carriers generated operating profits of $1.2 billion. By 1981, the trunk carriers had suffered operating losses of $672 million, a swing of $1.9 billion dollars.

Fare Wars

Coming off a fifty-eight-day machinist strike in 1979, United Air Lines initiated a half-fare–coupon promotion to try to win back some of the customers it had lost to new entrants. Retaliation followed, as other airlines not only matched fares but also created a variety of combinations of reduced fares that made proponents of deregulation smile at the windfall the paying passenger was receiving. With new, low-cost, nonunion carriers entering the marketplace, competition in the area of lower fares became increasingly disastrous to the unionized carriers. Price wars became commonplace. Price-cutting of as much as 75 percent of regulated-era fares became the norm. With wages established by contract, existing carriers were forced to match the prices of the new carriers without the ability to lower costs. These fare wars, promulgated by the new entrants' lower cost structures, caused the unionized carriers to seek immediate solutions. The fare wars set the stage for demands of wage and benefit concessions. Several carriers even formally requested their unions to open negotiations in advance of established contract amendment dates.

As the fare wars continued, market analysts were seeing airline losses so catastrophic that they questioned the ability of some airlines to ever recover. In an article for *Forbes Magazine*, Harold Seneker wrote, "So what this game is really about is: Who will have to draw back from the brink first; Who will have to choose first between owning the routes and owning the more fuel efficient planes the airlines must have in the future? It is a trench war whose Verdun is New York–California. If it long continues without some sort of de-facto truce, even winners may be bled white."[18]

Managing for Competitiveness

Aside from the price wars that developed, incumbent carriers were forced to adopt new managerial strategies. They now had to manage costs and generate revenues to achieve a profitable return, instead of collecting monopolistic revenues guaranteed by the CAB to return an acceptable profit irrespective of costs. During the initial years of deregulation, the airlines were faced with the challenge of new entrants in the marketplace and had to develop new plans for future viability. No one particular approach was followed by all airlines in answering questions of expansion, maintenance of market share, fares, and route structure. Instead, each airline followed its own path, based on its own management capabilities, experiences, and capital structure and on the conservative or liberal policies held by its management and boards of directors. But every airline had to take a hard look at its biggest cost: labor.

The Fuel Crisis of 1979

The depressed economic conditions and fuel crisis of 1979 were beyond direct control of the airlines, but many members of the industry made crippling strategic errors in other areas. The most prominent error was made by Braniff International Airways.[19] Braniff saw deregulation as an opportunity to expand its route structure. It was the first airline to apply for "automatic market entry" of unused routes made available by the sunsetting CAB. Although other airlines (Continental, North Central, Pan American, and Texas International) also followed an expansion philosophy, no one did so with the same vigor as Braniff. This monomaniacal approach, without consideration for costs, market surveys, and equipment, ended in the nation's first casualty of deregulation: Braniff's Chapter 11 bankruptcy two years later.

Another option pursued by many airlines was to utilize the financial mechanism that became the trademark of Texas International. The airlines began to form holding companies. This financial restructuring allowed the carriers to start up a low-cost nonunion airline, owned by the holding company that also owned a union carrier. Texas International started such an airline, New York Air, in 1980.

Very few contracts were scheduled to open for amendment during 1979. As a result, there were few changes in the collective bargaining process. But the stage was set for massive changes in 1980, when fourteen new carriers entered the marketplace, two existing carriers merged, and one airline exited the market (see table 8.2).

Table 8.1.
Section 401 carrier-certification activity in 1979

New carriers entering	Carriers exiting		
	Merged or sold	Waivers	Financial
Aeromech	National	Apollo	New York Airways
Air Cal	North Central		
Air Florida	Southern Airlines		
Air Wisconsin			
Altair			
Apollo			
Big Sky			
Empire			
Golden West			
Mackey			
Mid South			
Midway			
Mississippi Valley			
Pacific Southwest			
Republic			
Sky West			
Southeast			
Southwest			
Swift Aire Lines			

Table 8.2.
Section 401 carrier-certification activity in 1980

New carriers entering	Carriers exiting		
	Merged or sold	Waivers	Financial
Air North	Hughes Airwest	None	Mackey
American Eagle	Seaboard		
Cascade			
Flagship			
Golden Gate			
Great American			
Imperial			
International			
New Air			
New York Air			
Rocky Mountain			
Southern Air Trans			
Sun Land			
T-Bird			

Double-Breasting

The most controversial new entrant in 1980 was New York Air, a subsidiary of Texas Air Corporation (see fig. 8.2). The impact of the creating of New York Air as a nonunion entity of Texas Air, a highly unionized carrier, was felt almost immediately. Existing carriers embraced the concept, the National Mediation Board (NMB) was perplexed by the novelty, and the airline unions fought to curtail this approach. They viewed it as a threat by management to transfer, through manipulation, bargained work, corporate assets, and jobs. This complaint existed into the late 1980s at Eastern Airlines. The chairman of Eastern, Frank Lorenzo, transferred routes, equipment, and assets to Eastern's parent company, the same Texas Air Corporation.

This *double-breasting*, as it was called, was not a new phenomenon in the labor arena. The practice of transferring union work to nonunion companies owned by the same corporation has existed in other business sectors, and the National Labor Relations Board (NLRB) had addressed the situation numerous times in those sectors. But the concept gained wide acceptance in the airline industry as one airline after another took measures to capitalize on the new windfall, seeing the potential to rid themselves of the unions.

Indicative of the popularity of the approach were some of the changes made and holding companies created. Name changes and corporate identities took on new meanings. Alaska Airlines Inc. became Alaska Air Group Inc.; American Airlines became AMR Corporation; Northwest Orient became NWA Inc.; Ozark Air Lines Inc. became Ozark Holdings Inc.; Pan Am World Airlines became Pan Am Corporation; Peoples Express and Frontier Airlines became Peoples Express Inc.; Piedmont Airlines became Piedmont Aviation Inc.; Trans World Airlines became Trans World Corp.; USAir became USAir Group Inc.; and Continental Airlines, New York Air, Texas International, and Eastern Air became Texas Air Corporation.

Although some of the former corporations and holding companies existed in form before the creation of New York Air, the methods were put in place to ensure the ability of the corporations to assume new arrangements when and if the time came to form a new, nonunion carrier. Ozark Air Lines formed Ozark Holdings without any intention to operate a subsidiary carrier, intending, instead, to use the ploy as negotiating leverage with all their unions—in particular with the Aircraft Mechanics Fraternal Association (AMFA), which represented the mechanics and which had struck the airline on numerous occasions. So intent was the airline to use such strategy that Ozark Holdings was formalized and signed while the parties were in direct negotiations, and within one hour of its birth, the issue was presented at the negotiating table by management.

Figure 8.2. New York Air DC-9. New York Air's first flight was between New York and Boston in December 1980. The airline initially expanded rapidly, but mounting losses created a commercial crisis in early 1982. The airline employed over two thousand people before it was acquired by Continental Airlines in 1986. In February 1987, New York Air, People Express, and several commuter carriers were integrated into Continental Airlines to create the sixth-largest airline in the world. New York Air operated about forty aircraft painted in a red color scheme with an apple on the aircraft tail and the FAA-assigned radio call sign "Apple" evoking New York City's nickname "the Big Apple." Source: Wikimedia Commons; photo by Eduard Marmet; GNU Free Documentation License, Version 1.3.

Texas Air's establishment of the nonunion New York Air was challenged by the unions, particularly by the Air Line Pilots Association. The ALPA sought to dismantle the maneuver in federal court, contending that Texas Air Corporation had violated the tenets of the RLA. The ALPA's contention was that it was the certified collective bargaining representative for Texas International Airlines and that New York Air was simply an alter ego or extension of that airline. The ALPA cited transference of landing slots at various airports by Texas Air to New York Air. The ALPA also cited management, technical assistance, financial resources, and cross-leased aircraft as indications that the two airlines were for all purposes one and the same.

The court granted Texas Air's motion to dismiss the case, and this decision was affirmed by a court of appeals, which contended that the issue was one of representation under the RLA and therefore fell within the purview of the NMB. The board was to rule on the issue in case 8 NMB 217, but prior to the ruling, the merger of Texas International Air and Continental and

Continental's subsequent filing for bankruptcy protection completely overshadowed the original issue, and no NMB decision was ever rendered.

The First Two-Tier Wage Scales

Meanwhile, the failed union challenge to Texas Air's establishment of the nonunion New York Air left the unions with only one viable approach to counter such tactics: to negotiate scope language that would recognize the unions for any alter-ego carrier established under the holding-company concept. But such negotiations were not accomplished without a price, because management demanded an extensive quid pro quo. The eventual costs were concessions and the establishment of B scales for new employees on a number of airlines, whereby new hires began work at a lower rate of pay than in the past, usually catching up with the old (A) pay scale—typically in two to five years.

In 1981, thirteen new carriers entered the market, two existing carriers were sold or merged, and five carriers ceased operation for financial reasons (see table 8.3). The difficult labor relations

Table 8.3.
Section 401 carrier-certification activity in 1981

New carriers entering	Carriers exiting		
	Merged or sold	Waivers	Financial
Air Nevada	Aeromech	None	Air New England
Aerostar International	Aspen		American Eagle
American Transair			Apollo
Arrow			Golden Gate
Challenge			Swift Aire
Colgan			
Global			
Gulf			
Jet America			
Midstates			
Muse/Transtar			
Peoples Express			
South Pacific			

environment was exacerbated by a continuing economic recession. The financial position of the industry had worsened, with major carrier losses of $550 million for the year. Prospects were also grim for airline employees. Despite union attempts to curtail layoffs, seventeen thousand employees received furlough papers that year.

Enter Concessionary Bargaining

The fare wars continued, and as with any war ever fought, the costs to wage the battle had to be funded somehow. Financially vulnerable carriers sought to attack the only variable cost that could offset their losses: labor costs. Labor concessions and lower labor costs became the major focus of contractual negotiations. Management sought concessions and work-rule changes for cost reduction. Unions sought to preserve the status quo. In general, neither party concerned itself with the other's needs or well-being. The "piper" of past negotiations was beginning to be paid.

Several financially vulnerable carriers were able to secure concessions and lower labor costs from unions desiring to reduce expected employment losses. As encouraging as these achievements were from a cooperation standpoint, it created a bandwagon effect as the more financially stable carriers were placed at a cost disadvantage. The bandwagon now called for concessions from unions at all carriers, and union concessions became the byline of the management position.

A Perceptive and Prophetic Assessment

In 1980, New York market analyst Robert J. Joedicke wrote one of the most insightful and accurate assessments of the impact of deregulation, an analysis titled "The Goose That Laid Golden Eggs."[20] Although the analysis was written for the benefit of investors interested and concerned about the future financial outlook of the air transport sector, Joedicke had no way of knowing the profound impact deregulation would have. His observations were based only on the first two years of the deregulated environment. Joedicke did not know how accurate his predictions would turn out to be.

Excerpts of Joedicke's analysis appear in case study 8.1. This analysis provides the reader not only with an appreciation of Joedicke's views but also with an understanding of the historical developments that impact the air transport industry. Aside from providing a snapshot of the industry in 1980, it examines the industry's responses to deregulation as the airlines moved from the closed environment of stringent economic regulation to a laissez-faire, open-market environment. This article also serves as a backdrop for examining the status of the industry as it exists today.

Case Study 8.1: The Goose That Laid Golden Eggs

Once upon a time, so the story goes, a goose that laid golden eggs was killed by its owner, who hoped to get all the gold at once. The moral of this parable might aptly be applied to the airline industry today. The major losers could be management and employees of the large carriers. In fact, they may find their goose is cooked if a new industry danger is not faced squarely. Meanwhile, many shareholders in recent times have been receiving only goose eggs as far as dividends are concerned.

Nor is the gold flowing to produce necessary profits, since cash flow has already dried up to a mere trickle. This financial weakness is sharply restricting funds available for most carriers to modernize their capital plant for greater efficiency.

The problem is productivity, and the only long-term solution is greater effort by the workforce and better utilization of existing capital plant. More efficient new generation jets of medium size will become available within a couple of years, but these planes will have a high capital cost per seat as a result of inflation, as well as inclusion of advanced technology equipment. As a result, increasing debt commitments must also be served.

The airline industry today. The transportation area has always provided a labor of love for some, ever since lads ran away to sea on sailing ships. Then the railroads had their day when boomers roamed the High Iron throughout America. More recently, transportation buffs were attracted to the airlines following the derring-do of early aviators in the era of the leather cap, goggles, and white silk scarves.

Much of the romanticism in conquering the skies is long gone, and the airline field is now big business, generating $173 billion of annual revenue for U.S. carriers. The entire industry currently employs close to six hundred thousand people, while tens of thousands more work for ancillary and support operations. The U.S. Travel Data Center estimates that the overall travel field provides employment for over five million people, or 9 percent of all jobs in the United States.

Service industries are very labor intensive. Employee costs in the airline industry account for over 35 percent of cash operating expenses, and the average annual compensation per employee reached $33,580 by the end of September 1980. A majority of the workforce has been unionized for some time; several craft unions, such as the thirty-three thousand member Air Line Pilots Association (ALPA), trace their founding back to the early 1930s.

As a result, the organized airline labor field is also big business, with total union membership near the quarter-million mark. Union officers administer noteworthy assets, and executive-type jets are available to whisk them to meetings around the country.

Much has already been written about changes following the Airline Deregulation Act of 1978 as it has affected route networks and fare structures, since these trends actually began to emerge before passage of the act. Little has been said about the way in which the new climate is markedly altering the airline labor picture. The intent of deregulation was to foster competition in the airline industry, with the result that the number of carriers on many important routes has increased over the past two years and pricing flexibility is evident on all fronts.

However, few industry observers appreciate the fact that this legislation has also produced a competitive labor situation as a result of the emergence of new nonunion airlines. In this regard, CAB Chairman Kahn stated in a recent speech in New York that "There is a revolution at hand, and that revolution has been made possible by deregulation." He also noted that "the combined effect of government intervention, in all its forms, permitted labor costs to increase at a rate which, while within the productivity gains made possible by technological advances, was far in excess of the market for comparable skills."

We expect the industry may well face a peck of trouble in this area over the next several years until a new modus Vivendi is achieved in labor relations, one based on management and union leadership working together.

The latest industry challenge. Adjustment to the changed circumstances under deregulation is proving particularly difficult for all parties since the airline industry is already encrusted with some diehard traditions. In addition, the problem of transition is being exacerbated by rampant cost inflation, paced by price escalation of fuel which now accounts for 32 percent of industry cash operating expenses. This dilemma is necessitating acceleration in retirement of fuel-inefficient jets at a time when cash flow is inadequate to meet the massive capital expenditures required for their replacement.

Sagging traffic demand, accentuated by erosion of discretionary income for the populace, is also another important factor at the moment. Passenger volume in 1980 was down around 5 percent from the prior year. Records back to 1927 indicate only two years of decline (1948 and 1975), but these annual downturns were both less than one half of one percent. No one expects a sharp upturn of volume in the near future.

This story may not be a tale wherein "everyone lives happily ever after," since we foresee a period of major labor unrest for the airlines until the realities of the new order are recognized by unions and management alike. Some union leaders have belatedly been petitioning the Federal government to take a critical look at the effects of deregulation, but it is clearly too late to "put Humpty Dumpty back on the wall."

. . . Deregulation can be viewed as a two-edged sword capable of drawing blood. We look for some blood-letting affecting most parties involved, but hope that a blood bath will not occur. Nevertheless, some airlines may not survive under the current laissez-faire attitude fostered by Washington, while others are likely to prosper by achieving new peak earnings, and we are already seeing indications of this dichotomy. Whichever the case, the astute investor should be interested in the details of the new labor situation since it will become an increasingly important consideration in shaping investment selections within the airline group.

Labor climate before deregulation: The history of union activity. Since 1936 interstate airlines have come under the jurisdiction of the Railway Labor Act, with its provisions for mediation and arbitration through the National Mediation Board, as well as for "cooling-off" periods before legal work stoppages can take place. Thus, it has not been unusual that union members continue to work for months beyond an amendable contract date until a new accord is achieved. Union agreements under the Railway Labor Act only become amendable but do not expire as in the case of most other industries, unless a strike occurs.

Organization of the workforce within the airline field has traditionally been based on separate representations for most of the major crafts, as opposed to companywide memberships such as exist in the automobile and steel industries. As a result, many of the large trunks have a dozen or more labor contracts in force, with varying renewal dates. The degree of employee membership varies among the established scheduled carriers, but active union organization over the years in this labor intensive field has produced coverage ranging from around 60 percent of the headcount to over 90 percent unionization today.

There are 21 separate unions certified within the airline industry, although several (e.g., Air Line Pilots Association; International Association of Machinists; and the Transport Workers Union) hold broad certification embracing numerous carriers. The ten trunks alone have a total of 173 individual contracts in effect today, but some are negotiated on a group basis by a single union. This fragmentation of representation has sharply increased the potential for strikes over the years. The average 2–3-year contract period produces incessant labor negotiation for most airlines.

Historically, Delta was the only major exception to this widespread unionization of the airline industry prior to deregulation. The company continues to have very limited union membership, which is restricted to the pilot cadre and a small group of dispatchers. Even its organized flight officers have a unique rapport with the company. This relationship was evident in early 1974 when jet-fuel allocation required a major cutback in operations. No layoffs were made, but many pilots temporarily took on other chores, including the fueling of aircraft and handling of baggage.

This lack of union representation at Delta may partially reflect a traditional disinclination toward organized labor in the South, particularly since the company has always provided wage levels comparable to or better than those of its peers. However, the main reason was paternalistic guidance in the formative years by the company's founder and unique long-time leader, who molded an esprit de corps among the staff to the point that employees view themselves more as a family working together.

The end result is that Delta has not been faced with the same degree of restrictive and costly contract conditions resulting from work rules and duty assignments embodied in most union agreements. In return, its employees enjoy job security without layoffs and benefit from a policy of promotion from within the ranks. It is of interest to note that a recently retired chief executive officer of Delta was one of the original organizers of its pilots union in the 1930s.

It was no accident that Delta led the industry in profits during 1980, while many other trunk airlines were generating record losses. An entente cordiale with labor is a key factor in its continuing financial success.

There was a rather unique arrangement within the airline industry for twenty years prior to deregulation. The Mutual Aid Pact among a majority of the large scheduled airlines was first approved by the CAB in 1958 to permit financial aid to a struck airline under a formula basis intended to defray the fixed expenses and compensate for diverted traffic during a work stoppage. Over half a billion dollars in mutual aid was paid under this agreement until its demise under provisions of the Airline Deregulation Act of 1978.

The success of labor bargaining. Airline labor negotiations involve three distinct considerations. The most visible aspect is basic wage rates, although fringe benefits paid by the employer have increased even more sharply in recent years and are very expensive, particularly when applied retroactively on a length of service basis. The third major area is work rules, but the cost importance of this feature is not widely appreciated. Restrictive work rules do not increase the average compensation per employee, but they do inflate the number of employees required to run an operation by decreasing the average productivity per employee—a real concern of American industry today.

In any case, there is no doubt as to the success of airline union negotiators in gaining above-average increases for their members, at least up to the time of deregulation. The average annual percentage increase in compensation per employee was 9.9 percent for the airline industry in the 1969–79 period, as compared with an 8.1 percent average for all U.S. industry. This differential added $1.5 billion to total airline labor costs in 1979 alone.

Unfortunately, one measure of a successful labor leader is the gains he can achieve for the rank and file, irrespective of whether the company can make sufficient profit to cover the increases. It is more difficult for an airline to accept a strike than for most other industries because of an inability to maintain market presence by selling its products from inventory during a shutdown. . . .

. . . [S]uffice to say at this point that the pervasive deregulation legislation is not protecting those airlines with inordinately high unit labor costs. The CAB does not require uniform fares pegged at levels high enough to compensate carriers with an above-average cost structure.

In other words, the "closed shop" situation that existed prior to deregulation has evaporated, and the necessary gains in employee productivity now required by unionized carriers cannot be achieved solely by acquisition of more efficient aircraft, if the established carriers are to compete successfully with the newer unorganized entrants. . . .

In spite of continuing wage escalation, it is obvious that fringe benefits have become an increasing proportion of total employee compensation, the expense of which is inflating unit operating costs of the established carriers. In addition, there are sizable liabilities for unfunded but vested past-service costs, which totaled around $1.5 billion for the trunk group of airlines at the end of 1979. . . .

The end result of these developments has been a steady gain in the average employee compensation within the airline industry that has outpaced the rise in the Consumer Price Index. It can also be noted that average passenger yields have not increased as rapidly to produce the commensurate gains in revenue required to support these escalating labor costs. . . .

The facts suggest it is high time for a new attitude by all parties to replace the traditional stance of adversaries on opposite sides of the bargaining table with a spirit of cooperation for mutual benefit. Such action has occurred in the past only when individual airlines have been in financial distress to such a degree that union membership has felt threatened as to its very livelihood.

Such brinkmanship indicates a lack of management ability to convey the seriousness of the problem and a lack of willingness on the part of union leaders to face the inevitable, before excessive financial deterioration occurs. Nevertheless, a company cannot solve the problem alone. Management does not negotiate from strength as in the past, so it must rely more on creating an appreciation of the critical situation.

Labor officials must exhibit leadership and integrity, even though internal union politics can make an unpopular stand difficult to gain acceptance. Changing union representation to naive candidates who promise unrealistic goals to the rank-and-file will not change the outcome in the long run since it will be impossible "to get blood out of a stone" under the existing climate. . . .

Thus it should be patently clear that the fallout effect of airline deregulation is now sifting down on labor to becloud its favorable climate of the past that permitted above average gains in total benefits without offsetting increases in productivity.

It is to be hoped that the proverb "None so blind as those who do not want to see" will not prevail in this murky situation.

Make no mistake, the proliferation of non-union airlines is already producing an increasing threat to the financial viability of some mature trunks, and further deterioration will take place if steps are not taken promptly to improve profitability. Neither wishing nor blustering will change the inexorable trends, even though some may not be willing to accept the verity of the harsh facts facing the airline industry under deregulation. . . .

Trade unionists may believe that the solution is to organize the labor forces of all new entrants, and some success in this is to be expected. However, many of the employees recognize that their financial future depends on gaining market share from the higher-cost incumbents. Managements of the new airlines also understand this threat and are taking great care to relate to their employees in order to retain higher productivity. There are already cases where national certification of union groups within the new carriers has been withdrawn at the request of the local membership.

In any case, it is to be expected under deregulation that new entrants will keep popping up wherever there is an opportunity for a low-cost operation to make profits. Some union leaders may believe that strikes will be necessary to solve the problem, but such action is more likely to hasten the demise of larger airlines with high unit costs if a work stoppage is protracted.

Finally, in our underlying lighter vein of bird lore covering goose and phoenix, we would caution against a stance similar to the ostrich approach of burying its head in the sand when danger is at hand.

Joedicke's analysis in 1980 was prophetic. His call for new methodologies and a heightened awareness on the part of both management and unions to the necessary changes that deregulation demanded has still not been universally answered. Throughout the 1980s and 1990s, airline executives and labor leaders alike maintained an adversarial labor-management relationship. The parties remained deadlocked, fighting among themselves instead of facing the enemy of change together.

The Rate of Change Accelerates, Consequences Become More Harsh

During the three decades since deregulation, numerous changes have occurred in fundamental business philosophy. Leveraged buyouts, restructuring and downsizing, business failures, and mergers have modified the relationship between labor and management at the bargaining table. The only constant in this scenario has been the unchanged continuation of the RLA of 1926.

Deregulation and the plethora of nonunion new entrants to the industry were not the only factors that destabilized the labor relations process. The major events in the early 1980s that would shape the labor negotiations process for a long period of time in the future were the strike of the Professional Air Traffic Controllers (PAT-CO) and the dissolution of Braniff in Chapter 7 bankruptcy.

The year 1983 witnessed the first Chapter 11 bankruptcy of Continental Airlines and the formation of nonunion airlines by former unionized carriers through the use of holding companies. Carriers, as a result of this increased competition, began fighting for their economic survival by implementing draconian cost-cutting measures.

When Congress enacted deregulation, it believed that the competitive capabilities of the industry and the ability to adjust to the new environment would have been tested at the end of ten years. Now, in the beginning of deregulation's fourth decade, the modifications are still creating unrest and, in some cases, catharsis in the labor community. In 1989, Eastern Airlines was in the throes of a massive labor dispute driven by these fundamental changes (see fig. 8.3). The carrier experienced a major strike and subsequently filed a Chapter 11 bankruptcy to reorganize operations, presumably so that it might emerge as a nonunion carrier. The carrier was unable to achieve this goal, ceased operations, and dissolved in 1991.

Taken together, statements by a professor and by an industry insider reflect at the time the attitude taken by major carriers in their pursuit of, in some cases, a nonunion operating environment or, at least, an environment devoid of the crippling effect of huge labor costs. In January 1985, John T. Dunlop, Lamont University Professor at Harvard University, wrote, "The one word that best characterizes transportation labor relation is fragmented, and an extreme form pervades the airlines. There the separate system groups frustrate stronger national organizations of labor in many crafts. The crafts are isolated and often engage in intense rivalry to capture or to extinction; the carriers are divided

along many lines, and government labor policy in the air transportation sector can only be described in recent years as nihilistic and devoid of constructive leadership."[21] Three years prior to this, in a speech delivered at an airline industry conference, the then-president of Eastern Airlines, Frank Borman, stated, "In the final analysis, the Deregulation Act, if nothing else, was the greatest anti-labor act ever passed by an American Congress."[22]

As one contractual negotiator during this time commented, management viewed with a sigh of relief and respect in anticipation of its impact on airline negotiations the actions of President Ronald Wilson Reagan in the unilateral firing of PATCO members: "The firing of 11,000 air traffic controllers established clearly

Figure 8.3. Eastern Airlines L1011 on the tarmac in 1974. Under chairman Frank Lorenzo's tenure, Eastern was crippled by severe labor unrest. Asked to accept deep cuts in pay and benefits, Eastern's mechanics and ramp-service employees walked out on March 4, 1989. A sympathy strike called by the pilots and flight attendants effectively shut down the airline's domestic operations. Lorenzo sold Eastern's shuttle service to real-estate magnate Donald Trump in 1989 while selling other parts of Eastern to his Texas Air holding company and its major subsidiary, Continental Airlines, on disadvantageous terms to Eastern. As a result of the strike, weakened airline structure, inability to compete after deregulation, and other financial problems, Eastern filed for bankruptcy protection on March 9, 1989. With the airline collapsing from debt, it ran out of money to operate on January 18, 1991. Over eighteen thousand employees lost their jobs and pensions in one day, not including the thousands furloughed prior to the collapse. Source: Wikimedia Commons; GNU Free Documentation License, Version 1.3.

in the minds of businessmen and union leaders a pro management stance by government."[23] The action had two major influences on the negotiating process. First, airline negotiators schooled at preserving the most possible were now on the offensive, and their goal changed to getting the most possible from the union during contractual discussions. This philosophical change, never seen in the airline industry, fueled the demand for increased concessionary bargaining and work-rule-reduction talks and entrenched attitudes promoting management's right to manage. Second, in future negotiations, this new attitude in response to the government's actions, coupled with Lorenzo's seemingly cavalier approach toward unions, created in management a resolve never seen before by union negotiating committees. But PATCO also had its downside, and despite management's newfound freedoms, the scheduling restrictions placed on various airports by the FAA caused many of the existing carriers, particularly those who followed a path of expansion, severe economic hardship because of their inability to retreat from their costly route expansions.

The Braniff Bankruptcy

The air transport industry received another jolt in 1982 with the loss of a major carrier, Braniff International Airways (see fig. 8.4). In May, Braniff announced the filing of Chapter 11 bankruptcy. In its application, Braniff cited steadily slipping financial conditions amounting to debts of $733 million.[24]

This closure was devastating because until this point, airlines, unions, and employees believed it could not happen. At the table, comments were often made that the government would not permit an airline to go out of business—that someone would always take over and that most jobs would always be protected. This bankruptcy served notice to the entire industry that

it could happen to any airline. Braniff's demise also reinforced management's position that cost improvements and cash flow were of utmost importance. Immediate survival became the paramount issue. The short run became more important than any long-term strategies demanded by the industry deregulation.

The Quest for Job Security Begins

In late 1981, however, the unions achieved two important breakthroughs, and the two issues involved laid a pattern for negotiations that carried through the 1980s. At United Air Lines, the industry leader in 1981 in almost all aspects including labor relations, ALPA successfully negotiated a letter of agreement concerning alter-ego (double-breasting) operations. In August 1981, United agreed to broad guarantees for job security of the pilots. This agreement addressed the issue of alter ego. Part of the agreement, dubbed the "Blue Skies" contract, called for a no-furlough clause and an agreement that during the term of the contract, "neither United Airlines Inc., nor any organization which it or

Figure 8.4. Braniff Boeing 747 airliner. In 1928 an Oklahoma insurance salesman named Thomas Braniff and his brother Paul Braniff financed an aviation company named Paul R. Braniff Inc. The airline was named Tulsa–Oklahoma City Airways and offered passenger service between major cities in Oklahoma. Up to 1978, Braniff remained one of the fastest-growing and most profitable airlines in the U.S. But deregulation of the airline industry was to be introduced in 1978, and Braniff under Harding Lawrence misjudged this change. On May 12, 1982, Braniff Airways ceased all operations, a victim of escalating fuel prices, aggressive expansion, and fierce competition, thus ending fifty-four years of service in the airline industry.

its successors or assigns, control, manage or hold an equity interest in shall conduct commercial flight operation . . . unless such flying shall be performed by pilots on the United Airlines system . . . in accordance with . . . the Air Line Pilots Association, International." This letter of agreement became the benchmark for almost all future negotiations on scope protection where concessions were sought by management, and recognition of it as precedent was demanded by the unions before any agreement would be considered. The "Blues Skies" contract also finally enabled United to eliminate the flight engineer position on its B-737s.

Employees Buy the Company

The second issue negotiated at the bargaining table in 1981 was employee stock-ownership plans (ESOPs). This program was initially brought out by Texas Air Corporation's takeover of Continental Airlines. During the hostile takeover attempt, employees and management of Continental unsuccessfully attempted to prevent the acquisition by bidding for ownership themselves. This unsuccessful attempt planted a seed in the minds of employees at other beleaguered airlines, and several subsequent attempts at ESOP buyouts had a profound impact on negotiations and on the future of some airlines.

The 1987 buyout of Republic by Northwest led unions to give more attention to the potent power of ESOPs. In 1986, Northwest had bought Republic for $17 per share, up from an original value of $3.50 per share. Employees of Republic in the early 1980s had taken company stock in exchange for wage and benefit concessions. Disbursements totaled $150 million dollars for fifteen thousand employees-stockholders of Republic. The buyout demonstrated the potential of ESOP deals with management.[25]

Also in 1987, pilots at United Air Lines made the first of a series of proposals to purchase the airline via an ESOP. It would take eight years

for the drive to succeed, but United Airline employees on July 12, 1995, bought out the airline's parent company, UAL Corporation. Included were pilots, machinists and a large number of nonunion members, making United the largest employee-owned company in the world. Excluded were United's flight attendants as their union refused involvement in the ESOP.

The contract called for 55 percent ownership in the company in exchange for $4.9 billion in wage and work-rule concessions over the next six years, three seats on the twelve-member board, and restrictions on the new United Shuttle. In exchange, the company would receive wage cuts over the next six years.

Concessionary Bargaining Snowballs

Concessions remained the watchword in negotiations during 1982. Airlines and employee groups scrambled to preserve their existence. Among major carrier agreements, both Republic Airlines and Western settled with their unions on a 10 percent wage reduction for over eleven thousand workers. Pan American reached an agreement with their flight attendants calling for various wage increases followed by a 10 percent reduction that was to last for fifteen months. This agreement followed the lead of four other unions that had accepted 10 percent wage cuts. In exchange for wage reductions and a change in some work rules, Pan American employees received one dollar in company stock for every five dollars of earnings forgone. In addition, the union gained membership on the company's board of directors.

At Eastern Airlines, the airline pilots agreed to a wage freeze for twelve months followed by two wage increases totaling 10 percent. Interestingly, and as an indication of the impact of deregulation, Delta Air Lines, the darling of the industry, suffered its first fiscal loss ($86.7 million) in thirty-six years. This loss led Delta to concessionary talks in the following year.

Prior to this time, when concessions were given by the unions, the parties generally agreed on *snapback provisions*, or a date when the reductions and work rule changes would be returned. But the Chapter 11 bankruptcy of Braniff proved only a prelude to that airline's dissolution. Sensing a power shift from that and the September 1983 Chapter 11 bankruptcy filing by Continental, management bargained more strenuously, threatening extensive layoffs and/or Chapter 11 proceedings if concessions were not agreed on, and allowing no quid pro quo for snapback.

The bandwagon approach to negotiations gained full momentum in 1983. Each time a carrier received concessions, employees and unions at other carriers knew their management's demands would be similar or more intense. This bandwagon style of negotiation was not uncommon in the industry. Prior to deregulation, the unions practiced it with apparent success, seeking more in wages and benefits in the next contract, based on the figures of negotiations settled earlier.

In seeking concessions, management's approach varied in 1983 from strict wage and benefit reductions to additional demands of cross-utilization of employees (with customer-service agents and even pilots required to also handle the loading and unloading of baggage, for example—a task traditionally performed by a separate craft of workers represented by a different union, causing loss of jobs and conflict between unions), improved productivity, and the use of part-time employees. The latter had been desired for many years by management but had always been thwarted at the table by union negotiators. This state of affairs led unions to lobby Congress for aid. The unions were not able to convince Congress to restore some regulations of the industry. It was apparent that the parties would have to sort out the new environment themselves. The negotiation process would continue to evolve, guided by the only remaining controlling legislation, the RLA. Management used its leverage to gain concessions from its unions and to weaken the perception of labor's strength. While labor gave significant relief to many carriers during this period, much of it was used by management to subsidize the ongoing fare wars and to continue the corporations' diversification strategies rather than to improve airline operations.[26]

Fighting back against the concessionary trend, the unions pursued introduction of ESOPs as a countermeasure. Because of the expense of continuing ruinous price wars, management was failing to improve operations. Labor argued that concessions would not return the carriers to profitability and, as such, were not providing the employee with any hope of future security. The union position was that the carriers could not save their way back to profitability. Demands in return for concessions became commonplace. These returns could only be embraced under the ESOP programs, where the employee received a measure of company stock for his or her contribution. A variety of different programs emerged at this time, including total company buyouts in situations where management had given up hope of winning the ultimate battle of airline viability. Plans of an ESOP nature either had been previously introduced or entered the labor scene at this time at Eastern, Frontier, Pacific Southwest, Pan American, Republic, Trans World, and Western. A host of others were on the union drawing boards for introduction at a later date.

Among the concessions made in 1983, Eastern achieved an 18 percent pay cut (22 percent for pilots) and cost-reducing measures among three unions, Pan American negotiated extended pay cuts of 10 percent, Republic's ten thousand employees approved a 15 percent pay cut to last for nine months, and Western's employees approved 15 percent cuts for almost ten thousand workers. One model of labor-management cooperation stood out in 1983. Delta Air Lines employees, in appreciation for the carriers continuance of a no-furlough policy, purchased a new Boeing 767-200 christened "the Spirit of Delta," the company's first 767, for the airline. The costs of this acquisition were financed by an employee agreement to a 2.5 percent pay reduction during the year. Two other events of major significance occurred in 1983 that further improved management's hand at the bargaining table: the bankruptcy of Continental and development of the two-tier wage agreement.

Continental Airlines' Bankruptcy

The Continental bankruptcy in 1983 sent shock waves not only through the industry but also through all labor relations contracts in general, whether established under the RLA or the NLRA. Continental Airlines faced losses totaling over $471 million. Under Lorenzo's leadership, the carrier attempted various approaches, including negotiations with its unions, to find relief. In selecting the Chapter 11 bankruptcy alternative for reorganization, Lorenzo downsized the airline from twelve thousand employees to approximately four thousand, using the protection provisions to reopen as a low-fare carrier operating only a small portion of Continental's former route structure.

Seizing on provisions of the bankruptcy code that allowed for the abrogation of contracts, ostensibly designed to repudiate contracts with suppliers of goods and services, Lorenzo informed the unions at Continental that their employment contracts were no longer valid and that the airline would no longer honor the provisions of such previously negotiated agreements. Following this approach, he further advised employees that jobs were available but with modified wage rates and working conditions. Pilots were told that if they desired to retain employment, their new salaries would be reduced from the previous average of $77,000 to a flat

$43,000; flight attendants' salaries would be reduced from an average of $29,000 to $14,000. Because the International Association of Machinists (IAM), representing mechanics and baggage handlers, had been on strike against the carrier, no provisions were forthcoming for those workers except that the strikers may be rehired at company-approved rates, with selection at the company's discretion.

The bankruptcy of Braniff had released thousands of talented and trained employees, many of whom had not found airline work. This event had provided Continental and all other airlines with a ready supply of personnel from which to draw should their own airlines have need for strike replacements. This availability was not overlooked by existing managers and was used time and time again as a threat to unions that they were not irreplaceable as many had come to believe. Fully aware of this vast supply of trained workers, Continental also announced work-rule changes, including "emergency work rules" calling for increased pilot and flight attendant flight hours and modifications to rest periods.

In response to the company's decisions, the pilot and flight attendant unions joined the striking machinists. This action was not unanticipated, and Continental prevailed, drawing on the pool of available talent to continue operations while the unions and employees looked to the courts for relief. The abrogation of employment contracts was not a new occurrence. In 1980, Bildisco & Bildisco, a New Jersey building-and-supply company, had employed similar tactics with the Teamsters. But the situation at Continental prompted the first application of those rules in the airline industry.

In October 1983, the Supreme Court concluded hearing arguments in the Continental case. A decision was to be rendered sometime in early 1984. In the first court hearing of the bankruptcy, the U.S. Court of Appeals for the Third Circuit sided with Continental and Lorenzo, holding that an employer need only prove that a contract is a burden, leaving the bankruptcy court to balance the interests of the employers against those of the union-represented employee. The final decision was anticipated by labor to be in their favor, because no activity of this nature had taken place before in the airline industry.

The year 1984 opened with the awaited Supreme Court decision on *NLRB v. Bildisco & Bildisco*, in which the court held that employers filing for reorganization could temporarily terminate or alter labor contracts even before the bankruptcy judge had heard the case. Moreover, the termination or alteration could be made permanent if the employer could persuade the bankruptcy judge that the agreement burdened chances of recovery.[27]

Considering the *Bildisco* decision a striking blow to labor, the unions set a course of seeking legislation to alter that decision and to amend the bankruptcy laws to curtail the unilateral obliteration of negotiated agreements. With union support, amendments were eventually proposed to the bankruptcy code, and Section 1113 requiring court approval for any rejection or change to a collective bargaining under Chapter 11 was ultimately added. Further delineation of the requirements for abrogation of collective bargaining agreements was highlighted in a subsequent case in 1986, *Wheeling-Pittsburgh Steel Corporation v. United Steelworkers*, which set requirements that must be followed before any abrogation may take place. These requirements include the following:

- The abrogation cannot be unilateral; it must be discussed with the union, and a proposal must be made to the union permitting them to address the issue before any action may take place.
- Only those modifications necessary to permit reorganization can be considered and can be subjects of the above proposal.
- All relevant information must be supplied to the union.

- The company must meet with the union in an attempt to reach a good-faith agreement.
- The court can authorize abrogation only if the union has failed to accept the carrier's proposal without good cause.

The amendments to the code and the effects of *Wheeling* and other decisions curtailed the wanton abandon that management had employed and threatened in the heat of labor-management battles. The bankruptcy threat, so often used at the table, had now been neutralized.

Despite these activities, a bankruptcy judge in May 1984 upheld Continental's contract abrogation, and Continental later showed a profit of $17.6 million for the third quarter compared with a third quarter loss of $77.2 million one year earlier. During 1984, several airlines operated at a profit. But the continued erosion of profitability continued at most carriers, and the demands for concessions continued.

Viewed in the light of history, Lorenzo's use of bankruptcy at that moment can be seen as an act of diabolical genius. Until then, taking a company through bankruptcy was generally viewed as such an admission of managerial failure that it marked the end of a CEO's career. Faced with the need to deeply reduce labor costs and to do so quickly in order to compete with the nonunion upstart carriers but frustrated by the possibility of interminable negotiations, mediation, and other NMB Kabuki theater proceedings under the RLA, Lorenzo used bankruptcy filing like Alexander's sword to abruptly sever the RLA's Gordian knot, with Continental becoming freed of its union-bargained labor costs instantly. The startled and outraged reaction of the public, shocked by the perceived brutality of the unprecedented move, was not lost on Congress, which moved swiftly to amend the bankruptcy code to prevent anyone else (such as Continental's competition among the remaining legacy carriers) from mimicking Lorenzo's bold move. Though the termination of contracts is no longer automatic under the bankruptcy code, bankruptcy judges now routinely approve the termination of collective bargaining agreements as part of the reorganization process. What was once the kiss of death for a CEO's career is now more often deemed a shrewd business move, proof of executive courage, and reorganization in bankruptcy has become just another tool to be used as frequently as needed by management of airlines struggling for survival.

Two-Tier Wage Plans Proliferate

In November of 1983, American Airlines and the American Pilots Association agreed on a two-year contract that included a provision for reduced rates for new employees. The provision, for B-scale rates, or a two-tier pay system, provided that newly hired pilots would receive wage rates of approximately 50 percent of current pilot wage rates. The savings generated by such a plan did little to provide immediate cost relief but were thought to be a boon for future years. Since American was an airline that had developed specific strategic plans for deregulated operations, the agreement was seen as having significant consequences.

The unions abhorred the two-tier system, contending that it was both unfair and unhealthy for airlines to give different remuneration to employees who did the same work side by side. According to O. V. Delle-Femine of the Aircraft Mechanics Fraternal Association, this system would "cause chaos and dissension among employees." Delle-Femine's argument fell on deaf ears and did not deter other carriers from pursuing similar plans. Establishment of the B scale, in various forms, became a commonplace concessionary goal. Two-tier wage plans spread rapidly, with eight negotiated in 1983 alone. By 1985, that number had increased eightfold, to 63.[28]

By this point, the continued concessionary demands were creating solidarity among the industry's unions, and concession requests were invariably met with offsetting demands for ESOPs and alternative compensation programs. The focus of concessionary talks followed the bandwagon approach, and management's goals changed and centered on B-scale relief. Present or immediate cost reductions were now being slowly replaced by the need for future anticipated cost cuts. Airline reliance on pattern bargaining was replacing the strong push for immediate wage reductions. Industry negotiation practices had not changed appreciably from when the unions held the stronger negotiating position; they had only changed from one side of the table to the other. A follow-the-leader approach was still prevalent. In defense of the change of strategy, it might be noted that it was anticipated that the economy was going to recover appreciably and that a necessity for increased employment might occur in late 1984 and 1985.

The follow-the-leader approach to two-tier wage scales lacked the thought process that had been employed at American Airlines when the company and its unions agreed on implementation of its B-scale program. Under the aegis of that plan, new-hire rates were never intended to merge with current employees, and in return, American management made several agreements concerning job security and expansion to offset the union's agreement to the two-tier permanent arrangements. By the end of 1984, two-tier salary arrangements in the industry reached approximately forty in number, but none had the sophistication or forethought of the original agreement at American. Such two-tier wage scales had become the outcome of choice for airline negotiators.

Several 1984 settlements included concessionary provisions (which usually resulted in an overall decrease in compensation). At United Air Lines, the flight attendants agreed to a thirty-seven-month contract including a two-tier (B-scale) wage agreement for new employees at

25 percent of existing rates to remain in effect for seven years of hiring before merging with nonreduced (A-scale) rates; the mechanics agreed to a three-year contract with B-scale rates of pay to be in effect for five years before merging with existing A-scale rates. At Pacific Southwest Airlines, the Teamsters, the Southwest Airlines Pilots' Association, and other unions called for a 15 percent pay cut in return for a company agreement to place 15 percent of its stock into an employee trust fund. At Northwest Airlines, flight attendants represented by the Teamsters agreed to a six-month wage freeze, followed by a 6 percent increase in July of 1984 and 1985 and a 3 percent increase on July 1, 1986. The contract also established a dual-pay system under which newly hired attendants would be paid 30 percent of the current rates for six years, after which the A-scale rates would be applicable.

Piedmont Airlines negotiated contracts with four unions in which two-tier rates became applicable. Republic Airlines negotiated agreements with six unions that provided a two-tier system and an extension through 1986 of 15 percent pay reductions. In exchange, Republic agreed to establish profit sharing and to provide workers with shares of stock, increasing employee ownership of the company from 20 to 30 percent. At Western Airlines, four unions agreed to a 22.5 percent pay reduction through 1986. Management negotiated five contracts that called for changes in work rules to increase productivity. The company agreed to increase employee shares of company stock, establish a profit-sharing program, and increase union representation on the board of directors from two to four members. Frontier Airlines consummated agreements among five thousand workers calling for 11.5 percent reduction in wages and a two-tier pay system.

The airlines' successes in negotiating two-tier wage scales on the American Airlines model reached a turning point in 1985 in negotiations between United Air Lines and ALPA. In negotiations during late 1985, United's management had demanded a nonmerging two-tier pay scale for newly hired pilots. The ALPA refused to agree to the nonmerging aspect of the B scale, and the result was a twenty-nine-day strike that, when resolved, led to a two-tier scale that lasted for only a certain amount of years and then returned to the regular pilot pay rates. The nonmerging aspect of B scales had been defeated. Elsewhere in the industry, the ALPA's two-year-old strike against Continental Airlines ended on October 31 by order of a U.S. bankruptcy judge. The approach taken by the ALPA at United and the return at Continental marked a new beginning of union unity toward management's demands at the bargaining table.

In apparent reaction to its experience in the United and Continental strikes, the ALPA announced plans to build a $100 million "war chest" to repel employer attacks on the wages and benefits of its members. The fund, to be used for such purposes as strike benefits to the union members and loans and grants to other supporting unions, was accumulated by increasing membership dues by 1 percent. This fund later had a major impact in the strike against Eastern Airlines, which ended in the demise of that airline.

By 1989, two-tier wage scales had been negotiated away by the unions representing airline employees.

Trends, Issues, and Challenges in Airline Labor Relations

The metamorphosis of the last three decades is complex and not easily explained, nor can the final outcome (if any outcome in a living industry can be considered final) be predicted because airlines, government, and the unions still grapple with the hows and whys of their deregulated relationships. Management, with its newfound freedoms, has become more entrepreneurial.

The government, in its judicial capacity, has reversed many long-standing traditions. The National Mediation Board has seemingly taken a wait-and-see attitude. Many unions are still negotiating in an unenlightened manner, trying to desperately hold on to the ways of the past, while others seek to control their destinies through employee/union ownership of the very airlines with which they negotiate. This section examines some of the developments this new entrepreneurship, driven by free-market competition and challenged by dynamic market forces, has resorted to and the impacts on the airline labor force.

New Entrants

The most significant impact of deregulation on the existing carriers was the gradual removal of the restrictions placed on entry into the marketplace. Smaller carriers began to surface to provide scheduled service on selected routes in direct competition with established operators. Most of these new airlines started their services with smaller, two-engine aircraft. These new carriers for the most part operated on short- to medium-length routes that were in high-traffic areas. This enabled these airlines to generate profitable levels of traffic without having to compete in the long-haul markets with high capital cost. Since these new entrant airlines were almost exclusively nonunion, employee compensation levels were significantly lower for them than for the existing unionized carriers. These lower compensation levels equated directly to lower operating costs and allowed the new entrants to apply tremendous pressure on the larger, established carriers to adjust their fares downward.

Because of the nonunion nature of these new entrants, nontraditional job descriptions were developed, which meant greater efficiency in the use of personnel. Pilots were required to assist in the boarding of passengers and to spend non-flying hours in the airline sales or reservation offices. Ticket and gate personnel were required to assist in loading and off-loading passenger luggage. Flight attendants might assist in making seat assignments and in boarding procedures in the gate areas.

The new entrants did not generally offer the same level of service as did the existing carriers, so there was no need for them to invest in a full complement of ground services required by the larger carriers. These services, such as meal preparation, aircraft cleaning, fueling, and aircraft maintenance, were contracted to fixed-base operators, which reduced fixed costs drastically when compared to the costs of the existing carriers. Another important cost advantage was that without union contracts, the new entrants were at liberty to hire part-time or temporary workers to accomplish their goals. The existing union carriers were not afforded this luxury.

The new entrants were able to choose desired routes, dictate wages, and utilize contracted airline services to their profitable advantage. The smaller aircraft utilized by the new entrants required smaller crews and were much more efficient. The operating economies that the new entrants achieved by the use of smaller, more-efficient aircraft was put into perspective by Marvin Cohen, the chairman of the CAB in 1980:

> Incumbents must either concede many of these point to point markets to the new entrants or find a way to remain competitive. The magnitude of the problem is illustrated by the significant disparity in flight crew costs for the aircraft best suited to these markets as operated by various carriers. The average Boeing 737 labor cost for a trunk carrier in 1979 was about $418 per block hour. For the local service carriers, the cost was about $260. For Southwest, one of the oldest new entrants, flight crew costs were about $163 per block hour in

the year ending June 1980, approximately 65 percent below the trunk carrier costs. Southwest has generally lower costs for every phase of its operation. If the incumbents want to remain competitive in these markets, they must find ways to reduce costs. It is difficult to predict what will happen in these short-haul markets, but the pressure is now on the incumbents.[29]

This situation placed the trunk carriers in a precarious position. The necessity for lower fares was present, but the new entrants were able to establish fares at lower rates than the trunk carriers and still generate a profit. With their higher operating costs per unit, the larger airlines focused attention on preserving their market share of long-haul routes to fund lower rates on the routes where they competed with the new entrants. This approach did not create a profit, but it did make it more difficult for the new carriers.

Cost Reduction

The new watchword in the industry became cost control. The airlines began to turn inward in search of profits and took an introspective look at their internal organizations and cost structures. To produce a profit, adjustments and reductions needed to be made in operating costs. Fuel and labor costs are the two largest operating expenses for an airline. A variety of internal cost reduction programs were initiated.

Fuel-cost reduction. The airlines first looked at the need to reduce fuel costs. Short-term responses were to alter flight-planning and flight-operations procedures. Ozark Air Lines and North Central (later Republic) Airlines, for example, achieved fuel reductions by using only one engine on DC-9s during taxi and initiating complete engine shutdown when departure was delayed by air traffic control. Southwest and JetBlue Airlines have imposed slightly reduced cruise speeds to reduce fuel consumption. Longer-term responses include altering route structures and fleet compositions, eliminating the older, less fuel-efficient aircraft, and acquiring more-efficient transports (such as, initially, the MD-80 and B-737-300/400, later the B-737-700, B-767, and Airbus A-321, and now the B-787). Fuel cost increases in 1979 and beginning again in 2001 with marked escalation in 2007–8 have been major crisis points for the U.S. airline industry. This time, regional airlines are even reverting from jet to turboprop aircraft to reduce fuel costs. As more fully discussed in the next chapter, improved fuel economy has become a primary design goal for new airliner airframe and engine designs.

The unprecedented fuel price instability extant since 1979 made some of these approaches superfluous and ineffective, and these rapid fuel-price fluctuations did not fall on all carriers equally. Competitive advantage and the consequent ability to lower fares were available to those carriers who were able to negotiate more-favorable fuel contracts with their suppliers. The big carriers generally got a better price and could use this to competitive advantage. Southwest Airlines' innovative fuel-hedging program, since imitated by other financially able carriers, enabled that airline to effectively buffer rising fuel prices (see fig. 8.5). *Hedging* is a financial strategy that airlines and other fuel-dependent industries use to protect against rising prices by locking in (through a variety of forms of transaction) a price for fuel to be delivered in the future. Southwest's hedging program, begun in 1999, is credited with saving the airline $3.5 billion in its first nine years of operation, often making the difference between profit and loss. In 2008, for example, Southwest had hedged 70 percent of its fuel needs at $51 per barrel when the market price soared to over $140 per barrel.[30]

These fuel-cost-reduction programs, although generally effective, have been insufficient to return the carriers to profitability in and of themselves,

Figure 8.5. Southwest Airlines Boeing 737 jet. Fuel hedging has become a crucial part of business for the most-successful airlines. Since energy is usually an airline's second-highest cost (after labor), any tweaks in fuel costs or use can turn into big savings. All the major airlines have hedged fuel prices since the 1980s, but as the major carriers have run into financial difficulties in recent years, they have no longer had the cash (or the credit-worthiness) to play the oil-futures market. But that is not the case for Southwest Airlines. Southwest's impressive record of profitability was built with fuel hedging. With fuel being an airline's most important variable cost, Southwest's measures have become a model for the industry. Courtesy of Bob Harrington (BobQat.com).

particularly since the skyrocketing fuel costs that began in 2007 now threaten the very existence of the industry. Additional cost reductions had to be achieved. Labor costs also had to be reduced.

Labor-cost reduction. Financially stressed airlines turned to their employees for cost-saving concessions in bargained wages and benefits, and many unions responded positively in an effort to help employers weather the storm, expecting to recover the concessions "with interest" when profits returned. For example:

- In 2003, wage and benefit concessions totaling $1.6 billion annually were agreed to by unions representing pilots (Allied Pilots Association), flight attendants (Association of Professional Flight Attendants), and ground workers (Transport Workers Union), enabling American Airlines to avoid bankruptcy.[31]
- In 2005, Continental Airlines' pilots, represented by ALPA, agreed to concessions

in work rules, pensions, and pay, valued at about $213 million annually. Other employee unions also made concessions bringing the total cost savings up to $500 million annually after the carrier requested them to avoid a looming liquidity crisis.[32]

Once one airline's unions granted concessions, competing carriers immediately brought pressure to bear on their employee unions to grant similar concessions, giving rise to a period of *reverse pattern bargaining*, in which the tables were turned, with airlines using concessions granted by unions at other airlines as leverage to obtain similar concessions from their companies' unions.

Bankruptcies

The two types of bankruptcy proceedings are reorganization and dissolution. Chapter 11 of the bankruptcy code permits the bankrupt company to continue operating while it reorganizes under court supervision. Chapter 7 terminates operations, and the company's assets are sold off under court supervision to satisfy the debts of the business as the enterprise is dissolved. When airline unions were unwilling to agree to concessions, some found concessions forced upon them by the bankruptcy courts. According to the Air Transport Association of America, bankruptcy is endemic to the airline industry; approximately 180 airlines filed for bankruptcy since deregulation in 1978, including 43 airlines from 2000 to 2008. Not all of these have resulted in liquidation.[33] Chapter 8's supplemental readings in the study guide to the current volume includes a table of U.S. airline bankruptcies and service cessations since deregulation. By 2005, five of the six legacy carriers—Continental, Delta, Northwest, United, and US Airways— had shed $16 billion in annual operating costs through bankruptcy (among the legacy airlines, only American has never declared bankruptcy). For example:

- In 2002, United Airlines filed for reorganization in bankruptcy. The bankruptcy court allowed United to terminate employee pension plans and reduce health-care benefits. A new pilots' contract with ALPA, effective from 2003 through 2010, negotiated under bankruptcy-court supervision, included concessions valued at $1.4 billion annually for each of those years. Mechanics (represented by AMFA) also took deep pay cuts in the process.[34]
- In 2005, Northwest and Delta filed for reorganization in bankruptcy on the same day, October 14, within two hours of each other. Court-supervised renegotiation of collective bargaining agreements seeking reductions in wages and benefits and changes in work rules and deep reductions in labor forces enabled both carriers to emerge from bankruptcy (Delta in April 2007 and Northwest a month later), each with several $ billion in lower annual costs. In the process, Northwest mechanics went on strike, only to watch the airline continue to operate normally with replacement staff. Northwest flight attendants saw their contract voided and the bankruptcy court impose new terms dictated by the company. When the flight attendants threatened to strike, they were prohibited by a court injunction. At this writing, Delta has since acquired Northwest, merged it into Delta, although some details of the process, including merger of the two workforces into one, remain works in progress.[35]

In late 2008, with oil prices rapidly approaching $150 per barrel, and fuel outstripping labor as the airlines' biggest cost for the first time in history, industry analysts predicted that unless the price dropped back to about the $75 to $80 range by the end of 2009, most U.S. airlines would be driven to seek bankruptcy protection. In early 2009, the price plummeted to around

$35 before starting to climb again. By the end of 2010, oil prices were again approaching $100 per barrel, threatening the continued success of the airlines' recovery.[36] Such fluctuations play havoc with airline budgets, and no solution is in sight, although adding plant-based alternative fuels may add an element of price stability.

Pensions

Airline employees have seen major changes in their pension plans, with most switching from defined benefit plans (that afforded a predictable income stream upon retirement) to defined contribution plans such as private 401(k) plans (whose ultimate payoff is unforeseeable, depending entirely on the investment wisdom of fund managers and performance of the markets). Other pension plans were simply terminated as airlines reorganized in bankruptcy.

The Pension Benefit Guaranty Corporation (PBGC) is a federal corporation created by the Employee Retirement Income Security Act of 1974 (see fig. 8.6). It currently protects the pensions of nearly 44 million American workers and retirees in 30,330 private, single-employer- and multiemployer-defined–benefit pension plans. PBGC, which receives no funds from general tax revenues, is financed by insurance

Figure 8.6. Logo of the Pension Benefit Guaranty Corporation (PBGC) of the United States. In a devastating blow to 122,000 workers and retirees in May 2005, the bankruptcy court ruled that United Airlines could default on its pension obligations and turn over control of its pension funds to the PBGC. UAL's $9.8 billion pension-plan default is the largest in U.S. history. The highest-paid UAL workers, such as pilots, faced pension cuts of up to 50 percent.

premiums set by Congress and paid by sponsors of defined-benefit plans, investment income, assets from pension plans trusteed by PBGC, and recoveries from the companies formerly responsible for the plans. When pension plans are abandoned or allowed to be terminated in bankruptcy proceedings, the PBGC pays out far more limited amounts by default to covered employees. Pension plan terminations in the airlines and other U.S. industries in the first decade of the twenty-first century were so extensive that the PBGC itself was placed in financial peril.[37]

Downsizing

Soaring fuel costs motivate airlines to drop unprofitable routes, ground the less fuel-efficient aircraft in their fleets, close stations and facilities, and reduce their active workforces, all to cut costs. At this writing:

- United Airlines is selling its maintenance division, including its massive San Francisco maintenance base, along with its frequent flier plan and laying off 1,600 employees, including 950 pilots. UAL also grounded Ted, the low-cost airline-within-an-airline the company created in 2004.[38]
- Spirit Airlines has given notice required by the Worker Adjustment and Retraining Notification (WARN) Act of its intent to close hubs at New York's LaGuardia Airport and San Juan, Puerto Rico and downsize its main Ft. Lauderdale, Florida, hub. The downsizing may require up to 60 percent of the airline's 750 flight attendants and 45 percent of its 540 pilots to be furloughed or relocated to another base.[39]
- After emerging from bankruptcy, Delta Airlines offered voluntary severance payouts to about 30,000 employees (more than half of its workforce) as part of a program intended to eliminate up to 2,000 positions, including 700 in management. It is reported that more than 3,000 employees accepted

the buyout offer and Delta states that it will accept them all. The airline plans to cut U.S. domestic capacity by another 5 percent over and above previous cuts, grounding up to twenty mainline aircraft plus twenty-five regional jets in the process. Delta also announced cuts in its service to Mexico.[40]
- Continental Airlines has announced plans to shed 3,000 jobs and US Airways 1,700.[41]
- American Airlines announced plans to cut domestic capacity by 11 to 12 percent and cut about 8 percent of its workforce, an estimated 7,000 jobs.[42]
- AirTran Airways announced 15 percent pay cuts for corporate officers and cuts of from 5 to 8 percent for rank-and-file employees. However, almost half of AirTran's employees are represented by unions, so the company can unilaterally impose the cuts only on its unrepresented workers and must negotiate with the unions for concessions by the rest. The airline is also expected to announce furloughs and capacity reductions.[43]
- Oklahomans are finding it more difficult to book air travel due to flight cutbacks. In Oklahoma City, American Airlines has reduced its daily flight offerings to Chicago, while Continental Airlines has reduced or discontinued service to Cleveland. Regional carrier ExpressJet has pulled out of the Oklahoma City and Tulsa markets. In both Oklahoma City and Tulsa, flights to Chicago, Denver, Cleveland, San Diego, Sacramento, Los Angeles, and Albuquerque have been cancelled by United, American, Continental, Frontier, and ExpressJet. Oklahoma City director of airports Mark Kranenburg expected airlines to make more service cuts in the near future.[44]
- Connecticut's Bradley International Airport at Windsor Locks lost its only international service (to Amsterdam), along with its only nonstop service to Los Angeles and

Denver as Northwest Airlines, Northwest's transatlantic partner KLM Royal Dutch Airlines, and Frontier Airlines dropped unprofitable routes in the face of soaring fuel costs.[45]

Contracting Out and the Globalized Economy

Another tactic coming into increasing use by U.S. airlines to reduce costs in today's highly competitive global business environment is outsourcing (contracting out to other suppliers) of work, particularly to lower-cost nonunion businesses outside the United States. Heavy maintenance appears to be the principal function being outsourced, with such work being transferred from U.S. facilities operated by the airlines themselves to foreign repair stations in developing countries such as China, Dubai, El Salvador, Korea, and Singapore, where it can be accomplished cheaper, though American jobs are lost in the process.

A major U.S. carrier could expect to pay about $70 per hour in wages and benefits to an in-house union mechanic, about 25 percent less to a private maintenance contractor in the United States and even less to a contractor in a developing country. More than 60 percent of the heavy maintenance on U.S. airlines' aircraft, worth about $41 billion in 2008 and growing rapidly, is now being accomplished by foreign repair stations, according to a recent government audit. Foreign repair stations performing such work for U.S. airlines are required to be certified by the FAA, although some can avoid even that requirement by having the work signed off and the aircraft approved for return to service by individuals holding personal FAA airframe and power plant (A&P) certification and/or inspection authorization. FAA-certified foreign repair stations multiplied from 344 in 1994 to 700 in 70 countries in 2007.[46] Each of these repair stations is required to be inspected annually by the FAA, but such visits are announced

well in advance. Supervisors and inspectors who sign off work at foreign repair stations are not required to hold personal FAA repairman or A&P certification. Foreign repair stations are not subject to U.S. security requirements, and security is also a concern, particularly since a 2003 Department of Transportation inspector-general report found a member of the al-Qaida terrorist organization working at a Singapore repair station where work had been performed for at least one U.S. airline.[47]

U.S. airlines are required to monitor maintenance work performed at the vendor's site.[48] There is disagreement whether the skills and oversight of the workers at foreign repair stations (particularly those in developing countries, unlike those in Europe, for example) is really comparable to those that exist (or existed) in the airlines' own domestic maintenance shops. No U.S. airline accident has yet been attributed to any such difference, and because FAA rulemaking is more often motivated by lessons learned from a fatal accident or series of accidents, along with tight federal travel budgets, it seems unlikely to expect the FAA to take more initiative in this area unless compelled to do so by Congress.

One such FAA-certified foreign repair station performing work for U.S. airlines (including at least JetBlue and US Airways) is Aeroman, located in a modern facility at El Salvador International Airport, about thirty miles south of the capital city of San Salvador. Aeroman employs about thirteen hundred workers, who perform the nose-to-tail "C check" inspections the FAA requires every twelve to eighteen months on U.S. airliners, along with related repairs and cabin and avionics upgrades. Company employees include about six hundred mechanics holding Salvadoran licenses recognized by the European Aviation Safety Agency, and about one hundred of them also hold FAA certificates. Aeroman CEO Ernesto Ruiz says that all of the company's mechanics speak at least some English, the language in which they must complete all FAA-required paperwork and documentation, and are subject to random drug-and-alcohol tests and annual criminal-background checks. According to Ruiz, the company's entry-level aircraft-maintenance trainees are paid about $350 per month, while an experienced mechanic can earn over $1,000 a month and $120 in monthly bonuses, very good pay for Salvadorans. (El Salvador's minimum wage for service workers is $175/month.) Benefits for Aeroman workers include free bus transportation to and from work and subsidized lunches. Aeroman commercial director Andres Garcia says the FAA inspected the repair station four times in 2007. JetBlue maintenance representative Mitch Sine expressed the opinion that Aeroman beats U.S.-based manufacturers not just on price but also on performance and on-time delivery: "I can't buy this kind of quality in the United States. These Aeroman people really have pride in their work." Southwest Airlines was also on the verge of moving substantial work there but cancelled its plan when an uproar developed over improper deferral of inspections on its 737 fleet, apparently condoned by FAA inspectors who had too cozy a relationship with the airline.[49]

At this writing, Congress is considering legislation that would require the FAA to inspect all foreign repair stations performing work for U.S. airlines at least twice a year, that one of those inspections be unannounced, and that foreign repair station employees who perform "safety-sensitive functions" be subject to FAA regulations for mandatory drug-and-alcohol testing.[50] Given the necessity for FAA inspectors to obtain visas, clear customs, and otherwise deal with foreign governments in the performance of such inspections, and considering the close working relationships that typically exist between business and government, it seems naive to expect that the element of surprise could really be achieved in such inspections of foreign repair stations.

Meanwhile, within the United States, original-equipment manufacturers such as Pratt & Whitney, Honeywell, and General Electric provide extensive contract maintenance, as do outside repair stations.[51] American Airlines is striving to turn its maintenance operations, including the company's heavy-maintenance base at Kansas City International Airport, from a cost to a profit center by contracting to perform such work for other airlines that might find this an attractive alternative to flying the aircraft to another country to have the work performed.[52]

Airline reservations work has also largely been contracted out to overseas call centers and/or diverted to a largely online, automated function less dependent on human interaction.

Productivity

Considering the overwhelming cost-reduction pressures on airline management, it should be obvious that any recoupment of concessions previously given or advancement in pay or benefits of airline workers must be tied to improvements in worker productivity that will at least cover the added cost. Indeed, the Air Transport Association, trade association of the U.S. airline industry, credits labor restructuring with substantial gains in airline productivity that contributed enormously to the industry's remarkable recovery after 9/11 and continuing until overwhelmed by fuel-cost increases.[53] For example, Southwest Airlines pilots, represented by SWAPA, agreed to work the maximum duty and flight time allowed by FAA regulations in order to maximize their productivity and justify a pay raise.

Mergers and Acquisitions

At the dawn of deregulation, the trunk carriers held tremendous advantage over the new entrants in one area: the trunks had very deep pockets. The predominant approach ultimately taken by the trunk carriers in dealing with the new-entrant problem was given by the philosophy "If you can't beat 'em, buy 'em out." This approach led to a plethora of mergers and consolidations that effectively reduced competition in the industry.

Since its creation in 1938, the CAB controlled the airline industry with a velvet hammer, not allowing new airlines to enter and attempting to keep existing airlines viable by granting route monopoly in select markets. In the forty years before the enactment of deregulation, not a single new trunk carrier was established, and none went out of business. The early years of deregulation saw an explosion of new airlines. But by 1988, only a handful of these new-entrant carriers were still flying. Most went bankrupt; the balance was bought out by the major carriers. The predominant players in the merger game and the survivors of this dynamic period of activity were the remaining trunk carriers that had been in existence prior to deregulation.

Once the inherent inefficiencies in route structure and fare levels began to be corrected, management turned its attention toward labor costs. But just as the management of many airlines felt initially that they could ignore the presence of airlines like Southwest and Midway, labor reacted to deregulation just as passively, and a business-as-usual approach continued. Labor's inability to respond to the new market reality added to the demise of Braniff and Frontier Airlines and weakened both United Air Lines and Trans World Airlines with inflexible behavior. Labor unrest was evident throughout the airline industry.

The initial indifference of labor and management changed very quickly. In 1980, the pilots of Pacific Southwest Airlines (PSA), an intrastate carrier covered under the NLRA, struck for an extended period of time. The pilots, adamant in their demands, rejected several offers made by PSA. The PSA strike ventured into new territory regarding labor relations because the contract between the parties had expired under the NLRA. After seven weeks of strike activity, PSA advertised for replacements of flight deck officers. The company was inundated with applications from unemployed, and very well-qualified, pilots. Because of PSA's ability to hire trained pilots in large numbers, enough striking pilots crossed their own picket lines that the parties agreed on a contract settlement similar to the original offer made by PSA management. A new approach to contract negotiations had been discovered.[54]

Also significantly influential in the overall labor relations environment was the Professional Air Traffic Controllers Organization (PATCO) strike of 1981. The activities surrounding the handling and eventual outcome of this situation provided management with a new set of bargaining tools. The PATCO strike will long be remembered as a milestone in American labor history, as Frank H. Cassell and Frank A. Spencer comment: "The firing of 11,000 air traffic controllers established clearly in the minds of businessmen and union leaders a pro-management stance by government."[55]

Because of the PATCO strike, the Federal Aviation Administration imposed scheduling restrictions on traffic flow, airport usage, and gate usage at select airports. These restrictions lessened the market impact of the new entrants, but the continued competition for market share caused considerable erosion in airline profitability. New-entrant bankruptcies and mergers followed in rapid succession—a fortunate situation for the existing carriers.

A wave of mergers began in 1985, and the industry underwent major changes because of it. All prior mergers had taken place under the aegis of the CAB, and its demise left a void in future resolution of labor issues when mergers took place. Under the CAB's guidance, mergers involving unionized carriers traditionally contained *fence agreements*, agreements that allowed an orderly integration process of seniority and work rules to take place while the air operations continued. Mergers could have a destabilizing effect on workers, and the CAB had kept amalgamation problems at a minimum. The CAB had followed a policy of establishing labor-protective provisions to minimize the potential for severe disruption by providing a "floor," or standard, for employee protection during mergers and acquisitions.[56] This regulatory feature no longer exists. The Deregulation Act had transferred responsibility for airline merger approval from the CAB to the DOT, which performed that task for the first decade of deregulation. But when the word came down that the Department of Justice (DOJ) would soon take over the responsibility to review proposed mergers for antitrust (anticompetitive) effects, foreseeing a more rigorous review process, the airlines sought to complete all mergers that were contemplated before that shift in responsibility occurred.

Corporate moves during 1986 portended serious problems for airlines' unions in future years, as it became the year of the merger. Company after company sought to improve its balance sheet and eliminate competition through consolidation. These mergers fueled union desires to seek protective programs to preserve jobs. One of the most notable of such approaches was the unions' willingness to move from a position of protectionism to entrepreneurialism by attempting to obtain control of various companies through ESOPs.

Responding to the rash of mergers and acquisitions, the NMB acted to resolve some of the labor disputes resulting from questions about the bargaining status of unions absorbed in a merger. Rather than allowing questions of representation—that is, whether a carrier would be represented by one union or another or by no union at all—to be resolved carte blanche based on which group had the largest population at the time of merger, the board ruled that carriers must alert the NMB to possible employee-representation disputes before a merger takes place. Up to this time, there were no such requirements, and many airlines made no attempt to notify the NMB until after the mergers had been solidified. This laid-back approach on the part of airline management had worked toward the advantage of the airlines at the negotiating table.

The NMB established a new procedure that provided for earlier decision making about the representation status of a particular union. The board further established that when the certification status of a union was terminated, that same union could file for a new election for the combined craft or class within sixty days, if they could obtain union authorization cards from at least 35 percent of the new combined craft and class. This move almost ensured a reelection procedure if the absorbed or decertified union had an appreciable number of members.

Merger and representation disputes in 1987 were accentuated by activities at both USAir and Northwest Airlines. At USAir, the acquisition of PSA and Piedmont Airlines permitted the Association of Flight Attendants full representation of USAir and the acquired companies after the International Brotherhood of Teamsters (IBT) withdrew from an NMB election over the flight attendants at PSA. The Teamsters, adamant that no election should be held over the PSA/Piedmont merger until the USAir/PSA merger was actually completed, failed to convince the board of their position. Until that time, the Teamsters had been the certified bargaining agent for the PSA flight attendants. In the Northwest/Republic merger, the Teamsters gained the right to represent the flight attendants by defeating the Association of Flight Attendants, who represented Republic. Similarly, in the same merger, the IAM were certified to represent approximately twenty thousand Northwest employees. The former Republic employees had lower wage rates than Northwest employees. Because of the wage difference, the IAM sought parity wage increases, but Northwest refused to bargain, insisting that the agreements with these employees were still intact and were not subject to being amended under the RLA.

While Delta Air Lines was completing the acquisition of Western Airlines, the Air Transport Employees Union was in court attempting to stop the merger. At issue was the union's attempt to force Delta into honoring contracts it had previously negotiated with Western. Supreme Court Justice Sandra Day O'Connor vacated a lower-court ruling that mandated arbitration to resolve this dispute, citing that merger preparations were too costly to reverse. The lower-court ruling would have forced Delta to agree in advance to accept arbitration, and the merger would have been delayed until a decision was announced.[57]

Soon after the high-court decision, Delta made it known that the more than six thousand employees of the former Western Airlines would be nonunion after the merger because they were outnumbered in each respective job class by Delta employees, all of whom were nonunion. The only exception was the ALPA, which represented Western's pilots. That classification would remain union because Delta pilots were also members of the ALPA.

Later in the year, USAir Group, attempting to thwart a takeover bid by Trans World Airlines, set about acquiring other carriers. The negotiations and plans were put on a faster track when the Teamsters and PSA agreed to drop several provisions of their agreement. A crucial point that would have delayed the process was the Teamsters' right to bargain with any new owner of the airline. Once that provision had been dropped, USAir moved ahead with the purchase of PSA.

These events represent examples of how management was able to "wrestle" the unions into positive postures for the carrier. Unions were now used to severe financial problems on the part of the carriers. This financial trouble also had an impact on their members' security. The Braniff bankruptcy had shown the industry that it was not immune to free-market forces.

A new round of "merger mania" began with the 2005 merger between America West Airlines and US Airways, both of which had previously reorganized in Chapter 11 bankruptcy, with the new entity continuing under the US Airways name. The merger proved the challenges and obstacles posed by diverse union representation and existing collective bargaining agreements to melding two airlines into one functioning unit. It would be three years post merger before the two carriers were operationally unified under a single FAA Part 121 air carrier operating certificate and new collective bargaining agreements would be signed with all of the employee unions. In the process, conflict and animosity between old US Airways pilots and mechanics ("East," in the parlance of the process) and those of the former America West ("West") were often bitter and disruptive. The more numerous East pilots, feeling betrayed by their union, even succeeded in an NMB-supervised election to oust ALPA and install the newly organized US Airline Pilots Association as the collective bargaining agent of the merged company's pilots, rolling over the opposition of the West pilots.[58] The costs and difficulties that came to light in this merger caused the industry to become more gun-shy about mergers as a solution to their financial challenges.

Shortly after Delta and Northwest emerged from bankruptcy in 2007, the companies entered into merger negotiations that ultimately led to a 2008 merger, with Delta the surviving carrier becoming the world's largest airline. At this writing, in 2011, full consolidation of the two companies' workforces is still a work in progress.

Following on the heels of the Delta-Northwest merger, in 2010 United and Continental reached a merger agreement, with ownership of both companies transferred to a new holding company, United Continental Holdings Inc. Consolidation under the United name but with the Continental globe logo is progressing apace. Almost simultaneously, budget carrier Southwest announced that it had reached an agreement to purchase smaller rival AirTran (formerly ValueJet). American Airlines is also widely reported to be looking for a suitable merger partner, and pundits generally agree that this wave of industry consolidation will continue, both in the United States and globally.

Looming Issues
Foreign Ownership of U.S. Airlines

Seeking sources of fresh infusions of cash to enable them to ride out these challenging economic times, U.S. carriers have turned their eyes overseas. Many U.S. businesses (and much choice U.S. real estate) are now owned (in large, if not outright) by foreigner investors, but federal law limits foreign ownership of U.S. airlines to 25 percent (see fig. 8.7).[59] Increasing pressure is being brought on Congress by the industry to lower that barrier and welcome foreign investment in U.S. airlines. In April 2008, International Air Transport Association (IATA) director general and CEO Giovanni Bisignani encouraged globalization of the airlines: "Labor must see the good results of consolidation that we have seen in Europe and paint itself into the picture of even broader global consolidation. And governments must understand that the flag on the tail has lost its meaning. Airlines need to grow into global businesses, spreading risk and benefits in the same way that any other normal business would. Ownership and control restrictions must go."[60]

One obstacle to that line of thought may be Congress's concern that foreign ownership and control might undermine the willingness of U.S. carriers to participate in the Civil Reserve Air

Figure 8.7. Virgin America A319 jet at San Francisco International Airport. Virgin America, a U.S.-based low-cost airline, began service in August 2007. San Francisco International Airport is Virgin America's principal base of operations. Even though Virgin America, the brainchild of British entrepreneur Richard Branson (Virgin Atlantic), is a U.S. airline, no more than 25 percent of a U.S. airline, by law, may be owned by foreign interests and must be under the "actual control" of U.S. citizens. Virgin Group, which also licenses the Virgin brand to the airline, owns 25 percent of Virgin America. Conceived in 1970 by Branson, the Virgin Group has created more than two hundred branded companies worldwide, employing approximately fifty thousand people, in twenty-nine countries.

Fleet (CRAF) program, whereby U.S. airlines provide aircraft quickly convertible to all or partial cargo configuration to supplement military airlift capabilities as needed for the projection of force in the interest of national security. Bearing in mind the widespread opposition of many other nations (even many traditional U.S. allies) to the U.S. invasion and occupation of Iraq, an operation heavily dependent on CRAF airlift capacity, a person can't help but wonder what would have happened if those U.S. airlines had been under foreign control and opted out of CRAF participation due to disagreement with U.S. foreign policy.

Shortages of Pilots and Mechanics

A downturn in the training and retention of new, technologically qualified personnel, especially pilots and mechanics, coinciding with rampant economic growth in developing nations (particularly China and India) combined forces to cause a growing shortage of qualified employees in the industry globally. Employment levels in the airline industry have always been cyclical, generally tracking the rise and fall of the business cycle, and the sharp global economic downturn that began near the end of 2008 reduced the immediacy of the shortage, but it can reasonably be expected to return as the economy recovers and likely worse than before as a result of trends described below.

Many seasoned pilots and mechanics have chosen to leave the industry for nonairline careers, while prospects have ruled out the airlines as a career option worth training for in the first place because of the job insecurity and decreasing pay and benefits that have typified the unstable airline industry since deregulation. Other experienced flight crew members have found employment in the rapidly growing "fractional" business jet segment of the general aviation industry more attractive than the airlines (discussed more fully in chapter 10).[61]

In the period of growth immediately preceding the extreme fuel-price increases discussed above, major U.S. airlines were hiring increasingly larger numbers of pilots from regional carriers, generally with less flight experience than in the past, resulting in an extraordinary turnover rate and greater recruiting demand at the regional level.[62] Some major U.S carriers were even forced to cancel flights when they ran short of available flight crews.

It is not just the United States that is running up against a shortage of pilots. Airlines are increasingly searching globally for pilots, according to Marsha Bell, vice president for marketing of Boeing subsidiary Alteon Training. For example, in March of 2008, China's Jade Cargo Airlines was scheduled to launch weekly B-747 air freight flights from its Shenzen, China, base, through Shanghai, to Vancouver, Canada, and

on to Houston. It was planned to be the all-cargo carrier's first trans-Pacific service. Difficulties in finding and attracting qualified flight crews, however, put the airline's plans on hold. Indeed, in booming Asia, recruiting qualified pilots has emerged as one of the biggest challenges for growing airlines and start-ups. According to a 2008 statement by the Civil Aviation Administration of China (CAAC), China would need over nine thousand more pilots by 2010 to fly the new Boeing and Airbus airliners entering China's fleet at the rate of 150 aircraft per year. CAAC warned that China's flight schools could not meet the demand, being capable of training no more than seven thousand pilots in that time frame, leaving a shortfall of two thousand pilots. China's sticker shock at the wages and benefits expected by experienced U.S. airline pilots retiring under the FAA's mandatory (then age sixty) retirement rule also impeded the country from filling the shortfall with expatriates. In Australia, the country's largest regional carrier, Regional Express, reported a need for an additional eighteen pilots over that same two-year period but had the ability to train less than half that number. Emirates and other financially strong airlines from the oil-rich Middle East, along with Korean Air and growing airlines from India and Brazil, have been aggressively recruiting experienced pilots from North America.[63]

Not only regional airlines but also government agencies responsible for regulating aviation safety are being "hollowed out" by losses to the major airlines of experienced personnel. Indonesia's equivalent of the FAA lost 30 percent of its pilots to airline jobs in one year, according to Flight Safety Foundation president Bill Voss.[64] Flight schools, too, are being raided by the regional airlines for instructor pilots to such an extent that some schools have cut back their output or closed their doors. The situation is so serious, Kit Darby, president of aviation employment consultancy AIR Inc., publisher of

Airline Pilot Job Monthly, said, "The airlines are taking the instructors we need to train the next group of pilots. They're eating their young."[65]

In March 2008, IATA projected a worldwide requirement for seventeen thousand new pilots each year through 2025, based on Boeing, Airbus, and regional jet and turboprop aircraft already on order for delivery in that time frame.[66] Only five months later, International Civil Aviation Organization (ICAO), a U.N. organization charged with harmonizing technical standards for international commercial aviation, raised that figure to nineteen thousand pilots per year. IATA further projects that trend to continue through 2026, based on its forecast growth of the world airliner fleet by that year.[67] If these projections become reality, such increased demand coupled with the shortfall in supply of technologically skilled labor should empower labor unions representing pilots and mechanics. These projections may, however, prove overly optimistic if airline fuel costs are not radically reduced from 2008 levels or if the global economy descends into recession or worse, financially incapacitating air carriers from improving pay and benefits, no matter how otherwise justified.

At the very least, service cutbacks by U.S. carriers helped relieve the immediate pressures on domestic airlines resulting from the pilot shortage, as did the FAA's highly controversial December 13, 2007, rule change raising the mandatory retirement age for airline pilots from sixty to sixty-five (effective immediately upon President George W. Bush's signing on that date), enabling the most-experienced crew members to remain on the job for an additional five years. Any who retired under the FAA's previous age-sixty rule but had not yet reached age sixty-five were free to reapply for work with a U.S. carrier, though few did, because they would start over at the bottom of the seniority list, flying less-desirable equipment over less-desirable routes for minimal pay. Under the leadership of the ICAO, most nations of the world have moved or are moving to the mandatory retirement age of sixty-five.

The need for more pilots is changing the way pilots are trained. Traditionally, the approach focused on first preparing pilots to fly solo in small aircraft powered by piston engines and then gradually moved the student into more complex aircraft, typically over a period of years and at great expense. But what may prove to have greater appeal to the more tech-savvy and video-game–enjoying younger generation is accelerated, ab initio pilot-training programs based on the multicrew pilot-licensing training program endorsed by ICAO in 2006. The more airline-operations-oriented and simulator-based training may also improve marketers' ability to attract new trainees and may also produce pilots competent on graduation to perform safely and proficiently as first officers (copilots) in the airline environment at a much more rapid rate and at less cost. Ron Levy, past chair of the Flight Education Committee of the University Aviation Association (UAA), calculates the cost of a typical four-year university degree with a commercial pilot certificate with multiengine (piston), instrument, and flight instructor ratings in the $120,000 to $180,000 range.[68] Even this expenditure of time and money typically falls well short of producing graduates meeting the needs of even the regional airlines for pilots proficient in operating turbine-powered aircraft with advanced flight-management systems in a multicrew environment.

Environmental Impacts

Concerns over global warming have prompted a worldwide focus on reducing the emissions of "greenhouse gases" by human activities deemed largely responsible for the trend. Although commercial aviation is estimated to contribute only about 2 percent of the total of these emissions, a substantial portion of these emissions occur in the upper atmosphere, where they have a disproportionately adverse effect. With airline economics in an already fragile state, airlines, government agencies, airframe and engine manufacturers, and energy companies are seeking procedural and technological improvements in operations and maintenance, air traffic control, aerodynamics, structures, engine efficiencies, and alternative fuels to simultaneously reduce both the operating costs and carbon footprint of flight operations. The industry is meanwhile struggling to fend off proposed legislative and treaty initiatives (including so-called cap-and-trade carbon offsets styled after those first imposed by the European Union) that threaten to first impose environmental regulatory costs that many already financially strained airlines might not survive.

Summary

Deregulation has now passed its thirtieth anniversary, and numerous books and articles were written, both pro and con, about its impact and effectiveness. Initially, most carriers were against passage of the act, but several perceived it as a competitive godsend. In many cases, those who fought the change lost the ultimate battle because of an inherent inability to manage costs effectively in the new environment, partly because of the long-standing CAB security blanket of guaranteed profits. Some of the existing management teams were unable to play hardball. They had been brought up playing only softball.

In 1982 when Braniff International Airways went bankrupt after several last-ditch efforts at reducing costs, it was the first bankruptcy of a major airline, and it sent shock waves throughout the industry. By 1993, it was quite evident that management had the upper hand in negotiations and that operating costs had to be cut for economic survival. Forty-one thousand air transport workers were already unemployed. If

the unions remained standing on principle and continued the ways of the past, more job loss would occur. By the early twenty-first century, the flurry of punches including service disruptions caused by the terrorist attacks of September 11, 2001, a weak national and declining global economy, and unprecedented increases in fuel costs, most U.S. airlines found themselves if not already on the ropes, at least in the fight of their corporate lives, a fight that would be to the death for some. Labor, having granted concession after concession, found itself backed into the corner and could give no more.

Deregulation caused profound changes in the labor-relations environment. Prior to deregulation, the negotiation table was not a place of mutual problem-solving. Instead, the operative management attitude was "How little of what they want will we have to give them, and how soon can we petition the Civil Aeronautics Board to increase fares to recover those increases?" The unions, fully aware of the cost-recovery option available to management, generally demanded increases in wages and benefits that far outstripped the increases achieved in other industrial sectors. The unions were not concerned about the carriers' underlying financial condition. These bargaining approaches, fostered by the regulated financial protectionism of the CAB, created an industry with above-average wage and benefit levels and an adversarial labor-management relationship. These approaches also set the stage for the complex and disturbing changes that were to occur under deregulation.

The idea of mutual problem-solving was anathema to both management and unions. Both factions had grown up together believing that problem-solving was someone else's responsibility, namely, the CAB's. With the CAB rapidly backing away from full industry regulation, the carriers found themselves in a fight for survival. They would have to develop new ways of operating their businesses. They would also have to find new ways to resolve labor cost and productivity issues both at the table and with the unions in general. Those carriers that made inroads into this new managerial terrain survived; those that did not either have vanished or are close to extinction.

The unions also grew complacent under CAB regulation. They had become very big and very myopic businesses in and of themselves and were bureaucratic and trenchant in their responses to change. Also, they were unprepared for the onslaught of change brought about through deregulation. They had to either shift focus from patterned demand increases and seek new paths of negotiating or face catastrophic worker-displacement potentials. The realization that airline wages in 1978 were far too high (e.g., $26,000 to $30,000 a year for janitorial service employees, $14 to $16 per hour for baggage handlers, and average salaries of $89,000 a year for pilots) would be a bitter pill to swallow for employees and labor unions. On the other side, viewing the unions and their employees as active and necessary participants in the airline decision process was too great a change for many airline managers to accept.

Economically, deregulation could not have arrived at a worse time. Inflation and interest rates were at very high levels, and the country was heading into a severe recession. The industry was also experiencing extreme instability in the price of aviation kerosene, and some carriers' fuel allocations were being cut back. These factors would have been sufficient in and of themselves to cause disruption and change in the labor-management relationship, but an event with even more impact shook the very foundations of organized labor.

The public-policy goal of the Deregulation Act was to encourage development and attain an air transportation system that relies on competitive market forces to determine the quality, variety, and prices of air services. Regulatory changes were intended to promote more-competitive pricing, establish greater flexibility to respond to changing market demands, and improve overall efficiency of the industry. Little attention was paid by the framers of the act to the underlying reality that all collective bargaining agreements in the airline industry were based on the old regulatory system. The unions had captured a portion of, and were equally slaves to, the monopoly profits generated by the CAB regulatory process. As a consequence, deregulating the airlines also meant deregulating the air transport collective bargaining process—a reality evidently not noticed or ignored by the act's framers.

Whether deregulation has or has not worked is a moot point. It is, in the final analysis, a fait accompli. Even Alfred Kahn, the former chairman of the CAB and the "architect" of the act, had second thoughts regarding this grand experiment in economic theory. As early as 1986, Kahn stated that deregulation rather than fostering greater competition has produced a group of megacarriers with feeder networks offering potentially far less competition than had been intended.

Labor relations in the air transport sector did not change overnight with the passage of the Deregulation Act. Instead, an evolution in labor relations took place, fostered not only by the act but also by the exogenous market and political forces both extant and emerging, such as runaway fuel costs and economic fluctuations domestically and globally. What is emerging is a "new unionism" in the U.S. air transport sector as organized labor strives to find its footing to regain effectiveness in the face of these titanic forces to enable labor to help the airlines survive without bearing the entire brunt of these forces themselves.

9. The Aerospace Industry

The U.S. aerospace industry includes companies producing aircraft, missiles, spacecraft, aircraft engines, propulsion units, and related parts for both civil and military customers as well as companies performing aircraft overhaul, rebuilding, conversion, and salvaging. The industry is dominated by a few large firms, such as Boeing and Lockheed-Martin, that contract with private businesses and governments to produce aircraft and subcontract with smaller firms to produce component systems and parts.[1]

The industry employed approximately 652,000 workers in 2008, up from a fifty-year low of 579,700 in February 2004.[2] The high point of industry employment was 1.3 million jobs in 1989.[3] The majority of these jobs are highly technically skilled positions in aircraft production.[4] In 2006, the industry included 2,900 business establishments, the majority of which were subcontractors engaged in producing parts and employing fewer than 100 workers each. The vast majority of the jobs (62 percent), however, were in large manufacturing facilities that employed more than 1,000 workers each.[5] Major unions in the aerospace industry include the International Association of Machinists and Aerospace Workers (IAMAW); the United Automobile, Aerospace, and Agricultural Implement Workers of America (UAW); the Society of Professional Engineering Employees in Aerospace (SPEEA); and the International Union of Allied Industrial Workers of America (IAW).

The geographical distribution of these jobs is shown in figures 9.1 and 9.2.

According to the U.S. Bureau of Labor Statistics, in 2006, 21 percent of all workers in the aerospace industry were union members or covered by union contracts, compared with about 13 percent of all workers throughout private industry (see fig. 9.3). Production workers in the industry earned an average of $1,153 per week in 2006, compared with $691 in all manufacturing and $568 in all private industry. Nonproduction workers, such as engineering managers, engineers, and computer specialists, generally command higher pay because of their advanced education and training. All workers in the industry generally receive standard benefits, including health insurance, paid vacation, sick leave, and pension plans. The bureau forecasts that employment in the industry will continue to grow, though at a slower rate than other industries.[6] Employment levels are closely linked to levels of sales, which reached $198.8 billion in 2007 and were forecast to surpass $210 billion in 2008, the increase primarily attributable to increased deliveries of civil aircraft, engines, and related parts and components.[7] In 2007, the industry contributed a positive $56.6 billion to the U.S. balance of trade with exports of $92.7 billion, the largest of any manufacturing sector.[8]

Military contracts have sometimes tended to dampen the adverse economic effects of

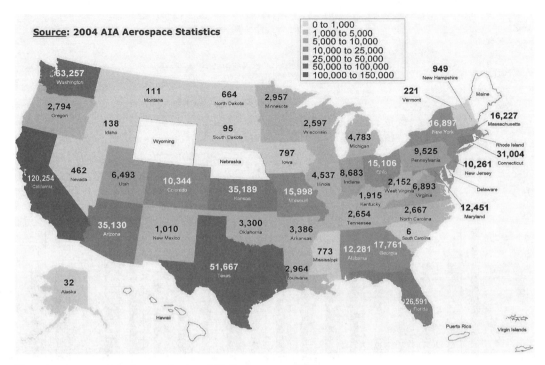

Figure 9.1. Aerospace employment by state. U.S. Department of Labor.

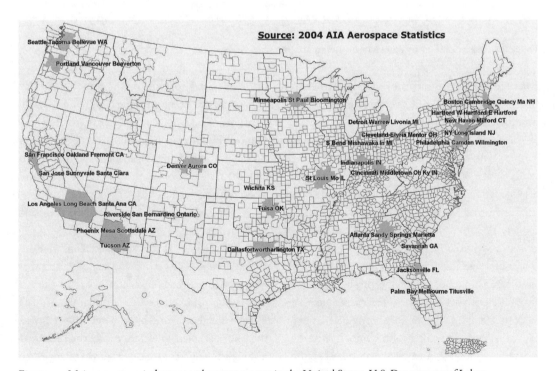

Figure 9.2. Major aerospace industry employment centers in the United States. U.S. Department of Labor.

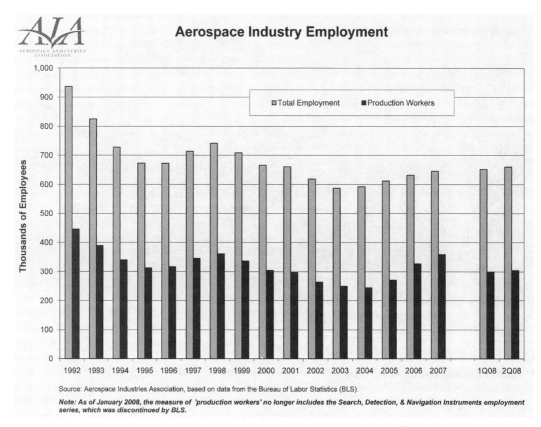

Figure 9.3. Aerospace industry employment. Aerospace Industries Association.

fluctuations in the fortunes of the airline industry, and vice-versa.[9] Case study 9.1 provides an illustrative example of this effect.

Case Study 9.1: Military Contracts Counterbalance Civilian Orders for Boeing

Boeing is the last U.S. aerospace company producing both civilian transport category aircraft and military aircraft, with the military and commercial divisions each accounting for about half of the company's business.

The Boeing company's military products include the T-45C Goshawk trainer; F-15E Strike Eagle, F/A-18 Hornet, and F-22 Raptor fighters; AV-8B Harrier II Plus attack jet; B-2 Spirit stealth bomber; airborne warning and control (AWACS) aircraft based on the commercial B-737, B-767, and Navy E-3 airframes, the P-8A Poseidon long-range antisubmarine warfare

(ASW) aircraft (also based on the commercial B-737 airframe); V-22 Osprey tilt-rotor; C-17 Globemaster III transport; KC-46A aerial refueling tanker; CH-47D/F Chinook medium-to-heavy lift helicopter; AH-64 Apache Longbow attack helicopter; and unmanned airborne systems, along with a variety of missiles and smart bombs (see fig. CS9.1.1).[10]

Boeing has acquired unmanned aerial vehicle (UAV) maker Insitu.

In July 2008, even as commercial airlines were deferring commercial jet orders and some industry analysts were forecasting cancellations of some airlines' orders, Boeing announced it will modernize AH-64D Apache Longbows for the U.S. Army, referred to as the "Block III" plan. In October 2010, the U.S. Army awarded Boeing a $247 million contract to begin low rate initial production of eight Apache Block III attack helicopters with a November 2012 completion date.

Figure CS 9.1.1. The AH-64D Longbow, which features a flexible M230 Chain Gun 30 mm cannon under the fuselage, providing a rate of fire of 625 rounds per minute. The AH-64D is also armed with the Longbow Hellfire air-to-surface missile, which has a range of 5 to 7.5 miles. However, the Apache can be equipped with air-to-air missiles and the Advanced Precision Kill Weapon System (APKWS), formerly known as Hydra, family of guided and unguided 70 mm rockets. From 2008, it has been armed with the AP-KWS II, a laser-guided version of the Hydra. In the close support role, the helicopter carries sixteen Hellfire missiles on four, four-rail launchers and four air-to-air missiles. Source: Wikimedia Commons; GNU Free Documentation License, Version 1.3.

The army plans to buy a total of 690 Apache Block III helicopters, which Boeing plans to assemble and test at its Mesa, Arizona, plant, providing secure employment for the plant's forty-seven hundred workers and adding to the stability and growth of the state's economy. Furthermore, Taiwan will receive thirty Apache Block III helicopters under a 2008 Bush administration weapons deal; Saudi Arabia could acquire thirty-six Apache Block IIIs, all built at the Mesa plant.[11]

The Block III version includes at least twenty-five major improvements, including composite rotor blades to improve high-altitude maneuverability in operating environments like Afghanistan, along with a more powerful engine and redesigned transmission. Improved sensors and computers better monitor the

health of aircraft systems to alert the pilot to developing problems and allow pilots to view terrain miles ahead (day or night) and transmit streaming video to other aircraft and command posts on the ground. The newly enhanced helicopter is capable of carrying, launching, and controlling an armed UAV capable of flying up to fifty miles ahead of the helicopter, relaying back video of terrain and activity, and launching missiles on command of the Apache's gunner.[12] Originally designed for service as a tank killer to face the Soviet threat in Europe, the Apache has evolved into a devastating weapons system providing close air support to troops on the ground engaged in combat in the Middle East, where soldiers say, "When the Apaches are flying, soldiers aren't dying."

Much like the airlines, the U.S. aerospace industry is facing increasingly fierce global competition, has undergone extensive consolidation, is resorting to outsourcing (along with extended global supply chains), and is reeling from spiking costs of raw materials. Labor is feeling the pressure as manufacturers seek improvements in productivity and strive to reduce costs. With the economic challenges facing the airlines discussed in the preceding chapter, Boeing (America's sole remaining manufacturer of large commercial aircraft) reports that although it has a substantial backlog of orders for new airliners, some financially stressed carriers deferred delivery pending recovery of the global economy.[13] Some industry experts foresaw cancellations if fuel prices did not abate soon; fuel prices did abate then but began a steady upward trend again in December 2010.[14]

Over a quarter of the industry's workforce is now eligible to retire, and the industry is facing a potential crisis in replacing them with qualified individuals, a situation paralleling the pilot shortage facing commercial aircraft operators discussed in the preceding chapter.[15]

Fuel costs and environmental concerns present short-term challenges whose technological

Figure 9.4. An Airbus A380 taking off during the Paris Air Show in 2007. Even though aerospace companies forecasted a drop in aircraft orders in 2008, the two largest plane makers, Boeing and Airbus, have a backlog of orders stretching so many years ahead, that if one ordered a new aircraft in 2008, it may not be ready until 2017.

solution is likely to deliver long-term payoffs to the industry.[16]

An Era of Industry Consolidation: Mergers and Acquisitions

Much like the airline industry, mergers and acquisitions have a long history in the aerospace industry, beginning no later than the mergers of companies founded by the Wright brothers and aviation pioneer Glen Curtiss to form the Curtiss-Wright Corporation and organization of the large aviation holding companies United Air Transport, North American Aviation, and the Aviation Corporation of America (AVCO) shortly before the stock market crash of 1929 triggered the Great Depression.[17]

As World War II approached, the U.S. industry was rapidly built up to produce over three hundred thousand aircraft, a record that still stands and appears unlikely to ever again even be approached, much less surpassed.[18] With the war's end, military aircraft contracts were abruptly cancelled, and defense spending declined sharply. Commercial aircraft markets simultaneously narrowed due to a glut of military surplus, modern transport–category aircraft entering the market. At the beginning of the war, only 365 transport aircraft were in the United States, but over eleven thousand, largely DC-3-/C-47 and DC-4/C-54 types, were built during the war.[19] Many of these aircraft soon appeared on the used-aircraft market as the armed forces began a major drawdown to peacetime levels.

Shrinking markets heightened competitive pressures, and U.S. aerospace companies sought ways to contain costs. A major solution seized upon was merger, which could enable former competitors to integrate their strengths, combining talents and other resources and reducing costs by eliminating redundant personnel and plants.

The First Wave Laps Gently

The first wave of the aerospace industry's postwar consolidation began shortly after the cessation of hostilities, as the cancellation of military aircraft orders, coupled with the challenges of the transformation to jet aircraft, began to overwhelm the financial capabilities of some companies.

The Curtiss-Wright Corporation, itself founded in a 1929 merger of a dozen aviation companies and once the largest aviation company in the United States, sold its airplane division to North American Aviation in 1948 after losing a critical U.S. Air Force competition for a jet interceptor to rival Northrop Aircraft (see fig. 9.5).[20] (Curtiss-Wright continues as a component manufacturer to this day.)

Convair, the product of a 1943 merger between Vultee Aircraft and Consolidated Aircraft (the latter of which was a product of a 1923 merger between the Dayton-Wright and Gaulladet Aircraft companies), was acquired by General Dynamics in 1953.[21]

The Second Wave Rolls In

The second wave of postwar consolidation of the U.S. aerospace industry began in 1960 with the acquisition by technology conglomerate Textron Inc. of Bell Aircraft to form the corporation's Bell Helicopter Textron division.[22] This was followed by the merger of veteran military

Figure 9.5. Curtiss-Wright Plant P-40 Warhawks being assembled in the early 1940s. As a result of Glenn Curtiss's early success, the Curtiss Aeroplane and Motor Company became the largest aircraft manufacturer in the world during World War I and went public in 1916. Curtiss had become the world's largest aviation company, employing twenty-one thousand workers. They produced ten thousand aircraft during World War I, more than a hundred in a single week. When Wright Aeronautical was incorporated in 1919, its charter was the design and manufacture of aero engines. As a result of the successes of the pioneers of the aviation industry, Curtiss-Wright Corporation was formed from the merger of twelve Wright and Curtiss–affiliated companies on July 5, 1929. On August 22 of that same year, Curtiss-Wright Corporation was listed on the New York Stock Exchange, where it still trades today. Courtesy of *Western New York Heritage Magazine.*

aircraft manufacturer Martin with the non–aerospace-materials company American Marietta to form Martin Marietta Corporation in 1961.[23]

In 1965, Fairchild Hiller (itself the result of previous mergers and acquisitions) acquired Republic Aviation.[24] In 1967, legendary military aircraft manufacturer North American Aviation merged with nonaerospace automotive-parts supplier Rockwell Standard to form North American Rockwell Corporation. The company was later renamed Rockwell International Corporation.[25]

Also in 1967, military aircraft manufacturer McDonnell Aircraft merged with the predominantly civil aircraft manufacturer Douglas Aircraft to form McDonnell Douglas Corporation (see fig. 9.6).[26] In 1968, Ryan Aeronautical, builder of Charles Lindbergh's *Spirit of St, Louis*, one of the most famous individual airplanes in history, was acquired by Teledyne Inc. and renamed Teledyne Ryan.[27] Teledyne (now Teledyne Technologies) also acquired light-aircraft-engine manufacturer Continental Motors in 1969, renaming it Teledyne Continental.[28]

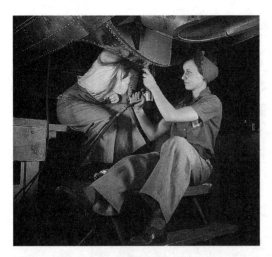

Figure 9.6. Women at work on bomber, Douglas Aircraft Company, Long Beach, California, in October 1942. Library of Congress.

In 1984, McDonnell Douglas acquired Hughes Helicopters. In 1985, Textron acquired aviation engine manufacturer Lycoming from its parent, Avco Corporation, renaming it Textron Lycoming.[29]

The Third Wave Crashes Ashore

The third wave of industry consolidation through mergers, acquisitions, and divestitures began in the early 1990s with General Dynamics selling off its general aviation aircraft manufacturing subsidiary, Cessna Aircraft, to the growing Textron.[30] General Dynamics went on to sell its tactical-fighter business to Lockheed, its missile business to General Motors subsidiary Hughes Electronics, and its space-systems division to Martin Marietta.[31] In 1991, Canadian firm Bombardier bought Learjet Corporation, continuing to manufacture the Learjet line of business jets in Wichita, Kansas.[32]

In 1992, Ford left the aerospace/defense sector by selling its division to Loral in 1992, with IBM following suit in 1994. In 1993, General Electric sold its aerospace division to Martin Marietta but retained its aircraft engines subsidiary.[33]

In 1994, driven primarily by defense considerations and with the strong support of the Department of Defense, airframe manufacturers Lockheed and Martin Marietta merged to form Lockheed Martin Corporation, America's largest defense company,[34] while McDonnell Douglas purchased General Dynamics' Convair division.[35] The following year, Northrop acquired both Grumman Corporation and the Vought Aircraft division of LTV Corporation to create the Northrop Grumman Corporation.[36]

In 1996, McDonnell Douglas closed its Convair division,[37] and Boeing acquired the space and defense units of Rockwell International.[38] In 1997, Boeing merged with McDonnell Douglas, creating the world's largest aerospace company, consolidating operations under the Boeing name.[39] Boeing was now the sole U.S. manufacturer of large civil jet-transport aircraft, Lockheed having bowed out of the market with the closing of the L-1011 TriStar production line in 1983, the company having lost over $2.5 billion on the aircraft.[40] Also in 1997, Lockheed Martin advised the U.S. Department of Justice (responsible for analysis of proposed mergers and acquisitions for compliance with the antitrust laws) of its intention to acquire Northrop Grumman. Based largely on Department of Defense objections that the proposed consolidation would have serious anticompetitive effects by concentrating defense-electronics production into a single company, the Justice Department announced that it considered the proposal anticompetitive. Rather than face antitrust litigation, Lockheed Martin withdrew.[41]

In 1999, Northrop Grumman acquired the Ryan Aeronautical division from Teledyne,[42] and a subsidiary of Dutch RDM Holdings Inc. purchased from Boeing the former Hughes commercial helicopter line that Boeing had acquired as part of its earlier merger with McDonnell Douglas, but the new owners continued production at the former Boeing MD Helicopters facility in Mesa, Arizona.[43] These mergers and acquisitions had left the United States with only two major airframe manufacturers: Boeing and Lockheed Martin.

In 2000, Boeing acquired Hughes Electronics' primary research facility, HRL Laboratories, along with Hughes Space and Communications Company, Hughes Electron Dynamics, and Spectrolab, combining all of these into a new subsidiary, Boeing Satellite Systems.[44] In 2001, GE attempted to buy Honeywell International, thinking Honeywell's advanced avionics made a good fit with GE, one of three leading global manufacturers of jet-aircraft engines, but the European Union's Commission blocked the proposed merger as anticompetitive. United Technologies Corporation acquired Schweizer Aircraft in 2004, merging it into UTC's Sikorsky Aircraft division.[45] In 2005, United Technologies aircraft-engine manufacturing division, Pratt & Whitney, acquired Boeing's space-propulsion division Rocketdyne, renaming the merged company the Pratt & Whitney Rocketdyne division of Pratt & Whitney.[46] UTC's Pratt & Whitney Rocketdyne is now the major U.S. manufacturer of rocket engines for space applications.[47]

In 2010, major aerospace manufacturers began selectively acquiring some (usually smaller) companies that had been suppliers, at least partially to resolve supply-chain problems by assuring more reliable quality and timely delivery.

Labor, Weakened, Responds

Each of these mergers and acquisitions had a direct disruptive effect on the lives of members of the workforces, particularly those of the merged or acquired company, as duplicative positions were eliminated, often among both labor and management. Often, government contracts had served to offset fluctuations in the civil aircraft market, but aerospace companies were hit with a double whammy in the mid-1990s,

seeing sweeping cancellations of large government programs at the same time as cutbacks in airline orders for new commercial aircraft. Thousands of aerospace workers were laid off, saw their plants close, and their jobs cease to exist. Union outrage raised the specter of potential job-security strikes.

In 1994 at Pratt & Whitney, the machinists, representing ten thousand workers, agreed to concessions to save twenty-three hundred jobs. Under the new contract, Pratt & Whitney agreed to close only one plant, rather than the five it had under consideration. Within minutes of a threatened machinists strike at McDonnell Douglas, the company and union signed a three-year contract covering eight thousand workers in St. Louis, Missouri. Work-rule changes and job loss through consolidation were the main points of argument.

That same year, Boeing and the International Association of Machinists and Aerospace Workers (IAMAW) also signed a new three-year agreement. The agreement provided the employees increased job security, along with a bonus, pay raise, and fully paid health care. Lockheed and the IAMAW also signed a new three-year contract covering eleven thousand workers.[48]

But the downturn in airline and government orders had weakened labor's bargaining position as it weakened the companies' ability to pay. Total aerospace-industry employment declined by 5.4 percent between September 1993 and September 1994. Boeing, McDonnell Douglas, United Technologies, and the Aerostructure Division of Textron were soon all in hardball negotiation with their unions, whose contracts were expiring in 1995, seeking concessions.[49]

Labor relations in the aerospace industry have since closely paralleled those in the airlines, though with a few years or even decades of time delay. Concessionary bargaining became the new standard as unions, desperate to save jobs (in part to preserve their own streams of income from membership dues), fell into a "save the company at any cost" mentality. Two-tier pay scales emerged, as they had at the airlines two decades earlier. In line with the trend sweeping all U.S. industries at the beginning of the twenty-first century, pensions shifted from defined-benefit to defined-contribution plans. Soaring health-care costs drove employers to cut back employees' health-insurance coverage, even to the extent of totally eliminating health-care coverage from employees' retirement benefits.

Lockheed Martin's Marietta, Georgia, factory, where the company manufactures military C-130J Hercules transports and F-22 Raptor fighters, employs about eight thousand workers, including about three thousand machinists. On the eve of an impending strike in March 2008, machinists represented by the IAMAW overwhelmingly voted in favor of ratifying a new three-year contract. Union president Jeff T. Goen reported that membership turnout for the vote was one of the largest the union had drawn in recent years, and about 88 percent of the members voted to approve the contract. Health care had been the final sticking point, with the company pressing for an increase in employee contributions to health-care costs, and the union refusing to agree or recommend ratification to its members. The union ultimately prevailed on that issue and recommended ratification to its members, with Goen stating that the deal "may be the best package we've ever gotten." Under the agreement, machinists at the plant received a 10 percent pay raise, with implementation spread over three years, along with a $2,000-per-worker bonus payable on contract ratification, and their contribution to plan health-care costs remained at 13 percent. Much of the cost of the agreement fell on new hires, who will be compensated at lower rates under a two-tier pay scale and who will not qualify for health-care benefits upon retirement. Another twenty-five hundred IAMAW

members employed by Lockheed at plants in other states, including California, Florida, and Mississippi, agreed to the same contract provisions shortly thereafter.[50]

Lean Manufacturing Boosts Productivity

Competitive pressures also brought widespread adoption by the aerospace industry of so-called *lean manufacturing*, with its focus on continuous improvement of manufacturing-process efficiency. Lean manufacturing is now typically combined with just-in time (JIT) inventory processes and Six Sigma total-quality-management (TQM) programs. Studies showed that at many aerospace plants, workers wasted time searching out needed parts, retrieving them, and carrying them back to the work station where they were needed. Lean manufacturing focuses on feeding needed parts to production-line workers just before the parts are needed, if sparingly, saving working time that would otherwise be wasted searching around the plant for the next part.[51] For example, at the Boeing Apache Longbow attack helicopter plant in Mesa, Arizona, some parts are brought to the work station for a particular phase of manufacture in open bins mounted on rolling racks, while others are made available at the work station in modified food-vending machines, accessible by a worker simply pushing the correct combination of buttons to select the desired part, then swiping his or her company ID card. In lean manufacturing, production workers are deeply personally involved in groups (called cells) focused on improving each step of the manufacturing process, always on the lookout for even the most minor changes that may improve production efficiency.[52]

Pratt & Whitney Canada (P&WC) implemented lean manufacturing in 1998 in combination with the Six Sigma approach to product quality control in a proprietary program the company calls ACE, short for achieving competitive excellence. P&WC credits the approach with reducing the company's lead time from customer order to engine delivery from twenty to twenty-four months in 1993 to ten to twelve months by 1998 to six to eight months by 2003. All United Technologies companies now use the ACE program.[53] When the company committed to opening a new final-assembly line in 2006 for its PW6000 family of engines designed to power the coming generation of very light jets (VLJ), the company set an astonishing goal to complete assembly within four hours or less per engine, with no more than eight hours elapsing from the moment parts are ready until engine testing is completed, compared to over forty-five hours typical of the then-current PW500 process for engine assembly and testing. The engine creeps along a sixty-foot-long conveyor at two inches per minute, enabling a single shift of workers to assemble and test four engines per day, sending a thousand new engines a year into the market. Addition of a second shift would easily double the output. P&WC is applying this one-piece flow approach (common to higher-volume manufacturing operations such as the automotive industry) not only to final assembly but also to parts production and component assembly, with production rates coordinated to eliminate wasteful backlog of parts inventory at one extreme and interruption of engine-assembly flow attributable to a component shortage at the other.[54]

Many production workers find this a more fulfilling, less-frustrating working environment. While justifying improvements in worker pay and benefits by the positive impact on the company's bottom line of efficiencies gained, lean manufacturing accomplishes that goal by reducing the number of workers (or worker hours) needed to accomplish the work. Thus, such programs are typically viewed by unions focused on maintaining and increasing their membership numbers and dues income as a mixed blessing, at best.

Outsourcing and Globalization: Impacts and Implications

At least from the early days of mass production, aircraft manufacturers have never been totally self-sufficient but have always relied on outside suppliers for materials, including components and subcomponents, such as engines, avionics, tires, and lights. As aircraft became increasingly complex, a subindustry of specialized-niche component manufacturers developed, producing increasingly major aircraft components, such as seats, landing gear, emergency-escape slides, and survival equipment. Likewise, many firms came to specialize in building airframe subassemblies, such as control surfaces, stabilizers, and flaps under contract to the manufacturer. The latter grew to include even major wing and fuselage sections. Until recently, U.S. aircraft manufacturers tended to buy these components from other U.S. companies, where available. So long as the U.S. airlines were the major customer for commercial aircraft, this practice went largely unchallenged.

But as foreign airlines came to represent a growing customer base and competition from foreign airframe manufacturers (particularly Europe's Airbus Industrie) grew, customer nations (which often owned the airline that was shopping for the new airliners) began to press manufacturers to agree to have suitable components of the aircraft manufactured by that nation's own companies to support their own national economic progress. Such international subcontracting can now be a deciding factor in whether the airline's order goes to Boeing or to Airbus.

The same competitive-cost pressures that motivated U.S. airlines to contract out their heavy maintenance to foreign repair stations (discussed in the preceding chapter) also came to bear on the aerospace industry, adding to pre-existing customer pressures to disperse more of the work globally. Some U.S. manufacturers have contracted out major structural subassembly work to foreign firms, while others have built plants in other countries or entered into licensing agreements for foreign firms to manufacture complete aircraft.

Where the Work Went

Mexico is one of several industrializing nations whose economy is benefiting from this trend. About 124 aeronautical companies are in Mexico. Aided by the U.S.-Mexico Bilateral Aviation Safety Agreement that allows design and production in Mexico to FAA standards while relieving the manufacturer of the requirement to send the item to a U.S. manufacturing or lab facility for certification, Mexican manufacturers are able to ship products directly to end users. Goodrich Aerostructures' new 350,000 square foot plant in Mexicali manufactures engine nacelles and thrust reversers for Boeing's new 787 Dreamliners and is competing for production work for Airbus, as well. The company operates another aircraft components plant in the neighboring state of Sonora. In the Mexican City of Queretaro, GE engineers at the company's research center design jet engines, while across town, workers earning $3.50 an hour build rudders and assemble wiring bundles for airliners. At Queretaro's airport, Bombardier workers build fuselages, rudders, and tail sections for the company's Global Express business jet and assemble wiring harnesses. The wiring-harness work was transferred there from Wichita, the rudder fabrication from Japan, and the fuselage building from Northern Ireland.[55] In 2008, Bombardier announced that it will manufacture the all-composite structure and other subcomponents for its new Learjet 85 at the Queretaro plant, though final assembly, interior completion, flight test, and customer delivery will be accomplished at the company's Wichita plant.[56]

Similar shifts of work from U.S. aerospace manufacturing plants are going to Asia. Cessna is fabricating its new model 162 SkyCatcher primary trainer in China, where Chinese contractor Shenyang Aircraft Company builds the fuselage. Cessna stated that it could not produce the aircraft in the United States and earn a profit.[57] To reduce costs and increase efficiency, Honeywell is transferring production of its autopilots, distance-measuring equipment, and other navigation equipment from Olathe, Kansas, to plants in Malaysia and Indonesia. The supply chain for Sikorsky's S-92 helicopter includes venture partners in Japan, China, Taiwan, Spain, and Brazil.[58] Boeing, though, took the biggest leap of all with its global supply chain for the 787 Dreamliner involving major-component manufacturing by partners in the United States, Japan, China, and Italy but with final assembly at Boeing's Everett, Washington, plant (see fig. 9.7). Boeing was already buying parts from about a dozen Chinese suppliers for its 737, 747, and 767 lines. For example, the 737's vertical fin, tail cone, aft fuselage section, and over-wing exit doors are all made in China by Shanghai Aircraft, part of the government-owned China Commercial Aircraft Company (CCAC). CCAC was established to develop and build a 150-seat, single-aisle jetliner to compete with Boeing and Airbus in the global market.[59]

Confrontation Time

Boeing's unionized labor force has a record of not shrinking from confrontation with the company. In the Seattle, Washington, area, Boeing's machinists, represented by the IAMAW, have gone out on strike seven times since the union was founded in 1935, and Boeing engineers, represented by the Society of Professional Engineering Employees in Aerospace (SPEEA, have stopped work twice. The machinists strike in 2005 stopped production of thirty aircraft. In the fall of 2008, with contracts for both employee groups soon to

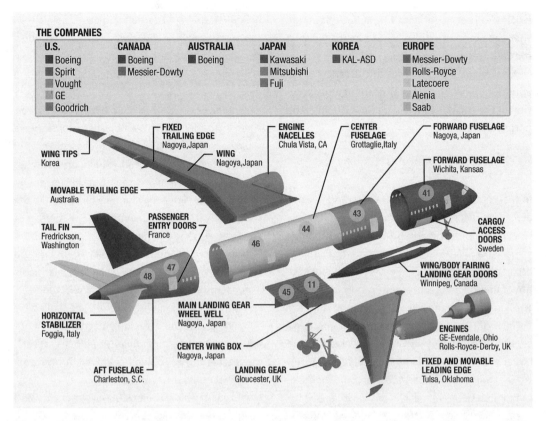

THE COMPANIES

U.S.	CANADA	AUSTRALIA	JAPAN	KOREA	EUROPE
■ Boeing	■ Boeing	■ Boeing	■ Kawasaki	■ KAL-ASD	■ Messier-Dowty
■ Spirit	■ Messier-Dowty		■ Mitsubishi		■ Rolls-Royce
■ Vought			■ Fuji		■ Latecoere
■ GE					■ Alenia
■ Goodrich					■ Saab

FIXED TRAILING EDGE
Nagoya, Japan

ENGINE NACELLES
Chula Vista, CA

CENTER FUSELAGE
Grottaglie, Italy

FORWARD FUSELAGE
Nagoya, Japan

WING TIPS
Korea

WING
Nagoya, Japan

FORWARD FUSELAGE
Wichita, Kansas

MOVABLE TRAILING EDGE
Australia

TAIL FIN
Fredrickson, Washington

PASSENGER ENTRY DOORS
France

CARGO/ ACCESS DOORS
Sweden

WING/BODY FAIRING LANDING GEAR DOORS
Winnipeg, Canada

HORIZONTAL STABILIZER
Foggia, Italy

MAIN LANDING GEAR WHEEL WELL
Nagoya, Japan

ENGINES
GE-Evendale, Ohio
Rolls-Royce-Derby, UK

CENTER WING BOX
Nagoya, Japan

AFT FUSELAGE
Charleston, S.C.

LANDING GEAR
Gloucester, UK

FIXED AND MOVABLE LEADING EDGE
Tulsa, Oklahoma

Figure 9.7. The Boeing 787, which represents a new way of assembling airplanes. Boeing will use nearly fifty outside partners and top-tier suppliers at 135 sites spanning four continents to fabricate about 70 percent of the Dreamliner, as opposed to 51 percent for existing planes. Only final assembly will be done in Everett, Washington. New plants in Italy, Japan, and South Carolina were built to manufacture the large composite pieces. Courtesy of the Boeing Company.

expire, negotiations began, and the unions began preparing to strike. The IAMAW was seeking improvements in wages and benefits (starting wages had not been raised since 1992, though others were raised in 2004) and blaming delays of well over a year in the B-787 production schedule on suppliers, arguing that the company would have been better off keeping the work in-house. Machinists were also up in arms about proposed changes to the company's medical plan that shifted more of the cost to the workers and about the company's announced desire to change its pension system. The union was feeling strong, expecting that Boeing would not want to risk a strike that would further delay the first 787 deliveries, in particular.[60] In 2002, SPEEA executive director Ray Goforth stated with reference to the 787 program: "Boeing outsourced everything it could to lower costs, and it's hurting this program and the company." Boeing Chairman and CEO Jim McNerney acknowledged that the global supply chain for the 787 program was "a very aggressive move" by the company. McNerney acknowledged that in some cases, Boeing outsourced more work than particular partners could handle and that those partners were "going through a painful learning curve." He did, however, defend the practice, stating his expectation that when Boeing develops its next commercial jetliner after the 787, the strategy will again rely extensively on global partners.[61] While strenuously disagreeing with the IAMAW position,

Boeing's chief negotiator Doug Knight stated that the company did plan to reward workers for the company's "great success."[62]

Case study 9.2 illustrates the interplay of negotiation, posturing, preparation for and execution of the IAMAW strike against Boeing, and pattern bargaining.

Case Study 9.2: Preparing for a Strike—2008

In the Puget Sound region surrounding Seattle, aerospace giant Boeing operates numerous facilities, many operating around the clock with three shifts, with final assembly of commercial airliners accomplished at plants in Seattle's southern suburb of Renton and its northern suburb of Everett. The company is financially strong, reporting a $4.1 billion profit in 2007, up 84 percent over 2006, and a seven-year backlog of aircraft orders valued at $346 billion, including 895 orders for its superefficient new 787 Dreamliner, the most successful commercial debut for a new commercial jet airliner ever (see fig. CS9.2.1). Final assembly of the 787 is done at the Everett plant. In 2001, Boeing had moved its corporate

Figure CS 9.2.1 The Boeing 787 Dreamliner, a midsized, wide-body, twin-engine jet airliner currently under development by Boeing Commercial Airplanes. It will carry between 210 and 330 passengers depending on variant and seating configuration. Boeing stated that it will be more fuel efficient than earlier Boeing airliners and will be the first major airliner to use composite materials for most of its construction. Source: Wikimedia Commons; photo by Mark J. Handel; Creative Commons Attribution 2.0 license.

headquarters from Seattle to Chicago, isolating its top executives from the company's actual production work and workers.

The International Association of Machinists and Aerospace Workers (IAM) represents about 25,000 Boeing employees in the region, up from 18,400 in 2005, when the company's airline-industry customers were still recovering from the economic consequences of the 9/11 attacks, leading Boeing to furlough thousands of workers and the union to agree to concessions on work rules and lower pay for new hires to help the company weather the downturn. In the summer of 2008, the average Boeing machinist earned $27 an hour, or about $56,000 a year, before overtime and incentives, already significantly higher than machinists in nonaerospace segments of U.S. manufacturing.[63]

Facing expiration of their three-year collective bargaining agreement, union and company negotiators began meeting regularly beginning several months before the September 4, 2008, contract-expiration date. Issues included job security, pensions, wages, incentives, vacations, survivor benefits, and health-care plans. Agreement is never a foregone conclusion, and in case no agreement is reached, the union must be prepared to strike immediately and in a well-organized and disciplined manner. Indeed, the specter of a strike and its potential impact on both the company and its employees is the main driving force on both sides to reach agreement in a timely manner. Boeing's lead negotiator, Doug Knight, promised the machinists that the company would make its "best and final offer" before the long Labor Day weekend (August 30 and 31 and September 1) to allow sufficient time for union members to review the proposal. The union scheduled a vote on the company's final offer for Wednesday, September 3. If two-thirds of the union's members voted to reject the offer, a strike would begin at 12:01 A.M. on the following day. With no more than a few hours between the strike vote and the initial work stoppage with commencement of picketing, both sides had to make preparations well in advance of the strike both hoped would prove unnecessary.

Strikes are not spontaneous events but require weeks, even months, of meticulous preparation. In this case, the union began at least a month before the potential strike date to prepare for its members to picket about one hundred Boeing gates across the region for twenty-four hours every day. The large number of union workers in the area would allow the union to staff the picket lines with each member having to spend only a four-hour shift once a week, but they would need support. Striking employees could not park on Boeing property while on strike, so it was arranged that union members would park at one of the four union halls (located in Everett, Seattle, Renton, and Auburn) and ride on union-provided shuttle buses or vans to the Boeing gates. The union ordered burn barrels for every gate, often the only source of heat and light, and members at each union hall took turns chopping wood to feed the barrels.

Picketing strikers would need signs, and the union ordered them, leaving only the detail of stapling each sign to a handle to be accomplished in the few hours between a strike vote and the first picket shift. Anticipating members' financial needs, the union scheduled locations and times for every member to pick up his or her weekly $150 strike-pay check required by union rules to be done in person. The union arranged for counselors at the credit union to advise striking members how best to deal with mortgage and other lenders and utility and credit-card companies during a strike and began talks with other area companies about arranging temporary work for members unable to afford to not work during the strike. (The union-provided strike pay covered only about 10 percent of a striking worker's average pay when not on strike.)

While acknowledging that it, too, was making prudent preparations for the possibility of a strike, Boeing declined to provide any details.[64]

As had become customary in previous IAMAW-Boeing negotiations, the negotiating teams moved en masse into a hotel during the final two weeks of the contract, to facilitate a near-continuous negotiation push to reach agreement by the expiration date.

On the Thursday before the Labor Day weekend, the company tendered its best and final offer, including pay raises averaging 11 percent (5 percent in the first year of the contract, then 3 percent in each of the next two years), pension increases, a 3 percent cost-of-living adjustment, and signing bonuses averaging $6,400 per worker, a package Boeing valued at $34,000 for the average worker. Boeing immediately posted the offer on its website for all to view and sponsored radio ads praising the generosity of the company's offer. The offer was generally viewed as a sweet deal for the union by outsiders, considering the general economic downturn, but it infuriated Boeing's machinists by including no limitations on the company's freedom to contract out work to others, demanding to shift a greater percentage of health-care costs onto the employees, changing the pension plan from a defined benefit to a 401(k)-style defined-contribution plan, and limiting death benefits for survivors. (The expiring contract guaranteed spouses of deceased Boeing workers monthly payments for life, but the company proposed to reduce this to a one-time payment of $4,000, insufficient for so much as a decent burial and leaving nothing to aid the spouse's own continued financial survival.) IAM representatives expressed outrage that Boeing would seek such concessions when the company was thriving.

On September 3, 2008, a stunning 87 percent of Boeing machinists rejected the offer and voted to strike. Washington governor Chris Gregoire and a federal mediator requested the parties agree to a forty-eight-hour contract extension to facilitate a last-ditch effort to reach agreement, and both the company and union agreed. When IAM chief negotiator Mark Blondin and Tom Wroblewski, president of Machinists District Lodge 751, announced the extension in a meeting of seven thousand members at the union hall in Everett, some union members already whipped up into a strike frenzy shouted them down with catcalls of "Sellout!" and "What was the strike vote for?"[65] The further talks were held at a Disney resort in Florida, where the negotiators flew to enable

IAM president Tom Buffenbarger, who was attending an IAM convention there, to participate. They failed to produce an agreement, and at 12:01 A.M. on Friday, September 5, hundreds of union members raised their strike signs outside the Boeing plants, cheering and blasting air horns at passing cars, many of which honked back. Boeing announced that it would not try to assemble planes during the strike.[66]

The first three weeks of the strike are reported to have cost Boeing about $1.4 billion in deferred delivery revenue and earnings, and industry analysts forecast that the strike could continue to cost Boeing about $100 million per day in deferred delivery revenue and $259 million per month in earnings.[67]

The outcome of the strike may signal the future direction of collective bargaining in the U.S. aerospace industry for years to come. Boeing machinists appear to have greater bargaining strength than those in other industries, filling a great variety of highly skilled and highly specialized positions. Boeing simply cannot build airplanes without them and could not find enough available and qualified replacements (particularly in the Puget Sound region, where these plants are located and where the cost of living is well above the national average). Other unions encouraged the IAM to hang tough, in hope of generating a rising tide that may lift all union boats, and Boeing's twenty-one thousand engineers in Washington, Oregon, California, and Utah, represented by SPEEA, followed close on the IAMAW's heels and presented their first proposal to Boeing for a new three-year contract to replace theirs that expired December 1, 2008. SPEEA's proposal also sought limitation of Boeing's ability to contract out work, pay raises, more vacation days, higher overtime pay, and improvements in health-care and pension plans. The *Chicago Tribune* newspaper quotes SPEEA executive Director Ray Goforth as saying, "The Boeing company's approach to the machinists is setting a pattern. Boeing could be facing back-to-back strikes."[68]

Richard Abulafia, vice president and aviation analyst for Teal Group, based in Fairfax, Virginia, sees the machinists having the upper hand in this match: "This is America's last successful major heavy industry. . . . As a result, the workers have a lot more power . . . and they're taking advantage of that power." Peter Morici, professor of international business at the University of Maryland, agrees but cautions, "This is a good example of why manufacturing is leaving the country. This is like the UAW in the '50s."[69]

This strike could be the tipping point, teetering to reversal of the trend of losses in wages and benefits of skilled labor in U.S. manufacturing or tottering as the last straw to break the back of America's last successful major heavy industry.

The strike ended after fifty-three days with a new collective bargaining agreement that included a 15 percent pay raise over four years, withdrawal of the company's proposed changes to the employee health-insurance plan, and a slight concession by Boeing on the outsourcing process.[70] Total costs of the strike to Boeing have not been revealed. A few weeks after the IAMAW strike ended, Boeing reached a new four-year agreement with SPEEA that included a pay increase averaging 5 percent per year over the term of the agreement, averting a second strike close on the heels of the IAMAW strike.[71] Less than two months later, in January 2009, the global economic downturn manifested itself, and Boeing announced plans to lay off 4,500 workers.[72] By the end of March, this would include 458 machinists and fewer than 20 engineers.[73] Then in October 2009, Boeing announced plans to move the B-787 production line to South Carolina (a right-to-work state) in an effort to reduce costs by shifting to nonunion labor in a locale with lower costs of living than the Puget Sound area. At this writing, Boeing is considering its next major airframe project: a replacement for the 737. Recognizing and learning from problems encountered with the global supply chain on the 787, Boeing is planning to truncate the supply chain for the next design at a "supersite," a cluster of major suppliers' plants near Boeing's final assembly site. That assembly site could be either in Washington or South Carolina, depending on whether Boeing decides to build the aircraft out of carbon-fiber composite-plastic (like the 787) or one of the new aluminum alloys (that use fabrication techniques similar to those long used to build metal aircraft such as the 737). The choice of metal for the medium would favor the Puget Sound area, while the choice of carbon-fiber composite-plastic would favor South Carolina.

A Judicial Rebuke

In April 1994, Textron Lycoming Reciprocating Engine Division entered into a three-year collective bargaining agreement with the United Automobile, Aerospace, and Agricultural Implement Workers of America (UAW) and its Local 187, representing about five hundred workers at the company's Williamsport, Pennsylvania, plant. A *no-strike clause* in the agreement prohibited the union from striking against the company for any reason during the term of the agreement. A separate memorandum agreement between the company and union required the company to give the union seven days' notice before subcontracting out work that would otherwise be performed by union members at the plant. About two months later, the company announced its intention to subcontract out a volume of work that would cause about half of the plant's union members to lose their jobs. Barred from striking over the issue by the new contract, the union sued in federal district court under section 301(a) of the Labor Management Relations Act, alleging that Textron Lycoming fraudulently induced the union to sign the collective bargaining agreement. The union claimed that before and during negotiations, it had repeatedly asked the company to provide any information it might have regarding plans to subcontract out work that would otherwise be performed by union members and

that during negotiations the company had in fact completed such a plan but despite the union's repeated inquiries said nothing about its existence. The union sought a declaratory judgment that the collective bargaining agreement was rendered voidable (by the union) and for compensatory and punitive damages for the company's misrepresentations and concealments.

Section 301(a) of the Act (29 U.S.C. sec. 185(a)) provides: "Suits for violation of contracts between an employer and a labor organization representing employees in an industry affecting commerce as defined in this Act, or between any such labor organizations, may be brought in any district court of the United States having jurisdiction of the parties, without respect to the amount in controversy or without regard to the citizenship of the parties."

The company moved to dismiss the complaint for lack of subject-matter jurisdiction, and the district court dismissed the complaint for lack of subject-matter jurisdiction because the company's actions were not alleged to violate the contract. On appeal in 1997, the U.S. Court of Appeals for the Third Circuit reversed. The U.S. Supreme Court granted certiorari, exercising its discretion to review the decision (always a long shot, as the court receives four thousand to five thousand petitions for writ of certiorari each year but typically selects from among them only about eighty cases to consider). In its 1998 opinion, written by Justice Antonin Scalia, the Supreme Court reversed, agreeing with the district court's plain reading of the first five words of Section 301(a).[74] The effect of this strict construction was that although the company may have pulled a fast one on the union in what no person of ordinary understanding would characterize as good-faith bargaining, the federal courts would take no action to prevent the company's reaping the benefits of that deceit. It was shades of the Supreme Court's 1921 evisceration of the Clayton Act, discussed in chapter 2.

Materials Costs Spike, Currency Fluctuates

In 2008, blessed with unprecedented backorders for new aircraft, global supply chains discussed above were already straining to meet the demand when the aerospace industry experienced raw-materials-cost spikes on a scale comparable to the fuel-cost spike that threatened the airline industry. The major materials used in aircraft manufacturing all saw substantial increases, with aluminum up 90 percent, carbon fiber up 60 percent, and titanium up 30 percent, knocking the foundation out from under manufacturing cost projections.

A characteristic of the industry worldwide is that aircraft sales (revenues) are in U.S. dollars, while costs (expenses) are paid in local currencies. According to Philip Troy, a managing director of global business-advisory firm AlixPartners, "[t]he combination of the spike in raw materials cost, the drop in the U.S. dollar, and the difficulties faced by aircraft OEMs [original-equipment manufacturers] and suppliers to deliver their huge backlogs could be a wind shear awaiting the aerospace industry globally." It should be noted, however, that the currency fluctuations fell most heavily on European aerospace companies such as Airbus because the euro appreciated 20 percent against the dollar in the year preceding this statement.[75]

A Labor Shortage Looms

The aerospace workforce is aging, with the average worker in his or her fifties, far older than the levels that prevail in other high-technology sectors. Twenty-eight percent, almost 160,000 workers, became eligible to retire in 2008. For example, roughly 6,000 Lockheed Martin Aeronautics employees, 27 percent of the company's workforce, became eligible to retire in 2008.[76] At Boeing, 15 percent of the company's engineers were already eligible to retire.[77]

Both Lockheed Martin Corporation and Northrop Grumman estimate that half of their workers will be eligible for retirement over the next decade, a potential total loss of approximately 131,000 workers.[78] Wichita, which bills itself as "the air capital of the world," with five major aircraft plants and hundreds of suppliers and vendors, faces the potential loss of 40 percent of its aerospace workforce to retirement over the next five years, with a need for 12,000 more aerospace workers by 2018.[79]

There is rare agreement between the companies and the unions on the seriousness of the shortage. The Aerospace Industries Association (AIA), the industry's trade association, listed the potential skills drain as one of its top-ten priorities in the 2008 presidential election. Former FAA Administrator Marion Blakey, now AIA president and CEO, commented, "It's a looming issue that's getting more serious year by year. These are real veterans. It's a hard workforce to replace."[80] Noting China's 2007 success in shooting down one of its own satellites and the retirement of the U.S. space-shuttle fleet as signals that the United States cannot afford to take its technological and military superiority for granted, Blakey said the country could be facing another "wake-up call" similar to the 1957 Soviet launch of Sputnik, the world's first artificial satellite, an event that shocked the nation and energized a fervor of scientific education and activity.[81] Edward Lazear, chairman of President George W. Bush's Council of Economic Advisers, warns that the skills shortage will eventually cut into U.S. economic growth.[82] IAM spokesman Frank Larkin agrees, except to state, "It's not a problem that's coming, it's here."[83]

John Dalrymple, president of Hamill Manufacturing in Pennsylvania, agrees. The company manufactures precision parts for military helicopters and submarines and has no shortage of orders, but only half its machines are running, due to a shortage of skilled workers. Millions of production jobs have moved to rapidly industrializing nations such as China in the past decade, but precision manufacturing remains a crucial niche in the United States, one in which the country can still compete effectively but for a chronic shortage of skilled workers. In one 2005 study, 90 percent of manufacturers reported suffering a moderate-to-severe shortage of qualified workers. Those skilled manufacturing jobs remaining in all U.S. industries pay well (an average of $60,000 a year, about double the service industries, and hourly wage workers in the aerospace industry typically earn 50 percent more than other production workers). The jobs also have good benefits and reasonable job security, yet many are going unfilled despite vigorous recruiting efforts by employers.[84] Among technical employees such as engineers and scientists, only the computer and software industry pays more than aerospace, and that difference is only slight.

As early as 1988, the Massachusetts Institute of Technology (MIT) established the Labor Aerospace Research Agenda (LARA) to conduct research and education centered on this workforce. LARA's research is focused on the impact of the kinds of instability discussed in this chapter on employment and work practices, the diffusion of new work systems, investment in intellectual capital, and global employment dynamics in the aerospace industry. In November of 2001, LARA published a white paper entitled *Developing a 21st Century Aerospace Workforce*, for submission to the Human Capital Task Force of the U.S. Commission on the Future of the Aerospace Industry. In the foreword to the report, Sheila Widnall, MIT Institute Professor and former Secretary of the Air Force, states in part:

> In recent years, the aerospace industry has been undergoing a set of dramatic transformations that have affected every facet of our professional lives and our industrial base. These transformations include moving from a focus on aircraft that flew "higher, faster, farther" to the industry providing value to its customers through the provision of a wide variety of aerospace goods and services. It includes the change in focus of the industry and its customers from a platform-centric view—focusing on individual airframes, their development and use—to a network view, aerospace vehicles as nodes in a network of information and capability. And it includes moving from an industry with a preeminent place in the competition for societal resources—as we saw in the Apollo era—to an industry that competes with many sectors for societal resources.

> These changes have given rise to a cruel dilemma. It is people's knowledge, skills and mindsets that are essential to addressing the transformation: transformations of skills and capabilities, of tools and approaches, of expectations and opportunities. At the same time, it is these same people who must deal with skill gaps, mixed messages, displacements, and various forms of instability inherent in the way the industry operates today.

> The aerospace industry has long been able to count on the passion of its employees for the accomplishments of the field. However, for too long, we have counted on this passion to sustain their commitment to aerospace without taking affirmative steps to sustain and develop skills on this base. We took it for granted that there would always be a ready pool of people coming into aerospace. And it is the experience base of the people in aerospace today that will make possible the advances of the future—a resource not to be squandered.[85]

Figure 9.8 illustrates the declining experience level of aerospace engineers and production workers involved in military aircraft projects over a forty-year career span. Perhaps the greatest insight into the cause of this recruiting shortfall came in report's statement of the problem, reporting the results of a recent survey of almost five hundred aerospace engineers, managers, production workers, and technical specialists. One of the survey questions was whether they would "highly recommend that their children work in this industry." Overall, 80 percent of respondents indicated that they would *not* recommend it to their children. In individual interviews, people said that while they were very proud of the industry and their own contributions, the instability was a major factor that led them to what was a personally heart-wrenching conclusion.[86]

In 2006, Congress passed a bill establishing an Interagency Aerospace Revitalization Task Force to further examine the problem and recommend solutions. President George W. Bush signed it into law on December 20, 2006. The task force completed its work and submitted

its report in February 2008, characterizing the potential retirements as a "demographic cliff" the aerospace industry was about to fall off. The report noted that many students are discouraged from entering the industry because of job instability and that although once the employer of choice for the "best and brightest" technically trained workers, aerospace now presents a negative image to such prospects.[87] Education is identified as a component cause. By twelfth grade, U.S. high school students rank near the bottom internationally in math and science performance, a problem being compounded by a shortage of teachers in those subjects. Fewer students are earning engineering and science degrees (from undergraduate to doctorate) at U.S. colleges and universities, and about 40 percent of those who do are foreigners who often return to their homelands or are barred by security rules from working on sensitive defense programs.[88] Case study 9.3 discusses some initiatives to address the educational system's shortcomings. In

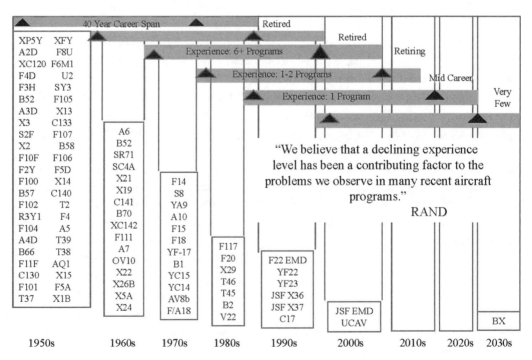

Figure 9.8. Declining experience levels in military aircraft programs.

mid-2007, a study by *Aviation Week & Space Technology* found forty thousand job openings in the aerospace/defense industry.[89]

Case Study 9.3: Addressing the Aerospace Labor Shortage—Educational Initiatives

America's businesses are facing the dual crises of an aging workforce and a shrinking pool of skilled talent. According to federal government data, 40 percent of all U.S. workers were fifty-five years of age or older by 2010. More than sixty million U.S. workers will retire within the next thirty years. The retirement of the American workforce is not affecting just one or two industries; it is a systemic problem. These retirements will place the United States in the position of having a severe shortage of workers, especially skilled workers.[90]

To make the matter worse, prospects for replacing retiring workers with younger individuals who have equal and greater skills do not look promising. As competition continues to intensify globally, the American labor force will increasingly need to acquire new skills and aptitudes. America faces a crisis in the workplace as the gap widens between the inadequate skill level of the nation's emerging workforce and the higher-skill needs of the changing workplace.

In a 2001 report, M. A. Chell, business-development executive with Ameren Services, reported that 60 percent of the new jobs in the early twenty-first century will require skills that are today possessed by only 20 percent of workers. Making up this skills gap will be a tremendous challenge for American workers and employers. Chell also predicted that by 2010, as many as three hundred thousand jobs would be taken internationally because of the lack of appropriately skilled workers in the United States.[91] Moreover, survey results show that 60 percent of U.S. manufacturers typically reject between one-half of and all applicants as unqualified, 62 percent of these manufacturers reported that job applicants have inadequate technical skills, and one-third reported that job applicants have inadequate communication (reading and writing) skills.

One specific industry facing acute shortages of skilled workers is aerospace. A 2005 U.S. government report on the aerospace industry indicated that 26 percent of aerospace workers would be eligible to retire in 2008. The average aerospace production worker is fifty-three years old, and the average aerospace engineer is fifty-four years of age.[92] It is widely believed that more than half of the nation's science and engineering workers will reach retirement age by 2015. This said, there is an increasing realization across the nation that aerospace industries will face serious problems hiring workers with needed skill sets.

This lack of supply of skilled workers is forcing existing employees to work overtime and causing two-year vocational schools to relaunch training programs that were canceled after the aerospace market started weakening in 2000. In 2007, International Association of Machinists and Aerospace Workers (IAMAW) released the results of a national survey that found widespread support among likely U.S. voters for two years of tuition-free, postsecondary education for every qualified American. According to the survey, 97 percent of respondents agreed that it was very important or somewhat important to increase the level of training and skills development. Surprisingly, the combined figure was greater than the importance given to assuring affordable health care, keeping mortgage rates down, and increasing the minimum wage.[93]

Fingerhut Granados Opinion Research, the organization that conducted the survey, states, "Persons of every income, education, and political affiliation would all support a national education policy that included two years of tuition-free education at a community college, vocational or high-tech institute, or apprentice program for qualified Americans. They rightly view this type of education policy as critical for the United States to compete successfully in today's skills-based global marketplace."[94]

Most will agree that education and skills are increasingly becoming the ticket to upward mobility and increased earnings in the aerospace industry.

This especially resonates in aircraft-manufacturing centers such as Wichita, Kansas.

Community leaders in Wichita, which has five major aircraft plants and hundreds of suppliers and vendors, are also pursuing countermeasures to offset the potential loss of more than 40 percent of the aeronautics workforce over the next five years. The Board of Sedgwick County Commissioners in Kansas is building a world-class aviation training center to help meet the need for twelve thousand more aerospace workers by 2018 (see fig. CS9.3.1). The proposed National Center for Aviation Training will focus on the immediate needs of the aerospace and general manufacturing industries to ensure the community can supply highly skilled, qualified workers. Business and government leaders believe this larger skilled, educated, and creative workforce is imperative to retain their existing employers and attract future businesses to their region.

The demand for specific-educated aerospace disciplines was expected to be double what it was ten years before, which is a positive since the literature finds that tomorrow's young workers are far more apt to attend a two- or four-year college rather than learn the skilled trades. However, the industry states that colleges and universities are turning out far too few aerospace-specific graduates to fill future vacancies. Although production workers in aerospace earn higher pay than those in most other manufacturing industries, Harry Holzer, a Georgetown University professor, says the industry does not have the recruitment appeal that it did decades ago during the Cold War. Many young job-seekers now regard aerospace plants as "old-fashioned" industries.[95]

The undergraduate-program enrollment always rises and falls in cycles. "It depends on the students' perception," says Richard W. Heckel, PhD, founder and technical director of Engineering Trends. "For example, many of the students who study engineering in this country do it in terms of personal financial reward. Only if it looks like personal financial reward will they pick engineering. If they think that times are tough for engineers, then they will go elsewhere." Some industry experts say it is only a matter of time before the decline of students in engineering programs hits the real world. Tighter requirements for visas and more investment in engineering programs internationally also have cut into foreign-student enrollment in American universities.[96]

Figure CS 9.3.1. The proposed National Center for Aviation Training, which will feel more like a business center than an educational institution. Workers for the county's five aircraft manufacturers and hundreds of businesses that support them will receive training at this new campus. A few of the programs selected for the new campus are various kinds of aviation training, manufacturing, welding, and robotics. Courtesy of Sedgwick County (Kansas) government.

Rumors of jobs being moved offshore have also discouraged students from entering engineering programs. "Regardless of the number of actual jobs sent overseas, when the media reports on it, the number of enrollments in engineering continues to decline," says Heckel. "Every time that comes up, the parents of high school students will look at this and ask, 'Should I recommend engineering to my son or my daughter?' ...When people keep getting infiltrated with information about offshoring, they hear about plants closing, and we have very little that shows up in the news as new engineering achievements these days. There is no counterbalance to these offshoring rumors. What is going to have an impact as well is whether U.S. companies are going to go on campus and hire this upcoming graduating class."[97]

With the aging of the labor force and unmet need for skilled younger workers, the U.S. aerospace industry realizes that it will be facing a labor shortage within the next decade. These shortages will become even more critical if leaders in the aerospace industry ignore them and fail to develop action plans for their own businesses. And the same exists for the educational institutions in this country.

Environmental Factors: Greening the Sky

It has been said that in the Chinese language, consisting of thousands of characters representing words and concepts, the character for *crisis* is a combination of the characters for *danger* and *opportunity*. While this may be a misconception,[98] it may nonetheless be an appropriate frame of reference for looking at the current destabilizing challenges to the aerospace industry presented by high fuel costs (and the impending depletion of fossil fuels) and the need to reverse the human carbon footprint on the environment by substantially decreasing aircraft emissions.

Current aerospace industry approaches to the problem include development of:

- Airframes with lighter weight and less drag, needing less thrust to achieve the same or higher speed

- More-efficient engines, burning less fuel to deliver the same or greater thrust
- Maintenance procedures to maximize sustained engine fuel efficiency
- Alternative fuels, burning cleaner while delivering equal or greater power per unit of weight and at equal or lesser cost

A major selling point for Boeing's new 787 Dreamliner is the aircraft's promised fuel efficiency. With its sleek, lightweight construction (at least 50 percent composites) and fuel-efficient engines designed specifically for the plane by GE and Rolls-Royce, Boeing claims the aircraft will use 20 percent less fuel for comparable missions than any previous, similarly sized airplane.[99] At the July 2008 international air show in Farnborough, England, Bombardier announced a new hundred-seat jet, called the C-series, also claimed to be 20 percent more fuel efficient than competing aircraft.[100]

At the Eco-Aviation conference in Washington, D.C., in June 2008, UTC's Hartford, Connecticut-based Pratt & Whitney unveiled its new "Pure Power"™ model PW 1000G geared turbofan engine that has been in development for two decades. P&WC claims the engine, now in flight test on a B-747, will burn up to 25 percent less fuel than existing engines of the same thrust, reducing annual operating costs by about $1.5 million per plane while running more than 50 percent more quietly. According to the company, the engine will be available in 2013. Airbus has promised to offer greener planes by 2020, and P&WC is looking to them as a potential customer for the new engine. P&WC is also marketing an engine-washing system that uses atomized water to prevent contaminant runoff. Regular washing can help turbine engines maintain their fuel efficiency.[101]

At the other end of an aircraft's useful life, even the jetliner salvage business is going green. Airbus's PAMELA (an acronym for process for advanced management of end-of-life aircraft) project recently concluded that about 85 percent of the dry weight of an airliner can be recycled, compared to the previously accepted maximum of 60 percent. Sorted metals can join a reverse supply chain, being recycled for sale as reusable raw materials. (Current processes for recycling composites are not economical and, unlike metals, do not produce a product that would be reusable in aerospace applications, though they can be crushed and incorporated into some plastics and concrete or burned to generate heat.) Aware that twelve hundred of their aircraft will be retired in the next twenty years, Airbus management has made planet-friendly aircraft dismantling part of the consortium's general environmental policy and is now looking for ways to encourage the establishment of green airliner-dismantling companies around the world.[102]

All of these initiatives presage new and exciting work opportunities in the aerospace industry, opportunities for scientists, engineers, and production workers to make real and meaningful personal contributions to saving the planet and the airline industry.

Summary

The aerospace industry is crucial to the economic and defense needs of the United States. The industry has been highly unstable for decades, characterized by cutthroat global competition, mergers and acquisitions, layoffs and reductions in force, leaner manufacturing regimes, outsourcing of work (particularly to overseas contractors or venture partners), and spiking costs of raw materials. Its customers, too, are reeling from spiking fuel costs. Both are affected by instabilities in the national and global economies.

Yet, the industry also enjoys a record backlog of orders (not counting World War II production demands), although the economic downturn is beginning to cause some cancellations and deferred deliveries and still offers pay and benefits better than most. But job openings go unfilled.

Granted, the industry, having matured along with its product line, lacks the instant gratification of the days when, for example, North American's engineers and production workers designed and built the first P-51 Mustang fighter in 117 days, and their counterparts at Lockheed designed and built America's first operational jet fighter (the P-80 Shooting Star) in six months. By comparison, an engineer could have been working on the F-22 Raptor for twenty years by the time the design was completed and the first aircraft completed.

Nonetheless, the best jobs are still here, and they are going begging. "Productivity in the United States has increased generation after generation, creating ever-rising standards of living," commented Alan Greenspan, chairman of the Federal Reserve Board, in 2004. "Our knowledge-based skills in a business environment, supported by a rule of law, have enabled our workforce to create ever-greater value added—irrespective of what goods and services we have chosen to produce at home and what and how much we have chosen to import."[103]

By young people not becoming prepared to fill these vacancies, not applying, as individuals, for these jobs, are we not as a nation choosing to not produce aircraft, spacecraft, and other aerospace products here in the United States? Are we not in effect voting to abandon this industry, too, to whatever other countries want it? And if we choose to allow this industry that contributes the greatest part of all to the positive side of our balance of payments to go elsewhere by default, what direction then may we reasonably expect our national and personal standards of living to turn?

10. General Aviation

General aviation (GA) is a broad term from the Federal Aviation Act of 1958 encompassing all but military and airline aviation operations. The industry is characterized by its remarkable diversity, which includes flight training, personal flying in private aircraft for transportation or recreation, crop spraying, aerial firefighting, emergency medical transport, air freight feeders, search and rescue, disaster relief, aerial imaging, law enforcement, transportation of business and government executives, air sightseeing, news gathering and entertainment, along with maintaining and servicing aircraft.[1]

According to the Aircraft Owners and Pilots Association (AOPA), 221,943 general aviation aircraft were in the United States in 2007. These included 145,036 piston single-engine airplanes, 18,708 piston multiengine airplanes, 8,063 turboprops, 10,379 jets, 9,159 rotorcraft, and 23,047 experimental aircraft.[2] These are flown by over 650,000 FAA-certified pilots utilizing over 20,000 landing facilities nationwide (including airports, heliports, and seaplane bases).[3]

While general aviation has its historical roots in small businesses such as mom-and-pop fixed-base operations providing flight training, aircraft rental, and servicing, (hardly fertile ground for union organizing), many GA operations today are major business enterprises where union representation is growing. Some of these corporations are international in scope.

While some elements of the industry fall within the jurisdiction of the National Labor Relations Board (NLRB), National Mediation Board (NMB) jurisdiction under the Railway Labor Act (RLA) extends beyond the airlines to include operators of nonairline aircraft including helicopters transporting persons or property for hire as well as some fractional operators of business jets

Jurisdictional Determination

Given the diverse services offered by general aviation businesses and changes in the developing industry, it is frequently unclear whether the NLRB has jurisdiction under the NLRA or the NMB's jurisdiction under the RLA applies. It has been a long-standing practice in matters involving aviation for the NLRB to request the NMB determine in doubtful cases whether the company involved is a "common carrier by air engaged in interstate or foreign commerce" within the meaning of section 181 of the RLA.[4] In such cases, the NLRB gives substantial deference to the NMB's opinion (see fig. 10.1).[5] If the NMB is of the opinion that the company in question meets the definition of a common carrier by air engaged in interstate or foreign commerce, the NLRB will decline to acknowledge jurisdiction and refer the parties to the NMB.[6]

As discussed in chapter 7, in such cases, the NMB applies a two-pronged test to determine

Figure 10.1. DHL B757. DHL, a subsidiary of Deutsche Post World Net, joined the competitive U.S. overnight business in 2003 when it purchased Airborne Freight for about $1 billion, rankling FedEx and UPS, which accused the monopoly Deutsche Post of investing in a U.S. carrier to fight them on their own turf. DHL came in promising a threat to the established carriers but in reality did very little to garner market share from either UPS or FedEx. In May 2008, the company announced it was scaling back its U.S. operations by closing hubs and terminals. By January 2009, DHL had ended domestic pickup and delivery service in the United States, effectively leaving UPS and FedEx as the two major express parcel delivery companies. Wikimedia Commons; GNU Free Documentation License, Version 1.3.

- A company engaged in operating, servicing, and storing aircraft at a county airport. *International Aviation Services*, 189 NLRB 75 (1971).
- A company operating an air ambulance service. *Air Methods Corp.*, 30 NMB 279 (2003); *Rocky Mountain Holdings, LLC d/b/a Eagle Airmed of Arizona*, 26 NMB 25 (1999).
- A company cleaning airline terminals. *Globe Aviation Services*, 334 NLRB 278 (2001).
- A company providing customer service, baggage service, and shuttle service for passengers and crews. *Worldwide Flight Services Inc.*, 31 NMB 386 (2004), and *John Menzies PLC, d/b/a Ogden Ground Services Inc.*, 30 NMB 405 (2003).

Case study 10.1 shows an example of a general aviation operator found to be a common carrier falling within NMB jurisdiction.

whether it has jurisdiction: whether the work is traditionally performed by employees of air and rail carriers (the "function test") and whether a common carrier exercises direct or indirect ownership or control (the "control test"). Applying this two-pronged test, the NMB has determined that it has jurisdiction over, among others:

- A company engaged in furnishing air travel service to its members. *Voyager 1000*, 202 NLRB 901 (1973).
- A company engaged in air taxi, charter, on-demand, and scheduled air transport plus aircraft refueling and maintenance work. *Skyway Aviation*, 194 NLRB 555 (1972).
- A company engaged in servicing and storing aircraft, selling fuel, providing pilots and service to an aircraft club, and running an air taxi. *Mark Aero Inc.*, 200 NLRB 304 (1972).

Case Study 10.1: Air Methods Corporation

Air Methods Corporation is the largest provider of air medical-emergency transport services and systems throughout the United States (see fig. CS10.1.1). The company, established in 1980, is dedicated exclusively to air medical transport, focusing on the quality of care to patients and safety in aviation operations. Headquartered in Englewood, Colorado, the company transports more than eighty-five thousand patients and operates a fleet of more than 340 helicopters and fixed-wing aircraft in forty-two states.[7]

The company provides air medical-emergency transport services under two separate operating models: the community-based model (CBM) and the

Figure CS 10.1.1. Logo of Air Methods Corporation. Courtesy of Air Methods Corporation.

hospital-based model (HBM). Under both CBM and HBM operations, the company transports persons requiring intensive medical care from either the scene of an accident or general-care hospital to highly skilled trauma centers or tertiary-care centers.

The community-based services segment provides medical care, aircraft operation and maintenance, twenty-four-hour communications and dispatch, and medical billing and collections. The division operates both helicopters and fixed-wing aircraft under both instrument flight rules and visual flight rules with concentrations in California, Arizona, the Midwest, the southeast, and the metropolitan areas.

The hospital-based services segment provides air medical transportation services to hospitals located in more than twenty-five states under operating agreements ranging from one to ten years. Under the HBM delivery model, the hospitals themselves provide in-flight medical personnel.

In 2002, Air Methods Corporation acquired 100 percent of Rocky Mountain Holdings, which conducts both CBM and HBM operations. Rocky Mountain (RMH), Mercy Air Service, (Mercy Air), and LifeNet operate as wholly owned subsidiaries of Air Methods (see fig. CS10.1.2 and fig. CS10.1.3).

Air Methods bought FSS Airholdings in late 2007 for $25 million in cash. FSS Airholdings provides medical transportation with helicopters and fixed-wing aircraft and offers aircraft charter and maintenance services. Other FSS units provide fixed-base operator (FBO) and helicopter maintenance services. The company operates from more than eighty-five locations across the United States.[8]

Air Methods Corporation's products division designs, manufactures, and installs aircraft medical interiors and other aerospace or medical transport products for domestic and international customers.

Air Methods' collective bargaining agreement with its flight deck crews is in the study guide.

Figure CS 10.1.3. The interior of a King Air 200 air ambulance.

Figure CS 10.1.2. LifeNet of New York Eurocopter EC-135. The helicopter has satellite tracking, dual GPS, radar, and an autopilot. Also installed are a wire strike-protection system and special lighting that enables the crew to perform night-vision-goggle operations. Courtesy of Air Methods Corporation.

The NMB has used that same two-pronged test to determine that it does not have jurisdiction over, among others:

- A company engaged solely in intrastate air transportation. *Panorama Air Tour*, 204 NLRB 45 (1973).
- A scheduled air carrier operating between several locations in California that made only one out-of-state flight within the preceding five years. *Air California*, 170 NLRB 18 (1968).
- A company engaged in airport and airline food catering. *Dobbs Houses v. NLRB*, 443 F.2d 1066 (6th Cir. 1971).
- A company that trains pilots and flight engineers. *Flight Safety Inc.*, 171 NLRB 146 (1968).

- A company providing such ground services to airlines as reservations, cleaning, and maintenance. *Evergreen Aviation Ground Logistics*, 327 NLRB 869 (1999).
- A company providing sky-cap services. *Servicemaster Aviation Services*, 325 NLRB 786 (1999) but contrast *Aviation Safeguards*, 338 NLRB 770 (2003).
- A company that leases and operates an airport. *Trans-East Air Inc.*, 189 NLRB 185 (1971).
- A company that performs aircraft fueling, baggage service, customer service, and ground-service-equipment maintenance for both common carriers and business aircraft operators. *Signature Flight Support*, 32 NMB 214 (2005).

The NMB will generally assert jurisdiction over companies providing services to airlines only where these companies are under the ownership or control of the airline. Contrast *Chelsea Catering Corp. and United Food & Commercial Workers International Union*, 309 NLRB 822 (1992) with *Dobbs Houses v. NLRB*, 443 F.2d 1066 (6th Cir. 1971).

Charter and Fractional Operators

For NMB jurisdictional purposes, the key to finding a company to be a common carrier by air is the company's representing ("holding out") to the public, either through advertising or by its course of conduct, that it will carry any member of the public who applies and pays for that service. Thus, the NMB considers all passenger-carrying commercial aircraft operators regularly conducting interstate operations to be covered by the RLA and thus under the jurisdiction of the NMB. This includes not only scheduled but also on-demand charter operations, such as air taxi operations under Federal Aviation Regulations (FAR) part 135. As seen in case study 4.1 on FedEx and UPS, the NMB and NLRB evaluations of statutory

and jurisdictional coverage for all-cargo carriers have been more nuanced.

As air taxi companies began to grow from their small-business roots as one of a variety of services offered by local fixed-base operators (FBOs), often called "flying services" or "air services," to stand-alone businesses operating regionally, then nationally, and now internationally, the unions found sufficient numbers of employees in these companies to justify organizing efforts. Applying its holding-out test, the NMB found such companies to be common carriers by air covered by the RLA and subject to the jurisdiction of the NMB. See, for example, *Executive Jet Aviation Inc.*, 28 NMB 471 (2001). Executive Jet has become NetJets, the largest fractional aircraft operator in the world. This segment of the industry includes not only conventional transportation of corporate executives and the wealthy but also growing niche operations such as emergency medical service (EMS) aviation companies. See, for example, *Air Methods Corp.*, 30 NMB 279 (2003). Air Methods is now the largest air-ambulance operator in the world.

With the cost of business jets growing along with their capacity and capabilities, in 1986 Executive Jet (now NetJets) pioneered the concept of fractional aircraft ownership. Fractional ownership of business jets has since become extremely popular, one of the fastest-growing segments of the general aviation industry. In a fractional program, companies and individuals purchase an undivided fractional interest in a specific, serial-numbered aircraft, with the size of the interest purchased being directly proportional to the number of hours the fractional owner expects to fly in a year, with a one-sixteenth interest representing fifty flight hours per year typically being the smallest fraction available. Through four legally complex, interlocking agreements between the fractional seller and buyer (aircraft-purchase agreement), among the fractional buyer/owners (joint-ownership agreement), between the fractional buyer/owners and an aircraft management company (aircraft-management agreement), and all of the program participants (master interchange agreement), each fractional owner is assured access to a program aircraft (not necessarily his or her own but comparable) with crew, scheduling services, insurance, inspection, maintenance, hangar, and other costs included.[9] In essence, fractional ownership outsources the functions and costs of a corporate flight department.

As mentioned in case study 7.1, the NMB has asserted jurisdiction over fractional aircraft operators, at least where such companies also operate air charter services under FAR Part 135. Two major U.S. fractional operators, NetJets and Flight Options, also hold FAA Part 135 or 121 certificates and conduct charter operations under them. It remains to be seen whether the NMB will attempt to assert jurisdiction over pure fractional companies, such as Bombardier's Flexjet, and the stronger argument appears against such companies being held to be common carriers by air, for two reasons:

- There is no holding out to the public that the fractional operator will sell them a ride. Fractional operators carry only those specified by co-owners of aircraft that are in the program ("program aircraft"). Thus, fractional operations are most like personal and corporate aircraft operations.
- Like personal and corporate aircraft operations, at least so long as these operations are conducted using program aircraft, the FAA regulates fractional aircraft operations under the general operating and flight rules of FAR Part 91, rather than the air carrier and commercial operator rules of FAR Parts 121 and 135. Subpart K of FAR Part 91 governs fractional aircraft operations.[10] Any use of

nonprogram aircraft supplied by a separate Part 135 or 121 certificate holder as a substitute to fill in when no program aircraft is available should be viewed as negligible or sporadic, so as to not to trigger a "common carrier by air" determination by the NMB against the pure fractional operator.

The NMB has previously determined that it does not have jurisdiction over Bombardier-operated JFK AirTrain, an electricity-powered light railway that began operation on December 17, 2003, from two locations in Queens, New York (Jamaica and Howard Beach), to John F. Kennedy International Airport (also in Queens, New York) (see fig. 10.2).[11]

Figure 10.2. AirTrain at JFK airport. AirTrain JFK is a three-line, 8.1 statute mile, people-mover system in New York City that connects John F. Kennedy International Airport (JFK) to the city's subway, commuter trains, and airport parking lots. Bombardier Transportation operates the train under contract to the Port Authority of New York and New Jersey. Source: Wikimedia Commons; GNU Free Documentation License, Version 1.3.

Both NetJets and Flight Options pilots have been represented by the International Brotherhood of Teamsters (IBT), Airline Division, Local 1108.[12] Although said to be the best-paid pilots in the fractional industry, the NetJets pilots voted overwhelmingly in July 2008 to replace the IBT with a new single-company union, the NetJets Association of Shared Aircraft Pilots

(NJASAP). Almost 82 percent of the NetJet pilots eligible to vote did so, and 97.7 percent of those who did vote voted for the NJASAP, with only 2.3 percent voting to remain with the IBT. The key issue appears to have been the percentage of membership dues going to the national union (25 percent, about $1.5 million) as compared to the amount retained by the union local actually responsible for the work involved in the contract negotiation and administration process. The IBT and NJASAP had agreed to resolve the representation issue by a secret ballot conducted by a mutually acceptable third party, with a simple majority to determine the winner. The agreement also provided that if the NetJets pilots voted to leave IBT Local 1108, executive-board slots held by NetJets pilots would be transferred to the Flight Options pilots, who remain represented by Local 1108.[13]

Flight Options LLC, an Ohio-based subsidiary of U.S. defense contractor Raytheon Company and founded in 1998, employs about fifteen hundred people, including about seven hundred pilots nationwide.[14] The IBT won a representation election at Flight Options in May 2006 and began bargaining with the company the following month. Issues included pay rates that the union claimed are the lowest in the industry and working conditions, such as burdensome crew-basing policies, company demands for the right to access and use FAA-mandated cockpit voice recorders for employee disciplinary purposes, and the company requirement that pilots cross the picket lines of colleagues engaged in a job action. After almost two years in negotiations, the IBT filed for NMB mediation on May 2, 2008, declaring that negotiations had broken down.[15] The company and union reached a tentative agreement in January 2010 and presented it to the pilots for ratification. The agreement was ratified in April 2010 by 88 percent of the pilots voting in favor agreement. The agreement gave pilots an almost 40 percent pay raise over five years, with 10 percent in the first year of the agreement, two months' retroactive pay amounting to a signing bonus, work-rule improvements similar to those at NetJets, job security provisions, overtime provisions, and limits on annual contributions to medical insurance plans.[16]

Ground Support and Maintenance

The business of servicing aircraft, particularly fueling, cargo handling, ground handling, catering, and maintenance, is another segment of the general aviation industry that has grown from its beginnings among of a variety of functions performed by local small-business FBOs, through the now-familiar pattern of mergers and acquisitions, to chains of major international corporations. With that growth has come union organizing of employees.

Signature Flight Support is an example of this trend. Signature is a subsidiary of London-based BBA Aviation PLC, which after divesting its electrical, automotive, rail, conveyor, industrial nonwoven fabric, and other subsidiaries by 2006 now calls itself a focused aviation-services company serving two primary markets: flight support and aftermarket services and systems. BBA and its subsidiaries have 10,700 employees in eleven countries on five continents. BBA subsidiary ASIG, acquired in 2001, operates the largest fuel consortium in the world, LAXFUEL, at Los Angeles International Airport (see fig. 10.3).[17]

Signature Flight Support came into being in 1992 as the result of BBA acquiring, then merging PageAvjet (best known for fabricating and installing special aircraft interiors and finishes for corporate and head-of-state customers) with FBO chain Butler Aviation. Signature is now the largest FBO in the world; providing fueling, hangar and office rentals, ground handling, passenger services, maintenance, and deicing at more than seventy-five locations throughout the

Figure 10.3. Skytanking USA providing an into-plane service at Philadelphia International Airport. Aircraft Service International Group (ASIG) is a recognized industry leader in aviation fueling services. ASIG handles nearly nineteen billion gallons of fuel a year and provides into-plane fueling services for major airlines and oil companies at more than fifty airports worldwide. Since April 1986, ASIG has operated the largest fuel consortium in the world, LAXFUEL, at Los Angeles International Airport. LAXFUEL is operated around the clock, receiving fuel from more than twenty suppliers, including Skytanking. Courtesy of Skytanking USA.

United States, Europe, South America, Africa, and Asia. Neither Signature nor its parent, BBA, flies aircraft or is directly or indirectly owned by an air carrier.[18]

In 2005, the NLRB requested an opinion from the NMB regarding whether Signature's operations at the Westchester County Airport (KHPN) in White Plains, New York, a major hub of business-jet activity in the northeastern United States, were subject to the RLA. The question arose out of a 2004 representation petition filed with the NLRB by the International Brotherhood of Teamsters, Local 478, seeking to represent all full-time and regular part-time concierges and customer-service representatives at Signature's White Plains facility.

Signature contended that under the two-prong test, it was subject to the RLA, claiming that its employees perform work of a type that is traditionally performed by airline employees (fueling, baggage handling, customer service, and ground-service-equipment maintenance) so as to satisfy the function test and that the majority of its work at KHPN is performed for customers NetJets and international charter-management company TAG Aviation, which exercise significant influence on Signature's daily operations and the manner in which its employees perform their duties. IBT countered that because many of Signature's clients at KHPN are nonfractional business jets wholly owned by such corporations as Tommy Hilfiger, CitiBank, and Xerox, the situation flunked the function test, and that since Signature hired, trained, supervised, and disciplined its employees, the situation flunked the control test. The NLRB had previously certified the United Auto Workers (UAW) as the exclusive bargaining representative for Signature's line-service technicians and facilities-maintenance employees, so the IBT also contended that by failing to raise the jurisdictional issue in that case, Signature had waived its claim of RLA jurisdiction.

Based on the record of facts developed in an NLRB hearing, together with submissions by the company and union, the NMB followed precedents cited above to hold that this work was traditionally performed by airline employees, thus satisfying the function test. Turning to the control test, the NMB found that although the scheduling of NetJets' flights affects the work schedules of Signature employees, Signature managers decide how many employees to call in or hold over and whether to authorize overtime. The board noted that Signature owns and maintains its own equipment. At KHPN, NetJets is not involved in Signature's hiring or personnel investigations, has not recommended the discipline or discharge of any Signature employee, does not provide office space or equipment to Signature, and does not directly supervise Signature employees or set their wage rates or ranges or authorize overtime. Neither does NetJets mandate personal-appearance standards or require Signature employees to wear the carrier's insignia. NetJets' access to Signature's records is limited to those necessary to verify compliance with FAA certification training, maintenance, security, and safety requirements. Signature hires, trains, pays, promotes, transfers, evaluates, and disciplines its workforce. Thus, the NMB found that Signature had failed to prove that air carrier NetJets exercises sufficient control over Signature's operations to pass the control test, so that jurisdiction lay with the NLRB under the NLRA, rather than the NMB under the RLA.[19]

Flight Training

Flight training, once predominately performed locally as one of the myriad services offered by small-business FBOs, is another segment of the U.S. general aviation industry that is becoming concentrated in increasingly fewer but larger enterprises. Indeed, the growing shortage of flight instructors (discussed in chapter 8) has proved the final straw for some FBOs, causing them to drop this service from their menus.

Perhaps the best example of the corporatization and globalization of flight training is Flight-Safety International Inc. (FSI), incorporated in 1951 as Flight Safety Inc. by legendary Pan Am flying-boat pilot Al Ueltshi, who kept his "day job" flying for Pan Am, living off his airline salary while plowing all of FSI's profits back into growing the company. Like NetJets, FSI is now a subsidiary of Berkshire Hathaway, acquired by Warren Buffett's $8 billion a year conglomerate for $1.5 billion in cash in 1997. The company is still headquartered at the Marine Air Terminal at La Guardia Airport in Flushing, New York, launching site for Pan Am's original fleet of "clipper" flying boats (see fig. 10.4).[20]

FSI is now the largest provider of pilot-training services to the general aviation, corporate,

and commercial airline markets. The company also trains military personnel through its Flight-Safety Services Corporation subsidiary. With a staff of 1,500 professional instructors and over 230 FAA-certified flight simulators located at over forty learning centers located in the United States, the United Kingdom, Canada, and France, FSI trains more than 75,000 people each year in more than three thousand courses for pilots, maintenance technicians, flight attendants, and dispatchers.[21]

In 1968, the NLRB, after consultation with the NMB, determined that FSI's business of training pilots is too far removed from interstate air transport to make the company a "common carrier by air" under the RLA subject to the NMB's jurisdiction. Beginning that year with a group of employees at Hayward, California, unionization and collective bargaining activities at FSI have been governed by the NLRB under the NLRA.[22] For a widely distributed company like FSI with employees distributed among many operating locations, with rarely any craft or class of employees represented in more than double digits at any one place of business, the NLRA process requiring separate union-recognition proceedings at each such location may tend to dampen union organizing zeal, especially if employees are well compensated and find their professional working environment agreeable.

Another increasing concentration of flight instructors is found at colleges and universities, such as private Embry-Riddle Aeronautical University (ERAU). Embry-Riddle employs flight instructors in primary and advanced flight-training programs at the university's two major brick-and-mortar campuses in Daytona Beach, Florida, and Prescott, Arizona. ERAU may open a third brick-and-mortar campus in either Houston, Texas, or Rockford, Illinois. In 2006, ERAU's Daytona Beach instructors became represented by the International Association of Machinists and Aerospace Workers (IAMAW),

Figure 10.4. The Boeing 314 (known erroneously as the "Clipper"), a long-range flying boat produced by the Boeing Airplane Company between 1938 and 1941. Twelve Clippers were built for Pan Am, but before delivery, three were sold to British Overseas Airways Corporation (BOAC) in 1941. Pan Am's Clippers were built for luxury, a necessity given the long duration of transoceanic flights. The seats could be converted into thirty-six bunks for sleeping accommodation; with a cruise speed of only two hundred mph, many flights lasted over twelve hours. The aircraft had a lounge and dining area, and men and women were provided with separate dressing rooms. Although the Clipper's transatlantic flights were short-lived, they were a form of travel for the super-rich, at $675 for a round trip. In today's dollars, this would be comparable to a round-trip international ticket costing approximately $8,000. Library of Congress.

ERAU Instructor Pilots Association, Local 501. The first contract between the university and union took effect on July 1, 2006.[23]

Summary

Once largely the domain of local small businesses, some elements of the diverse general aviation industry have undergone dramatic consolidation and growth, with a few companies emerging as major business enterprises with global reach. With growth and concentration of workforces in some general aviation companies, particularly those involved in charter and fractional flight operations, flight training, and ground support, union representation of employees is expanding. Other segments of the industry, such as agricultural aviation, aerial firefighting, sightseeing, and air-show performing, remain characterized by small-business operations not yet of sufficient scope to have attracted union organizing efforts.

Labor relations in the general aviation industry may be governed by either the NMB under the RLA or the NLRB under the NLRA, depending on the outcome of application of the two-pronged test to the factual details of a particular company's operations. The two agencies cooperate to resolve these jurisdictional issues, with the NLRB generally deferring to the NMB's determination in aviation and rail cases.

11. The Public Sector

A variety of government agencies, federal, state, and local, engage in civil aviation activities. At the federal level, the FAA has over 44,000 permanent employees, including over 33,000 in the agency's air traffic organization, almost 7,000 in aviation safety, 471 in airports, 56 in commercial space transportation, and almost 4,000 in staff offices (see fig. 11.1).[1] The National Transportation Safety Board (NTSB) employs air-safety

Figure 11.1. Logo of the Federal Aviation Administration (FAA). The FAA is responsible for the safety of civil aviation. Created by the Federal Aviation Act of 1958 under the name Federal Aviation Agency, the FAA adopted the present name in 1967 when it became a part of the Department of Transportation. The major roles of the FAA include regulating civil aviation to promote safety, encouraging and developing civil aeronautics, developing and operating a system of air traffic control and navigation, researching and developing the National Airspace System and civil aeronautics, developing and carrying out programs to control aircraft noise and other environmental effects of civil aviation, and regulating U.S. commercial space transportation.

investigators and engineers to conduct aircraft-accident investigations. Other federal civilian agencies with employees directly involved in aviation include NASA, which employs pilots, astronauts, engineers, and others involved in both aviation and space research; the Immigration and Customs Enforcement (ICE) and Coast Guard branches of the Department of Homeland Security (DHS), both of which operate numerous aircraft in law enforcement, border security, search and rescue, emergency service, and disaster relief roles; and the Transportation Security Administration (also under DHS), responsible for airline security.

Some state universities offer aviation degree programs employing classroom and flight instructors, aircraft-maintenance personnel, dispatchers, and staff. Some state vocational and technical institutions staff similar training programs for airframe, power plant, and avionics repair. Some states also have aviation departments. For example, California's Division of Aeronautics, a division of the California Department of Transportation (Caltrans), is a thirty-person office whose mission is to foster and promote the development of a safe, efficient, dependable, and environmentally compatible air transportation system for the state. The division issues permits for and annually inspects hospital heliports and public-use airports, makes recommendations regarding proposed school sites within two miles of an airport runway, and authorizes helicopter landing sites at or near schools. Aviation system planning by the division provides for the integration of aviation into transportation-system planning on a regional, statewide, and national basis. The Division of Aeronautics administers state noise-regulation and land-use-planning laws that foster compatible land use around airports and encourages environmental mitigation measures to lessen noise, air pollution, and other impacts caused by aviation. The Division of Aeronautics also provides state grants and loans for safety, maintenance, and capital improvement projects at California public airports.[2]

On the local level, the vast majority of the over five thousand public-use airports in the United States are owned and operated by local governments (cities and counties), with operations often coming under a political subdivision known as an airport authority.

While government pay scales are typically somewhat lower than those for comparable positions of responsibility in private industry, benefit packages (including health care and retirement) have tended to be better, along with job security. Many public employees are represented by unions, and some of the forces and trends identified in previous chapters as affecting labor relations in the private sector of the aviation industry are coming into play in the public sector now as well, if more slowly.

The Public-Sector Labor-Relations Environment

Although union membership in the U.S. private sector has been in decline since the late 1970s, union membership in the public sector (first made legal in 1959 by the socially progressive State of Wisconsin, followed quickly by the federal government and other states) has surged above 7.5 million and continues to grow steadily, even in the face of restrictive management-rights clauses narrowing the scope of bargaining and prohibitions against strikes, both of which serve to limit union power and influence on government employers.

Management-Rights Clauses

The federal Civil Service Reform Act and many state laws governing collective bargaining by employees of state and local governments limit the scope of bargaining. Issues on which most federal employees are precluded from bargaining include the agency's mission, budget, organization, number of employees, and internal-security practices; hiring, direction, discipline, and assignment of employees; wages and benefits; and even the contracting out of agency work. Thus, the scope of bargaining for covered federal employees is generally confined to agency policies and procedures, such as facility staffing and workload (including the numbers, types, and grades of employees or positions assigned along with the technology, methods, and means of performing the work). The FAA is unique among federal agencies in that its unions are able to negotiate wage rates. Even where not specified by statute, management-rights clauses restricting the scope of bargaining frequently appear in public-sector collective bargaining agreements.

Management Styles

Workers in private industry have generally gained a voice in the manner of performance of their work, such as through cooperative participation in *quality circles* that are a feature of the total quality management/continuous improvement and lean-manufacturing programs that have proven to reap improvements in productivity and product quality beneficial to employers. In contrast, government workplaces tend to more often feature militarily autocratic management styles, with orders flowing down the chain of command to the workers but few if any meaningful opportunities for worker input to flow in the opposite direction. Where workers are powerless, the ground is fertile for union organizing and labor-management confrontation.

Executive Orders

Clinton executive order. Recognizing that the same techniques that had proved so beneficial to the private sector might also improve government services, during the first year of his first term President Bill Clinton in 1993 issued an executive order mandating labor-management partnerships for agencies of the federal government:

> The involvement of Federal Government employees and their union representatives is essential to achieving the National Performance Review's Government reform objectives. Only by changing the nature of Federal labor-management relations so that managers, employees, and employees' elected union representatives serve as partners will it be possible to design and implement comprehensive changes necessary to reform Government. Labor-management partnerships will champion change in Federal Government agencies to transform them into organizations capable of delivering the highest quality services to the American people.[3]

The program was reaffirmed and expanded by a subsequent presidential memorandum in President Clinton's second term.[4] Over eight hundred thousand federal workers became involved in these cooperative partnerships,[5] and research indicates that they succeeded in creating a better labor-management climate that reduced disputes and improved such targeted performance outcomes as customer service.[6] This may prove to have been the high water–mark in federal labor-management relations.

Bush repeal. Despite the documented success of the partnerships, President George W. Bush revoked the Clinton executive order in February 2001 within weeks of his inauguration, citing no reason other than his presidential authority,[7] the first of many anti-union acts, particularly targeting the federal public sector, that would come to characterize this presidency. The courts have always given great deference to the executive branch in matters involving national security. Although the right of government employees to be represented by a union and bargain collectively has never been demonstrated to constitute a threat to national security, the Bush administration began in 2002, in the name of national security, to take away federal-employee collective bargaining rights, beginning with about one thousand employees of the Justice Department who had enjoyed those rights for almost three decades. The administration then succeeded, again under the mantle of national security, in obtaining legislation from the Republican-controlled Congress depriving about fifty-six thousand federal airport baggage screeners hired by the new Transportation Security Administration (TSA)—originally an agency of the Department of Transportation (DOT), then moved into the new Department of Homeland Security (DHS) as soon as the latter was created—of civil service rights and benefits, including the right to collective bargaining, workers compensation, equal employment opportunity, and veterans preference. No more than twenty days later, the administration terminated the long-standing collective bargaining rights of more than two thousand cartographers, digital imaging specialists, secretaries, and security guards in the National Imagery and Mapping Agency (NIMA).

The largest civilian federal agency by far is the Department of Defense (DOD). In 2003, Congress passed and President Bush signed into law the new Civil Service and National Security Personnel System Act that in one fell swoop removed almost seven hundred thousand civilian DOD employees from the civil service and placed them into a new personnel system that deprived them of the rights to union representation and collective bargaining that they had enjoyed for decades, again citing national security as justification.[8] At least 424,605 of these employees were represented by one of forty-three recognized labor unions and working under collective bargaining agreements the government considered abrogated by the stroke of the president's pen. The American Federation of Government Employees, AFL-CIO (AFGE), is the nation's largest federal-employee union, representing six hundred thousand workers in the federal government and the government of the District of Columbia.[9] AFGE, joined by at least ten other unions, filed suit challenging the constitutionality of the new law, thus far without effect.

The International Labour Organization (ILO), an organ of the United Nations headquartered in Geneva, Switzerland, is devoted to advancing opportunities for women and men to obtain decent and productive work in conditions of freedom, equity, security, and human dignity. The ILO's main aims are to promote rights at work, encourage decent employment opportunities, enhance social protection, and strengthen dialogue in handling work-related issues. In promoting social justice and internationally recognized human and labor rights, the organization continues to pursue its founding mission that labor peace is essential to prosperity.

Today, the ILO helps advance the creation of decent jobs and the kinds of economic and working conditions that give working people and businesspeople worldwide a stake in lasting peace, prosperity, and progress. The frustrated AFGE even went so far as to file a complaint with the ILO, alleging that the executive orders, legislation, and implementing orders issued by directors of U.S. federal agencies violate ILO conventions, treaties the United States agreed to. AFGE Deputy General Counsel Charles A. Hobbie asserted that while the national security

of the United States is critically important, "equally important, and without adverse effect on national security, is the protection of the rights of federal employees who are ultimately responsible for assuring national security."[10] The complaint has been referred to the ILO's Committee on Freedom of Association for consideration.

Outsourcing and Privatization

In government (particularly the federal government), as in industry, the outsourcing of work previously performed by its own employees to outside contractors swept boldly into vogue with the latest turn of the century. The trend and stated administration and agency objectives quickly shattered any illusion of job stability in federal employment. Unlike private industry, however, federal government outsourcing has been largely to the United States, rather than foreign, contractors.[11]

Although often characterized by the media as privatization, virtually all of these activities have in fact been contracting out (outsourcing). Privatization would be the government's abandonment of a particular area of activity (for example, air traffic control) to the private sector, while in contracting out, the government continues to provide the service but in part or in whole through the work of private-sector contractors performing under government supervision.

The A-76 Process

Through a series of policy statements dating back to 1955, the federal government has refined its policies for deciding whether a particular activity is an inherently governmental function that should be performed by federal employees or a commercial activity that should be performed by the private sector, either acting independently or under contract to the government. The most recent of these policy statements is Office of Management and Budget (OMB) Circular No. A-76, August 4, 1983, revised in 1999. The foundational philosophy of the policy is set forth concisely in the circular: "In the process of governing, the Government should not compete with its citizens. The competitive enterprise system, characterized by individual freedom and initiative, is the primary source of national economic strength. In recognition of this principle, it has been and continues to be the general policy of the Government to rely on commercial sources to supply the products and services the Government needs."[12]

The circular defines a *commercial activity* as one that is operated by a federal executive agency and that provides a product or service that could be obtained from a commercial source, excluding activities considered an inherently governmental function. Attachment A to the circular lists examples of activities deemed commercial, including the maintenance, overhaul, repair, and testing of aircraft and aircraft components, electronic equipment and systems, weapons and weapons systems, and space systems; the engineering, installation, operation, maintenance, and testing of communications systems, missile ranges, satellite tracking, and radar detection and tracking; and the air transportation of people and things. Federal agencies are, however, authorized to perform commercial activities where there is no commercial source available, if the activity

1. Is in the interest of the national defense
2. Is in the interest of patient care
3. Would result in lower costs to the government

According to the circular, it is the policy of the United States government to:

a) *Achieve economy and enhance productivity.* Competition enhances quality, economy, and productivity. Whenever commercial sector performance of a Government operated commercial activity is permissible, in accordance with this Circular and its Supplement, comparison of the cost of contracting and the cost of in-house performance shall be performed to determine who will do the work. When conducting cost comparisons, agencies must ensure that all costs are considered and that these costs are realistic and fair.

b) *Retain governmental functions in-house.* Certain functions are inherently Governmental in nature, being so intimately related to the public interest as to mandate performance only by Federal employees. These functions are not in competition with the commercial sector. Therefore, these functions shall be performed by government employees.

c) *Rely on the Commercial Sector.* The Federal Government shall rely on commercially available sources to provide commercial products and services. In accordance with the provisions of this Circular and its Supplement, the Government shall not start or carry on any activity to provide a commercial product or service if the product or service can be procured more economically from a commercial source.

These policies began to impact the federal workforce in significant numbers, with four hundred thousand civil service jobs eliminated during the Clinton administration, following the recommendations of Vice President Al Gore's National Performance Review, later known as the National Partnership for Reinventing Government. Labor and management positions alike were eliminated as the federal government moved toward a targeted 15-to-1 employee-to-supervisor ratio. The A-76 process rapidly snowballed under the George W. Bush presidency, beginning in 2001. President Bush was elected with a mandate to shrink the size, scope, and budget of the federal bureaucracy, and the A-76 process was seized upon as a tool to be used often and with gusto.

Within the defense department, at many U.S. military bases worldwide, operations and support functions including maintaining military aircraft were shifted from military personnel to outside civilian contractors who promised to accomplish the work at less cost to the government. As examples, DynCorp International won contracts to maintain military aircraft, while Flight Safety International won contracts to train military pilots at some bases.[13] While many of the federal employees and military personnel whose positions were eliminated when the work was outsourced to a private-sector contractor were promptly hired by that contractor to continue doing the same work (often at comparable salaries and benefits), a substantial number, especially among the older members of the federal workforce, elected to retire or simply found themselves unemployed. The effects have been generally destabilizing to the many labor unions that represented these employees, diminishing the union's power and influence, though some have successfully followed the displaced workers to organize them in their new places of employment.[14]

An example of a commercial enterprise heavily involved in providing outsourced services to the federal government through the A-76 process appears in case study 11.1.

committees that deal with defense issues. DynCorp also retains Washington lobbyists to funnel government contracts its way. In recent legislation negotiations, DynCorp hired two lobbying firms to block a congressional bill forcing federal agencies to justify private contracts on cost-saving grounds.[16]

DynCorp traces its origins to a small group of pilots returning from World War II and seeking to use their military contacts to start an air cargo business. In 1946, these pilots formed California Eastern Airways and were soon airlifting supplies to Asia for use in the Korean War. But two years after being organized, California Eastern Airways—despite being the second-largest independent air carrier in the United States—filed for bankruptcy in 1948.[17] Land-Air, an aircraft maintenance company, purchased the remnants of California Eastern Airways and went through a series of name changes, first to California Eastern Aviation and then in 1962 to Dynalectron Corporation before settling on DynCorp in 1987. DynCorp and other company subsidiaries were purchased by Computer Sciences Corporation (CSC), a technology-services company, for approximately $1 billion in March 2003.[18] Less than two years later, CSC sold three DynCorp units to Veritas Capital Fund for $850 million. In April 2010, DynCorp announced a conditional deal to be acquired by a private-equity

Case Study 11.1: DynCorp International

DynCorp is a private military company (PMC) and aircraft maintenance company relying on government contracts for over 95 percent of its business. For more than fifty years, Virginia-based DynCorp has been a worldwide force providing maintenance support to the U.S. military through contract field teams (see fig. CS11.1.1). As one of the federal government's top contractors, DynCorp has annual revenues of over $3 billion.[15] Similar to other PMCs, DynCorp has written numerous checks to political parties and has made other political contributions to specific congressional lawmakers on

Figure CS 11.1.1. DynCorp aviation-maintenance experts at work. Under the contract-field-teams system, teams are deployed anywhere around the world to provide fast, flexible maintenance services to aircraft at their home bases. Courtesy of DynCorp International.

firm, Cerberus Capital Management, for $17.55 per share (a total of $1 billion). The deal was finalized in July 2010.[19]

In 1951, Land-Air was awarded the first contract field team (CFT) contract by the Air Force Logistics Command. Since awarded that first contract, Dyn-Corp International has continuously been awarded a CFT contract in every round of competition (see fig. CS11.1.2). In addition, DynCorp has been the contract holder on the Logistics Civil Augmentation Program (LOGCAP) contract, which provides support to enhance the structure means of the U.S. Army to sufficiently support its forces using private military companies.[20] As a result, DynCorp has provided services for the U.S. military in several international arenas: Angola, Bolivia, Bosnia, Columbia, Haiti, Kosovo, and Somalia. When called upon, DynCorp International will provide security detail for international leaders and train fledgling police forces in countries such as Afghanistan and Iraq.[21] Overall, DynCorp has trained and deployed over six thousand civilian peacekeepers and police trainers to eleven countries for the U.S. State Department.[22]

DynCorp International continues to win the bulk of U.S. State Department's contracts as the company follows the succession of international conflicts to receive lucrative police-training contracts from Bosnia to Iraq and Afghanistan. In 2005, DynCorp was awarded a multimillion-dollar contract by the U.S. State Department to advise the Iraqi government on establishing law enforcement, judicial, and correctional agencies. DynCorp's work in Afghanistan began in 2003, two years after the fall of the Taliban. It was expanded in 2004 when the U.S. State Department issued DynCorp a contract to build seven regional training centers and provide police advisers across Afghanistan. This initial contract was replaced by a series of related contracts that did not expire until 2010.[23]

FAA Flight Service

The outsourcing of the work performed by the FAA's flight service stations (FSS) provides a recent example. At the FAA's flight service stations, air traffic specialists (not to be confused with air traffic controllers) provide important services. FSS personnel provide pilot weather briefings, issue warnings of flight restrictions and notices to airmen in effect regarding airspace and outages of radio aids to navigation along the route and at airports to be used, facilities out of service at destination and alternate airports (such as runways closed for paving), file flight plans, and initiate search efforts for overdue aircraft.

In the past, more than 350 flight service stations served the United States, staffed with personnel familiar with regional topography and weather phenomena. Aided by automation and computer technology, those had been consolidated into to 58 stations by 2005. Most FAA employees at these remaining facilities were represented by unions including the National

Figure CS 11.1.2. DynCorp International trainer at work. The company has recruited, trained, and deployed more than six thousand highly qualified civilian peacekeepers and police trainers to eleven countries, including Haiti, Bosnia, Afghanistan, and Iraq, for the Department of State. Courtesy of DynCorp International.

Association of Air Traffic Specialists (NAATS), with the technicians charged with maintaining, operating, and certifying the related FAA systems and equipment represented by the Professional Aviation Safety Specialists (PASS).

In June 2002, President Bush issued Executive Order 13624, deleting the phrase "an inherently government function" from an earlier executive order that President Clinton had issued in 2000 to block the outsourcing of the FSS function. Bush's action unlocked that door.

In what is believed to be the largest outsourcing project taken by the federal government to date not associated with a war, after a competitive bidding A-76 process, the FAA in early 2005 awarded a $1.9 billion contract to Lockheed Martin to further consolidate the flight services down to twenty automated flight service stations, closing thirty-eight, to upgrade FSS computers and other associated technology, and to staff and operate these facilities with Lockheed Martin employees (see fig. 11.2). Over two thousand federal jobs were eliminated in the process, which is now complete. The FAA projected the contract would save $2.2 billion over ten years.[24] In late September 2010, the FAA granted Lockheed Martin a three-year extension of the contract worth an additional $356 million.[25]

With elimination of the federal jobs went union representation and the collective bargaining agreements in place covering those workers. Lockheed Martin hired over a thousand of the former FAA FSS workers to continue to do the work, with no loss of salary and with comparable benefits, while many others were eligible to retire and elected to do so. Lockheed Martin hired recent graduates of college and university aviation programs to fill vacancies, and unions (including the IAMAW) sought to organize and gain recognition to represent this new craft of workers at the company.[26] In October 2009, the IAMAW succeeded in its bid to represent eight hundred Lockheed Martin flight service specialists at facilities across the country.[27] The fact that the pay and benefits are the same as the federal job is not necessarily indicative of any generosity on the part of the company but may be credited to the McNamara-O'Hara Service Contract Act, which requires federal contractors and subcontractors performing services on prime contracts over $2,500 to pay service employees in various classes at least the wage rates and fringe benefits found prevailing in the locality or the rates (including prospective increases) contained in a predecessor contractor's collective bargaining agreement.[28] For prime contracts over $100,000, contractors and subcontractors must also, under the Contract Work Hours and Safety Standards Act, as amended, pay laborers and mechanics, including guards and watchmen, at least one and one-half times their regular rate of pay for all hours worked over forty in a work week. The overtime

Figure 11.2. Lockheed Martin F-22A Raptor fighter jet. In 1995, the merger of Lockheed Corporation with Martin Marietta formed Lockheed Martin, a leading multinational aerospace manufacturer and advanced-technology company. Both companies contributed important products to the new portfolio. Lockheed products included the Trident missile, F-16 Fighting Falcon, F-22 Raptor, and the C-130 Hercules. Martin Marietta products included Titan rockets, Space Shuttle External Tank, Viking 1 and Viking 2 landers, and various satellite models. Lockheed Martin employed 140,000 in 2009 and had revenues of $45 billion in 2009. Lockheed Martin receives one of every fourteen dollars doled out by the Pentagon. Source: Wikimedia Commons; photo by Rob Shenk; Creative Commons Attribution 2.0 License.

provisions of the Fair Labor Standards Act may also apply to SCA-covered contracts.[29]

At this writing, several spending bills are pending before Congress that would require congressional approval before an agency could move ahead with an A-76 process competitive outsourcing.[30]

FAA Air Traffic Control

Outsourcing of flight service was generally viewed as a stalking horse for the big prize: air traffic control (ATC).[31] This hardly appears to have been a Chicken Little (The sky is falling! The sky is falling!) reaction, given that Robert W. Poole Jr., president of the Los Angeles–based Reason Foundation conservative think tank, who assisted George W. Bush in his 2000 presidential election campaign, had been strongly advocating commercialization of air traffic control as logical following airline deregulation.[32] Several major airlines were said to have contributed to fund the proposal, which included creation of a "non-profit, stakeholder controlled" ATC corporation funded by charging user fees for basic air traffic control services. Although the conservative Heritage Foundation continued to urge the privatization or commercialization of ATC at least as late as the fall of 2007,[33] as a result of a vigorous lobbying campaign by business and general aviation groups, that proposal appears tabled for now but may be revitalized as the Republican party regains power in Congress.

The National Air Traffic Controllers Association (NATCA) represents FAA air traffic controllers (see fig. 11.3). The union began contract negotiations with the FAA in July 2005 that included concessionary bargaining. By January 2006, NATCA said the negotiations were progressing well, with key issues resolved but for the most crucial one: pay.[34] The FAA was demanding pay concessions, and its final offer would save the agency $1.9 billion in labor costs over the five years of the contract. The union's final offer included $1.4 billion in savings.[35] At that point, the negotiation reached an impasse, and the Federal Mediation and Conciliation Service (FMCS) was called upon in hope of leading the parties to a breakthrough. That effort did not bear fruit, and the FMCS declared impasse in early April 2006.[36] The 1998 contract included a provision allowing the FAA, in the event an impasse was reached following good-faith negotiations, to impose a contract on the controllers, subject to congressional action within sixty days. On April 5, 2006, the FAA sent its proposed final contract, along with NATCA's final contract proposal and objections, to Congress.

Figure 11.3. Logo of the National Air Traffic Controllers Association (NATCA). Certified in 1987, NATCA is one of the strongest and most influential labor unions in the federal sector and is a direct affiliate of the AFL-CIO. NATCA represents over twenty thousand air traffic controllers, engineers, and other safety-related professionals. NATCA membership is found in every state, territory, and possession in the United States. Courtesy of National Air Traffic Controllers Association.

Despite a bill proposed by then-Senator Barack Obama (D–IL) and Representative Sue Kelly (R–NY) already being in the works that would amend the law to prohibit the FAA from imposing such a new contract without specific congressional authorization, Congress did not act to modify the FAA's final offer, which then took effect as the new contract.[37] NATCA subsequently filed unfair labor practice charges against the FAA with the Federal Labor

Relations Authority (FLRA). The FLRA dismissed those charges in August 2007, finding that the FAA had bargained in good faith and that the FAA's implementation of the contract was lawful. NATCA has also been lobbying Congress for legislation that would require the FAA to return to the bargaining table, though President Bush stated that he would veto any such legislation.[38] The House of Representatives did include a provision in H.R. 2881, the FAA Reauthorization Act of 2007, that would require binding arbitration in future contract negotiations between the FAA and NATCA to prevent such unilateral contract imposition. The House passed that bill in August 2007 but never came to a vote in the Senate.[39] In June 2008, Representative James Oberstar (D–MN), chairman of the house transportation and infrastructure subcommittee, and Representative Jerry Costello (D–IL), chairman of the house aviation subcommittee, introduced a new bill, the Air Service Improvement Act of 2008, which includes a requirement for the FAA and NATCA to return to the bargaining table "under the last mutual agreement." If they are unable to reach agreement within forty-five days, then the dispute would be resolved by binding arbitration. In the interim, affected employees would be eligible for back pay, subject to appropriations, not to exceed $20 million in the aggregate.[40]

Costello attributes the accelerated retirement rate of veteran air traffic controllers to low morale resulting from the agency's unilateral contract imposition and authoritarian handling of that workforce. In 2006, 583 controllers retired; in 2007, 828; and the FAA projects that between 2008 and 2017, 7,068 members of the current controller workforce will retire. The agency estimates from 2008 to 2017, an additional 5,316 fully qualified controllers will leave for other reasons, such as promotion, reassignment, resignation, and termination. The Government Accounting Office (GAO) forecasts that the FAA will need to hire and train nearly 17,000 replacement controllers to replace over 15,000 that GAO expects the FAA to lose to retirement and other reasons between 2008 and 2017. Meanwhile, the FAA is increasingly requiring controllers to work overtime as this accelerated retirement rate has created a shortage of fully qualified controllers at many major facilities. Costello believes this situation contributed to an increased rate of runway incursions in 2008, with obvious implications for aviation safety. Characterizing controller staffing as "reaching a crisis point," Costello called on the FAA to redouble its efforts to conclude a satisfactory labor contract with its controllers.[41]

At the request of U.S. Senator Richard Durbin (D–IL), DOT Inspector General Calvin Scovell III is reviewing factors that could affect controller fatigue. He told the House aviation subcommittee that factors identified early in the investigation as possible contributors to controller fatigue include agency scheduling practices with minimal time between shifts, conducting on-the-job training, requiring controllers to work six-day weeks, and requiring controllers to work an operational position for extended periods of time.[42] If airline activity continues to decline as a result of fuel-cost-driven service cutbacks and industry consolidation, this may relieve some of the staffing pressure for awhile.

Other FAA Employees

FAA air safety inspectors working at a flight standards district office (FSDO), air carrier district office (ACDO), and manufacturing inspection district office (MIDO), along with some computer specialists who support them and some other support staff, are represented by PASS or the National Association of Flight Standards Employees (NAFSE). There are long-standing concerns over the adequacy of the number of inspectors and budget available to meaningfully inspect the airlines, particularly given the trend toward airlines outsourcing maintenance work to foreign repair stations and the likelihood that Congress will require the FAA to double the frequency of inspection of those facilities.[43] With pay scales for information-technology workers steadily climbing in both the private and public sectors, PASS has been very active in striving to assure that those at FAA keep pace.[44]

Case study 11.2 takes a closer look at PASS and its activities on behalf of its members.

Case Study 11.2: Professional Aviation Safety Specialists (PASS)

The Professional Aviation Safety Specialists (PASS), AFL-CIO, was founded in 1977 by fifty Federal Aviation Administration (FAA) technicians to provide sole representation for their bargaining unit (see fig. CS11.2.1). The union was originally called the Professional Airways Systems Specialists, but in 2007, union members voted to change the name to the current one. PASS has grown significantly over the decades and now represents over eleven thousand FAA and Department of Defense (DOD) employees, encompassing five bargaining units within the FAA and DOD.[45]

The FAA filed an unfair labor practice (ULP) case against PASS in March 2006 after PASS informed the FAA they would oppose ratification of the tentative agreement with the FAA for their technical operations unit. In early 2006, after months of unsuccessful contract negotiations with the FAA, PASS realized that the agency had no intention of reaching a new labor agreement designed to satisfy both parties. Therefore, PASS accepted the FAA's proposal but made it clear that it would inform its members to vote against this pending agreement during the ratification process. The FAA alleged that PASS negotiated in bad faith, prompting the FAA to file the unfair labor practice complaint with the Federal Labor Relations Authority (FLRA). "PASS agreed to the FAA proposal knowing full well their membership would reject it," said a FAA spokesperson.[46]

According to PASS, the FAA insisted on major changes to work rules, including scheduling, that

were unacceptable to PASS employees. Furthermore, PASS said the FAA, which had declared over half of PASS's proposals as nonnegotiable, would not provide counterproposals when requested by the union. After witnessing the FAA's conduct at the bargaining table, PASS concluded that the FAA had no intention of reaching a new labor agreement favorable of both parties. Realizing that the FAA's final offer was their best option under current circumstances; PASS accepted the FAA's proposal in March 2006.[47]

Because PASS had theoretically accepted FAA's offer, the negotiations was shelved for approximately three months while the union members voted, which prevented the FAA from declaring an impasse. If an impasse had been reached, the FAA could have sent the contract dispute to Congress for resolution rather than submitting it for mediation; and if Congress

Figure CS 11.2.1. Professional Airways Systems Specialists 9/11 flag poster. Courtesy of Professional Aviation Safety Specialists, AFL-CIO (PASS).

Figure CS 11.2.2. Seal of the U.S. Federal Labor Relations Authority.

decided to take no action within sixty days, the FAA's final contract offer would be automatically imposed on PASS employees.[48]

After 98 percent of PASS members voted not to ratify the tentative agreement, the FAA filed the ULP case against PASS. Even though the case was initially dismissed by the FLRA regional director in July 2006, the FAA appealed the decision to the FLRA general counsel, who granted an appeal hearing in March 2007.[49]

In his August 2007 decision to dismiss all charges against PASS, the FLRA administrative law judge stated the union's tactic "may not have been the academic exercise of reasoned discussion that the FAA hoped for, but then neither was its threat to submit its final proposals to Congress and implement them. . . . [T]he FAA may be correct in its interpretation of title 49 [labor rules], but such an interpretation invited a response by the union, and the union's response in this case appears to me to be entirely lawful."[50]

After the FLRA's ruling that PASS did not fail to bargain in good faith, PASS President Tom Brantley stated, "Now that the judge has validated PASS's position, we look forward to returning to the negotiating table with the FAA and are hopeful that we can reach a mutually agreeable contract."[51] Legally, the FAA had the right to reject PASS's offer of returning to the bargaining table. In addition, the FAA could have legally appealed the judge's decision to

the FLRA, but it did not have a legal right to change the terms of the current labor agreement until PASS members successfully ratified a new collective bargaining agreement.

According to a September 2009 PASS report, the FAA chose to appeal the judge's decision; however, in November 2010, the FLRA granted requests by the FAA and the FLRA's general counsel to withdraw the FAA's exceptions in the ULP case against PASS regarding the failed ratification of a tentative agreement in August 2006 for PASS's technical-operations bargaining unit.[52] This meant that the original decision of the FLRA judge who ruled on the case stood. In his decision, the FLRA judge determined that PASS did not commit an unfair labor practice by recommending that its members vote against ratification of the tentative agreement. After more than four years of litigation, this ULP case ended.[53]

After the November 2010 request, Brantley stated, "The resolution of this case removes a major impediment to our ability to return to the bargaining table with the FAA to secure new collective bargaining agreements for all of our FAA bargaining units. I am optimistic that we will reach agreement in the near future to define how and when bargaining will occur."[54] On February 2, 2011, PASS and the FAA successfully negotiated ground rules to govern future negotiations in all PASS bargaining units. Under the newly defined ground rules, contract negotiations for PASS's technical-operations bargaining unit were scheduled to begin in April 2011.[55]

The American Federation of Government Employees (AFGE), the National Federation of Federal Employees (NFFE), and National Association of Government Employees (NAGE) also represent numerous FAA employees.

TSA Airport Security Officers

The Transportation Security Administration's treatment of its airport security officers has been nothing short of astonishing in its callous disregard for human rights, law, and reason (see fig. 11.4). As previously noted, when Congress created the TSA shortly after the terrorist attacks of September 11, 2001, it authorized the agency to ignore certain Civil Service laws for national-security reasons.

Figure 11.4. Logo of the Transportation Security Administration (TSA). The TSA is a U.S. government agency created by the Aviation and Transportation Security Act, which President George W. Bush signed into law November 19, 2001. The TSA, originally part of the U.S. Department of Transportation, was moved to the U.S. Department of Homeland Security on November 25, 2002. The agency is responsible for security in all modes of transportation; however, the bulk of TSA's efforts are in aviation security.

The Homeland Security Act (HSA) was enacted in November 2002.[56] It established the Department of Homeland Security (DHS), a cabinet-level agency whose mission is to "prevent and deter terrorist attacks, protect against and respond to threats and hazards to the nation, ensure safe and secure borders, welcome lawful immigrants and visitors, and promote the free-flow of commerce." The act merged twenty-two existing agencies from across the federal government (including the TSA, which was originally organized within the DOT), integrating 170,000 employees, seventeen unions, seven payroll systems, seventy-seven collective-bargaining units, and eighty personnel systems.

When Congress enacted HSA and established the DHS, it provided that "the Secretary of Homeland Security may, in regulations prescribed jointly with the Director of the Office of Personnel Management, establish, and from time to time adjust, a human resources management system."[57] Congress made it clear that this system is to—(1) be flexible; (2) be contemporary; (3) not waive, modify, or otherwise affect certain existing statutory provisions relating to merit hiring, equal pay, whistle-blowing, and prohibited personnel practices, and (4) ensure that employees may organize, bargain collectively, and participate through labor organizations of their own choosing in decisions which affect them, subject to any exclusion from coverage or limitation on negotiability established by law.[58] The act also mandated that DHS employees receive "fair treatment in any appeals that they bring in decisions relating to their employment."[59] Section 9701 does not mention chapter 71, which codifies the Federal Services Labor-Management Statute (FSLMS) and delineates the framework for collective bargaining for most federal-sector employees.[60]

In February 2005, the DHS and Office of Personnel Management (OPM) issued regulations establishing a human-resources-management system called MAXHR.[61] Unilaterally imposed on 160,000 DHS employees, MAXHR replaced decades of civil service pay grade and promotion rules with so-called performance-based job evaluations that would leave pay increases and promotions at the discretion of supervisors, opening the door to favoritism and political pressure being brought to bear on DHS employees. MAXHR also imposed draconian management rights, removing pay and work rules from the permissible scope of bargaining, effectively reducing union representation to dealing with individual employee grievances. The new HR system also authorized DHS to unilaterally abrogate lawfully negotiated and executed collective bargaining agreements. Taken together, these regulations in effect subordinated all collective bargaining–

agreement provisions to the prerogatives of DHS management.

A group of DHS employee unions banded together to file suit, challenging the legality of the new rules. In a fifty-page opinion dated June 27, 2006, in National Treasury Employees Union v. Chertoff, a three-judge panel of the U.S. Court of Appeals for the District of Columbia Circuit struck down the new DHS personnel-management rules as unlawful for failure to comply with the HSA's requirements and enjoined the agency from implementing the new system (see case study 11.3). When the DOD promulgated an extremely similar new personnel system called the National Security Personnel System (NSPS), a different three-judge panel of the same court found it lawful.[62]

Case Study 11.3: *National Treasury Employees Union v. Chertoff,* 452 F.3d 839 (D.C. Cir 2006)

When Congress enacted the Homeland Security Act of 2002 ("HSA" or the "Act") and established the Department of Homeland Security ("DHS" or the "Department"), it provided that "the Secretary of Homeland Security may, in regulations prescribed jointly with the Director of the Office of Personnel Management [OPM], establish, and from time to time adjust, a human resources management system." 5 U.S.C. § 9701(a). Congress made it clear, however, that any such system "shall—(1) be flexible; (2) be contemporary; (3) not waive, modify, or otherwise affect [certain existing statutory provisions relating to, inter alia, merit hiring, equal pay, whistle-blowing, and prohibited personnel practices, and] (4) ensure that employees may organize, bargain collectively, and participate through labor organizations of their own choosing in decisions which affect them, subject to any exclusion from coverage or limitation on negotiability established by law." *Id.* § 9701(b) (1)–(4). The Act also mandated that DHS employees receive "fair treatment in any appeals that they bring in decisions relating to their employment." Section 9701 does not

mention "Chapter 71," which codifies the Federal Services Labor-Management Statute (FSLMS), 5 U.S.C. §§ 7101–7106, 7111–7123, 7131–7135 (2000), and delineates the framework for collective bargaining for most federal sector employees.[63]

In February 2005, the Department and Office of Personnel Management ("OPM") issued regulations establishing a human resources-management system (codified at 5 C.F.R. Chapter XCVII and Part 9701) ("Final Rule" or "HR system"). The Final Rule, *inter alia,* defines the scope and process of collective bargaining for affected DHS employees, channels certain disputes through the Federal Labor Relations Authority ("FLRA" or the "Authority"), creates an in-house Homeland Security Labor Relations Board (HSLRB), and assigns an appellate role to the Merit Systems Protection Board (MSPB) in cases involving penalties imposed on DHS employees.

Unions representing many DHS employees (the "Unions") [challenged] aspects of the final rule. In a detailed and thoughtful opinion, *National Treasury Employees Union v. Chertoff,* 385 F.Supp.2d 1 (D.D.C.2005), the U.S. District Court for the District of Columbia found that the regulations would not ensure collective bargaining, would fundamentally and impermissibly alter FLRA jurisdiction, and would create an appeal process at MSPB that is not fair [see fig. CS11.3.1]. However, the district court rejected the unions' claims that the regulations impermissibly restricted the scope of bargaining and that DHS lacked authority to give MSPB an intermediate appellate function in cases involving mandatory removal offenses.

The district court held that the *"sine qua non* of good-faith collective bargaining is an enforceable contract once the parties reach an agreement." The court found that the final rule flouted this standard by allowing DHS to unilaterally abrogate agreements. Driving straight to the heart of the matter, the district court said:

> A contract that is not mutually binding is not a contract. Negotiations that lead to a contract that is not mutually binding are not true

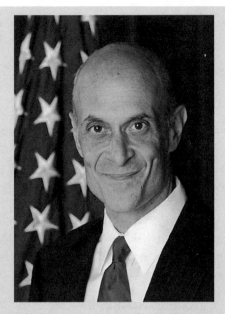

Figure CS 11.3.1. Michael Chertoff, second U.S. Secretary of Homeland Security (February 2005–January 2009) under President George W. Bush and coauthor of the USA PATRIOT Act.

found that "Congress gave the [Department] the authority to ignore the provisions of Chapter 71 and to establish new metes and bounds for collective bargaining at DHS."

The district court sustained the unions' objections to the role assigned to FLRA by the final rule. On this point, the court held that DHS could not "commandeer the resources of an independent agency and thereby fundamentally transform its functions, absent a clearer indication of congressional intent."

The district court also found that the final rule violated § 9701(f)(2) of the HSA because the restrictions on MSPB review "result in a system that is not fair." The court found that because the final rule specified that MSPB could modify penalties only when they are "so disproportionate as to be wholly without justification," review would become "almost a nullity."

On appeal, the U.S. Court of Appeals for the D.C. Circuit affirmed in part and reversed in part:

negotiations. A system of "collective bargaining" that permits the unilateral repudiation of agreements by one party is not collective bargaining. The Regulations fail because any collective bargaining negotiations pursuant to its terms are illusory: the Secretary retains numerous avenues by which s/he can unilaterally declare contract terms null and void, without prior notice to the Unions or employees and without bargaining or recourse.

Although courts normally defer to agencies' interpretations of their own rules, that inherent nonsense lead the district court to decline to follow the agency's interpretation in this case.

The district court also, however, declined to accept the unions' argument that the final rule impermissibly restricted the scope of bargaining. Although the court agreed that the regulations' "eradication of virtually all bargaining over 'operational' issues will have a dramatic effect upon the work lives of the employees the [Unions] represent," it nonetheless

We hold that the regulations fail in two important respects to "ensure that employees may bargain collectively," as the HSA requires. First, we agree with the District Court that the Department's attempt to reserve to itself the right to unilaterally abrogate lawfully negotiated and executed agreements is plainly unlawful. If the Department could unilaterally abrogate lawful contracts, this would nullify the Act's specific guarantee of collective bargaining rights, because the agency cannot "ensure" collective bargaining without affording employees the right to negotiate binding agreements.

Second, we hold that the Final Rule violates the Act insofar as it limits the scope of bargaining to employee-specific personnel matters. The regulations effectively eliminate all meaningful bargaining over fundamental working conditions (including even negotiations over procedural protections), thereby committing the bulk of decisions concerning conditions of employment to the Department's exclusive discretion. In no sense can such a limited scope of bargaining be viewed as consistent with the Act's mandate that DHS "ensure" collective bargaining rights for its employees. The Government argues that the HSA does not require the Department to adhere to the terms of Chapter 71 and points out that the Act states that the HR system must be "flexible," and from this concludes that a drastically limited scope of bargaining is fully justified. This contention is specious. Although the HSA does not compel the Government to adopt the terms of Chapter 71 as such, Congress did not say that Chapter 71 is irrelevant to an understanding of how DHS is to comply with its obligations under the Act. "Collective bargaining" is a term of art and Chapter 71 gives guidance to its meaning. It is also noteworthy that the HSA requires that the HR system be "contemporary" as well as flexible. We know of no contemporary system of collective bargaining that limits the scope of bargaining to employee-specific personnel matters, as does the HR system, and the Government cites to none. We therefore reverse the District Court on this point.

We affirm the District Court's judgment that the Department exceeded its authority in attempting to conscript FLRA into the HR system. The Authority is an independent administrative agency, operating pursuant to its own organic statute and long-established procedures. Although the Department was free to avoid FLRA altogether, it chose instead to impose upon the Authority a completely novel appellate function, defining FLRA's jurisdiction and dictating standards of review to be applied by the Authority. In essence, the Final Rule attempts to co-opt FLRA's administrative machinery, prescribing new practices in an exercise of putative authority that only Congress possesses. Nothing in the HSA allows DHS to disturb the operations of FLRA.

Finally, we reverse without prejudice the District Court's finding that DHS was without authority to change the standard by which the MSPB might mitigate a penalty for employee misconduct. This matter is not ripe for review.

In February 2007, the Senate homeland security committee voted to give airport screeners the same collective bargaining and whistle-blower–protection rights as most other federal employees. Committee chair Senator Joseph Lieberman (I–CT) said that TSA personnel management had been troubled from the beginning, with "unusually high rates of attrition, vacancy, workplace injury, discrimination complaints, and other indications of employee dissatisfaction." The 9-8 vote was strictly along party lines, with Democrats voting for and Republicans against the measure, which President Bush had threatened to veto.[64] The measure was included in Senate Bill S.4, Improving America's Security Act of 2007, passing the Senate on March 13, 2007, and disappearing into the House of Representatives, where it has not come to the floor.

Another case about TSA employees' rights, American Federation of Government Employees v. Stone, went to the court of appeals (see case study 11.4). In January 2007, the U.S. Court of Appeals for the Ninth Circuit, sitting in San Francisco, heard oral argument in this case that involved the constitutional rights of TSA employees to advocate union membership. In September, the court announced its decision, holding that "the fact that the TSA has banned collective bargaining does not mean that a union representing TSA employees has no useful function; nor does it mean that the TSA has free rein to retaliate against screeners who speak in favor of collective bargaining rights."

Case Study 11.4: *American Federation of Government Employees v. Stone*, Slip Opinion Dated September 5, 2007, in Case No. 05–15206, __ F.3d __ (9th Cir 2007)

John Gavello began work as a TSA security screener at Oakland International in March 2003. In October 2003, he spoke to his supervisor and a manager about his plans to distribute and post American Federation of Government Employees (AFGE) literature during break times. Throughout that November, Gavello posted union materials in the employee break room and made union forms available to fellow employees.

In response, TSA management apparently began "building a file" to justify terminating Gavello. On November 20, he received a warning for conducting union activities on the job. The following day, he was called to a manager's office and questioned about his union activities. When he refused to answer, he was placed on paid administrative leave pending an investigation into whether he had engaged in union activities while on duty. He was allowed to return to work on December 5 but received a memorandum of counseling and warning letter "for speaking on behalf of other employees, asking for written verification of policies, and posting union materials before receiving approval from TSA management."

In February 2004, Gavello submitted a written grievance requesting the TSA provide "written procedures regarding baggage inspection swiping and sampling" that were "not currently included in the [TSA's] standard operating procedures." At the bottom of the grievance appeared the phrase "cc: AFGE Legal Counsel." Six days later, the TSA terminated Gavello's employment on the grounds that he had improperly disclosed sensitive security information to an unauthorized person (AFGE's lawyer). Because Gavello had been employed by TSA for less than a year, he was considered a probationary screener. TSA had earlier issued a Human Resources Management Letter, HRM Letter 300–2 (July 29,2002), declaring that probationary screeners may be terminated at any time and that although the TSA would state

the reason for the termination, the employee had no right of reply or administrative appeal. In contrast, nonscreener TSA employees were covered by a separate personnel-management system that allowed employees, including those with less than one year of service, to appeal personnel actions to the MSPB.

Thus deprived of any avenue of administrative review, Gavello and AFGE filed suit in federal district court, claiming that the TSA had violated their First Amendment rights of freedom of speech and freedom of association "by penalizing Mr. Gavello's exercise of his legal right of advocacy of union membership." According to the complaint, approximately fifty Oakland security screeners had joined AFGE since Gavello began his organizing efforts, but his termination had a "chilling effect on other screeners." The government countered by filing a motion to dismiss for lack of subject-matter jurisdiction, arguing that by excluding TSA screeners from the protections of the Civil Service Reform Act and FAA personnel-management system, and by granting the TSA administrator unfettered discretion to determine screeners' terms and conditions of employment, Congress indicated its intention to preclude judicial review of screeners' constitutional claims. The government also argued that AFGE lacked standing to sue either on its own behalf or on behalf of its member Gavello.

The district court agreed with the government's positions and dismissed the complaint. AFGE and Gavello appealed that decision to the U.S. Court of Appeals for the Ninth Circuit in San Francisco. On the issue of AFGE's standing to sue, the court of appeals held that the complaint had set out sufficient facts showing the TSA's actions to have interfered with AFGE's ability to solicit membership and communicate its message to make the required threshold showing that the union:

1. Has suffered an "injury in fact" that is
   a. concrete and particularized, and
   b. actual or imminent, not conjectural or hypothetical

2. The injury is fairly traceable to the challenged action of the defendant; and
3. It is likely, as opposed to speculative, that the injury will be redressed by a favorable decision.

The appeals court noted that the Supreme Court has squarely held that a union may have standing to challenge governmental interference with organizing activities, citing *Allee v. Medrano*, 416 U.S.802 (1974), a case brought by the United Farm Workers against Texas state officials alleging that the state officials had conspired to deprive the union and others of their First Amendment rights. In that case, the Supreme Court stated:

> In this case the union has standing as a named plaintiff to raise any of the claims that a member of the union would have standing to raise . . . [I]t has been implicitly recognized that protected First Amendment rights flow to unions as well as their members and organizers. If, as alleged by the union in its complaint, its members were subject to unlawful arrests and intimidation for engaging in union organizational activity protected by the First Amendment, the union's capacity to communicate is unlawfully impeded, since the union can act only through its members. The union then has standing to complain of the arrests and intimidation and bring this action.

The government also argued that because the TSA had banned collective bargaining for screeners, "any interest that AFGE may have in representing TSA screeners is simply not legally cognizable." The appeals court noted that its counterpart District of Columbia Circuit had already held, in *American Federation of Government Employees v. Loy*, 367 F.3d 932 (D.C. Cir. 2004) that the TSA's ban on collective bargaining "does not prevent airport screeners from engaging in organizing activities or joining" AFGE. The Ninth Circuit went on to add that "the fact that the TSA has banned collective bargaining does not

mean that a union representing TSA employees has no useful function; nor does it mean that the TSA has free rein to retaliate against screeners who speak in favor of collective bargaining rights."

Turning to the issue of subject-matter jurisdiction, the court of appeals held that because the statutory scheme governing Gavello's employment does not clearly indicate an intention on the part of Congress to preclude judicial review of constitutional claims, Gavello and the union are entitled to seek judicial relief based on the alleged violation of their First Amendment rights. The appellate court reversed the district court's dismissal of the complaint and remanded the case to the district court to go forward with further proceedings not inconsistent with this opinion.

In Congress, the fiscal 2008 omnibus spending bill signed into law in December 2007 provided zero funding for the DHS personnel plan, instead granting the agency $10 million to turn around the results of a 2006 federal workforce study that rated the department at or near the bottom in leadership, performance management, and job satisfaction. With funding for the project cut off, DHS announced its intention to proceed no further with the new personnel regime for the time being.[65] In a May 2008 report, the DHS inspector general noted that TSA employees expressed their concerns about how the agency operates by historically filing formal complaints at rates significantly higher than other federal agencies of comparable size. Employees at some airports contacted the Congress, the DHS, OIG, and the media to report their frustrations with local management's lack of resolution of ongoing workplace problems. TSA employees, primarily transportation security officers (TSOs, also known as airport screeners), have criticized the agency for discrimination, selective hiring practices, nepotism, management misconduct, and other questionable activities. Although TSA reports that a stable, mature, and experienced workforce is the most effective tool it has to meet its mission, the agency currently experiences a 17 percent voluntary attrition rate and low employee morale.[66] Transportation security officers interviewed by the IG expressed concerns with:

- Inconsistent interpretation and implementation of TSA policies and procedures, such as operating procedures, leave policies, and overtime requirements
- Concerns with local management, such as lack of trust, fear of retaliation, authoritarian management style, mistreatment, and disrespect
- Poor communications and information sharing
- Insufficient time to complete all work-related responsibilities, such as training, collateral duties, and Performance Accountability and Standards System documentation
- Favoritism demonstrated through preferential scheduling and unfair promotion practices
- Insufficient staffing at passenger checkpoints

The AFGE TSA Local 1 represents some TSA screeners. Commenting on the OIG report, Local 1 spokesperson A. J. Castilla wrote in a statement to members: "This report, in its heartbreaking entirety, sums up the nightmare that has served to be the day-to-day workplace experience for most of TSA's airport screening inspector workforce." Local 1 president Tim Kriescher credits low morale to overly long shifts and a comparatively high injury rate.[67]

The IG expressed the opinion that given their level of frustration, screeners may be distracted and less focused on their security-and-screening responsibilities. Continuing workplace problems at the agency could in turn adversely affect the TSA's overall transportation-security mission by increasing turnover and decreasing workforce stability.

In February 2011, TSA Administrator John S. Pistole announced a policy change that allows TSA employees to bargain collectively. An election was held to determine whether a majority of TSA employees wanted to be represented by a union and, if so, to select the union to represent them in collective bargaining. The new policy allows the union to bargain over policies on shifts, dress code, break time, and awards but prohibits negotiation over wages, benefits, job qualifications, discipline standards, or anything relating to national security. A sizeable majority voted for union representation (the vote was 16,464 in favor of the two unions competing for recognition and divided almost equally between them, with only 3,111 votes against union representation), and the FLRA conducted a runoff election between the AFGE and NTEU to select the representative. Results of the runoff election were announced in late June 2011, with the AFGE winning the right to represent the TSA airport security workers by a vote of 8,903 to 8,447.[68]

State and Local Government Employees

At the local and regional levels of government, public airports are largely managed, operated, and maintained by public employees, with the contracting-out of work to private enterprise largely limited to construction projects, janitorial services, and at a few low-activity-level facilities, operation of air traffic control towers.

Airline Woes Straining Airport Budgets

While public-airport employment has experienced fairly stable growth at major hubs and reasonable stability at others, airport budgets are largely dependent on revenues received from the airlines using the facility, fuel sold to airlines and other aircraft, and leases to airport-terminal-building concessionaires and others doing business on the airport.

Concerns are that as airlines consolidate, reduce flights, and abandon service at some locations, airport revenues and the public jobs the airlines activities fund will be adversely affected, in some cases severely, particularly at nonhub airports.[69]

Outsourcing and Privatization of Airports

In 1987, Britain's government lead by conservative then-Prime Minister Margaret Thatcher sold what was then the British Airports Authority (BAA), owner and operator of the Heathrow, Gatwick, and Edinburgh Airports, via an initial public offering (IPO) of stock. Although initially viewed as an isolated transaction, about a dozen global airport companies (including BAA) are actively pursuing acquisitions and over a hundred airports have since gone over to private industry, including Europe's Belfast, Brussels, Budapest, Copenhagen, Dusseldorf, Frankfurt, Hamburg, and Rome; Australia's Auckland, Brisbane, Melbourne, and Sydney; some airports in South Africa, Argentina, Chile, Colombia, and Mexico. Hong Kong and Tokyo airports are also said to be in the works.[70]

In the United States, contractual restrictions included in the standard form of grant agreement required of recipients of federal airport-improvement monies precluded transfers of virtually all significant publicly owned airports to private ownership, at least unless all previous federal airport grants to the airport were repaid in the process. The grant agreements also require that airport revenues be used exclusively for airport purposes. But in 1996, Congress approved the Airport Privatization Pilot Program as part of that year's FAA Reauthorization Act, to explore privatization as a means to generate access to sources of private capital for airport improvement and development. The act authorized the FAA to permit up to five public-airport sponsors to sell or lease an airport (including only one large hub airport) and to exempt the airport sponsor, owner, and lease holder from repayment of federal grants and from the requirement

that the proceeds of the sale or lease, along with subsequent airport revenues, be used exclusively for airport purposes.[71]

The FAA program imposed a number of conditions, including that the private operator:

- prove its ability to comply with the public operator's grant obligations, including the obligation to ensure continued access to the airport(s) on reasonable terms
- provide assurance that it will operate the airport safely
- continue maintenance and improvement of the airport
- provide security (not including that now provided by TSA)
- mitigate noise and environmental impacts
- abide by any collective bargaining agreements already in place at the airport(s)

The public operator is also required to provide a plan for continued operation of the airport in case of the bankruptcy or other default of the private operator. At least 65 percent of the airport's air carriers (by number of carriers and by landed weight) must approve the airport sponsor's use of airport revenue for nonairport purposes. The private operator may not increase air carrier rates and charges at a rate that exceeds the consumer price index, unless approved by 65 percent of the air carriers at the airport (by the same measure).[72]

Six publicly owned-and-operated airports applied to participate in the pilot program: Brown Field Municipal Airport, San Diego, California; Chicago Midway International Airport, Chicago, Illinois; New Orleans Lakefront Airport, New Orleans, Louisiana; Niagara Falls International Airport, Niagara Falls, New York; Rafael Hernandez Airport, Aguadilla, Puerto Rico; and Stewart International Airport, Newburgh, New York. To date, the only one completed is Stewart Airport. The Port Authority of New York has already bought back the lease on that one from the private operator. Except for Chicago

Midway, the others withdrew or terminated their applications.

The City of Chicago owns and operates both the Chicago Midway International (MDW) and Chicago O'Hare International (ORD) large air carrier airports. Chicago Midway handles more than eighteen million passengers with 285,000 aircraft operations annually by seven airlines, including AirTran, ATA, Continental, Delta, Frontier, Northwest, and Southwest, operating about three hundred daily flights to fifty-five destinations (see fig. 11.5). In September 2006, the city submitted a preliminary application to the FAA for participation in the Airport Privatization Pilot Program to allow a long-term lease of MDW to a private operator. The FAA accepted it within two weeks.

At MDW are 190 city employees, with 165 under union collective bargaining agreements and 25 nonunion. Also in 2006, the Illinois State legislature enacted so-called best practices in labor protection into law to govern such privatization of public works. The state statute includes

Figure 11.5. Aerial view of Chicago Midway International Airport, aka the "world's busiest square mile." Today, Chicago Midway is dominated by low-cost carrier Southwest Airlines. AirTran Airways and Delta Air Lines are the airport's other major operators. In April 2009, a $2.5 billion deal to privatize Chicago Midway International Airport via a ninety-nine-year lease fell through when the consortium could not put together financing. The consortium operating under the name of Midway Investment and Development Company LLC would have operated the airport and collected airport parking, concession, and passenger facility charges. Source: Wikimedia Commons.

wage-and-benefit and job-security provisions requiring the city to offer employment under substantially similar terms and conditions to displaced airport workers in another location or department and also requires the private operator/lessee to offer such displaced workers employment under equivalent wages, benefits, terms, and conditions. The statute also prohibits expansion of Midway Airport's footprint.[73] In 2007, key player Southwest Airlines, which accounts for 70 percent of the airport's activity, reached agreement in principle with the city, leaving it to persuade at least four more of the seven carriers operating there.[74] The city went forward and solicited and received requests for qualification (RFQ) from firms and investment groups to demonstrate their qualifications to serve as the airport's private sponsor.

On April 1, 2008, the city announced that it had received RFQ statements from six teams.[75] It is estimated that a fifty-year lease on the airport could bring the city $3 billion, most of which it would use to repair other city infrastructure and fund pension plans for city employees. Most of the teams include foreign partners:

- Abertis Infraestructuras SA (Barcelona, Spain), Babcock & Brown Group (Sydney, Australia), and GE Commercial Aviation Services (Stamford, Connecticut)
- AirportsAmerica Group, consisting of Carlyle Infrastructure Partners LP (an investment fund managed by the Carlyle Group, headquartered in Washington, D.C.)
- Chicago Crossroads Consortium, consisting of Macquarie Capital Group Limited (Sydney, Australia), Macquarie Airports (Sydney, Australia), and Macquarie Infrastructure Partners (New York, New York), Macquarie Infrastructure Partners II (New York, New York)
- Chicago First Corp., consisting of HOCHTIEF AirPort GmbH (Essen, Germany), HOCHTIEF AirPort Capital GmbH &

Co. (Essen, Germany), and GS Global Infrastructure Partners I LP (New York, New York)

- Midway Investment and Development Corp., consisting of YVR Airport Services Ltd. (Vancouver, Canada), Citi Infrastructure Investors (New York, New York), and John Hancock Life Insurance Company (Boston, Massachusetts)
- Morgan Stanley Infrastructure Partners (New York, New York), Aeroports de Paris Management (Paris, France), and HMSHost Corporation (Bethesda, Maryland)[76]

This first privatization of a large U.S. airline hub was expected to be completed in the fall of 2008. Chicago selected the fifth of the groups listed above, but the global financial crisis that came to be known as the Great Recession intervened, causing months of delays until in June 2009, it was finally announced that the deal had fallen through because as a result of the drying-up of investment capital markets in the depression the winning bidder was unable to obtain the financing needed to complete the transaction.[77] The trend of privatization of air carrier airports internationally also paused for the same reason. It will be interesting to see if the Chicago Midway project is revived after the economic revival.

States Restrict Public-Employee Collective Bargaining

The November 2010 general elections yielded many ultraconservative "Tea Party" Republican candidate victories in state legislatures and governors' offices. Immediately upon taking their seats in January 2011, these new state legislators introduced proposed legislation in several states aimed at reducing, if not eliminating, the power of public employee unions, ostensibly as emergency state budget reduction moves necessitated by the adverse effects of the Great Recession on the states. Ironically, the first state to pass such legislation was Wisconsin, the first state that had allowed state employees to be represented by labor unions and to bargain collectively. That legislation passed only after weeks of massive public demonstrations staged by public-employee and other unions and others who opposed the change and procedural maneuvering by legislators on both sides of the issue. When the bill passed and was signed by the new governor, a lawsuit was filed challenging the procedure used by the legislature to pass the bill, and recall petitions began to be circulated against legislators who voted for the bill.

At this writing, several other states have passed similar, though generally more moderate, legislation limiting public employee collective bargaining rights, and others are considering such legislation.

Summary

While government pay scales are typically somewhat lower than those for comparable positions of responsibility in private industry, benefit packages (including health care and retirement) have tended to be better, along with job security. Many public employees are represented by unions, and some of the forces and trends identified in previous chapters as affecting labor relations in the private sector of the aviation industry are coming into play in the public sector now as well, if more slowly.

Collective bargaining in the public sector differs from the private sector mainly in that the scope of bargaining is often quite limited in the former by statutory management-rights clauses, and all federal and most state employees are prohibited from striking.

At the federal level, labor-management relations have reached extreme levels of strain, the escalation beginning in early 2001 when the administration of President George W. Bush, supported by a Republican-controlled Congress, citing only national security as a reason, imposed sweeping new restrictions on unionization and collective bargaining by hundreds of thousands of federal employees.

At the FAA, collective bargaining is credited with air traffic controllers enjoying a particularly generous pay scale for decades, until threatened by the Bush administration's unilateral imposition of pay cuts in 2006. Retention and morale of that segment of the federal workforce have since been on the decline.

Also in aviation, the TSA's airport security officers have borne the brunt of George W. Bush's administration's campaign to neutralize the power of organized labor in the federal sector, resulting in low morale and high turnover in this crucial segment of the federal workforce.

At the state and local levels, cutbacks in air service driven by excess capacity and made more urgent by soaring fuel costs, followed by a deep worldwide recession, threaten the revenues of public airports, particularly nonhub airports, and the public jobs they support. The Great Recession also caused state and local government revenues to plummet, and numerous states have enacted legislation to limit the power and scope of bargaining of state and local government employees. Such legislation is likely to reduce the attractiveness of public employment as wages are reduced, along with benefits and job security, though such a trend is unlikely to emerge (if at all) until the economy recovers and employment levels in both the public and private sectors return to prerecession levels.

Appendixes
Notes
Glossary
Index

Appendix A: The Railway Labor Act

Title 45—United States Code

Chapter 8—Railway Labor

*Subchapter 1—General Provisions,
Sections 151–88*

§151. Definitions; short title

When used in this chapter and for the purposes of this chapter—

First. The term "carrier" includes any railroad subject to the jurisdiction of the Surface Transportation Board, any express company that would have been subject to subtitle IV of title 49, "United States Code, as of December 31, 1995," and any company which is directly or indirectly owned or controlled by or under common control with any carrier by railroad and which operates any equipment or facilities or performs any service (other than trucking service) in connection with the transportation, receipt, delivery, elevation, transfer in transit, refrigeration or icing, storage, and handling of property transported by railroad, and any receiver, trustee, Or other individual or body, judicial or otherwise, when in the possession of the business of any such "carrier": Provided, however, That the term "carrier" shall not include any street, interurban, or suburban electric railway, unless such railway is operating as a part of a general steam-railroad system of transportation, but shall not exclude any part of the general steam-railroad system of transportation now or hereafter operated by any

other motive power. The Surface Transportation Board is authorized and directed upon request of the Mediation Board or upon complaint of any party interested to determine after hearing whether any line operated by electric power falls within the terms of this proviso. The term "carrier" shall not include any company by reason of its being engaged in the mining of coal, the supplying of coal to a carrier where delivery is not beyond the mine tipple, and the operation of equipment or facilities therefore, or in any of such activities.

Second. The term "Adjustment Board" means the National Railroad Adjustment Board created by this chapter.

Third. The term "Mediation Board" means the National Mediation Board created by this chapter.

Fourth. The term "commerce" means commerce among the several States or between any State, Territory, or the District of Columbia and any foreign nation, or between any Territory or the District of Columbia and any State, or between any Territory and any other Territory, or between any Territory and the District of Columbia, or within any Territory or the District of Columbia, or between points in the same State but through any other State or any Territory or the District of Columbia or any foreign nation.

Fifth. The term "employee" as used herein includes every person in the service of a carrier (subject to its continuing authority to supervise and direct the manner of rendition of his service) who performs any work defined as that of an employee or subordinate official in the orders of the Surface Transportation Board now in effect, and as the same may be amended or interpreted by orders hereafter entered by the Board pursuant to the authority which is conferred upon it to enter orders amending or interpreting such existing orders: Provided, however, That no occupational classification made by order of the Surface Transportation Board shall be construed to define the crafts according to which railway employees may be organized by their voluntary action, nor shall the jurisdiction or powers of such employee organizations be regarded as in any way limited or defined by the provisions of this chapter or by the orders of the Board.

The term "employee" shall not include any individual while such individual is engaged in the physical operations consisting of the mining of coal, the preparation of coal, the handling (other than movement by rail with standard railroad locomotives) of coal not beyond the mine tipple, or the loading of coal at the tipple.

Sixth. The term "representative" means any person or persons, labor union, organization, or corporation designated either by a carrier or group of carriers or by its or their employees, to act for it or them.

Seventh. The term "district court" includes the United States District Court for the District of Columbia; and the term "court of appeals" includes the United States Court of Appeals for the District of Columbia.

This chapter may be cited as the "Railway Labor Act."

(May 20, 1926, ch. 347, §1, 44 Stat. 577; June 7, 1934, ch. 426, 48 Stat. 926; June 21, 1934, ch. 691, §1, 48 Stat. 1185; June 25, 1936, ch. 804, 49 Stat. 1921; Aug. 13, 1940, ch. 664, §§2, 3, 54 Stat. 785, 786; June 25, 1948, ch. 646, §32(a), (b), 62 Stat. 991; May 24, 1949, ch. 139, §127, 63 Stat. 107.)

REFERENCES IN TEXT

This chapter, referred to in text, was in the original "this Act," meaning act May 20, 1926, ch. 347, 44 Stat. 577 as amended, known as the Railway Labor Act, which enacted this chapter and amended sections 225 and 348 of former Title 28, Judicial Code and Judiciary. Sections 225 and 348 of former Title 28 were repealed by section 39 of act June 25, 1948, ch. 646, 62 Stat. 992, section 1 of which enacted Title 28, Judiciary and Judicial Procedure. Section 225 of former Title 28 was reenacted as sections 1291 to 1294 of Title 28. For complete classification of this Act to the Code, see this section and Tables.

CODIFICATION

In par. First, "subtitle IV of title 49" substituted for "the Interstate Commerce Act [49 U.S.C. 1 et seq.]" on authority of Pub. L. 95-473, §3(b), Oct. 17, 1978, 92 Stat. 1466, the first section of which enacted subtitle IV of Title 49, Transportation.

Provisions of act Aug. 13, 1940, §2, similar to those comprising par. First of this section, limiting the term "employer" as applied to mining, etc., of coal, were formerly contained in section 228a of this title. Provisions of section 3 of the act, similar to those comprising par. Fifth of this section, limiting the term "employee" as applied to mining, etc., of coal, were formerly contained in sections 228a, 261, and 351 of this title, and section 1532 of former Title 26, Internal Revenue Code, 1939.

As originally enacted, par. Seventh contained references to the Supreme Court of the District of Columbia. Act June 25, 1936 substituted "the district court of the United States for the District of Columbia" for "the Supreme Court of the District of Columbia," and act June 25, 1948, as amended by act May 24, 1949, substituted "United States District Court for the District of Columbia" for "district court of the United States for the District of Columbia."

As originally enacted, par. Seventh contained references to the "circuit court of appeals." Act June 25, 1948, as amended by act May 24, 1949, substituted "court of appeals" for "circuit court of appeals."

As originally enacted, par. Seventh contained references to the "Court of Appeals of the District of Columbia." Act June 7, 1934, substituted "United States Court of Appeals for the District of Columbia" for "Court of Appeals of the District of Columbia."

AMENDMENTS

1940—Act Aug. 13, 1940, inserted last sentence of par. First, and second par. of par. Fifth.

1934—Act June 21, 1934, added par. Sixth and redesignated provisions formerly set out as par. Sixth as Seventh.

EFFECTIVE DATE OF 1996 AMENDMENT

Except as otherwise specifically provided, amendment by Pub. L. 104-264 applicable only to fiscal years beginning after Sept. 30, 1996, and not to be construed as affecting funds made available for a fiscal year ending before Oct. 1, 1996, see section 3 of Pub. L. 104-264, set out as a note under section 106 of Title 49, Transportation.

EFFECTIVE DATE OF 1995 AMENDMENT

Amendment by Pub. L. 104-88 effective Jan. 1, 1996, see section 2 of Pub. L. 104-88, set out as an Effective Date note under section 701 of Title 49, Transportation.

RESTRICTION ON ESTABLISHMENT OF NEW ANNUITIES OR PENSIONS

Pub. L. 91-215, Sec. 7, Mar. 17, 1970, 84 Stat. 72, provided that: "No carrier and no representative of employees, as defined in section 1 of the Railway Labor Act [this section], shall, before April 1, 1974, utilize any of the procedures of such Act [this chapter], to seek to make any changes in the provisions of the Railroad Retirement Act of 1937 [section 228a et seq. of this title] for supplemental annuities or to establish any new class of pensions or annuities, other than annuities payable out of the Railroad Retirement Account provided under section 15(a) of the Railroad Retirement Act of 1937 [subsection (a) of section 228o of this title], to become effective prior to July 1, 1974; nor shall any such carrier or representative of employees until July 1, 1974, engage in any strike or lockout to seek to make any such changes or to establish any such new class of pensions or annuities: Provided, That nothing in this section shall inhibit any carrier or representative of employees from seeking any change with respect to benefits payable out of the Railroad Retirement Account provided under section 15(a) of the Railroad Retirement Act of 1937 [subsection (a) of section 228o of this title]."

SOCIAL INSURANCE AND LABOR RELATIONS OF RAILROAD COAL-MINING EMPLOYEES; RETROACTIVE OPERATION OF ACT AUGUST 13, 1940; EFFECT ON PAYMENTS, RIGHTS, ETC.

Sections 4–7 of act Aug. 13, 1940, as amended by Reorg. Plan No. 2 of 1946, Sec. 4, eff. July 16, 1946, 11 F.R. 7873, 60 Stat. 1095, with regard to the operation and effect of the laws amended, provided: "Sec. 4. (a) The laws hereby expressly amended (section 1532 of Title 26, I.R.C. 1939 [former Title 26, Internal Revenue Code of 1939] and sections 151, 215, 228a, 261, and 351 of this title), the Social Security Act, approved August 14, 1935 (section 301 et seq. of Title 42), and all amendments thereto, shall operate as if each amendment herein contained had been enacted as a part of the law it amends, at the time of the original enactment of such law.

"(b) No person (as defined in the Carriers Taxing Act of 1937 [section 261 et seq. of this title]) shall be entitled, by reason of the provisions of this Act, to a refund of, or relief from liability for, any income or excise taxes paid or accrued, pursuant to the provisions of the Carriers Taxing

Act of 1937 or subchapter B of chapter 9 of the Internal Revenue Code [section 1500 et seq. of former Title 26, Internal Revenue Code of 1939], prior to the date of the enactment of this Act [Aug. 13, 1940] by reason of employment in the service of any carrier by railroad subject to part I of the Interstate Commerce Act [former 49 U.S.C. 1 et seq.], but any individual who has been employed in such service of any carrier by railroad subject to part I of the Interstate Commerce Act as is excluded by the amendments made by this Act from coverage under the Carriers Taxing Act of 1937 and subchapter B of chapter 9 of the Internal Revenue Code, and who has paid income taxes under the provisions of such Act or subchapter, and any carrier by railroad subject to part I of the Interstate Commerce Act which has paid excise taxes under the provisions of the Carriers Taxing Act of 1937 or subchapter B of chapter 9 of the Internal Revenue Code, may, upon making proper application therefor to the Bureau of Internal Revenue [now Internal Revenue Service], have the amount of taxes so paid applied in reduction of such tax liability with respect to employment, as may, by reason of the amendments made by this Act, accrue against them under the provisions of title VIII of the Social Security Act [section 1001 et seq. of Title 42] or the Federal Insurance Contributions Act (subchapter A of chapter 9 of the Internal Revenue Code) [section 1400 et seq. of former Title 26].

"(c) Nothing contained in this Act shall operate (1) to affect any annuity, pension, or death benefit granted under the Railroad Retirement Act of 1935 [section 215 et seq. of this title] or the Railroad Retirement Act of 1937 [section 228a et seq. of this title], prior to the date of enactment of this Act [Aug. 13, 1940], or (2) to include any of the services on the basis of which any such annuity or pension was granted, as employment within the meaning of section 210(b) of the Social Security Act or section 209(b) of such Act,

as amended [sections 410(b) and 409(b), respectively, of Title 42]. In any case in which a death benefit alone has been granted, the amount of such death benefit attributable to services, coverage of which is affected by this Act, shall be deemed to have been paid to the deceased under section 204 of the Social Security Act [section 404 of Title 42] in effect prior to January 1, 1940, and deductions shall be made from any insurance benefit or benefits payable under the Social Security Act, as amended [section 301 et seq. of Title 42], with respect to wages paid to an individual for such services until such deductions total the amount of such death benefit attributable to such services.

"(d) Nothing contained in this Act shall operate to affect the benefit rights of any individual under the Railroad Unemployment Insurance Act [section 351 et seq. of this title] for any day of unemployment (as defined in section 1(k) of such Act [section 351(k) of this title]) occurring prior to the date of enactment of this Act. [Aug. 13, 1940].

"Sec. 5. Any application for payment filed with the Railroad Retirement Board prior to, or within sixty days after, the enactment of this Act shall, under such regulations as the Federal Security Administrator may prescribe, be deemed to be an application filed with the Federal Security Administrator by such individual or by any person claiming any payment with respect to the wages of such individual, under any provision of section 202 of the Social Security Act, as amended [section 402 of Title 42].

"Sec. 6. Nothing contained in this Act, nor the action of Congress in adopting it, shall be taken or considered as affecting the question of what carriers, companies, or individuals, other than those in this Act specifically provided for, are included in or excluded from the provisions of the various laws to which this Act is an amendment.

"Sec. 7. (a) Notwithstanding the provisions of section 1605(b) of the Internal Revenue Code [section 1605(b) of former Title 26, Internal Revenue Code of 1939], no interest shall, during the period February 1, 1940, to the eighty-ninth day after the date of enactment of this Act [Aug. 13, 1940], inclusive, accrue by reason of delinquency in the payment of the tax imposed by section 1600 with respect to services affected by this Act performed during the period July 1, 1939, to December 31, 1939, inclusive, with respect to which services amounts have been paid as contributions under the Railroad Unemployment Insurance Act [section 351 et seq. of this title] prior to the date of enactment of this Act.

"(b) Notwithstanding the provisions of section 1601(a)(3) of the Internal Revenue Code [section 1601(a)(3) of former Title 26, Internal Revenue Code of 1939], the credit allowable under section 1601(a) against the tax imposed by section 1600 for the calendar year 1939 shall not be disallowed or reduced by reason of the payment into a State unemployment fund after January 31, 1940, of contributions with respect to services affected by this Act performed during the period July 1, 1939, to December 31, 1939, inclusive, with respect to which services amounts have been paid as contributions under the Railroad Unemployment Insurance Act [section 351 et seq. of this title] prior to the date of enactment of this Act [Aug. 13, 1940]: Provided, That this subsection shall be applicable only if the contributions with respect to such services are paid into the State unemployment fund before the ninetieth day after the date of enactment of this Act."

SECTION REFERRED TO IN OTHER SECTIONS

This section is referred to in sections 157, 182 of this title.

§151a. General purposes

The purposes of the chapter are: (1) to avoid any interruption to commerce or to the operation of any carrier engaged therein; (2) to forbid any limitation upon freedom of association among employees or any denial, as a condition of employment or otherwise, of the right of employees to join a labor organization; (3) to provide for the complete independence of carriers and of employees in the matter of self-organization to carry out the purposes of this chapter; (4) to provide for the prompt and orderly settlement of all disputes concerning rates of pay, rules, or working conditions; (5) to provide for the prompt and orderly settlement of all disputes growing out of grievances or out of the interpretation or application of agreements covering rates of pay, rules, or working conditions.

(May 20, 1926, ch. 347, §2, 44 Stat. 577; June 21, 1934, ch. 691, §2, 48 Stat. 1186.)

AMENDMENTS

1934—Act June 21, 1934, reenacted provisions comprising this section without change.

SECTION REFERRED TO IN OTHER SECTIONS

This section is referred to in sections 153, 157 of this title.

§152. General duties

First. Duty of carriers and employees to settle disputes

It shall be the duty of all carriers, their officers, agents, and employees to exert every reasonable effort to make and maintain agreements concerning rates of pay, rules, and working conditions and to settle all disputes, whether arising out of the application of such agreements or otherwise, in order to avoid any interruption to commerce or to the operation of any carrier growing out of any dispute between the carrier and the employees thereof.

Second. Consideration of disputes by representatives

All disputes between a carrier or carriers and its or their employees shall be considered, and, if possible, decided, with all expedition, in conference between representatives designated and authorized so to confer, respectively, by the carrier or carriers and by the employees thereof interested in the dispute.

Third. Designation of representatives

Representatives, for the purposes of this chapter, shall be designated by the respective parties without interference, influence, or coercion by either party over the designation of representatives by the other; and neither party shall in any way interfere with, influence, or coerce the other in its choice of representatives. Representatives of employees for the purposes of this chapter need not be persons in the employ of the carrier, and no carrier shall, by interference, influence, or coercion, seek in any manner to prevent the designation by its employees as their representatives of those who or which are not employees of the carrier.

Fourth. Organization and collective bargaining, freedom from interference by carrier, assistance in organizing or maintaining organization by carrier forbidden; deduction of dues from wages forbidden

Employees shall have the right to organize and bargain collectively through representatives of their own choosing. The majority of any craft or class of employees shall have the right to determine who shall be the representative of the craft or class for the purposes of this chapter. No carrier, its officers, or agents shall deny or in any way question the right of its employees to join, organize, or assist in organizing the labor organization of their choice, and it shall be unlawful for any carrier to interfere in any way with the organization of its employees, or to use the funds of the carrier in maintaining or assisting or contributing to any labor organization, labor representative, or other agency of collective bargaining, or in performing any work therefor, or to influence or coerce employees in an effort to induce them to join or remain or not to join or remain members of any labor organization, or to deduct from the wages of employees any dues, fees, assessments, or other contributions payable to labor organizations, or to collect or to assist in the collection of any such dues, fees, assessments, or other contributions: provided, that nothing in this chapter shall be construed to prohibit a carrier from permitting an employee, individually, or local representatives of employees from conferring with management during working hours without loss of time, or to prohibit a carrier from furnishing free transportation to its employees while engaged in the business of a labor organization.

Fifth. Agreements to join or not to join labor organizations forbidden

No carrier, its officers, or agents shall require any person seeking employment to sign any contract or agreement promising to join or not to join a labor organization; and if any such contract has been enforced prior to the effective date of this chapter, then such carrier shall notify the employees by an appropriate order that such contract has been discarded and is no longer binding on them in any way.

Sixth. Conference of representatives; time; place; private agreements

In case of a dispute between a carrier or carriers and its or their employees, arising out of grievances or out of the interpretation or application of agreements concerning rates of pay, rules, or working conditions, it shall be the duty of the designated representative or representatives of such carrier or carriers and of such employees, within ten days after the receipt of notice of a desire on the part of either party to confer in respect to such dispute, to specify a time and place at which such conference shall be held: Provided, (1) That the place so specified shall be situated upon the line of the carrier involved or as otherwise mutually agreed upon; and (2) that the time so specified shall allow the designated conferees reasonable opportunity to reach such place of conference, but shall not exceed twenty days from the receipt of such notice: And provided further, That nothing in this chapter shall be construed to supersede the provisions of any agreement (as to conferences) then in effect between the parties.

Seventh. Change in pay, rules, or working conditions contrary to agreement or to section 156 forbidden
No carrier, its officers, or agents shall change the rates of pay, rules, or working conditions of its employees, as a class, as embodied in agreements except in the manner prescribed in such agreements or in section 156 of this title.

Eighth. Notices of manner of settlement of disputes; posting
Every carrier shall notify its employees by printed notices in such form and posted at such times and places as shall be specified by the Mediation Board that all disputes between the carrier and its employees will be handled in accordance with the requirements of this chapter, and in such notices there shall be printed verbatim, in large type, the third, fourth, and fifth paragraphs of this section. The provisions of said paragraphs are made a part of the contract of employment between the carrier and each employee, and shall be held binding upon the parties, regardless of any other express or implied agreements between them.

Ninth. Disputes as to identity of representatives; designation by Mediation Board; secret elections
If any dispute shall arise among a carrier's employees as to who are the representatives of such employees designated and authorized in accordance with the requirements of this chapter, it shall be the duty of the Mediation Board, upon request of either party to the dispute, to investigate such dispute and to certify to both parties, in writing, within thirty days after the receipt of the invocation of its services, the name or names of the individuals or organizations that have been designated and authorized to represent the employees involved in the dispute, and

certify the same to the carrier. Upon receipt of such certification the carrier shall treat with the representative so certified as the representative of the craft or class for the purposes of this chapter. In such an investigation, the Mediation Board shall be authorized to take a secret ballot of the employees involved, or to utilize any other appropriate method of ascertaining the names of their duly designated and authorized representatives in such manner as shall insure the choice of representatives by the employees without interference, influence, or coercion exercised by the carrier. In the conduct of any election for the purposes herein indicated the Board shall designate who may participate in the election and establish the rules to govern the election, or may appoint a committee of three neutral persons who after hearing shall within ten days designate the employees who may participate in the election. The Board shall have access to and have power to make copies of the books and records of the carriers to obtain and utilize such information as may be deemed necessary by it to carry out the purposes and provisions of this paragraph.

Tenth. Violations; prosecution and penalties
The willful failure or refusal of any carrier, its officers or agents, to comply with the terms of the third, fourth, fifth, seventh, or eighth paragraph of this section shall be a misdemeanor, and upon conviction thereof the carrier, officer, or agent offending shall be subject to a fine of not less than $1,000, nor more than $20,000, or imprisonment for not more than six months, or both fine and imprisonment, for each offense, and each day during which such carrier, officer, or agent shall willfully fail or refuse to comply with the terms of the said paragraphs of this section shall constitute a separate offense. It shall be the duty of any United States attorney to whom any duly designated representative of a carrier's employees may apply to institute in the proper court and to prosecute under the direction of

the Attorney General of the United States, all necessary proceedings for the enforcement of the provisions of this section, and for the punishment of all violations thereof and the costs and expenses of such prosecution shall be paid out of the appropriation for the expenses of the courts of the United States: Provided, That nothing in this chapter shall be construed to require an individual employee to render labor or service without his consent, nor shall anything in this chapter be construed to make the quitting of his labor by an individual employee an illegal act; nor shall any court issue any process to compel the performance by an individual employee of such labor or service, without his consent.

Eleventh. Union security agreements; check-off
Notwithstanding any other provisions of this chapter, or of any other statute or law of the United States, or Territory thereof, or of any State, any carrier or carriers as defined in this chapter and a labor organization or labor organizations duly designated and authorized to represent employees in accordance with the requirements of this chapter shall be permitted

(a) to make agreements, requiring, as a condition of continued employment, that within sixty days following the beginning of such employment, or the effective date of such agreements, whichever is the later, all employees shall become members of the labor organization representing their craft or class: Provided, That no such agreement shall require such condition of employment with respect to employees to whom membership is not available upon the same terms and conditions as are generally applicable to any other member or with respect to employees to whom membership was denied or terminated for any reason other than the failure of the employee to tender the periodic dues, initiation fees, and assessments (not including fines and penalties) uniformly required as a condition of acquiring or retaining membership.

(b) to make agreements providing for the deduction by such carrier or carriers from the wages of its or their employees in a craft or class and payment to the labor organization representing the craft or class of such employees, of any periodic dues, initiation fees, and assessments (not including fines and penalties) uniformly required as a condition of acquiring or retaining membership: Provided, That no such agreement shall be effective with respect to any individual employee until he shall have furnished the employer with a written assignment to the labor organization of such membership dues, initiation fees, and assessments, which shall be revocable in writing after the expiration of one year or upon the termination date of the applicable collective agreement, whichever occurs sooner.

(c) The requirement of membership in a labor organization in an agreement made pursuant to subparagraph (a) of this paragraph shall be satisfied, as to both a present or future employee in engine, train, yard, or hostling service, that is, an employee engaged in any of the services or capacities covered in the First division of paragraph (h) of section 153 of this title defining the jurisdictional scope of the First Division of the National Railroad Adjustment Board, if said employee shall hold or acquire membership in any one of the labor organizations, national in scope, organized in accordance with this chapter and admitting to membership employees of a craft or class in any of said services; and no agreement made pursuant to subparagraph (b) of this paragraph shall provide for deductions from his wages for periodic dues, initiation fees, or assessments payable to any labor organization other than that in which he holds membership: Provided, however, That as to an employee in any of said services on a particular carrier at the effective date of any such agreement on a carrier, who is not a member of any one of the labor organizations, national in scope, organized in accordance with this chapter and admitting to membership employees of a craft or class in any of said services, such employee, as a condition of continuing his employment, may be required to become a member of the organization representing the craft in which he is employed on the effective date of the first agreement applicable to him: Provided, further, That nothing herein or in any such agreement or agreements shall prevent an employee from changing membership from one organization to another organization admitting to membership employees of a craft or class in any of said services.

(d) Any provisions in paragraphs Fourth and Fifth of this section in conflict herewith are to the extent of such conflict amended.
(May 20, 1926, ch. 347, §2, 44 Stat. 577; June 21, 1934, ch. 691, §2, 48 Stat. 1186; June 25, 1948, ch. 646, §1, 62 Stat. 909; Jan. 10, 1951, ch. 1220, 64 Stat. 1238.)

REFERENCES IN TEXT

The effective date of this chapter, referred to in par. Fifth, probably means May 20, 1926, the date of approval of act May 20, 1926, ch. 347, 44 Stat. 577.

AMENDMENTS

1951—Act Jan. 10, 1951, added par. Eleventh.
1934—Act June 21, 1934, substituted "by the carrier or carriers" for "by the carriers" in par. Second, generally amended pars. Third, Fourth, and Fifth, and added pars. Sixth to Tenth.

CHANGE OF NAME

Act June 25, 1948, eff. Sept. 1, 1948, substituted "United States attorney" for "district attorney of the United States." See section 541 of Title 28, Judiciary and Judicial Procedure, and Historical and Revision Notes thereunder.

SECTION REFERRED TO IN OTHER SECTIONS

This section is referred to in sections 153, 157 of this title; title 29 section 2101.

§153. National Railroad Adjustment Board

First. Establishment, composition, powers and duties, divisions, hearings and awards, judicial review
There is established a Board, to be known as the "National Railroad Adjustment Board," the members of which shall be selected within thirty days after June 21, 1934, and it is provided

(a) That the said Adjustment Board shall consist of thirty-four members, seventeen of whom shall be selected by the carriers and seventeen by such labor organizations of the employees, national in scope, as have been or may be organized in accordance with the provisions of sections 151a and 152 of this title.

(b) The carriers, acting each through its board of directors or its receiver or receivers, trustee or trustees, or through an officer or officers designated for that purpose by such board, trustee or trustees, or receiver or receivers, shall prescribe the rules under which its representatives shall be selected and shall select the representatives of the carriers on the Adjustment Board and designate the division on which each such representative shall serve, but no carrier or system of carriers shall have more than one voting representative on any division of the Board.

(c) Except as provided in the second paragraph of subsection (h) of this section, the national labor organizations, as defined in paragraph (a) of this section, acting each through the chief executive or other medium designated by the organization or association thereof, shall prescribe the rules under which the labor members of the Adjustment Board shall be selected and shall select such members and designate the division on which each member shall serve; but no labor organization shall have more than one voting representative on any division of the Board.

(d) In case of a permanent or temporary vacancy on the Adjustment Board, the vacancy shall be filled by selection in the same manner as in the original selection.

(e) If either the carriers or the labor organizations of the employees fail to select and designate representatives to the Adjustment Board, as provided in paragraphs (b) and (c) of this section, respectively, within sixty days after June 21, 1934, in case of any original appointment to office of a member of the Adjustment Board, or in case of a vacancy in any such office within thirty days after such vacancy occurs, the Mediation Board shall thereupon directly make the appointment and shall select an individual associated in interest with the carriers or the group of labor organizations of employees, whichever he is to represent.

(f) In the event a dispute arises as to the right of any national labor organization to participate as per paragraph (c) of this section in the selection and designation of the labor members of the Adjustment Board, the Secretary of Labor shall investigate the claim of such labor organization to participate, and if such claim in the judgment of the Secretary of Labor has merit, the Secretary shall notify the Mediation Board accordingly, and within ten days after receipt of such advice the Mediation Board shall request those national labor organizations duly qualified as per paragraph (c) of this section to participate in the selection and designation of the labor members of the Adjustment Board to select a representative. Such representative, together with a representative likewise designated by the claimant, and a third or neutral party designated by the Mediation Board, constituting a board of three, shall within thirty days after the appointment of the neutral member, investigate the claims of the labor organization desiring participation and decide whether or not it was organized in accordance with sections 151a and 152 of this title and is otherwise properly qualified to participate in the selection of the labor members of the Adjustment Board, and the findings of such boards of three shall be final and binding.

(g) Each member of the Adjustment Board shall be compensated by the party or parties he is to represent. Each third or neutral party selected under the provisions of paragraph (f) of this section shall receive from the Mediation Board such compensation as the Mediation Board may fix, together with his necessary traveling expenses and expenses actually incurred for subsistence, or per diem allowance in lieu thereof, subject to the provisions of law applicable thereto, while serving as such third or neutral party.

(h) The said Adjustment Board shall be composed of four divisions, whose proceedings shall be independent of one another, and the said divisions as well as the number of their members shall be as follows:

First division: To have jurisdiction over disputes involving train- and yard-service employees of carriers; that is, engineers, firemen, hostlers, and outside hostler helpers, conductors, trainmen, and yard-service employees. This division shall consist of eight members, four of whom shall be selected and designated by the carriers and four of whom shall be selected and designated by the labor organizations, national in scope and organized in accordance with sections 151a and 152 of this title and which represent employees in engine, train, yard, or hostling service: Provided, however, That each labor organization shall select and designate two members on the First Division and that no labor organization shall have more than one vote in any proceedings of the First Division or in the adoption of any award with respect to any dispute submitted to the First Division: Provided further, however, That the carrier members of the First Division shall cast no more than two votes in any proceedings of the division or in the adoption of any award with respect to any dispute submitted to the First Division.

Second division: To have jurisdiction over disputes involving machinists, boilermakers, blacksmiths, sheet-metal workers, electrical workers, car men, the helpers and apprentices of all the foregoing, coach cleaners, power-house employees, and railroad-shop laborers. This division shall consist of ten members, five of whom shall be selected by the carriers and five by the national labor organizations of the employees.

Third division: To have jurisdiction over disputes involving station, tower, and telegraph employees, train dispatchers, maintenance-of-way men, clerical employees, freight handlers, express, station, and store employees, signal men, sleeping-car conductors, sleeping-car porters, and maids and dining-car employees. This division shall consist of ten members, five of whom shall be selected by the carriers and five by the national labor organizations of employees.

Fourth division: To have jurisdiction over disputes involving employees of carriers directly or indirectly engaged in transportation of passengers or property by water, and all other employees of carriers over which jurisdiction is not given to the first, second, and third divisions. This division shall consist of six members, three of whom shall be selected by the carriers and three by the national labor organizations of the employees.

(i) The disputes between an employee or group of employees and a carrier or carriers growing out of grievances or out of the interpretation or application of agreements concerning rates of pay, rules, or working conditions, including cases pending and unadjusted on June 21, 1934, shall be handled in the usual manner up to and including the chief operating officer of the carrier designated to handle such disputes; but, failing to reach an adjustment in this manner, the disputes may be referred by petition of the parties or by either party to the appropriate division of the Adjustment Board with a full statement of the facts and all supporting data bearing upon the disputes.

(j) Parties may be heard either in person, by counsel, or by other representatives, as they may respectively elect, and the several divisions of the Adjustment Board shall give due notice of all hearings to the employee or employees and the carrier or carriers involved in any disputes submitted to them.

(k) Any division of the Adjustment Board shall have authority to empower two or more of its members to conduct hearings and make findings upon disputes, when properly submitted, at any place designated by the division: Provided, however, That except as provided in paragraph (h) of this section, final awards as to any such dispute must be made by the entire division as hereinafter provided.

(l) Upon failure of any division to agree upon an award because of a deadlock or inability to secure a majority vote of the division members, as provided in paragraph (n) of this section, then such division shall forthwith agree upon and select a neutral person, to be known as "referee," to sit with the division as a member thereof, and make an award. Should the division fail to agree upon and select a referee within ten days of the date of the deadlock or inability to secure a majority vote, then the division, or any member thereof, or the parties or either party to the dispute may certify that fact to the Mediation Board, which Board shall, within ten days from the date of receiving such certificate, select and name the referee to sit with the division as a member thereof and make an award. The Mediation Board shall be bound by the same provisions in the appointment of these neutral referees as are provided elsewhere in this chapter for the appointment of arbitrators and shall fix and pay the compensation of such referees.

(m) The awards of the several divisions of the Adjustment Board shall be stated in writing. A copy of the awards shall be furnished to the respective parties to the controversy, and the awards shall be final and binding upon both parties to the dispute. In case a dispute arises involving an interpretation of the award, the division of the board upon request of either party shall interpret the award in the light of the dispute.

(n) A majority vote of all members of the division of the Adjustment Board eligible to vote shall be competent to make an award with respect to any dispute submitted to it.

(o) In case of an award by any division of the Adjustment Board in favor of petitioner, the division of the Board shall make an order, directed to the carrier, to make the award effective and, if the award includes a requirement for the payment of money, to pay to the employee the sum to which he is entitled under the award on or before a day named. In the event any division determines that an award favorable to the petitioner should not be made in any dispute referred to it, the division shall make an order to the petitioner stating such determination.

(p) If a carrier does not comply with an order of a division of the Adjustment Board within the time limit in such order, the petitioner, or any person for whose benefit such order was made, may file in the District Court of the United States for the district in which he resides or in which is located the principal operating office of the carrier, or through which the carrier operates, a petition setting forth briefly the causes for which he claims relief, and the order of the division of the Adjustment Board in the premises. Such suit in the District Court of the United States shall proceed in all respects as other civil suits, except that on the trial of such suit the findings and order of the division of the Adjustment Board shall be conclusive on the parties, and except that the petitioner shall not be liable for costs in the district court nor for costs at any subsequent stage of the proceedings, unless they accrue upon his appeal, and such costs shall be paid out of the appropriation for the expenses of the courts of the United States. If the petitioner shall finally prevail he shall be allowed a reasonable attorney's fee, to be taxed and collected as a part of the costs of the suit. The district courts are empowered, under the rules of the court governing actions at law, to make such order and enter such judgment, by writ of mandamus or otherwise, as may be appropriate to enforce or set aside the order of the division of the Adjustment Board: Provided, however, That such order may not be set aside except for failure of the division to comply with the requirements of this chapter, for failure of the order to conform, or confine itself, to matters within the scope of the division's jurisdiction, or for fraud or corruption by a member of the division making the order.

(q) If any employee or group of employees, or any carrier, is aggrieved by the failure of any division of the Adjustment Board to make an award in a dispute referred to it, or is aggrieved by any of the terms of an award or by the failure of the division to include certain terms in such award, then such employee or group of employees or carrier may file in any United States district court in which a petition under paragraph (p) could be filed, a petition for review of the division's order. A copy of the petition shall be forthwith transmitted by the clerk of the court to the Adjustment Board. The Adjustment Board shall file in the court the record of the proceedings on which it based its action. The court shall have jurisdiction to affirm the order of the division, or to set it aside, in whole or in part, or it may remand the proceedings to the division for such further action as it may direct. On such review, the findings and order of the division shall be conclusive on the parties, except that the order of the division may be set aside, in whole or in part, or remanded to the division, for failure of the division to comply with the requirements of this chapter, for failure of the order to conform, or confine itself, to matters within the scope of the division's jurisdiction, or for fraud or corruption by a member of the division making the order.

The judgment of the court shall be subject to review as provided in sections 1291 and 1254 of title 28.

(r) All actions at law based upon the provisions of this section shall be begun within two years from the time the cause of action accrues under the award of the division of the Adjustment Board, and not after.

(s) The several divisions of the Adjustment Board shall maintain headquarters in Chicago, Illinois, meet regularly, and continue in session so long as there is pending before the division any matter within its jurisdiction which has been submitted for its consideration and which has not been disposed of.

(t) Whenever practicable, the several divisions or subdivisions of the Adjustment Board shall be supplied with suitable quarters in any Federal building located at its place of meeting.

(u) The Adjustment Board may, subject to the approval of the Mediation Board, employ and fix the compensations of such assistants as it deems necessary in carrying on its proceedings. The compensation of such employees shall be paid by the Mediation Board.

(v) The Adjustment Board shall meet within forty days after June 21, 1934, and adopt such rules as it deems necessary to control proceedings before the respective divisions and not in conflict with the provisions of this section. Immediately following the meeting of the entire Board and the adoption of such rules, the respective divisions shall meet and organize by the selection of a chairman, a vice chairman, and a secretary. Thereafter each division shall annually designate one of its members to act as chairman and one of its members to act as vice chairman: Provided, however, That the chairmanship and vice-chairmanship of any division shall alternate as between the groups, so that both the chairmanship and vice-chairmanship shall be held alternately by a representative of the carriers and a representative of the employees. In case

of a vacancy, such vacancy shall be filled for the unexpired term by the selection of a successor from the same group.

(w) Each division of the Adjustment Board shall annually prepare and submit a report of its activities to the Mediation Board, and the substance of such report shall be included in the annual report of the Mediation Board to the Congress of the United States. The reports of each division of the Adjustment Board and the annual report of the Mediation Board shall state in detail all cases heard, all actions taken, the names, salaries, and duties of all agencies, employees, and officers receiving compensation from the United States under the authority of this chapter, and an account of all moneys appropriated by Congress pursuant to the authority conferred by this chapter and disbursed by such agencies, employees, and officers.

(x) Any division of the Adjustment Board shall have authority, in its discretion, to establish regional adjustment boards to act in its place and stead for such limited period as such division may determine to be necessary. Carrier members of such regional boards shall be designated in keeping with rules devised for this purpose by the carrier members of the Adjustment Board and the labor members shall be designated in keeping with rules devised for this purpose by the labor members of the Adjustment Board. Any such regional board shall, during the time for which it is appointed, have the same authority to conduct hearings, make findings upon disputes and adopt the same procedure as the division of the Adjustment Board appointing it, and its decisions shall be enforceable to the same extent and under the same processes. A neutral person, as referee, shall be appointed for service in connection with any such regional adjustment board in the same circumstances and manner as provided in paragraph (1) of this section, with respect to a division of the Adjustment Board.

Second. System, group, or regional boards: establishment by voluntary agreement; special adjustment boards: establishment, composition, designation of representatives by Mediation Board, neutral member, compensation, quorum, finality and enforcement of awards

Nothing in this section shall be construed to prevent any individual carrier, system, or group of carriers and any class or classes of its or their employees, all acting through their representatives, selected in accordance with the provisions of this chapter, from mutually agreeing to the establishment of system, group, or regional boards of adjustment for the purpose of adjusting and deciding disputes of the character specified in this section. In the event that either party to such a system, group, or regional board of adjustment is dissatisfied with such arrangement, it may upon ninety days' notice to the other party elect to come under the jurisdiction of the Adjustment Board.

If written request is made upon any individual carrier by the representative of any craft or class of employees of such carrier for the establishment of a special board of adjustment to resolve disputes otherwise referable to the Adjustment Board, or any dispute which has been pending before the Adjustment Board for twelve months from the date the dispute (claim) is received by the Board, or if any carrier makes such a request upon any such representative, the carrier or the representative upon whom such request is made shall join in an agreement establishing such a board within thirty days from the date such request is made. The cases which may be considered by such board shall be defined in the agreement establishing it. Such board shall consist of one person designated by the carrier and one person designated by the representative of the employees. If such carrier or such representative fails to agree upon the establishment of such a board as provided herein, or to exercise its rights to designate a member of the board, the carrier or representative making the request for the establishment of the special board may request the Mediation Board to designate a member of the special board on behalf of the carrier or representative upon whom such request was made. Upon receipt of a request for such designation the Mediation Board shall promptly make such designation and shall select an individual associated in interest with the carrier or representative he is to represent, who, with the member appointed by the carrier or representative requesting the establishment of the special board, shall constitute the board. Each member of the board shall be compensated by the party he is to represent. The members of the board so designated shall determine all matters not previously agreed upon by the carrier and the representative of the employees with respect to the establishment and jurisdiction of the board. If they are unable to agree such matters shall be determined by a neutral member of the board selected or appointed and compensated in the same manner as is hereinafter provided with respect to situations where the members of the board are unable to agree upon an award. Such neutral member shall cease to be a member of the board when he has determined such matters. If with respect to any dispute or group of disputes the members of the board designated by the carrier and the representative are unable to agree upon an award disposing of the dispute or group of disputes they shall by mutual agreement select a neutral person to be a member of the board for the consideration and disposition of such dispute or group of disputes. In the event the members of the board designated by the parties are unable, within ten days after their failure to agree upon an award, to agree upon the selection of such neutral person, either member of the board may request the Mediation Board to appoint such neutral person and upon receipt of such request the Mediation Board shall promptly make such appointment. The neutral person

so selected or appointed shall be compensated and reimbursed for expenses by the Mediation Board. Any two members of the board shall be competent to render an award. Such awards shall be final and binding upon both parties to the dispute and if in favor of the petitioner, shall direct the other party to comply therewith on or before the day named. Compliance with such awards shall be enforceable by proceedings in the United States district courts in the same manner and subject to the same provisions that apply to proceedings for enforcement of compliance with awards of the Adjustment Board.
(May 20, 1926, ch. 347, §3, 44 Stat. 578; June 21, 1934, ch. 691, §3, 48 Stat. 1189; Pub. L. 89-456, §§1, 2, June 20, 1966, 80 Stat. 208, 209; Pub. L. 91-234, §§1–6, Apr. 23, 1970, 84 Stat. 199, 200.)

AMENDMENTS

1970—Par. First, (a). Pub. L. 91-234, §1, substituted "thirty-four members, seventeen of whom shall be selected by the carriers and seventeen" for "thirty-six members, eighteen of whom shall be selected by the carriers arid eighteen."

Par. First, (b). Pub. L. 91-234, §2, provided that no carrier or system of carriers have more than one voting representative on any division of the National Railroad Adjustment Board.

Par. First, (c). Pub. L. 91-234, §3, inserted "Except as provided in the second paragraph of subsection (h) of this section" before "the national labor organizations," and provided that no labor organization have more than one voting representative on any division of the National Railroad Adjustment Board.

Par. First, (h). Pub. L. 91-234, §4, decreased number of members on First division of Board from ten to eight members, with an accompanying decrease of five to four as number of members of such Board elected respectively by the carriers and by the national labor organizations satisfying the enumerated requirements, and set forth provisos which limited voting by each labor organization or carrier member in any proceedings of the division or in adoption of any award.

Par. First, (k). Pub. L. 91-234, §5, inserted "except as provided in paragraph (h) of this section" after proviso.

Par. First, (n). Pub. L. 91-234, §6, inserted "eligible to vote" after "Adjustment Board."

1966—Par. First, (m). Pub. L. 89-456, §2(a), struck out ", except insofar as they shall contain a money award" from second sentence.

Par. First, (o). Pub. L. 89-456, §2(b), inserted provision for a division to make an order to the petitioner stating that an award favorable to the petitioner should not be made in any dispute referred to it.

Par. First, (p). Pub. L. 89-456, §2(c), (d), substituted in second sentence "conclusive on the parties" for "prima facie evidence of the facts therein stated" and inserted in last sentence reasons for setting aside orders of a division of the Adjustment Board, respectively.

Par. First, (q) to (x). Pub. L. 89-456, §2(e), added par. (q) and redesignated former pars. (q) to (w) as (r) to (x), respectively.

Par. Second. Pub. L. 89-456, §1, provided for establishment of special adjustment boards upon request of employees or carriers to resolve disputes otherwise referable to the Adjustment Board and made awards of such boards final.

1934—Act June 21, 1934, amended provisions comprising this section generally.

§154. National Mediation Board

First. Board of Mediation abolished; National Mediation Board established; composition; term of office; qualifications; salaries; removal
The Board of Mediation is abolished, effective thirty days from June 21, 1934, and the members, secretary, officers, assistants, employees, and agents thereof, in office upon June 21, 1934, shall continue to function and receive their salaries for a period of thirty days from such date in the same manner as though this chapter had

not been passed. There is established, as an independent agency in the executive branch of the Government, a board to be known as the "National Mediation Board," to be composed of three members appointed by the President, by and with the advice and consent of the Senate, not more than two of whom shall be of the same political party. Each member of the Mediation Board in office on January 1, 1965, shall be deemed to have been appointed for a term of office which shall expire on July 1 of the year his term would have otherwise expired. The terms of office of all successors shall expire three years after the expiration of the terms for which their predecessors were appointed; but any member appointed to fill a vacancy occurring prior to the expiration of the term for which his predecessor was appointed shall be appointed only for the unexpired term of his predecessor. Vacancies in the Board shall not impair the powers nor affect the duties of the Board nor of the remaining members of the Board. Two of the members in office shall constitute a quorum for the transaction of the business of the Board. Each member of the Board shall receive necessary traveling and subsistence expenses, or per diem allowance in lieu thereof, subject to the provisions of law applicable thereto, while away from the principal office of the Board on business required by this chapter. No person in the employment of or who is pecuniarily or otherwise interested in any organization of employees or any carrier shall enter upon the duties of or continue to be a member of the Board. Upon the expiration of his term of office, a member shall continue to serve until his successor is appointed and shall have qualified.

All cases referred to the Board of Mediation and unsettled on June 21, 1934, shall be handled to conclusion by the Mediation Board.

A member of the Board may be removed by the President for inefficiency, neglect of duty, malfeasance in office, or ineligibility, but for no other cause.

Second. Chairman; principal office; delegation of powers; oaths; seal; report

The Mediation Board shall annually designate a member to act as chairman. The Board shall maintain its principal office in the District of Columbia, but it may meet at any other place whenever it deems it necessary so to do. The Board may designate one or more of its members to exercise the functions of the Board in mediation proceedings. Each member of the Board shall have power to administer oaths and affirmations. The Board shall have a seal which shall be judicially noticed. The Board shall make an annual report to Congress.

Third. Appointment of experts and other employees; salaries of employees; expenditures

The Mediation Board may (1) subject to the provisions of the civil service laws, appoint such experts and assistants to act in a confidential capacity and such other officers and employees as are essential to the effective transaction of the work of the Board; (2) in accordance with chapter 51 and subchapter III of chapter 53 of title 5, fix the salaries of such experts, assistants, officers, and employees; and (3) make such expenditures (including expenditures for rent and personal services at the seat of government and elsewhere, for law books, periodicals, and books of reference, and for printing and binding, and including expenditures for salaries and compensation, necessary traveling expenses and expenses actually incurred for subsistence, and other necessary expenses of the Mediation Board, Adjustment Board, Regional Adjustment Boards established under paragraph (w) of section 153 of this title, and boards of arbitration, in accordance with the provisions of this section and sections 153 and 157 of this title, respectively), as may be necessary for the execution of the functions vested in the Board, in the Adjustment Board and in the boards of arbitration, and as may be provided for by the Congress from time to time. All expenditures of the Board shall be allowed and paid on the presentation of itemized vouchers therefor approved by the chairman.

Fourth. *Delegation of powers and duties*

The Mediation Board is authorized by its order to assign, or refer, any portion of its work, business, or functions arising under this chapter or any other Act of Congress, or referred to it by Congress or either branch thereof, to an individual member of the Board or to an employee or employees of the Board to be designated by such order for action thereon, and by its order at any time to amend, modify, supplement, or rescind any such assignment or reference. All such orders shall take effect forthwith and remain in effect until otherwise ordered by the Board. In conformity with and subject to the order or orders of the Mediation Board in the premises, (and) such individual member of the Board or employee designated shall have power and authority to act as to any of said work, business, or functions so assigned or referred to him for action by the Board.

Fifth. *Transfer of officers and employees of Board of Mediation; transfer of appropriation*

All officers and employees of the Board of Mediation (except the members thereof, whose offices are abolished) whose services in the judgment of the Mediation Board are necessary to the efficient operation of the Board are transferred to the Board, without change in classification or compensation; except that the Board may provide for the adjustment of such classification or compensation to conform to the duties to which such officers and employees may be assigned.

All unexpended appropriations for the operation of the Board of Mediation that are available at the time of the abolition of the Board of Mediation shall be transferred to the Mediation Board and shall be available for its use for salaries and other authorized expenditures.

(May 20, 1926, ch. 347, §4, 44 Stat. 579; June 21, 1934, ch. 691, §4, 48 Stat. 1193; Oct. 28, 1949, ch. 782, title XI, §1106(a), 63 Stat. 972; Pub. L. 88-542, Aug. 31, 1964, 78 Stat. 748.)

REFERENCES IN TEXT

The civil service laws, referred to in par. Third, are set forth in Title 5, Government Organization and Employees. See, particularly, section 3301 et seq. of Title 5.

CODIFICATION

In par. First, provisions that prescribed the basic compensation of members of the Board were omitted to conform to the provisions of the Executive Schedule. See sections 5314 and 5315 of Title 5, Government Organization and Employees.

In par. Third, "subject to the provisions of the civil service laws, appoint such experts and assistants to act in a confidential capacity and such other officers and employees" substituted for "appoint such experts and assistants to act in a confidential capacity and, subject to the provisions of the civil-service laws, such other officers and employees." All such appointments are now subject to the civil service laws unless specifically excepted by such laws or by laws enacted subsequent to Executive Order 8743, Apr. 23, 1941, issued by the President pursuant to the Act of Nov. 26, 1940, ch. 919, title I, §1, 54 Stat. 1211, which covered most excepted positions into the classified (competitive) civil service. The Order is set out as a note under section 3301 of Title 5.

In par. Third, "chapter 51 and subchapter III of chapter 53 of title 5" substituted for "the Classification Act of 1949, as amended" on authority of Pub. L. 89-554, §7(b), Sept. 6, 1966, 80 Stat. 631, the first section of which enacted Title 5.

AMENDMENTS

1964—Par. First. Pub. L. 88-542 inserted sentences providing that each member of the Board in office on Jan. 1, 1965, shall be deemed to have been appointed for a term of office which shall expire on July 1 of the year his term would have otherwise expired, and that upon the expiration of his term of office a member shall continue to serve until his successor is appointed and shall have qualified, and struck out provisions which related to terms of office of members first appointed.

1949—Par. First. Act Oct. 15, 1949, increased basic rate of compensation for members of the board to $15,000 per year.

Par. Third. Act Oct. 28, 1949, substituted "Classification Act of 1949" for "Classification Act of 1923."

1934—Act June 21, 1934, amended section generally.

REPEALS

Act Oct. 28, 1949, ch. 782, cited as a credit to this section, was repealed (subject to a savings clause) by Pub. L. 89-554, Sept. 6, 1966, §8, 80 Stat. 632, 655.

TERMINATION OF REPORTING REQUIREMENTS

For termination, effective May 15, 2000, of provisions in par. Second relating to the requirement that the Board make an annual report to Congress, see section 3003 of Pub. L. 104-66, as amended, set out as a note under section 1113 of Title 31, Money and Finance, and the 6th item on page 184 of House Document No. 103-7.

SECTION REFERRED TO IN OTHER SECTIONS

This section is referred to in section 157 of this title.

§155. Functions of Mediation Board

First. Disputes within jurisdiction of Mediation Board
The parties, or either party, to a dispute between an employee or group of employees and a carrier may invoke the services of the Mediation Board in any of the following cases:

(a) A dispute concerning changes in rates of pay, rules, or working conditions not adjusted by the parties in conference.

(b) Any other dispute not referable to the National Railroad Adjustment Board and not adjusted in conference between the parties or where conferences are refused.

The Mediation Board may proffer its services in case any labor emergency is found by it to exist at any time.

In either event the said Board shall promptly put itself in communication with the parties to such controversy, and shall use its best efforts, by mediation, to bring them to agreement. If such efforts to bring about an amicable settlement through mediation shall be unsuccessful, the said Board shall at once endeavor as its final required action (except as provided in paragraph third of this section and in section 160 of this title) to induce the parties to submit their controversy to arbitration, in accordance with provisions of this chapter.

If arbitration at the request of the Board shall be refused by one or both parties, the Board shall at once notify both parties in writing that its mediatory efforts have failed and for thirty days thereafter, unless in the intervening period the parties agree to arbitration, or an emergency board shall be created under section 160 of this title, no change shall be made in the rates of pay, rules, or working conditions or established practices in effect prior to the time the dispute arose.

Second. Interpretation of agreement
In any case in which a controversy arises over the meaning or the application of any agreement reached through mediation under the provisions of this chapter, either party to the said agreement, or both, may apply to the Mediation Board for an interpretation of the meaning or application of such agreement. The said Board shall upon receipt of such request notify the parties to the

controversy, and after a hearing of both sides give its interpretation within thirty days.

Third. Duties of Board with respect to arbitration of disputes; arbitrators; acknowledgment of agreement; notice to arbitrators; reconvening of arbitrators; filing contracts with Board; custody of records and documents
The Mediation Board shall have the following duties with respect to the arbitration of disputes under section 157 of this title:

(a) On failure of the arbitrators named by the parties to agree on the remaining arbitrator or arbitrators within the time set by section 157 of this title, it shall be the duty of the Mediation Board to name such remaining arbitrator or arbitrators. It shall be the duty of the Board in naming such arbitrator or arbitrators to appoint only those whom the Board shall deem wholly disinterested in the controversy to be arbitrated and impartial and without bias as between the parties to such arbitration. Should, however, the Board name an arbitrator or arbitrators not so disinterested and impartial, then, upon proper investigation and presentation of the facts, the Board shall promptly remove such arbitrator.

If an arbitrator named by the Mediation Board, in accordance with the provisions of this chapter, shall be removed by such Board as provided by this chapter, or if such an arbitrator refuses or is unable to serve, it shall be the duty of the Mediation Board, promptly, to select another arbitrator, in the same manner as provided in this chapter for an original appointment by the Mediation Board.

(b) Any member of the Mediation Board is authorized to take the acknowledgment of an agreement to arbitrate under this chapter. When so acknowledged, or when acknowledged by the parties before a notary public or the clerk of a district court or a court of appeals of the United States, such agreement to arbitrate shall be delivered to a member of said Board or transmitted to said Board, to be filed in its office.

(c) When an agreement to arbitrate has been filed with the Mediation Board, or with one of its members, as provided by this section, and when the said Board has been furnished the names of the arbitrators chosen by the parties to the controversy it shall be the duty of the Board to cause a notice in writing to be served upon said arbitrators, notifying them of their appointment, requesting them to meet promptly to name the remaining arbitrator or arbitrators necessary to complete the Board of Arbitration, and advising them of the period within which, as provided by the agreement to arbitrate, they are empowered to name such arbitrator or arbitrators.

(d) Either party to an arbitration desiring the reconvening of a board of arbitration to pass upon any controversy arising over the meaning or application of an award may so notify the Mediation Board in writing, stating in such notice the question or questions to be submitted to such reconvened Board. The Mediation Board shall thereupon promptly communicate with the members of the Board of Arbitration, or a subcommittee of such Board appointed for such purpose pursuant to a provision in the agreement to arbitrate, and arrange for the reconvening of said Board of Arbitration or subcommittee, and shall notify the respective parties to the controversy of the time and place at which the Board, or the subcommittee, will meet for hearings upon the matters in controversy to be submitted to it. No evidence other than that contained in the record filed with the original award shall be received or considered by such reconvened Board or subcommittee, except such evidence as may be necessary to illustrate the interpretations suggested by the parties. If any member of the original Board is unable or unwilling to serve on such reconvened Board or subcommittee thereof, another arbitrator shall be named in the same manner and with the same powers and duties as such original arbitrator.

(e) Within sixty days after June 21, 1934, every carrier shall file with the Mediation Board a copy of each contract with its employees in effect on the 1st day of April 1934, covering rates of pay, rules, and working conditions. If no contract with any craft or class of its employees has been entered into, the carrier shall file with the Mediation Board a statement of that fact, including also a statement of the rates of pay, rules, and working conditions applicable in dealing with such craft or class. When any new contract is executed or change is made in an existing contract with any class or craft of its employees covering rates of pay, rules, or working conditions, or in those rates of pay, rules, and working conditions of employees not covered by contract, the carrier shall file the same with the Mediation Board within thirty days after such new contract or change in existing contract has been executed or rates of pay, rules, and working conditions have been made effective.

(f) The Mediation Board shall be the custodian of all papers and documents heretofore filed with or transferred to the Board of Mediation bearing upon the settlement, adjustment, or determination of disputes between carriers and their employees or upon mediation or arbitration proceedings held under or pursuant to the provisions of any Act of Congress in respect thereto; and the President is authorized to designate a custodian of the records and property of the Board of Mediation until the transfer and delivery of such records to the Mediation Board and to require the transfer and delivery to the Mediation Board of any and all such papers and documents filed with it or in its possession. (May 20, 1926, ch. 347, §5, 44 Stat. 580; June 21, 1934, ch. 691, §5, 48 Stat. 1195; June 25, 1948, ch. 646, §32(a), 62 Stat. 991; May 24, 1949, ch. 139, §127, 63 Stat. 107.)

CODIFICATION

As originally enacted, par. Third (b) contained a reference to the "circuit court of appeals." Act June 25, 1948, as amended by act May 24, 1949 substituted "court of appeals" for "circuit court of appeals."

AMENDMENTS

1934—Act June 21, 1934, amended generally par. First and par. Second, (e) and (f).

SECTION REFERRED TO IN OTHER SECTIONS

This section is referred to in sections 156, 157, 183 of this title.

§156. Procedure in changing rates of pay, rules, and working conditions

Carriers and representatives of the employees shall give at least thirty days' written notice of an intended change in agreements affecting rates of pay, rules, or working conditions, and the time and place for the beginning of conference between the representatives of the parties interested in such intended changes shall be agreed upon within ten days after the receipt of said notice, and said time shall be within the thirty days provided in the notice. In every case where such notice of intended change has been given, or conferences are being held with reference thereto, or the services of the Mediation Board have been requested by either party, or said Board has proffered its services, rates of pay, rules, or working conditions shall not be altered by the carrier until the controversy has been finally acted upon, as required by section 155 of this title, by the Mediation Board, unless a period of ten days has elapsed after termination of conferences without request for or proffer of the services of the Mediation Board. (May 20, 1926, ch. 347, §6, 44 Stat. 582; June 21, 1934, ch. 691, §6, 48 Stat. 1197.)

AMENDMENTS

1934—Act June 21, 1934, inserted "in agreements" after "intended change" in text, struck out provision formerly contained in text concerning changes requested by more than one class, and substituted "Mediation Board" for "Board of Mediation" wherever appearing.

WAGE AND SALARY ADJUSTMENTS

Ex. Ord. No. 9299, eff. Feb. 4, 1943, 8 F.R. 1669, provided procedure with respect to wage and salary adjustments for employees subject to this chapter.

SECTION REFERRED TO IN OTHER SECTIONS

This section is referred to in sections 152, 157, 726, 741, 797g, 1346 of this title; title 11 section 1167.

§157. Arbitration

First. Submission of controversy to arbitration
Whenever a controversy shall arise between a carrier or carriers and its or their employees which is not settled either in conference between representatives of the parties or by the appropriate adjustment board or through mediation, in the manner provided in sections 151–156 of this title such controversy may, by agreement of the parties to such controversy, be submitted to the arbitration of a board of three (or, if the parties to the controversy so stipulate, of six) persons: Provided, however, That the failure or refusal of either party to submit a controversy to arbitration shall not be construed as a violation of any legal obligation imposed upon such party by the terms of this chapter or otherwise.

Second. Manner of selecting board of arbitration
Such board of arbitration shall be chosen in the following manner:

(a) In the case of a board of three the carrier or carriers and the representatives of the employees, parties respectively to the agreement to arbitrate, shall each name one arbitrator; the two arbitrators thus chosen shall select a third arbitrator. If the arbitrators chosen by the parties shall fail to name the third arbitrator within five days after their first meeting, such third arbitra-

tor shall be named by the Mediation Board.

(b) In the case of a board of six the carrier or carriers and the representatives of the employees, parties respectively to the agreement to arbitrate, shall each name two arbitrators; the four arbitrators thus chosen shall, by a majority vote, select the remaining two arbitrators. If the arbitrators chosen by the parties shall fail to name the two arbitrators within fifteen days after their first meeting, the said two arbitrators, or as many of them as have not been named, shall be named by the Mediation Board.

Third. Board of arbitration; organization; compensation; procedure
(a) Notice of selection or failure to select arbitrators

When the arbitrators selected by the respective parties have agreed upon the remaining arbitrator or arbitrators, they shall notify the Mediation Board; and, in the event of their failure to agree upon any or upon all of the necessary arbitrators within the period fixed by this chapter, they shall, at the expiration of such period, notify the Mediation Board of the arbitrators selected, if any, or of their failure to make or to complete such selection.

(b) Organization of board; procedure

The board of arbitration shall organize and select its own chairman and make all necessary rules for conducting its hearings: Provided, however, That the board of arbitration shall be bound to give the parties to the controversy a full and fair hearing, which shall include an opportunity to present evidence in support of their claims, and an opportunity to present their case in person, by counsel, or by other representative as they may respectively elect.

(c) Duty to reconvene; questions considered

Upon notice from the Mediation Board that the parties, or either party, to an arbitration desire the reconvening of the board of arbitration (or a subcommittee of such board of arbitration appointed for such purpose pursuant to the agreement to arbitrate) to pass upon any controversy over the meaning or application of their award, the board, or its subcommittee, shall at once reconvene. No question other than, or in addition to, the questions relating to the meaning or application of the award, submitted by the party or parties in writing, shall be considered by the reconvened board of arbitration or its subcommittee.

Such rulings shall be acknowledged by such board or subcommittee thereof in the same manner, and filed in the same district court clerk's office, as the original award and become a part thereof.

(d) Competency of arbitrators

No arbitrator, except those chosen by the Mediation Board, shall be incompetent to act as an arbitrator because of his interest in the controversy to be arbitrated, or because of his connection with or partiality to either of the parties to the arbitration.

(e) Compensation and expenses

Each member of any board of arbitration created under the provisions of this chapter named by either party to the arbitration shall be compensated by the party naming him. Each arbitrator selected by the arbitrators or named by the Mediation Board shall receive from the Mediation Board such compensation as the Mediation Board may fix, together with his necessary traveling expenses and expenses actually incurred for subsistence, while serving as an arbitrator.

(f) Award; disposition of original and copies

The board of arbitration shall furnish a certified copy of its award to the respective parties to the controversy, and shall transmit the original, together with the papers and proceedings and a transcript of the evidence taken at the hearings, certified under the hands of at least a majority of the arbitrators, to the clerk of the district court of the United States for the district wherein the controversy arose or the arbi-

tration is entered into, to be filed in said clerk's office as hereinafter provided. The said board shall also furnish a certified copy of its award, and the papers and proceedings, including testimony relating thereto, to the Mediation Board to be filed in its office; and in addition a certified copy of its award shall be filed in the office of the Interstate Commerce Commission: Provided, however, That such award shall not be construed to diminish or extinguish any of the powers or duties of the Interstate Commerce Commission, under subtitle IV of title 49.

(g) Compensation of assistants to board of arbitration; expenses; quarters

A board of arbitration may, subject to the approval of the Mediation Board, employ and fix the compensation of such assistants as it deems necessary in carrying on the arbitration proceedings. The compensation of such employees, together with their necessary traveling expenses and expenses actually incurred for subsistence, while so employed, and the necessary expenses of boards of arbitration, shall be paid by the Mediation Board.

Whenever practicable, the board shall be supplied with suitable quarters in any Federal building located at its place of meeting or at any place where the board may conduct its proceedings or deliberations.

(h) Testimony before board; oaths; attendance of witnesses; production of documents; subpoenas; fees

All testimony before said board shall be given under oath or affirmation, and any member of the board shall have the power to administer oaths or affirmations. The board of arbitration, or any member thereof, shall have the power to require the attendance of witnesses and the production of such books, papers, contracts, agreements, and documents as may be deemed by the board of arbitration material to a just determination of the matters submitted to its arbitration, and may for that purpose request the clerk of the district court of the United States for the district wherein said arbitration is being conducted to issue the necessary subpoenas, and upon such request the said clerk or his duly authorized deputy shall be, and he is, authorized, and it shall be his duty, to issue such subpoenas.

Any witness appearing before a board of arbitration shall receive the same fees and mileage as witnesses in courts of the United States, to be paid by the party securing the subpoena. (May 20, 1926, ch. 347, §7, 44 Stat. 582; June 21, 1934, ch. 691, §7, 48 Stat. 1197; Pub. L. 91-452, title II, §238, Oct. 15, 1970, 84 Stat. 930.)

CODIFICATION

In par. Third (f), "subtitle IV of title 49" substituted for "the Interstate Commerce Act, as amended [49 U.S.C. 1 et seq.]" on authority of Pub. L. 95-473, §3(b), Oct. 17, 1978, 92 Stat. 1466, the first section of which enacted subtitle IV of Title 49, Transportation.

AMENDMENTS

1970—Par. Third, (h). Pub. L. 91-452 struck out provisions authorizing board to invoke aid of the United States courts to compel witnesses to attend and testify and to produce such books, papers, contracts, agreements, and documents to same extent and under same conditions and penalties as provided for in the Interstate Commerce Act.

1934—Act June 21, 1934, substituted "Mediation Board" for "Board of Mediation" wherever appearing.

EFFECTIVE DATE OF 1970 AMENDMENT

Amendment by Pub. L. 91-452 effective on sixtieth day following Oct. 15, 1970, and not to affect any immunity to which any individual is entitled under this section by reason of any testimony given before sixtieth day following Oct. 15, 1970, see section 260 of Pub. L. 91-452, set out as an Effective Date; Savings Provisions

note under section 6001 of Title 18, Crimes and Criminal Procedure.

ABOLITION OF INTERSTATE COMMERCE COMMISSION AND TRANSFER OF FUNCTIONS

Interstate Commerce Commission abolished and functions of Commission transferred, except as otherwise provided in Pub. L. 104-88, to Surface Transportation Board effective Jan. 1, 1996, by section 702 of Title 49, Transportation, and section 101 of Pub. L. 104-88, set out as a note under section 701 of Title 49. References to Interstate Commerce Commission deemed to refer to Surface Transportation Board, a member or employee of the Board, or Secretary of Transportation, as appropriate, see section 205 of Pub. L. 104-88, set out as a note under section 701 of Title 49.

WORK RULES DISPUTE

Pub. L. 88-108, Aug. 28, 1963, 77 Stat. 132, provided:

"[Sec. 1. Settlement of disputes]. That no carrier which served the notices of November 2, 1959, and no labor organizations which received such notices or served the labor organization notices of September 7, 1960, shall make any change except by agreement, or pursuant to an arbitration award as hereinafter provided, in rates of pay, rules, or working conditions encompassed by any of such notices, or engage in any strike or lockout over any dispute arising from any of such notices. Any action heretofore taken which would be prohibited by the foregoing sentence shall be forthwith rescinded and the status existing immediately prior to such action restored.

"Sec. 2. [Arbitration board]. There is hereby established an arbitration board to consist of seven members. The representatives of the carrier and organization parties to the aforesaid dispute are hereby directed, respectively, within five days after the enactment hereof [Aug. 28, 1963] each to name two persons to serve as members of such arbitration board. The four members thus chosen shall select three additional members. The seven members shall then elect a chairman. If the members chosen by the parties shall fail to name one or more of the additional three members within ten days, such additional members shall be named by the President. If either party fails to name a member or members to the arbitration board within the five days provided, the President shall name such member or members in lieu of such party and shall also name the additional three members necessary to constitute a board of seven members, all within ten days after the date of enactment of this joint resolution [Aug. 28, 1963]. Notwithstanding any other provision of law, the National Mediation Board is authorized and directed: (1) to compensate the arbitrators not named by the parties at a rate not in excess of $100 for each day together with necessary travel and subsistence expenses, and (2) to provide such services and facilities as may be necessary and appropriate in carrying out the purposes of this joint resolution.

"Sec. 3. [Decision of board]. Promptly upon the completion of the naming of the arbitration board the Secretary of Labor shall furnish to the board and to the parties to the dispute copies of his statement to the parties of August 2, 1963, and the papers therewith submitted to the parties, together with memorandums and such other data as the board may request setting forth the matters with respect to which the parties were in tentative agreement and the extent of disagreement with respect to matters on which the parties were not in tentative agreement. The arbitration board shall make a decision, pursuant to the procedures hereinafter set forth, as to what disposition shall be made of those portions of the carriers' notices of November 2, 1959, identified as 'Use of Firemen (Helpers) on Other Than Steam Power' and 'Consist of Road and Yard Crews' and that portion of the organiza-

tions' notices of September 7, 1960, identified as 'Minimum Safe Crew Consist' and implementing proposals pertaining thereto. The arbitration board shall incorporate in such decision any matters on which it finds the parties were in agreement, shall resolve the matters on which the parties were not in agreement, and shall, in making its award, give due consideration to those matters on which the parties were in tentative agreement. Such award shall be binding on both the carrier and organization parties to the dispute and shall constitute a complete and final disposition of the aforesaid issues covered by the decision of the board of arbitration.

"Sec. 4. [Award]. To the extent not inconsistent with this joint resolution the arbitration shall be conducted pursuant to sections 7 and 8 of the Railway Labor Act [this section and section 158 of this title], the board's award shall be made and filed as provided in said sections and shall be subject to section 9 of said Act [section 159 of this title]. The United States District Court for the District of Columbia is hereby designated as the court in which the award is to be filed, and the arbitration board shall report to the National Mediation Board in the same manner as arbitration boards functioning pursuant to the Railway Labor Act [this chapter]. The award shall continue in force for such period as the arbitration board shall determine in its award, but not to exceed two years from the date the award takes effect, unless the parties agree otherwise.

"Sec. 5. [Hearings]. The arbitration board shall begin its hearings thirty days after the enactment of this joint resolution [Aug. 28, 1963] or on such earlier date as the parties to the dispute and the board may agree upon and shall make and file its award not later than ninety days after the enactment of this joint resolution [Aug. 28, 1963]: Provided, however, That said award shall not become effective until sixty days after the filing of the award.

"Sec. 6. [Collective bargaining for issues not arbitrated]. The parties to the disputes arising from the aforesaid notices shall immediately resume collective bargaining with respect to all issues raised in the notices of November 2, 1959, and September 7, 1960, not to be disposed of by arbitration under section 3 of this joint resolution and shall exert every reasonable effort to resolve such issues by agreement. The Secretary of Labor and the National Mediation Board are hereby directed to give all reasonable assistance to the parties and to engage in mediatory action directed toward promoting such agreement.

"Sec. 7. [Considerations affecting award; enforcement.]

"(a) In making any award under this joint resolution the arbitration board established under section 2 shall give due consideration to the effect of the proposed award upon adequate and safe transportation service to the public and upon the interests of the carrier and employees affected, giving due consideration to the narrowing of the areas of disagreement which has been accomplished in bargaining and mediation.

"(b) The obligations imposed by this joint resolution, upon suit by the Attorney General, shall be enforcible through such orders as may be necessary by any court of the United States having jurisdiction of any of the parties.

"Sec. 8. [Expiration date]. This joint resolution shall expire one hundred and eighty days after the date of its enactment [Aug. 28, 1963], except that it shall remain in effect with respect to the last sentence of section 4 for the period prescribed in that sentence.

"Sec. 9. [Separability]. If any provision of this joint resolution or the application thereof is held invalid, the remainder of this joint resolution and the application of such provision to other parties or in other circumstances not held invalid shall not be affected thereby."

FEDERAL RULES OF CIVIL PROCEDURE

Subpoena, see rule 45, Title 28, Appendix, Judiciary and Judicial Procedure.

CROSS REFERENCES

Immunity of witnesses, see section 6001 et seq. of Title 18, Crimes and Criminal Procedure.

SECTION REFERRED TO IN OTHER SECTIONS

This section is referred to in sections 154, 155, 797g of this title; title 18 section 6001.

§158. Agreement to arbitrate; form and contents; signatures and acknowledgment; revocation

The agreement to arbitrate—

(a) Shall be in writing;

(b) Shall stipulate that the arbitration is had under the provisions of this chapter;

(c) Shall state whether the board of arbitration is to consist of three or of six members;

(d) Shall be signed by the duly accredited representatives of the carrier or carriers and the employees, parties respectively to the agreement to arbitrate, and shall be acknowledged by said parties before a notary public, the clerk of a district court or court of appeals of the United States, or before a member of the Mediation Board, and, when so acknowledged, shall be filed in the office of the Mediation Board;

(e) Shall state specifically the questions to be submitted to the said board for decision; and that, in its award or awards, the said board shall confine itself strictly to decisions as to the questions so specifically submitted to it;

(f) Shall provide that the questions, or any one or more of them, submitted by the parties to the board of arbitration may be withdrawn from arbitration on notice to that effect signed by the duly accredited representatives of all the parties and served on the board of arbitration;

(g) Shall stipulate that the signatures of a majority of said board of arbitration affixed to their award shall be competent to constitute a valid and binding award;

(h) Shall fix a period from the date of the appointment of the arbitrator or arbitrators necessary to complete the board (as provided for in the agreement) within which the said board shall commence its hearings;

(i) Shall fix a period from the beginning of the hearings within which the said board shall make and file its award: Provided, That the parties may agree at any time upon an extension of this period;

(j) Shall provide for the date from which the award shall become effective and shall fix the period during which the award shall continue in force;

(k) Shall provide that the award of the board of arbitration and the evidence of the proceedings before the board relating thereto, when certified under the hands of at least a majority of the arbitrators, shall be filed in the clerk's office of the district court of the United States for the district wherein the controversy arose or the arbitration was entered into, which district shall be designated in the agreement; and, when so filed, such award and proceedings shall constitute the full and complete record of the arbitration;

(l) Shall provide that the award, when so filed, shall be final and conclusive upon the parties as to the facts determined by said award and as to the merits of the controversy decided;

(m) Shall provide that any difference arising as to the meaning, or the application of the provisions, of an award made by a board of arbitration shall be referred back for a ruling to the same board, or, by agreement, to a subcommittee of such board; and that such ruling, when acknowledged in the same manner, and filed in the same district court clerk's office, as the original award, shall be a part of and shall have the same force and effect as such original award; and

(n) Shall provide that the respective parties to the award will each faithfully execute the same.

The said agreement to arbitrate, when properly signed and acknowledged as herein provided, shall not be revoked by a party to such agreement: Provided, however, That such agreement to arbitrate may at any time be revoked and canceled by the written agreement of both parties, signed by their duly accredited representatives, and (if no board of arbitration has yet been constituted under the agreement) delivered to the Mediation Board or any member thereof; or, if the board of arbitration has been constituted as provided by this chapter, delivered to such board of arbitration.

(May 20, 1926, ch. 347, §8, 44 Stat. 584; June 21, 1934, ch. 691, §7, 48 Stat. 1197; June 25, 1948, ch. 646, §32(a), 62 Stat. 991; May 24, 1949, ch. 139, §127, 63 Stat. 107.)

CODIFICATION

As originally enacted, par. (d) contained a reference to the "circuit court of appeals." Act June 25, 1948, as amended by act May 24, 1949, substituted "court of appeals" for "circuit court of appeals."

AMENDMENTS

1934—Act June 21, 1934, substituted "Mediation Board" for "Board of Mediation" wherever appearing.

SECTION REFERRED TO IN OTHER SECTIONS

This section is referred to in section 797g of this title.

§159. Award and judgment thereon; effect of chapter on individual employee

First. Filing of award

The award of a board of arbitration, having been acknowledged as herein provided, shall be filed in the clerk's office of the district court designated in the agreement to arbitrate.

Second. Conclusiveness of award; judgment

An award acknowledged and filed as herein provided shall be conclusive on the parties as to the merits and facts of the controversy submitted to arbitration, and unless, within ten days after the filing of the award, a petition to impeach the award, on the grounds hereinafter set forth, shall be filed in the clerk's office of the court in which the award has been filed, the court shall enter judgment on the award, which judgment shall be final and conclusive on the parties.

Third. Impeachment of award; grounds

Such petition for the impeachment or contesting of any award so filed shall be entertained by the court only on one or more of the following grounds:

(a) That the award plainly does not conform to the substantive requirements laid down by this chapter for such awards, or that the proceedings were not substantially in conformity with this chapter;

(b) That the award does not conform, nor confine itself, to the stipulations of the agreement to arbitrate; or

(c) That a member of the board of arbitration rendering the award was guilty of fraud or corruption; or that a party to the arbitration practiced fraud or corruption which fraud or corruption affected the result of the arbitration: Provided, however, That no court shall entertain any such petition on the ground that an award is invalid for uncertainty; in such case the proper remedy shall be a submission of such award to a reconvened board, or subcommittee thereof, for interpretation, as provided by this chapter: Provided further, That an award contested as herein provided shall be construed liberally by the court, with a view to favoring its validity, and that no award shall be set aside for trivial irregularity or clerical error, going only to form and not to substance.

Fourth. Effect of partial invalidity of award

If the court shall determine that a part of the award is invalid on some ground or grounds designated in this section as a ground of invalidity, but shall determine that a part of the award is valid, the court shall set aside the entire award: Provided, however, That, if the parties shall agree thereto, and if such valid and invalid parts are separable, the court shall set aside the invalid part, and order judgment to stand as to the valid part.

Fifth. Appeal; record

At the expiration of 10 days from the decision of the district court upon the petition filed as aforesaid, final judgment shall be entered in accordance with said decision, unless during said 10 days either party shall appeal therefrom to the court of appeals. In such case only such portion of the record shall be transmitted to the appellate court as is necessary to the proper understanding and consideration of the questions of law presented by said petition and to be decided.

Sixth. Finality of decision of court of appeals

The determination of said court of appeals upon said questions shall be final, and, being certified by the clerk thereof to said district court, judgment pursuant thereto shall thereupon be entered by said district court.

Seventh. Judgment where petitioner's contentions are sustained

If the petitioner's contentions are finally sustained, judgment shall be entered setting aside the award in whole or, if the parties so agree, in part; but in such case the parties may agree upon a judgment to be entered disposing of the subject matter of the controversy, which judgment when entered shall have the same force and effect as judgment entered upon an award.

Eighth. Duty of employee to render service
without consent; right to quit

Nothing in this chapter shall be construed to require an individual employee to render labor or service without his consent, nor shall anything in this chapter be construed to make the quitting of his labor or service by an individual employee an illegal act; nor shall any court issue any process to compel the performance by an individual employee of such labor or service, without his consent.

(May 20, 1926, ch. 347, §9, 44 Stat. 585; June 25, 1948, ch. 646, §32(a), 62 Stat. 991; May 24, 1949, ch. 139, §127, 63 Stat. 107.)

CODIFICATION

As originally enacted, pars. Fifth and Sixth contained references to the "circuit court of appeals." Act June 25, 1948, as amended by act May 24, 1949, substituted "court of appeals" for "circuit court of appeals."

FEDERAL RULES OF CIVIL PROCEDURE

Application of rules, see rule 81, Title 28, Appendix, Judiciary and Judicial Procedure.

§159a. Special procedure for commuter service

(a) Applicability of provisions

Except as provided in section 590(h) of this title, the provisions of this section shall apply to any dispute subject to this chapter between a publicly funded and publicly operated carrier providing rail commuter service (including the Amtrak Commuter Services Corporation) and its employees.

(b) Request for establishment of emergency board

If a dispute between the parties described in subsection (a) of this section is not adjusted under the foregoing provisions of this chapter and the President does not, under section 160 of this title, create an emergency board to investigate and report on such dispute, then any party to the

dispute or the Governor of any State through which the service that is the subject of the dispute is operated may request the President to establish such an emergency board.

(c) Establishment of emergency board

(1) Upon the request of a party or a Governor under subsection (b) of this section, the President shall create an emergency board to investigate and report on the dispute in accordance with section 160 of this title. For purposes of this subsection, the period during which no change, except by agreement, shall be made by the parties in the conditions out of which the dispute arose shall be 120 days from the day of the creation of such emergency board.

(2) If the President, in his discretion, creates a board to investigate and report on a dispute between the parties described in subsection (a) of this section, the provisions of this section shall apply to the same extent as if such board had been created pursuant to paragraph (1) of this subsection.

(d) Public hearing by National Mediation
Board upon failure of emergency board
to effectuate settlement of dispute

Within 60 days after the creation of an emergency board under this section, if there has been no settlement between the parties, the National Mediation Board shall conduct a public hearing on the dispute at which each party shall appear and provide testimony setting forth the reasons it has not accepted the recommendations of the emergency board for settlement of the dispute.

(e) Establishment of second emergency board

If no settlement in the dispute is reached at the end of the 120-day period beginning on the date of the creation of the emergency board, any party to the dispute or the Governor of any State through which the service that is the subject of the dispute is operated may request the

President to establish another emergency board, in which case the President shall establish such emergency board.

(f) Submission of final offers to second emergency board by parties

Within 30 days after creation of a board under subsection (e) of this section, the parties to the dispute shall submit to the board final offers for settlement of the dispute.

(g) Report of second emergency board

Within 30 days after the submission of final offers under subsection (f) of this section, the emergency board shall submit a report to the President setting forth its selection of the most reasonable offer.

(h) Maintenance of status quo during dispute period

From the time a request to establish a board is made under subsection (e) of this section until 60 days after such board makes its report under subsection (g) of this section, no change, except by agreement, shall be made by the parties in the conditions out of which the dispute arose.

(i) Work stoppages by employees subsequent to carrier offer selected; eligibility of employees for benefits

If the emergency board selects the final offer submitted by the carrier and, after the expiration of the 60-day period described in subsection (h) of this section, the employees of such carrier engage in any work stoppage arising out of the dispute, such employees shall not be eligible during the period of such work stoppage for benefits under the Railroad Unemployment Insurance Act [45 U.S.C. 351 et seq.].

(j) Work stoppages by employees subsequent to employees offer selected; eligibility of employer for benefits

If the emergency board selects the final offer submitted by the employees and, after the expiration of the 60-day period described in subsection (h)

of this section, the carrier refuses to accept the final offer submitted by the employees and the employees of such carrier engage in any work stoppage arising out of the dispute, the carrier shall not participate in any benefits of any agreement between carriers which is designed to provide benefits to such carriers during a work stoppage.

(May 20, 1926, ch. 347, §9A, as added Pub. L. 97-35, title XI, §1157, Aug. 13, 1981, 95 Stat. 681.)

REFERENCES IN TEXT

Section 590(h) of this title, referred to in subsec. (a), was repealed by Pub. L. 103-272, Sec. 7(b), July 5, 1994, 108 Stat. 1379.

The Railroad Unemployment Insurance Act, referred to in subsec. (i), is act June 25, 1938, ch. 680, 52 Stat. 1094, as amended, which is classified principally to chapter 11 (§351 et seq.) of this title. For complete classification of this Act to the Code, see section 367 of this title and Tables.

EFFECTIVE DATE

Section effective Aug. 13, 1981, see section 1169 of Pub. L. 97-35, set out as a note under section 1101 of this title.

§160. Emergency board

If a dispute between a carrier and its employees be not adjusted under the foregoing provisions of this chapter and should, in the judgment of the Mediation Board, threaten substantially to interrupt interstate commerce to a degree such as to deprive any section of the country of essential transportation service, the Mediation Board shall notify the President, who may thereupon, in his discretion, create a board to investigate and report respecting such dispute. Such board shall be composed of such number of persons as to the President may seem desirable: Provided, however, That no member appointed shall be pecuniarily or otherwise interested in any organization of employees or any carrier. The compensation of the members of any such board shall be fixed by the President. Such board shall be created separately in each instance and it shall investigate promptly the facts as to the dispute and make a report thereon to the President within thirty days from the date of its creation.

There is authorized to be appropriated such sums as may be necessary for the expenses of such board, including the compensation and the necessary traveling expenses and expenses actually incurred for subsistence, of the members of the board. All expenditures of the board shall be allowed and paid on the presentation of itemized vouchers therefor approved by the chairman.

After the creation of such board and for thirty days after such board has made its report to the President, no change, except by agreement, shall be made by the parties to the controversy in the conditions out of which the dispute arose. (May 20, 1926, ch. 347, §10, 44 Stat. 586; June 21, 1934, ch. 691, §7, 48 Stat. 1197.)

AMENDMENTS

1934—Act June 21, 1934, substituted "Mediation Board" for "Board of Mediation" wherever appearing.

SECTION REFERRED TO IN OTHER SECTIONS

This section is referred to in sections 155, 159a of this title.

§161. Effect of partial invalidity of chapter

If any provision of this chapter, or the application thereof to any person or circumstance, is held invalid, the remainder of the chapter, and the application of such provision to other persons or circumstances, shall not be affected thereby. (May 20, 1926, ch. 347, §11, 44 Stat. 587.)

SEPARABILITY; REPEAL OF INCONSISTENT PROVISIONS

Section 8 of act June 21, 1934, provided that: "If any section, subsection, sentence, clause, or phrase of this Act [amending sections 151 to 158, 160, and 162 of this title] is for any reason held to be unconstitutional, such decision shall not affect the validity of the remaining portions of this Act. All Acts or parts of Acts inconsistent with the provisions of this Act are hereby repealed."

§162. Authorization of appropriations

There is authorized to be appropriated such sums as may be necessary for expenditure by the Mediation Board in carrying out the provisions of this chapter. (May 20, 1926, ch. 347, §12, 44 Stat. 587; June 21, 1934, ch. 691, §7, 48 Stat. 1197.)

AMENDMENTS

1934—Act June 21, 1934, substituted "Mediation Board" for "Board of Mediation."

§163. Repeal of prior legislation; exception

Chapters 6 and 7 of this title, providing for mediation, conciliation, and arbitration, and all Acts and parts of Acts in conflict with the provisions of this chapter are repealed, except that the members, secretary, officers, employees, and agents of the Railroad Labor Board, in office on May 20, 1926, shall receive their salaries for a period of 30 days from such date, in the same manner as though this chapter had not been passed. (May 20, 1926, ch. 347, §14, 44 Stat. 587.)

REFERENCES IN TEXT

Chapters 6 and 7 of this title, referred to in text, were in the original references to the act of July 15, 1913, and title III of the Transportation Act, 1920, respectively.

§164. Repealed. Oct. 10, 1940, ch. 851, §4, 54 Stat. 1111

Section, act Feb. 11, 1927, ch. 104, §1, 44 Stat. 1072, related to advertisements for proposals for purchases or services rendered for Board of Mediation, including arbitration boards. See section 5 of Title 41, Public Contracts.

SUBCHAPTER II—CARRIERS BY AIR

SUBCHAPTER REFERRED TO IN OTHER SECTIONS

This subchapter is referred to in title 26 section 410; title 29 section 213; title 49 App. section 1371.

§181. Application of subchapter I to carriers by air

All of the provisions of subchapter I of this chapter except section 153 of this title are extended to and shall cover every common carrier by air engaged in interstate or foreign commerce, and every carrier by air transporting mail for or under contract with the United States Government, and every air pilot or other person who performs any work as an employee or subordinate official of such carrier or carriers, subject to its or their continuing authority to supervise and direct the manner of rendition of his service.

(May 20, 1926, ch. 347, §201, as added Apr. 10, 1936, ch. 166, 49 Stat. 1189.)

§182. Duties, penalties, benefits, and privileges of subchapter I applicable

The duties, requirements, penalties, benefits, and privileges prescribed and established by the provisions of subchapter I of this chapter except section 153 of this title shall apply to said carriers by air and their employees in the same manner and to the same extent as though such carriers and their employees were specifically included within the definition of "carrier" and "employee," respectively, in section 151 of this title.

(May 20, 1926, ch. 347, §202, as added Apr. 10, 1936, ch. 166, 49 Stat. 1189.)

§183. Disputes within jurisdiction of Mediation Board

The parties or either party to a dispute between an employee or a group of employees and a carrier or carriers by air may invoke the services of the National Mediation Board and the jurisdiction of said Mediation Board is extended to any of the following cases:

(a) A dispute concerning changes in rates of pay, rules, or working conditions not adjusted by the parties in conference.

(b) Any other dispute not referable to an adjustment board, as hereinafter provided, and not adjusted in conference between the parties, or where conferences are refused.

The National Mediation Board may proffer its services in case any labor emergency is found by it to exist at any time.

The services of the Mediation Board may be invoked in a case under this subchapter in the same manner and to the same extent as are the disputes covered by section 155 of this title.

(May 20, 1926, ch. 347, §203, as added Apr. 10, 1936, ch. 166, 49 Stat. 1189.)

§184. System, group, or regional boards of adjustment

The disputes between an employee or group of employees and a carrier or carriers by air growing out of grievances, or out of the interpretation or application of agreements concerning rates of pay, rules, or working conditions, including cases pending and unadjusted on April 10, 1936 before the National Labor Relations Board, shall be handled in the usual manner up to and including the chief operating officer of the carrier designated to handle such disputes; but, failing to reach an adjustment in this manner, the disputes may be referred by petition of the parties or by either party to an appropriate adjustment board, as hereinafter provided, with a full statement of the facts and supporting data bearing upon the disputes.

It shall be the duty of every carrier and of its employees, acting through their representatives, selected in accordance with the provisions of this subchapter, to establish a board of adjustment of jurisdiction not exceeding the jurisdiction which may be lawfully exercised by system, group, or regional boards of adjustment, under the authority of section 153 of this title.

Such boards of adjustment may be established by agreement between employees and carriers either on any individual carrier, or system, or group of carriers by air and any class or classes of its or their employees; or pending the establishment of a permanent National Board of Adjustment as hereinafter provided. Nothing in this chapter shall prevent said carriers by air, or any class or classes of their employees, both acting through their representatives selected in accordance with provisions of this subchapter, from mutually agreeing to the establishment of a National Board of Adjustment of temporary duration and of similarly limited jurisdiction. (May 20, 1926, ch. 347, §204, as added Apr. 10, 1936, ch. 166, 49 Stat. 1189.)

§185. National Air Transport Adjustment Board

When, in the judgment of the National Mediation Board, it shall be necessary to have a permanent national board of adjustment in order to provide for the prompt and orderly settlement of disputes between said carriers by air, or any of them, and its or their employees, growing out of grievances or out of the interpretation or application of agreements between said carriers by air or any of them, and any class or classes of its or their employees, covering rates of pay, rules, or working conditions, the National Mediation Board is empowered and directed, by its order duly made, published, and served, to direct the said carriers by air and such labor organizations of their employees, national in scope, as have been or may be recognized in accordance with the provisions of this chapter, to select and designate four representatives who shall constitute a board which shall be known as the "National Air Transport Adjustment Board." Two members of said National Air Transport Adjustment Board shall be selected by said carriers by air and two members by the said labor organizations of the employees, within thirty days after the date of the order of the National Mediation Board, in the manner and by the procedure prescribed by section 153 of this title for the selection and des-

ignation of members of the National Railroad Adjustment Board. The National Air Transport Adjustment Board shall meet within forty days after the date of the order of the National Mediation Board directing the selection and designation of its members and shall organize and adopt rules for conducting its proceedings, in the manner prescribed in section 153 of this title. Vacancies in membership or office shall be filled, members shall be appointed in case of failure of the carriers or of labor organizations of the employees to select and designate representatives, members of the National Air Transport Adjustment Board shall be compensated, hearings shall be held, findings and awards made, stated, served, and enforced, and the number and compensation of any necessary assistants shall be determined and the compensation of such employees shall be paid, all in the same manner and to the same extent as provided with reference to the National Railroad Adjustment Board by section 153 of this title. The powers and duties prescribed and established by the provisions of section 153 of this title with reference to the National Railroad Adjustment Board and the several divisions thereof are conferred upon and shall be exercised and performed in like manner and to the same extent by the said National Air Transport Adjustment Board, not exceeding, however, the jurisdiction conferred upon said National Air Transport Adjustment Board by the provisions of this subchapter. From and after the organization of the National Air Transport Adjustment Board, if any system, group, or regional board of adjustment established by any carrier or carriers by air and any class or classes of its or their employees is not satisfactory to either party thereto, the said party, upon ninety days' notice to the other party, may elect to come under the jurisdiction of the National Air Transport Adjustment Board.
(May 20, 1926, ch. 347, §205, as added Apr. 10, 1936, ch. 166, 49 Stat. 1190.)

Application of rules, see rule 81, Title 28, Appendix, Judiciary and Judicial Procedure.

Effect of rules on this section, see note by Advisory committee under rule 81.

SECTION REFERRED TO IN OTHER SECTIONS

This section is referred to in title 26 section 410; title 29 section 213; title 49 section 1371.

§186. Omitted

CODIFICATION

Section, act May 20, 1926, ch. 347, §206, as added Apr. 10, 1936, ch. 166, 49 Stat. 1191, transferred certain pending cases before National Labor Relations Board to Mediation Board.

§187. Separability

If any provision of this subchapter or application thereof to any person or circumstance is held invalid, the remainder of such sections and the application of such provision to other persons or circumstances shall not be affected thereby.

(May 20, 1926, ch. 347, §207, as added Apr. 10, 1936, ch. 166, 49 Stat. 1191.)

§188. Authorization of appropriations

There is authorized to be appropriated such sums as may be necessary for expenditure by the Mediation Board in carrying out the provisions of this chapter.

(May 20, 1926, ch. 347, §208, as added Apr. 10, 1936, ch. 166, 49 Stat. 1191.)

REFERENCES IN TEXT

This chapter, referred to in text, was in the original, this Act, meaning act May 20, 1926, ch. 347, 44 Stat. 577, as amended, known as the Railway Labor Act, which enacted this chapter and amended sections 225 and 348 of former Title 28, Judicial Code and Judiciary. Sections 225 and 348 of former Title 28 were repealed by section 39 of act June 25, 1948, ch. 646, 62 Stat. 992, section 1 of which enacted Title 28, Judiciary and Judicial Procedure. Section 225 of former Title 28 was reenacted as sections 1291 to 1294 of Title 28. For complete classification of this Act to the Code, see this section and Tables.

Appendix B: The National Labor Relations Act

Also cited NLRA or the Act; 29 U.S.C. §§151–69

[Title 29, Chapter 7, Subchapter II, United States Code]

FINDINGS AND POLICIES

Section 1 [§151.] The denial by some employers of the right of employees to organize and the refusal by some employers to accept the procedure of collective bargaining lead to strikes and other forms of industrial strife or unrest, which have the intent or the necessary effect of burdening or obstructing commerce by (a) impairing the efficiency, safety, or operation of the instrumentalities of commerce; (b) occurring in the current of commerce; (c) materially affecting, restraining, or controlling the flow of raw materials or manufactured or processed goods from or into the channels of commerce, or the prices of such materials or goods in commerce; or (d) causing diminution of employment and wages in such volume as substantially to impair or disrupt the market for goods flowing from or into the channels of commerce.

The inequality of bargaining power between employees who do not possess full freedom of association or actual liberty of contract and employers who are organized in the corporate or other forms of ownership association substantially burdens and affects the flow of commerce, and tends to aggravate recurrent business depressions, by depressing wage rates and the purchasing power of wage earners in industry and by preventing the stabilization of competitive wage rates and working conditions within and between industries.

Experience has proved that protection by law of the right of employees to organize and bargain collectively safeguards commerce from injury, impairment, or interruption, and promotes the flow of commerce by removing certain recognized sources of industrial strife and unrest, by encouraging practices fundamental to the friendly adjustment of industrial disputes arising out of differences as to wages, hours, or other working conditions, and by restoring equality of bargaining power between employers and employees.

Experience has further demonstrated that certain practices by some labor organizations, their officers, and members have the intent or the necessary effect of burdening or obstructing commerce by preventing the free flow of goods in such commerce through strikes and other forms of industrial unrest or through concerted activities which impair the interest of the public in the free flow of such commerce. The elimination of such practices is a necessary condition to the assurance of the rights herein guaranteed

It is declared to be the policy of the United States to eliminate the causes of certain substantial obstructions to the free flow of commerce and to mitigate and eliminate these obstructions when they have occurred by encouraging the practice and procedure of collective bargaining and by protecting the exercise by workers of full freedom of association, self-organization, and designation of representatives of their own choosing, for the purpose of negotiating the terms and conditions of their employment or other mutual aid or protection.

DEFINITIONS

Sec. 2. [§152.] When used in this Act [subchapter]—

(1) The term "person" includes one or more individuals, labor organizations, partnerships, associations, corporations, legal representatives, trustees, trustees in cases under title 11 of the United States Code [under title 11], or receivers.

(2) The term "employer" includes any person acting as an agent of an employer, directly or indirectly, but shall not include the United States or any wholly owned Government corporation, or any Federal Reserve Bank, or any State or political subdivision thereof, or any person subject to the Railway Labor Act [45 U.S.C. §151 et seq.], as amended from time to time, or any labor organization (other than when acting as an employer), or anyone acting in the capacity of officer or agent of such labor organization. [Pub. L. 93-360, §1(a), July 26, 1974, 88 Stat. 395, deleted the phrase "or any corporation or association operating a hospital, if no part of the net earnings inures to the benefit of any private shareholder or individual" from the definition of "employer."]

(3) The term "employee" shall include any employee, and shall not be limited to the employees of a particular employer, unless the Act [this subchapter] explicitly states otherwise, and shall include any individual whose work has ceased as a consequence of, or in connection with, any current labor dispute or because of any unfair labor practice, and who has not obtained any other regular and substantially equivalent employment, but shall not include any individual employed as an agricultural laborer, or in the domestic service of any family or person at his home, or any individual employed by his parent or spouse, or any individual having the status of an independent contractor, or any individual employed as a supervisor, or any individual employed by an employer subject to the Railway Labor Act [45 U.S.C. §151 et seq.], as amended from time to time, or by any other person who is not an employer as herein defined.

(4) The term "representatives" includes any individual or labor organization.

(5) The term "labor organization" means any organization of any kind, or any agency or employee representation committee or plan, in which employees participate and which exists for the purpose, in whole or in part, of dealing with employers concerning grievances, labor disputes, wages, rates of pay, hours of employment, or conditions of work.

(6) The term "commerce" means trade, traffic, commerce, transportation, or communication among the several States, or between the District of Columbia or any Territory of the United States and any State or other Territory, or between any foreign country and any State, Territory, or the District of Columbia, or within the District of Columbia or any Territory, or between points in the same State but through any other State or any Territory or the District of Columbia or any foreign country.

(7) The term "affecting commerce" means in commerce, or burdening or obstructing commerce or the free flow of commerce, or having led or tending to lead to a labor dispute burdening or obstructing commerce or the free flow of commerce.

(8) The term "unfair labor practice" means any unfair labor practice listed in section 8 [section 158 of this title].

(9) The term "labor dispute" includes any controversy concerning terms, tenure or conditions of employment, or concerning the association or representation of persons in negotiating, fixing, maintaining, changing, or seeking to arrange

terms or conditions of employment, regardless of whether the disputants stand in the proximate relation of employer and employee.

(10) The term "National Labor Relations Board" means the National Labor Relations Board provided for in section 3 of this Act [section 153 of this title].

(11) The term "supervisor" means any individual having authority, in the interest of the employer, to hire, transfer, suspend, lay off, recall, promote, discharge, assign, reward, or discipline other employees, or responsibly to direct them, or to adjust their grievances, or effectively to recommend such action, if in connection with the foregoing the exercise of such authority is not of a merely routine or clerical nature, but requires the use of independent judgment.

(12) The term "professional employee" means—

(a) any employee engaged in work (i) predominantly intellectual and varied in character as opposed to routine mental, manual, mechanical, or physical work; (ii) involving the consistent exercise of discretion and judgment in its performance; (iii) of such a character that the output produced or the result accomplished cannot be standardized in relation to a given period of time; (iv) requiring knowledge of an advanced type in a field of science or learning customarily acquired by a prolonged course of specialized intellectual instruction and study in an institution of higher learning or a hospital, as distinguished from a general academic education or from an apprenticeship or from training in the performance of routine mental, manual, or physical processes; or

(b) any employee, who (i) has completed the courses of specialized intellectual instruction and study described in clause (iv) of paragraph (a), and (ii) is performing related work under the supervision of a professional person to qualify himself to become a professional employee as defined in paragraph (a).

(13) In determining whether any person is acting as an "agent" of another person so as to make such other person responsible for his acts, the question of whether the specific acts performed were actually authorized or subsequently ratified shall not be controlling.

(14) The term "health care institution" shall include any hospital, convalescent hospital, health maintenance organization, health clinic, nursing home, extended care facility, or other institution devoted to the care of sick, infirm, or aged person.
[Pub. L. 93-360, §1(b), July 26, 1974, 88 Stat. 395, added par. (14).]

NATIONAL LABOR RELATIONS BOARD

Sec. 3. [§153.] (a) [Creation, composition, appointment, and tenure; Chairman; removal of members] The National Labor Relations Board (hereinafter called the "Board") created by this Act [subchapter] prior to its amendment by the Labor Management Relations Act, 1947 [29 U.S.C. §141 et seq.], is continued as an agency of the United States, except that the Board shall consist of five instead of three members, appointed by the President by and with the advice and consent of the Senate. Of the two additional members so provided for, one shall be appointed for a term of five years and the other for a term of two years. Their successors, and the successors of the other members, shall be appointed for terms of five years each, excepting that any individual chosen to fill a vacancy shall be appointed only for the unexpired term of the member whom he shall succeed. The President shall designate one member to serve as Chairman of the Board. Any member of the Board may be removed by the President, upon notice and hearing, for neglect of duty or malfeasance in office, but for no other cause.

(b) [Delegation of powers to members and regional directors; review and stay of actions of regional directors; quorum; seal] The Board is authorized to delegate to any group of three or more members any or all of the powers which it may itself exercise. The Board is also authorized to delegate to its regional directors its powers under section 9 [section 159 of this title] to determine the unit appropriate for the purpose of collective bargaining, to investigate and provide for hearings, and determine whether a question of representation exists, and to direct an election or take a secret ballot under subsection (c) or (e) of section 9 [section 159 of this title] and certify the results thereof, except that upon the filling of a request therefor with the Board by any interested person, the Board may review any action of a regional director delegated to him under this paragraph, but such a review shall not, unless specifically ordered by the Board, operate as a stay of any action taken by the regional director. A vacancy in the Board shall not impair the right of the remaining members to exercise all of the powers of the Board, and three members of the Board shall, at all times, constitute a quorum of the Board, except that two members shall constitute a quorum of any group designated pursuant to the first sentence hereof. The Board shall have an official seal which shall be judicially noticed.

(c) [Annual reports to Congress and the President] The Board shall at the close of each fiscal year make a report in writing to Congress and to the President summarizing significant case activities and operations for that fiscal year.

(d) [General Counsel; appointment and tenure; powers and duties; vacancy] There shall be a General Counsel of the Board who shall be appointed by the President, by and with the advice and consent of the Senate, for a term of four years. The General Counsel of the Board shall exercise general supervision over all attorneys employed by the Board (other than administrative law judges and legal assistants to Board members) and over the officers and employees in the regional offices. He shall have final authority, on behalf of the Board, in respect of the investigation of charges and issuance of complaints under section 10 [section 160 of this title], and in respect of the prosecution of such complaints before the Board, and shall have such other duties as the Board may prescribe or as may be provided by law. In case of vacancy in the office of the General Counsel the President is authorized to designate the officer or employee who shall act as General Counsel during such vacancy, but no person or persons so designated shall so act (1) for more than forty days when the Congress is in session unless a nomination to fill such vacancy shall have been submitted to the Senate, or (2) after the adjournment sine die of the session of the Senate in which such nomination was submitted.

[The title "administrative law judge" was adopted in 5 U.S.C. §3105.]

Sec. 4. [§154. Eligibility for reappointment; officers and employees; payment of expenses] (a) Each member of the Board and the General Counsel of the Board shall be eligible for reappointment, and shall not engage in any other business, vocation, or employment. The Board shall appoint an executive secretary, and such attorneys, examiners, and regional directors, and such other employees as it may from time to time find necessary for the proper performance of its duties. The Board may not employ any attorneys for the purpose of reviewing transcripts of hearings or preparing drafts of opinions except that any attorney employed for assignment as a legal assistant to any Board member may for such Board member review such transcripts and prepare such drafts. No administrative law judge's report shall be reviewed, either before or after its publication, by any person other than a member of the Board or his legal assistant, and no administrative law judge shall advise or consult with the Board with respect to exceptions taken to his findings, rulings, or recommendations. The Board may establish or utilize such regional, local, or other agencies, and utilize such voluntary and uncompensated services, as may from time to time be needed. Attorneys appointed under this section may, at the direction of the Board, appear for and represent the Board in any case in court. Nothing in this Act [subchapter] shall be construed to authorize the Board to appoint individuals for the purpose of conciliation or mediation, or for economic analysis.

[The title "administrative law judge" was adopted in 5 U.S.C. §3105.]

(b) All of the expenses of the Board, including all necessary traveling and subsistence expenses outside the District of Columbia incurred by the members or employees of the Board under its orders, shall be allowed and paid on the presentation of itemized vouchers therefor approved by the Board or by any individual it designates for that purpose.

Sec. 5. [§155. Principal office, conducting inquiries throughout country; participation in decisions or inquiries conducted by member] The principal office of the Board shall be in the District of Columbia, but it may meet and exercise any or all of its powers at any other place. The Board may, by one or more of its members or by such agents or agencies as it may designate, prosecute any inquiry necessary to its functions in any part of the United States. A member who participates in such an inquiry shall not be disqualified from subsequently participating in a decision of the Board in the same case.

Sec. 6. [§156. Rules and regulations] The Board shall have authority from time to time to make, amend, and rescind, in the manner prescribed by the Administrative Procedure Act [by subchapter II of chapter 5 of title 5], such rules and regulations as may be necessary to carry out the provisions of this Act [subchapter].

RIGHTS OF EMPLOYEES

Sec. 7. [§157.] Employees shall have the right to self-organization, to form, join, or assist labor organizations, to bargain collectively through representatives of their own choosing, and to engage in other concerted activities for the purpose of collective bargaining or other mutual aid or protection, and shall also have the right to refrain from any or all such activities except to the extent that such right may be affected by an agreement requiring membership in a labor organization as a condition of employment as authorized in section 8(a)(3) [section 158(a)(3) of this title].

UNFAIR LABOR PRACTICES

Sec. 8. [§158.] (a) [Unfair labor practices by employer] It shall be an unfair labor practice for an employer—

(1) to interfere with, restrain, or coerce employees in the exercise of the rights guaranteed in section 7 [section 157 of this title];

(2) to dominate or interfere with the formation or administration of any labor organization or contribute financial or other support to it: *Provided*, That subject to rules and regulations made and published by the Board pursuant to section 6 [section 156 of this title], an employer shall not be prohibited from permitting employees to confer with him during working hours without loss of time or pay;

(3) by discrimination in regard to hire or tenure of employment or any term or condition of employment to encourage or discourage membership in any labor organization: *Provided*, That nothing in this Act [subchapter], or in any other statute of the United States, shall preclude an employer from making an agreement with a labor organization (not established, maintained, or assisted by any action defined in section 8(a) of this Act [in this subsection] as an unfair labor practice) to require as a condition of employment membership therein on or after the thirtieth day following the beginning of such employment or the effective date of such agreement, whichever is the later, (i) if such labor organization is the representative of the employees as provided in

section 9(a) [section 159(a) of this title], in the appropriate collective-bargaining unit covered by such agreement when made, and (ii) unless following an election held as provided in section 9(e) [section 159(e) of this title] within one year preceding the effective date of such agreement, the Board shall have certified that at least a majority of the employees eligible to vote in such election have voted to rescind the authority of such labor organization to make such an agreement: *Provided further,* That no employer shall justify any discrimination against an employee for non-membership in a labor organization (A) if he has reasonable grounds for believing that such membership was not available to the employee on the same terms and conditions generally applicable to other members, or (B) if he has reasonable grounds for believing that membership was denied or terminated for reasons other than the failure of the employee to tender the periodic dues and the initiation fees uniformly required as a condition of acquiring or retaining membership;

(4) to discharge or otherwise discriminate against an employee because he has filed charges or given testimony under this Act [subchapter];

(5) to refuse to bargain collectively with the representatives of his employees, subject to the provisions of section 9(a) [section 159(a) of this title].

(b) [Unfair labor practices by labor organization] It shall be an unfair labor practice for a labor organization or its agents—

(1) to restrain or coerce (A) employees in the exercise of the rights guaranteed in section 7 [section 157 of this title]: *Provided,* That this paragraph shall not impair the right of a labor organization to prescribe its own rules with respect to the acquisition or retention of membership therein; or (B) an employer in the selection of his representatives for the purposes of collective bargaining or the adjustment of grievances;

(2) to cause or attempt to cause an employer to discriminate against an employee in violation of subsection (a)(3) [of subsection (a)(3) of this section] or to discriminate against an employee with respect to whom membership in such organization has been denied or terminated on some ground other than his failure to tender the periodic dues and the initiation fees uniformly required as a condition of acquiring or retaining membership;

(3) to refuse to bargain collectively with an employer, provided it is the representative of his employees subject to the provisions of section 9(a) [section 159(a) of this title];

(4)(i) to engage in, or to induce or encourage any individual employed by any person engaged in commerce or in an industry affecting commerce to engage in, a strike or a refusal in the course of his employment to use, manufacture, process, transport, or otherwise handle or work on any goods, articles, materials, or commodities or to perform any services; or (ii) to threaten, coerce, or restrain any person engaged in commerce or in an industry affecting commerce, where in either case an object thereof is—

(A) forcing or requiring any employer or self-employed person to join any labor or employer organization or to enter into any agreement which is prohibited by section 8(e) [subsection (e) of this section];

(B) forcing or requiring any person to cease using, selling, handling, transporting, or otherwise dealing in the products of any other producer, processor, or manufacturer, or to cease doing business with any other person, or forcing or requiring any other employer to recognize or bargain with a labor organization as the representative of his employees unless such labor organization has been certified as the representative of such employees under the provisions of section 9 [section 159 of this title]: *Provided,* That nothing contained in this clause (B) shall be construed to make unlawful, where not otherwise unlawful, any primary strike or primary picketing;

(C) forcing or requiring any employer to recognize or bargain with a particular labor organization as the representative of his employees if another labor organization has been certified as the representative of such employees under the provisions of section 9 [section 159 of this title];

(D) forcing or requiring any employer to assign particular work to employees in a particular labor organization or in a particular trade, craft, or class rather than to employees in another labor organization or in another trade, craft, or class, unless such employer is failing to conform to an order or certification of the Board determining the bargaining representative for employees performing such work:

Provided, That nothing contained in this subsection (b) [this subsection] shall be construed to make unlawful a refusal by any person to enter upon the premises of any employer (other than his own employer), if the employees of such employer are engaged in a strike ratified or approved by a representative of such employees whom such employer is required to recognize under this Act [subchapter]: *Provided further*, That for the purposes of this paragraph (4) only, nothing contained in such paragraph shall be construed to prohibit publicity, other than picketing, for the purpose of truthfully advising the public, including consumers and members of a labor organization, that a product or products are produced by an employer with whom the labor organization has a primary dispute and are distributed by another employer, as long as such publicity does not have an effect of inducing any individual employed by any person other than the primary employer in the course of his employment to refuse to pick up, deliver, or transport any goods, or not to perform any services, at the establishment of the employer engaged in such distribution;

(5) to require of employees covered by an agreement authorized under subsection (a)(3) [of this section] the payment, as a condition precedent to becoming a member of such organization, of a fee in an amount which the Board finds excessive or discriminatory under all the circumstances. In making such a finding, the Board shall consider, among other relevant factors, the practices and customs of labor organizations in the particular industry, and the wages currently paid to the employees affected;

(6) to cause or attempt to cause an employer to pay or deliver or agree to pay or deliver any money or other thing of value, in the nature of an exaction, for services which are not performed or not to be performed; and

(7) to picket or cause to be picketed, or threaten to picket or cause to be picketed, any employer where an object thereof is forcing or requiring an employer to recognize or bargain with a labor organization as the representative of his employees, or forcing or requiring the employees of an employer to accept or select such labor organization as their collective-bargaining representative, unless such labor organization is currently certified as the representative of such employees:

(A) where the employer has lawfully recognized in accordance with this Act [subchapter] any other labor organization and a question concerning representation may not appropriately be raised under section 9(c) of this Act [section 159(c) of this title],

(B) where within the preceding twelve months a valid election under section 9(c) of this Act [section 159(c) of this title] has been conducted, or

(C) where such picketing has been conducted without a petition under section 9(c) [section 159(c) of this title] being filed within a reasonable period of time not to exceed thirty days from the commencement of such picketing: *Provided*, That when such a petition has been filed the Board shall forthwith, without regard to the provisions of section 9(c)(1) [section 159(c)(1) of this title] or the absence of a showing of a substantial interest on the part of the labor organization, direct an election in such unit as the Board finds to be appropriate and shall certify the results thereof: *Provided further,* That nothing in this subparagraph (C) shall be construed to prohibit any picketing or other publicity for the purpose of truthfully advising the public (including consumers) that an employer does not employ members of, or have a contract with, a labor organization, unless an effect of such picketing is to induce any individual employed by any other person in the course of his employment, not to pick up, deliver or transport any goods or not to perform any services.

Nothing in this paragraph (7) shall be construed to permit any act which would otherwise be an unfair labor practice under this section 8(b) [this subsection].

(c) [Expression of views without threat of reprisal or force or promise of benefit] The expressing of any views, argument, or opinion, or the dissemination thereof, whether in written, printed, graphic, or visual form, shall not constitute or be evidence of an unfair labor practice under any of the provisions of this Act [subchapter], if such expression contains no threat of reprisal or force or promise of benefit.

(d) [Obligation to bargain collectively] For the purposes of this section, to bargain collectively is the performance of the mutual obligation of the employer and the representative of the employees to meet at reasonable times and confer in good faith with respect to wages, hours, and other terms and conditions of employment, or the negotiation of an agreement or any question arising there under, and the execution of a written contract incorporating any agreement reached if requested by either party, but such obligation does not compel either party to agree to a proposal or require the making of a concession: *Provided,* That where there is in effect a collective-bargaining contract covering employees in an industry affecting commerce, the duty to bargain collectively shall also mean that no party to such contract shall terminate or modify such contract, unless the party desiring such termination or modification—

(1) serves a written notice upon the other party to the contract of the proposed termination or modification sixty days prior to the expiration date thereof, or in the event such contract contains no expiration date, sixty days prior to the time it is proposed to make such termination or modification;

(2) offers to meet and confer with the other party for the purpose of negotiating a new contract or a contract containing the proposed modifications;

(3) notifies the Federal Mediation and Conciliation Service within thirty days after such notice of the existence of a dispute, and simultaneously therewith notifies any State or Territorial agency established to mediate and conciliate disputes within the State or Territory where the dispute occurred, provided no agreement has been reached by that time; and

(4) continues in full force and effect, without resorting to strike or lockout, all the terms and conditions of the existing contract for a period of sixty days after such notice is given or until the expiration date of such contract, whichever occurs later:

The duties imposed upon employers, employees, and labor organizations by paragraphs (2), (3), and (4) [paragraphs (2) to (4) of this subsection] shall become inapplicable upon an intervening certification of the Board, under which the labor organization or individual, which is a party to the contract, has been superseded as or ceased to be the representative of the employees subject to the provisions of section 9(a) [section 159(a) of this title], and the duties so imposed shall not be construed as requiring either party to discuss or agree to any modification of the terms and conditions contained in a contract for a fixed period, if such modification is to become effective before such terms and conditions can be reopened under the provisions of the contract. Any employee who engages in a strike within any notice period specified in this subsection, or who engages in any strike within the appropriate period specified in subsection (g) of this section, shall lose his status as an employee of the employer engaged in the particular labor dispute, for the purposes of sections 8, 9, and 10 of this Act [sections 158, 159, and 160 of this title], but such loss of status for such employee shall terminate if and when he is re-employed by such employer. Whenever the collective bargaining involves employees of a health care institution, the provisions of this section 8(d) [this subsection] shall be modified as follows:

(A) The notice of section 8(d)(1) [paragraph (1) of this subsection] shall be ninety days; the notice of section 8(d)(3) [paragraph (3) of this subsection] shall be sixty days; and the contract period of section 8(d)(4) [paragraph (4) of this subsection] shall be ninety days.

(B) Where the bargaining is for an initial agreement following certification or recognition, at least thirty days' notice of the existence of a dispute shall be given by the labor organization to the agencies set forth in section 8(d)(3) [in paragraph (3) of this subsection].

(C) After notice is given to the Federal Mediation and Conciliation Service under either clause (A) or (B) of this sentence, the Service shall promptly communicate with the parties and use its best efforts, by mediation and conciliation, to bring them to agreement. The parties shall participate fully and promptly in such meetings as may be undertaken by the Service for the purpose of aiding in a settlement of the dispute.

[Pub. L. 93-360, July 26, 1974, 88 Stat. 395, amended the last sentence of Sec. 8(d) by striking the words "the sixty-day" and inserting the words "any notice" and by inserting before the words

"shall lose" the phrase ", or who engages in any strike within the appropriate period specified in subsection (g) of this section." It also amended the end of paragraph Sec. 8(d) by adding a new sentence "Whenever the collective bargaining . . . aiding in a settlement of the dispute."]

(e) [Enforceability of contract or agreement to boycott any other employer; exception] It shall be an unfair labor practice for any labor organization and any employer to enter into any contract or agreement, express or implied, whereby such employer ceases or refrains or agrees to cease or refrain from handling, using, selling, transporting or otherwise dealing in any of the products of any other employer, or cease doing business with any other person, and any contract or agreement entered into heretofore or hereafter containing such an agreement shall be to such extent unenforceable and void: *Provided*, That nothing in this subsection (e) [this subsection] shall apply to an agreement between a labor organization and an employer in the construction industry relating to the contracting or subcontracting of work to be done at the site of the construction, alteration, painting, or repair of a building, structure, or other work: *Provided further*, That for the purposes of this subsection (e) and section 8(b)(4)(B) [this subsection and subsection (b)(4)(B) of this section] the terms "any employer," "any person engaged in commerce or an industry affecting commerce," and "any person" when used in relation to the terms "any other producer, processor, or manufacturer," "any other employer," or "any other person" shall not include persons in the relation of a jobber, manufacturer, contractor, or subcontractor working on the goods or premises of the jobber or manufacturer or performing parts of an integrated process of production in the apparel and clothing industry: *Provided further*, That nothing in this Act [subchapter] shall prohibit the enforcement of any agreement which is within the foregoing exception.

(f) [Agreements covering employees in the building and construction industry] It shall not be an unfair labor practice under subsections (a) and (b) of this section for an employer engaged primarily in the building and construction industry to make an agreement covering employees engaged (or who, upon their employment, will be engaged) in the building and construction industry with a labor organization of which building and construction employees are members (not established, maintained, or assisted by any action defined in section 8(a) of this Act [subsection (a) of this section] as an unfair labor practice) because (1) the majority status of such labor organization has not been established under the provisions of section 9 of this Act [section 159 of this title] prior to the making of such agreement, or (2) such agreement requires as a condition of employment, membership in such labor organization after the seventh day following the beginning of such employment or the effective date of the agreement, whichever is later, or (3) such agreement requires the employer to notify such labor organization of opportunities for employment with such employer, or gives such labor organization an opportunity to refer qualified applicants for such employment, or (4) such agreement specifies minimum training or experience qualifications for employment or provides for priority in opportunities for employment based upon length of service with such employer, in the industry or in the particular geographical area: *Provided*, That nothing in this subsection shall set aside the final proviso to section 8(a)(3) of this Act [subsection (a)(3) of this section]: *Provided further*, That any agreement which would be invalid, but for clause (1) of this subsection, shall not be a bar to a petition filed pursuant to section 9(c) or 9(e) [section 159(c) or 159(e) of this title].

(g) [Notification of intention to strike or picket at any health care institution] A labor organization before engaging in any strike, picketing, or other concerted refusal to work at any health care institution shall, not less than ten days prior to such action, notify the institution in writing and the Federal Mediation and Conciliation Service of that intention, except that in the case of bargaining for an initial agreement following certification or recognition the notice required by this subsection shall not be given until the expiration of the period specified in clause (B) of the last sentence of section 8(d) of this Act [subsection (d) of this section]. The notice shall state the date and time that such action will commence. The notice, once given, may be extended by the written agreement of both parties.

[Pub. L. 93-360, July 26, 1974, 88 Stat. 396, added subsec. (g).]

REPRESENTATIVES AND ELECTIONS

Sec. 9 [§159.] (a) [Exclusive representatives; employees' adjustment of grievances directly with employer] Representatives designated or selected for the purposes of collective bargaining by the majority of the employees in a unit appropriate for such purposes, shall be the exclusive representatives of all the employees in such unit for the purposes of collective bargaining in respect to rates of pay, wages, hours of employment, or other conditions of employment: *Provided*, That any individual employee or a group of employees shall have the right at any time to present grievances to their employer and to have such grievances adjusted, without the intervention of the bargaining representative, as long as the adjustment is not inconsistent with the terms of a collective-bargaining contract or agreement then in effect: *Provided further*, That the bargaining representative has been given opportunity to be present at such adjustment.

(b) [Determination of bargaining unit by Board] The Board shall decide in each case whether, in order to assure to employees the fullest freedom in exercising the rights guaranteed by this Act [subchapter], the unit appropriate for the purposes of collective bargaining shall be the employer unit, craft unit, plant unit, or subdivision thereof: *Provided*, That the Board shall not (1) decide that any unit is appropriate for such purposes if such unit includes both professional employees and employees who are not professional employees unless a majority of such professional employees vote for inclusion in such unit; or (2) decide that any craft unit is inappropriate for such purposes on the ground that a different unit has been established by a prior Board determination, unless a majority of the employees in the proposed craft unit votes against separate representation or (3) decide that any unit is appropriate for such purposes if it includes, together with other employees, any individual employed as a guard to enforce against employees and other persons rules to protect property of the employer or to protect the safety of persons on the employer's premises; but no labor organization shall be certified as the representative of employees in a bargaining unit of guards if such organization admits to membership, or is affiliated directly or indirectly with an organization which admits to membership, employees other than guards.

(c) [Hearings on questions affecting commerce; rules and regulations] (1) Whenever a petition shall have been filed, in accordance with such regulations as may be prescribed by the Board—

(A) by an employee or group of employees or any individual or labor organization acting in their behalf alleging that a substantial number of employees (i) wish to be represented for collective bargaining and that their employer declines to recognize their representative as the representative defined in section 9(a) [subsection (a) of this section], or (ii) assert that the individual or labor organization, which has been certified or is being currently recognized by their employer as the bargaining representative, is no longer a representative as defined in section 9(a) [subsection (a) of this section]; or

(B) by an employer, alleging that one or more individuals or labor organizations have presented to him a claim to be recognized as the representative defined in section 9(a) [subsection (a) of this section]; the Board shall investigate such petition and if it has reasonable cause to believe that a question of representation affecting commerce exists shall provide for an appropriate hearing upon due notice. Such hearing may be conducted by an officer or employee of the regional office, who shall not make any recommendations with respect thereto. If the Board finds upon the record of such hearing that such a question of representation exists, it shall direct an election by secret ballot and shall certify the results thereof.

(2) In determining whether or not a question of representation affecting commerce exists, the same regulations and rules of decision shall apply irrespective of the identity of the persons filing the petition or the kind of relief sought and in no case shall the Board deny a labor organization a place on the ballot by reason of an order with respect to such labor organization or its predecessor not issued in conformity with section 10(c) [section 160(c) of this title].

(3) No election shall be directed in any bargaining unit or any subdivision within which, in the preceding twelve-month period, a valid election shall have been held. Employees engaged in an economic strike who are not entitled to reinstatement shall be eligible to vote under such regulations as the Board shall find are consistent with the purposes and provisions of this Act [subchapter] in any election conducted within twelve months after the commencement of the strike. In any election where none of the choices on the ballot receives a majority, a runoff shall be conducted, the ballot providing for a selection between the two choices receiving the largest and second largest number of valid votes cast in the election.

(4) Nothing in this section shall be construed to prohibit the waiving of hearings by stipulation for the purpose of a consent election in conformity with regulations and rules of decision of the Board.

(5) In determining whether a unit is appropriate for the purposes specified in subsection (b) [of this section] the extent to which the employees have organized shall not be controlling.

(d) [Petition for enforcement or review; transcript] Whenever an order of the Board made pursuant to section 10(c) [section 160(c) of this title] is based in whole or in part upon facts certified following an investigation pursuant to subsection (c) of this section and there is a petition for the enforcement or review of such order, such certification and the record of such investigation shall be included in the transcript of the entire record required to be filed under section 10(e) or 10(f) [subsection (e) or (f) of section 160 of this title], and thereupon the decree of the court enforcing, modifying, or setting aside in whole or in part the order of the Board shall be made and entered upon the pleadings, testimony, and proceedings set forth in such transcript.

(e) [Secret ballot; limitation of elections] (1) Upon the filing with the Board, by 30 per centum or more of the employees in a bargaining unit covered by an agreement between their employer and labor organization made pursuant to section 8(a)(3) [section 158(a)(3) of this title], of a petition alleging they desire that such authorization be rescinded, the Board shall take a secret ballot of the employees in such unit and certify the results thereof to such labor organization and to the employer.

(2) No election shall be conducted pursuant to this subsection in any bargaining unit or any subdivision within which, in the preceding twelve-month period, a valid election shall have been held.

PREVENTION OF UNFAIR LABOR PRACTICES

Sec. 10. [§160.] (a) [Powers of Board generally] The Board is empowered, as hereinafter provided, to prevent any person from engaging in any unfair labor practice (listed in section 8 [section 158 of this title]) affecting commerce. This power shall not be affected by any other means of adjustment or prevention that has been or may be established by agreement, law, or otherwise: *Provided*, That the Board is empowered by agreement with any agency of any State or Territory to cede to such agency jurisdiction over any cases in any industry (other than mining, manufacturing, communications, and transportation except where predominately local in character) even though such cases may involve labor disputes affecting commerce, unless the provision of the State or Territorial statute applicable to the determination of such cases by such agency is inconsistent with the corresponding provision of this Act [subchapter] or has received a construction inconsistent therewith.

(b) [Complaint and notice of hearing; six-month limitation; answer; court rules of evidence inapplicable] Whenever it is charged that any person has engaged in or is engaging in any such unfair labor practice, the Board, or any agent or agency designated by the Board for such purposes, shall have power to issue and cause to be served upon such person a complaint stating the charges in that respect, and containing a notice of hearing before the Board or a member thereof, or before a designated agent or agency, at a place therein fixed, not less than five days after the serving of said complaint: *Provided*, That no complaint shall issue based upon any unfair labor practice occurring more than six months prior to the filing of the charge with the Board and the service of a copy thereof upon the person against whom such charge is made, unless the person aggrieved thereby was prevented from filing such charge by reason of service in the armed forces, in which event the six-month period shall be computed from the day of his discharge. Any such complaint may be amended by the member, agent, or agency conducting the hearing or the Board in its discretion at any time prior to the issuance of an order based thereon. The person so complained of shall have the right to file an answer to the original or amended complaint and to appear in person or otherwise and give testimony at the place and time fixed in the complaint. In the discretion of the member, agent, or agency conducting the hearing or the Board, any other person may be allowed to intervene in the said proceeding and to present testimony. Any such proceeding shall, so far as practicable, be conducted in accordance with the rules of evidence applicable in the district courts of the United States under the rules of civil procedure for the district courts of the United States, adopted by the Supreme Court of the United States pursuant to section 2072 of title 28, United States Code [section 2072 of title 28].

(c) [Reduction of testimony to writing; findings and orders of Board] The testimony taken by such member, agent, or agency, or the Board shall be reduced to writing and filed with the Board. Thereafter, in its discretion, the Board upon notice may take further testimony or hear argument. If upon the preponderance of the testimony taken the Board shall be of the opinion that any person named in the complaint has engaged in or is engaging in any such unfair labor practice, then the Board shall state its findings of fact and shall issue and cause to be served on such person an order requiring such person to cease and desist from such unfair labor practice, and to take such affirmative action including reinstatement of employees with or without backpay, as will effectuate the policies of this Act [subchapter]: *Provided*, That where an order directs reinstatement of an employee, backpay may be required of the employer or labor organization, as the case may be, responsible for the discrimination suffered by him: *And provided further*, That in determining whether a complaint shall issue alleging a violation of section 8(a)(1) or section 8(a)(2) [subsection (a)(1) or (a)(2) of section 158 of this title], and in deciding such cases, the same regulations and rules of decision shall apply irrespective of whether or not the labor organization affected is affiliated with a labor organization national or international in scope. Such order may further require such person to make reports from time to time showing the extent to which it has complied with the order. If upon the preponderance of the testimony taken the Board shall not be of the opinion that the person named in the complaint has engaged in or is engaging in any such unfair labor practice, then the Board shall state its findings of fact and shall issue an order dismissing the said complaint. No order of the Board shall require the reinstatement of any individual as an employee who has been suspended or discharged, or the payment to him of any backpay, if such individual was suspended or discharged for cause. In case the evidence is presented before a member of the Board, or before an administrative law judge or judges thereof, such member, or such judge or judges, as the case may be, shall issue and cause to be served on the parties to the proceeding a proposed report, together with a recommended order, which shall be filed with the Board, and if no exceptions are filed within twenty days after service thereof upon such parties, or within such further period as the Board may authorize, such recommended order shall become the order of the Board and become affective as therein prescribed.

[The title "administrative law judge" was adopted in 5 U.S.C. §3105.]

(d) [Modification of findings or orders prior to filing record in court] Until the record in a case shall have been filed in a court, as hereinafter provided, the Board may at any time, upon reasonable notice and in such manner as it shall deem proper, modify or set aside, in whole or in part, any finding or order made or issued by it.

(e) [Petition to court for enforcement of order; proceedings; review of judgment] The Board shall have power to petition any court of appeals of the United States, or if all the courts of appeals to which application may be made are in vacation, any district court of the United States, within any circuit or district, respectively, wherein the unfair labor practice in question occurred or wherein such person resides or transacts business, for the enforcement of such order and for appropriate temporary relief or restraining order, and shall file in the court the record in the proceeding, as provided in section 2112 of title 28, United States Code [section 2112 of title 28]. Upon the filing of such petition, the court shall cause notice thereof to be served upon such person, and thereupon shall have jurisdiction of the proceeding and of the question determined therein, and shall have power to grant such temporary relief or restraining order as it deems just and proper, and to make and enter a decree enforcing, modifying and enforcing as so modified, or setting aside in whole or in part the order of the Board. No objection that has not been urged before the Board, its member, agent, or agency, shall be considered by the court, unless the failure or neglect to urge such objection shall be excused because of extraordinary circumstances. The findings of the Board with respect to questions of fact if supported by substantial evidence on the record considered as a whole shall be conclusive. If either party shall apply to the court for leave to adduce additional evidence and shall show to the satisfaction of the court that such additional evidence is material and that there were reasonable grounds for the failure to adduce such evidence in the hearing before the Board, its member, agent, or agency, the court may order such additional evidence to be taken before the Board, its member, agent, or agency, and to be made a part of the record. The Board may modify its findings as to

the facts, or make new findings, by reason of additional evidence so taken and filed, and it shall file such modified or new findings, which findings with respect to question of fact if supported by substantial evidence on the record considered as a whole shall be conclusive, and shall file its recommendations, if any, for the modification or setting aside of its original order. Upon the filing of the record with it the jurisdiction of the court shall be exclusive and its judgment and decree shall be final, except that the same shall be subject to review by the appropriate United States court of appeals if application was made to the district court as hereinabove provided, and by the Supreme Court of the United States upon writ of certiorari or certification as provided in section 1254 of title 28.

(f) [Review of final order of Board on petition to court] Any person aggrieved by a final order of the Board granting or denying in whole or in part the relief sought may obtain a review of such order in any United States court of appeals in the circuit wherein the unfair labor practice in question was alleged to have been engaged in or wherein such person resides or transacts business, or in the United States Court of Appeals for the District of Columbia, by filing in such court a written petition praying that the order of the Board be modified or set aside. A copy of such petition shall be forthwith transmitted by the clerk of the court to the Board, and thereupon the aggrieved party shall file in the court the record in the proceeding, certified by the Board, as provided in section 2112 of title 28, United States Code [section 2112 of title 28]. Upon the filing of such petition, the court shall proceed in the same manner as in the case of an application by the Board under subsection (e) of this section, and shall have the same jurisdiction to grant to the Board such temporary relief or restraining order as it deems just and proper, and in like manner to make and enter a decree enforcing, modifying and enforcing as so modified, or setting aside in whole or in part the order of the Board; the findings of the Board with respect to questions of fact if supported by substantial evidence on the record considered as a whole shall in like manner be conclusive.

(g) [Institution of court proceedings as stay of Board's order] The commencement of proceedings under subsection (e) or (f) of this section shall not, unless specifically ordered by the court, operate as a stay of the Board's order.

(h) [Jurisdiction of courts unaffected by limitations prescribed in chapter 6 of this title] When granting appropriate temporary relief or a restraining order, or making and entering a decree enforcing, modifying and enforcing as so modified, or setting aside in whole or in part an order of the Board, as provided in this section, the jurisdiction of courts sitting in equity shall not be limited by sections 101 to 115 of title 29, United States Code [chapter 6 of this title] [known as the "Norris–La Guardia Act"].

(i) Repealed.

(j) [Injunctions] The Board shall have power, upon issuance of a complaint as provided in subsection (b) [of this section] charging that any person has engaged in or is engaging in an unfair labor practice, to petition any United States district court, within any district wherein the unfair labor practice in question is alleged to have occurred or wherein such person resides or transacts business, for appropriate temporary relief or restraining order. Upon the filing of any such petition the court shall cause notice thereof to be served upon such person, and thereupon shall have jurisdiction to grant to the Board such temporary relief or restraining order as it deems just and proper.

(k) [Hearings on jurisdictional strikes] Whenever it is charged that any person has engaged in an unfair labor practice within the meaning of paragraph (4)(D) of section 8(b) [section 158(b) of this title], the Board is empowered and directed to hear and determine the dispute out

of which such unfair labor practice shall have arisen, unless, within ten days after notice that such charge has been filed, the parties to such dispute submit to the Board satisfactory evidence that they have adjusted, or agreed upon methods for the voluntary adjustment of, the dispute. Upon compliance by the parties to the dispute with the decision of the Board or upon such voluntary adjustment of the dispute, such charge shall be dismissed.

(l) [Boycotts and strikes to force recognition of uncertified labor organizations; injunctions; notice; service of process] Whenever it is charged that any person has engaged in an unfair labor practice within the meaning of paragraph (4)(A), (B), or (C) of section 8(b) [section 158(b) of this title], or section 8(e) [section 158(e) of this title] or section 8(b)(7) [section 158(b)(7) of this title], the preliminary investigation of such charge shall be made forthwith and given priority over all other cases except cases of like character in the office where it is filed or to which it is referred. If, after such investigation, the officer or regional attorney to whom the matter may be referred has reasonable cause to believe such charge is true and that a complaint should issue, he shall, on behalf of the Board, petition any United States district court within any district where the unfair labor practice in question has occurred, is alleged to have occurred, or wherein such person resides or transacts business, for appropriate injunctive relief pending the final adjudication of the Board with respect to such matter. Upon the filing of any such petition the district court shall have jurisdiction to grant such injunctive relief or temporary restraining order as it deems just and proper, notwithstanding any other provision of law: *Provided further*, That no temporary restraining order shall be issued without notice unless a petition alleges that substantial and irreparable injury to the charging party will be unavoidable and such temporary restraining order shall be effective for no longer than five days and will become void at the expiration of such period: *Provided further*, That such officer or regional attorney shall not apply for any restraining order under section 8(b)(7) [section 158(b)(7) of this title] if a charge against the employer under section 8(a)(2) [section 158(a)(2) of this title] has been filed and after the preliminary investigation, he has reasonable cause to believe that such charge is true and that a complaint should issue. Upon filing of any such petition the courts shall cause notice thereof to be served upon any person involved in the charge and such person, including the charging party, shall be given an opportunity to appear by counsel and present any relevant testimony: *Provided further*, That for the purposes of this subsection district courts shall be deemed to have jurisdiction of a labor organization (1) in the district in which such organization maintains its principal office, or (2) in any district in which its duly authorized officers or agents are engaged in promoting or protecting the interests of employee members. The service of legal process upon such officer or agent shall constitute service upon the labor organization and make such organization a party to the suit. In situations where such relief is appropriate the procedure specified herein shall apply to charges with respect to section 8(b)(4)(D) [section 158(b)(4)(D) of this title].

(m) [Priority of cases] Whenever it is charged that any person has engaged in an unfair labor practice within the meaning of subsection (a)(3) or (b)(2) of section 8 [section 158 of this title], such charge shall be given priority over all other cases except cases of like character in the office where it is filed or to which it is referred and cases given priority under subsection (1) [of this section].

INVESTIGATORY POWERS

Sec. 11. [§161.] For the purpose of all hearings and investigations, which, in the opinion of the Board, are necessary and proper for the exercise of the powers vested in it by section 9 and section 10 [sections 159 and 160 of this title]—

(1) [Documentary evidence; summoning witnesses and taking testimony] The Board, or its duly authorized agents or agencies, shall at all reasonable times have access to, for the purpose of examination, and the right to copy any evidence of any person being investigated or proceeded against that relates to any matter under investigation or in question. The Board, or any member thereof, shall upon application of any party to such proceedings, forthwith issue to such party subpoenas requiring the attendance and testimony of witnesses or the production of any evidence in such proceeding or investigation requested in such application. Within five days after the service of a subpoena on any person requiring the production of any evidence in his possession or under his control, such person may petition the Board to revoke, and the Board shall revoke, such subpoena if in its opinion the evidence whose production is required does not relate to any matter under investigation, or any matter in question in such proceedings, or if in its opinion such subpoena does not describe with sufficient particularity the evidence whose production is required. Any member of the Board, or any agent or agency designated by the Board for such purposes, may administer oaths and affirmations, examine witnesses, and receive evidence. Such attendance of witnesses and the production of such evidence may be required from any place in the United States or any Territory or possession thereof, at any designated place of hearing.

(2) [Court aid in compelling production of evidence and attendance of witnesses] In case on contumacy or refusal to obey a subpoena issued to any person, any United States district court or the United States courts of any Territory or possession, within the jurisdiction of which the inquiry is carried on or within the jurisdiction of which said person guilty of contumacy or

refusal to obey is found or resides or transacts business, upon application by the Board shall have jurisdiction to issue to such person an order requiring such person to appear before the Board, its member, agent, or agency, there to produce evidence if so ordered, or there to give testimony touching the matter under investigation or in question; and any failure to obey such order of the court may be punished by said court as a contempt thereof.

(3) Repealed.

[Immunity of witnesses. See 18 U.S.C. §6001 et seq.]

(4) [Process, service and return; fees of witnesses] Complaints, orders and other process and papers of the Board, its member, agent, or agency, may be served either personally or by registered or certified mail or by telegraph or by leaving a copy thereof at the principal office or place of business of the person required to be served. The verified return by the individual so serving the same setting forth the manner of such service shall be proof of the same, and the return post office receipt or telegraph receipt therefore when registered or certified and mailed or when telegraphed as aforesaid shall be proof of service of the same. Witnesses summoned before the Board, its member, agent, or agency, shall be paid the same fees and mileage that are paid witnesses in the courts of the United States, and witnesses whose depositions are taken and the persons taking the same shall severally be entitled to the same fees as are paid for like services in the courts of the United States.

(5) [Process, where served] All process of any court to which application may be made under this Act [subchapter] may be served in the judicial district wherein the defendant or other person required to be served resides or may be found.

(6) [Information and assistance from departments] The several departments and agencies of the Government, when directed by the President, shall furnish the Board, upon its request, all records, papers, and information in their possession relating to any matter before the Board.

Sec. 12. [§162. Offenses and penalties] Any person who shall willfully resist, prevent, impede, or interfere with any member of the Board or any of its agents or agencies in the performance of duties pursuant to this Act [subchapter] shall be punished by a fine of not more than $5,000 or by imprisonment for not more than one year, or both.

LIMITATIONS

Sec. 13. [§163. Right to strike preserved] Nothing in this Act [subchapter], except as specifically provided for herein, shall be construed so as either to interfere with or impede or diminish in any way the right to strike or to affect the limitations or qualifications on that right.

Sec. 14. [§164. Construction of provisions] (a) [Supervisors as union members] Nothing herein shall prohibit any individual employed as a supervisor from becoming or remaining a member of a labor organization, but no employer subject to this Act [subchapter] shall be compelled to deem individuals defined herein as supervisors as employees for the purpose of any law, either national or local, relating to collective bargaining.

(b) [Agreements requiring union membership in violation of State law] Nothing in this Act [subchapter] shall be construed as authorizing the execution or application of agreements requiring membership in a labor organization as a condition of employment in any State or Territory in which such execution or application is prohibited by State or Territorial law.

(c) [Power of Board to decline jurisdiction of labor disputes; assertion of jurisdiction by State and Territorial courts] (1) The Board, in its discretion, may, by rule of decision or by published rules adopted pursuant to the Administrative Procedure Act [to subchapter II of chapter 5 of title 5], decline to assert jurisdiction over any labor dispute involving any class or category of employers, where, in the opinion of the Board, the effect of such labor dispute on commerce is not sufficiently substantial to warrant the exercise of its jurisdiction: *Provided*, That the Board shall not decline to assert jurisdiction over any labor dispute over which it would assert jurisdiction under the standards prevailing upon August 1, 1959.

(2) Nothing in this Act [subchapter] shall be deemed to prevent or bar any agency or the courts of any State or Territory (including the Commonwealth of Puerto Rico, Guam, and the Virgin Islands), from assuming and asserting jurisdiction over labor disputes over which the Board declines, pursuant to paragraph (1) of this subsection, to assert jurisdiction.

Sec. 15. [§165.] Omitted.

[Reference to repealed provisions of bankruptcy statute.]

Sec. 16. [§166. Separability of provisions] If any provision of this Act [subchapter], or the application of such provision to any person or circumstances, shall be held invalid, the remainder of this Act [subchapter], or the application of such provision to persons or circumstances other than those as to which it is held invalid, shall not be affected thereby.

Sec. 17. [§167. Short title] This Act [subchapter] may be cited as the "National Labor Relations Act."

Sec. 18. [§168.] Omitted.

[Reference to former sec. 9(f), (g), and (h).]

INDIVIDUALS WITH RELIGIOUS CONVICTIONS

Sec. 19. [§169.] Any employee who is a member of and adheres to established and traditional tenets or teachings of a bona fide religion, body, or sect which has historically held conscientious objections to joining or financially supporting labor organizations shall not be required to join or financially support any labor organization as a condition of employment; except that such employee may be required in a contract between such employee's employer and a labor organization in lieu of periodic dues and initiation fees, to pay sums equal to such dues and initiation fees to a nonreligious, non-labor organization charitable fund exempt from taxation under section 501(c)(3) of title 26 of the Internal Revenue Code [section 501(c)(3) of title 26], chosen by such employee from a list of at least three such funds, designated in such contract or if the contract fails to designate such funds, then to any such fund chosen by the employee. If such employee who holds conscientious objections pursuant to this section requests the labor organization to use the grievance-arbitration procedure on the employee's behalf, the labor organization is authorized to charge the employee for the reasonable cost of using such procedure.

[Sec. added, Pub. L. 93-360, July 26, 1974, 88 Stat. 397, and amended, Pub. L. 96-593, Dec. 24, 1980, 94 Stat. 3452.]

LABOR MANAGEMENT RELATIONS ACT
Also cited LMRA; 29 U.S.C. §§141–97

[Title 29, Chapter 7, United States Code]

SHORT TITLE AND DECLARATION OF POLICY

Section 1. [§141.] (a) This Act [chapter] may be cited as the "Labor Management Relations Act, 1947." [Also known as the "Taft-Hartley Act."]

(b) Industrial strife which interferes with the normal flow of commerce and with the full production of articles and commodities for commerce, can be avoided or substantially minimized if employers, employees, and labor organizations each recognize under law one another's legitimate rights in their relations with each other, and above all recognize under law that neither party has any right in its relations with any other to engage in acts or practices which jeopardize the public health, safety, or interest.

It is the purpose and policy of this Act [chapter], in order to promote the full flow of commerce, to prescribe the legitimate rights of both employees and employers in their relations affecting commerce, to provide orderly and peaceful procedures for preventing the interference by either with the legitimate rights of the other, to protect the rights of individual employees in their relations with labor organizations whose activities affect commerce, to define and proscribe practices on the part of labor and management which affect commerce and are inimical to the general welfare, and to protect the rights of the public in connection with labor disputes affecting commerce.

TITLE I, Amendments to
NATIONAL LABOR RELATIONS ACT

29 U.S.C. §§151–69 (printed above)

TITLE II

[Title 29, Chapter 7, Subchapter III, United States Code]

CONCILIATION OF LABOR DISPUTES IN INDUSTRIES AFFECTING COMMERCE; NATIONAL EMERGENCIES

Sec. 201. [§171. Declaration of purpose and policy] It is the policy of the United States that—

(a) sound and stable industrial peace and the advancement of the general welfare, health, and safety of the Nation and of the best interest of employers and employees can most satisfactorily be secured by the settlement of issues between employers and employees through the processes of conference and collective bargaining between employers and the representatives of their employees;

(b) the settlement of issues between employers and employees through collective bargaining may by advanced by making available full and adequate governmental facilities for conciliation, mediation, and voluntary arbitration to aid and encourage employers and the representatives of their employees to reach and maintain agreements concerning rates of pay, hours, and working conditions, and to make all reasonable efforts to settle their differences by mutual agreement reached through conferences and collective bargaining or by such methods as may be provided for in any applicable agreement for the settlement of disputes; and

(c) certain controversies which arise between parties to collective bargaining agreements may be avoided or minimized by making available full and adequate governmental facilities for furnishing assistance to employers and the representatives of their employees in formulating for inclusion within such agreements provision for adequate notice of any proposed changes in the terms of such agreements, for the final adjustment of grievances or questions regarding the application or interpretation of such agreements, and other provisions designed to prevent the subsequent arising of such controversies.

Sec. 202. [§172. Federal Mediation and Conciliation Service]

(a) [Creation; appointment of Director] There is created an independent agency to be known as the Federal Mediation and Conciliation Service (herein referred to as the "Service," except that for sixty days after June 23, 1947, such term shall refer to the Conciliation Service of the Department of Labor). The Service shall be under the direction of a Federal Mediation and Conciliation Director (hereinafter referred to as the "Director"), who shall be appointed by the President by and with the advice and consent of the Senate. The Director shall not engage in any other business, vocation, or employment.

(b) [Appointment of officers and employees; expenditures for supplies, facilities, and services] The Director is authorized, subject to the civil service laws, to appoint such clerical and other personnel as may be necessary for the execution of the functions of the Service, and shall fix their compensation in accordance with sections 5101 to 5115 and sections 5331 to 5338 of title 5, United States Code [chapter 51 and subchapter III of chapter 53 of title 5], and may, without regard to the provisions of the civil service laws, appoint such conciliators and mediators as may be necessary to carry out the functions of the Service. The Director is authorized to make such expenditures for supplies, facilities, and services as he deems necessary. Such expenditures shall be allowed and paid upon presentation of itemized vouchers therefor approved by the Director or by any employee designated by him for that purpose.

(c) [Principal and regional offices; delegation of authority by Director; annual report to Congress] The principal office of the Service shall be in the District of Columbia, but the Director may establish regional offices convenient to localities in which labor controversies are likely to arise. The Director may by order, subject to revocation at any time, delegate any authority and discretion conferred upon him by this Act [chapter] to any regional director, or other officer or employee of the Service. The Director may establish suitable procedures for cooperation with State and local mediation agencies. The Director shall make an annual report in writing to Congress at the end of the fiscal year.

(d) [Transfer of all mediation and conciliation services to Service; effective date; pending proceedings unaffected] All mediation and conciliation functions of the Secretary of Labor or the United States Conciliation Service under section 51 [repealed] of title 29, United States Code [this title], and all functions of the United States Conciliation Service under any other law are transferred to the Federal Mediation and Conciliation Service, together with the personnel and records of the United States Conciliation Service. Such transfer shall take effect upon the sixtieth day after June 23, 1947. Such transfer shall not affect any proceedings pending before the United States Conciliation Service or any certification, order, rule, or regulation theretofore made by it or by the Secretary of Labor. The Director and the Service shall not be subject in any way to the jurisdiction or authority of the Secretary of Labor or any official or division of the Department of Labor.

FUNCTIONS OF THE SERVICE

Sec. 203. [§173. Functions of Service] (a) [Settlement of disputes through conciliation and mediation] It shall be the duty of the Service, in order to prevent or minimize interruptions of the free flow of commerce growing out of labor disputes, to assist parties to labor disputes in industries affecting commerce to settle such disputes through conciliation and mediation.

(b) [Intervention on motion of Service or request of parties; avoidance of mediation of minor disputes] The Service may proffer its services in any labor dispute in any industry affecting commerce, either upon its own motion or upon the request of one or more of the parties to the dispute, whenever in its judgment such dispute threatens to cause a substantial interruption of commerce. The Director and the Service are directed to avoid attempting to mediate disputes which would have only a minor effect on interstate commerce if State or other conciliation services are available to the parties. Whenever the Service does proffer its services in any dispute, it shall be the duty of the Service promptly to put itself in communication with the parties and to use its best efforts, by mediation and conciliation, to bring them to agreement.

(c) [Settlement of disputes by other means upon failure of conciliation] If the Director is not able to bring the parties to agreement by conciliation within a reasonable time, he shall seek to induce the parties voluntarily to seek other means of settling the dispute without resort to strike, lockout, or other coercion, including submission to the employees in the bargaining unit of the employer's last offer of settlement for approval or rejection in a secret ballot. The failure or refusal of either party to agree to any procedure suggested by the Director shall not be deemed a violation of any duty or obligation imposed by this Act [chapter].

(d) [Use of conciliation and mediation services as last resort] Final adjustment by a method agreed upon by the parties is declared to be the desirable method for settlement of grievance disputes arising over the application or interpretation of an existing collective-bargaining agreement. The Service is directed to make its conciliation and mediation services available in the settlement of such grievance disputes only as a last resort and in exceptional cases.

(e) [Encouragement and support of establishment and operation of joint labor management activities conducted by committees] The Service is authorized and directed to encourage and support the establishment and operation of joint labor management activities conducted by plant, area, and industry wide committees designed to improve labor management relationships, job security and organizational effectiveness, in accordance with the provisions of section 205A [section 175a of this title].

[Pub. L. 95-524, §6(c)(1), Oct. 27, 1978, 92 Stat. 2020, added subsec. (e).]

Sec. 204. [§174. Co-equal obligations of employees, their representatives, and management to minimize labor disputes] (a) In order to prevent or minimize interruptions of the free flow of commerce growing out of labor disputes, employers and employees and their representatives, in any industry affecting commerce, shall—

(1) exert every reasonable effort to make and maintain agreements concerning rates of pay, hours, and working conditions, including provision for adequate notice of any proposed change in the terms of such agreements;

(2) whenever a dispute arises over the terms or application of a collective-bargaining agreement and a conference is requested by a party or prospective party thereto, arrange promptly for such a conference to be held and endeavor in such conference to settle such dispute expeditiously; and

(3) in case such dispute is not settled by conference, participate fully and promptly in such meetings as may be undertaken by the Service under this Act [chapter] for the purpose of aiding in a settlement of the dispute.

Sec. 205. [§175. National Labor-Management Panel; creation and composition; appointment, tenure, and compensation; duties] (a) There is created a National Labor-Management Panel which shall be composed of twelve members appointed by the President, six of whom shall be elected from among persons outstanding in the field of management and six of whom shall be selected from among persons outstanding in the field of labor. Each member shall hold office for a term of three years, except that any member appointed to fill a vacancy occurring prior to the expiration of the term for which his predecessor was appointed shall be appointed for the remainder of such term, and the terms of office of the members first taking office shall expire, as designated by the President at the time of appointment, four at the end of the first year, four at the end of the second year, and four at the end of the third year after the date of appointment. Members of the panel, when serving on business of the panel, shall be paid compensation at the rate of $25 per day, and shall also be entitled to receive an allowance for actual and necessary travel and subsistence expenses while so serving away from their places of residence.

(b) It shall be the duty of the panel, at the request of the Director, to advise in the avoidance of industrial controversies and the manner in which mediation and voluntary adjustment shall be administered, particularly with reference to controversies affecting the general welfare of the country.

Sec. 205A. [§175a. Assistance to plant, area, and industry wide labor management committees]

(a) [Establishment and operation of plant, area, and industry wide committees] (1) The Service is authorized and directed to provide assistance in the establishment and operation of plant, area and industry wide labor management committees which—

(A) have been organized jointly by employers and labor organizations representing employees in that plant, area, or industry; and

(B) are established for the purpose of improving labor management relationships, job security, organizational effectiveness, enhancing economic development or involving workers in decisions affecting their jobs including improving communication with respect to subjects of mutual interest and concern.

(2) The Service is authorized and directed to enter into contracts and to make grants, where necessary or appropriate, to fulfill its responsibilities under this section.

(b) [Restrictions on grants, contracts, or other assistance] (1) No grant may be made, no contract may be entered into and no other assistance may be provided under the provisions of this section to a plant labor management committee unless the employees in that plant are represented by a labor organization and there is in effect at that plant a collective bargaining agreement.

(2) No grant may be made, no contract may be entered into and no other assistance may be provided under the provisions of this section to an area or industry wide labor management committee unless its participants include any labor organizations certified or recognized as the representative of the employees of an employer participating in such committee. Nothing in this clause shall prohibit participation in an area or industry wide committee by an employer whose employees are not represented by a labor organization.

(3) No grant may be made under the provisions of this section to any labor management committee which the Service finds to have as one of its purposes the discouragement of the exercise of rights contained in section 7 of the National Labor Relations Act (29 U.S.C. §157) [section 157 of this title], or the interference with collective bargaining in any plant, or industry.

(c) [Establishment of office] The Service shall carry out the provisions of this section through an office established for that purpose.

(d) [Authorization of appropriations] There are authorized to be appropriated to carry out the provisions of this section $10,000,000 for the fiscal year 1979, and such sums as may be necessary thereafter.

[Pub. L. 95-524, §6(c)(2), Oct. 27, 1978, 92 Stat. 2020, added Sec. 205A.]

NATIONAL EMERGENCIES

Sec. 206. [§176. Appointment of board of inquiry by President; report; contents; filing with Service] Whenever in the opinion of the President of the United States, a threatened or actual strike or lockout affecting an entire industry or a substantial part thereof engaged in trade, commerce, transportation, transmission, or communication among the several States or with foreign nations, or engaged in the production of goods for commerce, will, if permitted to occur or to continue, imperil the national health or safety, he may appoint a board of inquiry to inquire into the issues involved in the dispute and to make a written report to him within such time as he shall prescribe. Such report shall include a statement of the facts with respect to the dispute, including each party's statement of its position but shall not contain any recommendations. The President shall file a copy of such report with the Service and shall make its contents available to the public.

Sec. 207. [§177. Board of inquiry]

(a) [Composition] A board of inquiry shall be composed of a chairman and such other members as the President shall determine, and shall have power to sit and act in any place within the United States and to conduct such hearings either in public or in private, as it may deem necessary or proper, to ascertain the facts with respect to the causes and circumstances of the dispute.

(b) [Compensation] Members of a board of inquiry shall receive compensation at the rate of $50 for each day actually spent by them in the work of the board, together with necessary travel and subsistence expenses.

(c) [Powers of discovery] For the purpose of any hearing or inquiry conducted by any board appointed under this title, the provisions of sections 49 and 50 of title 15, United States Code [sections 49 and 50 of title 15] (relating to the attendance of witnesses and the production of books, papers, and documents) are made applicable to the powers and duties of such board.

Sec. 208. [§178. Injunctions during national emergency]

(a) [Petition to district court by Attorney General on direction of President] Upon receiving a report from a board of inquiry the President may direct the Attorney General to petition any district court of the United States having jurisdiction of the parties to enjoin such strike or lockout or the continuing thereof, and if the court finds that such threatened or actual strike or lockout—

(i) affects an entire industry or a substantial part thereof engaged in trade, commerce, transportation, transmission, or communication among the several States or with foreign nations, or engaged in the production of goods for commerce; and

(ii) if permitted to occur or to continue, will imperil the national health or safety, it shall have jurisdiction to enjoin any such strike or lockout, or the continuing thereof, and to make such other orders as may be appropriate.

(b) [Inapplicability of chapter 6] In any case, the provisions of sections 101 to 115 of title 29,

United States Code [chapter 6 of this title] [known as the "Norris–La Guardia Act"] shall not be applicable.

(c) [Review of orders] The order or orders of the court shall be subject to review by the appropriate United States court of appeals and by the Supreme Court upon writ of certiorari or certification as provided in section 1254 of title 28, United States Code [section 1254 of title 28].

Sec. 209. [§179. Injunctions during national emergency; adjustment efforts by parties during injunction period]

(a) [Assistance of Service; acceptance of Service's proposed settlement] Whenever a district court has issued an order under section 208 [section 178 of this title] enjoining acts or practices which imperil or threaten to imperil the national health or safety, it shall be the duty of the parties to the labor dispute giving rise to such order to make every effort to adjust and settle their differences, with the assistance of the Service created by this Act [chapter]. Neither party shall be under any duty to accept, in whole or in part, any proposal of settlement made by the Service.

(b) [Reconvening of board of inquiry; report by board; contents; secret ballot of employees by National Labor Relations Board; certification of results to Attorney General] Upon the issuance of such order, the President shall reconvene the board of inquiry which has previously reported with respect to the dispute. At the end of a sixty-day period (unless the dispute has been settled by that time), the board of inquiry shall report to the President the current position of the parties and the efforts which have been made for settlement, and shall include a statement by each party of its position and a statement of the employer's last offer of settlement. The President shall make such report available to the public. The National Labor Relations Board, within the succeeding fifteen days, shall take a secret ballot of the employees of each employer involved in the dispute on the question of whether they wish to accept the final offer of settlement made by their employer, as stated by him and shall certify the results thereof to the Attorney General within five days thereafter.

Sec. 210. [§180. Discharge of injunction upon certification of results of election or settlement; report to Congress] Upon the certification of the results of such ballot or upon a settlement being reached, whichever happens sooner, the Attorney General shall move the court to discharge the injunction, which motion shall then be granted and the injunction discharged. When such motion is granted, the President shall submit to the Congress a full and comprehensive report of the proceedings, including the findings of the board of inquiry and the ballot taken by the National Labor Relations Board, together with such recommendations as he may see fit to make for consideration and appropriate action.

COMPILATION OF COLLECTIVE-BARGAINING AGREEMENTS, ETC.

Sec. 211. [§181.] (a) For the guidance and information of interested representatives of employers, employees, and the general public, the Bureau of Labor Statistics of the Department of Labor shall maintain a file of copies of all available collective bargaining agreements and other available agreements and actions thereunder settling or adjusting labor disputes. Such file shall be open to inspection under appropriate conditions prescribed by the Secretary of Labor, except that no specific information submitted in confidence shall be disclosed.

(b) The Bureau of Labor Statistics in the Department of Labor is authorized to furnish upon request of the Service, or employers, employees, or their representatives, all available data and factual information which may aid in the settlement of any labor dispute, except that no specific information submitted in confidence shall be disclosed.

EXEMPTION OF RAILWAY LABOR ACT

Sec. 212. [§182.] The provisions of this title [subchapter] shall not be applicable with respect to any matter which is subject to the provisions of the Railway Labor Act [45 U.S.C. §151 et seq.], as amended from time to time.

CONCILIATION OF LABOR DISPUTES IN THE HEALTH CARE INDUSTRY

Sec. 213. [§183.] (a) [Establishment of Boards of Inquiry; membership] If, in the opinion of the Director of the Federal Mediation and Conciliation Service, a threatened or actual strike or lockout affecting a health care institution will, if permitted to occur or to continue, substantially interrupt the delivery of health care in the locality concerned, the Director may further assist in the resolution of the impasse by establishing within 30 days after the notice to the Federal Mediation and Conciliation Service under clause (A) of the last sentence of section 8(d) [section 158(d) of this title] (which is required by clause (3) of such section 8(d) [section 158(d) of this title]), or within 10 days after the notice under clause (B), an impartial Board of Inquiry to investigate the issues involved in the dispute and to make a written report thereon to the parties within fifteen (15) days after the establishment of such a Board. The written report shall contain the findings of fact together with the Board's recommendations for settling the dispute, with the objective of achieving a prompt, peaceful and just settlement of the dispute. Each such Board shall be composed of such number of individuals as the Director may deem desirable. No member appointed under this section shall have any interest or involvement in the health care institutions or the employee organizations involved in the dispute.

(b) [Compensation of members of Boards of Inquiry] (1) Members of any board established under this section who are otherwise employed by the Federal Government shall serve without compensation but shall be reimbursed for travel, subsistence, and other necessary expenses incurred by them in carrying out its duties under this section.

(2) Members of any board established under this section who are not subject to paragraph (1) shall receive compensation at a rate prescribed by the Director but not to exceed the daily rate prescribed for GS-18 of the General Schedule under section 5332 of title 5, United States Code [section 5332 of title 5], including travel for each day they are engaged in the performance of their duties under this section and shall be entitled to reimbursement for travel, subsistence, and other necessary expenses incurred by them in carrying out their duties under this section.

(c) [Maintenance of status quo] After the establishment of a board under subsection (a) of this section and for 15 days after any such board has issued its report, no change in the status quo in effect prior to the expiration of the contract in the case of negotiations for a contract renewal, or in effect prior to the time of the impasse in the case of an initial bargaining negotiation, except by agreement, shall be made by the parties to the controversy.

(d) [Authorization of appropriations] There are authorized to be appropriated such sums as may be necessary to carry out the provisions of this section.

TITLE III

[Title 29, Chapter 7, Subchapter IV, United States Code]

SUITS BY AND AGAINST LABOR ORGANIZATIONS

Sec. 301. [§185.] (a) [Venue, amount, and citizenship] Suits for violation of contracts between an employer and a labor organization representing employees in an industry affecting commerce as defined in this Act [chapter], or between any such labor organization, may be brought in any district court of the United States having jurisdiction of the parties, without respect to the amount in controversy or without regard to the citizenship of the parties.

(b) [Responsibility for acts of agent; entity for purposes of suit; enforcement of money judgments] Any labor organization which represents employees in an industry affecting commerce as defined in this Act [chapter] and any employer whose activities affect commerce as defined in this Act [chapter] shall be bound by the acts of its agents. Any such labor organization may sue or be sued as an entity and in behalf of the employees whom it represents in the courts of the United States. Any money judgment against a labor organization in a district court of the United States shall be enforceable only against the organization as an entity and against its assets, and shall not be enforceable against any individual member or his assets.

(c) [Jurisdiction] For the purposes of actions and proceedings by or against labor organizations in the district courts of the United States, district courts shall be deemed to have jurisdiction of a labor organization (1) in the district in which such organization maintains its principal offices, or (2) in any district in which its duly authorized officers or agents are engaged in representing or acting for employee members.

(d) [Service of process] The service of summons, subpoena, or other legal process of any court of the United States upon an officer or agent of a labor organization, in his capacity as such, shall constitute service upon the labor organization.

(e) [Determination of question of agency] For the purposes of this section, in determining whether any person is acting as an "agent" of another person so as to make such other person responsible for his acts, the question of whether the specific acts performed were actually authorized or subsequently ratified shall not be controlling.

RESTRICTIONS ON PAYMENTS TO EMPLOYEE REPRESENTATIVES

Sec. 302. [§186.] (a) [Payment or lending, etc., of money by employer or agent to employees, representatives, or labor organizations] It shall be unlawful for any employer or association of employers or any person who acts as a labor relations expert, adviser, or consultant to an employer or who acts in the interest of an employer to pay, lend, or deliver, or agree to pay, lend, or deliver, any money or other thing of value—

(1) to any representative of any of his employees who are employed in an industry affecting commerce; or

(2) to any labor organization, or any officer or employee thereof, which represents, seeks to represent, or would admit to membership, any of the employees of such employer who are employed in an industry affecting commerce;

(3) to any employee or group or committee of employees of such employer employed in an industry affecting commerce in excess of their normal compensation for the purpose of causing such employee or group or committee directly or indirectly to influence any other employees in the exercise of the right to organize and bargain collectively through representatives of their own choosing; or

(4) to any officer or employee of a labor organization engaged in an industry affecting commerce with intent to influence him in respect to any of his actions, decisions, or duties as a representative of employees or as such officer or employee of such labor organization.

(b) [Request, demand, etc., for money or other thing of value]

(1) It shall be unlawful for any person to request, demand, receive, or accept, or agree to receive or accept, any payment, loan, or delivery of any money or other thing of value prohibited by subsection (a) [of this section].

(2) It shall be unlawful for any labor organization, or for any person acting as an officer, agent, representative, or employee of such labor organization, to demand or accept from the operator of any motor vehicle (as defined in part II of the Interstate Commerce Act [49 U.S.C. §301 et seq.]) employed in the transportation of property in commerce, or the employer of any such operator, any money or other thing of value payable to such organization or to an officer, agent, representative or employee thereof as a fee or charge for the unloading, or in connection with the unloading, of the cargo of such vehicle: *Provided,* That nothing in this paragraph shall be construed to make unlawful any payment by an employer to any of his employees as compensation for their services as employees.

(c) [Exceptions] The provisions of this section shall not be applicable (1) in respect to any money or other thing of value payable by an employer to any of his employees whose established duties include acting openly for such employer in matters of labor relations or personnel administration or to any representative of his employees, or to any officer or employee of a labor organization, who is also an employee or former employee of such employer, as compensation for, or by reason of, his service as an employee of such employer; (2) with respect to the payment or delivery of any money or other thing of value in satisfaction of a judgment of any court or a decision or award of an arbitrator or impartial chairman or in compromise, adjustment, settlement, or release of any claim, complaint, grievance, or dispute in the absence of fraud or duress; (3) with respect to the sale or purchase of an article or commodity at the prevailing market price in the regular course of business; (4) with respect to money deducted from the wages of employees in payment of membership dues in a labor organization: *Provided,* That the employer has received from each employee, on whose account such deductions are made, a written assignment which shall not be irrevocable for a period of more than one year, or beyond the termination date of the applicable collective agreement, whichever occurs sooner; (5) with respect to money or other thing of value paid to a trust fund established by such representative, for the sole and exclusive benefit of the employees of such employer, and their families and dependents (or of such employees, families, and dependents jointly with the employees of other employers making similar payments, and their families and dependents): *Provided,* That (A) such payments are held in trust for the purpose of paying, either from principal or income or both, for the benefit of employees, their families and dependents, for medical or hospital care, pensions on retirement or death of employees, compensation for injuries or illness resulting from occupational activity or insurance to provide any of the foregoing, or unemployment benefits or life insurance, disability and sickness insurance, or accident insurance; (B) the detailed basis on which such payments are to be made is specified in a written agreement with the employer, and employees and employers are equally represented in the administration of such fund, together with such neutral persons as the representatives of the employers and the representatives of employees may agree upon and in the event the employer and employee groups deadlock on the administration of such fund and there are no neutral persons empowered to break such deadlock, such agreement provides that the two groups shall agree on an impartial umpire to decide such dispute, or in event of their failure to agree within a reasonable length of time, an impartial umpire to decide such dispute shall, on petition of either group, be appointed by the district court of the United States for the district where the trust fund has its principal office, and shall also contain provisions for an annual audit of the trust fund, a statement of the results of which shall be available for inspection by interested persons at the principal office of the trust fund and at

such other places as may be designated in such written agreement; and (C) such payments as are intended to be used for the purpose of providing pensions or annuities for employees are made to a separate trust which provides that the funds held therein cannot be used for any purpose other than paying such pensions or annuities; (6) with respect to money or other thing of value paid by any employer to a trust fund established by such representative for the purpose of pooled vacation, holiday, severance or similar benefits, or defraying costs of apprenticeship or other training programs: *Provided,* That the requirements of clause (B) of the proviso to clause (5) of this subsection shall apply to such trust funds; (7) with respect to money or other thing of value paid by any employer to a pooled or individual trust fund established by such representative for the purpose of (A) scholarships for the benefit of employees, their families, and dependents for study at educational institutions, (B) child care centers for preschool and school age dependents of employees, or (C) financial assistance for employee housing: *Provided,* That no labor organization or employer shall be required to bargain on the establishment of any such trust fund, and refusal to do so shall not constitute an unfair labor practice: *Provided further,* That the requirements of clause (B) of the proviso to clause (5) of this subsection shall apply to such trust funds; (8) with respect to money or any other thing of value paid by any employer to a trust fund established by such representative for the purpose of defraying the costs of legal services for employees, their families, and dependents for counsel or plan of their choice: *Provided,* That the requirements of clause (B) of the proviso to clause (5) of this subsection shall apply to such trust funds: *Provided further,* That no such legal services shall be furnished: (A) to initiate any proceeding directed (i) against any such employer or its officers or agents except in workman's compensation cases, or (ii) against such labor organization, or its parent or subordinate bodies, or their officers or agents, or (iii) against any other employer or labor organization, or their officers or agents, in any matter arising under the National Labor Relations Act, or this Act [under subchapter II of this chapter or this chapter]; and (B) in any proceeding where a labor organization would be prohibited from defraying the costs of legal services by the provisions of the Labor-Management Reporting and Disclosure Act of 1959 [29 U.S.C. §401 et seq.]; or (9) with respect to money or other things of value paid by an employer to a plant, area or industry wide labor management committee established for one or more of the purposes set forth in section 5(b) of the Labor Management Cooperation Act of 1978.

[Sec. 302(c)(7) was added by Pub. L. 91-86, Oct. 14, 1969, 83 Stat. 133; Sec. 302(c)(8) by Pub. L. 93-95, Aug. 15, 1973, 87 Stat. 314; Sec. 302(c)(9) by Pub. L. 95-524, Oct. 27, 1978, 92 Stat. 2021; and Sec. 302(c)(7) was amended by Pub. L. 101-273, Apr. 18, 1990, 104 Stat. 138.]

(d) [Penalty for violations] Any person who willfully violates any of the provisions of this section shall, upon conviction thereof, be guilty of a misdemeanor and be subject to a fine of not more than $10,000 or to imprisonment for not more than one year, or both.

(e) [Jurisdiction of courts] The district courts of the United States and the United States courts of the Territories and possessions shall have jurisdiction, for cause shown, and subject to the provisions of rule 65 of the Federal Rules of Civil Procedure [section 381 (repealed) of title 28] (relating to notice to opposite party) to restrain violations of this section, without regard to the provisions of section 7 of title 15 and section 52 of title 29, United States Code [of this title] [known as the "Clayton Act"], and the provisions of sections 101 to 115 of title 29, United States Code [chapter 6 of this title] [known as the "Norris–La Guardia Act"].

(f) [Effective date of provisions] This section shall not apply to any contract in force on June 23, 1947, until the expiration of such contract, or until July 1, 1948, whichever first occurs.

(g) [Contributions to trust funds] Compliance with the restrictions contained in subsection (c)(5)(B) [of this section] upon contributions to trust funds, otherwise lawful, shall not be applicable to contributions to such trust funds established by collective agreement prior to January 1, 1946, nor shall subsection (c)(5)(A) [of this section] be construed as prohibiting contributions to such trust funds if prior to January 1, 1947, such funds contained provisions for pooled vacation benefits.

BOYCOTTS AND OTHER UNLAWFUL COMBINATIONS

Sec. 303. [§187.] (a) It shall be unlawful, for the purpose of this section only, in an industry or activity affecting commerce, for any labor organization to engage in any activity or conduct defined as an unfair labor practice in section 8(b)(4) of the National Labor Relations Act [section 158(b)(4) of this title].

(b) Whoever shall be injured in his business or property by reason of any violation of subsection (a) [of this section] may sue therefor in any district court of the United States subject to the limitation and provisions of section 301 hereof [section 185 of this title] without respect to the amount in controversy, or in any other court having jurisdiction of the parties, and shall recover the damages by him sustained and the cost of the suit.

RESTRICTION ON POLITICAL CONTRIBUTIONS

Sec. 304. Repealed.

[See sec. 316 of the Federal Election Campaign Act of 1972, 2 U.S.C. §441b.]

Sec. 305.[§188.] Strikes by Government employees. Repealed.

[See 5 U.S.C. §7311 and 18 U.S.C. §1918.]

TITLE IV
[Title 29, Chapter 7, Subchapter V, United States Code]

CREATION OF JOINT COMMITTEE TO STUDY AND REPORT ON BASIC PROBLEMS AFFECTING FRIENDLY LABOR RELATIONS AND PRODUCTIVITY

Secs. 401-407. [§§191–97.] Omitted.

TITLE V
[Title 29, Chapter 7, Subchapter I, United States Code]

DEFINITIONS

Sec. 501. [§142.] When used in this Act [chapter]—

(1) The term "industry affecting commerce" means any industry or activity in commerce or in which a labor dispute would burden or obstruct commerce or tend to burden or obstruct commerce or the free flow of commerce.

(2) The term "strike" includes any strike or other concerted stoppage of work by employees (including a stoppage by reason of the expiration of a collective-bargaining agreement) and any concerted slowdown or other concerted interruption of operations by employees.

(3) The terms "commerce," "labor disputes," "employer," "employee," "labor organization," "representative," "person," and "supervisor" shall have the same meaning as when used in the National Labor Relations Act as amended by this Act [in subchapter II of this chapter].

SAVING PROVISION

Sec. 502. [§143.] [Abnormally dangerous conditions] Nothing in this Act [chapter] shall be construed to require an individual employee to render labor or service without his consent, nor shall anything in this Act [chapter] be construed to make the quitting of his labor by an individual employee an illegal act; nor shall any court issue any process to compel the performance by an individual employee of such labor or service, without his consent; nor shall the quitting of labor by an employee or employees in good faith because of abnormally dangerous conditions for work at the place of employment of such employee or employees be deemed a strike under this Act [chapter].

SEPARABILITY

Sec. 503. [§144.] If any provision of this Act [chapter], or the application of such provision to any person or circumstance, shall be held invalid, the remainder of this Act [chapter], or the application of such provision to persons or circumstances other than those as to which it is held invalid, shall not be affected thereby.

Notes

Preface

1. Railway Labor Act, at 45 USC sec. 181.

1. Public Policy and Labor Law

1. J. Berkeley, J. Rouse, and R. Begovich, *The Craft of Public Administration* (Dubuque, IA: Brown, 1984), 99.

2. *Webster's Encyclopedia Unabridged Dictionary of the English Language*, 10th ed., s.v. "policy."

3. T. R. Dye, *Understanding Public Policy*, 3rd ed. (Englewood Cliffs, NJ: Prentice Hall, 1978), 3.

4. C. E. Cochren, L. C. Mayer, T. R. Carr, and N. Joseph Cayer, *American Public Policy*, 3rd ed. (New York: St. Martin's, 1990), 2.

5. Morrison Waite quoted in A. P. Melone, *Researching Constitutional Law* (New York: Harper Collins, 1990), 137–38.

6. *Wabash, St. Louis, and Pacific Railroad Company v. Illinois*, 118 U.S. 557 (1886), 563–77.

7. "Interstate Commerce Commission." *West's Encyclopedia of American Law*, vol. 6 (St. Paul, MN: West, 1998), 209–10.

8. A. Millbrooke, *Aviation History* (Englewood, CO: Jeppesen Sanderson, 1999).

9. S. H. Beer, "The Modernization of American Federalism," *Publius: The Journal of Federalism* (Fall 1973): 65.

10. R. M. Kane, *Air Transportation*, 14th ed. (Dubuque, IA: Kendall Hunt, 2003).

11. T. A. Heppenheimer, *Turbulent Skies: The History of Commercial Aviation* (New York: Wiley, 1995).

12. S. Morrison and C. Winston, *The Evolution of the Airline Industry* (Washington, DC: Brookings Institution, 1995).

13. S. Morrison and C. Winston, *The Economic Effects of Airline Deregulation* (Washington, DC: Brookings Institution, 1986).

14. "A Chronology of Dates Significant in the Background, History and Development of the Department of Transportation," *U.S. Department of Transportation Office of the Historian*, 2008, http://dotlibrary.dot.gov/Historian/chronology.htm (July 3, 2008).

15. D. Altman, "Airline Shock Waves: The Process; Others Failed, but This Bankruptcy Is Given a Chance," *New York Times*, August 13, 2002, http://query.nytimes.com/gst/fullpage.html?res=980 7E7D7103AF930A2575BC0A9649C8B63&sec= &spon=&pagewanted=1 (July 2, 2008).

16. G. W. Miller, *Problems of Labor* (New York: Macmillan, 1951), 493.

17. "Air Transportation," *Bureau of Labor Statistics*, March 12, 2008, http://www.bls.gov/oco/cg/cgs016.htm (September 22, 2008).

18. D. A. Borer, "Doing Battle: Flight Attendant Labor Relations in the 1990s," in Handbook of Airline Economics, ed. Darryl Jenkins (New York: Aviation Week, 1999), 567.

19. P. Lane, "Striking Flight Attendants Suspended—Union Delays Its First Alaska Trip," *Seattle (WA) Times*, August 23, 1993, http://community.seattletimes.nwsource.com/archive/?date=19930823 &slug=1717322 (July 8, 2008).

20. "Alaska Airline Workers Delay Las Vegas Flight," *Seattle (WA) Times*, August 25, 1993, http://community.seattletimes.nwsource.com/archive/?date=19930825&slug=1717643 (August 8, 2008).

21. "Alaska Suspends 17 More Attendants After Flights Disrupted," *Seattle (WA) Times*, September 14, 1999, http://community.seattletimes.nwsource.com

/archive/?date=19930914&slug=1720989 (July 9, 2008).

22. "US Airways Flight Attendants Hold News Conference," *CNN*, 11:03 A.M. ET, March 24, 2000, http://transcripts.cnn.com/TRANSCRIPTS/0003/24/se.02.html.

23. G. Meyer, "UAL Flight Attendants Threaten CHAOS," *Crain's Chicago Business*, April 29, 2005, http://www.chicagobusiness.com/cgi-bin/news.pl?id=16328 (July 8, 2008).

24. D. Russakoff, "Cabin Pressure—The Union Promises to Wreak 'Chaos' As Another Carrier Downsizes a Career," *Washington Post*, August 26, 2006, http://www.washingtonpost.com/wp-dyn/content/article/2006/08/24/AR2006082402002.html?nav=rss_business/special/1 (July 9, 2008).

25. P. Cassidy, "Court Upholds Strike Ban on Northwest's Flight Attendants," *Market Watch*, March 29, 2007, http://www.marketwatch.com/news/story/court-upholds-strike-ban-northwests/story.aspx?guid=%7BF746479D-9C47-43B7-9E11-BE1C01645990%7D (July 8, 2008).

26. "Northwest Flight Attendants Okay Bargaining Agreement," *Reuters*, May 29, 2007, http://www.reuters.com/article/businessNews/idUSWEN844920070530 (July 9, 2008).

27. "Northwest Airlines," *Answers.com*, 2011, http://www.answers.com/topic/northwest-airlines-corporation (January 28, 2011).

28. A. T. Wells, *Air Transportation: A Management Perspective* (Belmont, CA: Wadsworth, 1989), 164–65.

29. "Annual Report," *Regional Airline Association*, 1991, 10.

30. "U.S. Regional Airline Fact Sheet," *Regional Airline Association*, 2008.

31. "Annual Report," 12.

32. "Regional Carrier Full-time Equivalent Employees," Research and Innovative Technology Administration, Bureau of Transportation Statistics, *U.S. Department of Transportation*, (2006).

33. "Annual Report," *Regional Airline Association*, 1991, 12.

34. "U.S. Regional Airline Fact Sheet," *Regional Airline Association*, 2008.

35. "FAA Aviation Forecasts: Fiscal Years 1991–2002," U.S. Department of Transportation, Federal Aviation Administration (Washington, DC: GPO, 1991), 101.

36. Ibid., 99.

37. "AOPA's 2006 Fact Card," *Aircraft Owners and Pilots Association*, http://www.aopa.org/whatsnew/factcard.pdf (July 2, 2008).

38. "GA: Serving Your Community," *Aircraft Owners and Pilots Association*, 2008, http://www.gaservingamerica.org/Serving_Your_Community/jobs.htm (July 2, 2008).

39. "NATA Fact Sheet," *National Air Transportation Association*, 2008, http://www.nata.aero/pressroom/factsheet.jsp (July 2, 2008).

40. Berkeley, Rouse, and Begovich, *Craft of Public Administration*, 111.

41. Ibid., 112.

42. D. Lewin and S. B. Goldenberg, "Public Sector Unionism in the U.S. and Canada," *Industrial Relations* 19, no. 3 (Fall 1980): 239–56.

43. J. Wurf, "Establishing the Legal Right of Public Employees to Bargain," *Monthly Labor Review* (October 1978): 13–23, 67–69, 106.

44. J. Wurf, "Labor's Battle with Itself," *Washington Post*, October 14, 1973, C3.

45. H. C. Black, *Black's Law Dictionary*, 4th ed. (St. Paul, MN: West, 1968), 1568, s.v. "sovereignty."

46. William Adelman, "Pullman, 1894," *theunionsteward.com*, http://www.theunionsteward.com/Shop_Steward_Labor_History.html.

47. R. M. Tobias, "The Future of Federal Government Labor Relations and the Mutual Interest of Congress, the Administration and Unions," *Journal of Labor Research* 25, no. 1 (Winter 2004): 19–42.

48. D. H. Rosenbloom, *Public Administration: Understanding Management, Politics, and Law in the Public Sector*, 2d ed. (New York: Random, 1989), 232.

49. "Professional Air Traffic Controllers Organization Records, 1968–1982," no. L1986–45, Manuscript Collection, Special Collections and Archives Department, Georgia State University Library.

50. Berkeley, Rouse, and Begovich, *Craft of Public Administration*, 148.

51. A. Sloane and F. Witney, *Labor Relations*, 12th ed. (Upper Saddle River, NJ: Prentice Hall, 2007).

52. George Meany quoted in Chester A. Newland, "Collective Bargaining Concepts: Applications in

Government," *Public Administration Review* 28, no. 2 (March–April 1968): 135.

2. The Violent Beginnings of U.S. Labor Law

1. T. G. Moore, *Freight Transport Regulation* (Washington, DC: American Enterprise Institute, 1972), 23.

2. Selig Perlman, *A History of Trade Unionism in the United States* (New York: Macmillan, 1922), 3–18.

3. Fred Knee, "Revolt of Labor," *Social Democrat*, November 1910, 144.

4. Arthur Sloane, *Labor Relations*, 3rd ed. (Englewood Cliffs, NJ: Prentice Hall, 1977), 59–60.

5. Richard Rosecrance, "Why England Slipped," *Wilson Quarterly* 11, no. 4 (Fall 1987): 101.

6. Jerre S. Williams, *Labor Relations & the Law*, 3rd ed. (Boston: Little, Brown, 1965), 20.

7. Daniel Q. Mills, *Labor-Management Problems* (New York: McGraw-Hill, 1980), 31.

8. *West's Encyclopedia of American Law*, n.d., s.v. "Lemuel Shaw," http://www.answers.com/topic/lemuel-shaw (February 26, 2007).

9. Omar Swartz, "Defending Labor in *Commonwealth v. Pullis*: Contemporary Implications for Rethinking Community," *Murdoch University Electronic Journal of Law*, 11, no. 1 (March 2004).

10. Charles O. Gregory and Harold A. Katz, *Labor and the Law*, 3rd ed. (New York: Norton, 1979), 29.

11. 45 Mass. 111 (1842).

12. Charles M. Rehmus, "Evolution of Legislation Affecting Collective Bargaining in the Railroad and Airline Industries," in *The Railway Labor Act at Fifty*, ed. Rehmus (Washington, DC: GPO, 1977), 1.

13. Sloane, *Labor Relations*, 58.

14. Frank N. Wilner, *The Railway Labor Act & the Dilemma of Labor Relations* (Omaha, NE: Simmons-Boardman), 25.

15. Sloane, *Labor Relations*, 58–59.

16. Mills, *Labor-Management Problems*, 33.

17. Sanford Cohen, *Labor in the United States* (Columbus, OH: Merrill, 1960), 59.

18. Jonathan Grossman, *William Sylvis, Pioneer of American Labor* (New York: Columbia University Press, 1945), 56.

19. Philip S. Foner, *History of the Labor Movement in the United States. Vol. 1: From Colonial Times to the Founding of the American Federation of Labor* (New York: International, 1947), 39.

20. Melvyn Dubofsky, *Industrialism and the American Worker: 1865–1920*, 2nd ed. (Arlington Heights, IL: Davidson, 1985), 135–36.

21. Foster R. Dulles, *Labor in America* (New York: Crowell, 1966), 140.

22. Melvyn Dubofsky and Foster Dulles, *Labor in America: A History*, 6th ed. (Wheeling IL: Davidson, 1999), 86–88.

23. Fred A. Perlman, *A History of Trade Unionism in the United States* (New York: Macmillan, 1929), 68.

24. Dubofsky and Dulles, *Labor in America*, 78.

25. Ibid., 95.

26. Perlman, *History of Trade Unionism in the United States*, 123–24.

27. John A. Fossum, *Labor Relations: Development, Structure, Process*, 7th ed. (Boston: McGraw-Hill, 1999), 213.

28. Sigmund A. Lavine, *Allan Pinkerton—America's First Private Eye* (New York: Dodd, Mead, 1963), 71.

29. Dubofsky and Dulles, *Labor in America*, 96.

30. J. Mackay, *Allan Pinkerton: The First Private Eye* (New York: Wiley, 1996).

31. C. M. Robinson, *American Frontier Lawmen 1850–1930* (Oxford, UK: Osprey, 2005).

32. F. Voss and J. Barber, *We Never Sleep: The First Fifty Years of the Pinkertons* (Washington, DC: Smithsonian Institution, 1941).

33. J. P. Josephson, *Allan Pinkerton: The Original Private Eye* (Minneapolis: Lerner, 1996).

34. A. Axelrod, *The War between the Spies* (New York: Atlantic Monthly, 1992).

35. J. D. Horan and H. Swiggett, The Pinkerton Story (New York: Putnam, 1951).

36. F. Morn, *The Eye That Never Sleeps: A History of the Pinkerton National Detective Agency* (Bloomington: Indiana University Press, 1982).

37. D. R. Williams, *Call in Pinkerton's: American Detectives at Work for Canada* (Toronto: Dundurn, 1998).

38. David Wallechinsky and Irving Wallace, *The Peoples Almanac* (Garden City, NY: Doubleday, 1975), 206.

39. Florence Peterson, *Strikes in the U.S.* (Washington, DC: GPO, 1938), 30.

40. Wilner, *Railway Labor Act*, 28.

41. "American Experience: The Rockefellers," *PBSOnline*, 2000, http://www.pbs.org/wgbh/amex/rockefellers/sfeature/sf_8.html (September 5, 2008).

42. "Colorado Coal Field War Project, *University of Denver*, http://www.du.edu/anthro/ludlow (September 5, 2008).

43. Alex Aspden, "1914—The Ludlow Massacre," *libcom.org*, September 11, 2006, http://libcom.org/history/1914-the-ludlow-massacre (September 4, 2008).

44. L. Stein and P. Taft, *Massacre at Ludlow: Four Reports* (New York: Arno, 1971), 22–23.

45. "The Ludlow Massacre," *United Mine Workers of America*, n.d., http://www.umwa.org/jistory/ludlow.shtml (September 5, 2008).

46. Gerald G. Eggert, *Railroad Labor Disputes* (Ann Arbor: University of Michigan Press, 1967), 59.

47. Rehmus, "Evolution of Legislation," 4.

48. C. Nash, M. Wardman, K. Button, and P. Nijkamp, eds., *Classics in Transportation Analysis: Railroads* (Northampton, MA: Elgar, 2002), 191.

49. Eric Bashers, *Conrail: Government Creation and Privatization of an American Railroad*, INU Discussion Paper 38 (Washington, DC: Infrastructure and Urban Development, 1989), 1.

50. 25 Stat. 209 (1890) 15 U.S.C. 1–7.

51. *Plant v. Woods*, 57 N.E. 1011(Mass. 1900).

52. Ibid.

53. Wilner, *Railway Labor Act*, 13.

54. Edwin E. White, *The Government in Labor Disputes* (New York: McGraw Hill, 1931), 234.

55. *Loewe v. Lawler*, 208 U.S. 274 (1908).

56. *Hitchman Coal & Coke Company v. Mitchell*, 245 U.S. 229.

57. Mills, *Labor-Management Problems*, 35–36.

58. 245 U.S. 229 (1917).

59. *Adair v. United States*, 208 U.S. 161 (1908).

60. Nash, Wardman, Button, and Nijkamp, *Classics in Transportation Analysis*, 192.

61. Wilner, *Railway Labor Act*, 34.

62. John F. Stover, *The Life and Decline of the American Railroad* (New York: Oxford University Press, 1970), 120.

63. *Wilson v. New*, 243 U.S. 382 (1917).

64. *Loechner v. United States*, 198 U.S. 45 (1905).

65. Edwin Witte, *The Government in Labor Disputes* (New York: McGraw-Hill, 1932), 68–69.

66. Clayton Act, 38 Stat. 730 (1914).

67. Melvyn Dubofsky, *The State and Labor in Modern America* (Chapel Hill: University of North Carolina Press, 1994).

68. *Duplex Printing v. Deering*, 254 U.S. 443 (1921).

69. *Bedford Cut Stone Co. v. Journeymen Stone Cutters Association of North America*, 274 U.S. 37 (1927).

70. 39 Stat. 619, 643 (1916).

71. John F. Stover, *The Life and Decline of the American Railroad* (New York: Oxford University Press, 1970), 166.

72. Rehmus, "Evolution of Legislation," 6.

73. Harry D. Wolf, *The Railroad Labor Board* (New York: Columbia University Press, 1971), 58.

74. Leonard Lecht, *Experience under Railway Labor Legislation* (New York: Columbia University Press, 1955), 36.

75. Wolf, *Railroad Labor Board*, 58. The authors extrapolated the information concerning railroad unionization statistics.

76. Nash, Wardman, Button, and Nijkamp, *Classics in Transportation Analysis*, 192.

77. Austin K. Kerr, *American Railroad Politics* (Pittsburgh: University of Pittsburgh Press, 1968), 204.

78. *Pennsylvania RR. v. United States Railway Labor Board*, 261 U.S. 72.

79. *Pennsylvania Railroad System v. Pennsylvania Railroad Company*, 267 U.S. 203; 45 SCt 307; 69 LEd 574.

80. Jacob J. Kaufman, *Collective Bargaining in the Railroad Industry* (New York: Kings Crown, 1954), 65.

81. Wilner, *Railway Labor Act*, 46.

3. Major Collective Bargaining Legislation

1. K. Austin Kerr, *American Railroad Politics* (Pittsburgh: University of Pittsburgh Press, 1968), 41.

2. Irving Bernstein, *The New Deal Collective Bargaining Policy* (Los Angeles: University of California Press, 1950), 41.

3. Irving Bernstein, *The Lean Years* (Boston: Houghton Mifflin, 1960), 216.

4. Charles M. Rehmus, "Evolution of Legislation Affecting Collective Bargaining in the Railroad and Airline Industries," in *The Railway Labor Act at Fifty*, ed. Rehmus (Washington, DC: GPO, 1976), 8.

5. *Texas and New Orleans Railroad v. the Brotherhood of Railway and Steamship Clerks*, 281 U.S. 548 (1930).

6. *Adair v. United States*, 208 U.S. 161 (1908).

7. Charles O. Gregory, *Labor Laws and Legislation* (New York: Norton, 1958), 253.

8. Beatrice M. Burgoon, "Mediation under the Railway Labor Act," in *The Railroad Labor Act at Fifty*, ed. Charles Rehmus (Washington, DC: GPO, 1976), 23.

9. National Mediation Board, *Fifty-Third and Fifty-Fourth Report* (Washington, DC: GPO, 1989), 15.

10. "Rules, Title 29, Chapter X," *National Mediation Board*, n.d., http://www.nmb.gov/documents/nmbrules1099.html (February 7, 2008).

11. John W. Gohmann, *Air and Rail Labor Relations* (Dubuque, IA: Kendall Hunt, 1979), 5.

12. 45 USC sec. 154.

13. 45 USC sec. 155.

14. 45 USC sec. 155–60.

15. Bernstein, *Lean Years*, 43.

16. Leonard Lecht, *Experience under Railway Labor Legislation* (New York: Columbia University Press, 1955), 79.

17. H. Lawrence, *Aviation and the Role of the Government* (Dubuque, IA: Kendall Hunt, 2004).

18. John M. Baitsell, *Airline Industrial Relations: Pilots and Flight Engineers* (Cambridge, MA: Harvard University Press, 1966), 32.

19. Lindley H. Clark, "Airlines and Railroads: A Weird Marriage," *Wall Street Journal*, March 15, 1988.

20. *Railway Employees' Department v. Hanson*, 351 U.S. 225 (1956).

21. *Norris–La Guardia Act*, 47 Stat. 70 (1932).

22. Edward L. Barrett Jr., *Constitutional Law* (Westbury, NY: Foundation, 1989), 213.

23. National Industrial Recovery Act, 48 Stat. 198 (1933).

24. *Schechter Poultry Corp. v. United States*, 295 U.S. 495 (1935).

25. John Stern, "Collective Bargaining Legislation or Negotiation," *Harvard Law Review* 59 (June–July 1955), 657–63.

26. Barrett, *Constitutional Law*, 222.

27. 29 USC sec. 159–60.

28. *Schechter Poultry Corp. v. United States*, 295 U.S. 495 (1935).

29. *NLRB v. Jones and Laughlin Steel Corp.*, 301 U.S. 1 (1937). In addition to the *Jones & Laughlin* decision, four companion cases involving the constitutionality of the Wagner Act were decided by the Supreme Court: *NLRB v. Fruehauf Trailer Co.*, *NLRB v. Friedman-Harry Marks Clothing Co.*, *Washington, Virginia & Maryland Coach Co. v. NLRB*, and *Associated Press v. NLRB*.

30. Reed C. Richardson, *Collective Bargaining Objectives* (Englewood Cliffs, NJ: Prentice Hall, 1971), 37.

31. Ibid., 64.

32. Daniel Quinn Mills, *Labor-Management Relations*, 3rd ed. (New York: McGraw-Hill, 1986), 41.

33. *Retail Clerks, Local 1625 v. Schermerhorn*, 375 U.S. 96 (1963).

34. Kathleen Schalch, "1981 Strike Leaves Legacy for American Workers," *NPR.com*, August 3, 2006, http://www.npr.org/templates/story/story.php?storyId=5604656 (February 7, 2008).

35. S. Early, "An Old Lesson Still Holds for Unions," *Boston Globe*, July 31, 2006, http://www.boston.com/news/globe/editorial_opinion/oped/articles/2006/07/31/an_old_lesson_still_holds_for_unions?mode=PF (March 13, 2008).

36. Laura Mills-Alcott, "It's Always Morning in America," *Romance Club*, June 2004, http://www.theromanceclub.com/reagan/ (March 12, 2008).

37. Elizabeth Schulte, "The Defeat of PATCO: Signal of the Employers' Offensive," *SocialistWorker.org*, September 8, 2006, http://www.socialistworker.org/2006-2/600/600_08_PATCO.shtml (accessed March 14, 2008; link no longer available).

38. R. Pels, "The Pressures of PATCO: Strikes and Stress in the 1980s," *Essays in History* 37 (1995), http://etext.lib.virginia.edu/journals/EH/EH37?Pels.html (March 18, 2008).

39. J. Manning, "The Politics and Pop Culture of the 1980s: The Air Traffic Controllers' Strike," *Eighties Club*, 2000, http://eightiesclub.tripod.com/id296.htm (March 12, 2008).

40. A. Shostak and D. V. Skocik, *The Air Controllers' Controversy: Lessons from the PATCO Strike* (New York: Human Sciences, 1986).

41. Elizabeth Schulte, "Lessons of the PATCO Strike," August 3, 2001, reprint, *Socialistworker.org*, February 25, 2011, http://www.peacewww.socialistworker.org/2011/02/25/lessons-of-the-patco-strike (March 14, 2008).

42. Manning, *Politics and Pop Culture of the 1980s*.

43. Mills-Alcott, *It's Always Morning in America*.

44. R. Alton Lee, *Truman and Taft-Hartley* (Garden City, NY: Doubleday, 1980).

45. C. Northcote Parkinson, *Internal Disruption* (London: Leviathan, 1981), 131.

46. Landrum-Griffin Act, 73 Stat. 519, Section 2(b) (1959).

47. "Compliance Assistance—Fair Labor Standards Act (FLSA)," *U.S. Department of Labor: Employment Standards Administration Wage and Hour Division*, n.d., http://www.dol.gov/esa/whd/flsa/ (February 7, 2008).

48. Jay P. Lechner, "The New FLSA White-Collar Regulations—Analysis of Changes," *Florida Bar Journal* 79 (2005) www.floridabar.org/.../06A4630683BB9A20852570C70057ECF4 (February 6, 2008).

49. John Fraser, Monica Gallagher, and Gail Coleman, "Observations on the Department of Labor's Final Regulations: Defining and Delimiting the Exemptions for Executive, Administrative, Professional, Outside Sales, and Computer Employees," *AFL-CIO*, July 2004, http://www.aflcio.org/issues/jobseconomy/overtimepay/upload/OvertimeStudyTextfinal.pdf (February 7, 2008).

50. *NLRB v. Bildisco & Bildisco*, 104 U.S. 118 (1984).

51. "A Brief History of Bankruptcy in the U.S.," *Ruth Technology Corporation*, n.d., http://www.lawfirmsoftware.com/learning_center/bankruptcy/history.htm (February 4, 2008).

52. "Bankruptcy Terms," *BankruptcyHome.com*, n.d., http://www.bankruptcyhome.com/glossary.htm (February 5, 2008).

53. "The Equal Pay Act of 1963," *U.S. Equal Employment Opportunity Commission*, n.d., http://www.eeoc.gov/policy/epa.html (February 4, 2008).

4. Elections, Certifications, and Procedures

1. *Gibbons v. Ogden*, 22 U.S. 1 (1824).

2. *Champion v. Ames*, 188 U.S. 100 (1902); *Schechter Corp. v. U.S.*, 295 U.S. 495 (1935); *NLRB v. Jones and Laughlin Steel Corp.*, 301 U.S. 1 (1937); *U.S. v. Darby*, 312 U.S. 100 (1941).

3. *Virginia Ry. v. System Federation*, 300 U.S. 515, 556, 81 L. Ed. 789, 57 S. Ct. 592 (1937).

4. *Verret v. SABRE Group Inc.*, 70 F.Supp.2d 1277, 1282 (N.D. Okla. 1999).

5. 32 NMB no. 42.

6. Paul, Hastings, Janofsky, and Walker LLP, *An Introduction to the Railway Labor Act* (Washington, DC: Paul, Hastings, Janofsky, and Walker, 2005), http://www.bna.com/bnabooks/ababna/annual/2005/015.pdf.

7. *Chelsea Catering Corporation*, 19 NMB 301 (1992).

8. *Aeroguard Inc.*, 28 NMB 1996.

9. Ibid.

10. *System One Corp.*, 322 NLRB 732 (1996).

11. *Verret v. SABRE Group Inc.*, 70 F.Supp.2d 1277, 1282 (N.D. Okla. 1999).

12. *Federal Express Corp.*, 23 N.M.B. 32, 69–70 (1995).

13. *United Parcel Service Inc.*, 318 NLRB 778, 150 LRRM 1049 (1995).

14. *United Parcel Service Inc. v. NLRB*, 92 F.3d 1221, 153 LRRM 2001 (D.C. Cir. 1996).

15. J. Roberts, "FedEx Dealt Blow on Unionizing," *Commercialappeal.com*, June 29, 2007, http://www.commercialappeal.com/mca/business/article/0,1426,MCA_440_5607525,00.html (September 22, 2008).

16. "UPS Works to Hobble Its Rival FedEx," July 11, 2007, *Hill*, http://republicanpartyconvention.com/homenews/news/12512-ups-works-to-hobble-its-rival-fedex.

17. Ibid.

18. Bartholomew Sullivan, "Smith Defends Railway Labor Act Jurisdiction," *Commercialappeal.com*, July 20, 2007 http://www.commercialappeal.com/news/2007/jul/20/smith-defends-railway-labor-act-jurisdiction/.

19. Roberts, "FedEx Dealt Blow on Unionizing."

20. *Northwest Airlines Inc.*, 2 NMB 19 (1948); *Northwest Airlines Inc.*, 2 NMB 25 (1948).

21. *Braniff Airways*, 5 NMB 6 (1968); *Frontier Airlines Inc.*, 5 NMB 88 (1970).

22. *International Brotherhood of Teamsters & Midway Airlines Inc.*, 18 NMB 42, NMB R-6021 (1991).

23. *Nelson v. Piedmont Aviation*, 750 F.2d 1234 (4th Cir. 1984), cert denied, 471 U.S. 1116 (1985).

24. *IFFA v. Trans World Airlines*, 819 F.2d 839 (8th Cir. 1987).

25. 45 U.S.C. 152, Ninth (1982).

26. 45 U.S.C. 151, Sixth (1988).

27. 45 U.S.C. 151a, Ninth (1988).

28. *Brotherhood of Railway & Steamship Clerks, Freight Handlers, Express & Station Employees v. Association for the Benefit of Non-Contract Employees*, 380 U.S. 650 (1965).

29. 29 CFR 101.4 (1991).

30. 29 CFR 1203.2 (1991).

31. Ibid.

32. National Mediation Board, *Administration of the Railway Labor Act* (Washington, DC: GPO, 1970), 66.

33. *Erie Railroad Company*, 3 NMB 187 (1955).

34. 29 CFR 1206.4 (1991).

35. 45 U.S.C. 152, Ninth (1988).

36. *National Federation of Railroad Workers v. NMB*, 110 2d 529 (1940).

37. *International In-Flight Catering Co. v. NMB*, 121 DLRA-6 (9th Cir., 1977).

38. Ibid.

39. *Virginian Railroad Company v. System Federation*, 300 U.S. 515 (1937).

40. 29 CFR 1202.5 (1991).

41. 29 CFR 1202.7 (1991).

42. 45 U.S.C. 152, Ninth (1988).

43. Ibid.

44. 1 NMB 167 (1940).

45. *Switchman's Union v. NMB*, 320 U.S. 297 (1943).

46. Ibid.

47. 29 CFR 1202.8 (1991).

48. 45 U.S.C. 151a, Ninth (1988).

49. *American Airlines Inc.*, 1 NMB 394, 399 (1945).

50. 6 NMB 180 (1977).

51. *American Airlines Inc.*, 1 NMB 371 (1944).

52. *United Airlines Inc.*, 3 NMB 56 (1961).

53. *American Airlines*, 1 NMB 394 (1945).

54. *Continental Airlines*, NMB R-2714 (1953); *Pan American World Airways*, NMB R-2777 (1953).

55. 45 U.S.C. 152, Fourth (1988).

56. *Virginian Railroad Company v. System Federation*, no. 40, 300 U.S. 515, 547 (1937).

57. 45 U.S.C. sec. 152.

58. James Ott, "Board Decisions Muddle Rules on Unions' Role after Mergers," *Aviation Week and Space Technology*, August 28, 1989.

59. "Current Labor Statistics," *Monthly Labor Review*, April 1990, 49–100.

60. Kate Bronfenbrenner, *Prepared Statement for the National Mediation Board Open Meeting Re; RLA Rulemaking Docket No. C 6964*, December 7, 2009, http://www.nmb.gov/representation/proposed-rulemaking/bronfenbrenner.pdf.

61. Ibid.

62. 75 Fed. Reg. 90 (May 11, 2010), 26062–89.

63. Jad Mouawad, "In a Narrow Vote, Delta Flight Attendants Reject a Unionization Effort," *New York Times*, November 3, 2010, http://www.nytimes.com/2010/11/04/business/04delta.html.

64. *Russell v. NMB*, 1983.

65. *Chamber of Commerce*, 14 NMB 347 (1987).

66. *Ohio Power Company & Utility Workers Union of America*, 23 LRRM 1242, 80 NLRB 205 (1948).

67. Ibid.

68. *NLRB v. Textron Inc.*, 85 LRRM 2945 (1974).

69. *B. F. Goodrich & Co. and Local No. 281*, 37 LRRM 1383, 115 NLRB 103 (1956).

70. National Labor Relations Board, *A Guide to Basic Law and Procedures under the National Labor Relations Act* (Washington, DC: GPO, 1990), 43.

71. *Advance Pattern Co. & Printing Specialists and Paper Converters Union*, no. 363, 23 LRRM 1022, 80 NLRB 10 (1948).

72. *Kennecott Copper Corp.*, 29 LRRM 1300, 98 NLRB 14 (1952).

73. *J. C. Penney & Retail Clerks Intl.*, 25 LRRM 1039, 86 NLRB 109 (1949).

74. Daniel Quinn Mills, *Labor-Management Relations*, 4th ed. (New York: McGraw-Hill, 1989), 118.

75. *NLRB v. Metropolitan Life Ins. Co.*, 58 LRRM 2721, 380 U.S. 438 (1965).

76. *B. F. Goodrich & Co. and Local No. 281*, 37 LRRM 1383, 115 NLRB 103 (1956).

77. *National Torch Tip Co.*, 33 LRRM 1369, 107 NLRB 269 (1954).

78. *Booth Broadcasting Co.*, 49 LRRM 1278, 134 NLRB 80 (1961).

79. *Sportswear Industries Inc.*, 56 LRRM 1307, 147 NLRB 79 (1964).

80. Mills, *Labor-Management Relations*, 117.

81. *National Tube Co.*, 21 LRRM 1292, 76 NLRB 169 (1948).

82. *American Potash & Chemical Corp.*, 33 LRRM 1380, 107 NLRB 290 (1954).

83. *Mallinckrodt Chemical Works*, 64 LRRM 1011 (1966).

84. Michael Ballot, *Labor Management Relations in a Changing Environment* (New York: Wiley, 1992), 170.

85. *Brooks v. NLRB*, 348 U.S. 96 (1954).

5. Negotiating the Collective Bargaining Agreement

1. Robert N. Corley, *The Legal Environment of Business* (New York: McGraw-Hill, 1977).

2. Leonard R. Saleys and George Strauss, *Managing Human Resources* (Englewood Cliffs, NJ: Prentice Hall, 1981).

3. Daniel Quinn Mills, *Labor-Management Relations*, 3rd ed. (New York: McGraw-Hill, 1986).

4. International Brotherhood of Teamsters Professional Aviators Local 1108 (2008), *International Brotherhood of Teamsters Professional Aviators Local 1108*, http://www.ibt1108.org (July 10, 2008).

5. "NetJets Aviation and Teamsters Announce Approved Amendment," *Fractional News* (December 10, 2007), http://www.fractionalnews.com/fractional-aircraft-news/netjets-aviation-and-teamsters-announce-approved-amendment.html.

6. B. Spangler, "Integrative or Interest-Based Bargaining," *BeyondIntractability.org,* June 2003, http://www.beyondintractability.org/essay/interest-based_bargaining (July 10, 2008).

7. C. Trautvetter, "NetJets Pilots Set Another High Salary Standard," February 1, 2008, *AINOnline*, http://www.ainonline.com/news/single-news-page/article/netjets-pilots-set-another-high-salary-standard/?no_cache=1&cHash=20823d4ca3 (July 10, 2008).

8. Ibid.

9. "NetJets Pilots' Contract Amended and Extended," *Professional Pilot News*, January 5, 2008 http://propilotnews.com/2008/01/netjets-pilots-contract-amended-and.html (July 10, 2008).

10. Trautvetter, "NetJets Pilots Set Another High Salary Standard."

11. "American Flight Attendants Call for Execs to Defer Bonuses," *Dallas Business Journal*, April 1, 2008, http://www.bizjournals.com/dallas" /stories/2008/03/31/daily19.html (July 11, 2008).

12. 18 NMB 89, R-6040 (1991).

13. O. V. Delle-Femine, in interview with coauthor Kaps, August 1985.

14. Robert W. Kaps, *Air Transport Labor Relations* (Carbondale: Southern Illinois University Press, 1997), 100.

15. Ibid.

16. *Machinists v. National Mediation Board*, 73 LRRM 2278 (1970).

17. A. von Nordenflycht and T. A. Kochan, "Labor Contract Negotiations in the Airline Industry," *Monthly Labor Review*, July 2003, 8–28.

18. 70 FR 41440 (July 19, 2005).

19. William E. Simkin, *Mediation and the Dynamics of Collective Bargaining* (Washington, DC: Bureau of National Affairs, 1971), 77–106.

20. 45 U.S.C. 160 (1988).

21. U.S. General Accounting Office, *Airline Labor Relations: Information on Trends and Impact of Labor Actions*, GAO Report: GAO-03–652 (Washington, DC: GPO, June 2003).

22. Alexander Wells, *Air Transportation: A Management Perspective* (Belmont, CA: Wadsworth, 1984).

23. U.S. Government Accountability Office, *Airline Deregulation: Reregulating the Airline Industry Would Likely Reverse Consumer Benefits and Not Save Airline Pensions*, GAO report number GAO-06–630, *U.S. Government Accountability Office*, June 12, 2006, http://www.gao.gov/htext/d06630.html (July 8, 2008).

24. V. M. Briggs Jr., "The Mutual Aid Pact of the Airline Industry," *Industrial and Labor Relations Review* 19 (1965): 3–20, http://digitalcommons.ilr.cornell.edu/hr/21 (July 10, 2008).

25. S. H. Unterberger and E. Koziara, "The Demise of Airline Strike Insurance," *Industrial and Labor Relations Review* 34 (1980): 82–89.

26. J. T. Addison and C. Schnabel, *International Handbook of Trade Unions* (Northampton, MA: Elgar, 2003).

27. "Profits in Strikes," *Time Magazine*, October 16, 1972, http://www.time.com/time/magazine/article/0,9171,906607,00.html (July 9, 2008).

28. R. V. Foster, *Aviation Law: An Introduction* (Lanham, MD: Maryland Historical Press, 1985), 11.

29. Howard J. Anderson, *The Labor Board and the Collective Bargaining Process* (Washington, DC: GPO, 1971).

30. Reed C. Richardson, *Collective Bargaining Objectives* (Englewood Cliffs, NJ: Prentice Hall, 1971), 113.

31. Anderson, *Labor Board.*

32. 29 U.S.C. 158 (1988).

33. 29 U.S.C. 176 (1988).

34. 29 U.S.C. 177–78 (1988).

35. 29 U.S.C. 176 (1988).

36. Ibid.

37. Mills, *Labor-Management Relations.*

38. Ibid.

39. *Ottawa Silica Co. v. NLRB*, 482 F.2d 945 (1972).

40. Mills, *Labor-Management Relations.*

41. "Public Sector Collective Bargaining Laws," *American Federation of State, County, and Municipal Employees*, 2011, http://www.afscme.org//members /11075.cfm (February 20, 2011).

42. Ibid.

43. Ibid.

44. Steven Greenhouse, "Strained States Turning to Laws to Curb Labor Unions," *New York Times,* January 3, 2011. http://www.nytimes.com/2011/01 /04/business/04labor.html?.

45. Edmund Pinto, "Intelligence," *Aviation Daily*, April 11, 1991, 75.

46. Tom Bethel, "Labor Pains (Filibuster Stymies Enactment of Worker Replacement Bill)," *National Review*, July 11, 1994.

47. *NLRB v Mackay Radio & Telegraph Co.*, 304 U.S. 333 (1938).

48. Aaron Bernstein, "You Can't Bargain with a Worker Whose Job Is No More," *Business Week*, August 5, 1991.

49. Greenhouse, "Strained States," n45.

6. Unfair Labor Practices

1. National Labor Relations Act, 49 Stat. 449 (1935), amended P.L. 101, 80th Congress (1947), and P.L. 257, 86th Congress (1959); 29 U.S.C. 159–61.

2. Reed C. Richardson, *Collective Bargaining by Objectives* (Englewood Cliffs, NJ: Prentice Hall, 1947), 47.

3. P. Gilmore, "Taft-Hartley: A Workers' Nightmare," *Labor Party Press*, 1997, http://lpa.igc.org /lpv26/lp05.htm (July 19, 2008).

4. Sharon Smith, *Subterranean Fire: A History of Working-Class Radicalism in the United States* (Chicago: Haymarket, 2006), 170.

5. Gilmore, "Taft-Hartley: A Workers' Nightmare."

6. Ibid.

7. Ibid.

8. R. Nader, "Time to Repeal the Taft-Hartley Act," *Voice News*, August 2002, http://www.thevoice news.com/News/2002/0802/Features/F01_Nader-Taft-Hartley.html (July 21, 2008).

9. Ibid.

10. *NLRB v. Dale Industries Inc.*, 355 F.2d 851 (6th Cir., 1966).

11. *Master Touch Dental Laboratories*, 65 LRRM 1368, 165 NLRB 73 (1967).

12. *Darlington Manufacturing v. Amalgamated Clothing and Textile Workers Union*, 58 LRRM 2657, 380 U.S. 263 (1965).

13. *Medo Photo Supply Corp. v. NLRB*, 14 LRRM 581, 321 U.S. 678 (1944); *Standard Coil Products Inc.*, 30 LRRM 581, 99 NLRB 131 (1952); *NLRB v. Exchange Part Co.*, 55 LRRM 2098, 375 U.S. 405 (1965).

14. *Pacific Southwest Airlines*, 201 NLRB 647 (1973).

15. *Raleys Inc. v. NLRB*, 703 F.2d 410 (9th Cir., 1983).

16. *NLRB v. Collins & Aikman Corp.*, 15 LRRM 826, 146 F.2d 454 (4th Cir., 1944); *NLRB v. Swan Fastener Corp.*, 31 LRRM 2082, 199 F.2d 935 (1st Cir., 1952).

17. *Excelsior Laundry Co.*, 186 NLRB 914 (1970).

18. *General Engineering Inc.*, 131 NLRB 901 (1961).

19. *Montgomery Ward & Co. v. NLRB*, 385 F.2d 769 (8th Cir., 1967).

20. *NLRB v. Somerville Buick Inc.*, 29 LRRM 2379, 194 F.2d 935, 952 (1st Cir., 1952); *NLRB v. Swan Fastener Corp.*, 31 LRRM 2082, 199 F.2d 935 (1st Cir., 1952).

21. *Phelps Dodge Corp. v. NLRB*, 313 U.S. 177 (1941).

22. *Hoisting and Portable Engineers, Local 302*, 144 NLRB 1449 (1963).

23. *NLRB v. Hershey Foods Corp.*, 513 F.2d 1083 (9th Cir., 1975).

24. *Stoddard-Quirk Manufacturing Co.*, 51 LRRM 1110, 138 NLRB 75 (1962).

25. *J. P. Stevens & Company v NLRB*, 623 F.2d 322 (4th Cir., 1980).

26. *NLRB v. Gissel Packing Company*, 395 U.S. 575.

27. Kate Bronfenbrenner, *No Holds Barred: The Intensification of Employer Opposition to Organizing*, Economic Policy Institute briefing paper 235 (Washington, DC, May 20, 2009), 1–2, http://epi.3cdn.net/ edc3b3dc172dd1094f_0ym6ii96d.pdf.

28. Railway Labor Act, U.S. Code, Title 45, Ch. 8, Tenth, 45 U.S.C. 152 (1993).

29. *Texas & N.O.R. Co. v. Brotherhood of Railway & Steamship Clerks*, 281 U.S. 548 (1930).

30. *Virginian Railroad Co. v. System Federation*, No. 40, 300 U.S. 515 (1937).

31. *Allegheny Airlines Inc.*, NMB R-3470 (1962).

32. Ibid.

33. *Linea Aeropostal Venezolana*, NMB R-2938 (1955).

34. *Teamsters v. Braniff Airways Inc.*, 70 LRRM 3333 (1969).

35. *Association of Flight Attendants v. Horizon Air Industries*, U.S. Fed. District Ct. 017-5308, Oregon (1989).

36. *United States v. TACA Airways Agency Inc.*, Indictment 24270 E.D. LA (1952).

37. Kate Bronfenbrenner, *Prepared Statement for the National Mediation Board Open Meeting Re; RLA Rulemaking Docket No. C 6964*, December 7, 2009, http://www.nmb.gov/representation /proposed-rulemaking/bronfenbrenner.pdf.

38. *United States v. Jerry Winston & Broome County Aviation Inc. d/b/a Commuter Airlines Inc.*, Indictment 75-CR-83, Northern District, NY (1976).

39. D. Fadden, P. Morton, R. Taylor, and T. Lindberg, "First-Hand: Evolution of the 2-Person Crew Jet Transport Flight Deck," *IEEE Global History Network*, http://www.ieeeghn.org/wiki/index.php /First_Hand:Evolution_of_the_2-Person_Crew_ Jet_Transport_Flight_Deck (August 25, 2008).

40. G. E. Hopkins, *Flying the Line: The First Half-Century of the Air Line Pilots Association* (Washington, DC: Air Line Pilots Assoc., 1982), 175.

41. Civil Service Reform Act of 1978, 5 U.S.C. Sec. 7116.

42. Professional Airways Systems Specialists and United States Department of Transportation, Federal Aviation Administration, 18 FLRA no. 8.

43. *Pan American World Airways v. IBT*, 275 F.Supp 986 (S.D.N.Y. 1967).

7. Grievance Procedures

1. J. A. Lapp, *How to Handle Labor Grievances* (Deep Haven, CT: National Foreman's Institute, 1946).

2. H. W. Davey, *Contemporary Collective Bargaining* (Englewood Cliffs, NJ: Prentice Hall, 1972).

3. 16 NLRB 744.

4. Gerald Somers, *Grievance Settlement in Coal Mining* (Morgantown: West Virginia University, 1956).

5. *International Association of Machinists, AFL-CIO, v. Central Airlines Inc.*, 372 U.S. 682 (1963).

6. *Brotherhood of Railroad Trainmen v. Chicago River & Indiana Railroad Co.*, 353 U.S. 30 (1915).

7. *United Steelworkers v. Enterprise Wheel & Car Corp.*, 363 U.S. 593 (1960).

8. *Brotherhood of Railroad Trainmen v. Central of Georgia Railway Co.*, 415 F.2d 403 (1969).

9. Opinion and order, U.S. District Court, Southern District of Ohio, April 3, 2006, in *NetJets Aviation Inc. v. International Brotherhood of Teamsters*, case no. 2:05-CV-1049.

10. "Arbitration Provisions in Collective Agreements," *Monthly Labor Review*, March 1993, 262–66.

11. *United Steelworkers v. Warrior & Gulf Navigation Co.*, 363 U.S. 574 (1960).

12. *United Steelworkers v. Enterprise Wheel & Car Corp.*, 363 U.S. 593 (1960).

13. J. W. Friedman, "Individual Rights in Grievance Arbitration," *Arbitration Journal* 27, no. 4 (1972): 252–73.

14. A. B. Smith Jr., "The Impact on Collective Bargaining of Equal Employment Remedies," *Industrial & Labor Relations Review* 28, no. 3 (1975): 376–94.

15. A. H. Levy, "The Collective Bargaining Agreement as a Limitation on Union Control of Employees' Grievances," *Industrial Relations Law Digest* 13, no. 4 (1971): 27–54.

8. The Airline Industry

1. "When America Flies, It Works: 2010 Economic Report," *Airline Transport Association*, 2010, http:// www.airlines.org/Economics/ReviewOutlook/ Documents/2010AnnualReport.pdf (March 4, 2010).

2. "Energy/Fuel and U.S. Airlines—Coping with Sky-High Fuel Prices," *Air Transport Association*, 2008, http://www.airlines.org/economics/energy /default.htm (June 7, 2008).

3. Civil Aeronautics Act of 1938.

4. John R. Meyer and Clinton V. Oster Jr., eds., *Airline Deregulation: The Early Experience* (Boston: Auburn House, 1981).

5. Nawal K. Taneja, *The Commercial Airline Industry* (Lexington, MA: Heath, 1976), 124.

6. U.S. Civil Aeronautics Board, *Report No. 33*, 33 CAB 307 (1961).

7. Taneja, *Commercial Airline Industry*, 126.

8. J. S. Hamilton, *Practical Aviation Law*, 4th ed. (Ames, IA: Blackwell, 2005), 148.

9. Taneja, *Commercial Airline Industry*, 126.

10. John Dunlop, "Trends and Issues in Labor Relations," speech, Employee-Management Relations Committee of the National Academy of Sciences, Harvard University, January 14, 1985.

11. Gerald R. Ford, quoted in A. Brown, *The Politics of Airline Deregulation* (Knoxville: University of Tennessee Press, 1987), 2.

12. Meyer and Oster, *Airline Deregulation*, 8.

13. Dunlop, "Trends and Issues in Labor Relations," 2.

14. U.S. Senate, *Report No. 631*, 95th Cong., 2d sess. (1978), 2.

15. Brown quoted in *Politics of Airline Deregulation*, 2.

16. For a more detailed description of the regulatory impact of deregulation, see Harry P. Wolf and David A. NewMyer, *Aviation Industry Regulations*, 1st ed. (Carbondale: Southern Illinois University Press, 1985).

17. Meyer and Oster, *Airline Deregulation*, 211.

18. Harold Seneker, "Fare Wars," *Forbes Magazine*, September 1, 1980, 37.

19. Thomas S. Robertson and Scott Ward, "Management Lessons from Airline Deregulation," *Harvard Business Review* 61 (January–February 1983): 41.

20. Robert J. Joedicke, *The Goose That Laid Golden Eggs* (New York: Lehman, February 1981).

21. John T. Dunlop, "Trends and Issues in Labor Relations: Working towards Consensus," *Challenge* 25 (July–August 1985): 26–34.

22. Frank Borman, untitled presentation, Lehman Brothers–Kuhn Loeb–Airline Industry Seminar, New York, February 11–13, 1982.

23. George Rubin, "Labor Management Relations in 1988," *Monthly Labor Review* (January 1989): 26.

24. Alexander Wells, *Air Transportation: A Management Perspective* (Los Angeles: Wadsworth, 1984), 435.

25. S. Rosen, *Airline Collective Bargaining since Deregulation: Some Perspectives* (Washington, DC: Air Line Pilots Association, 1987).

26. Ibid.

27. *NLRB v. Bildisco & Bildisco*, 104 U.S. 118 (1984).

28. O. V. Delle-Femine, during concessionary negotiations between Ozark Airlines and AMFA, contained in Robert W. Kaps' minutes of negotiation, September 1983.

29. Marvin Cohen quoted in George Rubin, "Collective Bargaining in 1982," *Monthly Labor Review*, January 1983, 33.

30. D. Koenig, "Airlines Try to Hedge against Soaring Fuel Costs," *Houston (TX) Chronicle*, June 30, 2008, http://www.chron.com/disp/story.mpl/ap/business/5863632.html (July 2, 2008).

31. T. Banstetter, "How American Staved Off Bankruptcy," *Ft. Worth (TX) Star Telegram*, June 9, 2008, http://www.star-telegram.com/805/story/690296.html (June 10, 2008); T. Banstetter, "American Employees Unlikely to Accept Cuts," *Ft. Worth (TX) Star Telegram*, April 28, 2008, http://www.star-telegram.com/business/story/607945.html (April 29, 2008).

32. T. Reed, "Continental's Pilots Picket for Payback," *TheStreet.com*, March 13, 2008, http://www.thestreet.com/story/10407489.html (March 15, 2008).

33. "U.S. Airline Bankruptcies & Service Cessations," *Air Transport Association of America*, September 1, 2008, http://www.airlines.org/economics/specialtopics/USAirlineBankruptcies.htm (October 2, 2008).

34. C. Walsh, "United Pilots Will Picket at Airport," *Rocky Mountain News*, July 31, 2007, http://www.rockymountainnews.com (August 2, 2008).

35. "US Airline Unions Want to Recoup Losses," *Reuters AirWise News*, January 3, 2008, http://news.airwise.com/story/view/11993180045.html (January 3, 2008).

36. T. Maxon, "Fuel Costs May Ground More Airlines," *Dallas Morning News*, June 9, 2008, http://www.dallasnews.com (June 9, 2008).

37. O. Reed, P. Shedd, J. Morehead, and M. Pagnattaro, *The Legal and Regulatory Environment of Business*, 14th ed. (New York: McGraw-Hill, 2008), 463. See also www.pbgc.gov.

38. T. Reed, "UAL Plans Fly under the Radar," *TheStreet.com*, January 22, 2008, http://www.thestreet.com/newsanalysis/transportation/10399708.html (January 23, 2008); S. Freeman, "United to Ground Its Ted Carrier: Airline Announces Flight Reductions, Further Jobs Cuts," *Washing-*

ton Post, June 5, 2008, http://www.washington post.com/wp-dyn/content/article/2008/06/04/AR2008060400945 (June 6, 2008); J. Johnson, "United May Shed Repair Unit," *Chicago Tribune*, August 23, 2007, http://www.chicgaotribune.com/business/chi-thu_unitedaug23,0,5040865 (June 6, 2008).

39. A. Gonzales, "Spirit Airlines Proposes Job Cuts Due to Soaring Fuel Prices," *Miami Herald*, June 3, 2008, http://www.miamiherald.com/business/AP/story/556721.html (June 5, 2008).

40. B. Wilson, "Record Fuel Forces More Delta Cuts," *Aviation Week*, March 18, 2008, http://www.aviationweek.com/aw/generic/story_channel.jsp?channel=com&id=news/DAL03188.xml&headline=Record%20Fuel%20Forces%20More%20Delta%20Cuts%3E (March 19, 2008).

41. K. Peterson, "Airline Pilots Brace for Downsizing, Career Change," *Reuters*, July 2, 2008, http://www.reuters.com/article/articleId+UKN0237590120080702 (July 3, 2008).

42. T. Reed, "Oil's Attendant Job Cuts Weigh at American," *TheStreet.com*, July 9, 2008, http://www.thestreet.com/story/10424916.html (July 9, 2008).

43. K. Yamanouchi, "AirTran Plans 5 Percent to 15 Percent Pay Cuts; Furloughs Also Expected," *Atlanta Journal-Constitution*, July 2, 2008, http://www.ajc.com (July 3, 2008).

44. R. Jenkins, "Airlines Cancel Flights in Tulsa, Oklahoma City," *Associated Press*, June 30, 2008, http://www.forbes.com/feeds/ap/2008/06/30/ap5169569.html (July 2, 2008).

45. H. J. Levy, "Airlines Cutting Flights From Bradley Airport," *New York Times*, July 6, 2008, http://www.nytimes.com (July 7, 2008).

46. Marla Dickerson, "U.S. Airlines Flock to Foreign Repair Shops," *Los Angeles Times*, April 30, 2008, http://pqasb.pqarchiver.com/latimes/search.html (July 1, 2008).

47. "Airline Outsourcing Endangering Passengers, National Security, Say Aviation Mechanics, Industry Experts; Teamsters Union and Business Travel Coalition Sponsor Summit of Risks of Aircraft Maintenance Outsourcing," *Reuters*, February 11, 2008, http://www.reuters.com/article/idUS199638+11-Feb-2008+PRN20080211 (July 9, 2008).

48. "Questions and Answers on Contract Mainte-

nance," *Air Transport Association*, 2007, http://www.airlines.org/operationsandsafety/engineering/QandA (July 7, 2008).

49. Dickerson, "U.S. Airlines Flock to Foreign Repair Shops."

50. B. Wingfield, "Fighting over the Nuts and Bolts," *Forbes.com*, June 3, 2008, http://www.forbes.com (June 3, 2008); S. Holmes, "Danger in the Repair Shop," *Business Week*, July 30, 2007, http://www.businessweek.com/magazine/content/07_31/b4044056.htm (June 3, 2008).

51. "Questions and Answers on Contract Maintenance."

52. American Airlines, "American Airlines Maintenance Services, Allegiant Air Enter into Four-Year Contract," news release, *American Airlines*, December 18, 2006, http://www.aa.com/content/amrcorp/pressReleases/2006_12/18_allegiant.jhtml (July 9, 2008).

53. "ATA 2007 Economic Q&A and Industry Update," *Air Transport Association*, 2008, http://www.airlines.org/economice/review_and_outlook/ATA2007EconOutlookQandA.htm (June 6, 2008).

54. Kevin Trinkle, "The PSA History Page," *PSA Oldtimers Page*, 1995, http://www.psa-history.org/articles/hist.html (August 22, 2009).

55. Frank H. Cassell and Frank A. Spencer, *Airline Labor Relations under Deregulation: From Oligopoly to Competition—and Return?* (Evanston, IL: Northwestern University, 1986).

56. *International Brotherhood of Teamsters v. Texas International Airlines Inc.*, 8 NMB 217 (1981).

57. George Rubin, "Collective Bargaining in 1982," *Monthly Labor Review*, January 1983, 26–27.

58. J. Bailey, "Pilots' Battles over Seniority Play Havoc with Airline Mergers," *New York Times*, February 27, 2008, http://www.nytimes.com/2008/02/27/business/27pilots.html (June 9, 2008); C. Kahn, "US Airways Pilots Oust Union over Seniority Issues," *Washington Post*, April 18, 2008, http://www.washingtonpost.com/wp-dyn/content/article/2008/04/17/AR2008041702249 (April 18, 2008); T. Reed, "US Airways Pilots Veer Away from ALPA," *TheStreet.com*, September 10, 2007, http://www.thestreet.com/pf/newsanalysis/transportation/10378817.html (September 13, 2007).

59. J. Michels, "ALPA Questions Presidential Candidates on Issues," *Aviation Week*, January 8,

2008, http://www.aviationweek.com/aw/generic/story_generic.jsp?channel=aviationdaily&id=news/ALPA01087.xml (January 10, 2008).

60. "STW #446," *Speed News*, April 4, 2008, http://www.speednews.com (April 5, 2008).

61. I. Sheppard, "Pilot Shortage Respite Likely Short-lived," *Aviation International News*, May 2008, 101–8.

62. T. Banstetter, "Regional Airlines Lower Bar for Pilots," *Ft. Worth (TX) Star Telegram*, November 25, 2007, http://www.star-telegram.com/business/story/322928.html (June 6, 2008).

63. I. Putzger, "Beyond Crews Control: A Shortage of Pilots Is Tripping Up Freighter Expansion Plans in Asia, and Many Believe the Airlines' New Capacity Is Going to Get Worse," *Air Cargo World Online*, March 9, 2008, http://www.aircargoworld.com/features/0308_1.htm (March 10, 2008).

64. Sheppard, "Pilot Shortage Respite Likely Short-Lived."

65. T. Benenson, "Where Have All the Pilots Gone?" *Flying*, December 2007, 85–87.

66. Putzger, "Beyond Crews Control."

67. C. Epstein, "Pilot Shortage Ahead, IATA Plans to Bolster Numbers," *Aviation International News*, June 2008, 82; D. Pearson, "Pilot Shortage Could Curb Growth: Crunch May Increase Carriers' Labor Costs amid High Fuel Bills," *Wall Street Journal*, April 23, 2008, http://onlinewsj.com/article/SB120888629684535203.html (June 10, 2008).

68. Sheppard, "Pilot Shortage Respite Likely Short-Lived."

9. The Aerospace Industry

1. "Career Guide to Industries: Aerospace Product and Parts Manufacturing," *U.S. Bureau of Labor Statistics*, n.d., http://data.bls.gov/cgi-bin/print.pl/oco/cg/cgs006.htm (July 20, 2008).

2. "Total Employment: Annual—Calendar Years 1990 to 2008," *Aerospace Industries Association*, 2008, http://www.aia-aerospace.org/stats/aero_stats/stat12.pdf (July 20, 2008).

3. "Revitalization of the Aerospace Workforce," *Aerospace Industries Association*, 2008, http://www.aia-aerospace.org/issues/subject/employment_facts.cfm (July 20, 2008).

4. Table 9, "Aerospace Related Employment, 1993–2007," *Aerospace Industries Association*, 2008,

http://www.aia-aerospace.org (July 20, 2008).

5. "Career Guide to Industries."

6. Ibid.

7. "AIAA Releases Employment Figures, Issues Warning," *Speed News, STW #452*, May 16, 2008; "AIA Aerospace Research Center, 2007 Year-End Review and 2008 Forecast—An Analysis," 2008, and table 6, "Aerospace Balance of Trade, Calendar Years 2003–2007," *Aerospace Industries Association*, 2007, both at http://www.aia-aerospace.org (December 22, 2007).

8. *Career Guide to Industries.*

9. "Orders, Shipments and Backlog for Large Civil Jet Transport Aircraft," *Aerospace Industries Association*, 2008, http://www.aia-aerospace.org (July 22, 2008); J. Bowker, "Boeing Says Has Seen Order Deferrals in U.S. Market," *Reuters*, 2008, http://www.washingtonpost.com/wp-dyn/content/article/2008/07/09/AR2008070901448 (July 10, 2008).

10. "Defense, Space and Security," *Boeing*, 2011, http://www.boeing.com/bds/a_to_z.html (March 7, 2011).

11. G. Waldron, "Boeing Gets US Army Green Light for Apache IIIs," *FlightGlobal*, October 26, 2010, http://www.flightglobal.com/articles/2010/10/26/348907/boeing-gets-us-army-green-light-for-apache-block-iiis.html (March 7, 2011).

12. "AH-64A/D Apache Attack Helicopter, USA," *army-technology.com*, 2011, http://www.army-technology.com/projects/apache/ (March 7, 2011).

13. C. Brothers, "Brakes and Other Headaches at an Aircraft Show," *New York Times*, July 16, 2008, http://www.nytimes.com/2008/07/16/business/worldbusiness/16plane.html (July 17, 2008).

14. J. Tessler, "Likely Brain Drain Puts Aerospace Recruitment into High Gear," *Seattle (WA) Post-Intelligencer*, March 9, 2008, http://seattlepi.nwsource.com (March 10, 2008); D. Montgomery, "U.S. Aerospace Industry Facing Labor Shortage," *Ft. Worth (TX) Star-Telegram*, January 20, 2008, http://www.star-telegram.com/news/story/421119.html (January 21, 2008).

15. J. Millman, "Fuel-Efficient P&W Engine in the Lead," *Hartford Business.com*, July 7, 2008, http://www.hartfordbusiness.com (July 7, 2008).

16. H. Lawrence, *Aviation and the Role of Government* (Dubuque, IA: Kendall Hunt, 2004), 97–98.

17. Ibid., 136.

18. Ibid.

19. "Curtiss-Wright," *U.S. Centennial of Flight Commission*, 2003, http://www.centennialofflight.gov/essay/Aerospace/Curtiss-wright/Aero9.htm (July 23, 2008).

20. "Convair Division of General Dynamics," *U.S. Centennial of Flight Commission*, 2003, http://www.centennialofflight.gov/essay/Aerospace/convair/Aero36.htm (July 23, 2008).

21. "Consolidated Vultee Aircraft Corporation," *U.S. Centennial of Flight Commission*, 2003, http://www.centennialofflight.gov/essay/Aerospace/Consolidated_Vultee/Aero33.htm (July 23, 2008).

22. A. Pelletier, *Bell Aircraft since 1935* (Annapolis: Naval Institute Press, 1992); "Textron Business Overview: Bell Helicopter," *Textron*, 2008, http://www.textron.com/textron_businesses/bell/index.jsp (July 24, 2008).

23. "History," *Lockheed Martin*, 2008, http://www.centennialofflight.gov/essay/Aerospace/earlyU.S/Aero1.htm (July 23, 2008).

24. "Fairchild Aircraft Corporation," *U.S. Centennial of Flight Commission*, 2003, http://www.centennialofflight.gov/essay/Aerospace/Fairchild/Aero25.htm (July 23, 2008).

25. "North American Aviation," *U.S. Centennial of Flight Commission*, 2003, http://www.centennialofflight.gov/essay/Aerospace/NorthAmerican/Aero37.htm (July 24, 2008).

26. "McDonnell Douglas Corporation," *U.S. Centennial of Flight Commission*, 2003, http://www.centennialofflight.gov/essay/Aerospace/McDac/Aero32.htm (July 24, 2008).

27. "Ryan Aeronautical Company," *U.S. Centennial of Flight Commission*, 2003, http://www.centennialofflight.gov/essay/Aerospace/Ryan/Aero34.htm (July 24, 2008).

28. "Continental/Teledyne Continental: The Company," *KensAviation.com*, 2007, http://www.shanaberger.com/engines/continental.htm (July 24, 2008).

29. "Hughes Companies," *U.S. Centennial of Flight Commission*, 2003, http://www.centennialofflight.gov/essay/Aerospace/Hughes/Aero44.htm (July 23, 2008); "Our Company," *Lycoming*, n.d, http://www.lycoming.textron.com/company/ (July 24, 2008).

30. "The Cessna Story: Milestones, 1990–1999," *Cessna Aircraft*, 2008, http://www.cessna.com/story/milestones/1990s.chtml (July 24, 2008).

31. "General Dynamics Corporation," *U.S. Centennial of Flight Commission*, 2003, http://www.centennialofflight.gov/essay/Aerospace/generaldynamics/Aero35.htm (July 23, 2008).

32. "Bombardier: the Evolution of a Transportation Giant," *Canadian Broadcasting Corporation, CBC News*, 2006, http://www.cbc.ca/news/background/bombardier (July 25, 2008).

33. *Encyclopedia Britannica*, s.v. "Aerospace Industry History: Cooperation and Consolidation in a Global Economy, Mergers and Divestitures," 2008, http://www.britannica.com/EBchecked/topic/372aerospace-industry/225639/Mergers-and-divestitures (July 22, 2008).

34. J. McAleese, "Aerospace Industry Consolidation: News from the Front Lines," presentation, 1997 OEM/Supplier Symposium, http://www.mcaleese.com/papers/oem-97.pdf (July 22, 2008); "Lockheed since the 1950s," *U.S. Centennial of Flight Commission*, 2003, http://www.centennialofflight.gov/essay/Aerospace/lockheed-modern/Aero16.htm (July 23, 2008).

35. "Convair Division of General Dynamics," *U.S. Centennial of Flight Commission*, 2003, http://www.centennialofflight.gov/essay/Aerospace/convair/Aero36.htm (July 23, 2008).

36. "Northrop and Northrop Grumman," *U.S. Centennial of Flight Commission*, 2003, http://www.centennialofflight.gov/essay/Aerospace/Northrop_modern/Aero41.htm (July 23, 2008).

37. Ibid.

38. *Encyclopedia Britannica*, s.v. "Aerospace Industry History."

39. "McDonnell Douglas Corporation."

40. "Lockheed since the 1950s."

41. Ibid.

42. "Northrop and Northrop Grumman."

43. "Boeing Completes Sale of Commercial Helicopter Line," Reuters, February 19, 1999; "Boeing Completes Sale of Light Helicopter Product Lines to RDM," press release, *Boeing*, 1999, http://www.helis.com/news/1999/boeingsale.htm (July 23, 2008).

44. "Hughes Companies."

45. M. Elliott, "The Anatomy of the GE-Honeywell Disaster," *Time*, 2002, http://www.time.com/

time/printout/0,8816,166732,00.html (July 22, 2008); "EU Kills GE-Honeywell," 2001, *CNNMoney.com*, http://cnnmoney.com (July 22, 2008).

46. "Pratt & Whitney Rocketdyne Has Powered Missions to Nearly Every Planet in the Solar System," *Pratt & Whitney Space*, 2007, http://www.pw.utc.com/vgn-ext-templating/v/index.jsp?vgnextrefresh=1&vgnextoid=a4a307b06f5eb010VgnVCM1000000881000aRCRD (July 28, 2008).

47. Ibid.

48. Ibid.

49. Ibid.

50. P. Paul, "Lockheed Machinists Approve Three-year Contract," *Atlanta Journal Constitution*, March 2, 2008, http://www.ajc.com (March 10, 2008).

51. J. Demers, "The Lean Philosophy: Continuous Improvement by Any Name Can Boost a Company's Performance. The Choice Is Up to You," *Society of Managements Consultants of Canada*, 2005, http://www.managementmag.com/index.cfm/ci_id/1892/la_id/1/print/true.htm (June 5, 2008).

52. "Kaizen Philosophy of Continuous Incremental Improvements & Kaizen Method," *valuebasedmanagement.net*, 2005, http://www.valuebasedmanagement.net/methods_kaizen.html (June 5, 2008).

53. R. Olexa, "Jetting to Success," *Manufacturing Engineering*, May 2003, http://findarticles.com/p/articles/mi_qa3618/is_200305/ai_n9276970 (June 5, 2008).

54. M. Thurber, "The Soul of a New Engine," *Access Intelligence*, 2005, http://aviationtoday.com/cgi/am/show_mag.cgi?pub+am&mon+0405&file+soulofa.htm (May 11, 2008).

55. C. Hawley, "Aircraft Makers Flock to Mexico," *USA Today*, April 6, 2008, http://i.usatoday.net/news/2008/04/06/aerospacex (April 9, 2008); D. Lindquist, "Goodrich Opening Plant in Mexicali," *San Diego (CA) Tribune*, December 28, 2007, http://www.signonsandiego.com (January 1, 2008); "Learjet 85 Composite Work Goes South of the Border," *Aviation International News AIN Alerts*, June 3, 2008, http://www.ainalerts.com/alerts/060308_PF.html (June 3, 2008).

56. "Honeywell Moves Jobs to Asia," *AVwebBiz*, March 5, 2008.

57. "Cessna to Build Newest Aircraft in China," *Providence (RI) Journal*, November 29, 2007, http:

//www.projo.com/business/content/BZ_TEXTRON29_11-29-07_G582CMU_v12.1afbce9.html# (July 28, 2008).

58. M. Blakey, speech, annual Repair Symposium membership luncheon, Aeronautical Repair Station Association, Arlington, VA, March 15, 2008.

59. L. Spears, "Boeing to Extend Contract with Shanghai Maker of 737 Jet Parts," *Bloomberg.com*, May 13, 2008.

60. S. Ray, "Boeing Unions May Use 787 Delay for Contract Leverage (Update2)," *Bloomberg.com*, June 11, 2008.

61. J. Wallace, "Boeing Sticks to Global Plan," *Seattle (WA) Post-Intelligencer*, May 5, 2008, http://seattlepi.nwsource.com (May 28, 2008).

62. Ray, "Boeing Unions."

63. "Contract Talks Fail; Machinists Strike Boeing Co.," *Associated Press*, September 5, 2008, http://money.aol.com/news/articles/_a/bbdp/contract-talks-fail-machinists-strike/159999 (September 6, 2008).

64. M. Dunlop, "Boeing Machinists Plan for Possible Strike," *(Everett, WA) Daily Herald*, August 4, 2008, http://www.heraldnet.com/article/20080804/BIZ/823413578/1005 (August 6, 2008).

65. "Boeing Extends Pact Despite Strike Vote," *Associated Press*, September 4, 2008, http://money.aol.com/news/articles/_a/bbdp/boeing-extends-pact-despite-strike-vote/149135 (September 5, 2008); J. Weber, "Boeing Workers Are on the Brink," *Business Week*, September 5, 2008, http://www.businessweek.com/bwdaily/dnflash/content/sep2008/db2008094_317166.htm?chan=rss_topStories_ssi_5 (September 5, 2008).

66. "Contract Talks Fail."

67. S. Freeman, "Darling of the Jet Industry, Bane of the Picket Line: Dreamliner Outsourcing at the Heart of Boeing Strike," *Washington Post*, September 10, 2008, http://www.washingtonpost.com/wp-dyn/content/article/2008/09/09/AR2008090903262_pf.html (September 10, 2008).

68. T. Klass, "Unions Show Muscle in Aerospace and Steel: But Analysts Ask if Demands for More Job Security Are Realistic," *Houston (TX) Chronicle*, September 12, 2008, http://www.chron.com/disp/story.mpl/headline/biz/5997070.html (September 15, 2008); "Boeing Facing 2nd Labor Rift,"

chicagotribune.com, September 11, 2008, http://www.chicagotribune.com/business/chi-thu-boeing-strike-sep11,0,7885299.story (September 12, 2008).

69. Freeman, "Darling of the Jet Industry"; Klass, "Unions Show Muscle."

70. D. Gates, "Boeing, Machinists Reach Settlement; Pact Calls for 15 Percent Pay Raise over 4 Years," *Seattle (WA) Times*, October 28, 2008, http://seattletimes.nwsource.com/html/boeingaerospace/20083197_machinists28.html.

71. D. Gates, "Big Raises in SPEEA Contract with Boeing," *Seattle (WA) Times*, November 15, 2008, http://seattletimes.nwsource.com/html/boeingaerospace/2008390035_speea5.html.

72. D. Gates, "Boeing Plans Workforce Reduction of 4,500, with Layoff in Second Quarter," *Seattle (WA) Times*, January 9, 2009, http://seattletimes.nwsource.com/html/businesstechnology/2068609030_webboeing09.html.

73. D. Gates, "Latest Boeing Layoff Includes 458 Machinists," *Seattle (WA) Times*, March 20, 2009, http://seattletimes.nwsource.com/boeingaerospace/2008892949_webboeinglayoff20.html

74. D. Hedgpeth, "Boeing's S.C. Jobs a Setback for Unions," *Washington Post*, October 30, 2009.

75. D. Gates, "Boeing Considers 'Supersite' of Plants for New Jet," *Seattle (WA) Times*, March 10, 2011, http://seattletimes.nwsource.com/html/businesstechnology/2014461618_boeing11.html.

76. *Textron Lycoming v. UAW*, U.S. 97-463 (1998), http://www.law.cornell.edu/supct/html/97-463.ZO.html (July 26, 2008).

77. "Aerospace Industry Flying into Strong Turbulence Ahead, According to New AlixPartners Study," *PR-inside.com*, July 10, 2008, http://www.pr-inside.com/print696753.htm (July 22, 2008). Tessler, "Likely Brain Drain."

78. "Dassault Troubled over Effects of Weak Dollar," *Aviation International News*, July 2008, 14.

79. Montgomery, "U.S. Aerospace Industry."

80. Ibid.

81. Tessler, "Likely Brain Drain."

82. J. Morrison, "Small Manufacturers Desperately Seek Skilled Staff," *Reuters*, 2008, http://www.usatoday.com/money/industries/manufacturing/2008–01–21-manufacturing-jobs_N.htm (January 22, 2008).

83. Montgomery, "U.S. Aerospace Industry."

84. Morrison, "Small Manufacturers Desperately."

85. Sheila Widnall, foreword, in Joel Cutcher-Gershenfeld, Thomas Kochan, Betty Barrett, Eric Rebentisch, and Rob Scott, *Developing a 21st Century Aerospace Workforce*, presentation, MIT Center for Technology, Policy and Industrial Development, 2001, (slides available at http://web.mit.edu/ctpid/lara/pdfs/CTPIDLunch.pdf).

86. Ibid.

87. "Report of the Interagency Aerospace Revitalization Task Force," *USA Today*, January 21, 2008, 8, http://www.usatoday.com/money/industries/manufacturing/2008–01–21-manufacturing-jobs_N.htm (July 28, 2008).

88. "Revitalization of the Aerospace Workforce."

89. C. Hedden, "Aviation Week Workforce Study Finds Shortage of U.S. A&D Workers," *Aviation Week & Space Technology*, August 20, 2007, 80, http://www.aviationweek.com/workforce/awst08202007_01.htm (July 28, 2008).

90. S. Alexander, "Economic Changes Blamed for IT Labor Shortage," *CNN.com*, 1999, http://www.cnn.com/TECH/computing/9902/09/career.ent.idg/index.html (August 5, 2008).

91. M. A. Chell, "The American Workforce: Identifying Workforce Challenges, Trends, and Recommendations," *Economic Development Review* 17, no. 3 (2001): 76–81.

92. Ibid.

93. "Machinists Survey Finds Strong Voter Support for Tuition-Free Tech Training," *International Association of Machinists and Aerospace Workers*, 2008, http://www.goiam.org/content.cfm?cID=12612 (August 5, 2008).

94. Ibid.

95. "America's Aerospace Industry: Identifying and Addressing Workforce Challenges," *President's Commission on the Future of the United States Aerospace Industry*, 2005, http://63.88.32.17/brg/Indprof/Aerospace_Report.pdf (August 5, 2008).

96. B. Ireland, *Wanted: Skilled Labor*, 2007, http://ecmweb.com/mag/electric_wanted_skilled_labor/ (August 5, 2008).

97. Ibid.

98. V. Mair, "How a Misunderstanding about Chinese Characters Has Led Many Astray," *Pinyin*.

info, n.d, http://www.pinyin.info/chinese/crisis. html (July 28, 2008).

99. "Boeing Commercial Airplanes: About the 787 Family," *Boeing*, 2008, http://www.boeing.com /commercial/787family/background.html (July 28, 2008).

100. M. Maynard, "A New Bombardier Jet Draws Only Tepid Demand," *New York Times*, July 14, 2008.http://www.nytimes.com/2008/07/14/busi- ness/worldbusiness/14air.html (July 15, 2008).

101. Millman, "Fuel-Efficient P&W Engine in the Lead."

102. T. Dubois, "Airbus Studies Green Solution for Aircraft Dismantling Work," *Aviation Interna- tional News*, June 2008, 34–36.

103. Alan Greenspan, quoted in S. Sclafani. "New Expectations for a New Century: The Education Imperative," *Office of Vocational and Adult Educa- tion, United States Department of Education*, http: //www.aia-aerospace.org/pdf/ovae-dod_newexpect. pdf (July 20, 2008).

10. General Aviation

1. "GA Serving All Americans," *Aircraft Owners and Pilots Association*, 2008, http://www.gaserving america.org (July 30, 2008); "The Plane Facts," *Na- tional Air Transportation Association*, 2008, http:// www.nata.aero/about/index.jsp (July 30, 2008).

2. "Active General Aviation Aircraft in the U.S. 1973–2007," *Aircraft Owners and Pilots Association*, 2007, http://www.aopa.org/whatsnew/stats/air- craft.html (July 30, 2008).

3. "FAA Certificated Pilots by State and Certifi- cate Type," *Aircraft Owners and Pilots Association*, 2007, http://www.aopa.org/whatsnew/stats/pilots_ state.html (July 30, 2008); "Airports and Landing Areas 1965–2007," *Aircraft Owners and Pilots As- sociation*, 2008, http://www.aopa.org/whatsnew /stats/airports.html (July 30, 2008).

4. *Federal Express Corp.*, 317 NLRB 1115 (1995).

5. *DHL Worldwide Express*, NLRB 29-RC-9845, 340 NLRB 122 (2003).

6. *Flight Safety Inc., and International Brother- hood of Teamsters*, 171 NLRB 146 (1968).

7. "What We Do," *AirMethods.com*, n.d., http: //www.airmethods.com/content/index.cfm?fuse action=showContent&contentID=2&navID=2 (August 16, 2008).

8. "Air Methods Closes FSS Airholdings," *Boston. com*, October 1, 2007, http://www.boston.com/busi- ness/healthcare/articles/2007/10/01/air_methods_ closes_fss_airholdings_deal/ (August 16, 2008).

9. J. Hamilton, *Practical Aviation Law*, 5th ed. (Newcastle, WA: Aviation Supplies & Academics, 2007), 219–23.

10. 14 C.F.R. 91.1001–443 (2008).

11. *Independent Railway Supervisors Association and Bombardier Transit Systems Corp.*, 32 NMB 23 (2005).

12. *Flight Options, LLC Pilots*, 33 NMB 22 (2006); *NetJets Aviation Inc. v. International Brotherhood of Teamsters, Airline Division*, Opinion and Order of April 3, 1996, District Court for the Southern Dis- trict of Ohio) 2:05-cv-1049; *NetJets Pilots Break from IBT, Choose In-House Union*, Aviation International News, *AINalerts*, July 3, 2008, http://www.ainalerts. com/ainalerts/070308_PF.html (July 3, 2008).

13. "NetJets Pilots Seek Independent Union," *Avi- ation International News*, May 2008; "Our History," *NetJets Association of Shared Aircraft Pilots*, 2008, http: //www.njasap.com/history.html (August 4, 2008).

14. "Blame Management, Not the Canadians, Say the Teamsters: Pilots' Union Accuses Defense Contractor Subsidiary of Threatening Good Jobs," *Aviation Today*, May 7, 2007, http://www.aviation- today.com/pressreleases/11557.html (July 31, 2008).

15. "Teamsters File for Mediation with Flight Options," *International Brotherhood of Teamsters, Headline News*, May 4, 2008, http://www.teamster. org/08news/hn_080504_1.asp (July 31, 2008).

16. Alison Grant, "Flight Options Pilots OK Contract That Gives Them nearly 40% Raise over Five Years," April 2, 2010, *Plain Dealer* (Cleveland, OH), http://www.cleveland.com/business/index. ssf/2010/04/flight_options.html.

17. "History," *BBA Aviation*, 2010, http://www. bbaaviation.com/about-us/history/1990-2005.aspx (July 31, 2010).

18. "About Us," *Signature Flight Support*, http: //www.signatureflight.com/about/index.shtml (July 31, 2008).

19. *Signature Flight Support*, 32 NMB 214 (2005).

20. "Company History," *FlightSafety Interna- tional Inc.*, n.d., http://www.fundinguniverse.com /company-histories/FlightSafety-International-Inc- Company/History.html (July 30, 2008).

21. "About Us," *FlightSafety International Inc.*, http://www.flightsafety.com/fs_about_us_about-us.php (August 3, 2008).

22. *Flight Safety Inc.*, 171 NLRB 146 (1968).

23. "About Us," *ERAU Instructor Pilots Association*, 2008, http://riddleinstructors.org (August 4, 2008).

11. The Public Sector

1. "FAA Fact Book. FAA Resources: FAA Employment," *Federal Aviation Administration*, December 19, 2007, http://www.faa.gov/about/office_org/headquarters_offices/aba/admin_factbook/media/July_2008_Fact_Book.pdf (August 7, 2008).

2. "California Division of Aeronautics & Organizational Chart," *California Department of Transportation*, n.d., http://www.dot.ca.gov/hq/planning/aeronaut/index.html (August 7, 2008).

3. Executive Order 12871, signed October 1, 1993.

4. Presidential Memorandum dated October 28, 1999, Reaffirmation of Executive Order 12871—Labor-Management Partnerships.

5. J. Budd, *Labor Relations: Striking a Balance* (New York: McGraw-Hill, 2008), 404.

6. M. Masters, R. Albright, and D. Epilon, "What Did Partnerships Do? Evidence from the Federal Sector," *Industrial and Labor Relations Review* 59 (April 2006): 367–85.

7. Executive Order 13203, signed February 17, 2001.

8. P.L. 108–36, Title XI (November 24, 2003); C. Hobbie, "The U.S. Government's Attacks on the Collective Bargaining Rights of Federal Employees," *American Federation of Government Employees,* May 25, 2004, http://www.afge.org/Index.cfm (May 6, 2008); T. Kauffman, "Union-Busting, DOD Style: Work-Force Plan Would Slash Unions' Membership, Influence," *Federal Times*, February 16, 2004; "CRS Report to Congress: DOD's National Security Personnel System: Provisions of Law and Implementation Plans," *Congressional Research Service, the Library of Congress* (March 11, 2005).

9. Hobbie, "U.S. Government's Attacks."

10. Ibid.

11. A. Stanger, *One Nation under Contract: The Outsourcing of American Power and the Future of Foreign Policy* (New Haven: Yale University Press, 2009), 101–4.

12. "Performance of Commercial Activities," Circular No. A-76, *Office of Management and Budget*, August 4, 1983, revised 1999, http://www.whitehouse.gov/omb/circulars/a076/a076.html (August 14, 2008).

13. "Who We Are," *DynCorp International* (2008), http://www.dyn-intl.com/subpage aspx?id=13 (August 10, 2008).

14. "Texas Simulator Techs Win IAM Representation," *International Association of Machinists*, August 10, 2008, http://www.goiam.org/content.cfm?cID=6612 (August 10, 2008).

15. K. P. O'Meara, "US: DynCorp Disgrace," *Corpwatch.com* (January 14, 2002), http://www.corpwatch.org/article.php?id=11119 (March 14, 2011).

16. B. Yeoman, "Soldiers of Good Fortune," *MotherJones.com* (May/June 2003), http://motherjones.com/politics/2003/05/soldiers-good-fortune (March 14, 2011).

17. "California Eastern Files under Bankruptcy Act," *Wall Street Journal*, May 14, 1948, 9.

18. "DynCorp," *Sourcewatch.com*, n.d., http://www.sourcewatch.org/index.php?title=DynCorp (March 14, 2011).

19. "A Brief History of DynCorp International," *DynCorp International*, 2011, http://www.dyn-intl.com/history.aspx (March 14, 2011).

20. "DynCorp," http://dyncorp.co.tv/ (March 14, 2011).

21. "DynCorp International," *PMS PSC—Your Portal to Private Military Contract*, March 2009, http://pmcpsc.blogspot.com/2009/03/dyncorp-international.html (March 14, 2011).

22. "Building on 60 Years of Innovation and Trust," *DynCorp International*, 2011, http://www.dyn-intl.com/overview.aspx (March 14, 2011).

23. P. Chatterjee, "DynCorp Oversight in Afghanistan Faulted," *CorpWatch.org*, February 26, 2010, http://www.corpwatch.org/article.php?id=15540 (March 14, 2011).

24. S. Barr, "Lockheed Wins Flight Service Jobs from FAA," *Washington Post*, February 2, 2005, E01, http://www.washingtonpost.com/ac2/wp-dyn/A55583–2005Feb1 (August 10, 2008).

25. "Union Organizing Victories," *Dennis' Labor Solidarity*, August 7, 2009, http://www.laborsolidarity.info/index-12.html (January 18, 2011).

26. J. Wood, "Lockheed Martin Flight Service Contract Renewed," *General Aviation News*, September 29, 2010, http://www.generalaviationnews.com/?p=29783 (September 29, 2010); "Organizing Takes Center Stage in Orlando," *IAM Journal*, Fall 2007, 6–7.

27. "Union Organizing Victories."

28. J. Miller, "Unions Press Their Case against A-76," *Federal Computer World*, September 10, 2007.

29. 41 U.S.C. 351, et seq.

30. "McNamara-O'Hara Service Contract Act (SCA)," *U.S. Department of Labor, Employment Standards Administration, Wage and Hour Division*, n.d, http://www.dol.gov/ESA/WHD/contracts/sca.htm (August 15, 2008).

31. Noah Page, "Bush Administration Begins to Privatize the Skies," *World Socialist Web Site*, June 15, 2005, http://www.wsws.org/articles/2005/jun2005/air-j15.shtml (August 10, 2008).

32. See, for example, R. Poole and V. Butler, "How to Commercialize Air Traffic Control," policy study 278, *Policy Archive*, February 2001, https://www.policyarchive.org/bitstream/handle/10207/5917/ps278.pdf (August 14, 2008); R. Poole, "Commercializing Air Traffic Control: A New Window of Opportunity to Solve an Old Problem," *Regulation: The CATO Review of Business & Government*, 1997, http://www.cato.org/pubs/regulation/reg20n3a.html (August 14, 2008).

33. R. Utt, "Continuing the Effort to Curb Excessive FAA Salary Costs," WebMemo 1622, *Heritage Foundation*, September 19, 2007, http://www.hritage.org/research/labor/upload/wm_1622.pdf (August 15, 2008).

34. J. Bernstein, "FAA and Controller Union Wrangle," *New York Newsday*, January 27, 2006.

35. Daniel Pulliam, "FAA-Union Negotiations over Labor Contract Stall," *GovernmentExecutive.com*, April 5, 2006, http://www.govexec.com/story_page_pf.cfm?articleid=33766.

36. A. Schofield, "FAA Gets Mixed Bag in PASS and NATCA Decisions," *Aviation Week*, August 7, 2007, http://www.aviationweek.com/aw/generic/story.jsp?id=news/FLRA0877.xml&headline=FAA%20Gets%20Mixed%20Bag%20In%20PASS%20And%20NATCA%20Decisions%20&channel=comm (August 27, 2008); "Federal Labor Board Dismisses NATCA Unfair Labor Practice Charges," press release, *Federal Aviation Administration*, August 6, 2007, http://www.faa.gov/news/press_releases/news_story.cfm?newsId=9292.

37. "Statement on NATCA Contract by FAA Administrator Marion C. Blakey," press release, *Federal Aviation Administration*, June 5, 2006, http://www.faa.gov/news/press_releases/news_story.cfm?newsId=7202.

38. A. Rosenberg, "Aviation Groups Push Agenda as FAA Reauthorization Stalls," *GovernmentExecutive.com*, May 29, 2008, http://www.govexec.com/story_page_pf.cfm?articleid=40107 (May 29, 2008).

39. "H.R. 2881—110th Congress: FAA Reauthorization Act of 2007," *GovTrack.us* (database of federal legislation), http://www.govtrack.us/congress/bill.xpd?bill=h110-2881 (August 30, 2011).

40. Paul Lowe, "House Bill Seeks to Repair Rift between FAA, Natca," *Aviation International News*, August 2008, 6.

41. Paul Lowe, "Natca Blasts Controller Hiring Plan," *Aviation International News*, July 2008, http://www.ainonline.com/ain-and-ainalerts/aviation-international-news/single-publication-story/browse/0/article/natca-blasts-controller-hiring-plan-16726/?no_cache=1&tx_ttnews%5Bstory_pointer%5D=2&tx_ttnews%5Bmode%5D=1.

42. Ibid.

43. J. Cushman, "F.A.A. Staggers under Task of Monitoring Airline Safety," *New York Times*, February 13, 1990.

44. S. Menke, "FAA Union Sets Arbitration Date for IT Pay Increase," *Government Computer News*, March 9, 2001, http://www.gcn.com/online/vol1_no1/3786-1.html (November 4, 2007).

45. "What Is PASS?" *Professional Aviation Safety Specialists, AFL-CIO*, n.d. http://www.passnational.org/Public/what_is_pass_.html (March 9, 2011).

46. Adrian Schofield, "Union Sends FAA Proposal for Vote," *Aviation Week*, March 31, 2006, http://www.aviationweek.com/aw/generic/story_generic.jsp?channel=comm&id=news/FAAU03316.xml&headline=Union%20Sends%20FAA%20Proposal%20For%20Vote (March 9, 2011).

47. Adrian Schofield, "FAA Gets Mixed Bag in PASS and NATCA," *Aviation Week*, August 7, 2007, http://www.aviationweek.com/aw/generic/story_channel.jsp?channel=comm&id=news/FLRA0877.xml (March 9, 2011).

48. "FAA Employees and Collective Bargaining," *Professional Aviation Safety Specialists, AFL-CIO*, n.d., http://www.passnational.org/Public/issues_1.html (March 9, 2011).

49. "PASS Pride," *Professional Aviation Safety Specialists, AFL-CIO*, September 15, 2009, http://passregion2.typepad.com/files/pass-pride---september-2009.pdf (March 9, 2011).

50. Rosenberg, "Labor Board Rulings Highlight FAA-Union Tensions," *Government Executive.com*, August 7, 2007, http://www.govexec.com/dailyfed/0807/080707ar1.htm (March 9, 2011)

51. Kirby Harrison, "FAA Wins a Battle, Loses Another," *Aviation International News*, September 2007, http://www.ainonline.com/ain-and-ainalerts/aviation-international-news/single-publication-story/browse/0/article/faa-wins-a-battle-loses-another-9409/?no_cache=1&tx_ttnews%5Bstory_pointer%5D=4&tx_ttnews%5Bmode%5D=1 (March 9, 2011).

52. "PASS Pride."

53. T. Brantley, "FAA Withdraws Unfair Labor Practice (ULP) Case," *Professional Aviation Safety Specialists, AFL-CIO*, http://www.passcontractalert.org/ (March 9, 2011).

54. Ibid.

55. Ibid.

56. Pub. L. No. 107–296, 116 Stat. 2135 (2002).

57. 5 U.S.C. § 9701(a) (Supp. II, 2002).

58. 5 U.S.C. § 9701(b) (1)–(4).

59. 5 U.S.C. § 9701(f) (1) (A).

60. 5 U.S.C. §§ 7101–6, 7111–23, 7131–35 (2000).

61. 70 Fed. Reg. 5272 (February 1, 2005) (codified at 5 C.F.R. chapter 97 and part 9701), Department of Homeland Security Human Resources Management System; "DHS Ruling Deals Administration a Setback: Another Federal Court Victory for Collective Bargaining," *AFL-CIO*, June 27, 2006, http://www.aflcio.org/joinaunion/voiceatwork/d10_maxhr.cfm (May 6, 2008).

62. *American Federation of Government Employees v. Gates*, No. 06-5113, *uscourts.gov*, May 18, 2007, http://pacer.cadc.uscourts.gov/docs/common/opinions/200705/06-5113a.pdf (August 16, 2008).

63. 5 U.S.C. §9701(a); 5 U.S.C. §9701(b) (1)–(4); 5 U.S.C. §§7101–6, 7111–23, 7131–35 (2000).

64. B. Lumpkin, "Senators Give TSA Screeners Union Rights," *San Francisco Chronicle*, February 15, 2007, http://www.sfgate.com/cgi-bin/article.cgi?file=/n/a/2007/02/15/national/w140440S22.DTL&type=politics (May 6, 2008).

65. B. Ballenstedt, "Homeland Security Drops Proposed Labor Relations Plans," *GovernmentExecutive.com*, January 17, 2008, http://www.govexec.com/dailyfed/0108/011708b1.htm (February 10, 2008).

66. "Transportation Security Administration's Efforts to Proactively Address Employee Concerns," Office of the Inspector General, Management Report OIG-08-62, *Department of Homeland Security*, May 2008, http://www.dhs.gov/xoig/assets/mgmtrpts/OIG_08–06_May08.pdf (August 16, 2008).

67. A. J. Castilla and Tim Kriescher quoted in A. Kimery, "Airport Screeners Face Declining Morale, Other Problems," *Homeland Security Today*, July 14, 2008.

68. John Hughes, "U.S. Airport Screeners Pick Union," *Bloomberg*, June 23, 2011, http://www.bloomberg.com/news/print/2011-06-23/u-s-airport-screeners-pick-union.html (June 24, 2011).

69. J. Ritchie, "Airport in Mothballs?" *Pittsburgh (PA) Tribune-Review*, October 27, 2007, http://www.pittsburghlive.com/x/pittsburghtrib/news/s_534819.html (August 22, 2008).

70. R. Poole, "Will Midway Lease Re-start U.S. Airport Privatization?" *Reason Foundation Commentary: Public Works Financing*, January 2007, http://www.reason.org/commentaries/poole_20070100.shtml (August 28, 2008).

71. "Fact Sheet: Chicago Midway (MDW) Airport Privatization Pilot Program," *Federal Aviation Administration*, April 2008. http://www.aci-na.org/static/entransit/mdw_factsheet.pdf; "Airport Privatization Pilot Program," *Federal Aviation Administration*, n.d., http://www.faa.gov/airports_airtraffic/airports/airport_obligations/privatization/index.cfm (August 28, 2008).

72. 49 U.S.C. 47134.

73. Ill. Public Act 94-750 (2006).

74. G. Washburn, "Airline OKs, for Now, Privatizing Midway: Airline Tentatively Backs Daley's Plan," *Chicago Tribune*, November 16, 2007, http://www.chicagotribune.com/news/local/chi-midway-both16nov16,0,2918217.story (August 28, 2008).

75. "Fact Sheet."

76. Jerome R. Corsi, "For Lease: 1 Airport, Slightly Used: Plan Allows Foreign Investors to

Bid on Chicago's Midway," *WorldNetDaily*, April 4, 2008, http://www.wnd.com/?pageId=60744 (August 28, 2008).

77. S. Stanek, "2009 Budget & Tax News: Chicago's Midway Lease Falls Through," *Budget & Tax News*, July 2009, http://news.heartland.org /newspaper-article/2009/07/01/2009-july-budget-tax-news-chicago's-midway-lease-falls-through.

Glossary

administrative law judge (ALJ). In the United States, an official who presides at an administrative trial–type hearing to resolve a dispute between a government agency and someone affected by a decision of that agency. The initial trier of fact and decision maker. Can administer oaths, take testimony, rule on questions of evidence, and make factual and legal determinations.

affirmative-action programs. Programs that provide goals and timetables by which employers will target specific groups for hiring, promotion, and so on.

agency shop. A provision requiring nonmembers of a certified union to pay a sum equal to union dues when the union at a company serves as the agent for and receives dues and assessments from all employees in the bargaining unit, whether or not they are union members.

Airline Deregulation Act of 1978. Act relinquishing all governmental controls regulating the operation of airlines, except for safety requirements.

amendable date. Date at which the provisions of a contract are open to renegotiation. Under the NLRA, contracts terminable and contract termination date more a part of that terminology. More generally, a part of the terminology of the Railroad Labor Act, under which contracts are amendable but do not expire.

American Arbitration Association. Organization of professional arbitrators commonly used as third-party mediators and/or arbitrators in labor disputes and grievance hearings.

American Federation of Labor. Labor organization formed in 1886 by Samuel Gompers, who became known as the father of the American labor movement. The forerunner of the AFL-CIO.

American Federation of Labor and Congress of Industrial Organizations. Commonly called the AFL-CIO. Formed in 1955 by the merger of the AFL and the CIO to stave off the effects of the Taft-Hartley Act and bond labor to a cohesive front. Includes the majority of labor unions in the United States. Notable exceptions the Teamsters and the United Auto Workers.

arbitration. Method of determining a final solution to a dispute between parties to a labor agreement. The final decision from an outside disinterested party usually binding on the parties.

arbitrator. Third party neutral to a dispute. Employed jointly by union and management officials to make binding decisions on employee grievances.

attitudinal structuring. The process of developing close professional relationships between members of the negotiating teams, building the mutual respect and trust necessary to a more cooperative, less-adversarial working relationship.

authorization card. A statement signed by an employee designating a union to act on his or her behalf in collective bargaining or in requesting either the National Mediation Board or the National Labor Relations Board to hold a certification election.

award. Final decision rendered in various types of disputes. For example, an award of an arbitrator in a grievance decision.

back pay. Wages required to be paid to a worker who has been discharged and reinstated with full rights or wages required to be paid to a worker or workers because a contract is signed with a retroactive effective date.

bargaining unit. The defined area eligible to be represented by a particular union. Defined as *craft* or *class* under the Railway Labor Act.

bar rule. Refusal by the NMB to accept an application (bar filing of the application) under certain circumstances.

benefits. Portion of compensation other than direct wages, such as vacation time, health insurance, pension, and so on. Basically came into existence during World War II, when the federal government froze all wage increases.

binding arbitration. Agreement by both parties to a dispute to agree to the final decision of a disinterested third party, after both sides have had the opportunity to present arguments in favor of their particular position.

blue-collar worker. A worker whose job requires manual labor.

boycott. Refusal to deal with or purchase goods or services of a business in an attempt to exert pressure in a labor dispute.

B scale. A lower rate of pay for new hires than in the past, usually catching up with the old ("A") pay scale—typically in two to five years, although such merging is not required.

cease-and-desist order. A command issued by a labor board requiring either the employer or the union to refrain from an unfair labor practice.

certification. Official designation by either the National Labor Relations Board or National Mediation Board that a particular union is the exclusive bargaining representative of employees in a particular unit or class and craft.

check rides. Pilot-performance evaluations made by supervisory personnel during scheduled airline flights.

Civil Aeronautics Board (CAB). An independent federal agency that regulated carrier operations, including rates, routes, operating rights, and mergers, prior to the Deregulation Act of 1978.

class. A group of individuals ranked together as possessing common characteristics or as having the same status.

Clayton Act. Federal legislation passed in 1914 declaring that human labor is not an article of commerce.

closed shop. Arrangement between an employer and a union that only members of the union may be hired. Illegal under the Taft-Hartley Act, except in the construction industry. Not illegal under the Railway Labor Act.

coalition. A group of unions that makes a joint or cooperative effort for their common good in negotiation of contracts or methods of operation. Became pronounced in the airline industry during the late 1970s when wage concessions were requested from all unions.

collective bargaining. Attempt between union and management to resolve conflicting interests in a manner suitable to both parties.

common carrier. An individual or business that advertises to the public that it is available for hire to transport people or property in exchange for a fee.

Commonwealth v. Hunt. A landmark decision rendered in 1842 in the Commonwealth of Massachusetts that declared that the criminal conspiracy doctrine was not applicable in that state. The first decision rendered declaring that unions had a right to exist.

company union. Union organization that receives financial help and support from the company whose employees it represents. Illegal.

concessionary bargaining. Negotiation process wherein the company is generally seeking a reduction of wage and/or benefits or a change in work rules. The negotiation of pay freeze, pay cuts, rollbacks, and other work rule changes occurred frequently in the 1980s.

conciliation. Efforts by a third party to resolve opposing points of view and accommodate a voluntary settlement.

confidential workers. Those workers with access to personnel and labor relations records and files. See also *managerial employees.*

Congress of Industrial Organizations. Labor organization formed in 1938 to unionize employees on an industrial basis rather than a craft or trade basis. Merged with the American Federation of Labor in 1955 to become the AFL-CIO.

contract bar rule. Period of time and rules, applied by both the National Labor Relations Board and the National Mediation Board, determining when an existing contract between an employer and a union will stop a representation election by a rival or raiding union.

cooling-off period. Period of time during which employees are forbidden to strike and the employer is forbidden to lockout. Time for the parties to rethink their positions before they are permitted to utilize self-help methods. See also *thirty-day cooling-off period.*

craft. Those engaged in any trade, taken collectively.

craft and class determinations. Decisions rendered by the National Mediation Board as to workers following a particular craft or class in which they work.

craft union. Labor organization that seeks to include all workers who have a common skill, such as pilots or aerospace machinists.

craft unit. Bargaining unit consisting of workers following a particular craft (e.g., dispatchers) or using a particular type of skill.

criminal conspiracy. As defined in *Commonwealth v. Hunt,* "a combination of two or more persons, by some concerted action, to accomplish some criminal or unlawful purpose, or to accomplish some purpose, not in itself criminal or unlawful, by criminal or unlawful means."

decertification. The process of removing a union as the certified representative of employees within a bargaining unit.

decertification election. Election held by the National Labor Relations Board to determine employee desire to maintain union status.

de facto. Latin expression that means "of the fact" or "in practice" but not ordained by law. Commonly used in contrast to *de jure* ("by law") when referring to matters of law, governance, or technique (such as standards) that are found in the common experience as created or developed without or contrary to a regulation.

deregulation. Process of lifting artificial barriers or governmental control of an industry.

direct negotiations. The period of time when both the company and the union representatives are engaged in bargaining without the presence of a mediator.

distributive bargaining. Classic, old-school approach in which the parties (union and management) view the process of collective bargaining as negotiation to divide up a pie of a fixed size. Any gain by one side necessarily at the expense of the other, so the interests of each side are seen as being in direct conflict. Always highly adversarial and confrontational, typically characterized by mutual hostility, belligerency, posturing, histrionic ranting, table-pounding, threatening, bluffing, secrecy, deceit, and distrust. Also known as *zero-sum bargaining.* For opposite approach, see *integrative bargaining.*

double-breasting. The existence of separate union and nonunion divisions or companies in a single firm.

duty of fair representation. The responsibility of unions to represent fairly and impartially all union and nonunion members of a bargaining unit.

duty to bargain, legally mandated. Both the exclusive bargaining representative and the employer legally obligated to bargain in "good faith" (good-faith bargaining).

economic strike. An employee strike over the failure to negotiate economic issues such as wages or benefits.

emergency board. Board appointed by the president of the United States to investigate the effect potential strikes might have on commerce. Cooling-off periods implemented while the board considers the situations abetting the potential strikes. May be convened under both the Railway Labor Act and the National Labor Relations Act.

employee. A person currently on an employer's payroll; also a person whose work has ceased because of a current strike or an unfair labor practice. Excludes, under the Taft-Hartley Act, agricultural laborers, persons employed in the domestic service of a family or persons at their home, independent contractors, supervisors, persons covered under the RLA, and government employees.

employee ownership. A form of ownership in which employees of a firm also own and direct a sizable share of the company.

Employee Retirement Income and Security Act. Federal statute passed by Congress to ensure that employer pension plans meet minimum participation, vesting, and funding requirements.

employee stock-ownership plan. Program in which employer gives employees the opportunity to become shareholders in the company by matching employees' payment toward stock purchase or by providing matching stock for wages forgone in concessionary bargaining.

equitable remedy. An order for a defendant to do or refrain from doing something, as distinguished from a *remedy at law.*

exclusivity. Certified union's right to exclusively represent all of the employees in a unit or craft and class in collective bargaining.

externality. A consequence of the activity of an individual or firm that is incidental (or "external") to but indivisible from its main activity and that affects the utility of another individual or firm favorably or unfavorably.

fact-finding. Process used to determine facts and make recommendations in major disputes.

featherbedding. Contractual requirements that employees be hired into positions for which their services are not required. Made illegal under the National Labor Relations Act by the Taft-Hartley Act. No such proscription under the Railway Labor Act.

fence agreement. Provision in merger agreement to temporarily continue separate operation of the merging companies' workforces while an orderly integration process of seniority and work rules takes place, allowing operations continue. For example, in a merger of two airlines, flights will typically be operated

by flight deck and cabin crews composed entirely of workers from one or the other of the premerger companies until agreement is reached on these details.

fixed-base operators (FBO). Often called *flying services* or *air services.* Some provide a wide range of services, such as aircraft sales, rental, charter, fueling, and maintenance; flight training; and sales of aeronautical charts, literature, supplies, and gifts. Others limit their services. All operate from a fixed geographic location, as distinguished from the transient "barnstormers" of the early years of aviation business.

fractional ownership. An arrangement for partial ownership of an aircraft. An undivided fractional interest in a specific, serial-numbered aircraft. Size of the interest purchased by a company or individual directly proportional to the number of hours the fractional owner expects to fly in a year. A one-sixteenth interest, representing fifty flight hours per year, typically being the smallest fraction available.

furlough. As used in the airline industry, synonymous with layoff.

general aviation. A broad term from the Federal Aviation Act of 1958 encompassing all but military and airline aviation operations. Characterized by its remarkable diversity, which includes flight training, personal flying in private aircraft for transportation or recreation, crop spraying, aerial firefighting, emergency medical transport, air freight feeders, search and rescue, disaster relief, aerial imaging, law enforcement, transportation of business and government executives, air sightseeing, news gathering and entertainment, and maintaining and servicing aircraft.

good-faith bargaining. A sincere and honest effort by negotiators to reach a labor agreement.

grievance. An employee complaint alleging that a contract violation has occurred. May also be used by a union or an employer to voice allegations of a violation by the opposite party.

Haymarket Riot of 1886. Protest over the establishment of an eight-hour workday. Violence characterized its outcome, leading to the tide of public opinion against labor.

hedging. A financial strategy that airlines and other fuel-dependent industries use to protect against rising prices by locking in (through a variety of forms of transaction) a price for fuel to be delivered in the future.

impasse. Time in negotiations when no movement is either evident or obtainable. The parties unable to resolve issues among themselves. Third-party intervention usually required at this juncture.

injunction. Mandatory order by the court to perform or discontinue a specific activity. Can lead to fines, penalties, and/or jail terms for the party violating the terms of the injunction, if willful failure to comply determined.

integrative bargaining. Collective bargaining as a concerted effort to enlarge the pie so that labor's demands met and productivity improved to at least pay for labor's gains (or in a company in peril, to avoid labor's giving further concessions). A win for both labor and management. Also known as *interest-based bargaining.* For contrasting approach, see *distributive bargaining.*

intent. What the negotiators have in mind when they enter into some specific language. Usually, minutes of negotiation are maintained by the parties to indicate intent should a dispute arise over the contractual language.

interest-based bargaining. See *integrative bargaining.*

Kabuki theater. Somewhat sarcastic slang for the Railroad Labor Act–mandated and extremely time-consuming six- to eight-step process for resolution of major disputes. After the ancient Japanese style of drama that is so ritualized that a performance today would be indistinguishable from one delivered centuries ago, exalting form over substance.

labor agreement. A legal document negotiated between the union and the employer that states the terms and conditions of employment. Also called a *labor contract* or *collective bargaining agreement.*

laboratory conditions. The notion under both the Railway Labor Act and the National Labor Relations Act that workers should be free to decide in an environment free of coercion and misinformation whether they want union representation.

Labor-Management Relations Act. Basic law regulating labor relations of firms whose business affects interstate commerce. More commonly known as the Taft-Hartley Act of 1947. Incorporated into the National Labor Relations Act.

Labor-Management Reporting and Disclosure Act. Established a code of conduct for unions and required union constitutions and bylaws for the benefit of union members. More commonly known as the Landrum-Griffin Act. Incorporated into the National Labor Relations Act.

labor union. An organization of workers formed to bargain collectively with employers over wages and working conditions.

lean manufacturing. The practice of a theory of production that considers the expenditure of resources for any means other than the creation of value for the presumed customer to be wasteful and thus a target for elimination. Also called *lean production* and often known simply as *lean.*

lockout. An employer's closing down of a business to put economic pressure on the employees to accept the employer's contract proposals. The opposite of an economic strike.

management-rights clause. Contractual provision setting forth the rights of management under the terms of the working agreement. May include the right to hire, fire, control the workforce, make assignments, and so on.

managerial employee. An employee who formulates and executes management decisions. See also *confidential workers.*

mediation. Usage of a third party to attempt to find common ground for the settlement of a dispute. Acts on behalf of both parties, making proposals for settlement. Decisions and/or proposals not binding on the parties.

mediator. Third party to a dispute who attempts to coax or cajole the parties to come to terms. Has no binding authority as does an arbitrator.

National Industrial Recovery Act. Federal legislation passed in 1933 by the Roosevelt administration that included language giving employees the right to organize into unions.

National Labor Relations Act. Commonly known as the Wagner Act. Amended in 1947 by the Taft-Hartley Act and in 1959 by the Landrum-Griffin Act. All three acts incorporated to make up the National Labor Relations Act.

National Labor Relations Board. Five-member board appointed by the president of the United States and confirmed by the U.S. Senate to oversee representation and election questions, investigate unfair labor practice charges, and issue complaints over such charges.

National Mediation Board (NMB). Agency set up under the Railway Labor Act to mediate labor disputes in the railroad and air transportation industries and to conduct elections for choice of bargaining agents. The three board members appointed by the president of the United States and confirmed by the U.S. Senate.

national unions. The parent bodies that help organize, charter, guide, and assist affiliated local unions.

Norris–La Guardia Act. Eliminated yellow-dog contracts and made injunctions in labor matters more difficult to obtain. Popular name for the Federal Anti-Injunction Act of 1932.

no-strike clause. Portion of a contract in which a union agrees to not strike during the term of the contract for any reason. Usually also present, a company condition to prohibit the company from engaging a lockout.

opener. Formal proposal to begin negotiations. Details items to be considered during the process.

pattern bargaining. Occurs when the same or essentially the same contract is used as a guidepost for subsequent agreements for several companies, often in the same industry.

picketing. The establishment by union members of lines around the employer's premises for the purpose of achieving specific bargaining objectives.

proffer of arbitration. A formal offer by the National Mediation Board to resolve a dispute by binding arbitration after negotiation and mediation have reached impasse. Both parties must accept the offer for this process to go forward.

quality circles. Voluntary meetings of groups of workers with common work interests for the purpose of identifying, analyzing, and solving work-related problems, particularly in a production process.

Railway Labor Act (RLA). Legislation passed in 1926 that laid the foundation for the Wagner Act of 1935. Established administrative procedures for the prompt and orderly settlement of labor disputes between railroad unions and carriers. Guaranteed to unions the rights to self-organization and collective bargaining. Amended in 1936 to bring airlines under its jurisdiction.

rank-and-file employees. Generally, employees having no supervisory or management responsibilities. For purposes of ratification of a tentative contract, union members who are not officers of the union.

ratification. Approval required by the rank-and-file membership to implement a tentative contract agreed to by the negotiating committee of the union.

regulation. Laws that establish standards of conduct and affect the behavior of other governmental organizations, private organizations and individuals through legally enforceable methods; a rule by which conduct is regulated and which an authority develops to administer the principles of a given law.

remedy at law. An award by a court, such as a judgment that the defendant pay the plaintiff money for damages caused by the plaintiff's unlawful actions or inaction.

replacement worker. New, nonunion employees brought in by an employer during a strike to perform the work previously performed by striking employees. Also called a *scab* or *strikebreaker*.

representation election. A vote taken by employees in an election unit to determine whether a union is desired.

representative. Any person or persons, labor union, organization, or corporation designated either by a carrier or group of carriers or by its or their employees to act for it or them.

reverse pattern bargaining. Airlines using concessions granted by unions at other airlines as leverage to obtain similar concessions from their companies' unions.

right-to-work laws. Laws that ban union-security agreements by forbidding contracts that make employment conditional on union membership or nonmembership. Passed as a result of the Taft-Hartley Act and not applicable to the Railway Labor Act or the employees of the railroads or airlines.

run-off election. In a representation election where more than one union is competing to represent a bargaining unit, a second employee election held after no union received a majority of the votes cast in the first election.

scab. A strikebreaker or replacement worker.

scope of bargaining. All of the issues to be negotiated in a collective bargaining effort. May include both mandatory and permissive but not prohibited issues.

secondary boycott. Refusal to deal with or buy goods from a customer or supplier of an employer with whom strikers have a dispute. Can take the form of direct pressure by the establishment of picket lines against the supplier, which endeavors to stop the boycotted establishment's employees from working or to stop others from doing business with the boycotted employer.

Section 401 certification. Civil Aeronautics Board authorization permitting a carrier to engage in air transportation. Derived from Section 401 of the Federal Aviation Act of 1958.

Section 6 notice. The formal notification from either party to a major dispute under the Railway Labor Act that begins the process of negotiations.

self-help. A strike, a lockout, or any legal maneuvering designed to promote or force agreement with an opposition party.

seniority. Length of service with an employer or bargaining unit.

snapback provision. Automatically restores the cutbacks to preconcession levels on a certain future date or other specified contingency, such as the company's return to profitability, where labor has given concessions in wages, benefits, or work rules to help the company survive a crisis.

sovereignty. "The supreme, absolute, and uncontrollable power by which an independent state is governed." H. C. Black, *Black's Law Dictionary*, 4th ed. (St. Paul, MN: West, 1968), 1568, s.v. "sovereignty."

steward. A union steward, usually an elected employee whose position in the union is to help covered employees present their problems to management.

straw-man election. Voting for a person, rather than a union, in a decertification election held for the sole purpose of ousting the incumbent union and returning workers in the affected bargaining unit to unrepresented status upon that person's subsequent resignation. A ploy to circumvent Railway Labor Act provisions that do not enable railway and air carrier workers to return to unrepresented status once a union has been certified to represent them.

strike. Cessation of work by employees to gain economic benefit or changes in work rules. Generally is organized and occurs after contract termination or after termination of the cooling-off period.

strike benefit. Replacement income paid by the union to striking members during a strike.

strikebreaker. Employee who continues to work after the union has called a strike and who is willing to cross the union's picket lines. Also applied to employee hired specifically to work during a strike. Sometimes also applied to contractor engaged by management to use force and intimidation against strikers and to government agent tasked to disperse strikers.

strike deadline. The date announced by the union when a strike will commence if an agreement has not been reached.

supermediation. A period of "public interest" negotiations mediated by a member of the National Mediation Board during the cooling-off period following mediation to impasse in a further attempt to assist the parties to reach a settlement.

supervisor. An agent of management with the authority to hire and fire and make compensation decisions regarding employees. Under the National Labor Relations Act, supervisors enjoy no protection of bargaining rights. Such is not necessarily the case under the Railway Labor Act.

sympathy strike. Strike called to influence the outcome of a dispute in another company or industry.

system board of adjustment. Consists of one or more members from company management and an equal number from the union to decide grievances. May also include a third neutral party to break tie votes. The air carrier counterpart to the Railway Labor Act's National Railroad Adjustment Board.

Taft-Hartley Act. Popular term applied to the Labor-Management Relations Act of 1947.

tariff. A tax imposed on goods when they are moved across a political boundary. Usually associated with protectionism, the economic policy of restraining trade between nations. In airline terminology, a tariff encompasses the total agreement between the airline and the passenger or shipper.

thirty-day cooling-off period. A thirty-day period during which no strike or lockout may take place. Begins after a proffer of arbitration is refused by either party to a dispute and the National Mediation Board releases the case or after a Presidential Emergency Board has issued its findings. See also *cooling-off period*.

two-tier wage agreement. Wage settlement that decreases the pay rates of future hires while maintaining or increasing the pay rates of existing employees. Occurs when one group of employees (usually new hires) receives a different wage rate than other employees and may remain at a reduced rate for the life of their employment tenure or until some merge date. Employer achieves lower labor costs by paying new workers less than existing workers.

unfair labor practices. Actions employed by unions, management, or both that are prohibited by Section 8 of the Taft-Hartley Act.

union security clause. A contractual provision recognizing a union as the bargaining representative for a company. Makes it easier for unions to enroll and retain members.

union shop. Arrangement with a union where the employer may hire anyone desired, but a newly hired employee is required within a specified period of time to join the union certified on the property.

Wagner Act. The National Labor Relations Act, passed in 1935 and named after its sponsor Robert F. Wagner, a senator from New York. Recognized unions in industries other than the railroads and provided requirement for employers in dealing with unions.

walkout. Strike or other concerted effort in which employees leave the work area.

white-collar worker. A salaried professional or an educated worker who performs semi-professional office, administrative, and sales coordination tasks, as opposed to a blue-collar worker, whose job requires manual labor.

wildcat strike. Spontaneous work stoppage that takes place without the sanction of the union leadership and in violation of the labor contract.

work rules. Rules directly related to the terms and conditions negotiated between management and labor. Consist of all employment issues of a nonwage nature.

yellow-dog contract. Agreement in which an employee, in return for the opportunity to work, guarantees that he or she will not join a union or become involved with union activity. Declared illegal by the Norris–La Guardia Act and provisions of the Railway Labor Act.

zero-sum bargaining. See *distributive bargaining*.

Index

Page numbers in italics denote illustrations.

A-76 process, 239–42
Abulafia, Richard, 218
acquisitions, 101–2
Adair v. United States, 55
Adamson Act of 1916, 48
administrative law judge (ALJ), 8, 147, 297
Administrative Procedure Act, 98
Administrator of Aeronautics, 166
Administrator of Aviation, 6
advisory/interest arbitration, 128–29, 152–53
Aeroman, 194–95
Aerospace Industries Association (AIA), 220
aerospace industry, *9*, 9–10, *10*, 204–26; airframe
    manufacturers, 210–11, 213; declining experience
    level, 221–22, *222*; educational initiatives, 223–25;
    employment statistics, *205*; fuel prices and,
    207–8; health-care costs, 212, 215; labor shortage,
    220–25; lean manufacturing, 212–13; mergers
    and acquisitions, 208–12; military contracts,
    204–5; nonproduction workers, 204; number of
    employees, *205*; outsourcing and globalization,
    208, 213–19, 225; pensions, 212; retirement,
    208, 220, 223; sales, 204; strikes, 214–18;
    subcontractors, 204; suppliers, 211; unions, 211–12
affirmative action measures, 75–76, 138
Afghanistan, 242
African American workers, 31
aftermarket services and systems, 233
Age Discrimination in Employment Act (1967, 1984,
    and 1986), 75
agency shop, 67–68
age of workers, 22
Airborne Freight, *228*
Airbus Industrie, 213, 220, 225
Air California (NLRB), 229
air carrier operating certificate, 166–67, 198
Air Commerce Act of 1926, 5
aircraft: 162 Skycatcher, 214; Airbus A-321, 190;
    Airbus A380, *208*; Apache Block III attack

helicopters, 206–7, *207*; BAC-111, 145; Boeing 314
    ("Clipper"), *235*; Boeing 727–51C, *123*; Boeing
    737, 145, *191*; Boeing 787 Dreamliner, 190, 214,
    215, *216*, 216–18, 225; Bombardier C series, 225;
    C130J Hercules transport, 212; DC-9, 145;
    efficiency, 176, 177, 189–90, 225; F-22 Raptor, 212,
    243; Gulfstream IV-SP, *112*; L1011, *181*, 210; MD-
    80, 190; P-40 Warhawk, *209*; P-51 Mustang, 226;
    P-80 Shooting Star, 226; S-92 helicopter, 214;
    transport, 208; very light jets (VLJ), 213
Aircraft Mechanics Fraternal Organization
    (AMFA), 10, 95, 116–17, 120–21, 192; Ozark
    Holdings and, 174; two-tier system, view of, 187
Aircraft Owners and Pilots Association (AOPA), 227
Air Force Logistics Command, 242
airframe manufacturers, 210–11, 213
airframes, 225
AIR Inc., 200–201
Airline Deregulation Act of 1978 (ADA), 6–7, 101,
    109, 122, 123, 165; as anti-labor act, 181; enactment
    of, 168–69; labor protective provisions, 170;
    public-policy goal of, 203; sunset provision, 169.
    See also deregulation
airline industry, 165–203; bankruptcies, 181, 182,
    184–87, 191–92; certificates of public convenience,
    166–67; cost reduction, 190–91; deregulation,
    competition, and consequences, 169–88;
    downsizing, 193–94; environmental impacts, 201–
    2; era of economic regulation by CAB, 166–69;
    fares, 167, 170–72; fuel crisis of 1979, 172; globalized
    economy and, 194–95; legacy airlines, 69, 165, 170,
    191; looming issues, 199–202; megacarriers, 7, 132,
    203; move toward deregulation, 168–69; Mutual
    Aid Pact (MAP), 122–23, 168, 171, 179; new carriers,
    171–72, *173*, *175*, 180, 189–90, 195–96; pensions,
    192–93; RLA Amendment of 1936 and, 58, 165;
    shifting from regulation to competition, 170–71;
    trends, issues, and challenges in labor relations,
    188–99. *See also* bankruptcies; deregulation;
    mergers and acquisitions

Airline Pilot Job Monthly, 200–201

Air Line Pilots Association (ALPA), 10, 70, 101, *113*, 191, 198; Atlantic Southeast Airlines and, 119; deregulation and, 170, 175, 182, 188; early efforts, 8, 58, 177; featherbedding, 145; mergers and, 113; Northwest Airlines and, 123; Southern Airlines and, 167; United Air Lines and, 116, 182, 192

airlines: major and national, 10–15, *11*; regional, 10, *11*, 15–16, *140*, 200

Air Mail Act of 1925 (Kelly Act), 5, *5*

airmail carriers, 5, *5*, 8, 20, 58, 82

air medical-emergency transport services, 228–30

Air Methods Corp. (NMB), 230

Air Methods Corporation, *228*, 228–29, 230

Airport Privatization Pilot Program, 255–57

airports: budgets, 254–55; downsizing, 193–94; general aviation, 234–33; outsourcing and privatization, 255–57

Air Safety Board, 6, 166

air safety inspectors, 245–46

Air Service Improvement Act of 2008, 245

air taxi companies, 230

air traffic controllers, 244–45; PATCO strike, 23–24, *24*, 69, 69–71, 109, 130, 180–82, 196

air traffic specialists, 242–44

AirTrain (JFK Airport), 231, *231*

AirTran, 199

AirTran Airways, 193

Air Transport Association of America, 166, 191

air transportation, *9*, 10–16

Air Transport Employees Union, 198

Alaska Airlines, 12–14, 122

AlixPartners, 220

All-American Airways, *140*

All-American Aviation Company, *140*

Allee v. Medrano, 246

Allegheny Airlines, *140*, 140–41

Allied Pilots Association (APA), 14, 120, 191

Alteon Training, 200

Amalgamated Association of Iron, Steel, and Tin Workers, 35

amendments to the Constitution: First, 59, 143, 246; Fifth, 59; Tenth, 64; Fourteenth, 46, 48

Ameren Services, 223

American Airlines, 96, 113, 120, 193; avoidance of bankruptcy, 191; two-tier contracts, 187

American Arbitration Association, 160

American Federation of Government Employees (AFGE), 20, 254

American Federation of Labor (AFL), 31, 32, 33, 42, 53

American Federation of Labor–Congress of Industrial Organizations (AFL-CIO), 25, 67

American Federation of State, County, and Municipal Employees (AFSCME), 19, 131

American Postal Workers Union (APWU), 20

American Potash decision (NLRB), 106

American Railway Union (ARU), 31, 37, 42

Americans with Disabilities Act of 1990, 76, 161

America West Airlines, 101, 113, 119

America West case, 142

Amtrak, 4

anarchists (labor-union activists), 34, *34*

Apollo, 171

applicant, 87

arbitration, 8–9, 23, 25, 47, *60*, 110, 118–19; advisory/interest, 128–29, 152–53; binding, 22, 154; compulsory, 54–55; costs, 158–59, 161; final, 128–29; grievance type, 152–53, 154–56; under NLRA, 127–29; overruling decisions, 157–58, 159–60

Arbitration Act of 1888, 40–41, 42, 46

arbitrators, 154–56, 160, 282

Army Appropriation Act of 1916, 50

Association of Flight Attendants (AFA), 10, *12*, 12–14, 98, 119, *121*; America West, 1990, 142; Horizon Airlines case, 143; PSA/Piedmont merger and, 197

Association of Professional Flight Attendants (APFA), 96, 113, 191

Atlantic Southeast Airlines, 119

attitudinal structuring, 113–14

authorization cards, 89, 92, 104, *105*, 197

Aviation Corporation of America (AVCO), 208

aviation industry, *9*, 9–17, *10*. *See also* aerospace industry; airline industry

Aviation Safeguards case (NLRB), 230

bad faith, 124, 143

baggage loading, 184

Baldwin-Felts Detective Agency, 38

ballots, 87, 106, *108*; absentee, 142; Key, 98–101, *100*, 102; Laker, 98–100, *99*, 102. *See also* elections

Baltimore & Ohio Railroad, 43

bankruptcies, 7, 14, 102, 113, 124, 165, 191–92; abrogation of contracts, 185–86; Chapter 7, 74, 191; Chapter 11, 181, 182, 184, 191; Chapter 13, 74; debtor-in-possession status, 73; legislation, 72–74

Bankruptcy Amendment Act of 1984, 72–73, 74

Bankruptcy Reform Act of 1978, 73, 74

bargaining units, 23–25, 106; determination of, 21, 93–95; true craft group, 106; types of recognition, 20–21

Bashers, Eric, 41

BBA Aviation PLC, 232–33

Bedford Cut Stone Co. v. Journeymen Stone Cutters Association of North America, 50

Bell, Marsha, 200
Benoist Type XIV flying boat, 39, *39*
Berkley, Malcolm, 86
Berkshire Hathaway Company, 110, *111*, 234
Big Four brotherhoods, 31, 48
Bildisco & Bildisco, 185
Bill of Rights of union members, 71
Birth of Modern Public Employee Unions, The
    (Wechsler), 20
Bisignani, Giovanni, 199
Black, Chris, *121*
Black, Henry Campbell, 19
blacklists, 34
Blakey, Marion, 220
Blondin, Mark, 217
Blue Skies contract, 182–83
Board of Mediation and Conciliation, 48
Boeing, 204, 206–8; strikes at, 214–18
Bombardier, 214, 225, 231
Borman, Frank, 181
Boston Journeymen Bootmakers' Society, 28
boycotts, 42–43, 49, 321
Bradley International Airport, Connecticut, 193–94
Brandeis, Louis, 46
Braniff, Paul, *182*
Braniff, Thomas, *182*
Braniff Airways Inc., 7, 143
Braniff International Airways Inc., 172, 196;
    bankruptcy, 182, 184, 202
Branson, Richard, *199*
Britain, 255
British Airports Authority (BAA), 255
British Overseas Airways Corporation (BOAC), *235*
Bronczek, David J., 85
Bronfenbrenner, Kate, 97–98, 138–39, 145
Brotherhood of Locomotive Engineers, 31
Brotherhood of Locomotive Firemen and
    Enginemen, 31, 52
Brotherhood of Railroad Trainmen, 31
*Brotherhood of Railroad Trainmen v. Chicago River
    & Indiana Railroad Co.*, 157
Brotherhood of Railway and Steamship Clerks,
    96–97, 139–40
Brotherhood of Railway and Steamship Clerks case,
    96–97, 139–40
Buffenbarger, Tom, 217–18
Buffett, Warren, 110, *111*, 234
Bureau of National Affairs, 124
Bush, George W., 22, 120–21, 201; aerospace industry
    and, 222, 240, 243, 244, 245, 257–58
Bush, George W., administration, 72
Business and Professional Women, *75*
business-jet charters, 16, 110–12

Butler Aviation, 232
Button, K., 47

California Division of Aeronautics, 236–37
California Eastern Airways, 241
California Eastern Aviation, 241
campaigns, union contributions to, 71
cap-and-trade carbon offsets, 202
Capital Airlines, 167, 168
Carnegie, Andrew, 35
Carnegie Steel Company, 35
Carnegie, Phipps Steel Company, 36–37
Carpenters Union, 32
carriers: affiliates, 82–83; defined, 83–84, 230,
    231, 234, 261; foreign-flag carriers, 14–15, *60*;
    intrastate, 81; section 401 certification, 15, *173*, *175*
Carter, Jimmy, *6*, 70, 135, 169
case studies: aerospace labor shortage, 223–25;
    Air Methods Corporation, 228–29; *American
    Federation of Government Employees v. Stone*,
    252–53; assessment of deregulation, 176–80;
    Boeing strikes, 2008, 216–18; CHAOS, 12–14;
    Colorado Coal Field War, 37–40; *Commonwealth
    v. Hunt*, 28–30; DynCorp International, *241*,
    241–42, *242*; FedEx, 85–86; fractional ownership
    companies, 158; *Hitchman Coal & Coke Company
    v. Mitchell*, 43–46; military contracts, 206–8;
    Mutual Aid Pact—Northwest Orient Airlines,
    122–23; *National Treasury Employees Union
    v. Chertoff*, 249–51; NetJets Aviation, 110–12;
    PATCO strike, 60–71; Pinkerton Detective
    Agency, 35–37; Professional Aviation Safety
    Specialists, 246–47; Taft-Hartley, 134–36
Cassell, Frank H., 196
C check inspections, 194–95
cease-and-desist orders, 138, 143, 148
Cerberus Capital Management, 242
Certificates of Public Convenience and Necessity,
    166–67
certification: NLRA and, 102–14, *104*, 303–5; NMB
    and, 87–88; petition for, 104–5; Railway Labor
    Act (RLA) and, 81–102, *88*, *115*; unfair labor
    practices, 140–44. *See also* elections
Cesar Chavez Workforce Fairness Act of 1993, 132
Cessna, 214
Chamber of Commerce of the United States, 48, 102
CHAOS (create havoc around our system), 12–14
charter operations, 17, 110–12, 230–32
Chell, M. A., 223
*Chelsea Catering Corp. and United Food &
    Commercial Workers International Union*
    (NLRB), 230
Chicago, Burlington, and Quincy Railroad, 40

Chicago Midway International Airport, 255–56, *256*

China, 200, 214, 220

China Commercial Aircraft Company (CCAC), 214

Cigar Makers National Union, 32

CitationShares, 112

city pairs, 15, 166, 167, 171

Civil Aeronautics Act of 1938 (CAA), 5–6, 15, 166

Civil Aeronautics Authority, 6, 47, 166

Civil Aeronautics Board (CAB), 6, 15, 47, 122–23, 202–3; ceases operations, 169; era of regulation by, 166–69; fare levels and, 170–71; fence agreements, 196–97; new carriers and, 196

Civil Aviation Administration of China (CAAC), 200

Civil Reserve Air Fleet (CRAF), 199

Civil Rights Act of 1964, 74–75, 76

civil service. *See* federal civil service labor law

Civil Service and National Security Personnel System Act, 238–39

Civil Service Commission, 18

Civil Service Reform Act (CSRA) of 1978, 17, 18, 96, 129; free-speech provisions, 146–47; grievance procedures and, 151, 161, 162; Title VII, Federal Labor Relations Act, 21–22; unfair labor practices, 133, 145–48, 150. *See also* Federal Labor Relations Authority

Civil War, 36

class and craft determination, 23, 89, 93–95, 106

Clayton Antitrust Act of 1914, 49–50, 61, 219

Cleveland, Grover, 37

Clinton, William Jefferson, 22, 74, 120, *121*, 238, 243

closed shop, 59, 67, 68, 71, 179

coal mines, 59

code-sharing agreements, 15–16

Cohen, Marvin, 189–90

coin toss method, 160

collective bargaining, 317; concessionary, 176, 182, 183–85, 191, 211–12, 244; distributive (zero-sum), 110, 113; good-faith, 8, 21, 112, 124, 167; integrative (interest-based), 110–13; mandatory subject of, 77, *126*, 153; Norris–La Guardia Act and, 61; pattern, 116, 122, 191; positional, 111–12; provisions of Railway Labor Act, *60*; public-sector, 23–24; resistance and sovereignty doctrine, 18; reverse pattern, 191; scope of, 23, 130, 132, 175, 182–83, 237, 248–51, 257–58; state and local government, 130–31. *See also* bargaining units

collective bargaining agreement, negotiating, 109–32; approaches to bargaining, 110; arbitration, 118–19, 127–29; average duration, 117–18; bargaining topics, 124–25, *126*; contract-negotiation process, 125; emergency boards, 120–21; non-airline/railroad private sector under NLRA, 124–29; procedures

in the airlines under RLA, 114–24; public-sector procedures under other federal and state laws, 129–31; self-help, 126, 128; supermediation, 110, 119. *See also* mediation; Mutual Aid Pact; strikes

Colorado Coal Field War (1913–14), 37–40, 46

Colorado Fuel & Iron Corporation (CF&I), 37–40

Colored National Labor Union, 31

Command Airways, 96

commerce, defined, 261, 296

commerce clause, 3, 7, 46, 59, 62, 65, 81

Commonwealth v. Hunt, 27–30, 41

communications, interference through, 140–42

commuter airlines, 15–16

company stores, 38

company unions, 58, 88, 231–32

compromises, 111–12

Computer Sciences Corporation (CSC), 241

concessionary bargaining, 176, 182, 183–85, 191, 211–12, 244

conciliation, 110

confidential personnel, 103, 105

conspiracy, unions as, 27–31, 41

Continental Airlines, 109, 174, 175, *181*; bankruptcy, 7, 73–74, 181, 184–86, 188, 191; downsizing, 193; ESOPs, 183; merger with United, 198–99; unions and, 14, 95, 122, 188, 191

contract, liberty of, 48, 294

contract field team (CFT), 242

contract in perpetuity, 131

contracts: abrogation of, 185–86; amendable date, 114–17, 131, 178; ratification process, 151–52; suits for violation of, 219; yellow-dog (union-free agreements), 43–46, 48, 50, *54*, 58, *61*

Contract Work Hours and Safety Standards Act, 243

control, defined, 84

Coolidge, Calvin, *53*, 55

cooling-off periods, 9, 12, 55, *115*, 119, 127, 178

corruption, 71

Costello, Jerry, 245

counterproposals, 143

craft and class determination, 23, 89, 93–95, 106

craft unions, 10, 33

Curtiss, Glenn, 208, *209*

Curtiss-Wright Corporation, 208, *209*

Dalrymple, John, 220

Danbury Hatters (Loewe v. Lawlor), 42–43, 49

Darby, Kit, 200–201

"Death Special" armored car, 38

Debs, Eugene V., 37, 42

decertification, 70, *77*, 89

defined benefit plans, 192–93, 212, 217

Delle-Femine, O. V., 116, 187

Delta Air Lines, 98, 101, *102*, 178–79; bankruptcy, 192; concessionary bargaining, 183; downsizing, 193; wage cuts, 185

Delta-Northwest merger, 192, 198

Department of Defense (DOD), 210, 238–39

Department of Homeland Security (DHS), 236, 237

Department of Justice, 145, 197, 210

Department of Labor, 72, 75

Department of Transportation, 17, 197, *236*, 237

deregulation, 6, 69, 123, 169–88; accelerated rate of change, 180–82; assessment of, 176–80; concessionary bargaining, 176, 182–83; Continental bankruptcy, 185–87; double-breasting, 174–75, 182; ESOPs, 183; fare wars, 171–72; fuel crisis of 1979, 172; job security, 182–83; labor climate before, 178–79; labor protective provisions, 170; legacy airlines and, 170; managing for competitiveness, 172; move toward, 168–69; new carriers, 171–72, *173*, *175*, 180, 189–90, 195–96; shifting to competition, 170–71; small-community air service, 169–70; success of labor bargaining and, 179; two-tier contracts, 175–76, 187–88. *See also* Airline Deregulation Act of 1978 (ADA); airline industry

Deutsche Post World Net, *228*

Developing a 21st Century Aerospace Workforce (LARA), 221

developmental (subsidy) policy initiatives, 4–5

DHL, *228*

Disabilities Act of 1991, 75

distributive (zero-sum) bargaining, 110, 113

Dobbs Houses v. NLRB (NLRB), 229, 230

domestic servants, 105

double-breasting, 174–75, 182

due process of law, *4*, 46, *64*, 65

Dunlop, John T., 181

Duplex Printing v. Deering, 50

Durbin, Richard, 245

Duscoe, Rudolph O., 144

Dye, Thomas R., 3

Dynalectron Corporation, 241

DynCorp International, *241*, 241–42, *242*

Eastern Airlines, 74, 102, 171, 174, 183; 1989 dispute, 181, 188; wage cuts, 184

Eastman, Joseph, 94

Easton, Joseph B., 58

Eco-Aviation conference, 225

economic regulation, 5–7, 26, 41, 166–69

economy: 1830s depression, 27; 1873 depression, 36; currency fluctuation, 220; Great Depression, 55–56, 208; Great Recession, 131, 132, 257, 258; stock market crash of 1929, 208

education, 222, 236; initiatives, 223–25

eight-hour day movement, 33, 48, 50

elections, 17, 21, *64*, 71; absentee ballots, 142; ballots, 87, *97*, 98–102, *99*, *100*, 106, 142; certification without, 138; employer interference in, 97–98, 136–38; exceptions to rules, 98–101; NLRA certification process, 102–7; NLRB and, 106–7, *107*, *108*; NMB and, 90–92; participation, 93; petition for certification, 104–5; Railway Labor Act certification process, 81–102, *88*, *115*; representation disputes, 91–92; representation election, 95–98; straw-man, 102; treatment of non-votes, 96–97. *See also* certification; jurisdictional determination

Elkins Act of 1903, 47

El Salvador International Airport, 194

Embry-Riddle Aeronautical University (ERAU), 234–35

emergency boards, 68, 109, *115*, 120–21, 289–90, 315–17

emergency dispute resolutions, *54*, 57, *60*, 312–13

Employee Retirement Income Security Act (ERISA) of 1974, 76, 192

employees: class or craft, 89; clerical, 14–15, 139; declining experience level, 221–22, *222*; defined, 86, 87, 102–3, 105, 295; labor shortages, 199–201, 220–25; nontraditional job descriptions, 189; part-time, 105, 189; professional, 105, 204; protection of right to organize, 58; rights of, *66*, 298; subject to RLA, 86–87

employees at will, 16

employee stock-ownership plans (ESOPs), 183, 184, 197

employee trust funds, 188

employers: affirmative duties on, 63; interference in elections, 97–98, 136–38; petition for certification and, 104–5; representation disputes and, 88–89; subject to NLRA, 103; unfair labor practices charges against, *137*

engines, 190, 213, 214, 225

Enterprise Wheel & Car decision, 157, 158

environmental impacts: aerospace industry, 225–26; airline industry, 201–2

Equal Employment Opportunity (EEO), 75, 161

Equal Employment Opportunity Act of 1972, 74

Equal Employment Opportunity Commission (EEOC), 162

Equal Pay Act (EPA) of 1963, 74–75, *75*

equitable remedy, 44

Erdman Act of 1898, 46–47, 55

European Aviation Safety Agency, 194

Evergreen Aviation Ground Logistics (NLRB), 230

examiners, 74

exclusivity, 8

Executive Jet Aviation, 110, 230
Executive Jet Aviation Inc. (NMB), 230
Executive Order 10988 of 1962, 20–21
Executive Order 11246 (1965), 75
Executive Order 11491 of 1970, 21
Executive Order 12871 of 1993, 22
Executive Order 13203 of 2001, 22
Executive Order 13624 of 2002, 243
executive orders, 20–22, 75, 238–39
ex parte injunctive relief, 61
ExpressJet, 193
externalities, 5

fact-finding, 23, 25
fair competition, 62–63
Fair Labor Standards Act of 1938 (FLSA), *54*, 72,
    243–44
fares, 170–72
featherbedding, *66*, 68, *77*, 145
federal agencies, unfair labor practices and, 133,
    145–48
Federal Arbitration Act, 158
Federal Aviation Act of 1958, 167, 227, *236*;
    Reauthorization Acts, 85, 86, 245, 255
Federal Aviation Administration (FAA), *69*, 69–70,
    236, *236*; inspections and, 194–95; unfair labor
    practices and, 147–48
Federal Aviation Agency, *236*
Federal Aviation Regulations (FARs), 17; Part 91,
    subpart K, 158, 231; Part 121, 231; Part 135, 158,
    230–31
Federal Aviation Science and Technological
    Association (FASTA), 147
federal civil service labor law, 17–24; executive
    orders, 20–21, 22; merit system, 17–18; National
    Partnership Council, 22; political appointment,
    17; public-sector labor unions, 18–19, 22–24. *See
    also* Civil Service Reform Act (CSRA) of 1978
Federal Express (FedEx), 84–86, 102, 116, *228*
Federal Labor Relations Act (Title VII, Civil Service
    Reform Act of 1978), 21–22
Federal Labor Relations Authority (FLRA), 17,
    18, 21–22, 70, 130; unfair labor practices under,
    133, 147–48. *See also* Civil Service Reform Act
    (CSRA) of 1978Federal Labor Relations Board, 22
Federal Mediation and Conciliation Service (FMCS),
    22, *66*, 68, 117, 125, 127, 160, *160*, 244; references in
    text of NLRA, 301, 302, 312–15, 317–18
Federal Service Labor Management Relations
    statute, 129, 148
Federal Services Impasses Panel, 21, 130
Federation of Organized Trades and Labor Unions,
    32–33

fence agreements, 196–97
final arbitration, 128–29
Fingerhut Granados Opinion Research, 223
first strike method, 160
fixed-base operators (FBOs), 16, 189, 230, 232–34
Flexjet, 231
flight attendants, 10, *12*, 87, 96, 98, 113, 119; CHAOS,
    12–14; TWA strike, 1986, 87
flight engineer position, 183
Flight Options LLC, 231, 232
Flight Safety Foundation, 200
Flight Safety Inc., 234
Flight Safety Inc. (NLRB), 229
Flight Safety International Inc. (FSI), 234, 241
Flight Safety Services Corporation, 234
flight schools, 200–201, 234–35
flight service stations (FSS), 242–44
Florida East Coast Railway strike (1963), 129
flying boats, 234, *235*
*Flying the Line: The First Half-Century of the Air
    Line Pilots Association*, 145
Flying Tiger, 102
Ford, Gerald R., 168
foreign-flag carriers, 14–15, *60*
foreign investment partners, 256–57
foreign ownership of airlines, 199
foreign repair stations, 194–95, 213
fractional aircraft-ownership programs, 110, 158,
    230–32
free-speech provisions, 146–47
Frick, Henry Clay, 35, 37
Frontier Airlines, 157, 188, 196
FSS Airholdings, 229
fuel costs, 165–66, 190–92, 201; aerospace industry,
    207–8; crisis of 1979, 172; hedging, 190–91
function test, 228
furloughs, 176, 181, 182, 185, 193, 216

Garcia, Andres, 195
gender discrimination, 74, 75
General Accounting Office, 122
general aviation (GA), 16–17, 227–35; charter and
    fractional operators, 230–32; flight training, 234–
    35; ground support and maintenance, 232–34;
    jurisdictional determination, 227–30
general public, 109
Giant Cement Company strike (2005), 129
Gibbons v. Ogden, 81
Gilmore, Peter, 134
Glading, Laura, 113
globalization, 194–95; aerospace industry, 213–19, 225
Globe Aviation Services (NMB), 228
Goen, Jeff T., 212

Goforth, Ray, 215
Goldenberg, Shirley, 19
Gompers, Samuel, 32, *33*, 61
good-faith bargaining, 8, 21, 112, 124, 167
Goodrich Aerostructures, 214
"Goose That Laid Golden Eggs, The" (Joedicke), 176–80
Gore, Al, 240
Gould, Jay, 32
Government Accounting Office (GAO), 245
grandfather rights, 58
granger laws, *4*
Great Upheaval of 1886, 65
Greenspan, Alan, 226
Gregoire, Chris, 217
grievance, defined, 151
grievance procedures, 58, 151–62; arbitration, 152–53, 157–61; arbitration costs, 158–59, 161; arbitration under NLRA, *159*, 159–61; contract administration, 151–52; under CSRA and state laws, 161; NMB and, 152–53, 156; overruling arbitration decisions, 157–58, 159–60; statutory alternatives, 161–62; structural arrangements, 153–54; system board of adjustment, 156–57, 159, 162; Title VII, 22
ground services, 84, 95, 189, 230
guards, 105

Hamill Manufacturing, 220
Hamilton, J. Scott, 157
Hartley, Fred, 134
Hartley bill, 135
Haymarket Riot of 1886, 32, 34, *34*
health-care costs, 212, 215
health care industry, 317–18
Heckel, Richard W., 224, 225
hedging, 190–91
Hepburn Act of 1906, 47
history of U.S. labor law, 26–52; early judicial actions, 26–30; legislative beginnings, 40–48; national unions, 30–33; non-railroad labor activities, 48–50; Pinkerton National Detective Agency, 35–37; railroad labor gains, 50–51; strikes and the railroad industry, 34–35
Hitchman Coal & Coke Company v. Mitchell, 43–46
holding companies, 172, 181, 199, 208
holding-out test, 230
Holmes, Oliver Wendell, 42
Holzer, Harry, 224
Homestead Strike of 1892, 35, 36–37
Horizon Airlines, 143–44
hospital-based model (NBM), 228–29
Howell-Barkley Bill, 54–55

Hughes, Charles, *65*
Hughes, Thomas, 44–46
Hunt, John, 28

Icahn, Carl, 12, 89
Immigration Act of 1924, 53
impasses, 23
incarceration for striking, 70
independent contractors, 16, 105
indictments, 144–45
influence, 139–40
information services, 84
injunctions, 13, 14, 41–42, *54*, *77*, 308–9
Insitu, 206
inspectors, FAA, 245–46
integrative (interest-based) bargaining, 110–13
Interagency Aerospace Revitalization Task Force, 222
interest/advisory arbitration, 128–29, 152–53
interest-based (integrative) bargaining, 110–13
interference, 136–38; in certification elections, 142–43; through communications, 140–42; penalties for, 144–45
International Air Transport Association (IATA), 199, 200
International Association of Machinists (IAM), 50, 168, 178, 185
International Association of Machinists and Aerospace Workers (IAMAW), 9, 10, 14–15, 95, 120, 124; Boeing and, 204, 214–18; Embry-Riddle representation, 234–35; flight service specialists and, 243; Lockheed Martin and, 212; survey on education, 223
International Aviation Services (NMB), 228
International Brotherhood of Teamsters (IBT), 9, 14, 85, 86, 90, 100, 185; general aviation and, 231–32, 233; Local 1108, 110–12, 231–32; PSA/Piedmont merger and, 197; *Teamsters v. Braniff Airways Inc.*, 143; two-tier wage scales and, 188
International Civil Aviation Organization (ICAO), 201
International In-flight Catering Company, 92
International Labour Organization (ILO), 239
International Union of Allied Industrial Workers of America (IAW), 204
interpretation, problems of, 153
Interstate Commerce Act of 1887, 41, 60, 262, 264, 473–4
Interstate Commerce Commission (ICC), 4, 41, 47, 51, 283
Interstate Transportation of Strikebreakers Act (Byrnes Act) of 1936, 72
intrastate carriers, 81

investigation, 89, 105
Iraq, 199

Jackson, Andrew, 17
Jade Cargo Airlines (China), 200
Jannus, Tony, *39*
Japan Airlines, 92
JetBlue Airlines, 190, 194–95
job security, 182–83, 211
Joedicke, Robert J., 176–80
John F. Kennedy International Airport (New York), 231, *231*
John Menzies PLC, d.b.a Ogden Ground Services Inc. (NMB), 228
Johns-Manville Products Corporation, 129
Johnson, Lyndon Baines, 22
Jones, Mother, 38, *39, 53*
judiciary, 8, 21, *77*; administrative law judge (ALJ), 8, 147, 297; federal district court, 8–9
jump seat crewmember, 145
jurisdictional determination, 8, 47, 62; general aviation, 17, 227–30; National Labor Relations Act, 8–10, *83*, 102–5; NMB two-pronged test, 84, 158, 227–28, 235; Railway Labor Act, 8–10, 15, 81–86, *83*, 142–44, 158, 178; subject-matter, 219, 252, 253

Kabuki theater proceedings, 116, 186
Kahn, Alfred E., 169, 177, 203
Kansas City International Airport, 195
Kelly, Sue, 244
Kelly Act (Air Mail Act of 1925), 5, *5*
Kennedy, John F., 20, *75*
Key Airlines, 100
Key Airlines case, 98–101, *101*, 102, 142
Key ballot, 98–101, *100*
Kitty Hawk flight, 47
Knight, Doug, 216
Knights of Labor, 31–32
knowledge workers, 22, 296
Komaroff, Michael I., 153
Korean Air, 200
Kriescher, Tim, 254

Labor Aerospace Research Agenda (LARA), 221
Labor Board and the Collective Bargaining Process, The (BNA), 124
labor costs, 30, 109, 122, 176–77, 179, 186, 189–91, 244
Labor Day holiday, 33
Labor Day strike threat (1916), 48
labor-management partnerships, 22, 184–85, 238
Labor-Management Relations Act of 1947. *See* Taft-Hartley Act of 1947

Labor-Management Reporting and Disclosure Act of 1959. *See* Landrum-Griffin Act of 1959
labor shortages: aerospace industry, 220–25; pilots and mechanics, 199–201
La Follette, Robert M., 53
La Guardia, Henry Fiorello, 59, *61*
Laker election, 98–100, *99*, 102, 142
Landrum-Griffin Act of 1959, 54, 65, 72, 103; grievance procedures and, 151; Title I, 71–72
Larkin, Frank, 220
Lawrence, Harding, *182*
LAXFUEL, 232
layoffs, 75–76
Lazear, Edward, 220
lean manufacturing, 212–13
legacy airlines, 69, 165, 170, 191
legislation. *See individual bills and acts*
Levy, Ron, 201
Lewin, David, 19
Lewis, Drew, 71
liberty of contract, 48, 294
LifeNet, 229, *229*
Lincoln, Abraham, 35, 36, *36*
Lindbergh, Charles, 209
Linea Aeropostal Venzolana, 142
little Wagner acts, 130
lobbying, 18, 19
local government employees, 130–31
Lockheed Martin Aeronautics, 220
Lockheed Martin Corporation, 9, 10, 220, 243, *243*
lockouts, 8, 110, 121–22
Loewe and Company, 42–43
Loewe v. Lawlor (Danbury Hatters), 42–43, 49
Logistics Civil Augmentation Program (LOGCAP), 242
Lorenzo, Francisco A. (Frank), 73, *73*, 124, 174, *181*, 182, 186
Ludlow Massacre, 39–40

Machinists v. National Mediation Board, 116
mail carriers, 5, *5*, 8, 20, 58, 82
major airlines, 10–15, *11*
Mallinckrodt Chemical decision (NLRB), 106
management-rights clauses, 21, 23, 237
Management Strike Contingency Force, 70
management styles, 237–38
managerial personnel, 103
Mann Elkins Act of 1910, 47
manufacturing, aviation/aerospace, *9*, 9–10, *10*
Mark Aero Inc. (NMB), 228
Marshall, John, 81
Martin Marietta Corporation, 208–9, 210, *243*
Massachusetts Institute of Technology (MIT), 221

Massachusetts Supreme Judicial Court, 27–30
McGuire, Peter J., 32–33
McNamara-O'Hara Service Contract Act, 243
McNerney, Jim, 215
Meany, George, 25
mechanics, 10, 95, 192; shortages, 199–201
mediation, 23, 25, 57–58, 60, 77, 110, 116; Newlands
    Act of 1913, 47–48; NLRA and RLA differences,
    117–18; process, 118. See also Federal Mediation
    and Conciliation Service; National Mediation
    Board
mediators, 74, 118
megacarriers, 7, 132, 203
Mercy Air Service, 229
mergers and acquisitions, 101–2, 113, 167; aerospace
    industry, 208–12; deregulation and, 195–99; first
    wave, 171; seniority lists, 167
merit system, 17–18
Merit System Protection Board (MSPB), 18, 130, 162
Mexico, 214
Midway Investment and Development Company
    LLC, 256
Midwest Express (Midwest Airlines), 14
Miles' Law, 3
military aircraft capabilities, 199
military contracts, 204–8
military personnel, 76, 130
Military Selection Act of 1967, 76
Military Selective Service Act of 1967, 76
minutes of negotiation, 152
Missouri Pacific strike (1886), 32
Mitchell, John, 43
monopolies, regulation of, 5–6
monopoly route awards, 167
Monthly Labor Review, 19
Moody, G. R., 144
Moore, Thomas, 26
Morici, Peter, 218
Morrison, Steven, 6
Munn, Ira, 4
Munn Act, 41
Munn v. Illinois, 3
Mutual Aid Pact (MAP), 122–23, 168, 171, 179

Nader, Ralph, 135, 136
name changes, 174
Nash, C., 47
National Center for Aviation Training, 224, 224
National Airlines, 171
national airlines, 10–15, 11
National Airspace System, 236
National Air Traffic Controllers Association
    (NATCA), 68–69, 130, 244, 244–45

National Air Transport Adjustment Board
    (NATAB), 156, 162, 292
National Association of Air Traffic Specialists
    (NAATS), 242–43
National Association of Flight Standards Employees
    (NAFSE), 245
National Association of Letter Carriers (NALC), 20
National Association of Manufacturers, 55
National Bankruptcy Commission, 74
national defense, 4
National Emergency Board, 68
national health and safety, 66, 68, 71, 126–27, 312, 315,
    316
National Imagery and Mapping Agency (NIMA),
    238
National Industrial Recovery Act (NIRA), 58, 62–63
nationalized transport industries, 4
National Labor Board, 58, 62
National Labor Relations Act (NLRA) of 1935
    (Wagner Act), 7, 8–9, 18, 54, 62–72; activities
    prohibited under, 136; definitions, 295–96;
    election and certification process, 102–14, 104,
    303–5; employees subject to, 102–3; employers
    subject to, 103; Executive Order 10988 and,
    20–21; findings and policies, 294–95; grievance
    arbitration under, 159, 159–61; grievance
    procedures and, 151; judicial challenge to, 64–65;
    jurisdictional determination, 8–10, 83, 102–5;
    major provisions of, 64; managerial personnel
    subject to, 103; non-airline/railroad private sector,
    124–29; organized labor and, 9–10; origins of,
    63–65; regulatory aspects, 63; representation
    elections and, 96; RLA compared with, 76–77,
    77, 89, 108, 114, 141, 150, 162; Section 8, 63–64,
    129, 146; supervisory personnel subject to, 103;
    text of, 294–322; unfair labor practices under,
    63–65, 64, 77, 133–39, 205–9, 298–303. See also
    Landrum-Griffin Act of 1959; Taft-Hartley Act
    of 1947
National Labor Relations Board (NLRB), 8, 54, 63,
    64, 68, 81, 174, 291, 296–98; bargaining units
    and, 106; certification election under, 106–7, 107,
    108; deregulation and, 174; investigatory powers,
    309–10; jurisdictional standards, 83; limitations,
    310–11; notice of election, 107; procedures of,
    104–6, 105; unfair labor practices rulings, 138–39;
    UPS decision, 84–86
National Labor Union (NLU), 31
National League of Cities v. Usery, 24
National Mediation Board (NMB), 12, 54, 57–58, 60,
    81; application for investigation of representation
    dispute, 89, 90, 91; ballots, 97; certification
    procedures, 87–88; class and craft determination,

National Mediation Board (NMB) (*continued*)
89, 93–95; decision-making history, 86–87;
deregulation and, 174–75; discretionary power,
91–92, 108, 143–44; election-rule exceptions, 98–
101; functions of, 278–80; grievance procedures
and, 152–53, 156; jurisdictional determination,
8, 142–44; mediation process, 118; merger and
acquisitions cases, 101–2, 197; negotiation time
frame and, 114–17; not subject to judicial review,
143–44; procedures, *88*, 88–93; references in text
of RLA, 261, 267, 270, 275–78, 291; representation
elections and, 95–98; two-pronged test, 84, 158,
227–28, 235; unfair labor practices decisions, 133,
140–42. *See also* Railway Labor Act
National Partnership Council (NPC), 22
National Partnership for Reinventing Government,
240
National Performance Review, 238, 240
National Railroad Adjustment Board (NRAB),
56–57, 58, 153, 156, 162, 269–75
National Right-to-Work Committee, 67
national security: anti-union executive orders and,
238–39; foreign repair stations and, 194
National Security Personnel System Act, 238–39
National Transportation Safety Board (NTSB), 6, 236
National Tube decision (NLRB), 106
national unions, 30–33
negotiation. *See* collective bargaining agreement,
negotiating
NetJets Association of Shared Aircraft Pilots
(NJASAP), 231–32
NetJets Aviation, 110–12, 230, 231
NetJets Aviation v. Teamsters, 158
New Deal, 62
Newlands Act of 1913, 47–48, 55
New York Air, 171, 172, *174*, 174–75
Nijkamp, P., 47
Nixon, Richard M., 21
NLRB v. Bildisco & Bildisco, 73, 186
NLRB v. Gissel Packing Company, 138
NLRB v. Jones & Laughlin Steel Corporation, 64–65, *65*
NLRB v. Mackay Radio & Telegraph Co., 132
non-airline/railroad private sector, 124–29
Norris, George W., 59, *61*
Norris—La Guardia Act of 1932, 8, 43, *54*, 58, 76, *77*,
135, 308; provisions of, 59–62
North American Aviation, 208
North Central Airlines, 171, 190
Northrop Grumman Corporation, 220
Northwest Airlines, *12*, 14, 120–21, 123, 197;
bankruptcy, 192; ESOPs, 183; two-tier
contracts, 188
North-Western Police Agency, 35

Northwest Orient Airlines, 122–23
no-strike clauses, 219

Obama, Barrack, 244
Oberstar, James, 245
Occupational Safety and Health Act (OSHA) of
1970, 75, 161
O'Connor, Sandra Day, 198
Office of Federal Contract Compliance Programs
(OFCCP), 75
Office of General Counsel (OGC), 147
Office of Management and Budget (OMB), 239–42
Office of Personnel Management (OPM), 18, 130
*Ohio Power Company v. Utilities Workers Union of
America*, 103
oil prices, 165, 192
Oklahoma City and Tulsa markets, 193
oligopolistic conditions, 7
open-skies bilateral agreements, 14
Order No.8, 50
Order of Railway Conductors, 31
outsourcing and privatization, 194; aerospace
industry, 208, 213–19, 225; airports, 255–57; public
sector, 239–42, 243
Ozark Air Lines, 116–17, 174, 190
Ozark Holdings, 174

Pacific Southwest Airlines (PSA), 188, 196, 197
Page Avjet, 232
PAMELA (process for advances management of end-
of-life aircraft), 225–26
Pan American World Airways, 74, 150, 183, 184
Pan Am flying boats, 234
Panorama Air Tour (NLRB), 229
Part 298 operators, 15
passenger volume, 177
patronage system, 17
pattern bargaining, 116, 122, 191
Paul R. Braniff Inc., *182*
Pendleton Act of 1883, 17–18
Pension Benefit Guaranty Corporation (PBGC), *192*,
192–93
pensions, 192–93, 212, 263
People Express, *174*
petition for certification, 104–5
Philadelphia, early organizing efforts, 26
Piedmont Airlines, 188, 197
Piedmont Aviation, 87, 102
pilots, 10; shortages, 199–201, 207
Pinkerton, Allan, 35, *35*, *36*
Pinkerton National Detective Agency, 35–37
Pistole, John S., 254
plant closings, 75–76

Plant v. Woods, 41–42
Poli, Robert, 69, 70, 71
policy, definition, 3
political appointment and election, 17
Poole, Robert W., Jr., 244
positional bargaining, 111–12
Powderly, Terrence, 32, *32*
Pratt & Whitney, 211, 225
Pratt & Whitney Canada (P&WC), 212–13
presidential intervention, *66*, 68, 71, *115*, 120–21,
    126–27, 289–90
President's Task Force on Employee-Management
    Relations, 20
price discrimination, 49
private eye, as term, 36
private military companies (PMC), 241
productivity, 176, 180, 195
Professional Air Traffic Controllers (PATCO),
    23–24, *24*, *69*, 69–71, 109, 130, 180–82, 196
Professional Airways System Specialists (PASS), *147*,
    147–48
Professional Aviation Safety Specialists (PASS), 243,
    245–46
professional employees, 105, 204, 296
property law, 3–4, 18
protection of right of employees to organize, 58, 63
public interest, 3–4
Public Law 93–36 (health-care industry), 65
Public Law Boards, 153
public policy, 3, 158
public sector, 17, 22–24, 129–30, 236–58; air safety
    inspectors, 245–46; flight service stations
    (FSS), 242–44; labor-relations environment,
    237–39; management-rights clauses, 21, 237,
    257; management styles, 237–38; outsourcing
    and privatization, 239–42, 243; state and local
    government employees, 254–57
public-sector unions, 17; collective bargaining,
    23–24; rise of, 18–19, 22–23; state and local
    government laws, 24–25
Pullman, George, 37
Pullman Palace Car Company, 37, 42
Pullman strike (1894), 37, 40–41, 42, 46

racism, 31
Racketeering Influences and Corrupt Organizations
    Act (RICO) of 1970, 76
Railroad Administration, 50–51
railroad industry, 3–4, 18, 26; nationalization of,
    50–51; national unions, 30–31; strikes, 33, 34–35
Railroad Labor Board, 52, 53, 54
Railway Labor Act (RLA) of 1926, 7, 8–9, 18; airline
    provisions, 291–93; amendment of 1934, *54*, 58;

amendment of 1936 (Title II), *54*, 57, 58–59, 82,
    84, 165; amendment of 1940, *54*, 59; amendment
    of 1951, *54*, 59; arbitration, 281–85, 288; award and
    judgment, 286–88; class and craft determination,
    89, 93–95; commuter service procedure, 288–89;
    decertification, 102; Depression-era unionism,
    55–56; early judicial challenges, 55; election and
    certification process, 81–102, *88*, *115*; emergency
    boards, 68, 109, *115*, 120–21, 289–90, 315–17;
    employees subject to, 86–87; general duties,
    265–69; grievance procedures under, *156*, 156–59;
    jurisdiction, 8–10, 15, 81–86, *83*, 142–44, 158, 178;
    Landrum-Griffin Act and, 72; major and minor
    disputes, 56–57; National Railroad Adjustment
    Board, 269–75; negotiation time frame, 114–17;
    NLRA compared with, 76–77, *77*, 89, 108, 114,
    141, 150, 162; origins, 4, 53–54, 53–55; procedures
    in the airlines under, 114; provisions of, 56–57,
    60; public policy objectives, 56; rates of pay and
    working conditions, 280–81; representation
    elections and, 95–98; Section 2, 139; Section
    2, Eleventh, 59, 144; Section 2, Ninth, 88, 92,
    95, 141; Section 6, 119; Section 7, 118; social
    insurance, 263–65; text of, 261–93; Title I, 82;
    unchanged continuation of, 180; unfair labor
    practices under, 139–45; work rules, 283–85. *See
    also* National Mediation Board
rates, 41, 47, 51
Raytheon Company, 232
"R" docket number, 89
Reagan, Ronald Wilson, 24, *24*, 68, *70*, 70–71, 181
rebates, 47
recognition, 20–21, 23
regional airlines, 10, *11*, 15–16, *140*, 200
Regional Express (Australia), 200
regulation, 3–9; definition, 5; NLRA and, 63
regulatory policy initiatives, 4, 5–6
remedy at law, 44
Reorganization Plan No. 2 of 1978, 21
replacement workers, 13, 70, 124, 129, 131–32
representation disputes, 8–9, 21, 22, *77*, 88–89;
    application for investigation, 89, *90*, *91*; bar
    rules, 89–93; class and craft designation, 93–95;
    elections and, 91–92; mergers/acquisitions and,
    197–98
representative, defined, 87, 295
Republic Airlines, 171, 182, 184, 188, 190, 197
Republican party, 31, 244, 257
requests for qualification (RFQ), 256
retirement: 2007 rule change, 201; aerospace
    industry, 208, 220, 223; air traffic controllers, 245;
    expatriate pilots and, 200
revenues, *83*

reverse pattern bargaining, 191
right-to-work laws, *54*, 59, *59*, *66*, *67*, 67–68, 77, *77*, 218
Robson, John, 168–69
Rockefeller, John D., 37
Rocky Mountain Holdings (RMH), 229
Rocky Mountain Holdings, LLC d/b/a Eagles Airmed of Arizona (NMB), 228
Roosevelt, Franklin D., 62
route transfers, 167
Ruiz, Ernesto, 194–95

safety, 6, 10, 75, 245
Santulli, Richard, 110, 112
scabs. *See* replacement workers
Scalia, Antonin, 219
Schechter v. United States, 62
scheduling restrictions, 196
Scovell, Calvin, III, 245
scrip, 38
Seaboard Air Line Railroad, 93
secondary actions, 42–43, 56, 57–58, *65*, 77, *77*; Taft-Hartley ban on, 71
Section 401 certification, 15, *173*, *175*
self-help, 8, 12, 56, 110, 116, 119, 126, 128. *See also* strikes
Senate Committee on Labor, 40
Seneker, Harold, 172
seniority lists, 167
September 11, 2001 attacks, 165, *166*, 202
service industries, 177
Servicemaster Aviation Services (NLRB), 230
Shaw, Lemuel, *27*, 27–30, 41
Shenyang Aircraft Company, 214
Sherman Antitrust Act (1890), 41–43, 48, 49, 50
Signature Flight Support, 230, 232–34
Signature Flight Support (NMB), 230
Sikorsky, 214
Sine, Mitch, 195
Skytanking USA, *233*
Skyway Aviation (NMB), 228
Sloane, Arthur, 24
small businesses, 68
Smith, Frederick W., 86, 116
snapback provisions, 184
Social Security Act of 1935, 76
Society of Professional Engineering Employees in Aerospace (SPEEA), 204, 214–15, 218
Somers, Gerald G., 153
Southern Airlines, 167, 171
Southwest Airline Pilots' Association (SWAPA), 14
Southwest Airlines, *15*, 122, 189–90, 195
sovereignty doctrine, 19, 23, 64, 67
Soviet Union, 220

Special Boards of Adjustment, 153
Spencer, Frank A., 196
Spirit Airlines, 193
Spirit of St. Louis, 209
spoils system, 17
state and local government, 310–11; employees, 130–31, 154–55; executive orders and, 20; grievance procedures and, 161; labor-management relations and, 7–8; laws, 24–25; regulation of private enterprise, 3; restrictions on public-employee bargaining, 257; sovereignty, 64, 67; unfair labor practices and, 148–50, *149*
State Department, 242
statutory relief, 161–62
Stephens, Uriah S., 31
stereotypes, 56
Stewart International Airport (New York), 255
stocks and stores employees, 95
St. Petersburg-Tampa Airboat Line, 39
straw-man election, 102
strikebreakers, 12, 13, 72
strike pay, 217
strikes, 7, 8, 110, 300–302, 322; 1940s, 65, 135; 1955 law, 24; 1955 legislation, 70; actions during, 129; Adamson Act and, 48; aerospace industry, 214–18; Boeing, 214–18; CHAOS, 12–14; Colorado Coal Field War, 37–40, 46; costs of, 179, 180; grievance procedures and, 157, 159; Homestead, 35; incarceration for, 70; Missouri Pacific, 32; NMB and, 57; Pacific Southwest Airlines, 196; PATCO, 23–24, *24*, *69*, 69–71, 109, 130, 180–82, 196; preparation for, 216–17; protected, 19; Pullman, 37, 40–41, 42, 46; railroad industry, 33, 34–35; replacement workers, 13, 70, 124, 129, 131–32; restrictions on, 21, 23–24, 70, 121; under RLA, 121–22; state prohibitions, 25; UAW, mid-1930s, *82*; as ultimate weapon, 33, 121; Wabash Railroad, 32
subordinate official, 86–87
subsidiaries, 82, 174
subsidization of transportation, 4–6
supermediation, 110, 119
supervisory personnel, 68, 86, 103, 105, 296, 310
Supreme Court cases: *Adair v. United States*, 55; agency shop ruling, 67–68; on arbitration, 159, 162; bankruptcy, 74; *Bedford Cut Stone Co. v. Journeymen Stone Cutters Association of North America*, 50; *Brotherhood of Railroad Trainmen v. Chicago River & Indiana Railroad Co.*, 157; *Brotherhood of Railway and Steamship Clerks* case, 96–97; *Commonwealth v. Hunt*, 27–30, 41; *Danbury Hatters (Loewe v. Lawlor)*, 42–43, 49; *Duplex Printing v. Deering*, 50; *Enterprise Wheel & Car*, 157, 158; *Gibbons v. Ogden*, 81; *Hitchman*

Coal & Coke Company v. Mitchell, 43–46; *Munn v. Illinois*, 3, 4; *National Labor Relations Board v. Jones & Laughlin Steel Corporation*, 64, 64–65, 65; *National League of Cities v. Usery*, 24; *NetJets Aviation v. Teamsters*, 158; *NLRB v. Bildisco & Bildisco*, 73, 186; *NLRB v. Gissel Packing Company*, 138; *Plant v. Woods*, 41–42; *Schechter v. United States*, 62; *Texas and New Orleans Railroad v. the Brotherhood of Railway and Steamship Clerks*, 55, 139–40; *Virginian Railroad Company v. System Federation No. 40*, 96, 140, 414; *Wabash, St. Louis, & Pacific Railroad Company v. Illinois*, 3, 4; *Wheeling-Pittsburgh Steel Corporation v. United Steelworkers*, 186; writ of certiorari, 8

Switchman's Union of North America, 31

system boards of adjustment, 156–57, 159, 162, 291–92

Taft, Robert A., 134, *134*

Taft bill, 135

Taft-Hartley Act of 1947, 9, 24, 42, *54*, 65–69, 71, 77, 311–12; employee, defined, 102–3, 105; major provisions, *66*; right-to-work laws, 59, *59*; suits for violation of contracts, 219; unfair labor practices and, 134–36

TAG Aviation, 233

Taneja, Nawal K., 167

tariff, 167

Teal Group, 218

Teamsters vs. Braniff Airways Inc., 143

technical employees, 72, 221

Ted, 193

Texas Air Corporation, *73*, 124, 174–75, *181*

Texas and New Orleans Railroad v. the Brotherhood of Railway and Steamship Clerks, 55, 139–40, 141

Texas International Airlines, *73*, 169, 172, 175

Textron Lycoming Reciprocating Engine Division, 219

Thatcher, Margaret, 255

Tikas, Louis, 39

Title III (Transportation Act), 52, 55

Title VII, Civil Service Reform Act of 1978, 21–22, 24

Tobias, Robert, 22

trainee, 87

Trans-East Air Inc. (NLRB), 230

Transportation Act of 1920, 51–52, 53–54; Title III, 52, 55

transportation policy, 3–9

Transportation Security Administration (TSA), 236, 253–54

transportation security officers (TSOs, airport screeners), 253–54

Transport Workers Union (TWU), 14, 96, 178, 191

Trans World Airlines (TWA), 12, 87, 89, 132, 196, 198

Troy, Philip, 220

trucking, 84–85

true craft group, 106

Truman, Harry S., 59, 134

Trump, Donald, *181*

Tulsa–Oklahoma Airways, *182*

UAL Corporation, 183

Ueltshi, Al, 234

unfair labor practices (ULPs), 8, 21, *54*, 133–50, 295; activities prohibited under NLRA, 136; bankruptcy and, 73; court decisions, 143–44; under CSRA and state laws, 145–50; employer interference in elections, 97–98, 136–39; featherbedding, 145; federal agencies and, 133, 145–48; under Federal Labor Relations Authority, 133, 147–48; interference, 136–39; interference in certification elections, 142–43; interference through communications, 140–42; under NLRA, 63–65, *64*, *77*, 133–39, 298–303, 305–9; NLRB rulings, 138–39; penalties, 138; penalties for interference in elections, 144–45; under RLA, 139–45; state labor-relations agencies and, 148–50, *149*; surveillance actions, 136–38; Taft-Hartley Act and, 134–36; threats of plant closure, 137; by unions, *66*, 67, 134–36, *137*, 146

union-free agreements. *See* yellow-dog contracts

Union Intelligence Service, 36

union members, Bill of Rights, 71–72

unions, 9–10; aerospace industry, 211–12; company, 58, 88, 231–32; contributions to political campaigns, 71; craft, 10, 33; as criminal conspiracy, 27–30, 41; decertification, 70; duties under RLA, 265–66; employers as members, 33; national, 30–33; public, 17–19, 22–25; restrictions on payments to representatives, 319–21; suits by and against, 318; unfair labor practices by, *66*, 67, 134–36, *137*, 146

United Air Lines (UAL), 95, 116, *121*, 122–23, 196; bankruptcy, 192; Blue Skies contract, 182–83; Capital Airlines merger, 167; Continental merger, 198–99; downsizing, 193; featherbedding and, 145; machinist strike, 1979, 171; two-tier contracts, 187–88

United Air Transport, 208

United Automobile, Aerospace, and Agricultural Implement Workers of America (UAW), 204, 219

United Auto Workers (UAW), 9, *82*, 233

United Continental Holdings Inc., 199

United Hatters, 42

United Mine Workers of America (UMWA), 38–40; *Hitchman Coal & Coke Company v. Mitchell*, 43–46

United Nations, 239
United Parcel Services (UPS), 84–86, *228*
United States v. Jerry Winston & Broome County Aviation Inc. d/b/a Commuter Airlines Inc., 145
United States v. Taca Airways Agency Inc., 144
universities, 236
University Aviation Association (AA), 201
USAir, 102, *140*, 197
USAir Group, 198
US Airline Pilots Association, 113
US Airways, 113, *140*, 193, 194–95
U.S. Circuit Court of Appeals, 157
U.S. Commission on the Future of the Aerospace Industry, 221
U.S. Court of Appeals, 91–92, 147
U.S Court of Appeals for the Third Circuit, 73, 185–86, 219
U.S.-Mexico Bilateral Aviation Safety Agreement, 214
U.S. Secret Service, 36

ValueJet, 199
Veritas Capital Fund, 241
Vietnam Era Veteran Readjustment Assistance Act of 1974, 76
Virgin America, *199*
Virginian Railroad Company v. System Federation No. 40, 96, 140, 141
Vocational Rehabilitation Act of 1973, 75
Voss, Bill, 200
Voyager 1000 (NMB), 228

Wabash, St. Louis, & Pacific Railroad Company v. Illinois (Wabash case), 3, 4
Wabash Railroad strike (1885), 32
Wage and Hour Division, Department of Labor, 72
wage cuts, 184–85
wage rates, 179; increases during campaigns, 137–38
wages, 58; minimum-wage laws, 48, 72; overtime pay, 72, 243–44; two-tier contracts, 175–76, 187–88, 212
Wagner, Robert F., 63
Wagner Act. *See* National Labor Relations Act (NLRA) of 1935

Wagner Bill, 63
Wait, Isaac B., 28
Waite, Morrison, 3, *4*
walkouts, 119
Wardman, M., 47
Washington Post Pressmen strike (1975), 129
watch schedule, 147–48
Watson-Parker Bill, 55
Wechsler, Robert, 20
Westchester County Airport (KHPN), 233
Western Airlines, 101, *102*, 184, 198
Wheeling-Pittsburgh Steel Corporation v. United Steelworkers, 186
white-collar exemptions, 72
Whitney, Fred, 24
Wichita, Kansas, 220, 224
Widnall, Sheila, 221
Wien Air Alaska, 87
Wilson, Woodrow, 40, 48
windfall revenue, 122–23, 168
Winston, Clifford, 6
Winston, Jerry, 145
Worker Adjustment and Retraining Notification Act (WARN) of 1988, 75, 193
Workforce Fairness Act, 131–32
working conditions, 23, 38, 280–81
Workplace Fairness Act of 1993, 132
work rules, 12, 51, 58, 179, 185; Railway Labor Act, 283–85
work week, *54*, 72
World War I, 46, 48
World War II, 65
Worldwide Flight Services Inc. (NMB), 228
Wright brothers, 208
writ of certiorari, 8
Wroblewski, Tom, 217
Wurf, Jerry, 19

yellow-dog contracts (union-free agreements), 43–46, 48, 50, *54*; end of, 58, *61*

zero-sum (distributive) bargaining, 110, 113

Robert W. Kaps is a professor of aviation management in the Department of Aviation Management and Flight, Southern Illinois University Carbondale, and has more than thirty years' experience in labor and industrial relations, including work for a major airline. His background includes experience as a managerial negotiator for major air carriers and in the representation of labor unions in other industries and labor associations representing the interests of employees in the public sector. He is the author of *Fiscal Aspects of Aviation Management* and *Air Transport Labor Relations*.

J. Scott Hamilton is a professor of management at Embry-Riddle Aeronautical University and has more than thirty years' experience in the practice of law, including private practice specializing in aviation law (that included representing unions and union members in major and minor disputes in the airline industry), government service (as senior assistant attorney general), and in aviation management (as corporate general counsel, then chief operating officer). He is the author of *Practical Aviation Law*.

Timm J. Bliss holds the Roger Hardesty Endowed Chair in Aviation Science and is an associate professor of aviation management at Oklahoma State University with more than twenty years' experience in higher education and public service.